HISTORY OF THE HIGHLAND CLEARANCES.

First published by A. & W. MacKenzie, Inverness 1883.
© Introduction, John Prebble 1979

ISBN 0 9505884 7 4

THE
HISTORY
OF THE
HIGHLAND CLEARANCES

CONTAINING A REPRINT OF DONALD MACLEOD'S "GLOOMY
MEMORIES OF THE HIGHLANDS"; ISLE OF SKYE
IN 1882; AND A VERBATIM REPORT OF THE
TRIAL OF THE BRAES CROFTERS,

BY

ALEXANDER MACKENZIE, F.S.A. Scot.,

EDITOR OF THE *Celtic Magazine*; AUTHOR OF *The History of the Mackenzies*;
The History of the Macdonalds and Lords of the Isles; *The Macdonalds of
Glengarry*; *The Macdonalds of Clanranald*; *The History of the
Mathesons*; *The Prophecies of the Brahan Seer*; *Historical
Tales and Legends of the Highlands*, ETC.

FOREWORD BY JOHN PREBBLE

MELVEN PRESS

PERTH 1979

Acknowledgments are due to Rory Mackay of Inverness
for permission to print from his copy

Printed in Great Britain by
Billing & Sons Limited, Guildford, London and Worcester

PREFACE.

━━◦◦◦◦◦◦◦━━

THE late Robert Carruthers, LL.D., reviewing in
1878 in the *Inverness Courier*, a paper on the
Strathglass evictions, by Mr. Colin Chisholm, published
in the Transactions of the Gaelic Society of Inverness,
wrote :—"A good history of the changes in the Highlands, . . . and the 'Clearances,' since the great
Glengarry emigration, for the last century and a half,
would form a most interesting volume, and sufficient
materials exist for a diligent and honest enquirer.
We recommend the task to the editor of the *Celtic
Magazine*."

We had an idea long before this, that we might
possibly some day attempt a work such as our venerable friend here suggested, and the high compliment,
from such a quarter, implied in the terms of the
proposal, induced us to pay more attention to the
subject and keep a sharper eye than ever on anything which could throw light on the history of
the Highland Clearances. The result will be found
in the following pages. There is little attempt to

do more than place the facts before the reader, so far as they can be ascertained, accompanied by the views of contemporary writers, and others, whose opinions are sure to command respect. This we hold to be infinitely more valuable than anything original which we could have written on the subject.

Some people may ask "Why rake up all this iniquity just now?" We answer that the same laws which permitted the cruelties, the inhuman atrocities, described in this book, are still the laws of the country, and any tyrant who may be indifferent to the healthier public opinion which now prevails, may *legally* repeat the same proceedings whenever he may take it into his head to do so.

It is not in our power to alter the Laws of the Land so that a repetition of these evictions cannot take place, but the fear of getting pilloried, in a work like this, may possibly induce the tyrant to hold his hand, for very shame, until a more just and humane law shall make such mean and cruel work as the Highland Clearances for ever impossible ; and there is hope for such a result in the fact that the descendants of the oppressors of a past generation are so much ashamed of what was done by their predecessors that they would give much of what they at present possess if they could but recal the mean, indefensible, and harsh evictions of the past.

There is nothing in History so absolutely *mean* as the Eviction of the Highlanders by chiefs solely indebted for every inch of land they ever held to the strong arms and trusty blades of the progenitors of those whom the effeminate and ungrateful chiefs of the nineteenth century have so ruthlessly oppressed, evicted, and despoiled.

The interest in the subject of the Highland Evictions may be gathered from the fact, that of a pamphlet published by the present writer, in 1881, an edition of fifteen hundred copies went out of print in a few months, and that it has supplied the material for most of the speeches made, and many of the newspaper articles written, on the subject ever since, though seldom or ever acknowledged by those who had found it so useful and convenient!

It is hoped that the portion of this work relating to the Social state of the Isle of Skye in 1882, illustrated by the Trial of the Braes Crofters, and other proceedings connected with the Island, will be found both instructive and interesting.

The statistics of the population of the Highland Counties and Parishes, given in the Appendix, will be found in a convenient form for reference, and they may possibly prove useful, and perhaps interesting to those who concern themselves about the steady and rapid decrease of the rural population in the Highlands during the last fifty years.

For many items which we could not otherwise obtain (most of the Census Returns having gone out of print), we are indebted to the prompt and obliging courtesy of the Registrar-General for England ; for there are no copies prior to 1841 kept in the Scotch Office! All others to whom we are indebted—and to many of them we are under deep obligations—are mentioned in the body of the work, except Mr. Dugald Cowan, who, after considerable trouble and difficulty, succeeded in procuring for us some valuable information in the Library of the Royal College of Physicians, Edinburgh.

A. M.

Inverness, *January, 1883.*

An Introduction by
John Prebble

"How we enjoyed ourselves in those far away
days! Those were the happy days and there was
neither sin nor sorrow in the world for us. But
the clearances came upon us, destroying all . . .
turning our joy into misery, our gladness into
bitterness, our blessing into blasphemy . . . Oh,
dear man, the tears come on my eyes when I think
of all we suffered, and of the sorrows, hardships,
and oppressions we came through"

—Peigidh nic Cormaig

The words are an English translation. They are
more moving in the Gaelic which Peggy MacCormack used. She had been born a MacDonald and she
lived at Aird Bhuidhe, the yellow hill above Loch
Boisdale. In her old age, many years after the Clearances came upon her, she would still weep if reminded
of the time when her chief sold Uist and Benbecula
for £96,000, when his evicted and unwanted people
were driven to the loch shore and the waiting boats
of the emigrant ship *Admiral*. "Were you to see,"
said another witness of those days, "were you to see

the racing and chasing of policemen, you would think that you had been transported to the banks of the Gambia on the slave coast of Africa." It was the last great sale of the wide lands which the chiefs of Clanranald had once held in Arisaig and Moidart, in the westering islands of the Hebrides. By 1838, when Ranald George MacDonald, twentieth chief of Clanranald, sold South Uist and Benbecula to that great evictor John Gordon of Cluny, he had received more than £200,000 for the surrender of his inheritance. He was improvident, crippled by self-indulgent debts and the failure of the kelp industry, and it does not appear to have distressed him that the abandoned people of his clan might not be wanted by the new proprietors, that indeed they would be removed to make room for sheep. He had little recognisable feeling for them, being inclined to remove them himself if he thought their black stone cabins spoiled the view from his windows.

He lies now in a mouldering tomb in Brompton Cemetery, in London where he always preferred to reside, but the descendants of his clan are scattered across the world.

When Peggy MacCormack's sad lament first appeared in print at the turn of this century, the great waves of the Highland Clearances had subsided into the small tidal movements which still continue to-day. In 1881 the people of Glendale and other valleys on Skye had begun their long and ultimately victorious struggle against intransigent landlordism. In 1884 the

Crofters Commission had produced its monumental and influential report on the state of the Highlands, recording the evidence of old Highlanders who spoke with anguish of the days of eviction five, six, and seven decades before, their eloquent Gaelic literally translated into poetic English. In 1883, between the Battle of the Braes on Skye and the report of the Commission, the indefatigable editor of the *Celtic Magazine* had published this book, an indignant, impassioned and uncompromising indictment of Highland landlords and the diaspora of a people. It might be thought that these three events would have been strong and prevailing winds, blowing away the persuasive romance in which most men prefer their history to be cocooned. That they were not, that it was not until the second half of this century that a proper study of the Clearances was thought important, indeed imperative for a deeper understanding of the present state of Scotland, may also be an indictment—of our persistent and perilous indifference to the lessons of the past.

Alexander Mackenzie was forty-five when he published this account of the Clearances. Since 1875 he had edited the *Celtic Magazine*, "written almost entirely in English" and harmlessly devoted to Gaelic history, folk-lore and antiquities, "the Moral and Material interests of Celts at Home and Abroad." He had written or published several clan histories of a customary nature, and three editions of the Prophecies of the Brahan Seer. It may be—the thought is compelling if conjectural—that his first-hand experience as a journalist of the Glendale revolt, the trial of the Braes Crofters, turned his mind more actively to an obligatory work on the Clearances from the beginning. He was not the first polemicist to attack them. There had been others over the preceding seventy years upon whose work he greatly relied—men like Donald Macleod the stonemason of Strathnaver, Thomas Mulock the wayward father of the author of *John Halifax, Gentleman*, Donald Ross who got his information on the Strathcarron evictions from the bloodstained women who resisted them, and lastly an anonymous correspondent of the *Times*, who was sent to the Highlands after the Glencalvie removals of 1845.

The great strength of Mackenzie's narrative is its readable simplicity. However amateurish, even disjointed, it sometimes is, it is also a threnody for the abused and abandoned race to which he belonged. It is of no great consequence now that much of it is second or third-hand information, that a lack of referential dates produces occasional confusion, that truth is sometimes clouded by factual contradictions. Subsequent research has justified what Mackenzie was trying to tell his contemporaries, and his voice is still more powerful, more moving than the cautious confirmation of later scholars.

The wall of prejudice and ignorance he hoped to break was strong. He was attacking the sacred rights of wealth and property upon which Victorian Britain prospered, the belief that greater profit to the few must ease the deprivation of the many. This was probably not his intention in a general sense, and he did not condemn the Clearances as the Swiss social scientist, Simonde de Sismondi, had done forty years before, as an "absurd and revolting" contradiction of the arguments advanced in their defence. Mackenzie's sense of outrage was perhaps closer to the truth. He knew that they were a crime of betrayal, a deep and killing breach of faith. Whatever the gentry now thought their role in society to be, the common people of the Highlands still responded to older compulsions. The chief was the father of the clan, *ceann-cinnidh*, responsible for his children, obliged to protect them as they were to obey and defend him. This already obsolescent relationship had been blown away by cannon at Culloden, destroyed by punitive laws and reforming statutes, but the people still clung to their belief in it. When the Chief abandoned his obligations in favour of profit, they still responded to their own, and often walked to the emigrant ships with the meekness of the sheep that replaced them. Even their resistance, when it occurred, was despairingly brief, as if halted by guilt. That was the betrayal.

Mackenzie's book was a harsh intrusion upon the view of the Highlands enjoyed by southern Britain. Scotland was the land of romance, of Gothic tragedy, superb landscapes and stimulating climate. Its History, as it was understood, conspired to make it favoured by the English. The incredible expenditure of Highland lives in the Napoleonic wars, the publication of *Waverley*, the Balmorality of the monarchy and society, had replaced a bitter past with a romantic present. The clan system, once an omnipresent threat to the Lowlands and to the security of the realm, was thought to have survived the last Jacobite rebellion and was now, decently disinfected and respectfully loyal, the model of a quaintly archaic society. The thought of the Highland squares at Waterloo, of Sutherland men standing firm against Russian cavalry on Balaclava heights, staunch gillies on splendid moors, justified the English belief that the best had come from the worst of worlds and that it was the qualities of the English that had made it possible. So oppressive was this view that many Scots accepted their junior partnership in the Union to such a self-effacing degree that a Highland soldier in the Indian Mutiny could speak of the bravery of his regiment as being in the finest traditions of English valour.

Behind this gloss, which they enjoyed as much as others, Highland chiefs and proprietors in the early 19th century were greedy for the privileges and wealth of their southern peers. Land-rich and purse-poor, they had not shared in the increasing wealth of their class. Their glens were over-populated, and emigration had begun its drain as some small tacksmen escaped from the rack-renting of their chiefly cousins. Their tenants and sub-tenants, as their onetime clansmen now were, had no security of tenure, were annually dependent upon the will of the proprietor (to whom that fact would soon become most beneficial). Their mountain acres, thin soil on skeleton rock, scarcely supported a blackcattle economy and a run-rig husbandry. Their debts were becoming astronomical, their wives more eager for Edinburgh town-houses, their sons for expensive commission in English regiments, their daughters for marriages for which no dowries were available. Their problems seemed insoluble, and their wounded pride was only partly soothed by the elaborate Highland dress they some-times wore, monstrous caricatures of what had once been the simple dress of their people.

Providentially, if that is not an inapposite word, they were saved by an inoffensive, tractable, bleating animal which the people would soon call "the four-footed clansmen". The Great Cheviot Sheep, "finely-shaped, with countenance mild and pleasant", was man-made, the strain of its Border progenitors im-proved by Lincoln ewes, by Ryeland and Spanish rams, until it would not only survive in the Highlands but would actually flourish there. It was an answer to the dying black cattle economy, to recurring debt and eager ambition. By the end of the 18th century the Great Cheviot had reached the hills of Ross, and by the beginning of the next it had moved into Sutherland.

Few if any Highland landowners wished to become sheep-farmers. In the beginning they leased their lands to graziers from the Borders and Northumbria, only later would their improvidence or incompetence force them to sell the land itself. To free the required pastures, tenant and sub-tenant were evicted. Bred for centuries to accept the authority of the chief, in the customary belief that it was by definition benevolent, the people were willing victims of the great change. In 1792, *Bliadhna nan Caorach* the Year of the Sheep, there was indeed a spirited attempt to stop the northward flow of the Great Cheviot. The men of Ross drove the alien flocks from their glens, but they were quickly suppressed by armed gentry and men of the Black Watch, many of whom were their young kinsmen. Thenceforward, all resistance was brief and sporadic, and in the savage little encounters which did occur between the evicted and the sheriff's officers, it was the women of the glens who fought.

Sir John Sinclair of Ulbster, who had brought the Great Cheviot to Caithness, had warned Highland proprietors against any rash brutal change, any harsh removal of their tenantry before they considered how the people might share in a new prosperity. But his reasoned advocacy of sheep-farming also gave them good cause for greedy haste. Pasture which had once produced twopence an acre under lean cattle, he said, might now give two shillings under sheep. At its best, the annual yield of beef on the Highlands had never been more than £200,000, whereas the proprietors might now expect £900,000 from the sale of fine wool alone.

Although the majority of the Clearances were motivated by greed, some landlords in the beginning were genuinely moved by an obligation to improve the economy and society of the Highlands, believing that a duty to their conscience as much as to the fashionable theory that the richer a rich man grew, so must the poor become less poor. Without exception however, these men and their factors failed to understand the nature of a people who, they believed, should accept their eviction in the grand spirit of that improvement. The most dramatic Clearances recorded by Mackenzie are perhaps those which were the earliest, and which took place upon the Sutherland estates which the Marquess of Stafford, already one of the richest men in Britain, had acquired by marriage to Elizabeth Gordon, Countess of Sutherland. His Commissioner James Loch, who first used the word Improvement in this context, was a man of dangerous rectitude and consuming dedication, convinced that his work for his noble master would bring nothing but good to an ignorant, credulous, lazy and slothful people, as he believed the Highlanders to be.

The exercise of good intentions, where profit on private property is both cause and incentive, becomes more ruthless when it is resisted, and humane concern for those who suffer as a result decreases in inverse proportion to the self-righteousness of the executors. Thus brutality became a feature of all Clearances, whether modelled on Loch's Policy of Improvement or the result of a landlord's hunger for riches. To force a man from his cottage, to burn his roof-tree before him, is brutal enough, without the clubbing, the use of truncheon and bayonet which often became necessary before an estate could be cleared. To take a man from his mountain, to place him on a barren sea-coast as Loch did, to tell him that he must now be a fishermen, to tell his sons that they may not marry without permission, is also a brutal assault on the self-respect of inoffensive men. When the Policy failed, or when stubborn and bewildered men failed to do as it required, there was no return to their old life. Their townships were gone, and in their glens, said their bards, "nothing was heard but the bleating of sheep and the voices of English-speakers." For most of the evicted, on the mainland or the Isles, there were not even the alternative industries which Loch's Policy hopefully proposed. There were only the destitution roads south, the slums in Glasgow, the emigrant ships at Wick, at Thurso, Fort William, Loch Boisdale and Loch Broom.

The great Clearances came in three distinguishable waves, first rising in Sutherland, subsiding to rise again in the West and in the Isles, falling once more to rise again in Ross, Knoydart, Kintail and the Isles. By the sixth decade new dimensions had been added. Emigration, which had at first been resisted by Government and gentry because it robbed the nation of its "nursery of soldiers" and the landowners of a necessary tenantry, was now actively encouraged. Incoming proprietors wanted no estate encumbered by a pauper population for which they might be responsible under the Poor Laws; and famine, cholera and neglect had greatly increased poverty among the Highlanders. When a national Society was established, under Royal patronage, to facilitate emigration it was natural for the Victorians to see it as a humane and philanthropic venture. Although James Loch had once said that "the idle alone think of emigration", and others had protested against the departure of young men who should have been serving in the Army, it was now said that the colonies needed and would profit from the sturdy virtues of the Highland people. Vestigial Highland chiefs, like the MacDonell masters of Glengarry, wasted no time on such notions. They saw the Society for what it truly was, and asked it to send its emigrant ships to their sea-lochs even before they served writs of eviction upon their remaining people. And as before, men were chained and bound before they could be carried to the boats. "I see the bands departing," sang a Gaelic bard, "on the white-sailed ships. I see the Gael rising from his door, I see the people going . . ."

The Highlander had one blow he could strike against his chief, against Government and establishment. When the Crimean War began in 1854 it was confidently believed in Whitehall that the Highlands would again be the military nursery they had been in the past. But recruiters who went to the West and the Isles were met by angry men who baa-ed like sheep as the drums beat and the fifes played. On his own ground the Duke of Sutherland was bluntly told "Since you have preferred sheep to men, let sheep defend you." There were no replacements for the depleted Highland battalions of Alma and Balaclava.

Alexander Mackenzie was born too late to be a witness of the earlier Clearances, and he was only sixteen when the last great wave subsided on Glengarry's land. Yet he knew and talked with many of the victims, and this book is his response to the obligations they placed upon his professional conscience. He had the courage to defend himself defiantly when it was attacked. It makes great use of Donald Macleod's *Gloomy Memories*, a bitter personal account of the Sutherland evictions and an attack on Patrick Sellar, the Marquess's factor who was tried and acquitted of culpable homicide for his part in the Strathnaver evictions. Mackenzie believed, as many still do, that the trial and the verdict were an offence to justice. In March, 1883, shortly after his book was published, he received a letter from Sellar's son, complaining of his "disproved calumnies on a dead man", demanding a retraction and reserving the right to take action if it were not made. Mackenzie's response was spirited and unrepentant, he would not retract what he had written, he would not apologise.

> The great fact of the Sutherland Clearances, as described in McLeod's book, and fully corroborated by other writers, are as true historically as those of the massacre of Cawnpore, and I cannot understand how anyone, however closely interested,

can expect that such a chapter in the history of
the Highlands, with its various lessons, can be
permitted to fall into oblivion. Your father was
acquitted of the specific charges brought against
him in Court, but the object of my book is to make
it impossible that a law should be allowed to remain on the Statute Book which still permits the
same cruelties to be carried out in the Highlands
as were carried out in Sutherland during the first
half of the present century. I am of the opinion
that I have, in all the circumstances, simply done
my duty in republishing so much of McLeod's book.

The laws which had given the Highlander no
security of tenure, which had made him the helpless
victim of Clearance and eviction, were changed as a
result of the Crofters Commission Report. This did
not stop the draining of the Highlands of their ancient
people, it did not stop the transformation of that
once populous area into a beautiful desert of sheep-
walks, deer-forests and timber plantations.

This book is perhaps as much a valediction as it
was meant to be a protest. Despite its faults—and
they are pardonable errors of judgement and emotion—it has been and will remain a book to be read,
an essential part of any study of the Clearances.
There was a great need for it when it was first published, and in human terms that need remains. It
does not contain the words of Peggy MacCormack
quoted at the beginning of this Introduction. They
were printed in 1900, two years after Mackenzie's
death, and in Alexander Carmichael's *Carmina Gad-*

elica, but they echo much of the sorrow and despair that is to be found in this work. As do the words of Catherine MacPhee, another cottar of Uist whom Carmichael recorded:

> Many a thing I have seen in my own day and generation. Many a thing, O Mary Mother of the Black Sorrows. I have seen the townships swept and the big holdings being made of them, the people driven out of the countryside to the streets of Glasgow and to the wilds of Canada, such of them as did not die of hunger and plague and smallpox going across the ocean . . . I have seen the big strong men, the champions of the country-side, being bound on Loch Boisdale quay and cast into the ship as would be done to a batch of horses and cattle, the bailiffs and the ground-officers and the constables and the policemen behind them in pursuit of them. The God of Life, and He only, knows all the loathesome work of men on that day.

John P. Tee

1979.

CONTENTS.

THE ISLE OF SKYE IN 1882—

THE HIGHLAND CLEARANCES.

SUTHERLAND.

DONALD MACLEOD'S " Gloomy Memories," originally appeared as a series of Letters in the Edinburgh *Weekly Chronicle*. These letters were afterwards published separately in a thick pamphlet ; which has long become so rare in this country that no money will procure it. After a search of more than twenty years, we' were fortunate enough to pick up a copy of the enlarged Canadian edition in Nova Scotia, during a visit there, in 1879. The Letters originally published in this country, are given in the following pages in the form in which they first appeared, with the exception of a slight toning down in two or three instances.

LETTER I.

I AM a native of Sutherlandshire, and remember when the inhabitants of that country lived comfortably and happily, when the mansions of proprietors and the abodes of factors, magistrates, and ministers, were the seats of honour, truth, and good example—when people of quality were indeed what they were styled, the friends and benefactors of

all who lived upon their domains.   But all this is changed.
Alas, alas! I have lived to see calamity upon calamity
overtake the Sutherlanders.   For five successive years, on
or about the term day, has scarcely anything been seen but
removing the inhabitants in the most cruel and unfeeling
manner, and burning the houses which they and their forefathers had occupied from time immemorial.   The country
was darkened by the smoke of the burnings, and the descendants of those who drew their swords at Bannockburn,
Sheriffmuir, and Killicrankie—the children and nearest relations of those who sustained the honour of the British name in
many a bloody field—the heroes of Egypt, Corunna, Toulouse,
Salamanca, and Waterloo—were ruined, trampled upon,
dispersed, and compelled to seek an asylum across the
Atlantic ; while those who remained from inability to emigrate, deprived of all the comforts of life, became paupers—
beggars—a disgrace to the nation whose freedom and honour
many of them had maintained by their valour and cemented
with their blood.

   To these causes the destitution and misery that exists in
Sutherlandshire are to be ascribed ; misery as great, if not
the greatest to be found in any part of the Highlands, and
that not the fruit of indolence or improvidence, as some
would allege, but the inevitable result of the avarice and
tyranny of the landlords and factors for the last thirty or
forty years ; of treatment, I presume to say, without a
parallel in the history of this nation.   I know that a great
deal has been done to mitigate the sufferings of the Highlanders some years back, both by Government aid and public
subscriptions, but the unhappy county of Sutherland was
excluded from the benefits derived from these sources, by
means of false statements and public speeches, made by
hired agents, or by those whose interest it was to conceal

the misery and destitution in the country of which themselves were the authors. Thus the Sutherlandshire sufferers have been shut out from receiving the assistance afforded by Government or by private individuals ; and owing to the thraldom and subjugation in which this once brave and happy people are to factors, magistrates, and ministers, they durst scarce whimper a complaint, much less say plainly, " Thus and thus have you done ".

On the 20th of last April, a meeting of noblemen and gentlemen, connected with different districts of Scotland, was held in the British Hotel, Edinburgh, for the purpose of making inquiry into the misery and destitution prevailing in Scotland, and particularly in the Highlands, with a view to discover the causes and discuss means for meeting the prevailing evil. Gentlemen were appointed to make the necessary inquiry, and a committee named, with which these gentlemen were to communicate. At this meeting a Sutherlandshire proprietor made such representations regarding the inhabitants of that county, that, relying, I suppose, on his mere assertions, the proposed inquiry has never been carried into that district. Under these circumstances, I, who have been largely a sufferer, and a spectator of the sufferings of multitudes of my countrymen, would have felt myself deeply culpable if I kept silence, and did not take means to lay before the committee and the public the information of which I am possessed, to put the benevolent on their guard respecting the men who undertake to pervert, if they cannot stifle, the inquiry as to the causes and extent of distress in the shire of Sutherland. With a view to discharging this incumbent duty, I published a few remarks, signed " A Highlander," in the *Edinburgh Weekly Journal* of 29th May last, on the aforesaid proprietor's speech ; to which he made a reply, accusing me of singular ignorance and misrepresentation, and endeavouring to exonerate himself. Another letter has since appeared in the same paper, signed, "A Sutherlandshire Tenant," denying my assertions and challenging me to prove them by stating facts. To meet this challenge, aud to let these parties know that I am not so ignorant as they would represent; and also to afford information to the before-mentioned committee, it being impossible for those gentlemen to apply an adequate remedy till they know the real cause and nature of the disease, I addressed a second letter to the editor of the *Weekly Journal;* but, to my astonishment, it was refused insertion; through what influence I am not prepared to say. I have, in consequence, been subjected to much reflection and obloquy for deserting a cause which would be so much benefited by public discussion; and for failing to substantiate charges so publicly made. I have, therefore, now to request, that, through the medium of your valuable and impartial paper, the public may be made acquainted with the real state of the case; and I pledge myself not only to meet the two opponents mentioned, but to produce and substantiate such a series of appalling facts, as will sufficiently account for the distress prevailing in Sutherlandshire; and, I trust, have a tendency towards its mitigation.

LETTER II.

PREVIOUS to redeeming my pledge to bring before the Public a series of facts relating to the more recent oppressions and expatriation of the unfortunate inhabitants of Sutherlandshire, it is necessary to take a brief retrospective glance at the original causes.

Down from the feudal times, the inhabitants of the hills

and straths of Sutherlandshire, in a state of transition from vassalage to tenancy, looked upon the farms they occupied from their ancestors as their own, though subject to the arrangements as to rent, duties and services imposed by the chief in possession, to whom, though his own title might be equivocal, they habitually looked up with a degree of clannish veneration. Every thing was done "to please the Laird". In this kind of patriarchial dominion on the one side, and obedience and confidence on the other, did the late tenantry and their progenitors experience much happiness, and a degree of congenial comfort and simple pastoral enjoyment. But the late war and its consequences interfered with this happy state of things, and hence a foundation was laid for all the suffering and depopulation which has followed. This has not been peculiar to Sutherlandshire ; the general plan of almost all the Highland proprietors of that period being to get rid of the original inhabitants, and turn the land into sheep farms, though from peculiar circumstances this plan was there carried into effect with more revolting and wholesale severity than in any of the surrounding counties.

The first attempt at a general *Clearing* was partially made in Ross-shire, about the beginning of the present century ; but from the resistance of the tenantry and other causes, it has never been carried into general operation. The same was more or less the case in other counties. Effects do not occur without cause, nor do men become tyrants and monsters of cruelty all at once. Self-interest, real or imaginary, first prompts ; the moral boundary is overstepped, the oppressed offer either passive or active resistance, and, in the arrogance of power, the strong resort to such means as will effect their purpose, reckless of consequences, and enforcing what they call the rights of property, utterly neglect its duties. I do not pretend to represent the late Duchess or Duke of Sutherlandshire in particular, as destitute of the common attributes of humanity, however atrocious may have been the acts perpetrated in their name, or by their authority. They were generally absentees, and while they gave-in to the general clearing scheme, I have no doubt they wished it to be carried into effect with as little hardship as possible. But their prompters and underlings pursued a more reckless course, and, intent only on their own selfish ends, deceived these high personages, representing the people as slothful and rebellious, while, as they pretended, everything necessary was done for their accommodation.

I have mentioned above that the late war and its consequences laid the foundation of the evil complained of. Great Britain with her immense naval and military establishments, being in a great measure shut out from foreign supplies, and in a state of hostility or non-intercourse with all Europe and North America, almost all the necessaries of life had to be drawn from our own soil. Hence, its whole powers of production were required to supply the immense and daily increasing demand; and while the agricultural portions of the country were strained to yield an increase of grain, the more northern and mountainous districts were looked to for additional supplies of animal food. Hence, also, all the speculations to get rid of the human inhabitants of the Highlands, and replace them with cattle and sheep for the English market. At the conclusion of the war, these effects were about to cease with their cause, but the corn laws, and other food taxes then interfered, and the excluding of foreign animal food altogether, and grain till it was at a famine price, caused the increasing population to press against home produce, so as still to make it the interest of

the Highland lairds to prefer cattle to human beings, and to
encourage speculators with capital from England and the
south of Scotland to take the lands over the heads of the
original tenantry.   Thus Highland wrongs were continued,
and annually augmented, till the mass of guilt on the one
hand, and of suffering on the other, became so great as
almost to exceed description or belief.   Hence the difficulty
of bringing it fully before the public, especially as those
interested in suppressing inquiry are numerous, powerful,
and unsparing in the use of every influence to stop the
mouths of the sufferers.   Almost all the new tenants in
Sutherlandshire have been made justices of the peace, or
otherwise armed with authority, and can thus, under colour
of law, commit violence and oppression whenever they find
it convenient—the poor people having no redress and scarce
daring even to complain.   The clergy also, whose duty it is
to denounce the oppressors, and aid the oppressed, have all,
the whole seventeen parish ministers in Sutherlandshire,
with one exception, found their account in abetting the
wrong-doers, exhorting the people to quiet submission, helping to stifle their cries, telling them that all their sufferings
came from the hand of God, and was a just punishment for
their sins !   In what manner these reverend gentlemen were
benefited by the change, and bribed thus to desert the
cause of the people, I shall explain as I proceed.

The whole county, with the exception of a comparatively
small part of one parish, held by Mr. Dempster of Skibo,
and similar portions on the outskirts of the county held by
two or three other proprietors, is now in the hands of the
Sutherland family, who, very rarely, perhaps only once in
four or five years, visit their Highland estates.   Hence the
impunity afforded to the actors in the scenes of devastation
and cruelty—the wholesale expulsion of the people, and

pulling down and burning their habitations, which latter proceeding was peculiar to Sutherlandshire. In my subsequent communications I shall produce a selection of such facts and incidents, as can be supported by sufficient testimony, to many of which I was an eye-witness, or was otherwise cognizant of them. I have been, with my family, for many years, removed, and at a distance from those scenes, and have no personal malice to gratify, my only motive being a desire to vindicate my ill-used countrymen from the aspersions cast upon them, to draw public attention to their wrongs, and, if possible, to bring about a fair inquiry, to be conducted by disinterested men, as to the real causes, of their long-protracted misery and destitution, in order that the public sympathies may be awakened in their behalf, and something effected for their relief. With these observations I now conclude, and in my next letter I will enter upon my narration of a few of such facts as can be fully authenticated by living testimony.

LETTER III.

In my last letter, I endeavoured to trace the causes that led to the general clearing and consequent distress in Sutherlandshire, which dates its commencement from the year 1807. Previous to that period, partial removals had taken place, on the estates of Lord Reay, Mr. Honeyman of Armidale, and others: but these removals were under ordinary and comparatively favourable circumstances. Those who were ejected from their farms, were accommodated with smaller portions of land, and those who chose to emigrate had means in their power to do so, by the sale of their cattle, which then fetched an extraordinary high price. But in the year above mentioned, the system commenced on the Duchess of Sutherland's property; about 90 families were removed from the parishes of Farr and Larg. These people were, however, in some degree provided for, by giving them smaller lots of land, but many of these lots were at a distance of from 10 to 17 miles, so that the people had to remove their cattle and furniture thither, leaving the crops on the ground behind. Watching this crop from trespass of the cattle of the incoming tenants, and removing it in the autumn, was attended with great difficulty and loss. Besides, there was also much personal suffering, from their having to pull down their houses and carry away the timber of them, to erect houses on their new possessions, which houses they had to inhabit immediately on being covered in, and in the meantime, to live and sleep in the open air, except a few, who might be fortunate enough to get an unoccupied barn, or shed, from some of their charitable new-come neighbours.

The effects of these circumstances on the health of the aged and infirm, and on the women and children, may be readily conceived—some lost their lives, and others contracted diseases that stuck to them for life.

During the year 1809, in the parishes of Dornoch, Rogart, Loth, Clyne, and Golspie, an extensive removal took place; several hundred families were turned out, but under circumstances of greater severity than the preceding. Every means were resorted to, to discourage the people, and to persuade them to give up their holdings quietly, and quit the country; and to those who could not be induced to do so, scraps of moor, and bog lands, were offered in Dornoch moor, and Brora links, on which it was next to impossible to exist, in order that they may be scared into going entirely away. At this time, the estate was under the management of Mr. Young, a corn-dealer, as chief, and Mr. Patrick Sellar, a writer, as under-Factor, the latter of whom will make a conspicuous figure in my future communications. These gentlemen were both from Morayshire ; and, in order to favour their own country people, and get rid of the natives, the former were constantly employed in all the improvements and public works under their direction, while the latter were taken at inferior wages, and only when strangers could not be had.

Thus, a large portion of the people of these five parishes were, in the course of two or three years, almost entirely rooted out, and those few who took the miserable allotments above mentioned, and some of their descendants, continue to exist on them in great poverty. Among these were the widows and orphans of those heads of families who had been drowned in the same year, in going to attend a fair, when upwards of one hundred individuals lost their lives, while crossing the ferry between Sutherland and Tain. These destitute creatures were obliged to accept of any spot which afforded them a residence, from inability to go elsewhere.

From this time till 1812 the process of ejection was carried on annually, in a greater or less degree, and during this period the estates of Gordonbush and Uppet were added, by purchase, to the ducal property, and in the subsequent years, till 1829, the whole of the county, with the small exceptions before mentioned, had passed into the hands of this great family.

In the year 1811 a new era of depopulation commenced ; summonses of removal were served on large portions of the inhabitants. The lands were divided into extensive lots, and advertised to be let for sheep farms.

Strangers were seen daily traversing the country, viewing these lots, previous to bidding for them. They appeared to be in great fear of rough treatment from the inhabitants whom they were about to supersede ; but the event proved they had no cause ; they were uniformly treated with civility, and even hospitality, thus affording no excuse for the measures of severity to which the factors and their adherents afterwards had recourse. However, the pretext desired was soon found in an apparently concerted plan. A person from the south, of the name of Reid, a manager on one of the sheep farms, raised an alarm that he had been pursued by some of the natives of Kildonan, and put in bodily fear. The factors eagerly jumped as this trumped-up story ; they immediately swore-in from sixty to one hundred retainers, and the new inhabitants, as special constables ; trimmed and charged the cannon at Dunrobin Castle, which had reposed in silence since the last defeat of the unfortunate Stuarts. Messengers were then dispatched, warning the people to attend at the castle at a certain hour, under the pretence of making amicable arrangements. Accordingly, large numbers prepared to obey the summons, ignorant of their enemies' intentions, till, when about six miles from the castle, a large body of them got a hint of their danger from some one in the secret, on which they called a halt and held a consultation, when it was resolved to pass on to the Inn at Golspie, and there await the recontre with the factors. The latter were much disappointed at this derangement of their plans ; but on their arrival with the sheriff, constables, and others, they told the people, to their astonishment, that a number of them were to be apprehended, and sent to Dornoch Jail, on *suspicion* of an attempt to take Mr. Reid's life ! The people, with one voice, declared their innocence, and that they would not suffer any of their number to be imprisoned on such a pretence. Without further provocation, the sheriff proceeded to read the riot act, a thing quite new and unintelligible to the poor Sutherlanders so long accustomed to bear their wrongs patiently ; however, they immediately

dispersed and returned to their homes in peace.   The
factors, having now found the pretext desired, mounted their
horses and galloped to the castle in pretended alarm, sought
protection under the guns of their fortress, and sent an
express to Fort George for a military force to suppress the
rebellion in Sutherlandshire!   The 21st Regiment of foot
(Irish) was accordingly ordered to proceed by forced marches,
night and day, a distance of fifty miles, with artillery, and
cart-loads of ammunition.   On their arrival, some of them
were heard to declare they would now have revenge on the
Sutherlanders for the carnage of their countrymen at Tara-
hill and Ballynamuck; but they were disappointed, for they
found no rebels to cope with; so that, after having made a
few prisoners, who were all liberated on a precognition being
taken, they were ordered away to their barracks.   The
people, meantime, dismayed and spirit-broken at the array
of power brought against them, and seeing nothing but
enemies on every side, even in those from whom they should
have had comfort and succour, quietly submitted to their
fate.   The clergy, too, were continually preaching submission, declaring these proceedings were fore-ordained of
God, and denouncing the vengeance of Heaven and eternal
damnation on those who should presume to make the least
resistance.   No wonder the poor Highlanders quailed under
such influences; and the result was, that large districts of
the parishes before mentioned were dispossessed at the May
term, 1812.

The Earl of Selkirk hearing of these proceedings, came
personally into Sutherlandshire, and by fair promises of
encouragement, and other allurements, induced a number of
the distressed outcasts to enter into an arrangement with him,
to emigrate to his estates on the Red River, North America.
Accordingly, a whole shipful of them went thither; but on

their arrival, after a tedious and disastrous passage, they found themselves deceived and deserted by his lordship, and left to their fate in an inclement wilderness, without protection against the savages, who plundered them on their arrival, and, finally massacred them all, with the exception of a few who escaped with their lives, and travelled across trackless wilds till they at last arrived in Canada.

This is a brief recital of the proceedings up to 1813; and these were the only acts of riot and resistance that ever took place in Sutherlandshire.

LETTER IV.

In the month of March, 1814, a great number of the inhabitants of the parishes of Farr and Kildonan were summoned to give up their farms at the May term following, and, in order to ensure and hasten their removal with their cattle, in a few days after, the greatest part of the heath pasture was set fire to and burnt, by order of Mr. Sellar, the factor, who had taken these lands for himself. It is necessary to explain the effects of this proceeding. In the spring, especially when fodder is scarce, as was the case in the above year, the Highland cattle depend almost solely on the heather. As soon, too, as the grass begins to sprout about the roots of the bushes, the animals get a good bite, and are thus kept in tolerable condition. Deprived of this resource by the burning, the cattle were generally left without food, and this being the period of temporary peace, during Buonaparte's residence in Elba, there was little demand for good cattle, much less for these poor starving animals, who roamed about over their burnt pasture till a great part of them were lost, or sold for a mere trifle. The arable parts of the land were cropped by the outgoing tenants, as is customary, but the fences being mostly destroyed by the burning, the cattle of the incoming tenant were continually trespassing throughout the summer and harvest, and those who remained to look after the crop had no shelter; even watching being disallowed, and the people were hunted by the new herdsmen and their dogs from watching their own corn! As the spring had been severe, so the harvest was wet, cold, and disastrous for the poor people, who, under every difficulty, were endeavouring to secure the residue of their crops. The barns, kilns, and mills, except a few necessary to the new tenant, had, as well as the houses, been burnt or otherwise destroyed and no shelter left, except on the other side of the river, now overflowing its banks from the continual rains; so that, after all their labour and privations, the people lost nearly the whole of their crops, as they had already lost their cattle, and were thus entirely ruined.

But I must now go back to the May term and attempt to give some account of the ejection of the inhabitants; for to give anything like an adequate description I am not capable. If I were, its horrors would exceed belief.

The houses had been all built, not by the landlord as in the low country, but by the tenants or by their ancestors, and, consequently, were their property by right, if not by law. They were timbered chiefly with bog fir, which makes excellent roofing but is very inflammable: by immemorial usage this species of timber was considered the property of the tenant on whose lands it was found. To the upland timber, for which the laird or the factor had to be asked, the laird might lay some claim, but not so to the other sort, and in every house there was generally a part of both.

In former removals the tenants had been allowed to carry

away this timber to erect houses on their new allotments but now a more summary mode was adopted, by setting fire to the houses! The able-bodied men were by this time away after their cattle or otherwise engaged at a distance, so that the immediate sufferers by the general house-burning that now commenced were the aged and infirm, the women and children. As the lands were now in the hands of the factor himself, and were to be occupied as sheep-farms, and as the people made no resistance, they expected at least some indulgence, in the way of permission to occupy their houses and other buildings till they could gradually remove, and meanwhile look after their growing crops. Their consternation, was, therefore, the greater when, immediately after the May term day, and about two months after they had received summonses of removal, a commencement was made to pull down and set fire to the houses over their heads! The old people, women, and others, then began to try to preserve the timber which they were entitled to consider as their own. But the devastators proceeded with the greatest celerity, demolishing all before them, and when they had overthrown the houses in a large tract of country, they ultimately set fire to the wreck. So that timber, furniture, and every other article that could not be instantly removed, was consumed by fire, or otherwise utterly destroyed.

These proceedings were carried on with the greatest rapidity as well as with most reckless cruelty. The cries of the victims, the confusion, the despair and horror painted on the countenances of the one party, and the exulting ferocity of the other, beggar all description. In these scenes Mr. Sellar was present, and apparently, (as was sworn by several witnesses at his subsequent trial,) ordering and directing the whole. Many deaths ensued from alarm, from fatigue, and cold; the people being instantly deprived of shelter, and left to the mercy of the elements.   Some old men took to the woods and precipices, wandering about in a state approaching to, or of absolute insanity, and several of them, in this situation, lived only a few days.   Pregnant women were taken with premature labour, and several children did not long survive their sufferings.   To these scenes I was an eye-witness, and am ready to substantiate the truth of my statements, not only by my own testimony, but by that of many others who were present at the time.

In such a scene of general devastation it is almost useless to particularize the cases of individuals—the suffering was great and universal.   I shall, however, just notice a very few of the extreme cases which occur to my recollection, to most of which I was an eye-witness.   John MacKay's wife, Ravigill, in attempting to pull down her house, in the absence of her husband, to preserve the timber, fell through the roof. She was, in consequence, taken with premature labour, and in that state, was exposed to the open air and the view of the by-standers.   Donald Munro, Garvott, lying in a fever, was turned out of his house and exposed to the elements. Donald Macbeath, an infirm and bed-ridden old man, had the house unroofed over him, and was, in that state, exposed to wind and rain till death put a period to his sufferings.   I was present at the pulling down and burning of the house of William Chisholm, Badinloskin, in which was lying his wife's mother, an old bed-ridden woman of near 100 years of age, none of the family being present.   I informed the persons about to set fire to the house of this circumstance, and prevailed on them to wait till Mr. Sellar came.   On his arrival I told him of the poor old woman being in a condition unfit for removal.   He replied, "Damn her, the old witch, she has lived too long; let her burn".   Fire was immediately set to the house, and the blankets in which she was carried were in flames before she could be got out. She was placed in a little shed, and it was with great difficulty they were prevented from firing it also. The old woman's daughter arrived while the house was on fire, and assisted the neighbours in removing her mother out of the flames and smoke, presenting a picture of horror which I shall never forget, but cannot attempt to describe. She died within five days.

I could multiply instances to a great extent, but must leave to the reader to conceive the state of the inhabitants during this scene of general devastation, to which few parallels occur in the history of this or any other civilized country. Many a life was lost or shortened, and many a strong constitution ruined ;—the comfort and social happiness of all destroyed ; and their prospects in life, then of the most dismal kind, have, generally speaking, been unhappily realized.

LETTER V.

AT the spring assizes of Inverness, in 1816, Mr. Sellar was brought to trial, before Lord Pitmilly, for his proceedings, as partly detailed in my last letter. The indictment, charging him with culpable homicide, fire-raising, &c., was prosecuted by his Majesty's advocate. In the report of the trial, published by Mr. Sellar's counsel, it is said, " To this measure his lordship seems to have been induced, chiefly for the purpose of satisfying the public mind and putting an end to the clamours of the country ". If this, and not the ends of justice, was the intention, it was completely successful, for the gentleman was acquitted, to the astonishment of the natives, and the oppressors were thereby emboldened to proceed in their subsequent operations with a higher hand, and with perfect impunity, as will be seen in the sequel.

It is a difficult and hazardous attempt to impugn proceedings carried on by his Majesty's advocate, presided over by an honourable judge, and decided by a jury of respectable men; but I may mention a few circumstances which might have a tendency to disappoint the people. Out of forty witnesses examined at a precognition before the sheriff, there were only eleven, and those not the most competent, brought forward for the crown; and the rest, some of whom might have supported material parts of the indictment—as, for instance, in the case of Donald Monro—were never called at all. Besides, the witnesses for the prosecution, being simple, illiterate persons, gave their testimony in Gaelic, which was interpreted to the court; and, it is well known, much depends upon the translator, whether evidence so taken, retains its weight and strength or not. The jury, with very few exceptions, was composed of persons just similiarly circumstanced with the *new* tenants in Sutherlandshire, and consequently, might very naturally have a leaning to that side, and all the exculpatory witnesses were those who had been art and part, or otherwise interested, in the outrageous proceedings. Mr. Sellar was a man of talent, an expert lawyer, and a justice of the peace, invested with full powers, as factor and law agent to a great absentee proprietor, and strongly supported by the clergy and gentry in the neighbourhood: he was also the incoming tenant to the lands which were the scene of his proceedings—too great odds against a few poor simple Highlanders, who had only their wrongs to plead, whose minds were comparatively uncultivated, and whose pecuniary means were small.

The immediate cause which led to these legal proceedings was, that several petitions from the expelled tenants had been sent to the noble proprietors, representing the illegal and cruel treatment they had received; and, in consequence of the answers received expressing a wish that justice might be done, the case was laid before the sheriff-depute, Mr. Cranstoun, who sent an express injunction to Mr. Robert MacKid, sheriff-substitute for the county, to take a precognition of the case, and if there appeared sufficient cause, to take Mr. Sellar into custody. The sheriff-substitute was a man of acknowledged probity, but from the representations he had previously received, was considered unfavourable to the cause of the people. On examining the witnesses, however, a case of such enormity was made out as induced him to use some strong expressions contained in a letter to Lord Stafford, which I here subjoin, and which, with some false allegations, were urged against him on the trial, so that, under the direction of the court, the advocate-depute passed from his evidence on the grounds of malice and unduly expressed opinion, and thus Mr. MacKid's important testimony was lost. On the whole, this case furnishes an instance of "the glorious uncertainty of LAW".

TO LORD STAFFORD.

KIRKTOWN P. GOLSPIE, 30th May, 1815.

MY LORD,—I conceive it a duty I owe to your Lordship, to address you upon the present occasion, and a more distressing task I have seldom had to perform.

Your Lordship knows, that in summer last, a humble petition, subscribed by a number of tenants on Mr. Sellar's sheep farm in Farr and Kildonan, was presented to Lady Stafford, complaining of various acts of injury, cruelty and oppression, alleged to have been committed upon their persons and property, by Mr. Sellar, in the spring and summer of that year.

To this complaint, her ladyship, upon the 22nd of July last, was graciously pleased to return an answer in writing. In it, her Ladyship, with her usual candour and justice, with much propriety observes, "That if any person on the estate shall receive any illegal treatment, she will never consider it as hostile to her if they have recourse to legal redress, as a most secure way to receive the justice which she always desires they should have on every occasion". Her Ladyship also intimates, "That she had communicated the complaint to Mr. Sellar, that he may make proper inquiry and answer to her".

It would appear, however, that Mr. Sellar still refused, or delayed, to afford that redress to the removed tenants to which they conceived themselves entitled, which emboldened them to approach Earl Gower with a complaint, similar to the one they had presented to Lady Stafford.

To this complaint his Lordship graciously condescended, under date 8th February last, to return such an answer as might have been expected from his Lordship. His Lordship says that he has communicated the contents to your Lordship and Lady Stafford, who, as his Lordship nobly expresses himself, "Are desirous, that the tenants should know, that it is always their wish that justice should be impartially administered". His lordship then adds, that he has sent the petition, with directions to Mr. Young, that proper steps should be taken for laying the business before the sheriff-depute; and that the petitioners would therefore be assisted by Mr. Young, if they desired it, in having the precognition taken before the sheriff-depute, according to their petition.

Soon after receipt of Earl Gower's letter, it would appear that a copy of the petition, with his Lordship's answer, had been transmitted to the sheriff-depute by the tenants. Mr. Cranstoun, in answer, upon 30th March last, says, "that if the tenants mean to take a precognition immediately, it will proceed before the sheriff-substitute, as my engagement will not permit me to be in Sutherland until the month of July".

In consequence of these proceedings, on an express injunction from his Majesty's advocate-depute, and a similar one from the sheriff-depute, I was compelled to enter upon an investigation of the complaints.

With this view I was induced to go into Strathnaver, where, at considerable personal inconvenience and expense, and with much patient perseverance, I examined about forty evidences upon the allegations stated in the tenants' petition; and it is with the deepest regret I have to inform your lordship, that a more numerous catalogue of crimes, perpetrated by an individual, has seldom disgraced any country, or sullied the pages of a precognition in Scotland.

This being the case, the laws of the country imperiously call upon me to order Mr. Sellar to be arrested and incarcerated, in order for trial, and before this reaches your Lordship this preparatory legal step must be put in execution.

No person can more sincerely regret the cause, nor more feelingly lament the effect, than I do; but your Lordship knows well, and as Earl Gower very properly observed, "Justice should be impartially administered".

I have, in confidence, stated verbally to Mr. Young my fears upon this distressing subject, and I now take the liberty of stating my sentiments also to your lordship, in confidence.

The crimes of which Mr. Sellar stands accused are,—

1. Wilful fire-raising; by having set on fire, and reduced to ashes, a poor man's whole premises, including dwelling-house, barn, kiln, and sheep-cot, attended with most aggravated circumstances of cruelty, if not murder.

2. Throwing down and demolishing a mill, also a capital crime.

3. Setting fire to and burning the tenants' heath pasture, before the legal term of removal.

4. Throwing down and demolishing houses, whereby the lives of sundry aged and bed-ridden persons were endangered, if not actually lost.

5. Throwing down and demolishing barns, kilns, sheep-cots, &c., to the great hurt and prejudice of the owners.

6. Innumerable other charges of lesser importance swell the list.

I subjoin a copy of Mr. Cranstoun's letter to me upon this subject, for your lordship's information, and have the honour to be, &c.,

(Signed) ROBT. MACKID.

Here I must part with Messrs. Young and Sellar as agents for the noble family of Sutherland, for about this time they ceased to act as such. I shall in my next, proceed to describe the devastating removals of 1819 and '20—those which happened in the intermediate years between these and the year 1815, being similar in character to the removals I have already described. Mr. Sellar shall hereafter only figure in my narrative as a leviathan tenant, who individually supplanted scores of the worthy small farmers of the parish of Farr.

LETTER VI.

THE integrity manifested by the sheriffs, Cranstoun and MacKid, led to their dismissal from office, immediately after the trial. This dismissal operated as a sentence of banishment and ruin to Mr. MacKid—his business in Sutherlandshire was at an end; he retired to Caithness with a large family, and commenced business as a writer, where every malignant influence followed him from the ruling powers in the former county. It is to be hoped that this upright gentleman has since surmounted his difficulties; he must at all events have enjoyed a high reward in the testimony of a good conscience.

I have hitherto given the noble proprietors the title they bore at the time of the occurrences mentioned, but in order to avoid ambiguity, it may be necessary to give a very brief historical sketch of the family. The late Duchess of Sutherland, premier peeress of Scotland, in her own right, succeeded to the estates of her father, William, 21st Earl of Sutherland, with the title of Countess, in the year 1766, being then only one year old. In 1785 she married the Marquis of Stafford and took his title in addition.

In the year 1833, the Marquis was created a Duke, and his lady was subsequently styled Duchess-Countess of Sutherland. She was a lady of superior mind and attainments, but her great and good qualities were lost to her Highland tenantry, from her being non-resident, and having adopted the plan of removing the natives, and letting the lands to strangers. Their eldest surviving son, Lord Leveson Gower, also an eminent person, succeeded to the titles and estates of both parents on their decease, and is now the Duke of Sutherland.

The family mansion, Dunrobin Castle, is situated on the southern border of the county, and in the rare case of any of the noble family coming to the Highlands during the period of the removals, they only came to the castle and stopped there, where the old tenants were strictly denied access, while the new occupiers had free personal communication with the proprietors. When any memorial or petition from the former could be got introduced, there was no attention paid to them if not signed by a minister ; and this was next to impossible, as the clergy, with one honourable exception, had taken the other side. In every case it appeared that the factors and ministers were consulted, and the decision given according to their suggestions and advice.

On the resignation or dismissal of Messrs. Young and Sellar, Mr. Loch, now M.P. for the Northern Burghs, came into full power as chief, and a Mr. Suther as under factor. Mr. Loch is a Scotsman, but not a Highlander. He had previously been chief agent on the English estates, general adviser in the proceedings relative to the Sutherland tenantry, and cognizant of all the severities towards them. This gentleman has written a work entitled, "An Account of the Improvements on the estates of the Marquis of Stafford, in the counties of Stafford and Salop, and on the estate of Sutherland," in which he has attempted to justify or palliate the proceedings in which he bore a most important part. His book is, therefore, scarce ever to be relied on for a single fact, when the main object interfered; he vilifies the High-landers, and misrepresents every thing to answer his purpose. He has been fully answered, his arguments refuted, and his sophistries exposed by Major-General Stewart, in his "Sketches of the Character and Manners of the Highlanders of Scotland," to which excellent work I beg to call the attention of every friend to truth and justice, and especially those who take an interest in the fate of the expatriated tenantry. The General has completely vindicated the character of the Highland tenantry, and shown the impolicy, as well as cruelty, of the means used for their ejection. The removal of Messrs. Young and Sellar, particularly the latter, from the power they had exercised so despotically, was hailed with the greatest joy by the people, to whom their very names were a terror. Their appearance in any neighbour-hood had been such a cause of alarm, as to make women fall into fits, and in one instance caused a woman to lose her reason, which, as far as I know, she has not yet recovered; whenever she saw a stranger she cried out, with a terrific tone and manner, *Oh! sin Sellar!*—"Oh! there's Sellar!"

Bitter, however, was the people's disappointment when they found the way in which the new factors began to exercise their powers.   The measures of their predecessors were continued and aggravated, though, on account of unexpired leases, the removals were but partial till the years 1819 and 1820.   However, I must not pass over the expulsion and sufferings of forty families who were removed by Mr. Sellar, almost immediately after his trial.   This person, not finding it convenient to occupy the whole of the 6,000 or 7,000 acres, which he had obtained possession of, and partially cleared in 1814, had agreed to let these forty families remain as tenants at will; but he now proceeded to remove them in the same unfeeling manner as he had ejected the others, only he contented himself with utterly demolishing their houses, barns, &c., but did not, as before, set fire to them till the inmates were removed; they leaving their crops in the ground as before described.   This year (1816) will be remembered for its severity by many in Scotland.   The winter commenced by the snow falling in large quantities in the month of October, and continued with increasing rigour, so that the difficulty—almost impossibility—of the people, without barns or shelter of any kind, securing their crops, may be easily conceived.   I have seen scores of these poor outcasts employed for weeks together, with the snow from two to four feet deep, watching their corn from being devoured by the hungry sheep of the incoming tenants; carrying *on their backs*—horses being unavailable in such a case, across a country, without roads—on an average of twenty miles, to their new allotments on the sea-coast, any portion of their grain and potatoes they could secure under such dreadful circumstances.   During labour and sufferings, which none but a Highlander could sustain, they had to subsist entirely on potatoes dug out of the snow; cooking them as they could, in the open air, among the ruins of their once comfortable dwellings ! While alternate frosts and thaws, snow-storms and rain were succeeding each other in all the severity of mid-winter, the people might be seen carrying on their labours, and bearing their burdens of damp produce, under which many, especially the females, were occasionally sinking in a fainting state, till assisted by others little better off than themselves. In some very rare instances only, a little humane assistance was afforded by the shepherds; in general, their tender mercies, like those of their unfeeling masters, were only cruelties.

The filling up of this feeble outline must be left to the imagination of the reader, but I may mention that attendant on all previous and subsequent removals, and especially this one, many severe diseases made their appearance ; such as had been hitherto almost unknown among the Highland population ; viz., typhus fever, consumption, and pulmonary complaints in all their varieties, bloody flux, bowel complaints, eruptions, rheumatisms, piles, and maladies peculiar to females. So that the new and uncomfortable dwellings of this lately robust and healthy peasantry, "their country's pride," were now become family hospitals and lazar-houses of the sick and the dying ! Famine and utter destitution inevitably followed, till the misery of my once happy countrymen reached an alarming height, and began to attract attention as an almost national calamity.

Even Mr. Loch in his before-mentioned work, has been constrained to admit the extreme distress of the people. He says, (page 76,) " Their wretchedness was so great, that after pawning everything they possessed, to the fishermen on the coast, such as had no cattle were reduced to come down from the hills in hundreds, for the purpose of gathering cockles on the shore. Those who lived in the more remote situations

of the country were obliged to subsist upon broth made of
nettles, thickened with a little oatmeal. Those who had
cattle had recourse to the still more wretched expedient of
bleeding them, and mixing the blood with oatmeal, which
they afterwards cut into slices and fried. Those who had a
little money, came down and slept all night upon the beach,
in order to watch the boats returning from the fishing, that
they might be in time to obtain a part of what had been
caught." This gentleman, however, omits to mention, the
share he had in bringing things to such a pass, and also that,
at the same time, he had armed constables stationed at
Little-ferry, the only place where shell-fish were to be found,
to prevent the people from gathering them. In his next page
he gives an exaggerated account of the relief afforded by the
proprietors. I shall not copy his mis-statements, but proceed
to say what that relief, so ostentatiously put forth, really consisted of. As to his assertion that "£3,000 had been given
by way of loan to those who had cattle," I look upon it as
a fabrication, or, if the money really was sent by the noble
proprietors, it must have been retained by those intrusted
with its distribution ; for, to my knowledge, it never came to
the hands of any of the small tenants. There was, indeed, a
considerable quantity of meal sent, though far from enough
to afford effectual relief, but this meal represented to be given
in charity, was charged at the following Martinmas term, at
the rate of 50s. per boll. Payment was rigorously exacted,
and those who had cattle were obliged to give them up for
that purpose, but this latter part of the story was never sent
to the newspapers, and Mr. Loch has also forgotten to
mention it ! There was a considerable quantity of medicine
given to the ministers for distribution, for which no charge
was made, and this was the whole amount of relief afforded.

LETTER VII.

THE honourable acquittal of Mr. Sellar, and the compliments he received, in consequence, from the presiding judge, with the dismissal of the sheriffs, had the desired effect upon the minds of the poor Sutherlanders, and those who took an interest in their case. Every voice in their behalf was silenced and every pen laid down—in short, every channel for redress or protection from future violence was closed; the people were prostrated under the feet of their oppressors, who well knew how to take advantage of their position. It appeared, that, for a considerable interval, there were no regular sheriffs in the county, and that the authority usually exercised by them was vested in Captain Kenneth MacKay, a native of the county, and now one of its extensive sheep farmers. It was by virtue of warrants granted by this gentleman that the proceedings I am about to describe took place, and, if the sheriff-officers, constables, and assistants, exceeded their authority, they did so under his immediate eye and cognizance, as he was all the time residing in his house, situated so that he must have witnessed a great part of the scene from his own front windows. Therefore, if he did not immediately authorize the atrocities to the extent committed (which I will not assert), he at least used no means to restrain them.

At this period a great majority of the inhabitants were tenants-at-will, and therefore liable to ejectment on getting regular notice; there were, however, a few who had still existing tacks (although some had been wheedled or frightened into surrendering them), and these were, of course, unmolested till the expiration of their tacks; they were then turned out like the rest; but the great body of the tenantry were in the former condition. Meantime, the factors, taking advantage of the broken spirit and prostrate state of the people—trembling at their words or even looks—betook themselves to a new scheme to facilitate their intended proceedings, and this was to induce every householder to sign a bond or paper containing a promise of removal; and alternate threats and promises were used to induce them to do so. The promises were never realised, but, notwithstanding the people's compliance, the threats were put in execution. In about a month after the factors had obtained this promise of removal, and thirteen days before the May term, the work of devastation was begun. They commenced by setting fire to the houses of the small tenants in extensive districts—part of the parishes of Farr, Rogart, Golspie, and the whole parish of Kildonan. I was an eye-witness of the scene. This calamity came on the people quite unexpectedly. Strong parties, for each district, furnished with faggots and other combustibles, rushed on the dwellings of this devoted people, and immediately commenced setting fire to them, proceeding in their work with the greatest rapidity till about three hundred houses were in flames! The consternation and confusion were extreme; little or no time was given for removal of persons or property—the people striving to remove the sick and the helpless before the fire should reach them—next, struggling to save the most valuable of their effects. The cries of the women and children—the roaring of the affrighted cattle, hunted at the same time by the yelling dogs of the shepherds amid the smoke and fire—altogether presented a scene that completely baffles description: it required to be seen to be believed. A dense cloud of smoke enveloped the whole country by day, and even extended far on the sea; at night an awfully grand, but terrific scene presented itself—all the houses in an extensive district in flames at once! I myself ascended a height about eleven o'clock in the evening, and counted two hundred and fifty blazing houses, many of the owners of which were my relations, and all of whom I personally knew ; but whose present condition, whether in or out of the flames, I could not tell. The conflagration lasted six days, till the whole of the dwellings were reduced to ashes or smoking ruins. During one of these days a boat lost her way in the dense smoke as she approached the shore ; but at night she was enabled to reach a landing place by the light of the flames !

It would be an endless task to give a detail of the sufferings of families and individuals during this calamitous period ; or to describe its dreadful consequences on the health and lives of the victims.   I will, however, attempt a very few cases.   While the burning was going on, a small sloop arrived, laden with quick-lime, and while discharging her cargo, the skipper agreed to take as many of the people to Caithness as he could carry, on his return.   Accordingly, about twenty families went on board, filling deck, hold, and every part of the vessel.   There were childhood and age, male and female, sick and well, with a small portion of their effects, saved from the flames, all huddled together in heaps. Many of these persons had never been on sea before, and when they began to sicken a scene indescribable ensued. To add to their miseries, a storm and contrary winds prevailed, so that instead of a day or two, the usual time of passage, it was *nine days* before they reached Caithness.   All this time, the poor creatures, almost without necessaries, most of them dying with sickness, were either wallowing among the lime, and various excrements in the hold, or lying on the deck, exposed to the raging elements ! This voyage soon proved fatal to many, and some of the survivors feel its effects to this day.   During this time, also, typhus fever was raging in the country, and many in a critical state had to fly, or were carried by their friends out of the burning houses. Among the rest, a young man, Donald MacKay of Grumbmor, was ordered out of his parents' house; he obeyed, in a state of delirium, and (nearly naked) ran into some bushes adjoining, where he lay for a considerable time deprived of reason; the house was immediately in flames, and his effects burned. Robert MacKay, whose whole family were in the fever, or otherwise ailing, had to carry his two daughters on his back a distance of about twenty-five miles. He accomplished this by first carrying one, and laying her down in the open air, and returning, did the same with the other, till he reached the sea-shore, and then went with them on board the lime vessel before mentioned. An old man of the same name, betook himself to a deserted mill, and lay there unable to move; and to the best of my recollection, he died there. He had no sustenance but what he obtained by licking the dust and refuse of the meal strewed about, and was defended from the rats and other vermin, by his faithful *collie*, his companion and protector. A number of the sick, who could not be carried away instantly, on account of their dangerous situation, were collected by their friends and placed in an obscure, uncomfortable hut, and there, for a time, left to their fate. The cries of these victims were heart-rending—exclaiming in their anguish, " Are you going to leave us to perish in the flames ? " However, the destroyers passed near the hut, apparently without noticing it, and consequently they remained unmolested, till they could be conveyed to the shore, and put on board the before-mentioned sloop. George Munro, miller at Farr, residing within 400 yards of the minister's house, had his whole family, consisting of six or seven persons, lying in a fever; and being ordered instantly to remove, was enabled, with the assistance of his neighbours to carry them to a damp kiln, where they remained till the fire abated, so that they could be removed. Meantime the house was burnt. It may not be out of place here to mention generally, that the clergy, factors, and magistrates, were cool and apparently unconcerned spectators of the scenes I have been describing, which were indeed perpetrated under their immediate authority. The splendid and comfortable mansions of these gentlemen, were reddened with the glare of their neighbours' flaming houses, without exciting any compassion for the sufferers; no spiritual, temporal, or medical aid was afforded them; and this time they were all driven away without being allowed the benefit of their outgoing crop! Nothing but the sword was wanting to make the scene one of as great barbarity as the earth ever witnessed; and in my opinion, this would, in a majority of cases, have been mercy, by saving them from what they were afterwards doomed to endure. The clergy, indeed, in their sermons, maintained that the whole was a merciful interposition of Providence to bring them to repentance, rather than to send them all to hell, as they so richly deserved! And here I beg leave to ask those rev. gentlemen, or the survivors of them, and especially my late minister, Mr. MacKenzie of Farr, if it be true, as was generally reported, that during these horrors I have been feebly endeavouring to describe—there was a letter sent from the proprietors, addressed to him, or to the general body, requesting to know if the removed tenants were well provided for, and comfortable, or words to that effect, and that the answer returned was, that the people were quite comfortable in their new allotments, and that the change was greatly for their benefit. This is the report that was circulated and believed; and the subsequent conduct of the clergy affords too much reason for giving it credence, as I shall soon have occasion to show.

LETTER VIII.

THE depopulation I have been treating of, with its attendant horrors and miseries, as well as its impolicy, is so justly
reasoned upon by General Stewart, in the work formerly
alluded to, that I beg to transcribe a paragraph or two.
At page 168 he says :—" The system of overlooking the
original occupiers, and of giving every support to strangers,
has been much practised in the highland counties; and on
one great estate (the Sutherland) the support which was
given to farmers of capital, as well in the amount of sums
expended on improvements, as in the liberal abatement of
rents, is, I believe, unparalleled in the United Kingdom,
and affords additional matter of regret, that the delusions
practised on a generous and public-spirited landholder,
have been so perseveringly and successfully applied, that it
would appear as if all feeling of former kindness towards
the native tenantry had ceased to exist.   To them any
uncultivated spot of moorland, however small, was considered sufficient for the support of a family; while the
most lavish encouragement has been given to the new
tenants, on whom, and with the erection of buildings, the
improvement of lands, roads, bridges, etc., upwards of
£210,000 has been expended since the year 1808.   With
this proof of unprecedented liberality, it cannot be sufficiently lamented, that an estimate of the character of these
poor people was taken from the misrepresentations of interested persons, instead of judging from the conduct of
the same men when brought into the world, where they obtained a name and character which have secured the esteem
and approbation of men high in honour and rank, and,
from their talents and experience, perfectly capable of judging with correctness.   With such proofs of capability, and

with such materials for carrying on the improvements, and maintaining the permanent prosperity of the county, when occupied by a hardy, abstemious race, easily led on to a full exertion of their faculties, by a proper management, there cannot be a question but that if, instead of placing them, as has been done, in situations bearing too near a resemblance to the potato-gardens of Ireland, they had been permitted to remain as cultivators of the soil, receiving a moderate share of the vast sums lavished on their richer successors, such a humane and considerate regard to the prosperity of a whole people, would undoubtedly have answered every good purpose." In reference to the new allotments, he says : " when the valleys and higher grounds were let to the shepherds, the whole population was driven to the sea shore, where they were crowded on small lots of land, to earn their subsistence by labour and by sea fishing, the latter so little congenial to their former habits." He goes on to remark, in a note, that these *one or two acre lots*, are represented as an *improved* system. " In a country without regular employment and without manufactures, a family is to be supported on one or two acres ! ! " The consequence was and continues to be, that, " over the whole of this district, where the sea shore is accessible, the coast is thickly studded with wretched cottages, crowded with starving inhabitants." Strangers " with capital " usurp the land and dispossess the swain. " Ancient respectable tenants, who passed the greater part of life in the enjoyment of abundance, and in the exercises of hospitality and charity, possessing stocks of ten, twenty, and thirty breeding cows, with the usual proportion of other stock, are now pining on one or two acres of bad land, with one or two starved cows ; and for this accommodation, a calculation is made, that they must support their families and pay the rent of their lots, not from the produce but from the sea. When the herring fishery succeeds they generally satisfy the landlords, whatever privations they may suffer; but when the fishing fails, they fall in arrears and are sequestrated, and their stock sold to pay the rents, their lots given to others, and they and their families turned adrift on the world. There are still a few small tenants on the old system; but they are fast falling into decay, and sinking into the class just described." Again, "we cannot sufficiently admire their meek and patient spirit, supported by the powerful influence of moral and religious principle." I need not go further, but again beg the reader's attention to this most valuable work, especially the article "Change of Tenancy," as illustrative of the condition and exponent of the character and feelings of my poor countrymen, as well as corroborative of the facts to which I am endeavouring to call public attention, as causes of the distress and destitution still prevailing in Sutherlandshire.

By the means described, large tracts of country were depopulated, and converted into solitary wastes. The whole inhabitants of Kildonan parish (with the exception of three families), amounting to near 2,000 souls, were utterly rooted and burned out. Many, especially the young and robust, left the country; but the aged, the females and children, were obliged to stay and accept the wretched allotments allowed them on the sea shore, and endeavour to learn fishing, for which all their former habits rendered them unfit; hence their time was spent in unproductive toil and misery, and many lives were lost. Mr. Sage, of evergreen memory, was the parish minister—

Among the faithless, faithful only he !

This gentleman had dissented from his brethren, and, to

the best of his power, opposed their proceedings ; hence he was persecuted and despised by them and the factors, and treated with marked disrespect. After the burning out, having lost his pious elders and attached congregation, he went about mourning till his demise, which happened not long after. His son had been appointed by the people minister of a chapel of ease, parish of Farr, and paid by them ; but, when the expulsion took place, he removed to Aberdeen, and afterwards to a parish in Ross-shire. On account of his father's integrity he could not expect a kirk in Sutherlandshire.

After a considerable interval of absence, I revisited my native place in the year 1828, and attended divine worship in the parish church, now reduced to the size and appearance of a dove-cot. The whole congregation consisted of eight shepherds, with their *dogs*, to the number of between 20 and 30, the minister, three of his family, and myself ! I came in after the first singing, but, at the conclusion, the 120th psalm was given us, and we struck up to the famous tune Bangor ; when the four-footed hearers, became excited, got up on the seats and raised a most infernal chorus of howling. Their masters then attacked them with their crooks, which only made matters worse; the yelping and howling continued to the end of the service. I retired, to contemplate the shameful scene, and compare it with what I had previously witnessed in the large and devout congregations formerly attending in that kirk. What must the worthy Mr. Campbell have felt while endeavouring to edify such a congregation !

The Barony of Strathnaver, in the parish of Farr, 25 miles in length, containing a population as numerous as Kildonan, who had been all rooted out at the general conflagration, presented a similar aspect. Here, the church no longer found necessary, was razed to the ground, and the timber of it conveyed to Altnaharrow, to be used in erecting an Inn (one of the new *improvements*) there, and the minister's house converted into the dwelling of a fox-hunter. A woman, well known in that parish, happening to traverse the Strath the year after the burning, was asked, on her return, what news? "Oh," said she, "Sgeul bronach, sgeul bronach? sad news, sad news! I have seen the timber of our well-attended kirk, covering the Inn at Altnaharrow; I have seen the kirk-yard, where our friends are mouldering, filled with tarry sheep, and Mr. Sage's study room, a kennel for Robert Gunn's dogs; and I have seen a crow's nest in James Gordon's chimney head!" On this she fell into a paroxysm of grief, and it was several days before she could utter a word to be understood. During the late devastations, a Captain John MacKay was appointed sub-factor, under Mr. Loch, for the district of Strathnaver. This gentleman, had he been allowed his own way, would have exercised his power beneficially; but he was subject to persons cast in another mould, and had to sanction what he could not approve. He did all he could to mitigate the condition of the natives by giving them employment, in preference to strangers, at the public works and improvements, as they were called; but finding their enemies too powerful and malignant, and the misery and destitution too great to be even partially removed, he shrunk from his ungracious task and went to America, where he breathed his last, much regretted by all who knew him on both sides of the Atlantic.

LETTER IX.

I have already mentioned that the clergy of the Established Church (none other were tolerated in Sutherland), all but Mr. Sage, were consenting parties to the expulsion of the inhabitants, and had substantial reasons for their readiness to accept woolly and hairy animals—sheeps and dogs—in place of their human flocks. The kirks and manses were mostly situated in the low grounds, and the clergy hitherto held their pasturage in common with the tenantry; and this state of things, established by law and usage, no factor or proprietor had power to alter without mutual consent. Had the ministers maintained those rights, they would have placed in many cases, an effectual bar to the oppressive proceedings of the factors; for the strange sheep-farmers would not bid for, or take the lands where the minister's sheep and cattle would be allowed to co-mingle with theirs. But no! Anxious to please the "powers that be," and no less anxious to drive advantageous bargains with them, these reverend gentlemen found means to get their lines laid "in pleasant places," and to secure good and convenient portions of the pasture lands enclosed for themselves: many of the small tenants were removed purely to satisfy them in these arrangements. Their subserviency to the factors, in all things, was not for nought. Besides getting their hill pasturage enclosed, their tillage lands were extended, new manses and offices were built for them, and roads made specially for their accommodation, and every arrangement made for their advantage. They basked in the sunshine of favour: they were the bosom friends of the factors and new tenants (many of whom were soon made magistrates), and had the honour of occasional visits, at their manses, from the proprietors themselves. They were always employed to explain and interpret to the assembled people the orders and designs of the factors; and they did not spare their college paint on these occasions. Black was made white, or white black, as it answered their purpose, in discharging what they called their duty! They did not scruple to introduce the name of the Deity; representing Him as the author and abetter of all the foul and cruel proceedings carried on; and they had at hand another useful being ready to seize every soul who might feel any inclination to revolt. Indeed, the manifest works of the latter in their own hands, were sufficient to prove his existence; while the whole appearance of the country, and the state of its inhabitants at this period, afforded ample proof that the principle of evil was in the ascendant. The tyranny of one class, and the wrongs and sufferings of the other, had demoralising effects on both; the national character and manners were changed and deteriorated; and a comparatively degenerate race is the consequence. This was already manifest in the year 1822, when George IV. made his famous visit to Edinburgh. The brave, athletic and gallant men, who, in 1745, and again more recently, in 1800, rose in thousands at the call of their chief, were no longer to be traced in their descendants. When the clans gathered to honour His Majesty on the latter occasion, the Sutherland turn-out was contemptible. Some two or three dozen of squalid-looking, ill-dressed, and ill-appointed men, were all that Sutherland produced. So inferior, indeed, was their appearance to the other Highlanders, that those who had the management refused to allow them to walk in the procession, and employed them in some duty out of public view. If their appearance was so bad, so also were their accommodations. They were huddled together, in an old empty house, sleeping on straw, and fed with the coarsest fare, while the other clans were living in comparative luxury. Lord Francis Leveson Gower, and Mr. Loch, who were present, reaped little honour by the exhibition of their Sutherland retainers on that great occasion. Moral degradation also, to some extent, followed that of physical. Many vices, hitherto almost unknown, began to make their appearance; and though the people never resorted to "wild savage justice," like those of Ireland in similar circumstances, the minor transgressions of squabbling, drunkeness, and incontinency became less rare—the natural consequence of their altered condition. Religion also, from the conduct of the clergy, began to lose its hold on their minds—and who can wonder at it?—when they saw these holy men closely leagued with their oppressors. "Ichabod," the glory of Sutherland had departed—perhaps never to return!

LETTER X.

I NOW proceed to describe the "allotments" on which the expelled and burnt-out inhabitants were allowed to locate during the pleasure of the factors. These allotments were generally situated on the sea-coast, the intention being to force those who could not or would not leave the country, to draw their subsistence from the sea by fishing; and in order to deprive them of any other means, the lots were not only made small, (varying from one to three acres) but their nature and situation rendered them unfit for any useful purpose. If the reader will take the trouble to examine the map of Sutherlandshire by Mr. Loch, he will perceive that the county is bounded on the north by the Northern Ocean, on the south by the county of Ross, on the west by the Mynch, on the north-east by Caithness, and on the south-east by the Moray Firth. To the sea-coasts, then, which surround the greatest part of the country were the whole mass of the inhabitants, to the amount of several thousand families,

driven by unrelenting tyrants, in the manner I have
described, to subsist as they could, on the sea or the air;
for the spots allowed them could not be called land, being
composed of narrow stripes, promontories, cliffs and precipices, rocks, and deep crevices, interspersed with bogs and
deep morasses. The whole was quite useless to their
superiors, and evidently never designed by nature for the
habitation of man or beast. This was, with a few exceptions, the character of the allotments. The patches of soil
where anything could be grown, were so few and scanty that
when any dispute arose about the property of them, the
owner could almost carry them in a creel on his back and
deposit them in another place. In many places, the spots
the poor people endeavoured to cultivate were so steep that
while one was delving, another had to hold up the soil with
his hands, lest it should roll into the sea, and from its
constant tendency to slide downwards, they had frequently
to carry it up again every spring and spread it upon the
higher parts. These patches were so small that few of them
would afford room for more than a few handfuls of seeds, and
in harvest, if there happened to be any crop, it was in continual danger of being blown into the sea, in that bleak
inclement region, where neither tree nor shrub could exist to
arrest its progress. In most years, indeed, when any
mentionable crop was realised, it was generally destroyed
before it could come to maturity, by sea-blasts and mildew.
In some places, on the north coast, the sea is forced up
through crevices, rising in columns to a prodigious height and
scattering its spray upon the adjoining spots of land, to the
utter destruction of any thing that may be growing on them.
These were the circumstances to which this devoted people
were reduced, and to which none but a hardy, patient and
moral race, with an ardent attachment to their country,

would have quietly submitted; here they, with their cattle, had to remain for the present, expecting the southern dealers to come at the usual time (the months of June and July) to purchase their stocks ; but the time came and passed, and no dealers made their appearance; none would venture into the country ! The poor animals in a starving state, were continually running to and fro, and frequently could not be prevented from straying towards their former pasture grounds, especially in the night, notwithstanding all the care taken to prevent it. When this occurred, they were immediately seized by the shepherds and impounded without food or water, till trespass was paid ! this was repeated till a great many of the cattle were rendered useless. It was nothing strange to see the pinfolds, of twenty or thirty yards square, filled to the entrance with horses, cows, sheep and goats, promiscuously for nights and days together, in that starving state, trampling on and goring each other. The lamentable neighing, lowing, and bleating of these creatures, and the pitiful looks they cast on their owners when they could recognise them, were distressing to witness ; and formed an addition to the mass of suffering then prevailing. But this was not all that beset the poor beasts. In some instances when they had been trespassing, they were hurried back by the pursuing shepherds or by their owners, and in running near the precipices many of them had their bones broken or dislocated, and a great number fell over the rocks into the sea, and were never seen after. Vast numbers of sheep and many horses and other cattle which escaped their keepers and strayed to a distance to their former pastures, were baited by men and dogs till they were either partially or totally destroyed, or become meat for their hunters. I have myself seen instances of the kind, where the animals were lying partly consumed by the dogs, though still alive, and their eyes picked out by birds of prey. When the cattle were detained by the shepherds in the folds before mentioned, for trespass, to any amount the latter thought proper to exact, those of their owners who had not money—and they were the majority—were obliged to relieve them by depositing their bed and body-clothes, watches, rings, pins, brooches, etc., though many of these were the relics of dear and valued relatives, now no more, not a few of whom had shed their blood in defence of that country from which their friends were now ignominiously driven, or treated as useless lumber, to be got rid of at any price. The situation of the people with their families and cattle, driven to these inhospitable coasts, harassed and oppressed in every possible way, presented a lamentable contrast to their former way of life. While they were grudged those barren and useless spots—and at high rents too—the new tenants were accommodated with leases of as much land as they choose to occupy, and *at reduced rents;* many of them holding farms containing many thousand acres. One farm held by Messrs. Atkinson and Marshall, two gentlemen from Northumberland, contained a hundred thousand acres of good pasture-land! Mr. Sellar had three large farms, one of which was twenty-five miles long ; and, in some places, nine or ten miles broad, situated in the barony of Strathnaver. This gentleman was said to have lost, annually, large quantities of sheep; and others of the new tenants were frequently making complaints of the same kind; all these depredations, as well as every other, were laid to the charge of the small tenants. An association was formed for the suppression of sheep-stealing in Sutherlandshire, and large rewards were laid out—Lord Stafford himself offering £30 for the conviction of any of the offenders. But though every effort was used to bring the crime home to the natives (one gentleman, whom, for obvious reasons I will not name, said in my hearing, he would rather than £1000 get one conviction from among them): yet, I am proud to say, all these endeavours were ineffectual. Not one conviction could they obtain! In time, however, the saddle came to be laid on the right horse; the shepherds could rob their masters' flocks in safety, while the natives got the blame of all, and they were evidently no way sparing; but at last they were found out, and I have reason to know that several of them were dismissed, and some had their own private stocks confiscated to their masters to make good the damage of their depredations. This was, however, all done privately, so that the odium might still attach to the natives. In concluding this part of the subject, I may observe that such of the cattle as strayed on the ministers' grounds, fared no better than others; only that, as far as I know, these gentlemen did not follow the practice of the shepherds in working the horses all day and returning them to the pinfold at night: and I am very happy in being able to give this testimony in favour of these reverend gentlemen.

I must not omit to mention here an anecdote illustrative of the state of things prevailing at that time. One of the shepherds on returning home one Sabbath evening, after partaking of the Lord's Supper, in the church of Farr, observed a number of the poor people's sheep and goats trespassing at the outskirts of his master's hill-pasturage, and, with the assistance of his dogs, which had also been at the kirk, drove them home and impounded them. On Monday morning he took as many of the lambs and kids as he thought proper, and had them killed for the use of his own family! The owners complained to his master, who was a magistrate; but the answer was, that they should keep them off his property, or eat them themselves, and then his servants could not do it for them, or words to that effect. One way or other, by starvation, accidents, and the depredations of the shepherds and their dogs, the people's cattle to the amount of many hundred head, were utterly lost and destroyed.

LETTER XI.

I HAVE now endeavoured to shadow forth the cruel expulsion of my " co-mates and brothers in exile" from their native hearths, and to give a faint sketch of their extreme sufferings and privations in consequence. Few instances are to be found in modern European history, and scarce any in Britain, of such a wholesale extirpation, and with such revolting circumstances. It is impossible for me to give more than an outline; the filling up would take a large volume, and the sufferings, insult, and misery, to which this simple, pastoral race were exposed, would exceed belief. But if I can draw public attention to their case, so as to promote that authorised inquiry, so much deprecated by Highland proprietors, my end will be attained. If the original inhabitants could have been got rid of totally, and their language and memory eradicated, the oppressors were not disposed to be scrupulous about the means. Justice, humanity, and even the laws of the land, were violated with impunity, when they stood in the way of the new plans on " Change of Tenancy"; and these plans, with more or less severity, continue to be acted upon in several of the Highland counties, but more especially in Sutherland, to this day. But there is still a number left, abject, "scattered and peeled" as they are, in whose behalf I would plead, and to those wrongs I would wish to give a tongue, in hopes that the feeble remnant of a once happy and estimable people, may yet find some redress, or at least the comfort of public sympathy. I now proceed to give some account of the state of the Sutherlanders, on their maritime "allotments," and how they got on in their new trade of fishing.

People accustomed to witness only the quiet friths and petty heavings of the sea, from lowland shores, can form little conception of the gigantic workings of the Northern sea, which, from a comparatively placid state, often rises suddenly without apparent cause, into mountainous billows; and, when north winds prevail, its appearance becomes terrific beyond description. To this raging element, however, the poor people were now compelled to look for their subsistence, or starve, which was the only other alternative. It is hard to extinguish the love of life, and it was almost as hard to extinguish the love of country in a Highlandman in past times ; so that, though many of the vigorous and enterprising pursued their fortunes in other climes, and in various parts of Scotland and England, yet many remained, and struggled to accommodate themselves to their new and appalling circumstances. The regular fishermen, who had hitherto pursued the finny race in the northern sea, were, from the extreme hazard of the trade, extremely few, and nothing could exceed the contempt and derision—mingled sometimes with pity, even in their rugged breasts—with which they viewed the awkward attempts and sad disasters of their new landward competitors. Nothing, indeed, could seem more helpless, than the attempt to draw subsistence from such a boisterous sea with such means as they possessed, and in the most complete ignorance of all sea-faring matters ; but the attempt had to be made, and the success was such as might be expected in their circumstances ; while many—very many —lost their lives, some became in time expert fishermen.

Numerous as were the casualties, and of almost daily occurrence, yet the escapes, many of them extraordinary, were happily still more frequent; their disasters, on the whole, arose to a frightful aggregate of human misery. I shall proceed to notice a very few cases, to which I was a witness, or which occur to my recollection.

William MacKay, a respectable man, shortly after settling in his allotment on the coast, went one day to explore his new possession, and in venturing to examine more nearly the ware growing within the flood mark, was suddenly swept away by a splash of the sea, from one of the adjoining creeks, and lost his life, before the eyes of his miserable wife, in the last month of her pregnancy, and three helpless children who were left to deplore his fate. James Campbell, a man also with a family, on attempting to catch a peculiar kind of small fish among the rocks, was carried away by the sea, and never seen afterwards. Bell MacKay, a married woman, and mother of a family, while in the act of taking up salt water to make salt of, was carried away in a similar manner, and nothing more seen of her. Robert MacKay, who with his family was suffering extreme want, in endeavouring to procure some sea-fowls' eggs among the rocks, lost his hold, and falling from a prodigious height was dashed to pieces, and leaving a wife and five destitute children behind him. John MacDonald, while fishing, was swept off the rocks, and never seen again.

It is not my intention to swell my narrative, by reciting the " moving accidents " that befel individuals and boats' crews, in their new and hazardous occupation; suffice it to say, they were many and deplorable. Most of the boats were such as the regular fishermen had cast off as unserviceable or unsafe, but which those poor creatures were obliged to purchase and go to sea with, at the hourly peril of their lives ; yet they often not only escaped the death to which others became a prey, but were very successful. One instance of this kind, in which I bore a part myself, I will here relate. Five venturous young men, of whom I was one, having bought an old crazy boat, that had long been laid up as useless, and having procured lines of an inferior description for haddock fishing, put to sea, without sail, helm, or compass, with three patched oars ; only one of the party ever having been at sea before. This apparently insane attempt gathered a crowd of spectators, some in derision cheering us on, and our friends imploring us to come back. However, Neptune being then in one of his placid moods, we boldly ventured on, human life having become reduced in value; and, after a night spent on the sea, in which we freshmen suffered severely from sea-sickness, to the great astonishment of the people on shore, the *Heather-boat*, as she was called, reached land in the morning—all hands safe, with a very good take of fish. In these and similar ways, did the young men serve a dangerous and painful apprenticeship to the sea, " urged on by fearless want," in time became good fishermen, and were thereby enabled in some measure to support their families, and those dependent on them : but owing to peculiar circumstances, their utmost efforts were, in a great degree, abortive. The coast was, as I have said, extremely boisterous and destructive to their boats, tackle, etc. They had no harbours where they could land and secure their boats in safety, and little or no capital to procure sound boats, or to replace those which were lost. In one year, on the coast, between Portskerra and Rabbit Island (about 30 miles), upwards of one hundred boats had either been totally destroyed or so materially injured as to render them unserviceable ; and many of their crews had found a watery grave! It is lamentable to think, that while £210,000 were expended on the so-called improvements, besides £500 subscribed by the proprietors, for making a harbour, the most needful of all; not a shilling of the vast sum was ever expended for behoof of the small tenantry, nor the least pains taken to mitigate their lot! Roads, bridges, inns, and manses, to be sure, were provided for the accommodation of the new gentlemen tenantry and clergy, but those who spoke the Gaelic tongue were a proscribed race, and everything was done to get rid of them, by driving them into the forlorn hope of drawing subsistence from the sea, while squatting on their miserable allotments, where, in their wretched hovels, they lingered out an almost hopeless existence, and where none but such hardy " sons of the mountain and the flood" could have existed at all. Add to this, though at some seasons they procured abundance of fish, that they had no market for the surplus; the few shepherds were soon supplied, and they had no means of conveying them to distant towns, so that very little money could be realized to pay rent, or procure other necessaries, fishing tackle, etc., and when the finny race thought proper to desert their shores (as, in their caprice, they often did), their misery was complete! Besides those located on the sea-shore, there was a portion of the people sent to the moors, and these were no better off. Here they could neither get fish nor fowl, and the scraps of land given them were good for nothing—white or reddish gravel, covered with a thin layer of moss, and for this they were to pay rent, and raise food from it to maintain their families! By immense labour they did improve some spots in these moors, and raise a little very inferior produce, but not unfrequently, after all their toil, if they displeased the factors, or the shepherds, in the least, even by a word, or failed in paying the rent, they were unceremoniously turned out; hence, their state of bondage may be understood; they dare not even complain!* The people on the property of Mr. Dempster, of Skibo, were little, if anything, better off. They were driven out, though not by burning, and located on patches of moors, in a similiar way to those on the Sutherland property, with the only difference that they had to pay higher than the latter for their wretched allotments. Mr. Dempster says "he has kept his tenantry"; but how has he treated them? This question will be solved, I hope, when the authorised inquiry into the state of the poor Highlands takes place.

LETTER XII.

WERE it not that I am unwilling to occupy your valuable columns to a much greater extent, I could bring forward, in the history of many families, several interesting episodes to illustrate this narrative of my country's misfortunes. Numerous are the instances (some of the subjects of them could be produced even in this city) of persons, especially females, whose mental and bodily sufferings, during the scenes I have described, have entailed on them diseases which baffle medical skill, and which death only can put an end to; but I forbear to dwell on these at present, and pass on to the year 1827.

The depopulation of the county (with the exceptions I have described) was now complete. The land had passed into the hands of a few capitalists, and everything was done to promote their prosperity and convenience, while everything that had been promised to the small tenants, was, as

* For corroboration of these statements see quotations from Hugh Miller, and other high authorities, in the sequel.—A. M.

regularly, left undone. But yet the latter were so stubborn that they could not be brought to rob or steal, to afford cause for hanging or transporting them ; nor were they even willing to beg, though many of them were gradually forced to submit to this last degradation to the feelings of the high-minded Gael. It was in this year that her ladyship, the proprietrix, and suite, made a visit to Dunrobin Castle. Previous to her arrival, the clergy and factors, and the new tenants, set about raising a subscription throughout the county, to provide a costly set of ornaments, with compli-mentary inscriptions, to be presented to her ladyship in name of her tenantry. Emissaries were despatched for this purpose even to the small tenantry, located on the moors and barren cliffs, and every means used to wheedle or scare them into contributing. They were told that those who would subscribe would thereby secure her ladyship's and the factor's favour, and those who could not or would not, were given to understand, very significantly, what they had to expect, by plenty of menacing looks and ominous shakings of the head. This caused many of the poor creatures to part with their last shilling, to supply complimentary orna-ments to honour this illustrious family, and which went to purchase additional favour for those who were enjoying the lands from which they had been so cruelly expelled.

These testimonials were presented at a splendid entertain-ment, and many high-flown compliments passed between the givers and receiver ; but, of course, none of the poor victims were present ; no compliments were paid to them ; and it is questionable if her ladyship ever knew that one of them subscribed—indeed, I am almost certain that she never did. Three years after, she made a more length-ened visit, and this time she took a tour round the northern districts on the sea-shore, where the poor people were located, accompanied by a number of the clergy, the factors, etc. She was astonished and distressed at the destitution, nakedness, and extreme misery, which met her eye in every direction, made inquiries into their condition, and ordered a general distribution of clothing to be made among the most destitute; but unfortunately she confined her inquiries to those who surrounded her, and made them the medium for distributing her bounty—the very parties who had been the main cause of this deplorable destitution, and whose interest it was to conceal the real state of the people, as it continues to be to this day.

At one place she stood upon an eminence, where she had about a hundred of those wretched dwellings in view; at least she could see the smoke of them ascending from the horrid places in which they were situated. She turned to the parish minister in the utmost astonishment, and asked, "Is it possible that there are people living in yonder places?"—"O yes, my lady," was the reply. "And can you tell me if they are in any way comfortable?" "Quite comfortable, my lady." Now, sir, I can declare that at the very moment this reverend gentlemen uttered these words, he was fully aware of the horrors of their situation; and, besides that, some of the outcasts were then begging in the neighbouring county of Caithness, many of them carrying certificates from this very gentleman attesting that they were objects of charity!

Her ladyship, however, was not quite satisfied with these answers. She caused a general warning to be issued, directing the people to meet her, at stated places as she proceeded, and wherever a body of them met her, she alighted from her carriage, and questioned them if they were comfortable, and how the factors were behaving to them? [N.B. The factors were always present on these occasions.]

But they durst make little or no complaints. What they did say was in Gaelic, and of course, as in other cases, left to the minister's interpretation ; but their forlorn, haggard, and destitute appearance, sufficiently testified their real condition. I am quite certain, that had this great, and (I am willing to admit, when not misled) good woman remained on her estates, their situation would have been materially bettered, but as all her charity was left to be dispensed by those who were anxious to get rid of the people, root and branch, little benefit resulted from it, at least to those she meant to relieve. As I mentioned above, she ordered bed and body clothes to all who were in need of them, but, as usual, all was entrusted to the ministers and factors, and they managed this business with the same selfishness, injustice, and partiality, that had marked their conduct on former occasions. Many of the most needy got nothing, and others next to nothing. For an instance of the latter, several families, consisting of seven or eight, and in great distress, got only a yard and a half of coarse blue flannel, each family. Those, however, who were the favourites and toadies of the distributors, and their servants, got an ample supply of both bed and body clothes, but this was the exception; generally speaking, the poor people were nothing benefited by her ladyship's charitable intentions ; though they afforded hay-making seasons to those who had enough already, and also furnished matter for glowing accounts in the newspapers, of her ladyship's extraordinary munificence. To a decent highland woman, who had interested her ladyship, she ordered a present of a gown-piece, and the gentleman factor who was entrusted to procure it, some time after sent six yards of cotton stuff not worth 2s. in the whole. The woman laid it aside, intending to show it to her ladyship on her next visit, but her own death occurred in the meantime. Thus, in every way, were her ladyship's benevolent intentions frustrated or misapplied, and that ardent attachment to her family which had subsisted through so many generations, materially weakened, if not totally destroyed, by a mistaken policy towards her people, and an undue confidence in those to whose management she committed them, and who, in almost every instance, betrayed that confidence, and cruelly abused that delegated power. Hence, and hence only, the fearful misery and destitution in Sutherlandshire.

LETTER XIII.

IN the year 1832, and soon after the events I have been describing, an order was issued by Mr. Loch, in the name of the Duke and Duchess of Sutherland, that all the small tenants, on both sides of the road from Bighouse to Melness (about thirty miles), where their cottages were thickly studded, must build new houses, with stone and mortar, according to a prescribed plan and specification. The poor people, finding their utter inability, in their present condition, to erect such houses (which, when finished, would cost £30 to £40 each), got up petitions to the proprietors, setting forth their distressed condition, and the impossibility of complying with the requisition at present. These petitions they supplicated and implored the ministers to sign, well knowing that otherwise they had little chance of being attended to ; but these gentlemen could be moved by no entreaties, and answered all their applications by a contemptuous refusal. The petitions had, therefore, to be forwarded to London without ecclesiastical sanction, and, of course, effected nothing. The answer returned was, that if they did not immediately begin to build, they would be removed next term. The very word *removed* was enough; it brought back to their minds the recollection of former scenes, with all their attendant horrors. To escape was impossible, they had nowhere to go; and in such circumstances they would have consented to do anything, even to the making "bricks without straw," like their oppressed prototypes of old.

In the midst of hopeless misery, then, and many of them without a shilling in their pockets, did they commence the task of building houses, such as I have mentioned, on the barren spots, and without any security of retaining them, even when they were built. The edict was law; supplication or remonstrance was in vain; so to it they went, under circumstances such as perhaps building was never carried on before, in a country called Christian and civilized. Plans and specifications were published, and estimates required by the factors, directing the whole proceedings, and, as usual, without consulting the feelings of the poor people, or inquiring into the means they had for carrying them into effect. All was bustle and competition among masons and mechanics, of whom few resided in the county; most of them were strangers; and when they commenced work, the people were obliged to feed them, whether they had anything themselves to eat or not, and to pay them, even if they had to sell the last movable for that purpose. Some of the masons, however, showed great lenity, and are still unpaid. Previous to this, in the year 1829, I and my family had been forced away like others, being particularly obnoxious to those in authority for sometimes showing an inclination to oppose their tyranny; and therefore we had to be made examples of, to frighten the rest, but in 1833 I made a tour to the districts, when the building was going on, and shall endeavour to describe a small part of what met my eye on that occasion. In one district (and this was a fair specimen of all the rest), when the building was going on, I saw fourteen different squads of masons at work, the natives attending them. Old grey-headed men, worn down by previous hardship and present want, were to be seen carrying stones, and wheeling them and other materials on barrows, or carrying them on their backs to the buildings, and, with their tottering limbs and trembling hands straining to raise the stones, etc., to the walls. The young men also, after toiling all night at sea endeavouring to obtain subsistence, instead of rest, were obliged to yield their exhausted frames to the labours of the day. Even female labour could not be dispensed with; the strong as well as the weak, the delicate and sickly, and (shame to the nature of their oppressors!) even the pregnant, bare-footed, and scantily clothed and fed, were obliged to join in these rugged, unfeminine labours, carrying stones, clay, lime, wood, etc., on their backs or on barrows, their tracks often reddened with the blood from their hands and feet, and from hurts received by their awkwardness in handling the rude materials. In one instance I saw the husband quarrying stones, and the wife and children dragging them along in an old cart to the building. Such were the building scenes of that period. The poor people had often to give the last morsel of food they possessed to feed the masons, and subsist on shell-fish themselves when they could get them. The timber for their houses was furnished by the factors, and charged them about a third higher than it could be purchased at in any of the neighbouring sea-ports. I spent two melancholy days witnessing these scenes, which are now present to my mind, and which I can never forget. This went on for several years, in the course of which, many hundreds of houses were erected on inhospitable spots, unfit for human residence. It might be thought that the design of forcing the people to build such houses, was to provide for their comfort and accommodation; but there was another object, which I believe was the only true motive, and that was, to hide the misery that prevailed.   There had been a great sensation created in the public mind, by the cruelties exercised in these districts; and it was thought that a number of neat white houses, ranged on each side of the road, would take the eyes of strangers and visitors, and give a practical contradiction to the rumours afloat; hence, the poor creatures were forced to resort to such means, and to endure such hardships and privations as I have described, to carry the scheme into effect.   And after they had spent their all, and much more than their all, on the erection of these houses, and involved themselves in debt, for which they have been harassed and pursued ever since, they are still but whitened tombs; many of them now ten years in existence, and still without proper doors or windows, destitute of furniture, and of comfort; merely providing a lair for a heart-broken, squalid, and degenerated race.

LETTER XIV.

DURING the period in which the building was going on, I think in the year 1833, Lord Leveson Gower, the present Duke of Sutherland, visited the country, and remained a few weeks, during which he had an opportunity of witnessing the scenes I have described in my last; and such was the impression made on his mind, that he gave public orders that the people should not be forced to build according to the specific plan, but be allowed to erect such houses as suited themselves. These were glad tidings of mercy to the poor people, but they were soon turned to bitter disappointment; for no sooner had his lordship left the country, than Mr. Loch or his underlings issued fresh orders for the building to go on as before.

Shortly after this, in July, 1833, his Grace created first Duke of Sutherland, who had been some time in bad health, breathed his last in Dunrobin Castle, and was interred with great pomp in the family burying-place in the cathedral of Dornoch. The day of his funeral was ordered to be kept as a fast-day by all the tenantry, under penalty of the highest displeasure of those in authority, though it was just then herring-fishing season, when much depended on a day. Still this was a minor hardship. The next year a project was set on foot, by the same parties who formerly got up the expensive family ornaments presented to her Grace, to raise a monument to the Duke. Exactly similiar measures were resorted to, to make the small tenantry subscribe, in the midst of all their distresses, and with similiar results. All who could raise a shilling gave it, and those who could not, awaited in terror the consequences of their default. No doubt, the Duke deserved the highest posthumous honours from a portion of his tenantry—those who had benefited by the large sums he and the Duchess had lavished for their accommodation; but the poor small tenantry, what had been done for them? While the ministers, factors, and new tenantry, were rich and luxurious, basking in the sunshine of favour and prosperity, the miseries and oppressions of the natives remain unabated; *they* were emphatically in the shade, and certainly had little for which to be grateful to those whose abuse of power had brought them to such a pass—who had drained their cup of every thing that could sweeten life, and left only

A mass of sordid lees behind!

Passing the next two years, I now proceed to describe the failure of the harvest in 1836, and the consequences to the Highlands generally, and to Sutherland in particular. In this year the crops all over Britain were deficient, having had bad weather for growing and ripening, and still worse for gathering in. But in the Highlands they were an entire failure, and on the untoward spots occupied by the Sutherland small tenants there was literally nothing—at least nothing fit for human subsistence; and to add to the calamity, the weather had prevented them from securing the peats, their only fuel; so that, to their exhausted state from their disproportionate exertions in building, cold and hunger were now to be superadded. The sufferings of the succeeding winter, endured by the poor Highlanders, truly beggar description. Even the herring-fishing had failed, and consequently their credit in Caithness, which depended on its success, was at an end. Any little provision they might be able to procure was of the most inferior and unwholesome description. It was no uncommon thing to see people searching among the snow for the frosted potatoes to eat, in order to preserve life. As the harvest had been disastrous, so the winter was uncommonly boisterous and severe, and consequently little could be obtained from the sea to mitigate the calamity. The distress rose to such a height as to cause a universal sensation all over the island, and a general cry for government interference to save the people from death by famine; and the appeal, backed by the clergy of all denominations throughout the Highlands (with the exception of Sutherland), was not made in vain.

Dr. MacLeod of Glasgow was particularly zealous on this occasion. He took reports from all the parish ministers in the destitute districts, and went personally to London to represent the case to government and implore aid, and the case was even laid before both houses of parliament. In consequence of these applications and proceedings, money and provisions to a great amount were sent down, and the magistrates and ministers entrusted with the distribution of them : and in the ensuing summer, vessels were sent to take on board a number of those who were willing to emigrate to Australia. Besides this, private subscriptions were entered into, and money obtained to a very great amount. Public meetings were got up in all the principal cities and towns in Great Britain and Ireland, and large funds collected; so that effectual relief was afforded to every place that required it, with the single exception of that county which, of all others, was in the most deplorable state—the county of Sutherland! The reason of this I will explain presently ; but first let me draw the reader's attention for a moment to the new circumstances in which the Highlands were placed. Failure in the crops in those northern and north-western parts of Scotland was a case of frequent and common occurrence ; but famine, and solicitations for national aid and charitable relief, were something quite new. I will endeavour to account for the change. Previous to the " change of tenancy," as the cruel spoliation and expatriation of the native inhabitants was denominated, when a failure occurred in the grain and potato crops, they had recourse to their cattle. Selling a few additional head, or an extra score of sheep, enabled them to purchase at the sea-ports what grain was wanted. But now they had no cattle to sell ; and when the crops totally failed on their spots of barren ground, and when, at the same time, the fishing proved unprosperous, they were immediately reduced to a state of famine ; and hence the cry for relief, which, as I have mentioned, was so generously responded to. But, I would ask, who were the authors of all this mass of distress ? Surely, the proprietors, who, unmindful that

" property has its duties as well as its rights," brought about this state of things. They, in common with other landed legislators, enacted the food taxes, causing a competition for land, and then encouraged strange adventurers to supersede the natives, and drive them out, in order that the whole of the Highlands should be turned into a manufactory, to make beef and mutton for the English market. And when, by these means, they had reduced the natives to destitution and famine, they left it to the government and to charitable individuals to provide relief! Language is scarcely adequate to characterize such conduct; yet these are the great, the noble, and right honourable of the land! However, with the exception of my unfortunate native county, relief was afforded, though not by those whose right it was to afford it. Large quantities of oatmeal, seed oats, and barley, potatoes, etc., were brought up and forwarded to the North and West Highlands, and distributed among all who were in need; but nothing of all this for the Sutherlanders. Even Dr. Mac-Leod, in all the zeal of his charitable mission, passed from Stornoway to the Shetland Islands without vouchsafing a glance at Sutherland on his way. The reason of all this I will now explain. It was constantly asserted and reiterated in all places, that there was no occasion for government or other charitable aid to Sutherland, as the noble proprietors would themselves take in hand to afford their tenantry ample relief. This story was circulated through the newspapers, and repeated by the clergy and factors at all public meetings, till the public was quite satisfied on the subject. Meantime the wretched people were suffering the most unparalleled distress; famine had brought their misery to a frightful climax, and disease and death had commenced their work! In their agony they had recourse to the ministers, imploring them to represent their case to government, that they might partake of the relief afforded to other counties ; but all in vain ! I am aware that what I here assert is incredible, but not less true, that of the whole seventeen parish ministers, not one could be moved by the supplications and cries of the famishing wretches to take any steps for their relief ! They answered all entreaties with a cold refusal, alleging that the proprietors would, in their own good time, send the necessary relief ! but, so far as I could ever learn, they took no means to hasten that relief. They said in their sermons "that the Lord had a controversy with the land for the people's wickedness ; and that in his providence, and even in his mercy, he had sent this scourge to bring them to repentance," etc. Some people (wicked people, of course) may think such language, in such circumstances, savoured more of blasphemy than of religious truth. Meantime, the newspapers were keeping up the public expectations of the munificent donations the proprietors were sending. One journal had it that £9,000 worth of provisions were on the way ; others £8,000, and £7,000, etc. However, the other Highlanders had received relief at least two months before anything came to Sutherland. At last it did come ; the amount of relief, and the manner of its appropriation shall be explained in my next.

LETTER XV.

In my last I quoted an expression current among the clergy at the time of the famine " that God had a controversy with the people for their sins," but I contend—and I think my readers in general will agree with me—that the poor Sutherlanders were " more sinned against than sinning ". To the aspersions cast upon them by Mr. Loch, in his book (written

by an interested party, and evidently for a purpose), I beg
the public to contrast the important work by General Stewart
before mentioned, and draw their own conclusions.   The
truth is, that the Sutherlanders were examples of almost all
the humble virtues—a simple and uncorrupted, rural, and
pastoral population; even the unexampled protracted cruelty
with which they were treated, never stirred them to take wild
or lawless revenge.   During a period of 200 years, there had
been only three capital convictions, and very few crimes of
any description; the few that did occur were chiefly against
the excise laws.   But those who coveted the lands, which in
justice were their patrimony, like Queen Jezebel of old, got
false witnesses to defame them (in order that a pretext might
be afforded for expelling them from the possessions which
had been defended with the blood of their forefathers).   It
was the factors, the capitalists, and the clergy, that had a
controversy with the people, and not the Almighty, as they
blasphemously asserted.   The Sutherlanders had always
been a religious, a devout, and a praying people, and now
their oppressors, and not Divine Providence, had made
them a *fasting people.*   I proceed to give some account of
that mockery of relief which was so ostentatiously paraded
before the public in the newspapers, and at public meetings.

I have already observed that the relief afforded to the
Highland districts generally, by the government, and by
private charity, was not only effectual in meeting the exigency,
but it was a *bona-fide* charity, and was forthcoming in time;
while the pittance doled out to the Sutherlanders, was destitute of those characteristics.   How the poor people passed
the winter and spring under the circumstances already
mentioned, I must leave to the reader's imagination; suffice
it to say, that though worn to the bone by cold, hunger, and
nakedness, the bulk of them still survived.   The High-

landers are still proverbially tenacious of life. In the latter end of April, 1837, when news reached them that the long-promised relief, consisting of meal, barley, potatoes, and seed oats, had actually arrived, and was to be immediately distributed at Tongue and other stated places, the people at once flocked to these places, but were told that nothing would be given to anyone, till they produced a certificate from their parish minister that they were proper objects of charity. Here was a new obstacle. They had to return and implore those haughty priests for certificates, which were frequently withheld from mere caprice, or for some alleged offence or lack of homage in the applicant, who if not totally refused, had to be humbled in the dust, sickened by delay, and the boon only at last yielded to the intercession of some of the more humane of the shepherds. Those who were in the fishing trade were peremptorily refused. This is the way in which man, religious man, too! can trifle with the distress of his famishing brother.

The places appointed for distribution were distant from the homes of many of the sufferers, so that by the time they had waited on the ministers for the necessary qualification, and travelled again to places of distribution and back again, with what they could obtain, on their backs, several days were consumed, and in many cases from 50 to 100 miles traversed. And what amount of relief did they receive after all? From 7 to 28 ℔s. of meal, with seed oats and potatoes in the same proportion; and this not for individuals, but for whole families! In the fields, and about the dykes adjoining the places where these pittances were doled out, groups of famishing creatures might be lying in the mornings (many of them having travelled the whole day and night previous), waiting the leisure of the factors or their clerks, and no attention was paid to them till those gentlemen had breakfasted and dressed; by which time the day was far advanced.

Several subsequent distributions of meal took place; but in every new case, fresh certificates of continued destitution had to be procured from the ministers and elders of the respective parishes. This was the kind, and quantity, of relief afforded, and the mode of dispensing it; different indeed from what was represented in the glozing falsehoods so industriously palmed on public credulity.

In the month of September, her Grace being then on a visit in the country, the following proceedings took place, reported in the public papers of the day, which afforded a specimen of groundless assertions, clerical sycophancy, and fulsome adulation, for which it would be difficult to find a parallel:—

The Presbytery of Tongue, at their last meeting, agreed to present the following address to the Duchess of Sutherland. Her Grace being then at Tongue, the Presbytery waited on her: and the address being read by the Moderator, she made a suitable reply:—

"*May it please your Grace,*

"We, the Presbytery of Tongue, beg leave to approach your Grace with feelings of profound respect, and to express our joy at your safe arrival within our bounds.

"We have met here this day for the purpose of communicating to your Grace the deep sense which we entertain of your kindness during the past season to the people under our charge.

"When it pleased Providence by an unfavourable harvest to afflict the Highlands of Scotland with a scarcity of bread, and when the clergymen of other districts appealed to public charity on behalf of their parishioners, the confidence which we placed in your Grace's liberality led us to refrain from making a similar appeal.

"When we say that this confidence has been amply realised, we only express the feelings of our people; and participating strongly in these feelings, as we do, to withhold the expression of them from your Grace, would do injustice alike to ourselves and to them.

"In their name, therefore, as well as in our own, we beg to offer to your Grace our warmest gratitude. When other districts were left to the precarious supplies of a distant benevolence, your Grace took on yourself the charge of supporting your people; by a constant supply of meal, you not only saved them from famine, but enabled them to live in comfort; and by a seasonable provision of seed, you were the means, under God, of securing to them the blessing of the present abundant harvest.

"That Almighty God may bless your Grace,—that he may long spare you to be a blessing to your people,—and that He may finally give you the inheritance which is incorruptible, undefiled, and that fadeth not away, is the prayer of,

"May it please your Grace,
"THE MEMBERS OF THE PRESBYTERY OF TONGUE,
(Signed) "HUGH MACKENZIE, *Moderator.*"

The evident tendency of this document was to mislead her Grace, and by deluding the public, to allay anxiety, stifle inquiry, and conceal the truth. However, her Grace made a "suitable reply," and great favour was shown to the adulators. About a year before, the very clergyman whose signature is appended to this address exchanged part of his glebe for the lands of Diansad and Inshverry; but in consenting to the change, he made an express condition that the present occupiers, amounting to eight families, should be "removed," and accordingly they were driven out in a body! To this gentleman, then, the honour is due of having consummated the Sutherland ejections; and hence he was admirably fitted for signing the address. I must not omit to notice "the abundant harvest," said to succeed the famine. The family "allotments" only afforded the sowing of from a half firlot to two or three firlots of oats, and a like quantity of barley, which, at an average in good seasons, yielded about three times the quantity sown; in bad years little or nothing; and even in the most favourable cases, along with their patches of potatoes, could not maintain the people more than three months in the year. The crop succeeding the famine was anything but an abundant one to the poor people; they had got the seed too late, and the season was not the most favourable for bringing it

to even ordinary perfection.   Hence, that "abundance,"
mentioned in the address was like all the rest of its groundless assumption.   But I have still to add to the crowning
iniquity—the provisions distributed in charity had to be
paid for ! but this point—I must postpone till my next.

LETTER XVI.

IT would require a closer acquaintance with the recent
history of Sutherlandshire than I am able to communicate,
and better abilities than mine to convey to the reader an
adequate idea of the mournful contrast between the former
comfortable and independent state of the people and that
presented in my last.   They were now, generally speaking,
become a race of paupers, trembling at the very looks of
their oppressors, objects of derision and mockery to the
basest underlings, and fed by the scanty hand of those who
had been the means of reducing them to their present state ;
To their capability of endurance must, in a great measure,
be ascribed their surviving, in any considerable numbers,
the manifold inflictions they had to encounter.   During the
spring and summer many of the young and robust of both
sexes left the country in quest of employment ; some to the
neighbouring county of Caithness, but most of them went
to the Lowlands, and even into England, to serve as cattle
drivers, labourers, and in other menial occupations.   No
drudgery was too low for their acceptance, nor any means
left untried, by which they could sustain life in the most
frugal manner, and anything earned above this was carefully
transmitted to their suffering relations at home.   When
harvest commenced they were rather better employed, and
then the object was to save a little to pay the rent at the

approaching term; but there was another use they had never thought of, to which their hard and scanty earnings had to be applied.

Not long after the termination of the Duchess' visit (during which the address given in my last was presented), I think just about two months after, the people were astonished at seeing placards posted up in all public places, warning them to prepare to pay their rents, and also the meal, potatoes, and seed oats and barley they had got during the spring and summer! This was done in the name of the Duchess, by the orders of Mr. Loch and his under-factors. Ground-officers were despatched in all directions to explain and enforce this edict, and to inform the small tenants that their rents would not be received till the accounts for the provisions were first settled. This was news indeed!—astonishing intelligence this—that the pitiful mite of relief, obtained with so much labour and ceremony, and doled out by pampered underlings with more than the usual insolence of charity, was after all to be paid for! After government aid and private charity, so effectually afforded to other Highland districts had been intercepted by ostentatious promises of ample relief from the bounty of her Grace; after the clergy had lauded the Almighty, and her Grace no less, for that *bounty ;* the poor creatures were to be concussed into paying for it, and at a rate too, considerably above the current prices. I know this, to persons unacquainted with Highland tyranny, extortion and oppression, will appear incredible; but I am able to substantiate its truth by clouds of living witnesses.

The plan adopted deserves particular notice. The people were told, "their rents would not be received till the provisions were first paid for". By this time those who had procured a little money by labouring elsewere, were returning with their savings to enable their relatives to meet the rents, and this was thought a good time to get the "charity" paid up. Accordingly when the people, as usual, waited upon the factor with the rent, they were told distinctly that the meal, etc., must be paid first, and that if any lenity was shown, it would be for the rent, but none for the provisions! The meaning of this scheme seems to be, that by securing payment for the provisions in the first instance, they would avoid the odium of pursuing for what was given as charity, knowing that they could at any time enforce payment of the rent, by the usual summary means to which they were in the habit of resorting. Some laid down their money at once, and the price of all they had got was then deducted, and a receipt handed to them for the balance, in part of their rent. Others seeing this, remonstrated and insisted on paying their rents first, and the provisions afterwards, if they must be paid; but their pleading went for nothing, their money was taken in the same manner (no receipts in any case being given for the payment of the "charity,"), and they were driven contemptuously from the counting-table.

A few refused to pay, especially unless receipts were granted for the "charity," and returned home with their money, but most of them were induced by the terror of their families to carry it back and submit like the rest. A smaller portion, however, still continued refractory, and alternate threats and wheedlings were used by the underlings to make these comply; so that gradually all were made to pay the last shilling it was possible for them to raise. Some who had got certificates of destitution being unable, from age or illness, to undergo the fatigue of waiting on the factors for their portion, or of carrying it home, had to obtain the charitable assistance of some of their abler fellow sufferers for that purpose, but when there was any difficulty about the payment, the carriers were made accountable the same as if they had been the receivers! Hitherto, the money collected at the church doors, had been divided among the poor, but this year it was withheld; in one parish to my personal knowledge (and as far as my information goes the refusal was general), the parish minister telling them that they could not expect to get meal and money both, signifying that the deficient payments for the provisions had to be made up from the church collections. Whether this was the truth or not, it served for a pretext to deprive the poor of this slender resource; for, ever since—now four years—they have got nothing. This is one among many subjects of inquiry. Verily there is much need for light to be thrown on this corner of the land! A rev. gentleman from the west, whose failing it was to transgress the ten commandments, had, through some special favour, obtained a parish in Sutherlandshire, and thinking probably that charity should begin at home, had rather misapplied the poor's money which was left in his hand, for on his removal to another parish, there was none of it forthcoming. The elders of his new parish being aware of this, refused to entrust him with the treasureship, and had the collection-money kept in a locked box in the church, but when it amounted to some pounds, the box was broken up and the money was taken out. The minister had the key of the church.

Owing to the complete exhaustion of the poor people's means in the manner I have been describing, the succeeding year (1838) found them in circumstances little better than its predecessor. What any of them owed in Caithness and elsewhere, they had been unable to pay, and consequently their credit was at an end, and they were obliged to live from hand to mouth; besides, this year was unproductive in the fishing, as the years since have also been.

In the earlier part of this correspondence, I have treated of the large sums said to have been laid out on improvements (roads, bridges, inns, churches, manses, and mansions for the new tenants); but I have yet to mention a poll-tax called road-money, amounting to 4s. on every male of 18 years and upwards, which was laid on about the year 1810, most rigorously exacted, and continues to be levied on each individual in the most summary way, by seizure of any kind of moveables in or about the dwelling till the money is paid. To some poor families this tax comes to £1 and upwards every year, and be it observed that the capitalist possessing 50,000 acres, only pays in the same proportion, and his shepherds are entirely exempt! Those of the small tenantry or their families, who may have been absent for two or three years, on their return are obliged to pay up their arrears of this tax, the same as if they had been all the time at home; and payment is enforced by seizure of the goods of any house in which they may reside. The reader will perceive that the laws of Sutherlandshire are different, and differently administered, from what they are in other parts of the country—in fact those in authority do just what they please, whether legal or otherwise, none daring to question what they do. Nothwithstanding this burdensome tax, the roads, as far as the small tenants' interests are concerned, are shamefully neglected, while every attention is paid to suit the convenience and pleasure of the ruling parties and the new tenantry, by bringing roads to their very doors.

———

LETTER XVII.

IN my last letter I mentioned something about the with-holding and misappropriation of the money collected at church doors for the poor; but let it be understood that notwithstanding the iniquitous conduct of persons so acting, the loss to the poor was not very great. The Highlander abhors to be thought a pauper, and the sum afforded to each of the few who were obliged to accept of it, varied from 1s. 6d. to 5s. a year; the congregations being much diminished, as I had before occasion to observe. It is no wonder, then, that the poor, if at all able, flee from such a country and seek employment and relief in the various maritime towns in Scotland, where they arrive broken down and exhausted by previous hardship—meatless and money-less; and when unable to labour, or unsuccessful in obtain-ing work, they become a burden to a community who have no right to bear it, while those who have reduced them to that state escape scot-free. Any person acquainted gener-ally with the statistics of pauperism in Scotland will, I am sure, admit the correctness of these statements. The Highland landlords formerly counted their riches by the number of their vassals or tenants, and were anxious to retain them; hence the poem of Burns, addressed to the Highland lairds, and signed Beelzebub, by which the ever selfish policy of those gentlemen is celebrated in their endeavouring, by force, to restrain emigration to Canada. But since then the case is reversed. First the war, and then the food monopoly has made raising of cattle for the English markets, the more eligible speculation, against which the boasted feelings of clanship, as well as the claims of common humanity have entirely lost their force. Regard-ing the poll-tax or road money, it is also necessary to state, that in every case when it is not paid on the appointed day, expenses are arbitrarily added (though no legal progress has been entered) which the defaulter is obliged to submit to without means of redress. There are no tolls in the county; the roads, etc., being kept up by this poll-tax, paid by the small tenants for the exclusive benefit of those who have superseded them. In this way very large sums are screwed out of the people, even the poorest, and from the absentees, if they ever return to reside. So that if the population are not extirpated wholesale, a considerable portion of the sums laid out on improvements will ultimately return to the proprietors, from a source whence, of all others, they have no shadow of right to obtain it.

I have now arrived at an important event in my narrative; the death of an exalted personage to whom I have often had occasion to refer—the Duchess-Countess of Sutherland.

This lady who had, during a long life, maintained a high position in courtly and aristocratic society, and who was possessed of many great qualities, was called to her account on the 29th of January, 1839, in the 74th year of her age. Her death took place in London, and her body was conveyed to Sutherland by Aberdeen, and finally interred with great pomp in the family vault, beside the late Duke, her husband, in the Cathedral of Dornoch. The funeral was attended to Blackwell by many of the first nobility in England, and afterwards by her two grandsons, Lord Edward Howard, and the Honourable Francis Egerton, and by her friend and confidential servant, Mr. Loch, with their respective suites. The procession was met by Mr. Sellars, Mr. Young, and many of her under-factors and subordinate retainers, together with the whole body of the new occupiers, while the small tenantry brought up the rear of the solemn cavalcade. She was buried with the rites of the Church of

England. Mr. George Gunn, under-factor, was the only
gentleman native of the county who took a prominent part
in the management of the funeral, and who certainly did
not obtain that honour by the exercise of extraordinary virtues towards his poor countrymen : the rest were all those
who had taken an active part in the scenes of injustice and
cruelty which I have been endeavouring to represent to the
reader, in the previous part of my narrative. The trump of
fame has been seldom made to sound a louder blast, than
that which echoed through the island, with the virtues of the
Duchess ; every periodical, especially in Scotland, was for a
time literally crammed with them, but in those extravagant
encomiums few or none of her native tenantry could honestly
join. That she had many great and good qualities none
will attempt to deny, but at the same time, under the sanction or guise of her name and authority, were continually
perpetrated deeds of the most atrocious character, and her
people's wrongs still remained unredressed. Her severity
was felt, perhaps, far beyond her own intentions ; while her
benevolence was intercepted by the instruments she employed, and who so unworthily enjoyed her favour and confidence. Her favours were showered on aliens and strangers;
while few, indeed, were the drops which came to the relief of
those from whom she sprung, and whose co-eval, though
subordinate right to their native soil, had been recognised
for centuries.

The same course of draining the small tenants, under one
pretext or another, continued for some time after her Grace's
decease ; but exactions must terminate, when the means of
meeting them are exhausted. You cannot starve a hen and
make her lay eggs at the same time. The factors, having
taken all, had to make a virtue of necessity, and advise the
Duke to an act of high-sounding generosity—to remit all

arrears due by the small tenantry.   Due proclamation was
made of his Grace's benevolent intentions, with an express
condition annexed, that no future arrears would be allowed,
and that all future defaulters should be instantly removed,
and their holdings (not let to tenants, but) handed over to
their next neighbour, and failing him, to the next again, and
so on. This edict was proclaimed under the authority of
his Grace and the factors, in the year 1840, about twelve
months after the Duchess's decease, and continues the law
of the estate as regards the unfortunate natives, or small
tenantry as they are generally called.

It will be perceived that I have now brought my narrative
to an end. I may, however, with your permission, trouble
you with a few remarks in your next publication, by way of
conclusion.

LETTER XVIII.

In concluding my narrative, allow me to express—or rather
to declare my inability to express—the deep sense I entertain of your kindness in permitting me to occupy so large a
space of your columns, in an attempt to pourtray the wrongs
of my countrymen. I trust these feelings will be participated
by those whose cause you have thus enabled me to bring
before the public, as well as by all benevolent and enlightened minds, who abhor oppression, and sympathize with its
victims.   I am conscious that my attempt has been a feeble
one.   In many cases my powers of language fell short, and
in others I abstained from going to the full extent, when I
was not quite prepared with proof, or when the deeds of our
oppressors were so horrible in their nature and consequence
as to exceed belief.

Though nowhere in the North Highlands have such atrocities been practised in the wholesale way they have been in Sutherland, yet the same causes are producing like effects, more or less generally in most, if not all, the surrounding counties. Sutherland has served as a model for successfully "clearing" the land of its aboriginal inhabitants, driving them to the sea-shore, or into the sea,—to spots of barren moors—to the wilds of Canada—and to Australia ; or if unable to go so far, to spread themselves over Lowlands, in quest of menial employment among strangers, to whom their language seems barbarous, who are already overstocked with native labourers, besides those continually pouring in from Ireland. No wonder the Highland lairds combine to resist a government inquiry, which would lead to an exposure of their dark and daring deeds, and render a system of efficient poor laws (not sham, like those now existing) inevitable. Were all the paupers they have created, by "removing" the natives and substituting strangers and cattle in their places, enabled to claim that support from the soil they are justly entitled to, what would become of their estates ?

Hence their alarm and anxiety to stifle all inquiry but that conducted by themselves, their favourites and retainers, and their ever-subservient auxiliaries, the parochial clergy. Will these parties expose themselves by tracing the true causes of Highland destitution ? Oh, no ! What they cannot ascribe to Providence, they will lay to the charge of the "indolent, improvident, and intractable character," they endeavour to cover their own foul deeds by ascribing to their too passive victims. They say "the Highlanders would pay no rent". A falsehood on the very face of it. Were not the tenants' principal effects in cattle, the article of all others most convenient of arrest ? "The Highlanders were unteachable, enemies to innovation or improvement, and incorrigibly opposed to the will of their superiors." Where are the proofs? What methods were taken to instruct them in improved husbandry, or any other improvements? None! They were driven out of the land of their fathers, causelessly, cruelly, and recklessly. Let their enemies say what have been their crimes of revenge under the most inhumane provocation? Where are the records in our courts of law, or in the statistics of crime, of the fell deeds laid to the charge of the expatriated Highlander? They are nowhere to be found, except in the groundless accusations of the oppressors, who calculating on their simplicity, their patient, moral, and religious character, which even the base conduct of their clergy could not pervert, drove them unresisting, like sheep to the slaughter, or like mute fishes, unable to scream, on whom any violence could be practised with impunity. It was thought an illiterate people, speaking a lauguage almost unknown to the public press, could not make their wrongs heard as they ought to be, through the length and breadth of the land. To give their wrongs a tongue—to implore inquiry by official, disinterested parties into the cause of mal-practices which have been so long going on, so as if possible to procure some remedy in future— has been my only motive for availing myself of your kindness to throw a gleam of light on Highland misery, its causes and its consequences. And I cannot too earnestly implore all those in any authority, who take an interest in the cause of humanity, to resist that partial and close-conducted, sham inquiry to which interested parties would have recourse to screen themselves from public odium, and save their pockets. Some of these parties are great, wealthy, and influential. Several of them have talent, education, and other facilities for perverting what they cannot altogether suppress, making "the worst appear the better reason," and white-washing their blackest deeds—therefore, I say, beware! They want now a government grant, forsooth, to take away the redundant population! There is no redundant population but black cattle and sheep, and their owners, which the lairds have themselves introduced; and do they want a grant to rid of these? Verily, no! Their misdeeds are only equalled by their shameless impudence to propose such a thing. First, to ruin the people and make them paupers, and when their wrongs and miseries have made the very stones cry out, seek to get rid of them at the public expense! Insolent proposition! "Contumelious their humanity." No doubt there have been some new churches built, but where are the congregations? Some schools erected, but how can the children of parents steeped in poverty profit by them? The clergy say they dispense the bread of life, but if they do so, do they give it freely—do they not *sell it* for as much as they can get, and do the dirty work of the proprietors, instead of the behests of Him they pretend to serve? Did this precious article grow on any lands which the proprietors could turn into sheep walks, I verily believe they would do so, and the clergy would sanction the deed! They and the proprietors think the natives have no right to any of God's mercies, but what they dole out in a stinted and miserable charity. Mr. Dempster of Skibo, the orator and apologist of the Highland lairds, says he " keeps two *permanent* soup-kitchens on his estate "; if this were true (as I have reason to believe it is not), what is to be inferred but that the wholesome ruin inflicted on the natives has rendered such a degrading expedient necessary. Their forefathers, a stalwart and athletic race, needed no soup-kitchens, nor would their progeny, if they had not been inhumanely and unjustly treated. Mr. Loch says in his work, that the Sutherlanders

were "in a state of nature". Well; he and his coadjutors
have done what they could to put them in an unnatural
state—a state from which it would take an age to reclaim
them.   I admit there was great need of improvement in
Sutherland fifty years ago, as there was at that time in the
Lothians and elsewhere; but where, except in the Highlands,
do we find general expulsion and degradation of the inhabitants resorted to by way of improvement ?   But Mr. Loch
has improved—if not in virtue, at least in station—and
become a great man and a legislator, from very small beginnings ; he and his coadjutors have waxed fat on the
miseries of their fellow-creatures, and on the animals they
have substituted for human beings.   Well, I would not
incur their responsibility for all their grandeur and emolu-
ments.   Mr. Dempster has improved, and his factor from
being a kitchen boy, has become a very thriving gentleman.
These are the kind of improvements which have taken
place, and all would go merrily if they could get entirely
rid of the small tenants, "the redundant population," by a
grant of public money.   A redundant population in an
extensively exporting country !   This is *Irish* political economy.   The same cause (the food taxes) is in operation in
that unhappy country, and producing similar results ; but
the Irish do not always bear it so tamely; a little Lynch law,
a few-extra judicial executions is now and then administered,
by way of example.   This, however, is a wrong mode of
proceeding, and one which I trust my countrymen will never
imitate : better suffer than commit a crime.   No system of
poor law in the Highlands would be of any avail, but one
that would confer SETTLEMENT ON EVERY PERSON BORN IN
THE PARISH.   The lairds will evade every other, and to save
their pockets would be quite unscrupulous as to the means.
They could easily resort again to their burning and hunting,

but a settlement on the English plan would oblige them either to support the paupers they have made, or send them away at their own expense. This would be bare justice, and in my humble opinion nothing short of it would be of any avail. Comparatively few of the sufferers would now claim the benefit of such settlements; the greater part of them have already emigrated, and located elsewhere, and would not fancy to come back as paupers whatever their right might be. But there are still too many groaning and pining away in helpless and hopeless destitution in Sutherland, and in the surrounding counties, and I have reason to know that the West Highlands are much in the same situation. There is much need, then, for official inquiry, to prevent this mass of human misery from accumulating, as well as to afford some hope of relief to present sufferers. I have now made an end for the present; but should any contradiction appear, or any new event of importance to my countrymen occur, I shall claim your kind indulgence to resume the pen.

———

LETTER XIX.

I AM glad to find that some of my countrymen are coming forward with communications to your paper confirming my statements, and expressing that gratitude we ought all deeply to feel for the opportunity you have afforded of bringing our case before the public, by so humble an instrument as myself.

Nothing, I am convinced, but fear of further persecution, prevents many more from writing such letters, and hence you need not wonder if some of those you receive are anonymous. They express a wish, which from various sources of information, I am inclined to think general, that my narrative should appear, as it now will, in the form of a pamphlet, and that my own particular case should form an appendage to it. I had no intention originally of bringing my particular case and family sufferings before the public, but called on, as I am, it appears a duty to the public, as well as myself, to give a brief account of it, lest withholding it might lead to suspicion as to my motives and character.

I served an apprenticeship in the mason trade to my father, and on coming to man's estate I married my present wife, the partner of my fortunes, most of which have been adverse, and she, the weaker vessel, has largely partaken of my misfortunes in a life of suffering and a ruined constitution. Our marriage took place in 1818. My wife was the daughter of Charles Gordon, a man well known and highly esteemed in the parish of Farr, and indeed throughout the county, for his religious and moral character.

For some years I followed the practice of going south during the summer months for the purpose of improving in my trade and obtaining better wages, and returning in the winter to enjoy the society of my family and friends; and also, to my grief, to witness the scenes of devastation that were going on, to which, in the year 1820, my worthy father-in-law fell a victim. He breathed his last amid the scenes I have described, leaving six orphans in a state of entire destitution to be provided for; for he had lost his all, in common with the other ejected inhabitants of the county.

This helpless family now fell to my care, and, in order to discharge my duty to them more effectually, I wished to give up my summer excursions, and settle and pursue my business at home.

I, therefore, returned from Edinburgh in the year 1822, and soon began to find employment, undertaking mason work by estimate, etc., and had I possessed a less independent mind and a more crouching disposition, I might perhaps have remained. But stung with the oppression and injustice prevailing around me, and seeing the contrast my country exhibited to the state of the Lowlands, I could not always hold my peace ; hence I soon became a marked man, and my words and actions were carefully watched for an opportunity to make an example of me. After I had baffled many attempts, knowing how they were set for me, my powerful enemies at last succeeded in effecting my ruin after seven years' labour in the pious work ! If any chose to say I owed them money, they had no more to do than summon me to the court, in which the factor was judge, and a decreet, right or wrong, was sure to issue. Did any owe me money, it was quite optional whether they paid me or not, they well knew I could obtain no legal redress.

In the year 1827, I was summoned for £5 8s., which I had previously paid [in this case the factor was both pursuer and judge !]. I defended, and produced receipts and other vouchers of payment having been made; all went for nothing! The factor, pursuer and judge, commenced the following dialogue :—

Judge—Well, Donald, do you owe this money ?

Donald—I would like to see the pursuer before I would enter into any defences.

Judge—I'll pursue you.

Donald—I thought you were my judge, sir.

Judge—I'll both pursue and judge you—did you not promise me on a former occasion that you would pay this debt ?

Donald—No, Sir.

Judge—John MacKay (constable), seize the defender.

I was accordingly collared like a criminal, and kept a prisoner in an adjoining room for some hours, and afterwards placed again at the bar, when the conversation continued.

Judge—Well, Donald, what have you got to say now, will you pay the money?

Donald—Just the same, sir, as before you imprisoned me; I deny the debt.

Judge—Well, Donald, you are one of the damn'dest rascals in existence, but if you have the sum pursued for between heaven and hell, I'll make you pay it, *whatever receipts you may hold*, and I'll get you removed from the estate.

Donald—Mind, sir, you are in a magisterial capacity.

Judge—I'll let you know that—(with another volley of execrations).

Donald—Sir, your conduct disqualifies you for your office, and under the protection of the law of the land, and in presence of this court, I put you to defiance.

I was then ordered from the bar, and the case continued undecided. Steps were, however, immediately taken to put the latter threat—my removal—my banishment!—into execution.

Determined to leave no means untried to obtain deliverance, I prepared an humble memorial in my own name, and that of the helpless orphans, whose protector I was, and had it transmitted to the Marquis and Marchioness of Stafford, praying for an investigation. In consequence of this, on the very term day, on which I had been ordered to remove, I received a verbal message from one of the under-factors, that it was the noble proprietor's pleasure that I should retain possession, repair my houses and provide my fuel as usual, until Mr. Loch should come to Sutherlandshire, and then my case would be investigated. On this announcement becoming known to my opponent, he became alarmed, and the parish minister no less so, that the man he feasted with was in danger of being disgraced ; every iron was therefore put in the fire, to defeat and ruin Donald for his presumption in disputing the will of a factor, and to make him an example to deter others from a similar rebellion.

The result proved how weak a just cause must prove in Sutherland, or anywhere, against cruel despotic factors and graceless ministers ; my case was judged and decided before Mr. Loch left London ! I, however, got Jeddart justice, for on that gentleman's arrival, I was brought before him for examination, though, I had good reason to know, my sentence had been pronounced in London six weeks before, and everything he said confirmed what I had been told. I produced the receipts and other documents, and evidence, which proved fully the statements in my memorial, and vindicated my character apparently to his satisfaction. He dismissed me courteously, and in a soothing tone of voice bade me go home and make myself easy, and before he left the country he would let me know the result. I carried home the good news to my wife, but her fears, her dreams, and forebodings were not so easily got over, and the event proved that her apprehensions were too well founded, for, on the 20th October, 1830, about a month after the investigation by Mr. Loch, the concluding scene took place.

On that day a messenger with a party of eight men following entered my dwelling (I being away about forty miles off at work), about three o'clock just as the family were rising from dinner ; my wife was seized with a fearful panic at seeing the fulfilment of all her worst forebodings about to take place. The party allowed no time for parley, but, having put out the family with violence, proceeded to fling out the furniture, bedding, and other effects in quick time, and after extinguishing the fire, proceeded to nail up the doors and windows in the face of the helpless woman, with a sucking infant at her breast, and three other children, the eldest under eight years of age, at her side. But how shall I describe the horrors of that scene? Wind, rain and sleet were ushering in a night of extraordinary darkness and violence, even in that inclement region. My wife and children, after remaining motionless a while in mute astonishment at the ruin which had so suddenly overtaken them, were compelled to seek refuge for the night under some neighbour's roof, but they found every door shut against them! Messengers had been despatched warning all the surrounding inhabitants, at the peril of similar treatment, against affording shelter, or assistance, to wife, child, or animal belonging to Donald MacLeod. The poor people, well aware of the rigour with which such edicts were carried into execution, durst not afford my distressed family any assistance in such a night as even an "enemy's dog" might have expected shelter. After spending most part of the night in fruitless attempts to obtain the shelter of a roof or hovel, my wife at last returned to collect some of her scattered furniture, and to erect with her own hands a temporary shelter against the walls of her late comfortable residence, but even this attempt proved in vain; the wind dispersed her materials as fast as she could collect them, and she was obliged to bide the pelting of the pitiless storm with no covering but the frowning heavens, and no sound in her ears but the storm, and the cries of her famishing children. Death seemed to be staring them in the face, for by remaining where they were till morning, it was next to impossible that even the strongest of them could survive, and to travel any distance amid the wind, rain, and darkness, in that rugged district, seemed to afford no prospect but that of death by falling over some of the cliffs or precipices with which they were surrounded, or even into the sea, as many others had done before.

LETTER XX.

BEFORE proceeding to detail the occurrences of that memorable night in which my wife and children were driven from their dwelling, it seems necessary to guard against any misconception that might arise from my rather incredible statement, that the factor (whose name I omit for obvious reasons) was both pursuer and judge.

The pretended debt had been paid, for which I hold a receipt, but the person represented it as still due, and the factor advanced the amount, issued the summons, etc., and proceeded in court in the manner I have described in my last. But to proceed with my narrative.

The only means left my wife seemed to be the choice of perishing with her children where she was, or of making some perilous attempts to reach distant human habitations where she might hope for shelter. Being a woman of some resolution, she determined on the latter course. Buckling up her children, including the one she had hitherto held at her breast, in the best manner she could, she left them in charge of the eldest (now a soldier in the 78th regiment), giving them such victuals as she could collect, and prepared to take the road for Caithness, fifteen miles off, in such a night and by such a road as might have appalled a stout heart of the other sex ! And for a long while she had the cries of her children, whom she had slender hopes of seeing again alive, sounding in her ears. This was too much ! No wonder she has not been the same person since. She had not proceeded many miles when she met with a good Samaritan, and acquaintance, of the name of Donald MacDonald, who, disregarding the danger he incurred, opened his door to her, refreshed and consoled her, and (still under the cover of night), accompanied her to the dwelling of William Innes, Esq., of Sandside, Caithness, and through his influence, that gentlemen took her under his protection, and gave her permission to occupy an empty house of his at Armidale (a sheep farm he held of the Sutherland family), only a few miles from the dwelling she had been turned out of the day before. On arriving there she was obliged to take some rest for her exhausted frame, notwithstanding the horrible suspense she was in as to the fate of her children.

At this time I was working in Wick, and on that night had laboured under such great uneasiness and apprehension of something wrong at home that I could get no rest, and at last determined to set out and see how it fared with my family, and late in the evening I overtook my wife and her benevolent conductor proceeding from Sandside. After a brief recital of the events of the previous night, she implored me to leave her and seek the children, of whose fate she was ignorant. At that moment I was in a fit mood for a deed that would have served as a future warning to Highland tyrants, but the situation of my imploring wife, who suspected my intention, and the hope of saving my children, stayed my hand, and delayed the execution of justice on the miscreants, till they shall have appeared at a higher tribunal.

I made the best of my way to the place near our dwelling where the children were left, and to my agreeable surprise, found them alive; the eldest boy, in pursuance of his mother's instructions, had made great exertions, and succeeded in obtaining for them temporary shelter. He took the infant on his back, and the other two took hold of him by the kilt, and in this way they travelled in darkness, through rough and smooth, bog and mire, till they arrived at a grand-aunt's house, when, finding the door open, they bolted in, and the boy advancing to his astonished aunt, laid his infant burden in her lap, without saying a word, and proceeding to unbuckle the other two, he placed them before the fire without waiting for invitation. The goodman here rose, and said he must leave the house and seek a lodging for himself, as he could not think of turning the children out, and yet dreaded the ruin threatend to any that would harbour or shelter them, and he had no doubt his house would be watched to see if he should transgress against the order. His wife, a pious woman, upbraided him with cowardice, and declared that if a legion of devils were watching her, she would not put out the children or leave the house either. So they got leave to remain till I found them next day, but the man impelled by his fears, did go and obtain a lodging two miles off. I now brought the children to their mother, and set about collecting my little furniture and other effects, which had been damaged by exposure to the weather, and some of it lost or destroyed. I brought what I thought worth the trouble, to Armidale, and having thus secured them and seen the family under shelter, I began to cast about to see how they were to live, and here I found troubles and difficulties besetting us on every side.

I had no fear of being able by my work to maintain the family in common necessaries, if we could get them for money, but one important necessary, fuel, we could scarcely at all obtain, as nobody would venture to sell or give us peats (the only fuel used), for fear of the factors ; but at last it was contrived that they would allow us to take them by stealth, and under cover of night !

My employment obliging me to be often from home, this laborious task fell to the lot of my poor wife. The winter came on with more than usual severity, and often amidst blinding, suffocating drifts, and tempests unknown in the lowlands, had this poor, tenderly brought-up woman to toil through snow, wind, and rain, for miles, with a burden of peats on her back! Instances, however, were not few of the kind assistance of neighbours endeavouring by various ways to mitigate her hard lot, though, of course, all by stealth, lest they should incur the vengeance of the factors.

During the winter and following spring, every means was used to induce Mr. Innes to withdraw his protection and turn us out of the house; so that I at last determined to take steps for removing myself and family for ever from those scenes of persecution and misery. With this view, in the latter end of spring, I went to Edinburgh, and found employment, intending when I had saved as much as would cover the expenses, to bring the family away. As soon as it was known that I was away, our enemies recommenced their work. Mr.———, a gentleman, who fattened on the spoils of the poor in Sutherland, and who is now pursuing the same course on the estates of Sir John Sinclair in Caithness; this manager and factor bounced into my house one day quite unexpectedly, and began abusing my wife, and threatened her if she did not instantly remove, he would take steps that would astonish her, the nature of which she would not know till they fell upon her, adding that he knew Donald MacLeod was now in Edinburgh, and could not assist her in making resistance. The poor woman, knowing she had no mercy to expect, and fearing even for her life, removed with her family and little effects to my mother's house which stood near the parish church, and was received kindly by her. There she hoped to find shelter and repose for a short time, till I should come and take her and the family away, and this being the week of the sacrament, she was anxious to partake of that ordinance, in the house where her forefathers had worshipped, before she bade it farewell for ever. But on the Thursday previous to that solemn occasion, the factor again terrified her by his appearance, and alarmed my mother to such an extent that my poor family had again to turn out in the night, and had they not a more powerful friend, they would have been forced to spend that night in the open air. Next day she bade adieu to her native country and friends, leaving the sacrament to be received by her oppressors, from the hands of one no better than themselves, and, after two days of incredible toil, she arrived with the family at Thurso, a distance of nearly forty miles !

These protracted sufferings and alarms have made fatal inroads on the health of this once strong and healthy woman—one of the best of wives—so that instead of the cheerful and active helpmate she formerly was, she is now, except at short intervals, a burden to herself, with little or no hope of recovery. She has been under medical treatment for years, and has used a great quantity of medicine with little effect ; the injuries she received in body and mind, were too deep for even her good spirits and excellent constitution to overcome, and she remains a living monument of Highland oppression.

LETTER XXI.

I BEG leave, by way of conclusion, to take a retrospective glance at some of the occurrences that preceded the violent expulsion of my family, as described in my two last letters, and our final retirement from the country of our nativity.

For reasons before stated, nothing could have given more satisfaction to the factors, clergy, and all the Jacks-in-office under them, than a final riddance of that troublesome man, Donald MacLeod ; and hence their extreme eagerness to make an example of him, to deter others from calling their proceedings in question. I mentioned in letter XIX that on being unjustly and illegally imprisoned, and decerned to pay money I did not owe, I prepared and forwarded a memorial to the noble proprietors (the then Marquis and Marchioness of Stafford), setting forth the hardships of my case, and praying for investigation, alleging that I would answer the accusation of my enemies, by undeniable testimonials of honest and peaceful character. This memorial was returned with the deliverance that Mr. Loch, on his next visit to Sutherland, would examine into my case and decide. I then set about procuring my proposed certificate preparatory to the investigation, but here I found myself baffled and disappointed in a quarter from which I had no reason to expect such treatment. I waited on my parish minister, the Rev. Mr. Mackenzie, requesting him to give me a certificate, and then, after him, I could obtain the signatures of the elders and as many of the other parishoners as might be necessary. He made no objection at the time, but alleging that he was then engaged, said I could send my wife for it. I left directions with her accordingly, and returned to my work. The same night the factor (my pretended creditor and judge) *had the minister and his family to spend the evening with him*, and the consequence was that in the morning a messenger was dispatched from his reverence to my wife, to say, that she need not take the trouble of calling for the certificate, as he had changed his mind ! Some days after, I returned and waited on the Rev. gentleman to inquire the cause of this change. I had great difficulty in obtaining an audience, and when at last I did, it was little to my satisfaction. His manner was contemptuous and forbidding ; at last he told me that he could not give me a certificate as I was at variance with the factor; that my conduct was unscriptural, as I obeyed not those set in authority over me, etc. I excused and defended myself as well as I could, but all went for nothing, and at last he ordered me to be off, and shut the door in my face. This took place in June, 1830, and Mr. Loch was not expected till the September following, during which interval I had several rencounters with the minister. Many of his elders and parishioners pleaded and remonstrated with him on my behalf, well knowing that little attention would be paid in high quarters to my complaints, however just, without his sanction ; and considerable excitement prevailed in the parish about this dispute, but the minister remained im-moveable. Meantime the parish schoolmaster mentioned in confidence to one of the elders (who was a relation of my wife, and communicated it to us) that my case was already decided by Mr. Loch, though a sham trial would take place; that he had been told this, and he had it from good authority, and that the best thing I could do was to leave the place entirely. I could not believe this, but the result proved the truth of it. Matters continued in the same way till Mr. Loch's arrival, when I ventured to repeat my request to the minister, but found him still more determined, and I was dismissed with more than usual contempt. I then got a certificate prepared myself, and readily obtained the signatures of the elders and neighbouring parishioners to the number of several hundreds, which I presented to Mr. Loch, along with the before-mentioned memorial, when the following dialogue took place between that gentleman and me in presence of the factors, etc.

Mr. Loch.—Well, Mr. MacLeod, why don't you pay this £5 8s. you were summoned for ?

Donald.—Just, sir, because I don't consider myself entitled to pay it. I hold legal receipts to show that I paid it two years ago ; besides, that is a case to be legally decided before a competent court, and has no connection with my memorial.

Mr. L.—Will you pay it altogether or by instalments, if you are allowed to remain on the estate ?

D.—Let the case be withdrawn from the civil court or decided by the civil magistrate, before I answer that question.

Mr. L.—Well, can you produce the certificate of character mentioned in this memorial ?

I handed over to him the certificate mentioned above, with three or four sheets full of names attached to it. He looked at it for some time (perhaps surprised at the number of signatures) and then said,—

Mr. L.—I cannot see the minister's name here, how is this ?

D.—I applied to the minister and he would not sign it.

Mr. L.—Why ?

D.—He stated as his reason that I was at variance with the factors.

One of the Factors.—That is a falsehood.

Mr. L.—I will wait upon Mr. MacKenzie on the subject.

D.—Will you allow me, sir, to meet you and Mr. MacKenzie face to face, when he is asked to give his reasons ?

Mr. L.—Why will you not believe what he says ?

D.—I have got too much reason to doubt it ; but if he attempts to deny what I have stated, I hope you will allow him to be examined on oath ?

Mr. L.—By no means, we must surely believe the minister.

After asking me some further questions which had nothing to do with the matter in hand, he dismissed me in seeming good humour.

I pressed to know his decision in my case, but he said, "you will get to know it before I leave the country; make yourself easy, I will write to your parish minister in a few days". The result was the cruel expulsion of my family and the spoliation of my goods, as detailed in my two last letters.

Mr. Loch, in his judgment on my case, alleged as his principal reason for punishing me that Mr. MacKenzie denied my assertions in regard to himself, and represented me as a turbulent character.

During our temporary residence at Armidale, I took an opportunity of again waiting on the rev. gentleman when he was catechising in a neighbouring fishing village with several of his elders in company, and asked to speak with him in their presence. He attempted to meet me outside the door, but I pushed in where the elders were sitting at breakfast; saying, "No sir, I wish what passes between you and me to be before witnesses. I want a certificate of my moral character, or an explanation from you before your elders why it is withheld." Here my worthy friend Donald MacDonald (the preserver of my wife's life on the memorable night of her expulsion) interfered and expostulated with his reverence, who driven into a corner, found no excuse for refusal, except that he had not writing materials convenient. I directly met this objection by producing the articles required, yet, strange to say, he found means to shuffle the business over by a solemn promise, in presence of his elders, to do it on a certain mentioned day. I waited on him that day, and after long delay was admitted into his parlour and accosted with, "Well, MacLeod, I am not intending to give you a certificate." "Why so, sir?" "Because you have told false-hoods of me to Mr. Loch, and I cannot certify for a man that I know to be a liar," adding "Donald, I would favour you on your father's account, and much more on your

father-in-law's account, but after what you have said of me,
I cannot." I repelled the charge of being a liar, and said,
"I do believe that if my father and father-in-law, whom you
have mentioned with so much respect, stood at the gate of
Heaven seeking admittance, and nothing to prevent them
but a false accusation on the part of some of the factors, you
would join in refusing their entrance, to all eternity". He
rose up and said, "you are a Satan and not fit for human
society". I retired for that time; but ultimately forced him,
by incessant applications, to write and sign the following :—

> "This certifies that the bearer, DONALD MACLEOD, is a native of
> this parish, a married man, free from church censure ; therefore he,
> his wife and family may be *admitted as Gospel hearers* wherever
> Providence may order their lot.
>
> Given at Farr Manse.   (Signed)

Previous to granting this certificate, the minister proposed
to bind me up not to use it to the prejudice of the Marquis
of Stafford, or any of his factors. This point, however, he
did not carry, for when he submitted it to the session he was
overruled by their votes.

This concludes the narrative of what I have myself suffered
at the hands of the petty tyrants whom I had enraged by
denouncing their barbarous treatment of my countrymen,
and whose infamous deeds I have had the satisfaction of
exposing to public reprobation. I shall not resume the pen
on this subject unless I see that what I have written requires
to be followed up to prevent a continuation of such atrocities
as I have already recorded.

RIOTS IN DURNESS.

LETTER XXII.

When concluding that series of letters, descriptive of the woes of Sutherlandshire, which I now republish in the form of a pamphlet, I was not expecting so soon to find occasion to add important new matter to the sad detail. Another portion of my native county has fallen under the oppressor, and got into the fangs of law, which being administered by those interested, little mercy can be expected by the wretched defaulters.

All those conversant with the public papers will have seen an article, copied from the *Inverness Courier*, entitled, "Riot in Durness, Sutherlandshire," in which as usual a partial and one-sided account of the affair is given, and the whole blame laid on the unfortunate inhabitants. The violation of law, committed by the poor people, driven to desperation, and for which they will no doubt have to pay dear, is exaggerated, while their inhuman oppression and provocation are carefully left out of sight. The following facts of the case are a combination of my own knowledge, and that of trustworthy correspondents who were eye-witnesses of this unfortunate occurrence, which will yet be productive of much misery to the victims—perhaps end in causing their blood to be shed !

Mr. Anderson, the tacksman of Keenabin, and other farms under Lord Reay, which were the scene of the riot, was one of the earliest of that unhallowed crew of new tenants, or middle-men, who came in over the heads of the native farmers. He, with several others I could name, some of whom have come to an unhappy end, counting the natives as their slaves and prey, disposed without scruple of them and all that they had, just as it suited their own interest or convenience, reckless of the wrongs and misery they inflicted on these simple, unresisting people. They were removed from their comfortable houses and farms in the interior, to spots on the sea shore, to make room for the new comers with their flocks and herds, and to get their living, and pay exorbitant rents, by cultivating kelp, and deep-sea fishing. In these pursuits their persevering courage and industry enabled them to surmount appalling difficulties, though with much suffering and waste of health and life. The tacksman set up for a fish curer and *rented the sea to them* at his own pleasure, furnishing boats and implements at an exorbitant price, *while he took their fish at his own price*, and thus got them drowned in debt and consequent bondage, from which, by failures both in the kelp and fishing trades, they have never been able to relieve themselves. Seeing this, and thinking he could, after taking their all for thirty years, put their little holdings, improved by their exertions, to a more profitable use, this gentlemen *humanely* resolved to extirpate them, root and branch, after he had sucked their blood and peeled their flesh, till nothing more could be got from them, and regardless of the misery to which he doomed them, how they might fare, or which way they were to turn to procure a subsistence. To emigrate they were unable, and to repair to the manufacturing towns in quest of employment, when such multitudes are in destitution already, would afford no hope of relief. Where, then, were they to find refuge? To this question, so often urged by the poor outcasts in Sutherlandshire, the general answer of their tyrants was, "let them go to hell, but they must leave our boundaries".

Human patience and endurance have limits, and is it to be wondered at that poor creatures driven to such extremities should be tempted to turn on their oppressors, and violate the letter of the law? Hence it is true that the poor people gathered, and seized and burned the paper, which appeared as a death warrant to them (and may in one way or other prove so to them) and did their utmost, though without much personal violence, to scare away their enemies; and though law may punish, will humanity not sympathise with them? The story as represented in the papers, of severe beating and maltreatment of the officers is, to say the least, a gross exaggeration. The intention, however indefensible on the score of law, was merely to intimidate, not to injure. The military, it seems, is now to be called upon to wind up the drama in the way of their profession. I pray it may not end tragically. If the sword be unsheathed at Cape Wrath, let the Southrons look out! If the poor and destitute—made so by injustice—are to be cut down in Sutherland, it may only be the beginning; there are plenty of poor and destitute elsewhere, whose numbers the landlords, to save their monopoly, might find it convenient to curtail; and to do which they only want a colourable pretext. Meanwhile, I shall watch the progress of the affair at Durness, and beg to call on all rightly constituted minds to sympathise with the distress of the unfortunate people.

LETTER XXIII.

HAVING lately exposed the partial and exaggerated statements in the *Inverness Courier*, the organ of the oppressors of Sutherlandshire, my attention is again called to subsequent paragraphs in that paper, and which I feel it my duty to notice.

Since my last, I have received communications from correspondents on whom I can rely, which, I need scarcely say, give a very different colour to the proceedings from what appears in the *Courier*, emanating, as it evidently does, from the party inflicting the injury. The first notice in that paper represents the conduct of the poor natives in the blackest aspect, while the latter, that of the 27th October, is calculated to mislead the public in another way, by representing them as sensible of their errors, and acknowledging the justice of the severities practised upon them.

The *Courier* says, "We are happy to learn that the excitement that led to the disturbance by Mr. Anderson's tenants in Durness has subsided, and that the people are quiet, peaceful, and fully sensible of the illegality and unjustifiable nature of their proceedings. The Sheriff addressed the people in a powerful speech, with an effect which had the best consequences. They soon made written communications to the Sheriff and Mr. Anderson, stating their contrition, and soliciting forgiveness; promising to remove voluntarily in May next, if permitted in the meantime to remain and occupy their houses. An arrangement on this footing was then happily accomplished, which, while it vindicates the law, tempers justice with mercy. Subsequently, Mr. Napier, Advocate-Depute, arrived at the place to conduct the investigation."

Latterly, the *Courier* says—" The clergyman of the parish convinced the people, and Mr. Lumsden, the Sheriff, addressed them on the serious nature of their late proceed-ings; this induced them to petition Mr. Anderson, their landlord, asking his forgiveness ; and he has allowed them to remain till May next. We trust something will be done in the interval for the poor homeless Mountaineers." This is the subdued, though contemptuous tone of the *Courier*, owing doubtless to the noble and impartial conduct of the Advocate-Depute, Mr. Napier, who in conducting the inves-tigation, found, notwithstanding the virulent and railing accusations brought by those who had driven the poor people to madness, that their conduct was very different from what it had been represented. The *Courier*, in his first article, called for the military "to vindicate the law" by shedding the blood of the Sutherland rebels ; but now calls them "poor homeless mountaineers". His crocodile tears accord ill with the former virulence of him and his employers, and we have to thank Mr. Napier for the change. The local authorities who assisted at the precognition did the utmost that malice could suggest to exasperate that gentleman against the people, but he went through the case in his own way, probing it to the bottom, and qualifying their rage by his coolness and impartiality.

Notwithstanding a series of injuries and provocations un-paralleled, this is the first time the poor Sutherlanders, so famous in their happier days for defending their country and its laws, have been led to transgress ; and I hope when the day of trial comes, the very worst of them will be found "more sinned against than sinning". It is to be lamented that the law has been violated, but still more to be lamented that all the best attributes of our common nature—all the principles of justice, mercy, and religion, had been violated by the oppressors of this people, under colour of law! The poor victims, simple, ignorant, and heart-broken, have men of wealth, talent, and influence for their opponents and accusers—the very individuals who have been the authors of all their woes, are now their vindictive persecutors. Against the combination of landlords, factors, and other officials, there is none to espouse their cause. One of my correspondents says, that the only gentleman who seemed to take any interest in the people's cause was ordered by Sheriff Lumsden out of his presence. Another says, no wonder the Sheriff was so disposed, for when he arrived in Dornoch, the officials represented the people as savages in a state of rebellion, so that he at first declined proceeding without military protection, and in consequence, a detachment of the 53rd Regiment, in Edinburgh Castle, received orders to march; and could a steamboat have been procured at the time, which providence prevented, one hundred rank and file would have been landed on the shores of Sutherlandshire, and, under the direction of the people's enemies, would probably have stained their arms with innocent blood! But before a proper conveyance could be obtained, the order was countermanded, the Sheriff having found cause to alter his opinion, and the people, though goaded into momentary error, became immediately amenable to his advice. The clergyman of the parish, also made himself useful on this occasion, threatening the people with punishment here and hereafter, if they refused to bow their necks to the oppressor. According to him, all the evils inflicted upon them were ordained of God, and for their good, whereas any opposition on their part proceeded from the devil, and subjected them to just punishment here, and eternal torment hereafter. Christ says:—" Of how much more value is a man than a sheep?" The Sutherland clergy never preached this doctrine, but practically the reverse. They literally prefer flocks of sheep to their human flocks, and lend their aid to every scheme for extirpating the latter to make room for the former. They find their account in leaguing with the oppressors, following up the threatenings of fire and sword by the Sheriff with the terrors of the bottomless pit. They gained their end; the people prostrated themselves at the feet of their oppressors, "whose tender mercies are cruel". The *Courier* says, "the law has thus been vindicated". Is it not rather injustice and tyranny that have been vindicated, and the people made a prey? When they were ordered, in the manner described, to put themselves entirely in the wrong, and beg mercy, they were led to believe this would procure a full pardon and kinder treatment. But their submission was immediately followed up by the precognition, in which, as I said before, every means was used to criminate them, and exaggerate their offence, and it depends on the view the Lord Advocate may be induced to take, what is to be their fate. One thing is certain, Mr. Anderson and his colleagues will be content with nothing short of their expatriation, either to Van Dieman's Land or the place the clergy consigned them to; he cares not which. For the mercy which, as the *Courier* says, has been tempered with justice, of allowing the people to possess their houses till May, while their crop has been lost by the bad weather, or destroyed by neglect during the disturbance, they are mainly indebted to Mr. Napier. Anderson found himself shamed into a consent, which he would otherwise never have given. God knows, their miserable allotments, notwithstanding the toil and money they have expended on them, are not worth contending for, did the poor creatures know where to go when banished? but this with their attachment to the soil, makes them feel it like death itself, to think of removing.

Anderson craftily turned this feeling to his advantage, for, though he obtained the decrees of ejectment in April, he postponed their execution till the herring fishing was over, in order to drain every shilling the poor people had earned, exciting the hope, that if they paid up, they would be allowed to remain! The *Courier* hopes "something will be done for the poor mountaineers". O my late happy, high-minded countrymen, has it come to this? Represented as wild animals or savages, and hunted accordingly in your own native straths, so often defended by the sinews and blood of your vigorous ancestors!

Surely, your case must arouse the sympathy of generous Britons, otherwise the very stones will cry out! Surely, there is still so much virtue remaining in the country that your wrongs will be made to ring in the ears of your oppressors, till they are obliged to hide their heads for very shame, and tardy justice at length overtake them in the shape of public indignation.

———

LETTER XXIV.

SINCE my last communication was written, I have received letters from several correspondents in the north of Scotland, and I now proceed to lay a portion of the contents before the public. Much of the information I have received must be suppressed, from prudential considerations. Utter ruin would instantly overtake the individual, especially if he were an official, who dared to throw a gleam of light on the black deeds going on, or give a tongue to the people's wrongs. Besides, the language of some of the letters is too strong and justly indignant, to venture its publication, least I might involve myself and others in the toils of the law, with the meshes of which I am but little acquainted; hence my correspondence must, generally speaking, be suppressed or emasculated. From the mass of evidence received, I am fully satisfied that the feeble resistance to the instruments of cruelty and oppression at Durness—and which was but a solitary and momentry outbreak of feeling—owes its importance as a *riot* entirely to the inventive and colouring talents of the correspondent of the *Inverness Courier*. One of my correspondents says, "this affray must be a pre-concerted one on the part of the authorities"; another says "the Advocate-Depute asked me, why did the Duke of Sutherland's tenants join Mr. Anderson's tenants; my reply was (which he allowed to be true) that when Anderson would remove his, he and his either hand neighbours would directly use their influence to get the duke's small tenants removed likewise, as they now hate to see a poor man at all, and if any of the tenants would offer to say so much, they would not be believed. This is the way the offspring of the once valiant MacKays are now used; their condition is beyond what pen can describe, but we are here afraid to correspond with such a character as you: if it was known, we would be ruined at once." Another says, "there was not a pane of glass, a door, or railing, or any article of furniture broken within or without the inn at Durine, nor as much as a hair of the head of a Sheriff, Fiscal, or Constable touched. If it was the Sheriff or Fiscal Fraser who published the first article, entitled Durness Riot, in the *Inverness Courier*, indeed, they should be ashamed of their unpardonable conduct"; another says, "after all their ingenuity it was only one Judas they made in Durness, and if there was any one guilty of endeavouring to create disturbance, it was himself. Therefore, we may call him Donald Judas Mac an Diabhuil, fear casaid na braithrean, and the authorities should consider what credence his evidence deserved in criminating the people he was trying to mislead." Another correspondent says, " Fraser the Fiscal (a countryman himself, but an enemy, as all renegades are) inserted a most glaring and highly coloured mis-statement in the *Inverness Courier*, and is ever on the alert to publish anything that might serve his employers and injure his poor countrymen"; another says, "the Fiscal and Sheriff Lumsden were very severe on the people before the Advocate-Depute, but after he had gone through the business they found it prudent to alter their tone a good deal"; he adds, "I incurred the Fiscal's displeasure *for not giving the evidence he wanted for condemning the people*, and to punish me, he would pay me only 10s. for attending the precognition five days and a night. But when the Duke comes I will lay the case before him and tell him how Fraser was so anxious to get the people into a scrape. He is a little worth gentleman." The conduct of the Fiscal requires no comment, and his, it is said, is the *Courier's* authority for its mis-statements. The plan of the persecutors is not only to ruin and expel the natives, by any and every means, but to deprive them of public sympathy, by slandering their character, belying their actions, and harassing them in every possible way, so as to make them willing to leave their native soil before a regular authorised enquiry takes place, which would (in case their victims remain on the spot) not only expose their nefarious deeds, but also lead the way to a regular law for obliging them to provide in some way for the poor they have made.

These are now the two objects of their fears ; first, lest they should be shown up, and secondly, that a real—and not, as hitherto, a sham—poor-law should be established, to make them contribute to relieve the misery they have so recklessly and wickedly created. With these preliminaries, I present you with a large extract *verbatim,* from the letter of a gentleman, with whom, though I know his highly respectable connexions, I am personally unacquainted. Coming evidently from a person of education and character, it seems justly entitled to the consideration of all who are pleased to interest themselves in the woes and wrongs of Sutherland, and the outrages there offered to our common humanity :—

"You are aware that Anderson was a pretty considerable speculator in his time (but not so great a speculator as * * *), extensively engaged in the white and herring fishings, at the time he held out the greatest inducements to the poor natives who were expelled from other places in this parish, came and built little huts on his farm, and were entirely dependent on their fishings, and earnings with him. In this humble sphere they were maintaining themselves and families, until God in just retribution turned the scales upon Anderson ; his speculations proved unsuccessful, he lost his shipping, and his cash was fast following ; he broke down his herring establishments, and so the poor fishermen had to make the best of it they could with other curers. Anderson now began to turn his attention to sheep farming, and removed a great many of his former tenants and fishermen : however, he knew little or nothing of the details of sheep farming, and was entirely guided by the advice of his either hand neighbours, Alex. Clark, Erribol, and John Scobie, of Koldale (both sheep farmers) ; and it is notorious that it was at the instigation of these creatures that he adopted such severe measures against those remaining of his tenants —but, be this as it may, this last summer when the whole male adult population were away at the fishing in Wick, he employed a fellow of the name of C———l to summon and frighten the poor women in the absence of their husbands. The proceeding was both cowardly and illegal. However, the women (acting as it can be proved upon C———l's own suggestion!) congregated, lighted a fire, laid hands on C———l and compelled him to consign his papers to the flames! Anderson immediately reported the case to the Dornoch law-mongers, who, smelling a job, dispatched their officer;—off he set to Durness as big as a mountain, and together with one of Anderson's shepherds proceeded to finish what C———l had begun: however, he 'reckoned without his host,' for ere he got half through, the women fell in hot love with him also—and embraced him so cordially, that he left with them his waterproof Mackintosh, and 'cut' to the tune of Cabarfeidh. No sooner had he arrived in Dornoch, than the gentlemen there concluded that they themselves had been insulted and ill-used by proxy in Durness. Shortly afterwards they dispatched the same officer and a messenger-at-arms, with instructions to raise a trusty party by the way to aid them. They came by Tongue, went down to Farr on the Saturday evening, raised Donald MacKay, pensioner, and other two old veterans, whom they sent off before them on the Sabbath, *incog.*; however, they only advanced to the ferry at Hope when they were told that the Durness people were fully prepared to give them a warm reception, so they went no further, but returned to Dornoch, and told there a doleful Don Quixote tale. Immediately thereafter, a 'council of war' was held, and the sheriff-substitute, together with the fiscal and a band of fourteen special constables marched off to Durness. Before they arrived the people heard of their approach, and consulted among themselves what had best be done (the men were by this time all returned home). They allowed the whole party to pass through the parish till they reached the inn; this was on a Saturday evening about eight or nine o'clock;—the men of the parish to the amount of four dozen called at the inn, and wanted to have a conference with the sheriff. This was refused to them. They then respectfully requested an assurance from him that they would not be interfered with during the Sabbath, which was likewise refused to them. Then the people got a little exasperated, and, determined in the first place on depriving the sheriff of his sting. They took his constables one by one, and turned them out of the house *minus* their batons. There was not the least injury done, or violence shewn to the persons of any of the party. The natives now made their way to the sheriff's room and began to dictate (!) to him; however, as they could not get him to accede to their terms, they ordered him to march off; which, after some persuasion he did; they laid no hands on him or the fiscal. And, to show their civility, they actually harnessed the horses for them, and escorted them beyond the precincts of the parish ! ! !

The affair had now assumed rather an alarming aspect. The glaring and highly coloured statement already referred to, appeared in the *Inverness Courier*, and soon found its way into all the provincial and metropolitan prints; the parties referred to were threatened with a military force. The Duke of Sutherland was stormed on all hands with letters and petitions. The matter came to the ears of the Lord Advocate. Mr. Napier, the Depute-Advocate, was sent from Auld Reekie, and the whole affair investigated before him and the Sheriff, and Clerk and Fiscal of the County. How this may ultimately terminate I cannot yet say, but, one thing is certain, the investigators have discovered some informality in the proceedings on the part of the petty lawyers, which has for the present suspended all further procedure! I am glad to understand that the Duke of Sutherland expresses great sympathy with the poor people. Indeed, I am inclined to give his Grace credit for good intentions, if he only knew how his people are harassed; but this is religiously concealed from him.

I live at some distance from Tongue, but I satisfied myself of the certainty of the following extraordinary case which could have occurred nowhere but in Sutherland.

The present factor in Tongue is from Edinburgh. This harvest, a brother of his who is a clerk, or something in that city, came down to pay him a visit; they went out a-shooting one day in September, but could kill no birds. They, however, determined to have some sport before returning home, so, falling in with a flock of goats belonging to a man of the name of Manson, and within a few hundred yards of the man's own house, they set to, and after firing a number of ineffectual shots, succeeded at length, in taking down two of the goats, which they left on the ground! Satisfied and delighted with this manly sport they returned to Tongue. Next day when called upon by the poor man who owned the goats, and told that they were all he had to pay his rent with, this exemplary factor told him, "he did not care should he never pay his rent,"—"he was only sorry he had not proper ammunition at the time,"—as "he would not have left one of them alive!!!" Think you, would the Duke tolerate such conduct as this, or what would he say did the fact come to his ears? As Burns says:—

> This is a sketch of H———h's way,
> Thus does he slaughter, kill, and slay,
> And 's weel paid for 't.

The poor man durst not whisper a complaint for this act

of brutal despotism; but I respectfully ask, will the Duke of Sutherland tolerate such conduct? I ask will such conduct be tolerated by the legislature? Will Fiscal Fraser and the Dornoch law-mongers smell this job?"

LETTER XXV.

HAVING done my best to bring the wrongs of the Sutherlanders in general, and, latterly, those of Mr. Anderson's tenantry in particular, under the public eye in your valuable columns, I beg leave to close my correspondence for the present, with a few additional facts and observations. Before doing so, however, I must repeat my sense—in which I am confident my countrymen will participate—of your great kindness in allowing me such a vehicle as your excellent paper through which to vent our complaints and proclaim our wrongs. I also gratefully acknowledge the disinterested kindness of another individual, whose name it is not now necessary to mention, who has assisted me in revising and preparing my letters for the press. I hope such friends will have their reward.

It is unnecessary to spin out the story of the Durness Riot (as it is called) any longer. It evidently turns out what I believed it to be from the beginning—a humbug scheme for further oppressing and destroying the people; carrying out, by the most wicked and reckless means, the long prevailing system of expatriation, and, at the same time, by gross misrepresentations, depriving them of that public sympathy to which their protracted sufferings and present misery give them such strong claims. In my latest correspondence from that quarter the following facts are contained, which further justify my previous remarks, viz. :—

A gentleman who makes a conspicuous figure in the proceedings against the people is law-agent for Mr. Anderson, the lessee, from whose property the poor crofters were to be ejected; and C———l, the first officer sent to Durness, was employed by them. This C———l was an unqualified officer, but used as a convenient tool by his employers, and it was actually, as I am assured, this man who advised or suggested to the poor women and boys, in absence of the male adults, to kindle the fire, and lay hold of him, and compel him to consign his papers to the flames!—acting probably under the directions of his employers.

The next emissary sent was a qualified officer—qualified by having served an apprenticeship as a thief-catcher in the police establishment of Edinburgh, who, when he came in contact with the virtuous Durness women, behaved as he was wont to do among those of a different sort in Anchor Close and Halkerston's Wynd; and I am sorry to say some of the former were inhumanly and shamefully dealt with by him.—See *Inverness Courier* of 17th November. And here, I am happy to be able in a great degree to exonerate that journal from the charge brought against it in former letters. The Editor has at last put the saddle on the right horse—namely, his first informers, the advisers and actors in the cruel and vindictive proceedings against the poor victims of oppression.

It is lamentable to think that the Sheriff-substitute of Sutherland should arrive in Durness, with a formidable party and a train of carts, to carry off to Dornoch Jail the prisoners he intended to make, on the Sabbath-day! If this was not his intention, what was the cause of the resistance and defeat he and his party met with? Just this (according to the *Courier* and my own correspondents), that he would not consent to give his word that he would not execute his warrant on the Sabbath-day, although they were willing to give him every assurance of peaceably surrendering on the Monday following. Provoked by his refusal, the men of Durness, noted for piety as well as forbearance, chose rather to break the laws of man on the Saturday, than see the laws of God violated in such a manner on the Sabbath. He and his party, who had bagpipes playing before them on leaving Dornoch, told inquirers, that " they were going to a wedding in Durness". It was rather a divorce, to tear the people away from their dearly-loved, though barren, hills. Under all the circumstances, many, I doubt not will think with me that these willing emissaries of mischief got better treatment than they deserved. It is high time the law-breaking and law-wresting petifoggers of Sutherlandshire were looked after. This brings again to my mind the goat-shooting scene, described in my last, which was the more aggravated and diabolical from having been perpetrated during the late troubles, and while a military force was hourly expected to cut down such as should dare to move a finger against those in authority; knowing that, under these circumstances, no complaints of the people would be listened to. But this was not the only atrocity of the kind that took place in the country at this time. I have seen a letter from a respectable widow woman residing in Blairmore, parish of Rogart, to her son in Edinburgh, which, after detailing the harassment and misery to which the country is subject, says—" I had only seven sheep, and one of Mr. Sellar's shepherds drowned five of them in Lochsalchie, along with other five belonging to Donald MacKenzie; and many more, the property of other neighbours, sharing the same fate. We could not get so much as the skins of them." But they durst not say one word about it, or if they did no one would hearken to their complaints. God alone knows how they are used in that unfortunate country, and he will avenge it in his own time.

A correspondent of mine says—" At an early period of your narrative, you stated that the natives were refused employment at public works, even at reduced wages; but, if you believe me, sir, in the last and present year, masons, carpenters, etc., were brought here from Aberdeenshire, and employed at those works, while equally good, if not better native tradesmen were refused, and obliged to go idle. This, however, was not admitted as an excuse when house-rent, poll-tax, or road money was demanded, but the most summary and oppressive means were used for recovery. They have been paying these strangers four or five shillings a-day, when equally good workmen among the natives would be glad of eighteen-pence!"

In this way, the money drained from the natives in the most rigorous manner, is paid away to strangers before their eyes, while they themselves are refused permission to earn a share of it! My correspondent adds—"We know the late Duchess, some years before her demise, gave orders (and we cannot think the present Duke of Sutherland has annulled these orders) that no stranger should be employed, while natives could be found to execute the work. But it seems the officials, and their under-strappers, can do what they please, without being called to account; and this is but one instance among the many in which their tyranny and injustice is manifested." Every means, direct and indirect, are used to discourage the aborigines, to make them willing to fly the country, or be content to starve in it.

May I not ask, will the Duke of Sutherland never look into the state of his county? Will he continue to suffer such treatment of the people to whom he owes his greatness; proceedings so hazardous to his own real interest and safety? Is it not high time that that illustrious family should institute a searching inquiry into the past and present conduct of those who have wielded their power only to abuse it?

Their extensive domains are now, generally speaking, in the hands of a few selfish, ambitious strangers, who would laugh at any calamity that might befall the people as they do at the miseries of those faithful subjects whom they have supplanted. Many of these new tenants have risen from running about with hobnails in their shoes, and a collie dog behind them, their whole wardrobe being on their back—and all their other appointments and equipage bearing the same proportion—to be Esquires, Justices of the Peace, and gentlemen riding in carriages, or on blood-horses, and living in splendid mansions, all at the expense of his Grace's family, and of those whom they have despoiled of their inheritance. The time may come—I see it approaching already—when these gentlemen will say to his Grace, "If you do not let your land to us on our own terms, you may take it and make the best of it; who can compete with us?" This will be the case, especially when the natives are driven away, and the competition for land, caused by the food taxes, comes to an end. Let his Grace consider these things, and no longer be entirely guided by the counsels of his Ahitophel, nor adopt the system of Rehoboam towards the race of the devoted vassals of his ancestors, a portion of whose blood runs in his veins.

"Woe is me! the possessors of my people slay them, and hold themselves not guilty"; and they that sell them say, "blessed be the Lord, for I am rich; and their own shepherds pity them not". "Let me mourn and howl" for the pride of Sutherland is spoiled!"

In a former letter I put the question to the Sutherland clergy, "of how much more value is a man than a sheep?" No reply has been made.

I ask again, "You that have a thousand score of sheep feeding on the straths that formerly reared tens of thousand of as brave and virtuous men as Britain could boast of, ready to shed their blood for their country or their chief; were these not of more value than your animals, your shepherds, or yourselves? You that spend your ill-gotten gains in riotous living, in hunting, gaming, and debauchery, of how much more value were the men you have dispersed, ruined, and tortured out of existence, than you and your base companions?" But I must now cease to unpack my heart with words, and take leave of the subject for the present; assuring my kind correspondents, that their names will never be divulged by me, and pledging myself to continue exposing oppression so long as it exists in my native country.

In conclusion I implore the Government to make inquiry into the condition of this part of the empire, and not look lightly at the out-rooting of a brave and loyal people and the razing to the ground of that important portion of the national bulwarks, to gratify the cupidity of a few, to whose character neither bravery nor good feeling can be attributed.

REPLY TO MRS. BEECHER STOWE'S "SUNNY MEMORIES".

[*Abridged.*]

MACLEOD here apologises for his style in the following terms :—"I am quite aware that great allowance must be made by readers of education and literary taste, should these pages be honoured with a perusal by any such, I am not capable of writing to please critics; I had a higher aim, and my success in bringing out the case of my countrymen must now stand the ordeal of public opinion. For my own part, zeal and faithfulness are all I lay claim to, and if my conscience tells me true, I deserve to have both conceded to me, by both friends and foes." He then refers particularly to various acts of tyranny, one of these being the evictions from Coire-Bhuic, in Strathconan, and the case of Angus Campbell, Rogart, the particulars of which he relates thus :—

Angus Campbell possessed a small lot of land in the parish of Rogart, in the immediate neighbourhood of the parish minister, the Rev. Mr. Mackenzie. This rev. divine, it seems, had, like King Ahab, coveted this poor man's small possession, in addition to his own extensive glebe, and obtained a grant of it from the factor. Angus Campbell, besides his own numerous family, was the only support of his elder brother, who had laboured for many years under a painful and lingering disease, and had spent his all upon physicians.

Angus having got notice of the rev. gentleman's designs, had a memorial drawn up and presented to her grace the late Duchess, who, in answer, gave orders to the factor to the effect that, if Angus Campbell was to be removed for the convenience of Mr. Mackenzie, he should be provided with another lot of land equally as good as the one he possessed. But, like all the other good promised by her Grace, this was disregarded as soon as she turned her back : the process of removal was carried on, and to punish Angus for having applied to her, he was dealt with in the following manner, as stated in a memorial to his Grace the present Duke, dated 30th March, 1840.

In his absence, a messenger-at-arms, with a party, came from Dornoch to his house, and ejected his wife and family ; and having flung out their effects, locked the doors of the dwelling house, offices, etc., and carried the keys to the safe keeping of the Rev. Mr. Mackenzie, for his own behoof. These proceedings were a sufficient warning to all neighbours not to afford shelter or relief to the victims ; hence the poor woman had to wander about, sheltering her family as well as she could in severe weather, till her husband's arrival. When Angus came home, he had recourse to an expedient which annoyed his reverence very much ; he erected a booth on his own ground in the churchyard, and on the tomb of his father, and in this solitary abode he kindled a fire, endeavouring to shelter and comfort his distressed family, and showed a determination to remain, notwithstanding the wrath and threatenings of the minister and factors. But as they did not think it prudent to expel him thence by force, they thought of a stratagem, which succeeded. They spoke him fair, and agreed to allow him to resume his former possession, if he would pay the expenses, £4 13s., incurred in ejecting him. The poor man consented, but no sooner had he paid the money than he was turned out again, and good care taken this time to keep him out of the churchyard. He had then to betake himself to the open fields, where he remained with his family till his wife was seized with an alarming trouble, when some charitable friend at last ventured to afford him a temporary covering ; but no distress could soften the heart of his reverence, so as to make *him* relent !

This Campbell is a man of good and inoffensive character, to attest which he forwarded a certificate numerously signed, along with his memorial to the Duke, but received for answer, that, as the case was settled by his factor, his Grace could not interfere !

The second case is that of an aged woman of four-score— Isabella Graham, of the parish of Lairg, who was also ejected with great cruelty. She, too, sought redress at the hands of his Grace, but with no better success. A copy of the substance of her memorial, which was backed by a host of certificates, I here subjoin :—

That your Grace's humble applicant, who has resided with her husband on the lands of Toroball for upwards of fifty years, has been removed

from her possession for no other reason than that Robert Murray, holding
an adjoining lot, coveted her's in addition. That she is nothing in arrears
of her rent, and hopes from your Grace's generosity and charitable
disposition, that she will be permitted to remain in one of the houses
belonging to her lot, till by some means or other she may obtain another
place previous to the coming winter, and may be able to get her bed
removed from the open field, where she has had her abode during the last
fifteen weeks! Your Grace's humane interposition is most earnestly but respectfully implored on the present occasion, and your granting immediate
relief will confirm a debt of never-ending gratitude, and your memorialist
shall ever pray, etc.

In the enlarged edition of his work, published in Canada,
in 1857, MacLeod falls foul of Mrs. Beecher Stowe, who
had attacked him in her *Sunny Memories.* A great portion
of the controversy is personal and now of little interest
to any one. When it is not personal it is directed against
classes and institutions lauded to the skies by Mrs. Beecher
Stowe. Referring to her sympathies for the slaves of
America, MacLeod contrasts, in feeling and eloquent
language, her labours in their interest with her laudation of
those in high places in this country, who had treated their
dependents worse than the slaves of the Southern States.
" The American slave-owners," he says, "are to be pitied,
for they are the dupes or victims of false doctrine, or
rather, say, of the misinterpretation of sacred records.
They believe to have a divine right to sell and buy African
slaves ; to flog, hang, and shoot them for disobedience ;
and to chase them with bloodhounds and methodist
ministers if they run away. But the English aristocracy
maintain to still higher prerogatives, in direct opposition to
sacred records,—they believe to have divine right to mono-
polise the whole creation of God in Britain for their own
private use, to the exclusion of all the rest of His creatures.
They have enacted laws to establish these rights, and they

blush not to declare these laws sacred. And it is to be lamented that these laws and doctrines are generally believed. Let any one peruse their Parchment Rights of Property, and he will find that they include the surface of the earth, all the minerals below the surface to the centre, all that is above it up to the heavens, rivers of water, bays and creeks of mixed salt water and fresh water for one and one-fourth of a league out to sea, with all the fish of every description which spawn or feed therein, and all the fowls who lay and are raised on land,—a right to deprive the people of the least pretention of right to the creation of God but what they choose to give them,—a right to compel the people to defend their properties from invaders; to press and ballot as many of them as they choose; handcuff them if they are unwilling, and force them to swear by God to be true and faithful slaves,—a right to imprison, to flog, to hang, and shoot them, if refractory, or for the least disobedience. Yes, a right to force them away to foreign and unhealthy climes, to fight nations who never did them any injury, where they perish in thousands by disease, fatigue, and starvation, like brute beasts ; to hang, shoot, or flog them to death for even taking a morsel of food when dying for the want of it—all to gain more possessions and power for the British aristocracy.

"Slavery is damnable, and is the most disgusting word in the English or any other language; it is to be hoped that the Americans will soon discern its deformity, pollution and iniquity, and wipe away that old English polluted stain from their character. But there is not the least shadow of hope that ever the British aristocracy will think shame, or give up *their* system of slavery—for it is the most profitable now under heaven, the most admired, and is adopted by all other nations of the earth—at least, until the promised Millenium will arrive, whatever time that blessed era will take in coming—unless the people in their might will rise some morning early, and demand their rights and liberties with the united voice of thunder which will 'make the most hardened and stubborn of the aristocratic adamant hearts tremble and ache'."

Mrs. Beecher Stowe, referring to the so-called "Sutherland Improvements," wrote:—"To my view it is an almost sublime instance of the benevolent employment of superior wealth and power in shortening the struggles of civilisation, and elevating in a few years a whole community to a point of education and material prosperity, which, unassisted, they might never have obtained". To this remarkable statement MacLeod replies:—Yes, indeed, the shortest process of civilisation recorded in the history of nations. Oh, marvellous! From the year 1812 to 1820, the whole interior of the county of Sutherland—whose inhabitants were advancing rapidly in the science of agriculture and education, who by nature and exemplary training were the bravest, the most moral and patriotic people that ever existed—even admitting a few of them did violate the excise laws, the only sin which Mr. Loch and all the rest of their avowed enemies could bring against them—where a body of men could be raised on the shortest possible notice that kings and emperors might and would be proud of; and where the whole fertile valleys, and straths which gave them birth were in due season waving with corn; their mountains and hill-sides studded with sheep and cattle; where rejoicing, felicity, happiness, and true piety prevailed; where the martial notes of the bagpipes sounded and reverberated from mountain to glen, from glen to mountain. I say, marvellous! in eight years converted to a solitary wilderness, where the voice of man praising God is not to be heard, nor the image of God upon man to be seen; where you can set a compass with twenty miles of a radius upon it, and go round with it full stretched, and not find one acre of land within the circumference which has come under the plough for the last thirty years, except a few in the parishes of Lairg and Tongue,—all under mute brute animals. This is the advancement of civilisation, is is not, madam? Return now with me to the begining of your elaborate eulogy on the Duchess of Sutherland, and if you are open to conviction, I think you should be convinced that I never published nor circulated in the American, English, or Scotch public prints any ridiculous, absurd stories about her Grace of Sutherland. An abridgement of my lucubrations is now in the hands of the public, and you may peruse them. I stand by them as facts *(stubborn chiels)*. I can prove them to be so even in this country (Canada), by a cloud of living witnesses, and my readers will find that, instead of bringing absurd accusations against her Grace, that I have endeavoured in some instances to screen her and her predecessors from the public odium their own policy and the doings of their servants merited. Moreover, there is thirty years since I began to expostulate with the House of Sutherland for their short-sighted policy in dealing with their people as they were doing, and it is twenty years since I began to expose them publicly, with my real name, Donald MacLeod, attached to each letter, sending a copy of the public paper where it appeared, directed by post, to the Duke of Sutherland. These exposing and remonstrating letters were published in the Edinburgh papers, where the Duke and his predecessors had their principal Scotch law agent, and you may easily believe that I was closely watched, with the view to find one false accusation in my letters, but they were baffled. I am well aware that each letter I have written on the subject would, if untrue, constitute a libel, and I knew the editors, printers, and publishers of these papers were as liable or responsible for libel as I was. But the House of Sutherland could never venture to raise an action of damages against either of us. In 1841, when I published my first pamphlet, I paid $4 50c., for binding one of them, in a splendid style, which I sent by mail to his Grace the present Duke of Sutherland, with a complimentary note requesting him to peruse it, and let me know if it contained anything offensive or untrue. I never received a reply, nor did I expect it; yet I am satisfied that his Grace did peruse it. I posted a copy of it to Mr. Loch, his chief commissioner; to Mr. W. Mackenzie, his chief lawyer in Edinburgh; to every one of their underlings, to sheep-farmers, and ministers in the county of Sutherland who abetted the depopulators, and I challenged the whole of them, and other literary scourges who aided and justified their unhallowed doings, to gainsay one statement I have made. Can you or any other believe that a poor sinner like Donald MacLeod would be allowed for so many years to escape with impunity, had he been circulating and publishing calumnious, absurd falsehoods against such personages as the House of Sutherland. No, I tell you, if money could secure my punishment, without establishing their own shame and guilt, that it would be considered well-spent long ere now,—they would eat me in penny pies if they could get me cooked for them.

I agree with you that the Duchess of Sutherland is a beautiful accomplished lady, who would shudder at the idea of taking a faggot or a burning torch in her hand to set fire to the cottages of her tenants, and so would her predecessor, the first Duchess of Sutherland, her good mother; likewise would the late and present Dukes of Sutherland, at least I am willing to believe that they would. Yet it was done in their name, under their authority, to their knowledge, and with their sanction. The Dukes and Duchesses of Sutherland, and those of their depopulating order, had not, nor have they any call to defile their pure hands in milder work than to burn people's houses; no, no, they had, and have plenty of willing tools at their beck to perform their dirty work. Whatever amount of humanity and purity of heart the late or the present Duke and Duchess may possess or be ascribed to them, we know the class of men from whom they selected their commissioners, factors and underlings. I knew every one of the unrighteous servants who ruled the Sutherland estate for the last fifty years, and I am justified in saying that the most skilful phrenologist and physiognomist that ever existed could not discern one spark of humanity in the whole of them, from Mr. Loch down to Donald Sgrios, or, Damnable Donald, the name by which the latter was known. The most of those cruel executors of the atrocities I have been describing are now dead, and to be feared but not lamented. But it seems their chief was left to give you all the information you required about British slavery and oppression. I have read from speeches delivered by Mr. Loch at public dinners among his own party, "that he would never be satisfied until the Gaelic language and the Gaelic people would be extirpated root and branch from the Sutherland estate; yes, from the highlands of Scotland". He published a book, where he stated as a positive fact, "that when he got the management of the Sutherland estate he found 408 families on the estate who never heard the name of Jesus," —whereas I could make oath that there were not at that time, and for ages prior to it, above two families within the limits of the county who did not worship that Name

and holy Being every morning and evening. I know there
are hundreds in the Canadas who will bear me out in this
assertion. I was at the pulling down and burning of the
house of William Chisholm. I got my hands burnt taking
out the poor old woman from amidst the flames of her once
comfortable though humble dwelling, and a more horrifying
and lamentable scene could scarcely be witnessed. I may
say the skeleton of a once tall, robust, high-cheek-boned,
respectable woman, who had seen better days; who could
neither hear, see, nor speak; without a tooth in her mouth,
her cheek skin meeting in the centre, her eyes sunk out of
sight in their sockets, her mouth wide open, her nose standing
upright among smoke and flames, uttering piercing moans
of distress and agony, in articulations from which could be
only understood, "Oh, *Dhia, Dhia, teine, teine*—Oh God,
God, fire, fire". When she came to the pure air, her bosom
heaved to a most extraordinary degree, accompanied by a
deep hollow sound from her lungs, comparable to the sound
of thunder at a distance. When laid down upon the bare,
soft, moss floor of the roofless shed, I will never forget the
foam of perspiration which emitted and covered the pallid
death-looking countenance. This was a scene, madam,
worthy of an artist's pencil, and of a conspicuous place on
the stages of tragedy. Yet you call this a specimen of the
ridiculous stories which found their way into respectable
prints, because Mr. Loch, the chief actor, told you that
Sellar, the head executive, brought an action against the
sheriff and obtained a verdict for heavy damages. What a
subterfuge; but it will not answer the purpose, "*the bed is
too short to stretch yourself, and the covering too narrow and
short to cover you*". If you took the information and
evidence upon which you founded your *Uncle Tom's Cabin*
from such unreliable sources (as I said before), who can

believe the one-tenth of your novel? I cannot. I have at my hand here the grandchild of the slaughtered old woman, who recollects well of the circumstance. I have not far from me a respectable man, an elder in the Free Church, who was examined as a witness at Sellar's trial, at the Spring assizes of Inverness, in 1816, which you will find narrated in letters four and five of my work. Had you the opportunity, madam, of seeing the scenes which I, and hundreds more, have seen—the wild ferocious appearance of the infamous *gang* who constituted the burning party, covered over face and hands with soot and ashes of the burning houses, cemented by torch-grease and their own sweat, kept continually drunk or half-drunk while at work; and to observe the hellish amusements some of them would get up for themselves and for an additional pleasure to their leaders! The people's houses were generally built upon declivities, and in many cases not far from pretty steep precipices. They preserved their meal in tight-made boxes, or chests, as they were called, and when this fiendish party found any quantity of meal, they would carry it between them to the brink, and dispatch it down the precipice amidst shrieks and yells. It was considered grand sport to see the box breaking to atoms and the meal mixed with the air. When they would set fire to a house, they would watch any of the domestic animals making their escape from the flames, such as dogs, cats, hens, or any poultry; these were caught and thrown back to the flames—grand sport for demons in human form!

As to the vaunted letter which his "Grace received from one of the most determined opposers of the measures, who travelled in the north of Scotland as editor of a newspaper, regretting all that he had written on the subject, being convinced that he was misinformed," I may tell you, madam, that this man did not travel to the north or in the north of Scotland as editor; his name was Thomas Mulock; he came to Scotland a fanatic speculator in literature in search of money, or a lucrative situation, vainly thinking that he would be a dictator to every editor in Scotland. He first attacked the immortal Hugh Miller, of the *Witness*, Edinburgh, but in him he met more than his match. He then went to the north, got hold of my first pamphlet, and by setting it up in a literary style, and in better English than I, he made a splendid and promising appearance in the northern papers for some time; but he found out that the money expected was not coming in, and that the hotels, head inns, and taverns would not keep him up any longer without the prospect of being paid for the past or for the future. I found out that he was hard up, and a few of the Highlanders in Edinburgh and myself sent him from twenty to thirty pounds sterling. When he saw that that was all he was to get, he at once turned tail upon us, and instead of expressing his gratitude, he abused us unsparingly, and regretted that ever he wrote in behalf of such a hungry, moneyless class. He smelled (like others we suspect) where the gold was hoarded up for hypocrites and flatterers, and that one apologising letter to his Grace would be worth ten times as much as he could expect from the Highlanders all his lifetime; and I doubt not it was, for his apology for the sin of mis-information got wide circulation.

He then went to France and started an English paper in Paris, and for the service he rendered Napoleon in crushing republicanism during the besieging of Rome, etc., the Emperor presented him with a *gold pin*, and in a few days afterwards sent a *gendarme* to him with a brief notice that his service was not any longer required, and a warning to quit France in a few days, which he had to do. What became of him after I know not, but very likely he is dictating to young Loch, or some other Metternich.

No feelings of hostile vindictiveness, no desire to inflict chastisement, no desire to make riches, influenced my mind, pourtraying the scenes of havoc and misery which in those past days darkened the annals of Sutherland. I write in my own humble style, with higher aims, wishing to prepare the way for demonstrating to the Dukes of Sutherland, and all other Highland proprietors, great and small, that the path of selfish aggrandisement and oppression leads by sure and inevitable results, yea to the ruin and destruction of the blind and misguided oppressors themselves. I consider the Duke himself victimised on a large scale by an incurably wrong system, and by being enthralled by wicked counsellors and servants. I have no hesitation in saying, had his Grace and his predecessors bestowed one-half of the encouragement they had bestowed upon strangers on the aborigines—a hardy, healthy, abstemious people, who lived peaceably in their primitive habitations, unaffected with the vices of a subtle civilisation, possessing little, but enjoying much; a race devoted to their hereditary chief, ready to abide by his counsels; a race profitable in peace, and loyal, available in war; I say, his Grace, the present Duke of Sutherland, and his beautiful Duchess, would be without compeers in the British dominions, their rents, at least doubled; would be as secure from invasion and annoyance in Dunrobin Castle as Queen Victoria could, or can be, in her Highland residence, at Balmoral, and far safer than she is in her English home, Buckingham Palace; every man and son of Sutherland would be ready, as in the days of yore, to shed the last drop of their blood in defence of their chief, if required. Congratulations, rejoicings, dancing to the martial notes of the pipes, would meet them at the entrance to every glen and strath in Sutherlandshire, accompanied, surrounded, and greeted, as they proceeded, by the most grateful, devotedly attached, happy, and bravest peasantry that ever existed; yes, but alas! where there is nothing now, but desolation and the cries of famine and want, to meet the noble pair—the ruins of once comfortable dwellings—will be seen the land-marks of the furrows and ridges which yielded food to thousands, the footprints of the arch-enemy of human happiness, and ravager—before, after, and on each side, solitude, stillness, and the quiet of the grave, disturbed only at intervals by the yells of a shepherd, or fox-hunter, and the bark of a collie dog. Surely we must admit that the Marquises and Dukes of Sutherland have been duped and victimised to a most extraordinary and incredible extent; and we have Mr. Loch's own words for it in his speech in the House of Commons, June 21st, 1845:—"I can state, as from facts, that from 1811 to 1833, not one sixpence of rent has been received from that county; but, on the contrary, there has been sent there for the benefit and improvement of the people a sum exceeding sixty thousand pounds sterling". Now think you of this immense wealth which has been expended. I am not certain, but I think the rental of the county would exceed £60,000 a year; you have then from 1811 to 1833, twenty-two years, leaving them at the above figures, and the sum total will amount to £1,320,000 expended upon the self-styled Sutherland improvements; add to this £60,000 sent down to preserve the lives of the victims of those improvements from death by famine, and the sum total will turn out in the shape of £1,380,000. It surely cost the heads of the house of Sutherland an immense sum of money to convert the county into the state I have described it in a former part of this work (and I challenge contradiction). I say the expelling of the people from their glens and straths, and huddling them in motley groups on the sea-shore and barren moors, and to keep them alive there, and to make them willing to be banished from the nation when they thought proper, or when they could get a *haul* of the public money to pay their passage to America or Australia, cost them a great deal. This fabulous, incredible munificence of their Graces to the people I will leave the explanation of what it was, how it was distributed, and the manner in which payment and refunding of the whole of it was exacted from the people, to my former description of it in this work; yet I am willing to admit that a very small portion, if any, of the *refunding* of the amount sent down ever reached the Duke's or the Marquis's coffers. Whatever particle of good the present Duke might feel inclined to do will be ever frustrated by the counteracting energy of a prominent evil principle; I know the adopting and operations of the Loch policy towards the Sutherland peasantry cost the present Duke and his father many thousands of pounds, and, I predict, it will continue to cost them on a large scale while a Loch is at the head of their affairs, and is principal adviser. Besides, how may they endanger what is far more valuable than gold and silver; for those who are advised by men who never sought counsel or advice from God all their lifetime, as their work will testify, do hazard much, and are trifling with Omniscience.

You should be surprised to hear and learn, madam, for what purposes most of the money drained from the Duke's coffers yearly are expended since he became the Duke and proprietor of Sutherland, upholding the Loch policy. There are no fewer than seventeen who are known by the name of water bailiffs in the county who receive yearly salaries, what doing, think you? Protecting the operations of the Loch policy, watching day and night the freshwater lakes, rivers, and creeks, teeming with the finest salmon and trout fish in the world, guarding from the famishing people, even during the years of famine and dire distress, when many had to subsist upon weeds, sea-ware, and shellfish, yet guarded and preserved for the amusement of English anglers; and what is still more heart-rending, to prevent the dying by hunger to pick up any of the dead fish left by the sporting anglers rotting on the lake, creek, and river sides, when the smallest of them, or a morsel, would be considered by hundreds, I may say thousands, of the needy natives, a treat; but they durst not touch them, or if they did and were found out, to jail they were conducted, or removed summarily from his Grace's domains; (let me be understood, these gentlemen had no use for the fish, killing them for amusement, only what they required for their own use, and complimented to the factors; they were not permitted to cure them).

You will find, madam, that about three miles from Dunrobin Castle there is a branch of the sea which extends up the county about six miles, where shellfish, called mussels, abound. Here you will find two sturdy men, called mussel bailiffs, supplied with rifles and ammunition, and as many Newfoundland dogs as assistants, watching the mussel scalps, or beds, to preserve them from the people in the surrounding parishes of Dornoch, Rogart, and Golspie, and keep them, to supply the fishermen, on the opposite side of the Moray Firth, with bait, who come there every year and take away thousands of tons of this nutritive shellfish, when many hundreds of the people would be thankful for a diet per day of them, to pacify the cravings of nature. You will find that the unfortunate native fishermen, who pay a yearly rent to his Grace for bait, are only permitted theirs from the refuse left by the strangers of the other side of the Moray Firth, and if they violate the *iron* rule laid down to them, they are entirely at the mercy of the underlings.   There has been an instance of two of the fishermen's wives going on a cold, snowy, frosty day to gather bait, but on account of the boisterous sea, could not reach the place appointed by the factors; one took what they required from the forbidden ground, and was observed by some of the bailiffs, in ambush, who pursued them like tigers.   One came up to her unobserved, took out his knife and cut the straps by which the basket or creel on her back was suspended; the weight on her back fell to the ground, and she, poor woman, big in the family way, fell her whole length forward in the snow and frost.   Her companion turned round to see what had happened, when she was pushed back with such force that she fell; he then trampled their baskets and mussels to atoms, took them both prisoners, ordered one of them to call his superior bailiff to assist him, and kept the other for two hours standing, wet as she was, among frost and snow, until the superior came a distance of three miles.   After a short consultation upon the enormity of the crime, the two poor women were led, like convicted criminals, to Golspie, to appear before Licurgus Gunn, and in that deplorable condition were left standing before their own doors in the snow, until Marshall Gunn found it convenient to appear and pronounce judgment,— verdict: You are allowed to go into your houses this night; this day week you must leave this village for ever, and the whole of the fishermen of the village are strictly prohibited from taking bait from the Little Ferry until you leave; my bailiffs are requested to see this my decree strictly attended to.   Being the middle of winter and heavy snow, they delayed a week longer: ultimately the villagers had to expel the two families from among them, so that they would get bait, having nothing to depend upon for subsistence but the fishing, and fish they could not without bait. This is a specimen of the injustice to and subjugation of the Golspie fishermen, and of the people at large; likewise of the purposes for which the Duke's money is expended in that quarter. If you go, then, to the other side of the domain, you will find another Kyle, or a branch of the sea, which abounds in cockles and other shellfish, fortunately for the poor people, not forbidden by a Loch ukase. But in the years of distress, when the people were principally living upon vegetables, sea-weeds, and shellfish, various diseases made their appearance amongst them hitherto unknown. The absence of meal of any kind being considered the primary cause, some of the people thought they would be permitted to exchange shellfish for meal with their more fortunate neighbours in Caithness, to whom such shellfish were a rarity, and so far the understanding went between them, that the Caithness boats came up loaded with meal, but the Loch embargo, through his underling in Tongue, who was watching their movements, was at once placed upon it; the Caithness boats had to return home with the meal, and the Duke's people might live or die, as they best could. Now, madam, you have steeped your brains, and ransacked the English language to find refined terms for your panegyric on the Duke, Duchess, and family of Sutherland. (I find no fault with you, knowing you have been well paid for it.) But I would briefly ask you (and others who devoted much of their time and talents in the same strain), would it not be more like a noble pair,—if they did merit such noble praise as you have bestowed upon them—if they had, especially during years of famine and distress, freely opened up all these bountiful resources which God in His eternal wisdom and goodness prepared for His people, and which should never be intercepted nor restricted by man or men. You and others have composed hymns of praise, which it is questionable if there is a tune in heaven to sing them to.

So I returned, and considered all the oppressions that are done under the sun : and behold the tears of such as were oppressed, and they had no comforter ; and on the side of their oppressors there was power ; but they had no comforter.—ECCLES. iv. I.

> The wretch that works and weeps without relief
> Has one that notices his silent grief.
> He, from whose hands alone all pow'r proceeds,
> Ranks its abuse among the foulest deeds,
> Considers *all* injustice with a frown,
> But *marks* the man that treads his fellow down.
> Remember Heav'n has an avenging rod—
> To smite the poor is treason against God.—COWPER.

But you shall find the Duke's money is expended for most astonishing purposes ; not a little of it goes to hire hypocrites, and renowned literary flatterers, to vindicate the mal-administration of those to whom he entrusted the management of his affairs, and make his Grace (who is by nature a simple-minded man) believe his servants are innocent of all the charges brought against them, and doing justice to himself and to his people, when they are doing the greatest injustice to both ; so that instead of calling his servants to account at any time, and enquiring into the broad charges brought against them—as every wise landlord should do—it seems the greater the enormities of foul deeds they commit, and the louder their accusations may sound through the land, the farther they are received into his favour. The fact is, that James Loch was Duke of Sutherland, and not the "tall, slender man with rather a thin face, light brown hair, and mild blue eyes " who armed you up the extraordinary elegant staircase in Stafford House.

Allow me to allude to an historical parallel. After the conquest, the Norman kings afforested a large portion of the soil of conquered England, in much the same way as the landlords are now doing in the Highlands of Scotland. To such an extent was this practice carried on, that an historian informs us, that in the reign of King John "the greater part of the kingdom" was turned into forest, and that so multiform and oppressive were the forest laws, that it was impossible for any man who lived within the boundaries to escape falling a victim to them. To prepare the land for these forests, the people were required to be driven, in many cases, as in the Highlands, at the point of the bayonet; cultivated lands were laid waste, villages were destroyed, and the inhabitants extirpated. Distress ensued, and discontent followed as natural consequences. But observe, the Norman kings did all this in virtue of their feudal supremacy; and in point of law and right, were better entitled to do it than the Highland lairds are to imitate their example in the present day. Was it, however, to be tolerated? were the people to groan for ever under this oppression? No. The English Barons gave a practical reply to these questions at Runneymede, which it is unnecessary to detail. King John did cry out *utopian* at first, but was compelled to disafforest the land, and restore it to its natural and appropriate use; and the records of that great day's proceedings are universally esteemed as one of the brightest pages in English history. With this great example before their eyes, let the most conservative pause before they yield implicit faith in the doctrine that every one of them may do with his lands as he pleases. The fundamental principle of land tenure are unchanged since the days of Magna Charta; and however much the tendency of modern ideas may have cast these principles into oblivion, they are still deeply graven in the constitution, and if necessity called, would be found as strong and operative in the present day as they were five centuries ago. If the barons could compel the sovereign to open his forests, surely the sovereign may more orderly compel the barons to open theirs, and restore them to their natural and appropriate use; and there is a power behind the throne which impels and governs all. These are deep questions that should be stirred in the country, in the midst of extremities and abuse of power. For it is impossible for any one to travel in the Highlands of Scotland, and cast his eyes about him without feeling inwardly that such a crisis is approaching, and indeed consider it should have arrived long ago. Sufferings have been inflicted in the Highlands as severe as those occasioned by the policy of the brutal Roman kings in England; deer have extended ranges, while men have been hunted within a narrower and still narrower circle. The strong have fainted in the race for life; the old have been left to die. One after another of their liberties have been cloven down. To kill a fish in the stream, or a wild beast in the hill, is a transportable crime, even in time of famine. To travel through the fenceless forest is a crime; paths which at one time linked hamlet to hamlet for ages have been shut and barred. These oppressions are daily on the increase, and if pushed much farther, (I should say if not speedily and timely pushed back) it is obvious that the sufferings of the people will reach a pitch, when action will be the plainest duty, and the most sacred instinct. To prevent such forbidden calamity, permit me to address a few lines to Her Majesty.

Come Victoria, Queen of Great Britain, Berwick-upon-Tweed, and Ireland; thou, the most beloved of all Sovereigns upon earth, in whose bosom and veins the blood of the Stuarts, the legitimate Sovereigns of Scotland is freely circulating; who hath endeared thyself to thy Celtic lieges in a peculiar manner, stretch forth thy Royal hand to preserve that noble race from extirpation, and becoming extinct, and to protect them from the violence, oppression, and spoliation to which they have been subjected for many years. Bear in mind, that this is the race in whom your forefathers confided, trusted, and depended on so much at all times, especially when a foreign invader threatened and attempted to take possession of the Scottish throne; and never trusted to them in vain. And though they unfortunately divided upon who of the Stuart family was to rule over them, and much valuable blood shed on that account; yet the impartial investigator into that affair will find the zeal, patriotism and loyalty of each party meriting equal praise and admiration, though the *butchers* and literary scourges of the defeated party converted the praise and loyalty due to them into calumny and abuse. But these gloomy days of strife and murder are over, and the defeated consider that they sustained no loss but that they gained much; and I assure your Majesty that your name is now imprinted upon every Scotch Highlander's heart in letters more valuable than gold, and that the remnant of them still left, are as willing and as ready to shed their blood for the honour and dignity of your crown, and the safety of your person and family, as their fathers were for your grandsires. Then allow not this noble race to be extirpated, nor deteriorated in their soul, mind, chivalry, character, and persons: allow it not, your Majesty, to be told in Gath, nor published in the streets of Askelon, that other nations have to feed and keep alive your Highland Scotch warriors, while you require their service on the battle field; while the nursery where these brave men, who carried many a laurel to the British crown from foreign strands, are now converted into game preserves, hunting parks, and lairs for wild animals. Come then, like a God-fearing, God-loving and Christian queen ; like a subject-loving and beloved sovereign, and demand the restitution of their inalienable rights for your Highland lieges, and the restoration of the Highland straths and glens to their natural and appropriate use. Examine, like *Ahasuerus*, the book of records of the chronicles, and find what service the High-landers rendered you and your forefathers, and how they were requitted. "Who knoweth whether thou art come to the kingdom for such a time as this?" and "how can you endure to see the evil that came upon your people, or how can you endure to see the destruction of your kindred" people? and then like good Queen Esther, declare boldly and publicly that you shall not have a Hamanite or a Hamanitess about your person, in your household, or in your counsel. Highland proprietors hold the lands and other rights they plundered from the people, on the principle that Rob Roy maintained his right to the cattle he stole from his distant neighbours in Badenoch. But the day is drawing nigh when these rank delusions in high quarters will be dispelled. It is a Satanic imposture, that the stewardship of God's soil is freely convertible into a mis-chevious power of oppressing the poor. The proper use of property is to make property useful ; where this is not done, it were better for land owners to have been born beggars, than to live in luxury while causing the wretched to want and weep. I know that if our Sovereign Lady was to make such a demand as this, that she would incur the ire and displeasure of the turf and sporting classes, a consuming not a producing body, the most destructive, vicious, cruel, dis-orderly, unvirtuous, revelling, and the most useless of all her

Majesty's subjects. On the other hand her Majesty would gain for herself the praise and admiration of all the most wise, prudent, liberal, humane, virtuous, and most exemplary of the nation; the blessings of the people and of heaven would rest upon her, and remain with her, and Highland proprietors, their children, and children's children would have cause to hold her name and memory in grateful recollection. Their estates would in a few years double their rents, and they and their heirs would be redeemed from insolvency, and secured from beggary. The poor law would become a dead letter. The poaching game law expenditure, along with many other unrighteous laws, which are hanging heavily upon the nation, would fall to disuse; the people would prosper, and nothing would be lost but hunting grounds for the younger branches of the aristocracy and English snobs, and that could be easily supplied by Her Majesty directing the attention of this cruel cowardly class to the Hudson's Bay and North West Territories, where they might have plenty useful sport, destroying animals much of their own disposition, *though not half so injurious.*

The Duchess of Sutherland pays a visit every year to Dunrobin Castle, and has seen and heard so many supplicating appeals presented to her husband by the poor fishermen of Golspie, soliciting liberty to take mussels from the Little Ferry Sands to bait their nets—a liberty of which they were deprived by his factors, though paying yearly rent for it; yet returned by his Grace, with the brief deliverance, that he could do nothing for them. Can I believe that this is the same personage who can set out from Dunrobin Castle, her own Highland seat, and after travelling from it, then can ride in one direction over thirty miles, in another direction forty-four miles, in another, by taking the necessary circuitous route, sixty miles, and that over fertile glens, valleys, and straths, bursting with fatness, which gave birth to, and where were reared for ages, thousands of the bravest, the most moral, virtuous, and religious men that Europe could boast of; ready to a man, at a moment's warning from their chiefs, to rise in defence of their king, queen, and country; animated with patriotism and love to their chief, and irresistible in the battle contest for victory. But these valiant men had then a *country*, a *home*, and a *chief* worth the fighting for. But I can tell her that she can now ride over these extensive tracts in the interior of the county without seeing the image of God upon a man travelling these roads, with the exception of a wandering Highland shepherd, wrapped up in a gray plaid to the eyes, with a colly dog behind him as a drill serjeant to train his ewes and to marshal his tups. There may happen to travel over the dreary tract a geologist, a tourist, or a lonely carrier, but these are as rare as a pelican in the wilderness, or a camel's convoy caravan in the deserts of Arabia. Add to this a few English sportsmen, with their stag hounds, pointer dogs, and servants, and put themselves and their bravery together, and one company of French soldiers would put ten thousand of them to a disorderly flight, to save their own carcases, leaving their ewes and tups to feed the invaders! The question may arise, where those people, who inhabited this country at one period, have gone? In America and Australia the most of them will be found. The Sutherland family and the nation had no need of their services; hence they did not regard their patriotism or loyalty, and disregarded their past services. Sheep, bullocks, deer, and game, became more valuable than men. Yet a remnant, or in other words a *skeleton*, of them is to be found along the sea-shore, huddled together in motley groups upon barren moors, among cliffs and precipices, in the most impoverished, degraded, subjugated, slavish, spiritless condition that human beings could exist in. If this is really the lady who has "Glory to God in the highest, peace on earth, and good will to men," in view, and who is so religiously denouncing the American statute which "denies the slave the sanctity of marriage, with all its joys, rights, and obligations —which separates, at the will of the master, the wife from the husband, the children from the parents,"—I would advise her in God's name to take a tour round the sea-skirts of Sutherland, her own estate, beginning at Brora, then to Helmsdale, Portskerra, Strathy, Farr, Tongue, Durness, Eddrachillis, and Assynt, and learn the subjugated, degraded, impoverished, uneducated condition of the spiritless people of that sea-beaten coast, about two hundred miles in length, and let her with similar zeal remonstrate with her husband, that their condition be bettered; for the cure for all their misery and want is lying unmolested in the fertile valleys above, and all under his control; and to advice his Grace, her husband, to be no longer guided by his Ahitophel, Mr. Loch, but to discontinue his depopulating schemes, which have separated many a wife from her husband, never to meet—which caused many a premature death, and that separated many sons and daughters, never to see each other; and by all means to withdraw that mandate of Mr. Loch, which forbids marriage on the Sutherland estate, under pains and penalties of being banished from the county; for it has already been the cause of a great amount of prostitution, and his augmented illegitimate connections and issues fifty per cent. above what such were a few years ago—before this unnatural, ungodly law was put in force.

Let us see what the character of these ill-used people was! General Stewart of Garth, in his "Sketches of the Highlands," says :—In the words of a general officer by whom the 93rd Sutherlanders were once reviewed, "They exhibit a perfect pattern of military discipline and moral rectitude. In the case of such men disgraceful punishment would be as unnecessary as it would be pernicious." "Indeed," says the General "so remote was the idea of such a measure in regard to them, that when punishments were to be inflicted on others, and the troops in garrison assembled to witness their execution, the presence of the Sutherland Highlanders was dispensed with, the effects of terror as a check to crime being in their case uncalled for, as examples of that nature were not necessary for such honourable soldiers. When the Sutherland Highlanders were stationed at the Cape of Good Hope, anxious to enjoy the advantages of religious instruction agreeably to the tenets of their national church, and there being no religious service in the garrison except the customary one of reading prayers to the soldiers on parade, the Sutherland men," says the General, "formed themselves into a congregation, appointed elders of their own number, engaged and paid a stipend (collected among themselves) to a clergyman of the Church of Scotland, and had divine service performed agreeably to the ritual of the Established Church every Sabbath, and prayer meetings through the week." This reverend gentlemen, Mr. Thom, in a letter which appeared in the *Christian Herald* of October, 1814, writes thus :— "When the 93rd Highlanders left Cape Town last month, there were among them 156 members of the church, including three elders and three deacons, all of whom, so far as men can know the heart from the life, were pious men. The regiment was certainly a pattern of morality, and good behaviour to all other corps. They read their Bibles and observed the Sabbath. They saved their money to do good. 7,000 rix dollars, a sum equal to £1,200, the non-commissioned officers and privates saved for books, societies, and for the spread of the Gospel, a sum unparalleled in any other corps in the world, given in the short space of eighteen months. Their example had a general good effect on both the colonists and the heathen. If ever apostolic days were revived in modern times on earth, I certainly believe some of those to have been granted to us in Africa." Another letter of a similar kind, addressed to the Committee of the Edinburgh Gaelic School Society (fourth annual report), says:—" The 93rd Highlanders arrived in England, when they immediately received orders to proceed to North America; but, before they re-embarked, the sum collected for your society was made up and remitted to your treasurer, amounting to seventy-eight pounds sterling." " In addition to this," says the noble minded, immortal General, "such of them as had parents and friends in Sutherland did not forget their destitute condition, occasioned by the operation of the *(fire and faggot) mis*-improved state of the county." During the short period the regiment was quartered at Plymouth, upwards of £500 was lodged in one banking-house, to be remitted to Sutherland, exclusive of many sums sent through the Post-office and by officers; some of the sums exceeding £20 from an individual soldier. Men like these do credit to the peasantry of a country. " It must appear strange, and somewhat inconsistent," continues the General, " when the same men who are so loud in their profession of an eager desire to promote and preserve the religious and moral virtues of the people, should so frequently take the lead in removing them from where they imbibed principles which have attracted the notice of Europe and of measures which lead to a deterioration, placing families on patches of potato ground as in Ireland, a system pregnant with degradation, poverty, and disaffection." It is only when parents and heads of families in the Highlands are moral, happy, and contented, that they can instil sound principles into their children, who in their intercourse with the world may become what the men of Sutherland have already been, "an honourable example, worthy the imitation of all".

I cannot help being grieved at my unavoidable abbreviation of these heart-stirring and heart-warming extracts, which should ornament every mantel-piece and library in the Highlands of Scotland; but I could refer to other authors of similar weight; among the last (though not the least), Mr. Hugh Miller of the *Witness*, in his "Sutherland as it was and is : or, How a country can be ruined;" a work which should silence and put to shame every vile, malignant, calumniator of Highland religion and moral virtue in bygone years, who in their sophistical profession of a desire to promote the temporal and spiritual welfare of the people, had their own sordid cupidity and aggrandisement in view in all their unworthy lucubrations (as I will endeavour to show at a future period). Come then, ye perfidious declaimers and denouncers ; you literary scourges of Highland happiness, under whatever garb, whether political economist or theology mongers, answer for yourselves—What good have you achieved, after expending such enormous sums of money? Is it possible that the world will believe you, or put confidence in you any longer? Before I am done with you, come, you professing preachers of the everlasting Gospel of peace and of good will to men, stand alongside and on the same platform with the Highland Destitution Relief Board, exhibited before God and the

world, and accused of misapplying and squandering away
an enormous amount of money, and of having in your
league, and combination with political economists—treacherous professing civilizers and improvers of the Highlands
and Highland population,—produced the most truly deplorable results that ever were recorded in the history of any
nation, the utter ruin and destruction of as brave, moral,
religious, loyal, and patriotic a race of men as ever existed.
Spiritual and temporal destitution in the Highlands has been
a profitable field for you these many years back. Many a
scheme has been tried, hitherto successful, to extract money
from the pockets of the credulous benevolent public, who
unfortunately believed your fabulous accusation and misrepresentation of the Highlanders, and who confided in
your honesty; and although you, yourselves, may see, the
public, yea, and he that runneth may see, that the Lord,
not without a cause, has discountenanced you, still you continue pour appeals to the public, that your traffic may continue likewise; appeals from respectable quarters have lately
been made for Gaelic teachers, Gaelic bibles, and psalm
books, and tracts, for the poor Highlanders, who are dying
for want of food. Depend upon it that there is a squad of
students out of employment, and a great deal of these
books unsold somewhere, that must be turned to money. We
have now an association forming in Edinburgh, got up by
men from whom better things should be expected, who have
for their object to export these dying, penniless Highlanders
to Ireland, to mix location with the poor Irish—who have
gone through many a fiery ordeal for the last sixty years—
that the wastes of Ireland may be reclaimed from nature,
and cultivated by Highlanders; just as if there was no
waste land in the Highlands and Islands of Scotland to
reclaim and cultivate; or, as if there was something devilish

or unnatural in the Highland soil, detrimental to the progress of its inhabitants.

Britain will some day bewail the loss of her Highland sons, Highland bravery, loyalty, patriotism, and Highland virtue. May God hasten the day, that I may live to see it.

At the commencement of the Russian war a correspondent wrote MacLeod as follows :—" Your predictions are making their appearance at last, great demands are here for men to go to Russia, but they are not to be found. It seems that the Secretary of War has corresponded with all our Highland proprietors, to raise as many men as they could for the Crimean war, and ordered so many officers of rank to the Highlands to assist the proprietors in doing so —but it has been a complete failure as yet. The nobles advertised, by placards, meetings of the people ; these proclamations were attended to, but when they came to understand what they were about, in most cases the recruiting proprietors and staff were saluted with the ominous cry of ' Maa ! maa ! boo ! boo !' imitating sheep and bullocks, and, ' Send your deer, your roes, your rams, dogs, shepherds, and gamekeepers, to fight the Russians, they have never done us any harm'. The success of his Grace the Duke of Sutherland was deplorable; I believe you would have pitied the poor old man had you seen him.

" In my last letter I told you that his head commissioner, Mr. Loch, and military officer, was in Sutherland for the last six weeks, and failed in getting one man to enlist ; on getting these doleful tidings, the Duke himself left London for Sutherland, arriving at Dunrobin about ten days ago, and after presenting himself upon the streets of Golspie and Brora, he called a meeting of the male inhabitants of the parishes of Clyne, Rogart, and Golspie ; the meeting was well attended; upwards of 400 were punctual at the hour; his Grace in his carriage, with his military staff and factors appeared shortly after; the people gave them a hearty cheer; his Grace took the chair. Three or four clerks took their seats at the table, and loosened down bulky packages of bank notes, and spread out platefuls of glittering gold. The Duke addressed the people very seriously, and entered upon the necessity of going to war with Russia, and the danger of allowing the Czar to have more power than what he holds already; of his cruel, despotic reign in Russia, etc.; likewise praising the Queen and her government, rulers and nobles of Great Britain, who stood so much in need of men to put and keep down the tyrant of Russia, and foil him in his wicked schemes to take possession of Turkey. In concluding his address, which was often cheered, the Duke told the young able-bodied men that his clerks were ready to take down the names of all those willing to enlist, and everyone who would enlist in the 93rd Highlanders, that the clerk would give him, there and then, £6 sterling; those who would rather enter any other corps, would get £3, all from his own private purse, independently of the government bounty. After advancing many silly flattering decoyments, he sat down to see the result, but there was no movement among the people; after sitting for a long time looking at the clerks, and they at him, at last his anxious looks at the people assumed a somewhat indignant appearance, when he suddenly rose up and asked what was the cause of their non-attention to the proposals he made, but no reply; it was the silence of the grave. Still standing, his Grace suddenly asked the cause; but no reply; at last an old man leaning upon his staff, was observed moving towards the Duke, and when he approached near enough, he addressed his Grace something as follows:—" I am sorry for the response your Grace's proposals are meeting here to-day, so near the spot where your maternal grand-mother, by giving forty-eight hours' notice, marshalled fifteen hundred men to pick out of them the nine hundred she required, but there is a cause for it, and a grievous cause, and as your Grace demands to know it, I must tell you, as I see no one else are inclined in this assembly to do it. Your Grace's mother and predecessors applied to our fathers for men upon former occasions, and our fathers responded to their call; they have made liberal promises, which neither them nor you performed; we are, we think, a little wiser than our fathers, and we estimate your promises of to-day at the value of theirs, besides you should bear in mind that your predecessors and yourself expelled us in a most cruel and unjust manner from the land which our fathers held in lien from your family, for their sons, brothers, cousins, and relations, which were handed over to your parents to keep up their dignity, and and to kill the Americans, Turks, French, and the Irish; and these lands are devoted now to rear dumb brute animals, which you and your parents consider of far more value than men. I do assure your Grace that it is the prevailing opinion in this county, that should the Czar of Russia take possession of Dunrobin Castle and of Stafford House next term, that we could not expect worse treatment at his hands, than we have experienced at the hands of your family for the last fifty years. Your parents, yourself, and your commissioners, have desolated the glens and straths of Sutherland, where you should find hundreds, yea, thousands of men to meet you, and respond cheerfully to your call, had your parents and yourself kept faith with them. How could your Grace expect to find men where they are not, and the few of them which are to be found among the rubbish or ruins of the county, has more sense an to be decoyed by chaff to the field of slaughter; but one comfort you have, though you cannot find men to fight, you can supply those who will fight with plenty of mutton, beef, and venison." The Duke rose up, put on his hat and left the field.

Whether my correspondent added to the old man's reply to his Grace or not, I cannot say, but one thing is evident, it was the very reply his Grace deserved.

I know for a certainty this to be the prevailing feeling throughout the whole Highlands of Scotland, and who should wonder at it? How many thousands of them who served out their 21, 22, 25 and 26 years, fighting for the British aristocracy, and on their return—wounded, maimed, or worn out—to their own country, promising themselves to spend the remainder of their days in peace, and enjoying the blessings and comfort their fathers enjoyed among their Highland, healthy, delightful hills, but found to their grief, that their parents were expelled from the country to make room for sheep, deer, and game, the glens where they were born desolate, and the abodes which sheltered them at birth, and where they were reared to manhood, burnt to the ground; and instead of meeting the cheers, shaking-hands, hospitality, and affections of fathers, mothers, brothers, sisters, and relations, met with desolated glens, bleating of sheep, barking of dogs; and if they should happen to rest their worn-out frame upon the green sod which has grown upon their father's hearth, and a game-keeper, factor, or water bailiff, to come round, he would very unceremoniously tell them to absent themselves as smart as they could, and not to annoy the deer. No race on record has suffered so much at the hands of those who should be their patrons, and proved to be so tenacious of patriotism as the Celtic race, but I assure you it has found its level now, and will disappear soon altogether; and as soon as patriotism shall disappear in any nation, so sure that nation's glory is tarnished, victories uncertain, her greatness diminished, and decaying consumptive death will be the result. If ever the old adage, which says, "Those whom the gods determine to destroy, they first deprive them of reason," was verified, it was, and is, in the case of the British aristocracy, and Highland proprietors in particular. I am not so void of feeling as to blame the Duke of Sutherland, his parents, or any other Highland absentee proprietor for all the evil done in the land, but the evil was done in their name, and under the authority they have invested in wicked, cruel servants. For instance, the only silly man who enlisted from among the great assembly which his Grace addressed, was a married man, with three of a family and his wife; it was generally believed that his bread was baked for life, but no sooner was he away to Fort George to join his regiment, than his place of abode was pulled down, his wife and family turned out, and only permitted to live in a hut, from which an old female pauper was carried a few days before to the church-yard; there the young family were sheltered, and their names registered upon the poor roll for support; his Grace could not be guilty of such low rascality as this, yet he was told of it, but took no cognisance of those who did it in his name. It is likewise said that this man got a furlough of two weeks to see his wife and family before going abroad, and that when the factor heard he was coming, he ordered the ground-officer of the parish of Rogart, named MacLeod, to watch the soldier, and not allow him to see nor speak to his wife, but in his (the officer's) presence. We had at the same time, in the parish an old bachelor of the name of John Macdonald, who had three idiot sisters, whom he upheld, independent of any source of relief; but a favourite of George, the notorious factor, envied this poor bachelor's farm, and he was summoned to remove at next term. The poor fellow petitioned his Grace and Loch, but to no purpose; he was doomed to walk away on the term day, as the factor told him, " to America, Glasgow, or to the devil if he choosed". Seeing he had no other alternative, two days before the day of his removal he yoked his cart, and got neighbours to help him to haul the three idiots into it, and drove away with them to Dunrobin Castle. When he came up to factor Gunn's door, he capsized them out upon the green, and wheeled about and went away home. The three idiots finding themselves upon the top of one another so sudden, they raised an inhuman-like yell, fixed into one another to fight, and scratched, yelled, and screeched so terrific that Mr. Gunn, his lady, his daughters, and all the clerks and servants were soon about them; but they hearkened to no reason, for they had none themselves, but continued their fighting and inharmonious music. Messenger after messenger was sent after John, but of no use; at last the great Gunn himself followed and overtook him, asked him how did he come to leave his sisters in such a state? He replied, " I kept them while I had a piece of land to support them; you have taken that land from me, then take them along with the land, and make of them what you can; I must look out for myself, but I cannot carry them to the labour market". Gunn was in a fix, and had to give John assurance that he would not be removed if he would take his sisters, so John took them home, and has not been molested as yet.

I have here beside me (in Canada) a respectable girl of the name of Ann Murray, whose father was removed during the time of the wholesale *faggot* removals, but got a lot of a barren moor to cultivate. However barren-like it was, he was raising a family of industrious young sons, and by dint of hard labour and perseverance, they made it a comfortable home; but the young sons one by one left the country (and four of them are within two miles of where I sit); the result was, that Ann was the only one who remained with the parents. The mother, who had an attack of palsy, was left entirely under Ann's care after the family left; and she took it so much to heart that her daughter's attention was required day and night, until death put an end to her afflictions, after twelve years' suffering. Shortly after the mother's death, the father took ill, and was confined to bed for nine months; and Ann's labour re-commenced until his decease. Though Ann Murray could be numbered among the most dutiful of daughters, yet her incessant labour, for a period of more than thirteen years, made visible inroads upon her tender constitution; yet by the liberal assistance of her brothers, who did not loose sight of her and their parent (though upon a foreign strand), Ann Murray kept the farm in the best of order, no doubt expecting that she would be allowed to keep it after her parent's decease, but this was not in store for her; the very day after her father's funeral, the officer came to her, and told her that she was to be removed in a few weeks, that the farm was let to another, and that Factor Gunn wished to see her. She was at that time afflicted with jaundice, and told the officer she could not undertake the journey, which was only ten miles. Next day the officer was at her again, more urgent than before, and made use of extraordinary threats; so she had to go. When she appeared before this Bashaw, he swore like a trooper, and damned her soul, why she disobeyed his first summons; she excused herself, trembling, that she was unwell; another volley of oaths and threats met her response, and told her to remove herself from the estate next week, for her conduct; and with a threat, which well becomes a Highland tyrant, not to take away, nor sell a single article of furniture, implements of husbandry, cattle, or crop; nothing was allowed but her own body clothes; everything was to be handed over to her brother, who was to have the farm. Seeing there was neither mercy nor justice for her, she told him the crop, house, and every other thing belonging to the farm, belonged to her and brothers in America, and that the brother to whom he (the factor) intended to hand over the farm and effects never helped her father or mother while in trouble; and that she was determined that he should not enjoy what she laboured for, and what her other brothers paid for. She went and got the advice of a man of business, advertised a sale, and sold off, in the face of threats of interdict, and came to Canada, where she was warmly received by brothers, sisters, and friends, now in Woodstock, and can tell her tale better than I can. No one could think, nor believe that his Grace would ever countenance such doings as these; but it was done in his name.

I have here within ten miles of me, Mr. William Ross, once taxman of Achtomleeny, Sutherlandshire, who occupied the most convenient farm to the principal deer-stalking hills in the county. Often have the English and Irish lords, connected in marriage with the Sutherlands, dined and took their lunch at William Ross's table, and at his expense; and more than once passed the night under his roof. Mr. Ross being so well acquainted among the mountains and haunts of the deer, was often engaged as a guide and instructor to these noblemen on their deer-stalking and fishing excursions, and became a real favourite with the Sutherland family, which enabled him to erect

superior buildings to the common rule, and improve his
farm in a superior style; so that his mountain-side farm
was nothing short of a Highland paradise. But unfortunately for William, his nearest neighbour, one Major
Gilchrist, a sheep-farmer, coveted Mr. Ross's vineyard, and
tried many underhand schemes to secure the place for
himself, but in vain. Ross would hearken to none of his
proposals. But Ahab was a chief friend of Factor Gunn;
and William Ross got notice of removal. Ross prepared
a memorial to the first and late Duchess of Sutherland,
and placed it in her own hand. Her Grace read it, instantly went into the factor's office, and told him that
William Ross was not to be removed from Achtomleeny
while he lived; and wrote the same on the petition, and
handed it back to Ross, with a graceful smile, saying, "You
are now out of the reach of factors; now, William, go
home in peace". William bowed, and departed cheerfully;
but the factor and ground-officer followed close behind
him, and while Ross was reading her Grace's deliverance,
the officer, David Ross, came and snapped the paper out of
his hand, and ran to Factor Gunn with it. Ross followed,
but Gunn put it in his pocket, saying, "William, you would
need to give it to me afterwards, at any rate, and I will
keep it till I read it, and then return it to you," and with a
tiger-like smile on his face, said, "I believe you came good
speed to-day, and I am glad of it"; but William never got
it in his hand again. However, he was not molested during
her Grace's life. Next year she paid a visit to Dunrobin, when
Factor William Gunn advised Ross to apply to her for a
reduction of rent, under the mask of favouring him. He
did so, and it was granted cheerfully. Her Grace left
Dunrobin that year never to return; in the beginning of the
next spring, she was carried back to Dunrobin a corpse,

and a few days after was interred in Dornoch. William Ross was served with a summons of removal from Achtomleeny, and he had nothing to show. He petitioned the present Duke, and his commissioner, Mr. Loch, and related the whole circumstances to them, but to no avail, only he was told that Factor Gunn was ordered to give him some other lot of land, which he did : and having no other resource, William accepted of it to his loss ; for between loss of cattle, building and repairing houses, he was minus one hundred and fifty pounds sterling, of his means and substance, from the time he was removed from Achtomleeny till he removed himself to Canada. Besides, he had a written agreement or promise for melioration or valuation for all the farm improvements and house building at Achtomleeny, which was valued by the family surveyor at £250. William was always promised to get it, until they came to learn that he was leaving for America, then they would not give him a cent. William Ross left them with it to join his family in Canada ; but he can in his old age sit at as comfortable a table, and sleep on as comfortable a bed, with greater ease of mind and a clearer conscience, among his own dutiful and affectionate children, than the tyrant factor ever did, or ever will among his. I know as well as any one can tell me, that this is but one or two cases out of the thousand I could enumerate, where the liberality and benevolence of his Grace, and of his parents, were abused, and that to their patron's loss. You see in the above case that William was advised to plead for a reduction of rent, so that the factor's favourite, Ahab Gilchrist, would have the benefit of Naboth Ross's improvement, and the reduction he got on his rent, which would not be obtained otherwise. The unhallowed crew of factors and officials, from the highest to the lowest grade, employed by the family of Sutherland, got the corrupt portion of the public press on their side, to applaud their wicked doings and schemes, as the only mode of improvement and civilisation in the Highlands of Scotland. They have got what is still more to be lamented, all the Established ministers, with few exceptions, on their side; and in them they found faithful auxiliaries in crushing the people. Any of them could hold a whole congregation by the hair of their heads over hell-fire, if they offered to resist the powers that be, until they submitted. If a single individual resisted, he was denounced from the pulpit, and considered afterwards a dangerous man in the community; and he might depart as quick as he could. Any man, or men, may violate the laws of God, and violate the laws of heaven, as often as he chooses; he is never heeded, and has nothing to fear; but if he offends the Duke's factor, the lowest of his minions, or violates the least of their laws and regulations, it is an unpardonable sin. The present Duke's mother was no doubt a liberal lady of many good parts, and seemed to be much attached to the natives, but unfortunately for them, she employed for her factors, a vile, unprincipled crew, who were their avowed enemies; she would hearken to the complaints of the people, and would write to the ministers of the Gospel to ascertain the correctness of complaints, and the factor was justified, however gross the outrage was that he committed—the minister dined with the factor, and could not refuse to favour him. The present Duke is a simple, narrow-minded gentleman, who concerns himself very little even about his own pecuniary affairs; he entrusts his whole affairs to his factors, and the people are enslaved so much, that it is now considered the most foolish thing a man can do to petition his Grace, whatever is done to him, for it will go hard with the factor, or he will punish and make an example of him to deter others.

To detail what I knew myself personally, and what I have learned from others of their conduct, would, as I said before, fill a volume. For instance :—When a marriage in the family of Sutherland takes place, or the birth of an heir, a feast is ordered for the Sutherland people, consisting of whisky, porter, ale, and plenty of eatables. The day of feasting and rejoicing is appointed, and heralded throughout the country, and the people are enjoined in marshal terms to assemble—barrels of raw and adulterated whisky are forwarded to each parish, some raw adulterated sugar, and that is all. Bonfires are to be prepared on the tops of the highest mountains. The poorest of the poor are warned by family officers to carry the materials, consisting of peats and tar barrels, upon their backs ; the scene is lamentable to see groups of these wretched, half-clad and ill-shod, climbing up these mountains with their loads ; however, the work must be done, there is no denial, the evening of rejoicing is arrived, and the people are assembled at their different clachans. The barrels of whisky are taken out to the open field, poured into large tubs, a good amount of abominable-looking sugar is mixed with it, and a sturdy favourite is employed to stir it about with a flail handle, or some long cudgel—all sorts of drinking implements are produced, tumblers, bowls, ladles, and tin jugs. Bag-pipers are set up with great glee. In the absence of the factor, the animal called the ground-officer, and in some instances the parish minister, will open the jollification, and show an example to the people how to deal with this coarse beverage. After the first round, the respectable portion of the people will depart, or retire to an inn, where they can enjoy themselves ; but the *drouthies*, and ignorant youthful, will keep the field of revelling until tearing of clothes and faces comes to be the rule ; fists and cudgels supplant jugs and ladles, and this will continue until king Bacchus enters the field and hushes the most heroic brawlers, and the most ferocious combatants to sound snoring on the field of rejoicing, where many of them enter into contracts with death, from which they could never extricate themselves. With the co-operation and assistance of factors, ministers, and editors, a most flourishing account is sent to the world, and to the absentee family in London, who knows nothing about how the affair was conducted. The world will say how happy must the people be who live under such good and noble, liberal-minded patrons ; and the patrons themselves are so highly-pleased with the report, that however extraordinary the bill that comes to them on the rent day, in place of money, for roast beef and mutton, bread and cheese, London porter and Edinburgh ale, which was never bought, nor tasted by the people, they will consider their commissioners used great economy ; no cognizance is taken, the bill is accepted and discharged, the people are deceived, and the proprietors injured.

JOHN MACKIE.

Donald MacLeod continues his remarks on the Sutherland thus :—

"I am sorry that for the present I must lay aside many important communications bearing upon the clearing system of the Highlanders which corroborates and substantiates my description of it, such as letters published by Mr. Somers and Mr. Donald Ross, Glasgow, Mr. Donald Sutherland, which appeared in the *Woodstock Sentinel*, a few weeks ago; but above all I regret how little I can take from the pen of Mr. Mackie, editor of the *Northern Ensign*, Wick, Caithness, a gentleman who, since the appearance of his valuable paper, proved himself the faithful friend of the oppressed, the indefatigable exposer of their wrongs, the terror of their oppressors, and chastiser of their tools, apologisers and abettors, though his pecuniary benefits would be to sail in the same boat with his unprincipled contemporaries in the north of Scotland; but he chose the better part, and there is a higher promise of reward for him than worm Dukes, Lords, Esquires, and their vile underlings could bestow. The following is among the last of Mr. Mackie's productions on the subject" :—

WILLING HANDS FOR INDIA.

Over this title *Punch* of last week gives a very exciting illustration. A towering cart-load of ingathered grain, with a crowing cock on its summit, forms the background; while in front a recruiting officer and a party are cheered by the excited harvesters, coming forward with reaping-hooks in their hands, to volunteer for India, the banner borne by the officer representing the British lion in the act of springing on the Bengal tiger. The recruits, not yet returned from the harvest field, are all enthusiasm, and are eagerly rushing to enrol themselves among the avengers of the butcheries that have been perpetrated in our Indian empire.

The newspapers of the south report that the recruiting in certain districts had been most successful, and that already many thousand young men of promise have entered the line. It is remarkable, however, particularly so, that all reference to the districts from which the main strength of our regular army was formerly obtained is most studiously

avoided.   May we ask the authorities what success the
recruiting officer has now met with in the Highlands of
Scotland?   Time was, in former exigencies, when all eyes
were turned in that direction, and not in vain.   Time was
when, in only five days, the county of Sutherland alone
contributed one thousand young men ; and when, in fourteen days, no fewer than eleven times that number were
enrolled as recruits from the various Highland districts.
Time was when the immortal Chatham boasted that "he
had found upon the mountains of Caledonia a gallant
though oppressed race of heroes, who had triumphantly
carried the British banner into every quarter of the globe".
Time was when *Punch* would, in such an illustration as that
of last week, have included in his representation some half-
dozen kilted Celts, shoulder to shoulder, issuing from their
mountain homes, and panting to be let loose on the Indian
bloodhounds.

Why not now?   Answer the question, my Lord Duke of
Sutherland.   Tell Her Majesty, my Lord, why the bagpipes
of the recruiting party are silent in Sutherland, and why no
"willing hands for India" are found in your Grace's vast
Highland domain.   Tell her how it happens that the patriotic enthusiasm which at the close of the last century was
shown in the almost magical enrolment of thousands of
brawny Sutherlanders, who gained wide-world renown at
Corunna, at Fuentes d'Onor, at Vittoria, at Waterloo, and
elsewhere, is now unknown in Sutherland, and how the
enrolment of one man in that large county is a seven years'
wonder.   If your Grace is silent, the answer is not wanting,
nor is Her Majesty ignorant of it.

And yet the cursed system which has disheartened and
well-nigh destroyed that "race of heroes," is pertinaciously
persevered in by the very men who, of all others, should

be the first to come forward and denounce it. "Willing hands for India," says *Punch*. "No," says high-bred lords and coroneted peers; "give us game preserves, deer forests, and sheep walks. Perish your bold peasantry! and life to the pleasures of the forest and the mountain heath." And thus it is that landlord after landlord is yearly weeding out the aborigines, and converting Scotland into one ponderous deer forest. Not a year passes without seeing hundreds of unoffending men, women, and children, from Cape Wrath to Mull of Galloway, remorselessly unhoused, and their little crofts added to the vast waste. And now that Britain for the second time in four years has again to invoke the patriotism of her sons, and to call for aid in the eventful crisis in India, the blast of the recruiter's bugle evokes only the bleat of sheep, or the pitiful bray of the timid deer, in the greater part of these wide regions which formerly contributed their tens of thousands of men to fight their country's battles. Oh, had Chatham been alive now, what a feeling would have been awakened in his manly breast as he surveyed the wreck which the Loch policy had occasioned; and with what crushing eloquence would he have invoked the curse of heaven on that system. Meanwhile, Britain misses her Highland heroes, and the imperilled troops in India, with the unoffending women and children, must wait the tardy arrival of "willing hands" to assist them, while, had the Highlanders of Scotland been as they once were, in one week more men would have been raised for India than would have sufficed to have effectually crushed the Indian revolt, had it spread itself from the foot of the Himalaya mountains to the most distant district of our Indian empire.

Let Highland evictors, from Dukes to the meanest squires, beware. Popular patience has a limit; and it seems to me that the time is rapidly nearing when, if Parliament remains longer silent, the people of the country will arouse themselves, and, by one united expression of their will, drive back to its native den the foul and disastrous policy which has depeopled the Scottish Highlands.

MacLeod continues :—To detail individual deaths, sufferings, and oppressions in the Highlands of Scotland, would be an endless work. A few months ago a letter from Donald Sutherland, farmer, West Lorra, Canada West, appeared in the *Woodstock Sentinel,* detailing what his father and family suffered at the hands of the Sutherlandshire landlords ; all the offence his father was guilty of was that he, along with others, went and remonstrated with the house burners and made them desist until the people could remove their families and chattels out of their houses ; for this offence he would not be allowed to remain on the estate. He took shelter with his family under the roof of his father-in-law ; from this abode he was expelled, and his father-in-law made a narrow escape from sharing the same fate for affording him shelter. He was thus persecuted from one parish to another, until ultimately another proprietor, Skibo, took pity upon him, and permitted him, in the beginning of an extraordinary stormy winter, to build a house in the middle of a bog or swamp, during the building of which, he having no assistance, his family being all young, and far from his friends, and having all materials to carry on his back, the stance of his new house being inaccessible by horses or carts, he, poor fellow, fell a victim to cold and fever, and a combination of other troubles, and died before the house was finished, leaving a widow and six fatherless children in this half-finished hut, in the middle of a swamp, to the mercy of the world. Well might Donald Sutherland, who was the oldest of the family, and who recollects what his father suffered, and his death,

I say, charge the Sutherland family and their tools with his death.

But many were the hundreds who suffered alike, and died similar deaths in Sutherlandshire during the wholesale evictions and house-burnings of the County. But I must now cease to unpack my heart upon these revolting scenes and gloomy memories. I know many will say that I have dealt too hard with the House of Sutherland,—that such disclosures as I have made cannot be of any public service,—that the present Duke of Sutherland is a good man, and that in England he is called the Good Duke. I have in my own unvarnished way brought to light a great amount of inhumanity, foul, unconstitutional, and barbarous atrocities, committed and perpetrated in his name, and in the name of his parents, and by their authority. I stand by these as stern facts.

———————

The preceding pages are a reproduction of the Canadian edition of Donald MacLeod's "Gloomy Memories of the Highlands," published at Woodstock, in 1857. The "Letters" are, with very slight alterations, re-printed entire; but the author's Appendix, written in reply to Mrs. Beecher Stowe's "Sunny Memories" is considerably abridged and otherwise modified.

We shall next give the opinions of such eminent authors as General Stewart of Garth, Hugh Miller, Professor John Stuart Blackie, John Mackay C.E., born and bred in the County ; and others.

GENERAL STEWART OF GARTH,

REFERRING to the Sutherland evictions, in his first edition, writes :—On the part of those who instituted similar improvements, in which so few of the people were to have a share, conciliatory measures, and a degree of tenderness, beyond what would have been shown to strangers, were to have been expected towards the hereditary supporters of their families. It was, however, unfortunately the natural consequences of the measures which were adopted, that few men of liberal feelings could be induced to undertake their execution. The respectable gentlemen, who, in so many cases, had formerly been entrusted with the management of Highland property, resigned, and their places were supplied by persons cast in a coarser mould, and, generally, strangers to the country, who, detesting the people, and ignorant of their character, capability, and language, quickly surmounted every obstacle, and hurried on the change, without reflecting on the distress of which it might be productive, or allowing the kindlier feelings of landlords to operate in favour of their ancient tenantry. To attempt a new system, and become acceptable tenants, required a little time and a little indulgence, two things which it was resolved should not be conceded them : they were immediately removed from the fertile and cultivated farms ; some left the country, and others were offered limited portions of land on uncultivated moors, on which they were to form a settlement ; and thus, while particular districts have been desolated, the gross numerical population has, in some manner, been preserved. Many judicious men, however, doubt the policy of these measures, and dread their consequences on the condition and habits of the people. The following account of their situation is from the respectable and intelligent clergyman of an extensive parish in that county :—" When the valleys and higher grounds were let to the shepherds, the whole population was drawn down to the sea-shore, where they were crowded on small lots of land, to earn their subsistence by labour (where all are labourers and few employers) and by sea-fishing, the latter so little congenial to their former habits. This cutting down farms into lots was found so profitable, that over the whole of this district, the sea-coast, where the shore is accessible, is thickly studded with wretched cottages, crowded with starving inhabitants. Ancient respectable tenants, who passed the greater part of life in the enjoyment of abundance, and in the exercise of hospitality and charity, possessing stocks of ten, twenty, and thirty breeding cows, with the usual proportion of other stock, are now pining on one or two acres of bad land, with one or two starved cows, and, for this accommodation, a calculation is made, that they must support their families and pay the rent of their lots, which the land cannot afford. When the herring fishery (the only fishery prosecuted on this coast) succeeds, they generally satisfy the landlords, whatever privations they may suffer, but when the fishing fails, they fall in arrears, and are sequestrated, and their stock sold to pay the rents, their lots given to others, and they and their families turned adrift on the world. The herring fishery, always precarious, has, for a succession of years, been very defective, and this class of people are reduced to extreme misery. At first, some of them possessed capital, from converting their farm stock into cash, but this has been long exhausted. It is distressing to view the general poverty of this class of people, aggravated by their having once enjoyed abundance and independence; and we cannot sufficiently admire their meek and patient spirit, supported by the powerful influence of religious and moral principle. There are still a few small tenants on the old system, occupying the same farm jointly, but they are falling fast to decay, and sinking into the new class of cottars."

This mode of sub-dividing small portions of inferior land is bad enough certainly, and to propose the establishment of villages, in a pastoral country, for the benefit of men who can neither betake themselves to the cultivation of the land nor to commerce for earning the means of subsistence, is doubtless a refinement in policy solely to be ascribed to the enlightened and enlarged views peculiar to the new system. But, leaving out of view the consideration that, from the prevalence of turning corn lands into pasture, the demand for labour is diminished, while the number of labourers is increased, it can scarcely be expected that a man who had once been in the condition of a farmer, possessed of land, and of considerable property in cattle, horses, sheep, and money, often employing servants himself, conscious of his independence, and proud of his ability to assist others, should, without the most poignant feelings, descend to the rank of a hired labourer, even where labour and payment can be obtained, more especially if he must serve on the farms or in the country where he formerly commanded as a master. It is not easy for those who live in a country like England, where so many of the lower orders have nothing but what they acquire by the labour of the passing day, and possess no permanent property or share in the agricultural produce of the soil, to appreciate the nature of the spirit of independence, which is generated in countries where the free cultivators of the soil constitute the major part of the population. It can scarcely be imagined how proudly a man feels, however small his property may be, when he has a spot of arable land and pasture, stocked with corn, horses, and cows, a species of property which, more than any other, binds him, by ties of interest and attachment, to the spot with which he is connected. He considers himself an independent person, placed in a station in society far above the day-labourer, who has no stake in the permanency of existing circumstances, beyond the prospect of daily employment; his independence being founded on permanent property, he has an interest in the welfare of the state, by supporting which he renders his own property more secure, and, although the value of the property may not be great, it is every day in his view; his cattle and horses feed around him; his grass and corn he sees growing and ripening; his property is visible to all observers, which is calculated to raise the owner in general consideration; and when a passing friend or neighbour praises his thriving crops and his cattle, his heart swells with pleasure, and he exerts himself to support and to preserve that government and those laws which render it secure. Such is the case in many parts of the world; such was formerly the case in Scotland, and is still in many parts of the Highlands. Those who wish to see only the two castes of capitalists and day-labourers, may smile at this union of independence and poverty. But, that the opposite system is daily quenching the independent spirit of the Highlanders, is an undoubted fact, and gives additional strength to the arguments of those who object to the reduction of the agricultural population, and regret their removal to the great towns, and to the villages in preparation in some parts of the country.

It is painful to dwell on this subject, but as information, communicated by men of honour, judgment, and perfect veracity, descriptive of what they daily witness, affords the best means of forming a correct judgment, and as these gentlemen, from their situations in life, have no immediate interest in the determination of the question, beyond what is dictated by humanity and a love of truth, their authority may be considered as undoubted.

The following extract of a letter from a friend, as well as the extract already quoted, is of this description. Speaking of the settlers on the new allotments, he says :—" I scarcely need tell you that these wretched people exhibit every symptom of the most abject poverty, and the most helpless distress. Their miserable lots in the moors, notwithstanding their utmost labour and strictest economy, have not yielded them a sufficient crop for the support of their families for three months. The little money they were able to derive from the sale of their stock, has, therefore, been expended in the purchase of necessaries, and is now wholly exhausted. Though they have now, therefore, overcome all their scruples about leaving their native land, and possess the most ardent desire to emigrate, in order to avoid more intolerable evils of starvation, and have been much encouraged by the favourable accounts they have received from their countrymen already in America, they cannot possibly pay the expense of transporting themselves and their families thither."

It has been said that an old Highlander warned his countrymen " to take care of themselves, for the law had reached Ross-shire ". When his fears were excited by vague apprehensions of change, he could not well anticipate that the introduction of civil order, and the extension of legal authority, which in an enlightened age, tend to advance the prosperity as well as promote the security of a nation, should have been to his countrymen either the signals of banishment from their native country, or the means of lowering the condition of those who were permitted to remain. With more reason it might have been expected that the principles of an enlightened age would have gradually introduced beneficial changes among the ancient race ; that they would have softened down the harsher features of their character, and prepared them for habits better suited to the cultivation of the soil, than the indolent freedom of a pastoral life. Instead of this, the new system, whatever may be its intrinsic merits or defects, has, in too many cases, been carried into execution, in a manner which has excited the strongest and most indignant sensations in the breasts of those who do not overlook the present inconvenience and distress of the many, in the eager pursuit of a prospective advantage to the few. The consequences which have resulted, and the contrast between the present and past condition of the people, and between their present and past disposition and feelings toward their superiors, show, in the most striking light, the impolicy of attempting, with such unnatural rapidity, innovations, which it would require an age, instead of a few years, to accomplish in a salutary manner, and the impossibility of effecting them without inflicting great misery, endangering morals, and undermining loyalty to the king, and respect for constituted authority.

A love of change, proceeding from the actual possession of wealth, or from the desire of acquiring it, disturbs, by an ill-directed influence, the gradual and effectual progress of those improvements which, instead of benefiting the man of capital alone, should equally distribute their advantages to all. In the prosecution of recent changes in the north, it would appear that the original inhabitants were never thought of, nor included in the system which was to be productive of such wealth to the landlord, the man of capital, and the country at large,—and that no native could be intrusted with, or, perhaps, none was found hardy enough to act a part in the execution of plans which commenced with the ejectment of their unfortunate friends and neighbours.   Strangers were, therefore, called in, and whole glens cleared of their inhabitants, who, in some instances, resisted these mandates (although legally executed), in the hope of preserving to their families their ancient homes, to which all were enthusiastically attached.   These people, blameless in every respect, save their poverty and ignorance of modern agriculture, could not believe that such harsh measures proceeded from their honoured superiors, who had hitherto been kind, and to whom they themselves had ever been attached, and faithful.   The whole was attributed to the acting agents, and to them, therefore, their indignation was principally directed; and, in some instances, their resistance was so obstinate, that it became necessary to enforce the orders "vi et armis," and to have recourse to a mode of ejectment, happily long obsolete, by setting their houses on fire.   This last species of legal proceeding was so peculiarly conclusive and forcible, that even the stubborn Highlanders, with all their attachment to the homes of their fathers, were compelled to yield.

In the first instances of this mode of removing refractory tenants, a small compensation (six shillings), in two separate sums, was allowed for the houses destroyed.   Some of the ejected tenants were also allowed small allotments of land, on which they were to build houses at their own expense, no assistance being given for that purpose.   Perhaps it was owing to this that they were the more reluctant to remove till they had built houses on their new stations. The compensations allowed in the more recent removals are stated to have been more liberal; and the improvements which have succeeded those summary ejectments of the ancient inhabitants are highly eulogised both in pamphlets and newspapers. Some people may, however, be inclined to doubt the advantages of improvements which called for such frequent apologies; for, if more lenient measures had been pursued, vindication would have, perhaps, been unnecessary, and the trial of one of the acting agents might have been avoided. This trial was brought forward at the instance of the Lord Advocate, in consequence of the loud cry of indignation raised in the country against proceedings characterised by the sheriff of the county as "conduct which has seldom disgraced any country". But the trial ended (as was expected by every person who understood the circumstances) in the acquittal of the acting agent, the verdict of the jury proceeding on the principle that he acted under legal authority. This acquittal, however, did by no means diminish the general feeling of culpability; it only transferred the offence from the agent to a quarter too high and too distant to be directly affected by public indignation, if, indeed there be any station so elevated, or so distant, that public indignation, justly excited, will not, sooner or later, reach, so as to touch the feelings, however obtuse, of the transgressor of that law of humanity written on every upright mind, and deeply engraved on every kind and generous heart.

It must, however, be a matter of deep regret, that such a line of proceeding was pursued with regard to these brave, unfortunate, and well-principled people, as excited a sensation of horror, and a conviction of culpability, so powerful as only to be removed by an appeal to a criminal court. It is no less to be deplored, that any conduct sanctioned by authority, even although productive of ultimate advantage (and how it can produce any advantage beyond what might have been obtained by pursuing a scheme of conciliation and encouragement is a very questionable point), should have, in the first instance, inflicted such general misery. More humane measures would undoubtedly have answered every good purpose; and had such a course been pursued, as an enlightened humanity would have suggested, instead of depopulated glens, and starving peasantry, alienated from their superiors, and, in the exacerbation of their feelings, too ready to imbibe opinions hostile to the best interests of their country, we should still have seen a high-spirited and loyal people, ready, at the nod of their respected chiefs, to embody themselves into regiments, with the same zeal as in former times; and when enrolled among the defenders of their country, to exhibit a conduct honourable to that country and to their profession. Such is the acknowledged character of the men of these districts as soldiers, when called forth in the service of their country, although they be now described as irregular in their habits, and a burthen on the lands which gave them birth, and on which their forefathers maintained the honour, and promoted the wealth and prosperity, of the ancestors of those who now reject them. But is it conceivable that the people at home should be so degraded, while their brothers and sons who become soldiers maintain an honourable character? The people ought not to be reproached with incapacity or immorality without better evidence than that of their prejudiced and unfeeling calumniators. If it be so, however, and if this virtuous and honourable race, which has contributed to raise and uphold the character of the British peasantry in the eyes of all Europe, are thus fallen, and so suddenly fallen; how great and powerful must be the cause, and how heavy the responsibility of its authors?

But if at home they are thus low in character, how un-paralleled must be the improvement which is produced by difference of profession, as for example, when they become soldiers, and associate in barracks with troops of all characters, or in quarters, or billets, with the lowest of the people, instead of mingling with such society as they left in their native homes? Why should these Highlanders be at home so degenerate as they are represented, and as in recent instances they would actually appear to be? And why, when they mount the cockade, are they found to be so virtuous and regular, that one thousand men of Sutherland have been embodied four and five years together, at different and distant periods, from 1759 to 1763, from 1779 to 1783, and from 1793 to 1798, without an instance of military punishment? These men performed all the duties of soldiers to the perfect satisfaction of their commanders, and continued so unexceptionable in their conduct down to the latest period, when embodied into the 93rd regiment, that, according to the words of a distinguished general officer, "Although the youngest regiment in the service, they might form an example to all": and on general parades for punishment, the Sutherland Highlanders have been ordered to their quarters, as "examples of this kind were not necessary for such honourable soldiers".*

The same author adds the following, in the third edition of the same work, published in 1825:—

"The great changes which have taken place in the above parishes of Sutherland, and some others, have excited a warm and general interest. While the liberal expenditure of capital was applauded by all, many intelligent persons

* Sketches of the Character, Manners, and Present State of the High-landers of Scotland, with details of the Military Service of the Highland Regiments, by Colonel David Stewart, 1822.

lamented that its application was so much in one direction; that the ancient tenantry were to have no share in this expenditure; and that so small a portion was allotted for the future settlement of the numerous population who had been removed from their farms, and were placed in situations so new, and in many respects so unsuitable,—certain that, in the first instance, great distress, disaffection, and hostility towards the landlords and government, with a diminution of that spirit of independence, and those proper principles which had hitherto distinguished them, would be the inevitable result. So sudden and universal a change of station, habits, and circumstances, and their being reduced from the state of independent tenants to that of cottagers and day-labourers, could not fail of arresting the notice of the public.

Anxious to obtain the best information on this interesting subject, I early made the most minute inquiry, careful, at the same time, to form no opinion on intelligence communicated by the people of the district, or by persons connected with them, and who would naturally be interested in, and prejudiced against, or in favour of those changes. I was the more desirous for the best information, as the statements published with regard to the character, capability, and principles of the people, exhibited a perfect contrast to my own personal experience and knowledge of the admirable character and exemplary conduct of that portion of them that had left their native country; and I believe it improbable, nay impossible, that the sons of worthless parents, without religious or moral principle—as they have been described—could conduct themselves in such an honourable manner as to be held up as an example to the British army. But, indeed, as to information, so much publicity had been given, by various statements explanatory of, and in vindication of these proceedings, that little more was necessary, beyond what these publications afforded, to show the nature of the plans, and the manner in which they were carried into execution.

Forming my opinions, therefore, from those statements, and from information communicated by persons not immediately connected with that part of the country, I drew the conclusions which appeared in the former editions of these Sketches. But, with a strong desire to be correct and well informed in all I state, and with an intention of correcting myself, in this edition, should I find that I had been misinformed, or had taken up mistaken views of the subject, in the different statements I had produced, I embraced the first spare time I could command, and in autumn 1823, I travelled over the "improved" districts, and a large portion of those parts which had been depopulated and laid out in extensive pastoral farms, as well as the stations in which the people are placed. After as strict an examination as circumstances permitted, and a careful inquiry among those who, from their knowledge and judgment were enabled to form the best opinions, I do not find that I have one statement to alter, or one opinion to correct; though I am fully aware that many hold very different opinions. But however much I may differ in some points, there is one in which I warmly and cordially join; and that is, in expressing my high satisfaction and admiration at the liberality displayed in the immense sums expended on buildings, in enclosing, clearing, and draining land, in forming roads and communications, and introducing the most improved agricultural implements. In all these, the generous distribution of such exemplary encouragement stands unparalleled and alone. Equally remarkable is the great abatement of rents given to the tenants of capital—

abatements which it was not to be expected they would ask, considering the preference and encouragement given them, and the promises they had held out of great and unprecedented revenue, from their skill and exertions. But these promises seem to have been early forgotten; the tenants of capital were the first to call for relief; and so great and generous has this relief been, that the rents are reduced so low as to be almost on a level with what they were when the great changes commenced. Thus while upwards of £210,000 have been expended on improvements, no return is to be looked for from this vast expenditure; and in the failure of their promised rents, the tenants have sufficiently proved the unstable and fallacious nature of the system which they, with so much plausibility and perseverance, got established by delusions practised on a high minded, honourable individual, not aware of the evils produced by so universal a movement of a whole people. Every friend to a brave and valuable race, must rejoice that these evils are in progress of alleviation by a return of that kindness and protection which had formerly been so conspicuous towards that race of tenantry, and which could never have been interrupted had it not been for those delusions to which I have more than once alluded, and which have been prosecuted, within the last twenty years, in many parts of the Highlands, with a degree of assiduity and antipathy to the unfortunate inhabitants altogether remarkable.

But in the county in question, no antipathy to the people is now to be dreaded; a return of ancient kindness will cement with ancient fidelity and attachment; and if the people are rendered comfortable and contented, they will be kept loyal, warlike, and brave.

HUGH MILLER.

So MUCH has been already said about these disastrous Sutherland evictions that we greatly fear the reader is already sickened with the horrid narrative, but as it is intended to make the present record of these atrocious proceedings not only in Sutherland but throughout the whole Highlands, as complete as it is now possible to make it, we shall yet place before the reader at considerable length Hugh Miller's observations on this National Crime—especially as his remarks largely embody the philosophical views and conclusions of the able and far-seeing French writer Sismondi, who in his great work declares,—" It is by a cruel use of legal—it is by an unjust usurpation—that the tacksman and the tenant of Sutherland are considered as having no right to the land which they have occupied for so many ages. . . . A count or earl has no more right to expel from their homes the inhabitants of his county, than a king to expel from his country the inhabitants of his kingdom." Hugh Miller introduces his remarks on Sutherland by a reference to the celebrated Frenchman's work, and his opinion of the Sutherland Clearances, thus :—There appeared at Paris, about five years ago, a singularly ingenious work on political economy, from the pen of the late M. de Sismondi, a writer of European reputation. The greater part of the first volume is taken up with discussions on territorial wealth, and the condition of the cultivators of the soil ; and in this portion of the work there is a prominent place assigned to a subject which perhaps few Scotch readers would expect to see introduced through the medium of a foreign tongue to the people of a great continental state. We find this philosophic writer, whose works are known far beyond the limits of his language, devoting an entire essay to the case of the Duchess of Sutherland and her tenants, and forming a judgment on it very unlike the decision of political economists in our own country, who have not hesitated to characterise her great and singularly harsh experiment, whose worst effects we are but beginning to see, as at once justifiable in itself and happy in its results. It is curious to observe how deeds done as if in darkness and in a corner, are beginning, after the lapse of nearly thirty years, to be proclaimed on the house-tops. The experiment of the late Duchess was not intended to be made in the eye of Europe. Its details would ill bear the exposure. When Cobbett simply referred to it, only ten years ago, the noble proprietrix was startled, as if a rather delicate family secret was on the eye on being divulged; and yet nothing seems more evident now than that civilised man all over the world is to be made aware of how the experiment was accomplished, and what it is ultimately to produce.

In a time of quiet and good order, when law, whether in the right or the wrong, is all-potent in enforcing its findings, the argument which the philosophic Frenchman employs in behalf of the ejected tenantry of Sutherland is an argument at which proprietors may afford to smile. In a time of revolution, however, when lands change their owners, and old families give place to new ones, it might be found somewhat formidable,—sufficiently so, at least, to lead a wise proprietor in an unsettled age rather to conciliate than oppress and irritate the class who would be able in such circumstances to urge it with most effect. It is not easy doing justice in a few sentences to the facts and reasonings of an elaborate essay; but the line of the argument runs thus :—

Under the old Celtic tenures—the only tenures, be it remembered, through which the Lords of Sutherland derive their rights to their lands,—the *Klaan*, or children of the soil, were the proprietors of the soil;—"the whole of Sutherland," says Sismondi, belonged to "the men of Sutherland ". Their chief was their monarch, and a very absolute monarch he was. "He gave the different *tacks* of land to his officers, or took them away from them, according as they showed themselves more or less useful in war. But though he could thus, in a military sense, reward or punish the clan, he could not diminish in the least the property of the clan itself ";—he was a chief, not a proprietor, and had "no more right to expel from their homes the inhabitants of his county, than a king to expel from his country the inhabitants of his kingdom ". "Now, the Gaelic tenant," continues the Frenchman, "has never been conquered; nor did he forfeit, on any after occasion, the rights which he originally possessed";—in point of right, he is still a co-proprietor with his captain. To a Scotchman acquainted with the law of property as it has existed among us, in even the Highlands, for the last century, and everywhere else for at least two centuries more, the view may seem extreme; not so, however, to a native of the Continent, in many parts of which prescription and custom are found ranged, not on the side of the chief, but on that of the vassal. "Switzerland," says Sismondi, "which in so many respects resembles Scotland,—in its lakes, its mountains,—its climate,—and the character, manners, and habits of its children,—was likewise at the same period parcelled out among a small number of lords. If the

Counts of Kyburgh, of Lentzburg, of Hapsburg, and of Gruyeres, had been protected by the English laws, they would find themselves at the present day precisely in the condition in which the Earls of Sutherland were twenty years ago. Some of them would perhaps have had the same taste for *improvements*, and several republics would have been expelled from the Alps, to make room for flocks of sheep. But while the law has given to the Swiss peasant a guarantee of perpetuity, it is to the Scottish laird that it has extended this guarantee in the British empire, leaving the peasant in a precarious situation. The clan,—recognised at first by the captain, whom they followed in war, and obeyed for their common advantage, as his friends and relations, then as his soldiers, then as his vassals, then as his farmers,—he has come finally to regard as hired labourers, whom he may perchance allow to remain on the soil of their common country for his own advantage, but whom he has the power to expel so soon as he no longer finds it for his interest to keep them."

Arguments like those of Sismondi, however much their force may be felt on the Continent, would be formidable at home, as we have said, in only a time of revolution, when the very foundations of society would be unfixed, and opinions set loose, to pull down or re-construct at pleasure. But it is surely not uninteresting to mark how, in the course of events, that very law of England which, in the view of the Frenchman, has done the Highland peasant so much less, and the Highland chief so much more than justice, is bidding fair, in the case of Sutherland at least, to carry its rude equalising remedy along with it. Between the years 1811 and 1820, fifteen thousand inhabitants of this northern district were ejected from their snug inland farms, by means for which we would in vain seek a precedent, except, per-chance, in the history of the Irish massacre.

But though the interior of the county was thus improved into a desert, in which there are many thousands of sheep, but few human habitations, let it not be supposed by the reader that its general population was in any degree less-ened. So far was this from being the case, that the census of 1821 showed an increase over the census of 1811 of more than two hundred ; and the present population of Suther-land exceeds, by a thousand, its population before the change. The county has not been depopulated—its popula-tion has been merely arranged after a new fashion. The late Duchess found it, spread equally over the interior and the sea-coast, and in very comfortable circumstances ;—she left it compressed into a wretched selvage of poverty and suffering that fringes the county on its eastern and western shores, and the law which enabled her to make such an arrangement, maugre the ancient rights of the poor High-lander, is now on the eve of stepping in, in its own clumsy way, to make her family pay the penalty. The southern kingdom must and will give us a poor-law ; and then shall the selvage of deep poverty which fringes the sea-coasts of Sutherland avenge on the titled proprietor of the county both his mother's error and his own. If our British laws, unlike those of Switzerland, failed miserably in her day in protecting the vassal, they will more than fail, in those of her successor, in protecting the lord. Our political econo-mists shall have an opportunity of reducing their argu-ments regarding the improvements in Sutherland, into a few arithmetical terms, which the merest tyro will be able to grapple with.

There is but poor comfort, however, to know, when one sees a country ruined, that the perpetrators of the mischief

have not ruined it to their own advantage. We purpose
showing how signal in the case of Sutherland this ruin has
been, and how very extreme the infatuation which continues to
possess its hereditary lord. We are old enough to remember the county in its original state, when it was at once the
happiest and one of the most exemplary districts in Scotland, and passed, at two several periods, a considerable
time among its hills; we are not unacquainted with it now,
nor with its melancholy and dejected people, that wear out
life in their comfortless cottages on the sea-shore. The
problem solved in this remote district of the kingdom is not
at all unworthy the attention which it seems but beginning
to draw, but which is already not restricted to one kingdom,
or even one continent.

But what, asks the reader, was the economic condition—
the condition with regard to circumstances and means of
living—of these Sutherland Highlanders? How did they
fare? The question has been variously answered: much
must depend on the class selected from among them as
specimens of the whole,—much, too, taking for granted
the honesty of the party who replies, on his own condition
in life, and his acquaintance with the circumstances of the
poorer people of Scotland generally. The county had its
less genial localities, in which, for a month or two in the
summer season, when the stock of grain from the previous
year was fast running out, and the crops on the ground not
yet ripened for use, the people experienced a considerable
degree of scarcity—such scarcity as a mechanic in the
South feels when he has been a fortnight out of employment.
But the Highlander had resources in these seasons which
the mechanic has not. He had his cattle and his wild pot-
herbs, such as the mug-wort and the nettle. It has been
adduced by the advocates of the change which has ruined

Sutherland, as a proof of the extreme hardship of the Highlander's condition, that at such times he could have eaten as food broth made of nettles, mixed up with a little oatmeal, or have had recourse to the expedient of bleeding his cattle, and making the blood into a sort of pudding. And it is quite true that the Sutherlandshire Highlanders was in the habit, at such times, of having a recourse to such food. It is not less true, however, that the statement is just as little conclusive regarding his condition, as if it were alleged that there must always be famine in France when the people eat the hind legs of frogs, or in Italy when they make dishes of snails. With regard to the general comfort of the people in their old condition, there are better tests than can be drawn from the kind of food they occasionally ate. The country hears often of dearth in Sutherland now! every year in which the crop falls a little below average in other districts, is a year of famine there : but the country never heard of dearth in Sutherland then. There were very few among the holders of its small inland farms who had not saved a little money. Their circumstances were such, that their moral nature found full room to develop itself, and in a way the world has rarely witnessed. Never were there a happier or more contented people, or a people more strongly attached to the soil ; and not one of them now lives in the altered circumstances on which they were so rudely precipitated by the landlord, who does not look back on this period of comfort and enjoyment with sad and hopeless regret.

But we have not yet said how this ruinous revolution was effected in Sutherland,—how the aggravations of the *mode*, if we may so speak, still fester in the recollections of the people,—or how thoroughly that policy of the lord of the soil, through which he now seems determined to complete the work of ruin which his predecessor began, harmonizes with its worst details. We must first relate, however, a disastrous change which took place, in the providence of God, in the noble family of Sutherland, and which, though it dates fully eighty years back, may be regarded as pregnant with the disasters which afterwards befell the county.

The marriage of the young countess into a noble English family was fraught with further disaster to the county. There are many Englishmen quite intelligent enough to perceive the difference between a smoky cottage of turf, and a whitewashed cottage of stone, whose judgment on their respective inhabitants would be of but little value. Sutherland, as a county of men, stood higher at this period than perhaps any other district in the British Empire; but, as our descriptions have shown,—it by no means stood high as a county of farms and cottages. The marriage of the countess brought a new set of eyes upon it,—eyes accustomed to quite a different face of things. It seemed a wild, rude county, where all was wrong, and all had to be set right,—a sort of Russia on a small scale, that had just got another Peter the Great to civilize it,—or a sort of barbarous Egypt, with an energetic Ali Pasha at its head. Even the vast wealth and great liberality of the Stafford family militated against this hapless county! it enabled them to treat it as the mere subject of an interesting experiment, in which gain to themselves was really no object,—nearly as little so, as if they had resolved on dissecting a dog alive for the benefit of science. It was a still farther disadvantage, that they had to carry on their experiment by the hands, and to watch its first effects with the eyes, of others. The agonies of the dog might have had their softening influence on a dissecter who held the knife himself; but there could be no such influence exerted over him, did he merely issue orders to his footman that the dissection should be completed, remaining himself, meanwhile, out of sight and out of hearing. The plan of improvement sketched out by his English family was a plan exceedingly easy of conception. Here is a vast tract of land, furnished with two distinct sources of wealth. Its shores may be made the seats of extensive fisheries, and the whole of its interior parcelled out into productive sheep farms. All is waste in its present state ; it has no fisheries, and two-thirds of its internal produce is consumed by the inhabitants. It had contributed, for the use of the community and the landlord, its large herds of black cattle ; but the English family saw, and, we believe, saw truly, that for every one pound of beef which it produced, it could be made to produce two pounds of mutton, and perhaps a pound of fish in addition. And it was resolved, therefore, that the inhabitants of the central districts, who, as they were mere Celts, could not be transformed, it was held, into store farmers, should be marched down to the sea-side, there to convert themselves into fishermen, on the shortest possible notice, and that a few farmers of capital, of the industrious Lowland race, should be invited to occupy the new sub-divisions of the interior.

And, pray, what objections can be urged against so liberal and large-minded a scheme ? The poor inhabitants of the interior had very serious objections to urge against it. Their humble dwellings were of their own rearing ; it was they themselves who had broken in their little fields from the waste ; from time immemorial, far beyond the reach of history, had they possessed their mountain holdings,—they had defended them so well of old that the soil was still virgin ground, in which the invader had found only a grave ; and their young men were now in foreign lands, fighting, at the command of their chieftainess, the battles of their country, not in the character of hired soldiers, but of men who regarded these very holdings as their stake in the quarrel. To them, then, the scheme seemed fraught with the most flagrant, the most monstrous injustice. Were it to be suggested by some Chartist convention in a time of revolution, that Sutherland might be still further improved —that it was really a piece of great waste to suffer the revenues of so extensive a district to be squandered by one individual—that it would be better to appropriate them to the use of the community in general—that the community in general might be still further benefited by the removal of the one said individual from Dunrobin to a road-side, where he might be profitably employed in breaking stones— and that this new arrangement could not be entered on too soon—the noble Duke would not be a whit more aston- ished, or rendered a whit more indignant, by the scheme, than were the Highlanders of Sutherland by the scheme of his predecessor.

The reader must keep in view, therefore, that if atrocities unexampled in Britain for at least a century were perpet- rated in the clearing of Sutherland, there was a species of at least passive resistance on the part of the people (for active resistance there was none), which in some degree provoked them. Had the Highlanders, on receiving orders, marched down to the sea-coast, and become fishermen, with the readiness with which a regiment deploys on review day, the atrocities would, we doubt not, have been much fewer. But though the orders were very distinct, the High- landers were very unwilling to obey; and the severities formed merely a part of the means though which the ne- cessary obedience was ultimately secured. We shall instance a single case, as illustrative of the process.

In the month of March, 1814, a large proportion of the

Highlanders of Farr and Kildonan, two parishes in Sutherland, were summoned to quit their farms in the following
May. In a few days after, the surrounding heaths on which
they pastured their cattle, and from which at that season,
the sole supply of herbage is derived (for in those northern
districts the grass springs late, and the cattle-feeder in the
spring months depends chiefly on the heather), were set on
fire and burnt up. There was that sort of policy in the stroke
which men deem allowable in a state of war. The starving
cattle went roaming over the burnt pastures, and found
nothing to eat. Many of them perished, and the greater
part of what remained, though in miserable condition, the
Highlanders had to sell perforce. Most of the able-bodied
men were engaged in this latter business at a distance from
home, when the dreaded term-day came on. The pasturage
had been destroyed before the legal term, and while in
even the eye of the law, it was still the property of the poor
Highlanders ; but ere disturbing them in their dwellings,
term-day was suffered to pass. The work of demolition
then began. A numerous party of men, with a factor at
their head, entered the district, and commenced pulling
down the houses over the heads of the inhabitants. In an
extensive tract of country not a human dwelling was left
standing, and then, the more effectually to prevent their
temporary re-erection, the destroyers set fire to the wreck.
In one day were the people deprived of home and shelter,
and left exposed to the elements. Many deaths are said to
have ensued from alarm, fatigue, and cold.

Our author then corroborates in detail the atrocities,
cruelties, and personal hardships already described by
Donald MacLeod and proceeds :—But to employ the language of Southey,

> Things such as these, we know, must be
> At every famous victory.

And in this instance the victory of the lord of the soil over the children of the soil was signal and complete. In little more than nine years a population of fifteen thousand individuals were removed from the interior of Sutherland to its sea-coasts or had emigrated to America. The inland districts were converted into deserts, through which the traveller may take a long day's journey, amid ruins that still bear the scathe of fire, and grassy patches betraying when the evening sun casts aslant its long deep shadows, the half-effaced lines of the plough.

After pointing out how at the Disruption sites for churches were refused, Hugh Miller proceeds:—We have exhibited to our readers, in the *clearing* of Sutherland a process of ruin so thoroughly disastrous, that it might be deemed scarcely possible to render it more complete. And yet with all its apparent completeness, it admitted of a supplementary process. To employ one of the striking figures of Scripture, it was possible to grind into powder what had been previously broken into fragments,—to degrade the poor inhabitants to a still lower level than that on which they had been so cruelly precipitated,—though persons of a not very original cast of mind might have found it difficult to say how the Duke of Sutherland has been ingenious enough to fall on exactly the one proper expedient for supplementing their ruin. All in mere circumstance and situation that could lower and deteriorate had been present as ingredients in the first process; but there still remained for the people, however reduced to poverty or broken in spirit, all in religion that consoles and ennobles. Sabbath-days came round with their humanising influences; and, under the teachings of the gospel, the poor and the oppressed looked longingly forward to a future scene of being, in which there is no poverty or oppression. They still posessed, amid their misery, something positively good, of which it was impossible to deprive them ; and hence the ability derived to the present lord of Sutherland of deepening and rendering more signal the ruin accomplished by his predecessor.

These harmonise but too well with the mode in which the interior of Sutherland was cleared, and the improved cottages of its sea-coasts erected. The plan has its two items. No sites are to be granted in the district for Free Churches, and no dwelling-houses for Free Church ministers. The climate is severe,—the winters prolonged and stormy, —the roads which connect the chief seats of population with the neighbouring counties, dreary and long. May not ministers and people be eventually worn out in this way? Such is the portion of the plan which his Grace and his Grace's creatures can afford to present to the light. But there are supplementary items of a somewhat darker kind. The poor cotters are, in the great majority of cases, tenants-at-will ; and there has been much pains taken to inform them, that to the crime of entertaining and sheltering a Protesting minister, the penalty of ejection from their holdings must inevitably attach. The laws of Charles have again returned in this unhappy district, and free and tolerating Scotland has got, in the nineteenth century, as in the seventeenth, its intercommuned ministers. We shall not say that the intimation has emanated from the Duke. It is the misfortune of such men, that there creep around them creatures whose business it is to anticipate their wishes ; but who, at times, doubtless, instead of anticipating misinterpret them ; and who, even when not very much mistaken, impart to whatever they do the impress of their own low and menial natures, and thus exaggerate in the act, the intention of their masters. We do not say, therefore, that the intimation has emanted from the Duke; but this we say, that an exemplary Sutherlandshire minister of the Protesting Church, who resigned his worldly all for the sake of his principles, had lately to travel, that he might preach to his attached people, a long journey of forty-four miles outwards, and as much in return, and all this without taking shelter under cover of a roof, or without partaking of any other refreshment than that furnished by the slender store of provisions which he had carried with him from his new home. Willingly would the poor Highlanders have received him at any risk; but knowing from experience what a Sutherlandshire removal means he preferred enduring any amount of hardship rather than that the hospitality of his people should be made the occasion of their ruin. We have already adverted to the case of a lady of Sutherland threatened with ejection from her home because she had extended the shelter of her roof to one of the Protesting clergy,—an aged and venerable man, who had quitted the neighbouring manse, his home for many years, because he could no longer enjoy it in consistency with his principles; and we have shown that that aged and venerable man was the lady's own father. What amount of oppression of a smaller and more petty character may not be expected in the circumstances, when cases such as these are found to stand but a very little over the ordinary level?

The meanness to which ducal hostility can stoop in this hapless district, impress with a feeling of surprise. In the parish of Dornoch for instance, where his Grace is fortunately not the sole landowner, there has been a site procured on the most generous terms from Sir George Gunn Munro of Poyntzfield; and this gentleman, believing himself possessed of a hereditary right to a quarry, which, though on the Duke's ground, had been long resorted to by the proprietors of the district generally, instructed the builder to take from it the stones which he needed. Never had the quarry been prohibited before, but on this occasion, a stringent interdict arrested its use. If his Grace could not prevent a hated Free Church from arising in the district, he could at least add to the expense of its erection. We have even heard that the portion of the building previously erected had to be pulled down and the stones returned.

How are we to account for a hostility so determined, and that can stoop so low? In two different ways, we are of opinion, and in both have the people of Scotland a direct interest. Did his Grace entertain a very intense regard for Established Presbytery, it is probably that he himself would be a Presbyterian of the Establishment. But such is not the case. The church into which he would so fain force the people has been long since deserted by himself. The secret of the course which he pursues can have no connection therefore with religious motive or belief. It can be no proselytising spirit that misleads his Grace. Let us remark, in the first place, rather however, in the way of embodying a fact, than imputing a motive, that with his present views, and in his present circumstances, it may not seem particularly his Grace's interest to make the county of Sutherland a happy or desirable home to the people of Scotland. It may not be his Grace's interest that the population of the district should increase. The clearing of the sea-coast may seem as little prejudicial to his Grace's welfare now, as the clearing of the interior seemed adverse to the interests of his predecessor thirty years ago; nay, it is quite possible that his Grace may be led to regard the clearing of the coast as the better and more important clearing of the two. Let it not be forgotten that a poor-law hangs over Scotland,—that the shores of Sutherland are covered with

what seems one vast straggling village, inhabited by an impoverished and ruined people,—and that the coming assess-
ment may yet fall so weighty that the extra profits accruing
to his Grace from his large sheep-farms, may go but a small
way in supporting his extra paupers. It is not in the least
improbable that he may live to find the revolution effected
by his predecessor taking to itself the form, not of a crime,—
for that would be nothing,—but of a disastrous and very
terrible blunder.

There is another remark which may prove not unworthy
the consideration of the reader. Ever since the completion
of the fatal experiment which ruined Sutherland, the noble
family through which it was originated and carried on have
betrayed the utmost jealousy of having its real results made
public. Volumes of special pleading have been written on
the subject,—pamphlets have been published, laboured
articles have been inserted in widely-spread reviews,—
statistical accounts have been watched over with the most
careful surveillance. If the misrepresentations of the press
could have altered the matter of fact, famine would not be
gnawing the vitals of Sutherland in a year a little less abundant than its predecessors, nor would the dejected and
oppressed people be feeding their discontent, amid present
misery, with the recollections of a happier past. If a
singularly well-conditioned and wholesome district of
country has been converted into one wide ulcer of
wretchedness and woe, it must be confessed that the sore
has been carefully bandaged up from the public eye,—that
if there has been little done for its cure, there has at least
been much done for its concealment. Now, be it remembered, that a Free Church threatened to insert a *tent* into
this wound, and so keep it open. It has been said that the
Gaelic language removes a district more effectually from the

influence of English opinion than an ocean of three thousand miles, and that the British public know better what is doing in New York than what is doing in Lewis or Skye. And hence one cause, at least, of the thick obscurity that has so long enveloped the miseries which the poor Highlander has had to endure, and the oppressions to which he has been subjected. The Free Church threatens to translate her wrongs into English, and to give them currency in the general mart of opinion. She might possibly enough be no silent spectator of conflagrations such as those which characterised the first general improvement of Sutherland,— nor yet of such Egyptian schemes of house-building as that which formed part of the improvements of a later plan. She might be somewhat apt to betray the real state of the district, and thus render laborious misrepresentation of little avail. She might effect a diversion in the cause of the people, and shake the foundations of the hitherto despotic power which has so long weighed them down. She might do for Sutherland what Cobbett promised to do, but what Cobbett had not character enough to accomplish, and what he did not live even to attempt. A combination of circumstances have conspired to vest in a Scottish proprietor, in this northern district, a more despotic power than even the most absolute monarchs of the Continent possess; and it is, perhaps, no great wonder that that proprietor should be jealous of the introduction of an element which threatens, it may seem, materially to lessen it. And so he struggled hard to exclude the Free Church, and, though no member of the Establishment himself, declares warmly in its behalf. Certain it is, that from the Establishment, as now constituted, he can have nothing to fear, and the people nothing to hope.

After what manner may his grace the Duke of Sutherland

be most effectually met in this matter, so that the case of toleration and freedom óf conscience may be maintained in the extensive district which God, in his providence, has consigned to his stewardship? We are not unacquainted with the Celtic character, as developed in the Highlands of Scotland. Highlanders, up to a certain point, are the most docile, patient, enduring of men; but that point once passed, endurance ceases, and the all too gentle lamb starts up an angry lion. The spirit is stirred and maddens at the sight of the naked weapon, and that in its headlong rush upon the enemy, discipline can neither check nor control. Let our oppressed Highlanders of Sutherland beware. They have suffered much; but, so far as man is the agent, their battles can be fought on only the arena of public opinion, and on that ground which the political field may be soon found to furnish.

Such of our readers as are acquainted with the memoir of Lady Glenorchy, must remember a deeply melancholy incident which occurred in the history of this excellent woman, in connection with the noble family of Sutherland. Her only sister had been married to William, seventeenth Earl of Sutherland,—"the first of the good Earls"; "a nobleman," says the Rev. Dr. Jones in his Memoir, "who to the finest person united all the dignity and amenity of manners and character which give lustre to greatness". But his sun was destined soon to go down. Five years after his marriage, which proved one of the happiest, and was blessed with two children, the elder of the two, the young Lady Catherine, a singularly engaging child, was taken from him by death, in his old hereditary castle of Dunrobin. The event deeply affected both parents, and preyed on their health and spirits. It had taken place amid the gloom of a severe northern winter, and the soli-

tude of the Highlands ; and, acquiescing in the advice of
friends, the Earl and his lady quitted the family seat, where
there was so much to remind them of their bereavement,
and sought relief in the more cheerful atmosphere of Bath.
But they were not to find it there. Shortly after their
arrival, the Earl was seized by a malignant fever, with which,
upheld by a powerful constitution, he struggled for fifty-four
days, and then expired. "For the first twenty-one days and
nights of these," says Dr. Jones, " Lady Sutherland never
left his bedside ; and then, at last, overcome with fatigue,
anxiety, and grief, she sank an unavailing victim to an
amiable but excessive attachment, seventeen days before the
death of her lord." The period, though not very remote,
was one in which the intelligence of events travelled
slowly ; and in this instance the distraction of the family
must have served to retard it beyond the ordinary time.
Her ladyship's mother, when hastening from Edinburgh to
her assistance, alighted one day from her carriage at an inn,
and on seeing two hearses standing by the wayside, inquired of an attendant whose remains they contained ? The
reply was, the remains of Lord and Lady Sutherland, on
their way for interment to the Royal Chapel of Holyrood
House. And such was the first intimation of which the
lady received of the death of her daughter and son-in-
law.

The event was pregnant with disaster to Sutherland,
though many years elapsed ere the ruin which it involved
fell on that hapless country. The sole survivor and heir of
the family was a female infant of but a year old. Her
maternal grandmother, an ambitious, intriging woman of
the world, had the chief share in her general training and
education ; and she was brought up in the south of Scotland, of which her grandmother was a native, far removed

from the influence of those genial sympathies with the
people of her clan, for which the old lords of Sutherland
had been so remarkable, and, what was a sorer evil still,
from the influence of the vitalities of that religion which,
for five generations together, her fathers had illustrated and
adorned.   The special mode in which the disaster told first,
was through the patronage of the county, the larger part of
which was vested in the family of Sutherland.   Some of the
old Earls had been content, as we have seen, to place themselves on the level of the Christian men of their parishes,
and thus to unite with them in calling to their churches the
ministers of their choice.   They know,—what regenerated
natures can alone know, with the proper emphasis, that in
Christ Jesus the vassal ranks with his lord, and they con-
scientiously acted on the conviction.   But matters were now
regulated differently.   The presentation supplanted the
call, and ministers came to be placed in the parishes of
Sutherland without the consent, and contrary to the will of
the people.   Churches, well-filled hitherto, were deserted by
their congregations, just because a respectable woman of the
world, making free use of what she deemed her own, had
planted them with men of the world, who were only tolerably
respectable ; and in houses and barns, the devout men of
the district learned to hold numerously-attended Sabbath
meetings for reading the Scriptures, and mutual exhortation
and prayer, as a sort of substitute for the public services, in
which they found they could no longer join with profit.
The spirit awakened by the old Earls had survived themselves, and ran directly counter to the policy of their
descendant.   Strongly attached to the Establishment, the
people, though they thus forsook their old places of worship,
still remained members of the national Church, and
travelled far in the summer season to attend the better

ministers of their own and the neighbouring counties. We have been assured, too, from men whose judgment we respect, that, under all their disadvantages, religion continued peculiarly to flourish among them;—"a deep-toned evangelism prevailed; so that perhaps the visible Church throughout the world at the time could furnish no more striking contrast than that which obtained between the cold, bald, common-place service of the pulpit in some of these parishes, and the fervid prayers and exhortations which give life and interest to these humble meetings of the people." What a pity it is that differences such as these the Duke of Sutherland cannot see!

Let us follow, for a little, the poor Highlanders of Sutherland to the sea-coast. It would be easy dwelling on the terrors of their expulsion, and multiplying facts of horror; but had there been no permanent deterioration effected in their condition, these, all harrowing and repulsive as they were, would have mattered less. Sutherland would have soon recovered the burning up of a few hundred hamlets, or the loss of a few bed-ridden old people, who would have died as certainly under cover, though perhaps a few months later, as when exposed to the elements in the open air. Nay, had it lost a thousand of its best men in the way in which it lost so many at the storming of New Orleans, the blank ere now would have been completely filled up. The calamities of fire or of decimation even, however distressing in themselves, never yet ruined a country: no calamity ruins a country that leaves the surviving inhabitants to develop, in their old circumstances, their old character and resources.

In one of the eastern eclogues of Collins, where two shepherds are described as flying for their lives before the troops of a ruthless invader, we see with how much of the terrible the imagination of a poet could invest the evils of war, when aggravated by pitiless barbarity. Fertile as that imagination was, however, there might be found new circumstances to heighten the horrors of the scene—circumstances beyond the reach of invention—in the retreat of the Sutherland Highlanders from the smoking ruins of their cottages to their allotments on the coast. We have heard of one man, named Mackay, whose family, at the time of the greater conflagration referred to by Macleod, were all lying ill of fever, who had to carry two of his sick children on his back a distance of twenty-five miles. We have heard of the famished people blackening the shores, like the crew of some vessel wrecked on an inhospitable coast, that they might sustain life by the shell-fish and sea-weed laid bare by the ebb. Many of their allotments, especially on the western coast, were barren in the extreme—unsheltered by bush or tree, and exposed to the sweeping sea-winds, and in time of tempest, to the blighting spray ; and it was found a matter of the extremest difficulty to keep the few cattle which they had retained, from wandering, especially in the night-time into the better sheltered and more fertile interior. The poor animals were intelligent enough to read a practical comment on the nature of the change effected ; and, from the harshness of the shepherds to whom the care of the interior had been entrusted, they served materially to add to the distress of their unhappy masters. They were getting continually impounded ; and vexatious fines, in the form of trespass-money, came thus to be wrung from the already impoverished Highlanders. Many who had no money to give were obliged to relieve them by depositing some of their few portable articles of value, such as bed or body-clothes, or, more distressing still, watches, and rings, and pins,—the only relics, in not a few instances, of brave men whose bones were mouldering under the fatal rampart at New Orleans, or in the arid sands of Egypt—on that spot of proud recollection, where the invincibles of Napoleon went down before the Highland bayonet. Their first efforts as fishermen were what might be expected from a rural people unaccustomed to the sea. The shores of Sutherland, for immense tracts together, are iron-bound, and much exposed —open on the Eastern coast to the waves of the German Ocean, and on the North and West to the long roll of the Atlantic. There could not be more perilous seas for the unpractised boatmen to take his first lessons on ; but though the casualties were numerous, and the loss of life great, many of the younger Highlanders became expert fishermen. The experiment was harsh in the extreme, but so far, at least, it succeeded. It lies open, however, to other objections than those which have been urged against it on the score of its inhumanity.*

PROFESSOR JOHN STUART BLACKIE.

PROFESSOR BLACKIE in his recently published and splendid work, "Altavona," sums up his chapter on the Sutherland Clearances in appropriate terms. Having listened to the leading character in the book—the Professor himself— giving both sides of the question at length, Bücherblume, the German scholar, exclaimed :—

"If all this is true, the power of a factor, under one of your gigantic landowners in Scotland, and wielding laws, made for the most part by landlords in their own interests, and manipulated by lawyers and judges, who were them-

* Hugh Miller's leading articles on " *Sutherland as it was and is*",

selves mostly landowners, must have been tremendous, not a whit less galling than the domination of the police in Prussia, under the Government of the old unqualified bureaucracy."

MAC.—"Tremendous, indeed. Even now the factor of an absentee landlord, or of a resident landlord, who may be feeble, or careless, or asleep, is the most absolute of despots. In many matters of vital importance to the poor peasant there is neither law nor public opinion to lay a check on his high-handedness."

The Professor then reproduces the conversation which took place between Donald Macleod and his judge at Dornoch, already printed at pp. 81-82 of this work, when Bücherblume again exclaims :—

"Good heavens! And this is British liberty in the year 1827. Our Teutonic Michel must learn to admire the glorious British Constitution less from a moral point of view."

MAC.—"Very wise. There are rats sometimes in the biggest palaces, as well as in the lowest hovels;" and he sums up by laying down the following propositions :—

I. I hold it to be quite certain, as a consequence of the altered relation of the Highlands to the Government occasioned by the rebellion of '45, and the gradual opening up of "the rough boundaries" to Lowland influences thereupon following, that some very considerable changes would require to take place in the management of Highland properties.

II. Among these changes, I consider it proven that the introduction of sheep-farming was one of the most obvious, and has proved one of the most beneficial.

III. I lay it down as an axiom of social science, that all changes affecting the welfare and comfort of large classes of men ought not to be made hastily, and in the way of a sharp revolution, but gradually, moderately, and with great tenderness : and this especially when the sufferers by any social changes are not to be the few rich and prosperous, but the many poor and industrious of the land.

IV. As a deduction from this axiom, it is plain that the introduction of sheep-farming in the wholesale manner practised by the managers of the Sutherland estates at the commencement of the present century was harsh, cruel, and tyrannical, and in the circumstances altogether unjustifiable.

V. I hold it proven, that by the use and wont of clan law, and the practice of their recognised chiefs, the Highland peasantry had a right to expect, that, unless convicted of gross misconduct, they were not to be ejected from their holdings : certainly not in favour of strangers, who had no interest in the country, but to extrude the native population, and make money by the wholesale substitution of sheep for men.

VI. I hold it *not* proven, that for the introduction of sheep-farming into the Sutherland estates, it was necessary to hand over the whole glens to the tender mercies of Lowland adventurers, and men of business eager to make money ; and that it would have been more politic and more wise, not to say more human, to have gradually enlarged the holdings, as the holders might die out, or, at all events, to have attached to each new sheep farm of more moderate dimensions, a certain number of small crofts for the supply of labour, or finally to have kept the peasantry on the property by the introduction of club-farms, or otherwise, according to circumstances ; *not* proven also, that sheep-farming cannot be carried on beneficially in conjunction with the other forms of rural economy ; but generally rather proven, that eagerness to make money, combined with a fashionable *doctrinaire* mania for large farms, and a natural desire in the factors to get clear returns with as little trouble as possible, was the real cause of the atrocious proceedings commonly known as the Sutherland Clearances.

VII. I hold it proven that in Sutherland, as in other parts of the Highlands, there existed a large population, beyond what the district could profitably support, who dragged on their tenure from father to son without any capacity of progress; but, as this population had been allowed to grow up under the eye and even with the encouragement of the proprietor and the Goverment, it was not the people who ought to have been made to suffer from the neglect and the misconduct of their natural heads; and this state of the case furnished an additional reason why any changes that took place should have been made with peculiar tenderness and delicacy.

VIII. I hold it proven that the government of large Highland estates by absentee landlords, English Commissioners, and Lowland factors, utterly ignorant of the language, the feelings, and the consuetudinary rights of the people from whom they draw their rents, is the form of economical administration naturally the best calculated to produce those harsh, inhuman, and impolitic agrarian changes commonly called the Sutherland Clearances.

Are you satisfied? asks the Professor, and the German replies:—

" I am: so far, at least, as one may be, who has not, like you, carefully read all the documents. I must say, however, that my own convictions on the general question are so strongly on your side, arising partly from my practical knowledge of the condition of rural economy in Westphalia and other parts of my fatherland, partly from the recollections I have of the admirable prelections on this subject delivered by Professor Roscher in Leipzig, that no evidence that I am likely to get from the detailed consideration of the documents from which you have quoted so copiously, would have any power to rebut the moral and political presumptions, which from the beginning have led me to condemn the whole ugly process by which your selfish, anti-social, or ignorant and short-sighted oligarchs have turned the green glens of Alba, smoking with rows of bonnie white cottages, into banks of investment for Dumfriesshire farmers, and braes of browsing ground for wild beasts. My German opinion on this big British blunder is expressed in one short classical sentence—

LATIFUNDIA PERDIDERE CALEDONIAM!"

The Professor, *alias* "Macdonald," expresses the following "sentiments," as he terms them, to which the philosophical German, in each case, adds his hearty AMEN :—

If there be any person who maintains that money, rather than men, constitutes the wealth of a healthy and well-ordered State, let him be anathema-maranatha !

If there be any person who maintains that it is better to make one big Lowland farmer rich than a hundred Highlanders happy and prosperous in a Highland glen, let him be anathema-maranatha !

If any man maintain that landlords have no duties but to gather rents, and that they may, without sin before God, and without injury to society, neglect the condition and the distribution of the people, from whom they draw their rents, let him be anathema-maranatha !

If any say that cash payment is and ought to be the only bond of cement between the different classes of society, let him be anathema-maranatha !

If any one maintain that it is better for the land of a country to be held by a few large proprietors, than to be distributed into many properties, of various sizes and qualities, let him be anathema-maranatha !

If any man maintain that a lord of the soil is justified in extruding an old and faithful tenantry, and making a deer forest of their cultivable lots, merely because he can make more money of it, or indulge himself in a wild pleasure, let him be anathema-maranatha!

If any man maintain that the distinctive glory of a landed proprietor in Scotland consists in the number of grouse which he can shoot, the number of deer which he can stalk, and the number of salmon which he can hook during the season, let him be anathema-maranatha!

If any man maintain that Scotland is only a northern province of England, and the sooner all local distinctions between the two peoples are merged in the universal dominance of purely English manners, customs, and institutions, let him be anathema-maranatha!

If any man maintain that the Highlands of Scotland are fit for nothing but being hired out as hunting-ground to the English aristocracy and plutocracy, let him be anathema-maranatha!*

To all of which we also say— AMEN!

The Sutherland Clearances Professor Blackie finally condemns as "a social crime and a blunder" for which he holds the land laws principally to blame.

JOHN MACKAY, C.E.,

REFERRING to the Sutherland Clearances, Mr. John Mackay, C.E., Hereford, said at a recent meeting of the Edinburgh Sutherland Association :—

* *Altavona; Fact and Fiction from my Life in the Highlands.* By John Stuart Blackie, F.R.S.E., Professor of Greek, Edinburgh: David Douglas, 1882.

We still helplessly condemn the fatuity that caused the m we hopelessly deplore the national blunder that permitted such barbaric acts to be perpetrated upon such a generous, loyal, and unoffending people, the most moral, the most religious population in the Highlands of Scotland, leaving the remnant of it that could not take itself away, struck and benumbed with a terror from which it has not yet recovered, and never will.

> Gus an till an gràdh 's an t-iochd
> 'S dual do athair thoirt d'a shliochd
> 'S gu'm faic na triath gur fearr na treun
> Na milte uan am mile treud.

Thrust out of their ancient homes in fertile plains and sheltered valleys on to sterile hill-sides, or equally sterile sea shores, to make new habitations for themselves, if they could or would, out of moory, mossy, heathery hillsides, or lead an amphibious life on sandy, rocky, stormy sea shores, without aid, without even encouragement being given or extended to them, to live or not to live, to dig or not to dig, to improve or not to improve, often without sufficient sustenance, need it be surprising that the population has dwarfed and dwindled away? The greater surprise is that it has not died out of existence altogether, and that it has in spite of oppression, repression, contumely, and neglect, maintained itself as it has. Surely such facts as these speak volumes for the tenacity and morals of that people. What was the condition of the population thus treated in so barbarous a manner in a civilized country, vaunting so much of its civilization? I will give it you in the words of a Sutherland lady, put by her on record upwards of fifty years ago. She says :—"I have of late frequently heard strangers coming amongst us express their surprise at the marked intelligence evinced by the old people of this district, devoid of any degree of early cultivation. To this it may be answered that the state of society was very different then from what it is now, progressively retrograding as it has been for the last few years, at least in this part of the country. At the time I allude to the lords, lairds, and gentleman of the county not only interested themselves in the welfare and happiness of their clan and dependants, but they were always solicitous that their manners, and customs, and intelligence, should keep pace with their personal appearance. The fact was the chief knew his clansmen, and it was deemed no inconsiderable part of duty in the higher classes of the community to elevate the minds as well as to assist in increasing the means of their humbler relatives and clansmen. I am aware that many unacquainted with the close ties of such a system argue largely that the distinction of rank appointed by God could not be maintained by such indiscriminate intercourse—still the habits of that day never produced a contrary effect. The chiefs here for many generations had been 'men fearing God and hating covetousness'. Iniquity was ashamed and obliged to hide its face. A dishonourable action excluded the guilty person from the invaluable privilege enjoyed by his equals in the kind notice and approbation of their superiors. Grievances of any kind were minutely inquired into and redressed, and the humble orders of the community had a degree of external polish and manly mildness of deportment in domestic life that few of the present generation have attained to, much as had been said of modern improvements." That is a picture to you of the civilization and morality existing and reigning in Sutherland, and other districts of the Highlands, at the beginning of this century, before the dark and dread days of the evictions were seen or thought of, and it may be asked what was the result of such kind and considerate conduct on the part of chiefs, lords, and lairds? History has a ready reply. From 1760 to 1810, a period of only half a century, the Highlands of Scotland, under the regime which the Sutherland lady so graphically described, sent forth 80,000 of its best and bravest men to defend the country, and fight its battles, and when they did go forth, they restored the prestige of the country, retrieved its laurels, and brought victory to crown British banners in every quarter of the globe. There is not a village round Paris, nor round Brussels, in which I have been, and conversed with their oldest inhabitants, but still revere the conduct of those Highland soldiers; so different it was to that of the other regiments of the British army. Were this the time and place, I could keep you long relating anecdotes I gathered from French and Belgians of the grand " *soldats Ecossais,*" lambs in the house, lions in the field of battle. It was from that grand population in the Highlands, nurtured and reared in the way the Sutherland lady describes so truly, that those gallant, brave soldiers went forth in legions to conquer or to die. What has Sutherland itself done in that eventful period of our history, before sheep became to be of greater value in the estimation of lairds, than a brave and loyal population of happy, contented, and hardy peasantry! In the '45 the chiefs of Sutherland had 2550 men under arms in the defence of the Throne and the country. In 1760, in the short space of nine days, 1100 Sutherland men responded to the call of their chiefs and served their country for four years. In 1777, when the country was in dire need of men, gallant and true, an equal number answered the call to arms, and served under their chiefs for five years. In 1794, the Sutherland chiefs again appealed to their clansmen, and 1800 men followed them into the field, Sutherlands and Mackays. These men, sons of crofters and tacksmen, behaved themselves in England, Ireland, and the Channel Islands in a manner that drew forth from commanding generals the highest enconiums for their good conduct and military bearing in quarters, and in the field. General Lake, on his defeat by the French at Castlebar, said of the Mackay Regiment of Fencibles, "If I had my brave and honest Reays here this would not have happened". In 1800, the 93rd Highlanders was raised, 1000 strong ; 800 of them were Sutherland men, and how that regiment comported itself whenever it had an opportunity of showing the stern stuff of which it was composed, its history nobly tells. In the Cape Colony all the Dutchmen spoke of it with raptures. By its conciliatory and gentle, and considerate conduct, it alleviated conquest to the conquered. Such were the sons and brothers of the evicted of Sutherland.

> Where are they now? Tell us where are thy sons and daughters,
>   Sutherland ! sad mother ! no more in thy bosom they dwell ;
> Far, far away, they have found a new home o'er the waters,
>   Yearning for thee with a love that no language can tell.
> Nimrods and hunters are now lords of the mount and forest.
>   Men but encumber the soil where their forefathers trod ;
> Tho' for their country they fought when its need was the sorest,
>   Forth they must wander, their hope not in man, but in God.

I need not enlarge upon this theme, but I may be permitted to ask what are loyalty and affection ? Are they virtues to be held cheap by the country ? It is said that loyalty in the subject is the stability and safety of the throne, the palace, and the castle ; but after all, loyalty and affection are simply the development of our best sentiments, which can be cultivated, which can be increased or diminished by kind or harsh treatment, by good or bad government, exactly as the Sutherland lady described in the past, and as we ourselves, most unfortunately, see in our own day in the Highlands and in Ireland—grievances unheeded and unredressed, till agitation and outrage bring them to the light of day. Then remedies more or less drastic have to be applied, and loud complaints heard of confiscation and cries for compensation. Was any compensation ever heard of for the evicted of the Highlands? Highlanders carried the spirit of loyalty with them even when evicted. They were proud of the sentiment, and maintained it, from the furnace of fire on the field of Culloden, so glorious to the vanquished, so humiliating to the conquerors, to the fires of the evictions and through them to the present day, in spite of the divorce from their chiefs, in spite of the want of sympathy that might reasonably have been expected from chiefs whom they so implicitly trusted, and whom they so well served, little conscious of what was their own due for such elevated services, and in spite, too, of after neglect, harsh treatment, and want of any encouragement when the evil day overtook them. Greed of gold, love of display in the hearts and minds of Highland chiefs, led to the national disaster of the extirpation of the heroic population of the Highlands of seventy years ago, the boast and the pride of Scotland, the safety of England and the terror of her foes. Shall we see its like again? No, not for another century or more. Wealth, with its concomitant vices—pride, luxury, tyranny, oppression, and disregard of the golden rule—lead to nihilism, socialism, communism, as it has led to the decline and fall of empires and kingdoms, ancient and modern. Well will it be for us and for themselves if our aristocracy and plutocracy, imitating the bright and grand example of the best and most beloved monarch that ever ruled the destinies of our country, to exercise the rights conferred upon them by the Crown, and by Acts of Parliament framed by themselves, that from them to us might flow a stream of affection, pure and unalloyed, and from us to them course its way back in veins of true loyalty and attachment, as a return for the proper exercise of duties implied and understood in the conferring of rights. This done and observed, the throne and the castle are secure ; this not done, both are insecure—a breath can unmake them, as a breath has made. Both are in danger of being swept away here as elsewhere, and in other countries :

> Remember, man, the universal cause
> Acts not by partial, but by general laws.

The eternal law of right and justice to all classes and between all classes must ultimately prevail. The British Government is no longer at the dictation of the rich and powerful. Was not the great principle of National Education in Scotland wrung from rapacious noblemen by John Knox ? Was not political power wrenched from an unwilling oligarchy half a century ago ? Has not free trade in corn been made the law of the land in spite of the opposition of the landed interest ? Were not civil and religious freedom secured to us by the best blood of our countrymen, in the face of much opposition and bloodshed ? Frequently evil is done by want of thought as much as by want of heart. I have attempted to describe what was the happy and contented condition of the Highland people, and the state of civilization that ruled at the beginning of this century, before the terrible change came that tore them from their homes, and thrust them out totally unprepared for such a dire catastrophe. Humanity shudders at the scene. Need it be surprising that a people so accustomed to gentle, kind, considerate treatment and cultivation from former chiefs, were absolutely stunned by such a sudden and terrible revolutionary visitation. No wonder that the people reeled

GLENCALVIE.

Great cruelties were perpetrated at Glencalvie, Ross-shire, where the evicted had to retire into the parish churchyard, where for more than a week they found the only shelter obtainable in their native land, no one daring to succour them, under a threat of receiving similar treatment to those whose hard fate had driven them thus among the tombs. Many of them, indeed, wished that their lot had landed them under the sod with their ancestors and friends, rather than be treated and driven out of house and home in such a ruthless manner. A special Commissioner sent down by the London *Times* describes the circumstances as follows :—

ARDGAY, NEAR TAIN, ROSS-SHIRE,
15th May, 1845.

Those who remember the misery and destitution to which large masses of the population were thrown by the systematic " Clearances " (as they are here called) carried on in Sutherlandshire some 20 years ago, under the direction and on the estate of the late Marchioness of Stafford—those who have not forgotten to what an extent the ancient ties which bound clansmen to their chiefs were then torn asunder—will regret to learn the heartless source with all its sequences of misery, of destitution, and of crime, is again being resorted to in Ross-shire. Amongst an imaginative people like the Highlanders, who, poetic from dwelling amongst wild and romantic scenery, shut out from the world and clinging to the traditions of the past, it requires little, with fair treatment, to make them almost idolise their heritor. They would spend the last drop of their blood in his service. But this feeling of respectful attachment to the landowners, which money cannot buy, is fast passing away. This change is not without cause ; and perhaps if the dark deeds of calculating "feelosophy" transacted through the instrumentality of factors in some of these lonely glens ; if the almost inconceivable misery and hopeless destitution in which, for the expected acquisition of a few pounds, hundreds of peaceable and generally industrious and contented peasants are driven out from the means of self-support to become wanderers and starving beggars, and in which a brave and valuable population is destroyed—are exposed to the gaze of the world, general indignation and disgust may effect what moral obligations and humanity cannot. One of these clearances is about to take place in the parish of Kincardine, from which I now write ; and throughout the whole district it has created the strongest feeling of indignation. This parish is divided into two districts each of great extent ; one is called the parliamentary district of Croick. The length of this district is about 20 miles, with a breadth of from 10 to 15 miles. It extends amongst the most remote and unfrequented parts of the country, consisting chiefly of hills of heather and rock, peopled only in a few straths and glens. This district was formerly thickly peopled ; but one of those clearances many years ago nearly swept away the population, and now the whole number of its inhabitants amounts, I am told, to only 370 souls. These are divided into three straths or glens, and live in a strath called Amatnatua, another strath called Greenyard, and in Glencalvie. It is the inhabitants of Glencalvie, in number 90 people, whose turn it is now to be turned out of their homes, all at once, the aged and the helpless as well as the young and strong; nearly the whole of them without hope or prospect for the future. The proprietor of this glen is Major Charles Robertson of Kindeace, who is at present out with his regiment in Australia; and his factor or steward who acts for him in his absence is Mr. James Gillanders of Highfield Cottage, near Dingwall. Glencalvie is situated about 25 miles from Tain, eastward. Bleak rough hills, whose surface are almost all rock and heather, closed in on all sides, leaving in the valley a gentle declivity of arable land of a very poor description, dotted over by cairns of stone and rock, not, at the utmost computation, of more than 15 to 20 acres in extent. For this piece of indifferent land with a right of pasturage on the hills impinging upon it—and on which, if it were not a fact that sheep do live, you would not credit that they could live, so entirely does it seem so devoid of vegetation beyond the brown heather, whilst its rocky nature makes it dangerous and impossible even for a sheep walk—the almost increditable rent of £55 10s., has been paid. I am convinced that for the same land no farmer in England would give £15 at the utmost.

Even respectable farmers here say they do not know how the people raise the rent for it. Potatoes and barley were grown in the valley, and some sheep and a few black cattle find provender amongst the heather. Eighteen families have each a cottage in the valley; they have always paid their rent punctually, and they have contrived to support themselves in all ordinary seasons. They have no poor on the poor roll, and they help one another over the winter. I am told that not an inhabitant of this valley has been charged with any offence for years back. During the war it furnished many soldiers; and an old pensioner, 82 years of age, who has served in India, is now dying in one of these cottages, where he was born. For the convenience of the proprietor, some ten years ago, four of the principal tenants became bound for the rest, to collect all the rents and pay the whole in one sum.

The clearance of this valley, having attracted much notice, has been thoroughly enquired into, and a kind of defence has been entered upon respecting it, which I am told has been forwarded to the Lord Advocate. Through the politeness of Mr. Mackenzie, writer, Tain, I have been favoured with a copy of it. The only explanation or defence of the clearance, that I can find in it, is that shortly after Mr. Gillanders assumed the management of Major Robertson's estate, he found that it became absolutely necessary to adopt a different system, in regard to the lands of Glencalvie " from that hitherto pursued ".

The " different system " as it appears was to turn the barley and potato grounds into a sheep walk; and the "absolute necessity" for it is an alleged increase of rent.

It was accordingly, in 1843, attempted to serve summonses of removal upon the tenants. They were in no arrears of rent, they had no burdens in poor; for 500 years their fathers had peaceably occupied the glen, and the people were naturally indignant. Who can be surprised that on the constables going amongst them with the summonses, they acted in a manner which, while it showed their excitement, not the less evinced their wish to avoid breaking the law. The women met the constables beyond the boundaries, over the river, and seized the hand of the one who held the notices : whilst some held it out by the wrist, others held a live coal to the papers and set fire to them. They were afraid of being charged with destroying the notices, and they sought thus to evade the consequences.

This act of resistance on their part has been made the most of. One of the men told me, hearing they were to be turned out because they did not pay rent enough, that they offered to pay £15 a-year more, and afterwards to pay as much rent as any other man would give for the place. The following year (1844) however, the four chief tenants were decoyed to Tain, under the assurance that Mr. Gillanders was going to settle with them, they believing that their holdings were to be continued to them. The notices were then, as they say, in a treacherous and tricky manner, served upon them, however. Having been served, "a decreet of removal" was obtained against them under which, of course, if they refused to turn out they would be put out by force. Finding themselves in this position, they entered into an arrangement with Mr. Gillanders, in which after several propositions on either side, it was agreed that they should remain until the 12th of May, to give them time to provide themselves with holdings elsewhere, Mr. Gillanders agreeing to pay them £100 on quitting, and to take their stock on at a valuation. They were also to have liberty to carry away the timber of their houses, which was really worthless except for firewood. On their part they agreed to leave peaceably, and not to lay down any crop. Beyond the excessive harshness of removing the people at all, it is but right to say that the mode of proceeding in the removal hitherto has been temperate and considerate.

Two respectable farmers became bound for the people that they would carry out their part of the agreement, and the time of removal has since been extended to the 25th of this month. In the defence got up for this proceeding it is stated that all have been provided for; this is not only not the case, but seems to be intentionally deceptive. In speaking of all, the four principal tenants only are meant; for, according to the factor, these were all he had to do with; but this is not the case even in regard to the four principal tenants. Two only, a father and son, have got a piece of black moor, near Tain, 25 miles off, without any house or shed on it, out of which they hope to obtain subsistence. For this they are to pay £1 rent for 7 acres the first year; £2 for the second year; and £3 for a continuation. Another old man with a family has got a house and a small lot of land in Edderton, about 20 miles off. These three, the whole who have obtained places where they may hope to make a living. The old pensioner, if removing does not kill him, has obtained for himself and family, and for his son's family, a house at a rent of £3 or £4, some ten miles off, without any land or means of subsistence attached to it. This old soldier has been offered 2s. a-week by the factor to support him while he lived. He was one of the four principal tenants bound for the rent; and he indignantly refused to be kept as a pauper.

A widow with four children, two imbecile, has obtained two small apartments in a bothie or turf hut near Bonar Bridge, for which she is to pay £2 rent, without any land or means of subsistence. Another, a man with a wife and four children, has got an apartment at Bonar Bridge, at £1 rent. He goes there quite destitute, without means of living. Six only of eighteen households therefore have been able to obtain places in which to put their heads; and of these, three only have any means of subsistence before them. The rest are hopeless and helpless. Two or three of the men told me they have been round to every factor and proprietor in the neighbourhood, and they could obtain no place, and nothing to do, and they did not know where to go to, nor what to do to live.

Speaking of the cottages the Commissioner says:—The

fire is on a stone in the middle of the family or centre room, and warms the whole cottage. Though the roofs and sides are blackened with the peat smoke, everything within is clean and orderly.

And for what are all these people to be reduced from comfort to beggary? For what is this virtuous and contented community to be scattered? I confess I can find no answer. It is said that the factor would rather have one tenant than many, as it saves him trouble! But so long as the rent is punctually paid as this has been, it is contrary to all experience to suppose that one large tenant will pay more rent than many small ones, or that a sheep walk can pay more rent than cultivated land.

Let me add that so far from the clearance at Glencalvie being a solitary instance in this neighbourhood, it is one of many. The tenants of Newmore, near Tain, who I am told, amount to 16 families, are to be weeded out (as they express it here) on the 25th, by the same Mr. Gillanders. The same factor manages the Strathconon estate, about 30 miles from Newmore, from which during the last four years, some hundreds of families have been weeded. The Government Church of that district, built eighteen years ago, to meet the necessities of the population, is now almost unnecessary from the want of population. At Black Isle, near Dingwall, the same agent is pursuing the same course, and so strong is the feeling of the poor Highlanders at these outrageous proceedings, so far as they are concerned wholly unwarranted from any cause whatever, that I am informed on the best authority, and by those who go amongst them and hear what they say, that it is owing to the influence of religion alone that they refrain from breaking out into open and turbulent resistance of the law. I enclose you the defence of this proceeding, with a list of the names and numbers of each family in Glencalvie—in all 92 persons.*

Mr. Gillanders has been severely hit off for his conduct here, in Strathconon, and elsewhere, by Duncan Mackenzie, the Kenlochewe Bard, in a long Gaelic poem, from which we extract the following stanzas :—

'S dhearbh Seumas a dhuthchas,
A bhi na shiamarlan bruideal,
Mar bha sheanair bho thus,
A creach, 's a rusgadh nam bochd.
Am fior-anmhaidh, gun churam,
Gun Dia, gun chreideamh, gun umhlachd,
Gun chliu, gun tuigse, gun diulam,
Ach na ùmaidh gun tlachd ;
Gheibh e bhreitheanas dubailt,
Air son na Rosaich a sgiursadh,
A Gleann-a-Chalbhaidh le dhurachd,
Na daoine ionraic gun lochd,
Bha riamh onarach, sumhail,
Gun sgilig fhiachan air chul orr',
'S na màil paight' aig gach aon diubh,
'S gach cis shaoghalt bha orr'.

Bu truagh, cianail, a dh-fhag e,
Gleann-a-Chalbhaidh na fhasach,
An sluagh sgaipte anns gach aite,
Gun cheo, gun larach, gun tigh,
Air an ruagadh le tamailt,
'S olc a fhuair iad an caradh,
Gun aite fuirich na tamh ac',
Gun truas, gun chairdeas, gun iochd.
Chaidh cuid a chomhnuidh fuidh sgail dhiubh,
Ann an cladh Chinn a-Chairdin ;
Thug sud masladh, 'us taire,
Dha 'n t-Siorr'achd ghaidh'leach so 'm feasd ;
'S bi' Seumas mor air a phaigheadh,
An lath a' ghairmeas am bàs e,
'S cha bhi bron air na Gaidheil,
Nuair theid a charadh fuidh lic.

*London *Times* of Tuesday, 20th of May, 1845.

Rinn am buamasdair grannda,
Obair eile, bha graineil,
A chur air ruaig Cloinn-'ic-Thearlaich,
Bha paigheadh mal Choirre-bhuic,
An tuath chothromach, laidir,
Nach dh-fhuair masladh, no taire,
Gus an d-thainig an namhaid
Nach deanadh fabhar air bith.
Chaidh an Sgaoileadh 's gach aite ;
Cha robh trocair 'na nadurs',
Fear gun choguis, gun naire,
Air an laidh an càineadh is mios',
'S iomadh athchuimhnich araidh,
'Chaidh a ghuidhe d' a chnaimhean ;
'S cha 'n urrainn es' a bhi sabhailt
Ann an aite sam bith.

THE EVICTION OF THE ROSSES.

IN a "Sermon for the Times," the Rev. Richard Hibbs, of the Episcopal Church, Edinburgh, referring to these evictions says :—"Take first, the awful proof how far in oppression men can go—men highly educated and largely gifted in every way—property, talents, all; for the most part indeed, they are so-called noblemen. What, then, are they doing in the Highland districts, according to the testimony of a learned professor in this city? Why, depopulating those districts in order to make room for red deer. And how? by buying off the cottars, and giving them money to emigrate? Not at all, but by starving them out; by rendering them absolutely incapable of procuring subsistence for themselves and families ; for they first take away from them their apportionments of poor lands, although they may have paid their rents ; and if that don't suffice to eradicate from their hearts that love of the soil on which they have been born and bred—a love which

the great Proprietor of all has manifestly implanted in our
nature—why, then, these inhuman landlords, who are far
more merciful to their very beasts, take away from these
poor cottars the very roofs above their defenceless heads,
and expose them, worn down with age and destitute of
of everything, to the inclemencies of a northern sky; and
this, forsooth, because they must have plenty of room for
their dogs and deer. For plentiful instances of the most
wanton barbarities under this head we need only point to
the Knoydart evictions. Here were perpetrated such
enormities as might well have caused the very sun to hide
his face at noon-day." Macleod, referring to this sermon,
says :—

"It has been intimated to me by an individual who heard
this discourse on the first occasion that the statements
referring to the Highland landlords have been controverted.
I was well aware, long before the receipt of this intimation,
that some defence had appeared; and here I can truly say,
that none would have rejoiced more than myself to find
that a complete vindication had been made. But, unhappily, the case is far otherwise. In order to be fully
acquainted with all that had passed on the subject, I have
put myself during the week in communication with the
learned professor to whose letter, which appeared some
months ago in the *Times*, I referred. From him I learn
that none of his statements were invalidated—nay, not even
impugned; and he adds, that to do this was simply impossible, as he had been at great pains to verify the facts. All
that could be called in question was the theory that he had
based upon those facts—namely, that evictions were made
for the purpose of making room for more deer. This, of
course, was open to contradiction on the part of those landlords who had not openly avowed their object in evicting

the poor Highland families.   As to the evictions themselves
—and this was the main point—no attempt at contradiction
was made."

In addition to all that the benevolent Professor [Black]
has made known to the world under this head, who has not
heard of "The Massacre of the Rosses," and the clearing
of the glens.   "I hold in my hand," Mr. Hibbs continued, "a
little work thus entitled, which has passed into the second
edition.   The author, Mr. Donald Ross—a gentleman
whom all who feel sympathy for the down-trodden and
oppressed must highly esteem.   What a humiliating picture
of the barbarity and cruelty of fallen humanity does this
little book present!   The reader, utterly appalled by its
horrifying statements finds it difficult to retain the recollection that he is perusing the history of his own times, and
country too.   He would fain yield himself to the tempting
illusion that the ruthless atrocities which are depicted were
enacted in a fabulous period, in ages long past ; or at all
events, if it be contemporaneous history, that the scene of
such heart-rending cruelties, the perpetrators of which were
regardless alike of the innocency of infancy and the helplessness of old age, is some far distant, and as yet not merely
unchristianized, but wholly savage and uncivilized region of
of our globe.   But alas! it is Scotland, in the latter half of
the nineteenth century, of which he treats.   One feature of
the heart-harrowing case is the shocking and barbarous
cruelty that was practised on this occasion upon the female
portion of the evicted clan.   Mr. D. Ross, in a letter
addressed to the Right Hon. the Lord Advocate, Edinburgh, dated April 19, 1854, thus writes in reference to one
of those clearances and evictions which had just then taken
place, under the authority of a certain sheriff of the district,
and by means of a body of policemen as executioners :—

"The feeling on this subject, not only in the district, but in Sutherlandshire and Ross-shire is, among the great majority of the people, one of universal condemnation of the Sheriff's reckless conduct, and of indignation and disgust at the brutality of the policemen. Such, indeed, was the sad havoc made on the females on the banks of the Carron, on the memorable 31st March last, that pools of blood were on the ground—that the grass and earth were dyed red with it—that the dogs of the district came and licked up the blood; and at last, such was the state of feeling of parties who went from a distance to see the field, that a party (it is understood by order or instructions from head-quarters) actually harrowed the ground during the night to hide the blood!

"The affair at Greenyard, on the morning of the 31st March last, is not calculated to inspire much love of country, or rouse the martial spirit of the already ill-used Highlanders. The savage treatment of innocent females on that morning, by an enraged body of police, throws the Sinope butchery into the shade; for the Ross-shire Haynaus have shown themselves more cruel and more blood-thirsty than the Austrian women-floggers. What could these poor men and women—with their wounds, and scars, and broken bones, and disjointed arms, stretched on beds of sickness, or moving on crutches, the result of the brutal treatment of them by the police at Greenyard—have to dread from the invasion of Scotland by Russia?"

Commenting on this incredible atrocity, committed in the middle of the nineteenth century! Donald Macleod says truly that :—It was so horrifying and so brutal that he did not wonder at the rev. gentleman's delicacy in speaking of it, and directing his hearers to peruse Mr. Ross's pamphlet for full information. Mr. Ross went from Glasgow to Greenyard,

all the way to investigate the case upon the spot, and found
that Mr. Taylor, a native of Sutherland, well educated in the
evicting schemes and murderous cruelty of that county,
and Sheriff-substitue of Ross-shire, marched from Tain upon
the morning of the 31st March, at the head of a strong
party of armed constables, with heavy bludgeons and fire
arms, conveyed in carts and other vehicles, allowing them as
much ardent drink as they chose to take before leaving and
on their march, so as to qualify them for the bloody work
which they had to perform; fit for any outrage, fully
equipped, and told by the Sheriff to show no mercy to any
one who would oppose them, and not allow themselves to
be called cowards, by allowing these mountaineers victory
over them. In this excited, half-drunken state, they came
in contact with the unfortunate women of Greenyard, who
were determined to prevent the officers from serving the
summonses of removal upon them, and keep their holding of
small farms where they and their forefathers lived and died
for generations. But no time was allowed for parley; the
Sheriff gave the order to clear the way, and, be it said to his
everlasting disgrace, he struck the first blow at a woman,
the mother of a large family, and large in the family way at
the time, who tried to keep him back; then a general
slaughter commenced; the women made noble resistance,
until the bravest of them got their arms broken; then they
gave way. This did not allay the rage of the murderous
brutes, they continued clubbing at the protectless creatures
until every one of them was stretched on the field, weltering
in their blood, or with broken arms, ribs, and bruised limbs.
In this woful condition many of them were hand-cuffed
together, others tied with coarse ropes, huddled into carts,
and carried prisoners to Tain. I have seen myself
in the possession of Mr. Ross, Glasgow, patches or scalps

of the skin with the long hair adhering to them, which was found upon the field a few days after this inhuman affray.   I did not see the women, but I was told that gashes were found on the heads of two young female prisoners in Tain jail, which exactly corresponded with the slices of scalps which I have seen, so that Sutherland and Ross-shire may boast of having had the Nana Sahib and his chiefs some few years before India, and that in the persons of some whose education, training, and parental example should prepare their minds to perform and act differently.   Mr. Donald Ross placed the whole affair before the Lord Advocate for Scotland, but no notice was taken of it by that functionary, further than that the majesty of the law would need to be observed and attended to.

In this unfortunate country, the law of God and humanity may be violated and trampled under foot, but the law of wicked men which sanctions murder, rapine, and robbery must be observed.   From the same estate (the estate of Robertson of Kindeace, if I am not mistaken in the date) in the year 1843 the whole inhabitants of Glencalvie were evicted in a similar manner, and so unprovided and unprepared were they for removal at such an inclement season of the year, that they had to shelter themselves in a Church and a burying-ground.   I have seen myself nineteen families within this gloomy and solitary resting abode of the dead, they were there for months.   The London *Times* sent a commissioner direct from London to investigate into this case, and he did his duty; but like the Sutherland cases, it was hushed up in order to maintain the majesty of the law, and in order to keep the right, the majesty of the people, and the laws of God in the dark.

In the year 1819 or '20, about the time when the depopulation of Sutherlandshire was completed, and the annual conflagration of burning the houses ceased, and when there was not a glen or strath in the county to let to a sheep farmer, one of these insatiable monsters of Sutherlandshire sheep farmers fixed his eyes upon a glen in Ross-shire, inhabited by a brave race, hardy for time immemorial. Summonses of removal were served upon them at once. The people resisted—a military force was brought against them —the military and the women of the glen met at the entrance to the glen—a bloody conflict took place; without reading the riot act or taking any other precaution, the military fired (by the order of Sheriff MacLeod) ball cartridge upon the women; one young girl of the name of Mathieson was shot dead on the spot; many were wounded. When this murder was observed by the survivors, and some young men concealed in the background, they made a heroic sudden rush upon the military, when a hand-to-hand melee or fight took place. In a few minutes the military were put to disorder by flight; in their retreat they were unmercifully dealt with, only two of them escaping with whole heads. The Sheriff's coach was smashed to atoms, and he made a narrow escape himself with a whole head. But no legal cognisance was taken of this affair, as the Sheriff and the military were the violators. However, for fear of prosecution, the Sheriff settled a pension of £6 sterling yearly upon the murdered girl's father, and the case was hushed up likewise. The result was that the people kept possession of the glen, and that the proprietor, and the oldest and most insatiable of Sutherlandshire scourges went to law, which ended in the ruination of the latter, who died a pauper.

Hugh Miller, describing a " Highland Clearing," in one of his able leading articles in the *Witness*, since published in volume form, quotes freely from an article by John Robertson, which appeared in the *Glasgow National* in August, 1844, on the evictions of the Rosses of Glencalvie. When the article from which Hugh Miller quotes was written, the inhabitants of the glen had just received notices of removal, but the evictions had not yet been carried out. Commenting on the proceedings our authority says :—

"In an adjacent glen (to Strathcarron), through which the Calvie works its headlong way to the Carron, that terror of the Highlanders, a summons of removal, has been served within the last few months on a whole community : and the graphic sketch of Mr. Robertson relates both the peculiar circumstances in which it has been issued, and the feelings which it has excited. We find from his testimony that the old state of things which is so immediately on the eve of being broken up in this locality, lacked not a few of those sources of terror to the proprietary of the county, that are becoming so very formidable to them in the newer states."

The constitution of society in the Glen, says Mr. Robertson, is remarkably simple. Four heads of families are bound for the whole rental. The number of souls was about ninety, sixteen cottages paid rent ; they supported a teacher for the education of their own children ; they supported their own poor. "The laird has never lost a farthing of rent in bad years, such as 1836 and 1837, the people may have required the favour of a few weeks' delay, but they are not now a single farthing in arrears ;" that is, when they are in receipt of summonses of removal. "For a century," Mr. Robertson continues, speaking of the Highlanders, "their privileges have been lessening ; they dare not now hunt the deer, or shoot the grouse or the blackcock ; they have no longer the range of the hills for their cattle and their sheep ; they must not catch a salmon in the stream : in earth, air, and water, the rights of the laird are greater, and the rights of the people are smaller, than they were in the days of their forefathers." The same writer eloquently concludes :—

"The father of the laird of Kindeace bought Glencalvie. It was sold by a Ross two short centuries ago. The swords of the Rosses of Glencalvie did their part in protecting this little glen, as well as the broad lands of Pitcalvie, from the ravages and the clutches of hostile septs. These clansmen bled and died in the belief that every principle of honour and morals secured their descendants a right to subsisting on the soil. The chiefs and their children had the same charter of the sword. Some Legislatures have made the right of the people superior to the right of the chief ; British law-makers made the rights of the chief everything, and those of their followers nothing. The ideas of the morality of property are in most men the creatures of their interests and sympathies. Of this there cannot be a doubt, however, the chiefs would not have had the land at all, could the clansmen have foreseen the present state of the Highlands— their children in mournful groups going into exile—the faggot of legal myrmidons in the thatch of the feal cabin— the hearths of their homes and their lives the green sheep-walks of the stranger. Sad it is, that it is seemingly the will of our constituencies that our laws shall prefer the few to the many. Most mournful will it be, should the clansmen of the Highlands have been cleared away, ejected, exiled, in deference to a political, a moral, a social, and an economical mistake,—a suggestion not of philosophy, but of mammon,— a system in which the demon of sordidness assumed the shape of the angel of civilization and of light."

That the Eviction of the Rosses was of a most brutal character is amply corroborated by the following account, extracted from the *Inverness Courier :*—"We mentioned last week that considerable obstruction was anticipated in the execution of the summonses of removal upon the tenants of Major Robertson of Kindeace, on his property of Green-yards, near Bonar Bridge. The office turned out to be of a very formidable character. At six o'clock on the morning of Friday last, Sheriff Taylor proceeded from Tain, accompanied by several Sheriff's officers, and a police force of about thirty more, partly belonging to the constabulary force of Ross-shire, and partly to that of Inverness-shire,— the latter under the charge of Mr. Mackay, inspector, Fort-William. On arriving at Greenyards, which is nearly four miles from Bonar Bridge, it was found that about three hundred persons, fully two-thirds of whom were women, had assembled from the county round about, all apparently prepared to resist the execution of the law. The women stood in front, armed with stones, and the men occupied the background, all, or nearly all, furnished with sticks.

"The Sheriff attempted to reason with the crowd, and to show them the necessity of yielding to the law: but his efforts were fruitless ; some of the women tried to lay hold of him and to strike him, and after a painful effort to effect the object in view by peaceable means—which was renewed in vain by Mr. Cumming, the superintendent of the Ross-shire police—the Sheriff was reluctantly obliged to employ force. The force was led by Mr. Cumming into the crowd, and after a sharp resistance, which happily lasted only a few minutes, the people were dispersed, and the Sheriff was enabled to execute the summonses upon the four tenants. The women, as they bore the brunt of the battle, were the principal sufferers. A large number of them—fifteen or sixteen, we believe, were seriously hurt, and of these several are under medical treatment ; one woman, we believe, still lies in a precarious condition. The policemen appear to have used their batons with great force, but they escaped themselves almost unhurt.   Several correspondents from the district, who do not appear, however, to make sufficient allowance for the critical position of affairs, and the necessity of at once impressing so large a multitude with the serious nature of the case, complain that the policemen used their batons with wanton cruelty.   Others state that they not only did their duty, but that less firmness might have proved fatal to themselves.   The instances of violence are certainly, though very naturally, on the part of the attacking force ; several batons were smashed in the melee, a great number of men and women were seriously hurt, especially about the head and face, while not one of the policemen, so far as we can learn, suffered any injury in consequence.   As soon as the mob was fairly dispersed, the police made active pursuit, in the hope of catching some of the ringleaders.   The men had, however, fled, and the only persons apprehended were some women, who had been active in the opposition, and who had been wounded.   They were conveyed to the prison at Tain, but liberated on bail next day, through the intercession of a gallant friend, who became responsible for their appearance."

" A correspondent writes," continues the *Courier*, "ten young women were wounded in the back of the skull and other parts of their bodies. . . . . . The wounds on these women show plainly the severe manner in which they were dealt with by the police when they were retreating.   It was currently reported last night that one of them was dead ; and the feeling of indignation is so strong against the manner in which the constables have acted, that I fully believe the life of any stranger, if he were supposed to be an officer of the law, would not be worth twopence in the district.   This unfortunate affair reminds me of an Irishman who was successful in a law suit, and after all, said he had only 'gained a loss'; and truly the authority of the law has fared in a similar way in the parish of Kincardine. The fact is that the authority of the law has served to clear an estate of paupers at the public expense; for if the relation that ought to exist between landlord and tenant existed in this case, neither law nor blows would be required in the removal of the poor crofters. If we refer to your paper in the spring of 1845 we shall find summonses peaceably served on 70 or 80 tenants in Glencalvie. Repeated applications were then made for the military and refused. Could not our Lord-Advocate introduce some short measure that would do away with these harrowing Clearances?"

The *Northern Ensign*, referring to the same case, says:— "One day lately a preventive officer with two cutter men made their appearance on the boundaries of the estate and were taken for Tain Sheriff-officers. The signals were at once given, and in course of half-an-hour the poor gauger and his men were surrounded by 300 men and women, who would not be remonstrated with, either in English or Gaelic; the poor fellows were taken and denuded of their clothing, all papers and documents were extracted and burnt, amongst which was a purse with a considerable quantity of money. In this state they were carried shoulder-high off the estate, and left at the Braes of Downie, where the great Culrain riot took place thirty years ago."

THE HEBRIDES.

THE people of Skye and the Uist, where the Macdonalds for centuries ruled in the manner of princes over a loyal and devoted people, were treated not a whit better than those on the mainland, when their services were no longer required to fight the battles of the Lords of the Isles, or to secure to them their possessions, their dignity, and power. *Bha latha eile ann!* There was another day! When possessions were held by the sword, those who wielded them were highly valued, and well cared for. Now that sheep-skins are found sufficient, what could be more appropriate in the opinion of some of the sheepish chiefs of modern times than to displace the people who anciently secured and held the lands for real chiefs worthy of the name, and replace them by the animals that produced the modern sheep-skins by which they hold their lands; especially when these were found to be better titles than the old ones—the blood and sinew of their ancient vassals.

Prior to 1849, the manufacture of kelp in the Outer Hebrides had been for many years a large source of income to the proprietors of those islands, and a considerable revenue to the inhabitants; the lairds, in consequence, for many years encouraged the people to remain, and it is alleged that they multiplied to a degree quite out of proportion to the means of subsistance within reach when kelp manufacture failed. To make matters worse for the poor tenants, the rents were meanwhile raised by the proprietors to more than double—not because the land was considered worth more by itself, but because the possession of it enabled the poor tenants to earn a certain sum a year from kelp made out of the sea-ware to which their holdings entitled them, and out of which the proprietor pocketed a profit of from £3 to £4 per ton, in addition to the enhanced rent obtained from the crofter for the land. In these circumstances one would have thought that some consideration would have been shown to the people, who, it may perhaps be admitted, were found in the altered circumstances, too numerous to obtain a livelihood in those islands; but such consideration does not appear to have been given—indeed the very reverse.

NORTH UIST.

IN 1849, Lord Macdonald determined to evict between 600 and 700 persons from Sollas, in North Uist, of which he was then proprietor. They were at the time in a state of great misery from the failure of the potato crop for several years previously in succession, many of them having had to work for ninety-six hours a week for a pittance of two stones of Indian meal once a fortnight. Sometimes even that miserable dole was not forthcoming, and families had to live for weeks solely on shell-fish picked up on the sea-shore. Some of the men were employed on drainage works, for which public money was advanced to the proprietors; but here, as in most other places throughout the Highlands, the money earned was applied by the factors to wipe off old arrears, while the people were permitted generally to starve. His lordship having decided that they must go, notices of ejectment were served upon them, to take effect on the 15th of May, 1849. They asked for delay, to enable them to dispose of their cattle and other effects to the best advantage at the summer markets, and offered to work meanwhile making kelp, on terms which would prove remunerative to the proprietors, if only, in the altered circumstances, they might get their crofts on equitable terms—for their value, as such—apart from the kelp manufacture, on account of which the rents had previously been raised. Their petitions were ignored. No answers were received, while at the same time they were directed to sow as much corn and potatoes as they could during that spring, and for which they were told, they would be fully compensated, whatever happened. They sold much of their effects to procure seed, and continued to work and sow up to and even after the 15th of May. They then began to cut their peats as usual, thinking they were after all to be allowed to get the benefit. They were, however, soon disappointed—their goods were hypothecated. Many of them were turned out of their houses, the doors locked, and everything they possessed—cattle, crops, and peats—seized. Even their bits of furniture were thrown out of doors in the manner which had long become the fashion in such cases. The season was too far advanced—towards the end of July —to start for Canada. Before they could arrive there the cold winter would be upon them, without means or money to provide against it. They naturally rebelled, and the principal Sheriff-Substitute, Colquhoun, with his officers and a strong body of police left Inverness for North Uist, to eject them from their homes. Naturally unwilling to proceed to extremes, on the arrival of the steamer at Armadale, they sent a messenger ashore to ask for instructions to guide them in case of resistance, or if possible to obtain a modification of his lordship's views. Lord Macdonald had no instructions to give, but referred the Sheriff to Mr.

Cooper, his factor, whose answer was that the whole population of Sollas would be subject to eviction if they did not at once agree to emigrate. A few men were arrested who obstructed the evictors on a previous occasion. They were marched off to Lochmaddy by the police. The work of destruction soon commenced. At first no opposition was made by the poor people. An eye-witness, whose sympathies were believed to be favourable to the proprietor, describes some of the proceedings as follows :—" In evicting Macpherson, the first case taken up, no opposition to the law officers was made. In two or three minutes the few articles of furniture he possessed—a bench, a chair, a broken chair, a barrel, a bag of wool, and two or three small articles, which comprised his whole household of goods and gear—were turned out to the door, and his bothy left roofless. The wife of the prisoner Macphail (one of those taken to Lochmaddy on the previous day) was the next evicted. Her domestic plenishing was of the simplest character—its greatest, and by far its most valuable part, being three small children, dressed in nothing more than a single coat of coarse blanketing, who played about her knee, whilst the poor woman, herself half-clothed, with her face bathed in tears, and holding an infant in her arms, assured the Sheriff that she and her children were totally destitute and without food of any kind. The Sheriff at once sent for the Inspector of Poor, and ordered him to place the woman and her family on the poor's roll." The next house was occupied by very old and infirm people, whom the Sheriff positively refused to evict. He also refused to eject eight other families, where an irregularity was discovered by him in the notices served upon them. The next family ejected led to the almost solitary instance hitherto in the history of Highland evictions where the people made anything like real resistance.

This man was a crofter and weaver, having a wife and nine children to provide for. At this stage a crowd of men and women gathered on an eminence a little distance from the house, and gave the first indications of a hostile intention by raising shouts, as the police advanced to help in the work of demolition, accompanied by about a dozen men who came to their assistance in unroofing the houses from the other end of the island. The crowd, exasperated at the conduct of their own neighbours, threw some stones at the latter. The police were then drawn up in two lines. The furniture was thrown outside, the web was cut out of the loom, and the terrified woman rushed to the door with an infant in her arms, exclaiming in a passionate and wailing voice—"Tha mo chlann air a bhi' air a muirt" (My children are to be murdered). The crowd became excited, stones were thrown at the officers, their assistants were driven from the roof of the house, and they had to retire behind the police for shelter. Volleys of stones and other missiles followed. The police charged in two divisions. There were some cuts and bruises on both sides. The work of demolition was then allowed to go on without further opposition from the crowd.

Several heart-rending scenes followed, but we shall only give a description of the last which took place on that occasion, and which brought about a little delay in the cruel work. In one case it was found necessary to remove the women out of the house by force. "One of them threw herself upon the ground and fell into hysterics, uttering the most doleful sounds, and barking and yelling like a dog for about ten minutes. Another, with many tears, sobs, and groans put up a petition to the Sheriff that they would leave the roof over part of her house, where she had a loom with cloth in it, which she was weaving ; and a third woman, the eldest of the family made an attack with a stick on an officer, and, missing him, she sprang upon him, and knocked off his hat. So violently did this old woman conduct herself that two stout policemen had great difficulty in carrying her outside the door. The excitement was again getting so strong that the factor, seeing the determination of the people, and finding that if he continued and took their crops away from those who would not leave, even when their houses were pulled down about their ears, they would have to be fed and maintained at the expense of the parish during the forthcoming winter, relaxed and agreed to allow them to occupy their houses until next spring, if the heads of families undertook and signed an agreement to emigrate any time next year, from the 1st of February to the end of June. Some agreed to these conditions, but the majority declined; and, in the circumstance, the people were permitted to go back to their unroofed and ruined homes for a few months longer. Their cattle were, however, mostly taken possession of, and applied to the reduction of old arrears."

Four of the men were afterwards charged with deforcing the officers, and sentenced at Inverness Court of Justiciary each to four months' imprisonment. The following year the district was completely and mercilessly cleared of all its remaining inhabitants, numbering 603 souls.*

The Sollas evictions did not satisfy the evicting craze which his lordship afterwards so bitterly regretted, In 1851-53 he, or rather his trustee, determined to evict the people from the villages of

BORERAIG AND SUISINISH, ISLE OF SKYE.

His Lordship's position in regard to the proceedings was

---

* A very full account of these proceedings, written on the spot, appeared at the time in the *Inverness Courier*, to which we are indebted for the above facts.

most unfortunate. Donald Ross, writing as an eye-witness of these evictions, says—"Some years ago Lord Macdonald incurred debts on his property to the extent of £200,000 sterling, and his lands being entailed, his creditors could not dispose of them, but they placed a trustee over them in order to intercept certain portions of the rent in payment of the debt. Lord Macdonald, of course, continues to have an interest and a surveillance over the property in the matter of removals, the letting of the fishings and shootings, and the general improvement of his estates. The trustee and the local factor under him have no particular interest in the property, nor in the people thereon, beyond collecting their quota of the rents for the creditors; consequently the property is mismanaged, and the crofter and cottar population are greatly neglected. The tenants of Suisinish and Boreraig were the descendants of a long line of peasantry on the Macdonald estates, and were remarkable for their patience, loyalty, and general good conduct." The only plea made at the time for evicting them was that of over population. Ten families received the usual summonses, and passages were secured for them in the *Hercules*, an unfortunate ship which sailed with a cargo of passengers under the auspices of a body calling itself "The Highland and Island Emigration Society". A deadly fever broke out among the passengers, the ship was detained at Cork in consequence, and a large number of the passengers died of the epidemic. After the sad fate of so many of those previously cleared out, in the ill-fated ship, it was generally thought that some compassion would be shown for those who had still been permitted to remain. Not so, however. On the 4th of April, 1853, they were all warned out of their holdings. They petitioned and pleaded with his Lordship to no purpose. They were ordered to remove their cattle from the pasture, and themselves from their houses and lands. They again petitioned his Lordship for his merciful consideration. For a time no reply was forthcoming. Subsequently, however, they were informed that they would get land on another part of the estate—portions of a barren moor, quite unfit for cultivation.

In the middle of September following, Lord Macdonald's ground-officer, with a body of constables, arrived, and at once proceeded to eject, in the most heartless manner, the whole population, numbering thirty-two families, and that at a period when the able-bodied male members of the families were away from home trying to earn something by which to pay their rents, and help to carry their families through the coming winter. In spite of the wailing of the helpless women and children, the cruel work was proceeded with as rapidly as possible, and without the slightest apparent compunction. The furnitute was thrown out in what had now become the orthodox fashion. The aged and infirm, some of them so frail that they could not move, were pushed or carried out. " The scene was truly heart-rending. The women and children went about tearing their hair, and rending the heavens with their cries. Mothers with tender infants at the breast looked helplessly on, while their effects, and their aged and infirm relatives, were cast out, and the doors of their houses locked in their faces." The young children, poor, helpless, little creatures, gathered in groups, gave vent to their feelings in loud and bitter wailings. " No mercy was shown to age or sex—all were indiscriminately thrust out and left to perish on the hills." Untold cruelties were perpetrated on this occasion on the helpless creatures during the absence of their husbands and other principal bread-winners. Donald Ross in his pamphlet, " Real Scottish Grievances," published in

1854, and who not only was an eye-witness, but generously supplied the people with a great quantity of food and clothing, describes several of the cases. I can only find room here, however, for his first, that of

Flora Robertson or Matheson, a widow, aged ninety-six years, then residing with her son, Alexander Matheson, who had a small lot of land in Suisinish. Her son was a widower, with four children; and shortly before the time for evicting the people arrived, he went away to labour at harvest in the south, taking his oldest boy with him. The grandmother and the other three children were left in the house. "When the evicting officers and factor arrived, the poor old woman was sitting on a couch outside the house. The day being fine, her grandchildren lifted her out of her bed and brought her to the door. She was very frail; and it would have gladdened any heart to have seen how the two youngest of her grandchildren helped her along; how they seated her where there was most shelter; and then, how they brought her some clothing and clad her, and endeavoured to make her comfortable. The gratitude of the old woman was unbounded at these little acts of kindness and compassion; and the poor children, on the other hand, felt highly pleased at finding their services so well appreciated. The sun was shining beautifully, the air was refreshing, the gentle breeze wafted across the hills, and, mollified by passing over the waters of Loch Slapin, brought great relief and vigour to poor old Flora. Often with eyes directed towards heaven, and with uplifted hands, did she invoke the blessings of the God of Jacob on the young children who were ministering so faithfully to her bodily wants. Nothing could now exceed the beauty of the scene. The sea was glittering with millions of little waves and globules, and looked like a lake of silver, gently agitated. The hills, with the heather in full bloom, and with the wild flowers in their beauty, had assumed all the colours of the rainbow, and were most pleasant to the eye to look upon. The crops of corn in the neighbourhood were beginning to get yellow for the harvest; the small patches of potatoes were under flower, and promised well; the sheep and cattle, as if tired of feeding had lain down to rest on the face of the hills; and the dogs, as if satisfied their services were not required for a time, chose for themselves pleasant, well-sheltered spots and lay basking at full length in the sun; even the little boats on the loch, though their sails were spread, made no progress, but lay at rest, reflecting their own tiny shadows on the bosom of the deep and still waters. The scene was most enchanting; and although old Flora's eyes were getting dim with age, she looked on the objects before her with great delight. Her grandchildren brought her a cup of warm milk and some bread from a neighbour's house, and tried to feed her as if she had been a pet bird; but the old woman could not take much, although she was greatly invigorated by the change of air. Nature seemed to take repose. A white fleecy cloud now and then ascended, but the sun soon dispelled it; thin wreaths of cottage smoke went up and along, but there was no wind to move them, and they floated on the air; and, indeed, with the exception of a stream which passed near the house, and made a continuous noise in its progress over rocks and stones, there was nothing above or around to disturb the eye or the ear for one moment. While the old woman was thus enjoying the benefit of the fresh air, admiring the beauty of the landscape, and just when the poor children had entered the house to prepare a frugal meal for themselves and their aged charge, a sudden barking of dogs gave signal intimation of the approach of strangers. The native inquisitiveness of the young ones was immediately set on edge, and off they set across the fields, and over fences, after the dogs. They soon returned, however, with horror depicted in their countenances; they had a fearful tale to unfold; the furniture and other effects of their nearest neighbours, just across the hill, they saw thrown out; they heard the children screaming, and they saw the factor's men putting bars and locks on the doors. This was enough. The heart of the old woman, so recently revived and invigorated, was now like to break within her. What was she to do? What could she do? Absolutely nothing! The poor children, in the plenitude of their knowledge of the humanity of lords and factors, thought that if they could only get their aged grannie inside before the evicting officers arrived, that all would be safe,—as no one, they thought, would interfere with an old creature of ninety-six, especially when her son was not there to take charge of her; and, acting upon this supposition, they began to remove their grandmother into the house. The officers, however, arrived before they could get this accomplished; and in place of letting the old woman in, they threw out before the door every article that was inside the house, and then they placed large bars and padlocks on the door! The grandchildren were horror-struck at this procedure—and no wonder. Here they were, shut out of house and home, their father and elder brother several hundred miles away from them, their mother dead, and their grandmother, now aged, frail, and unable to move, sitting before them, quite unfit to help herself,—and with no other shelter than the broad canopy of heaven. Here then was a crisis, a predicament, that would have twisted the strongest nerve and tried the stoutest heart and healthiest frame,—with nothing but helpless infancy and

old age and infirmities to meet it. We cannot comprehend the feelings of the poor children on this occasion;
and cannot find language sufficiently strong to express
condemnation of those who rendered them houseless.
Shall we call them savages? That would be paying them
too high a compliment, for among savages conduct such as
theirs is unknown. But let us proceed. After the grandchildren had cried until they were hoarse, and after their
little eyes had emptied themselves of the tears which
anguish, sorrow, and terror had accumulated within them,
and when they had exhausted their strength in the general
wail, along with the other children of the district, as house
after house was swept of its furniture, the inmates evicted,
and the doors locked,—they returned to their poor old
grandmother, and began to exchange sorrows and consola-
tions with her. But what could the poor children do?
The shades of evening were closing in, and the air, which
at mid-day was fresh and balmy, was now cold and freezing.
The neighbours were all locked out, and could give no shelter,
and the old woman was unable to travel to where lodgings
for the night could be got. What were they to do? We
may rest satisfied that their minds were fully occupied with
their unfortunate condition, and that they had serious con-
sultations as to future action. The first consideration,
however, was shelter for the first night, and a sheep-cot
being near, the children prepared to remove the old woman
to it. True, it was small and damp, and it had no door,
no fire-place, no window, no bed,—but then, it was better
than exposure to the night air; and this they represented to
their grandmother, backing it with all the other little bits of
arguments they could advance, and with professions of
sincere attachment which, coming from such a quarter, and
at such a period, gladdened her old heart. There was a

difficulty, however, which they at first overlooked. The grandmother could not walk, and the distance was some hundreds of yards, and they could get no assistance, for all the neighbours were similarly situated, and were weeping and wailing for the distress which had come upon them. Here was a dilemma; but the children helped the poor woman to creep along, sometimes she walked a few yards, at other times she crawled on her hands and knees, and in this way, and most materially aided by her grandchildren, she at last reached the cot.

The sheep-cot was a most wretched habitation, quite unfit for human beings, yet here the widow was compelled to remain until the month of December following. When her son came home from the harvest in the south, he was amazed at the treatment his aged mother and his children had received. He was then in good health; but in a few weeks the cold and damp of the sheep-cot had a most deadly effect upon his health, for he was seized with violent cramps, then with cough; at last his limbs and body swelled, and then he died! When dead, his corpse lay across the floor, his feet at the opposite wall, and his head being at the door, the wind waved his long black hair to and fro until he was placed in his coffin.

The inspector of poor, who, be it remembered, was ground-officer to Lord Macdonald, and also acted as the chief officer in the evictions, at last appeared, and removed the old woman to another house; not, however, until he was threatened with a prosecution for neglect of duty. The grand-children were also removed from the sheep-cot, for they were ill; Peggy and William were seriously so, but Sandy, although ill, could walk a little. The inspector for the poor gave the children, during their illness, only 14 lbs. of meal and 3 lbs. of rice, as aliment for three weeks, and nothing else. To the grandmother he allowed two shillings and sixpence per month, but made no provision for fuel, lodgings, nutritious diet, or cordials—all of which this old woman much required.

When I visited the house where old Flora Matheson and her grand-children reside, I found her lying on a miserable pallet of straw, which, with a few rags of clothing, are on the bare floor. She is reduced to a skeleton, and from her own statement to me, in presence of witnesses, coupled with other inquiries and examinations, I have no hesitation in declaring that she was then actually starving. She had no nourishment, no cordials, nothing whatever in the way of food but a few wet potatoes and two or three shell-fish. The picture she presented, as she lay on her wretched pallet of black rags and brown straw, with her mutch as black as soot, and her long arms thrown across, with nothing on them but the skin, was a most lamentable one—and one that reflects the deepest discredit on the parochial authorities of Strath. There was no one to attend to the wants or infirmities of this aged pauper but her grandchild, a young girl, ten years of age. Surely in a country boasting of its humanity, liberty, and Christianity, such conduct should not be any longer tolerated in dealing with the infirm and help-less poor. The pittance of 2s 6d a month is but a mockery of the claims of this old woman ; it is insulting to the com-monsense and every-day experience of people of feeling, and it is a shameful evasion of the law. But for accidental charity, and that from a distance, Widow Matheson would long ere this have perished of starvation.

Three men were afterwards charged with deforcing the officers of the law, before the Court of Justiciary at Inver-ness. They were first imprisoned at Portree, and afterwards marched on foot to Inverness, a distance of over a 100 miles, where they arrived two days before the date of their trial. The factor and sheriff-officers came in their conveyances, at the public expense, and lived right royally, never dreaming but they would obtain a victory, and get the three men sent to the Penitentiary, to wear hoddy, break stones, or pick oakum for at least twelve months. The accused, through the influence of charitable friends, secured the services of Mr. Rennie, solicitor, Inverness, who was able to show to the jury the unfounded and farcical nature of the charges made against them. His eloquent and able address to the jury in their behalf was irresistible, and we cannot better explain the nature of the proceedings than by quoting it in part from the report given of it, at the time, in the *Inverness Advertiser* :—

"Before proceeding to comment on the evidence in this case, he would call attention to its general features. It was one of a fearful series of ejectments now being carried through in the Highlands ; and it really became a matter of serious reflection, how far the pound of flesh allowed by law was to be permitted to be extracted from the bodies of the Highlanders. Here were thirty-two families, averaging four members each, or from 130 to 150 in all, driven out from their houses and happy homes, and for what ? For a tenant who, he believed, was not yet found. But it was the will of Lord Macdonald and of Messrs. Brown and Ballingal, that they should be ejected ; and the civil law having failed them, the criminal law with all its terrors, is called in to overwhelm these unhappy people. But, thank God, it has come before a jury—before you, who are sworn to return, and will return, an impartial verdict ; and which verdict will, I trust, be one that will stamp out with ignominy the cruel actors in it. The Duke of Newcastle had querulously asked, 'Could he not do as he liked with his own ?' but a greater man had answered, that 'property had its duties as well as its rights,' and the concurrent opinion of an admiring age testified to this truth. Had the factor here done his duty? No! He had driven the miserable inhabitants out to the barren heaths and wet mosses. He had come with the force of the civil power to dispossess them, and make way for sheep and cattle. But had he provided adequate refuge? The evictions in Knoydart, which had lately occupied the attention of the press and all thinking men, were cruel enough; but there a refuge was provided for a portion of the evicted, and ships for their conveyance to a distant land. Would such a state of matters be tolerated in a country where a single spark of Highland spirit existed? No! Their verdict that day would proclaim, over the length and breadth of the land, an indignant denial. Approaching the present case more minutely, he would observe that the prosecutor, by deleting from this libel the charge of obstruction, which was passive, had cut away the ground from under his feet. The remaining charge of deforcement being active, pushing, shoving, or striking, was essential. But he would ask, What was the character of the village and the household of Macinnes? There were mutual remonstrances; but was force used? The only things the officer, Macdonald, seized were carried out. A spade and creel were talked of as being taken from him, but in this he was unsupported. The charge against the panel, Macinnes, only applied to what took place inside his house. As to the other panels, John Macrae was merely present. He had a right to be there; but he touched neither man nor thing, and he at any rate must be acquitted. Even with regard to Duncan Macrae, the evidence *quoad* him was contemptible. According to Alison in order to constitute the crime of deforcement, there must be such violence as to intimidate a person of ordinary firmness of character. Now, there was no violence here, they did not even speak aloud, they merely stood in the door; that might be obstruction, it was certainly no deforcement. Had Macdonald, who it appeared combined in his single person the triple offices of sheriff-officer, ground-officer, and inspector of poor, known anything of his business, and gone about it in a proper and regular manner, the present case would never have been heard of. As an instance of his irregularity, whilst his execution of deforcement bore that he read his warrants, he by his own mouth stated that he only read part of them. Something was attempted to be made of the fact of Duncan Macrae seizing one of the constables and pulling him away; but this was done in a good-natured manner, and the constable admitted he feared no violence. In short, it would be a farce to call this a case of deforcement. As to the general character of the panels, it was unreproached and irreproachable, and their behaviour on that day was their best certificate."

The jury immediately returned a verdict of "Not guilty," and the poor Skyemen were dismissed from the bar, amid the cheers of an Inverness crowd. The families of these men were at the next Christmas evicted in the most spiteful and cruel manner, delicate mothers, half-dressed, and recently-born infants, having been pushed out into the drifting snow. Their few bits of furniture, blankets and other clothing lay for days under the snow, while they found shelter themselves as best they could in broken-down, dilapidated out-houses and barns. These latter proceedings were afterwards found to have been illegal, the original summonses, on which the second proceedings were taken, having been exhausted in the previous evictions, when the Macinnesses and the Macraes were unsuccessfully charged with deforcing the sheriff-officers. The proceedings were

universally condemned by every right-thinking person who
knew the district, as quite uncalled for, most unjustifiable
and improper, as well as for "the reckless cruelty and inhumanity with which they were carried through". Yet, the
factor issued a circular in defence of such horrid work in
which he coolly informed the public that these evictions
were "prompted by motives of benevolence, piety, and
humanity," and that the cause for them all was "because
they (the people) were too far from Church". Oh God!
what crimes have been committed in Thy name, and in that
of religion? Preserve us from such piety and humanity as
were exhibited by Lord Macdonald and his factor on this
and other occasions.

A Contrast.

Before leaving Skye, it will be interesting to see the difference of opinion which existed among the chiefs regarding
the eviction of the people at this period and a century
earlier. We have just seen what a Lord Macdonald has
done in the present century, little more than thirty years
ago. Let us compare his proceedings and feelings to those
of his ancestor, in 1739, a century earlier. In that year a
certain Norman Macleod managed to get some islanders to
emigrate, and it was feared that Government would hold
Sir Alexander Macdonald of Sleat reponsible, as he was
reported to have encouraged Macleod. The baronet being
from home, his wife, Lady Margaret, wrote to Lord Justice-
Clerk Milton on the 1st of January, 1740, pleading with
him to use all his influence against a prosecution of her
husband, which, "tho' it cannot be dangerouse to him, yett
it cannot faill of being both troublsome and expensive".
She begins her letter by stating that she was informed " by

different hands from Edinburgh that there is a currant report of a ships haveing gon from thiss country with a greate many people designed for America, and that Sir Alexander is thought to have concurred in forceing these people away ". She then declares the charge against her husband to be " a falsehood," but she " is quite acquainted with the danger of a report " of that nature. Instead of Sir Alexander being a party to the proceedings of this " Norman Macleod, with a number of fellows that he had picked up to execute his intentions," he " was both angry and concern'd to hear that some of his oune people were taken in thiss affair". What a contrast between the sentiments here expressed and those which carried out the modern evictions ; and yet it is well known that, in other respects no more humane man ever lived than he who was nominally responsible for the cruelties in Skye and at Sollas. He allowed himself to be imposed upon by others, and completely abdicated his high functions as landlord and chief of his people. We have the most conclusive testimony and assurance from one who knew his lordship intimately, that, to his dying day, he never ceased to regret what had been done in his name, and at the time, with his tacit approval, in Skye and in North Uist. This should be a warning to other proprietors, and induce them to consider carefully proposals submitted to them by heartless or inexperienced subordinates. It is very generally believed that to this same dependence on and belief in subordinates some of the more recent evictions in the Highlands can be traced; but matters had proceeded so far that it was found impossible to retrace without an appearance of giving way to the clamour raised by outsiders. These are only specimens of the proceedings carried out on an extensive scale in the Western Islands.

SOUTH UIST AND BARRA.

Napoleon Bonaparte, at one time, took 500 prisoners and was unable to provide food for them; let them go he would not, though he saw that they would perish by famine. His ideas of mercy suggested to him to have them all shot. They were by his orders formed into a square, and 2000 French muskets with ball cartridge was simultaneously levelled at them, which soon put the disarmed mass of human beings out of pain. Donald Macleod refers to this painful act as follows :—" All the Christian nations of Europe were horrified, every breast was full of indignation at the perpetrator of this horrible tragedy, and France wept bitterly for the manner in which the tender mercies of their wicked Emperor were exhibited. Ah! but guilty Christian, you Protestant law-making Britain, tremble when you look towards the great day of retribution. Under the protection of your law, Colonel Gordon has consigned 1500 men, women, and children, to a death a hundred-fold more agonising and horrifying. With the sanction of your law he (Colonel Gordon) and his predecessors, in imitation of His Grace the Duke of Sutherland and his predecessors, removed the people from the land created by God, suitable for cultivation, and for the use of man, and put it under brute animals ; and threw the people upon bye-corners, precipices, and barren moors, there exacting exorbitant rack-rents, until the people were made penniless, so that they could neither leave the place nor better their condition in it. The potato-blight blasted their last hopes of retaining life upon the unproductive patches—hence they became clamourous for food. Their distress was made known through the public press ; public meetings were held, and it was managed by some known knaves to saddle the God of providence with the whole misery—a job in which many of God's professing and well-paid servants took a very active part. The generous public responded; immense sums of money were placed in the hands of Government agents and other individuals, to save the people from death by famine on British soil. Colonel Gordon and his worthy allies were silent contributors, though terrified. The gallant gentleman solicited Government, through the Home Secretary, to purchase the Island of Barra for a penal colony, but it would not suit; yet our humane Government sympathised with the Colonel and his coadjutors, and consulted the honourable and brave MacNeil, the chief pauper gauger of Scotland, upon the most effective and speediest scheme to relieve the gallant Colonel and colleagues from this clamour and eye-sore, as well as to save their pockets from able-bodied paupers. The result was, that a liberal grant from the public money, which had been granted a twelvemonth before for the purpose of improving and cultivating the Highlands, was made to Highland proprietors to assist them to drain the nation of its best blood, and to banish the Highlanders across the Atlantic, there to die by famine among strangers in the frozen regions of Canada, far from British sympathy, and far from the resting place of their brave ancestors, though the idea of mingling with kindred dust, to the Highlanders, is a consolation at death, more than any other race of people I have known or read of under heaven. Oh! Christian people, Christian people, Christian fathers and mothers, who are living at ease, and never experienced such treatment and concomitant sufferings; you Christian rulers, Christian electors, and representatives, permit not Christianity to blush and hide her face with shame before heathenism and idolatry any longer. I speak with reverence when I say, permit not Mahomet Ali to deride our

Saviour with the conduct of His followers—allow not demons to exclaim in the face of heaven, 'What can you expect of us, when Christians, thy chosen people, are guilty of such deeds of inhumanity to their own species?' I appeal to your feelings, to your respect for Christianity and the cause of Christ in the world, that Christianity may be redeemed from the derision of infidels, Mahomedans, idolaters, and demons—that our beloved Queen and constitutional laws may not be any longer a laughing stock and derision to the despots of the Continent, who can justly say, 'You interfere with us for our dealings with our people; but look at your cruel conduct toward your own. Ye hypocrites, first cast out the beam out of your own eye, before you meddle with the mote in ours.' Come, then, for the sake of neglected humanity and prostrated Christianity, and look at this helpless, unfortunate people ; place yourselves for a moment in their hopeless condition at their embarkation, decoyed, in the name of the British Government, by false promises of assistance, to procure homes and comforts in Canada, which were denied to them at home—decoyed I say, to an unwilling and partial consent—and those who resisted or recoiled from this conditional consent, and who fled to the caves and mountains to hide themselves from the brigands, look at them, chased and caught by policemen, constables, and other underlings of Colonel Gordon, handcuffed, it is said, and huddled together with the rest on an emigrant vessel. Hear the sobbing, sighing, and throbbings of their guileless, warm Highland hearts, taking their last look, and bidding a final adieu to their romantic mountains and valleys, the fertile straths, dales, and glens, which their forefathers from time immemorial inhabited, and where they are now lying in undisturbed and everlasting repose, in spots endeared and sacred to the memory of their unfortunate offspring, who must now bid a mournful farewell to their early associations, which were as dear and as sacred to them as their very existence, and which had hitherto made them patient in suffering. But follow them on their six weeks' dreary passage, rolling upon the mountainous billows of the Atlantlc, ill fed, ill clad, among sickness, disease and excrements. Then come a-shore with them where death is in store for them—hear the Captain giving orders to discharge the cargo of live stock—see the confusion, hear the noise, the bitter weeping and bustle; hear mothers and children asking fathers and husbands, where are we going? hear the reply, ' cha neil fios againn'—we know not; see them in groups in search of the Government Agent, who, they were told, was to give them money; look at their despairing countenances when they come to learn that no agent in Canada is authorised to give them a penny; hear them praying the Captain to bring them back that they might die among their native hills, that their ashes might mingle with those of their forefathers; hear this request refused, and the poor helpless wanderers bidding adieu to the Captain and crew, who showed them all the kindness they could, and to the vessel to which they formed something like an attachment during the voyage; look at them scantily clothed, destitute of food, without implements of husbandry, consigned to their fate, carrying their children on their backs, begging as they crawl along in a strange land, unqualified to beg or buy their food for want of English, until the slow moving and mournful company reach Toronto and Hamilton, in Upper Canada, where according to all accounts, they spread themselves over their respective burying-places, where famine and frost-bitten deaths were awaiting them. Mothers in Christian Britain, look, I say, at these Highland mothers, who conceived and gave birth, and who are equally as fond of their offspring as you can be ; look at them by this time, wrapping their frozen remains in rags and committing them to a frozen hole—fathers, mothers, sons, and daughters, participants of similar sufferings and death, and the living who are seeking for death (yet death fleeing from them for a time) performing a similar painful duty.   This is a painful picture, the English language fails to supply me with words to describe it.   I wish the spectrum would depart from me to those who could describe it and tell the result.   But how can Colonel Gordon, the Duke of Sutherland, James Loch, Lord Macdonald, and others of the unhallowed league and abettors, after looking at this sight, remain in Christian communion, ruling elders in Christian Churches, and partake of the emblems of Christ's broken body and shed blood?   But the great question is, Can we as a nation be guiltless, and allow so many of our fellow creatures to be treated in such a manner, and not exert ourselves to put a stop to it and punish the perpetrators?   Is ambition, which attempted to dethrone God, become omnipotent, or so powerful, when incarnated in the shape of Highland dukes, lords, esquires, colonels, and knights, that we must needs submit to its revolting deeds?   Are parchment rights of property so sacred that thousands of human beings must be sacrificed year after year, till there is no end of such, to preserve them inviolate?   Are sheep walks, deer forests, hunting parks, and game preserves, so beneficial to the nation that the Highlands must be converted into a hunting desert, and the aborigines banished and murdered?   I know that thousands will answer in the negative; yet they will fold their arms in criminal apathy until the extirpation and destruction of my race shall be completed.   Fearful is the catalogue of those who have already become the victims of the cursed clearing system in the Highlands, by famine, fire, drowning, banishment, vice, and crime."

He then publishes the following communication from an eye-witness, of the enormities perpetrated in South Uist and in the Island of Barra in the summer of 1851 :—The unfeeling and deceitful conduct of those acting for Colonel Gordon cannot be too strongly censured. The duplicity and art which was used by them in order to entrap the unwary natives, is worthy of the craft and cunning of an old slave-trader. Many of the poor people were told in my hearing, that Sir John McNeil would be in Canada before them, where he would have every necessary prepared for them. Some of the officials signed a document binding themselves to emigrate, in order to induce the poor people to give their names ; but in spite of all these stratagems, many of the people saw through them and refused out and out to go. When the transports anchored in Loch Boisdale these tyrants threw off their masks, and the work of devastation and cruelty commenced. The poor people were commanded to attend a public meeting at Loch Boisdale, where the transports lay, and, according to the intimation, any one absenting himself from the meeting was to be fined in the sum of two pounds sterling. At this meeting some of the natives were seized and, in spite of their entreaties, sent on board the transports. One stout Highlander, named Angus Johnston, resisted with such pith that they had to hand-cuff him before he could be mastered ; but in consequence of the priest's interference his manacles were removed, and he was marched between four officers on board the emigrant vessel. One morning, during the transporting season, we were suddenly awakened by the screams of a young female who had been re-captured in an adjoining house ; she having escaped after her first capture. We all rushed to the door, and saw the broken-hearted creature, with dishevelled hair and swollen face, dragged away by two constables and a ground-officer. Were you to see the racing and chasing of policemen, constables, and ground-officers, pursuing the outlawed natives, you would think, only for their colour, that you had been, by some miracle, transported to the banks of the Gambia, on the slave coast of Africa.

The conduct of the Rev. H. Beatson on that occasion is deserving of the censure of every feeling heart. This 'wolf in sheep's clothing,' made himself very officious, as he always does, when he has an opportunity of oppressing the poor Barra-men, and of gaining the favour of Colonel Gordon. In fact, he is the most vigilant and assiduous officer Colonel Gordon has. He may be seen in Castle Bay, the principal anchorage in Barra, whenever a sail is hoisted, directing his men, like a game-keeper with his hounds, in case any of the doomed Barra-men should escape. He offered one day to board an Arran boat, that had a poor man concealed, but the master, John Crawford, lifted a hand-spike and threatened to split the skull of the first man who would attempt to board his boat, and thus the poor Barra-man escaped their clutches.

I may state in conclusion that, two girls, daughters of John Macdougall, brother of Barr Macdougall, whose name is mentioned in Sir John McNeill's report, have fled to the mountains to elude the grasp of the expatriators, where they still are, if in life. Their father, a frail, old man, along with the rest of the family, has been sent to Canada. The respective ages of these girls are 12 and 14 years. Others have fled in the same way, but I cannot give their names just now.

We shall now take the reader after these people to

Canada, and witness their deplorable and helpless condition and privations in a strange land. The following is extracted from a Quebec newspaper :—

We noticed in our last the deplorable condition of the 600 paupers who were sent to this country from the Kilrush Unions. We have to-day a still more dismal picture to draw. Many of our readers may not be aware that there lives such a personage as Colonel Gordon, proprietor of large estates in South Uist and Barra, in the Highlands of Scotland ; we are sorry to be obliged to introduce him to their notice, under circumstances which will not give them a very favourable opinion of his character and heart.

It appears that his tenants on the above-mentioned estates were on the verge of starvation, and had probably become an eye-sore to the gallant Colonel ! He decided on shipping them to America. What they were to do there? was a question he never put to his conscience. Once landed in Canada, he had no further concern about them. Up to last week, some 1100 souls from his estates had landed at Quebec, and begged their way to Upper Canada ; when in the summer season, having only a daily morsel of food to procure, they probably escaped the extreme misery which seems to be the lot of those who followed them.

On their arrival here, they voluntarily made and signed the following statement :—" We the undersigned passengers per *Admiral*, from Stornoway, in the Highlands of Scotland, do solemnly depose to the following facts :—that Colonel Gordon is proprietor of estates in South Uist and Barra ; that among many hundreds of tenants and cottars whom he has sent this season from his estates to Canada, he gave directions to his factor, Mr. Fleming of Cluny Castle, Aberdeenshire, to ship on board of the above-named vessel a number of nearly 450 of said tenants and cottars, from the estate in Barra ; that accordingly, a great majority of these people, among whom were the undersigned, proceeded voluntarily to embark on board the *Admiral*, at Loch Boisdale, on or about the 11th August, 1851 ; but that several of the people who were intended to be shipped for this port, Quebec, refused to proceed on board, and, in fact, absconded from their homes to avoid the embarkation. Whereupon Mr. Fleming gave orders to a policeman, who was accompanied by the ground-officer of the estate in Barra, and some constables, to pursue the people, who had run away, among the mountains ; which they did, and succeeded in capturing about twenty from the mountains and islands in the neighbourhood ; but only came with the officers on an attempt being made to handcuff them ; and that some who ran away were not brought back, in consequence of which four families at least have been divided, some having come in the ships to Quebec, while the other members of the same families are left in the Highlands.

"The undersigned further declare, that those who voluntarily embarked, did so under promises to the effect, that Colonel Gordon would defray their passage to Quebec ; that the Government Emigration Agent there would send the whole party free to Upper Canada, where, on arrival, the Government agents would give them work, and furthermore, grant them land on certain conditions.

"The undersigned finally declare, that they are now landed in Quebec so destitute, that if immediate relief be not afforded them, and continued until they are settled in employment, the whole will be liable to perish with want."

(Signed)   "HECTOR LAMONT,
and 70 others."

This is a beautiful picture ! Had the scene been laid in

Russia or Turkey, the barbarity of the proceeding would have shocked the nerves of the reader ; but when it happens in Britain, emphatically the land of liberty, where every man's house, even the hut of the poorest, is said to be his castle, the expulsion of these unfortunate creatures from their homes—the man-hunt with policemen and bailiffs—the violent separation of families—the parent torn from the child, the mother from her daughter, the infamous trickery practised on those who did embark—the abandonment of the aged, the infirm, women, and tender children, in a foreign land—forms a tableau which cannot be dwelt on for an instant without horror.   Words cannot depict the atrocity of the deed.   For cruelty less savage, the slave-dealers of the South have been held up to the execration of the world.

And if, as men, the sufferings of these our fellow-creatures find sympathy in our hearts, as Canadians their wrongs concern us more dearly.   The fifteen hundred souls whom Colonel Gordon has sent to Quebec this season, have all been supported for the past week at least, and conveyed to Upper Canada at the expense of the colony ; and on their arrival in Toronto and Hamilton, the greater number have been dependent on the charity of the benevolent for a morsel of bread.   Four hundred are in the river at present, and will arrive in a day or two, making a total of nearly 2000 of Colonel Gordon's tenants and cottars whom the province will have to support.   The winter is at hand, work is becoming scarce in Upper Canada.   Where are these people to find food ? *

We take the following from an Upper Canadian paper describing the position of the same people after finding their way to Ontario :—We have been pained beyond measure for some time past, to witness in our streets so

* *Quebec Times.*

many unfortunate Highland emigrants, apparently destitute of any means of subsistence, and many of them sick from want and other attendant causes. It was pitiful the other day, to view a funeral of one of these wretched people. It was, indeed, a sad procession. The coffin was constructed of the rudest material; a few rough boards nailed together, was all that could be afforded to convey to its last resting-place the body of the homeless emigrant. Children followed in the mournful train; perchance they followed a brother's bier, one with whom they had sported and played for many a healthful day among their native glens. Theirs were looks of indescribable sorrow. They were in rags; their mourning weeds were the shapeless fragments of what had once been clothes. There was a mother, too, among the mourners, one who had tended the departed with anxious care in infancy, and had doubtless looked forward to a happier future in this land of plenty. The anguish of her countenance told too plainly these hopes were blasted, and she was about to bury them in the grave of her child.

There will be many to sound the fulsome noise of flattery in the ear of the generous landlord, who had spent so much to assist the emigration of his poor tenants. They will give him the misnomer of a *benefactor*, and for what? Because he has rid his estates of the encumbrance of a pauper population.

Emigrants of the poorer class, who arrive here from the Western Highlands of Scotland, are often so situated, that their emigration is more cruel than banishment. Their last shilling is spent probably before they reach the upper province—they are reduced to the necessity of begging. But again, the case of those emigrants of which we speak, is rendered more deplorable from their ignorance of the

English tongue. Of the hundreds of Highlanders in and around Dundas at present, perhaps not half-a-dozen understand anything but Gaelic.

In looking at these matters, we are impressed with the conviction, that so far from emigration being a panacea for Highland destitution, it is fraught with disasters of no ordinary magnitude to the emigrant whose previous habits, under the most favourable circumstances, render him unable to take advantage of the industry of Canada, even when brought hither free of expense. We may assist these poor creatures for a time, but charity will scarcely bide the hungry cravings of so many for a very long period. Winter is approaching, and then—but we leave this painful subject for the present.*

———

The Island of Rum.

This Island, at one time, had a large population, all of whom were weeded out in the usual way. The Rev. Donald Maclean, Minister of the Parish of Small Isles, informs us in *The New Statistical Account*, that "in 1826 all the inhabitants of the Island of Rum, amounting at least to 400 souls, found it necessary to leave their native land, and to seek for new abodes in the distant wilds of our Colonies in America. Of all the old residenters, only one family remained upon the island. The old and the young, the feeble and the strong were all united in this general emigration—the former to find tombs in a foreign land—the latter to encounter toils, privations, and dangers, to become familiar with customs, and to acquire that to which they had been

* *Dundas Warder*, 2nd October, 1851.

entire strangers. A similar emigration took place in 1828, from the Island of Muck, so that the parish has now become much depopulated."

In 1831, the population of the whole parish was 1015, while before that date it was much larger. In 1851, it was 916. In 1881, it was reduced to 550. The total population of Rum, in 1881, was 89 souls.

Hugh Miller, who visited the Island afterwards, describes it and the evictions thus :—The evening was clear, calm, golden-tinted ; even wild heaths and rude rocks had assumed a flush of transient beauty ; and the emerald-green patches on the hill-sides, barred by the plough lengthwise, diagonally, and transverse, had borrowed an aspect of soft and velvety richness, from the mellowed light and the broadening shadows. All was solitary. We could see among the deserted fields the grass-grown foundations of cottages razed to the ground ; but the valley, more desolate than that which we had left, had not even its single inhabited dwelling : it seemed as if man had done with it for ever. The Island eighteen years before, had been divested of its inhabitants, amounting at the time to rather more than four hundred souls, to make way for one sheep-farmer and eight thousand sheep. All the aborigines of Rum crossed the Atlantic ; and, at the close of 1828, the entire population consisted of but the sheep-farmer, and a few shepherds, his servants : the Island of Rum reckoned up scarce a single family at this period for every five square miles of area which it contained. But depopulation on so extreme a scale was found inconvenient ; the place had been rendered too thoroughly a desert for the comfort of the occupant ; and on the occasion of a clearing which took place shortly after in Skye, he accommodated some ten or twelve of the ejected families with sites for cottages, and pasturage for a few cows, on the bit of morass beside Loch Scresort, on which I had seen their humble dwellings. But the whole of the once peopled interior remains a wilderness, without inhabitants,—all the more lonely in its aspect—from the circumstance that the solitary valleys, with their plough-furrowed patches, and their ruined heaps of stone, open upon shores every whit as solitary as themselves, and that the wide untrodden sea stretches drearily around. The armies of the insect world were sporting in the light this evening by the million ; a brown stream that runs through the valley yielded an incessant poppling sound, from the myriads of fish that were ceaselessly leaping in the pools, beguiled by the quick glancing wings of green and gold that fluttered over them : along a distant hillside there ran what seemed the ruins of a gray-stone fence, erected, says tradition, in a remote age, to facilitate the hunting of the deer ; there were fields on which the heath and moss of the surrounding moorlands were fast encroaching, that had borne many a successive harvest ; and prostrate cottages, that had been the scenes of christenings, and bridals, and blythe new-year's days ;—all seemed to bespeak the place of fitting habitation for man, in which not only the necessaries, but also a few of the luxuries of life, might be procured.; but in the entire prospect, not a man nor a man's dwelling could the eye command. The landscape was one without figures. I do not much like extermination carried out so thoroughly and on system ;—it seems bad policy ; and I have not succeeded in thinking any the better of it though assured by the economists that there are more than people enough in Scotland still. There are, I believe, more than enough in our workhouses—more than enough on our pauper-rolls—more than enough muddled up, disreputable, useless, and unhappy, in their miasmatic valleys and typhoid courts of our large towns ; but I have yet to learn how arguments for local depopulation are to be drawn from facts such as these. A brave and hardy people, favourably placed for the development of all that is excellent in human nature, form the glory and strength of a country ;—a people sunk into an abyss of degradation and misery, and in which it is the whole tendency of external circumstances to sink them yet deeper, constitute its weakness and its shame ; and I cannot quite see on what principle the ominous increase which is taking place among us in the worse class, is to form our solace or apology for the wholesale expatriation of the better. It did not seem as if the depopulation of Rum had tended mnch to anyone's advantage. The single sheep-farmer who had occupied the holdings of so many had been unfortunate in his speculations, and had left the island ; the proprietor, his landlord, seemed to have been as little fortunate as the tenant, for the island itself was in the market, and a report went current at the time that it was on the eve of being purchased by some wealthy Englishman, who purposed converting it into a deer-forest. How strange a cycle ! Uninhabited originally, save by wild animals, it became at an early period a home of men, who, as the gray wall on the hillside testified, derived in part at least, their sustenance from the chase. They broke in from the waste the furrowed patches on the slopes of the valleys,—they reared herds of cattle and flocks of sheep,—their number increased to nearly five hundred souls,—they enjoyed the average happiness of human creatures in the present imperfect state of being,—they contributed their portion of hardy and vigorous manhood to the armies of the country, and a few of their more adventurous spirits, impatient of the narrow bounds which confined them, and a course of life little varied by incident, emigrated to America. Then came the change of system so general in the Highlands; and the island lost all its original inhabitants, on a wool and mutton speculation,—inhabitants, the descendants of men who had chased the deer on its hills five hundred years before, and who, though they recognised some wild island lord as their superior, and did him service, had regarded the place as indisputably their own. And now yet another change was on the eve of ensuing, and the island was to return to its original state, as a home of wild animals, where a few hunters from the mainland might enjoy the chase for a month or two every twelvemonth, but which could form no permanent place of human abode. Once more a strange, and surely most melancholy cycle! *

In another place the same writer asks, " Where was the one tenant of the island, for whose sake so many others had been removed?" and he answers, "We found his house occupied by a humble shepherd, who had in charge the wreck of his property,—property no longer his, but held for the benefit of his creditors. The great sheep-farmer had gone down under circumstances of very general bearing, and on whose after development, when in their latent state, improving landlords had failed to calculate."

HARRIS and the other Western Islands suffered in a similar manner. Mull, Tiree, and others in Argyleshire, will be noticed when we come to deal with that county.

GLENGARRY.

GLENGARRY was peopled down to the end of last century with a fine race of men. In 1745, six hundred stalwart vassals followed the chief of Glengarry to the battle of

* Leading Articles from the *Witness.*

Culloden. Some few years later they became so disgusted with the return made by their chief that many of them emigrated to the United States, though they were almost all in comfortable, some indeed, in affluent circumstances. Notwithstanding this semi-voluntary exodus, Major John Macdonell of Lochgarry, was able in 1777, to raise a fine regiment—the 76th, or Macdonald Highlanders—numbering 1086 men, 750 of whom were Highlanders mainly from the Glengarry property. In 1794, Alexander Macdonell of Glengarry, raised a Fencible regiment, described as "a handsome body of men," of whom one-half were enlisted on the same estate. On being disbanded in 1802, these men were again so shabbily treated, that they followed the example of the men of the "Forty-five," and emigrated in a body, with their families, to Canada, taking two Gaelic-speaking ministers along with them to their new home. They afterwards distinguished themselves as part of the "Glengarry Fencibles" of Canada, in defence of their adopted country, and called their settlement there after their native glen in Scotland. The chiefs of Glengarry drove away their people, only, as in most other cases in the Highlands, to be themselves ousted soon after them.

The Glengarry property at one time covered an area of nearly 200 square miles, and to-day, while many of their expatriated vassals are landed proprietors and in affluent circumstances in Canada, not an inch of the old possessions of the ancient and powerful family of Glengarry remains to the descendants of those who caused the banishment of a people who, on many a well-fought field, shed their blood for their chief and country. In 1853, every inch of the ancient heritage was possessed by the stranger, except Knoydart in the west, and this has long ago become the property of one of the Bairds. In the year named, young

Glengarry was a minor, his mother, the widow of the late chief, being one of his trustees. She does not appear to have learned any lesson of wisdom from the past misfortunes of her house. Indeed, considering her limited power and possessions, she was comparatively the worst of them all.

The tenants of Knoydart, like all other Highlanders, had suffered severely during and after the potato famine in 1846 and 1847, and some of them got into arrear with a year and some with two years' rent, but they were fast clearing it off. Mrs. Macdonell and her factor determined to evict every crofter on her property, to make room for sheep. In the spring of 1853, they were all served with summonses of removal, accompanied by a message that Sir John Macneil, chairman of the Board of Supervision, had agreed to convey them to Australia. Their feelings were not considered worthy of the slightest consideration. They were not even asked whether they would prefer to follow their countrymen to America and Canada. They were to be treated as if they were nothing better than Africans, and the laws of their country on a level with those which regulated South American slavery. The people, however, had no alternative but to accept any offer made to them. They could not get an inch of land on any of the neighbouring estates, and any one who would give them a night's shelter was threatened with eviction.

It was afterwards found not convenient to transport them to Australia, and it was then intimated to the poor creatures, as if they were nothing but common slaves to be disposed of at will, that they would be taken to North America, and that a ship would be at Isle Ornsay, in the Isle of Skye, in a few days, to receive them, and that they *must* go on board. The *Sillery* soon arrived. Mrs. Macdonell and her factor came all the way from Edinburgh to see the people hounded across in boats, and put on board this ship whether they would or not. An eye-witness who described the proceeding at the time, in a now rare pamphlet, and whom we met a few years ago in Nova Scotia, characterises the scene as heart-rending. "The wail of the poor women and children as they were torn away from their homes would have melted a heart of stone." Some few families, principally cottars, refused to go, in spite of every influence brought to bear upon them; and the treatment they afterwards received was cruel beyond belief. The houses, not only of those who went, but of those who remained, were burnt and levelled to the ground. The Strath was dotted all over with black spots, showing where yesterday stood the habitations of men. The scarred, half-burned wood—couples, rafters, and cabars—were strewn about in every direction. Stooks of corn and plots of unlifted potatoes could be seen on all sides, but man was gone. No voice could be heard. Those who refused to go aboard the *Sillery* were in hiding among the rocks and the caves, while their friends were packed off like so many African slaves to the Cuban market.

No mercy was shown to those who refused to emigrate; their few articles of furniture were thrown out of their houses after them—beds, chairs, tables, pots, stoneware, clothing, in many cases, rolling down the hill. What took years to erect and collect were destroyed and scattered in a few minutes. "From house to house, from hut to hut, and from barn to barn, the factor and his menials proceeded carrying on the work of demolition, until there was scarcely a human habitation left standing in the district. Able-bodied men who, if the matter would rest with a mere trial of physical force, would have bound the factor and his party hand and foot, and sent them out of the district, stood aside as dumb spectators. Women wrung their hands and cried aloud, children ran to and fro dreadfully frightened ; and while all this work of demolition and destruction was going on no opposition was offered by the inhabitants, no hand was lifted, no stone cast, no angry word was spoken." The few huts left undemolished were occupied by the paupers, but before the factor left for the south even they were warned not to give any shelter to the evicted, or their huts would assuredly meet with the same fate. Eleven families, numbering in all over sixty persons, mostly old and decrepit men and women, and helpless children, were exposed that night, and many of them long afterwards, to the cold air, without shelter of any description beyond what little they were able to save out of the wreck of their burnt dwellings.

We feel unwilling to inflict pain on the reader by the recitation of the untold cruelties perpetrated on the poor Highlanders of Knoydart ; but doing so may, perhaps, serve a good purpose. It may convince the evil-doer that his work shall not be forgotten, and any who may be disposed to follow the example of past evictors may hesitate before they proceed to immortalise themselves in such a hateful manner. We shall therefore quote a few cases from the pamphlet already referred to :—

John Macdugald, aged about 50, with a wife and family, was a cottar, and earned his subsistence chiefly by fishing. He was in bad health, and had two of his sons in the hospital, at Elgin, ill of smallpox, when the *Sillery* was sent to convey the Knoydart people to Canada. He refused to go on that occasion owing to the state of his health, and his boys being at a distance under medical treatment. The factor and the officers, however, arrived, turned Macdugald and his family adrift, put their bits of furniture out on the field, and in a few minutes levelled their house to the ground. The whole family had now no shelter but the broad canopy of heaven. The mother and the youngest of the children could not sleep owing to the cold, and the father, on account of his sickness, kept wandering about all night near where his helpless family lay down to repose. After the factor and the officers left the district Macdugald and his wife went back to the ruins of their house, collected some of the stones and turf into something like walls, threw a few cabars across, covered them over with blankets, old sails, and turf, and then, with their children, crept underneath, trusting that they would be allowed, at least for a time, to take shelter under this temporary covering. But, alas! they were doomed to bitter disappointment. A week had not elapsed when the local manager, accompanied by a *posse* of officers and menials, traversed the country and levelled to the ground every hut or shelter erected by the evicted peasantry. Macdugald was at this time away from Knoydart; his wife was at Inverie, distant about six miles, seeing a sick relative; the oldest children were working at the shore; and in the hut, when the manager came with the 'levellers,' he found none of the family except Lucy and Jane, the two youngest. The moment they saw the officers they screamed and fled for their lives. The demolition of the shelter was easily accomplished—it was but the work of two or three minutes; and, this over, the officers and menials of the manager amused themselves by seizing hold of chairs, stools, tables, spinning-wheels, or any other light articles, by throwing them a considerable distance from the hut. The mother, as I said, was at Inverie, distant about six or seven miles, and Lucy and Jane proceeded in that direction hoping to meet her. They had not gone far, however, when they missed the footpath and wandered far out of the way. In the interval the mother returned from Inverie and found the hut razed to the ground, her furniture scattered far and near, her bedclothes lying under turf, clay, and *debris*, and her children gone ! Just imagine the feelings of this poor Highland mother on the occasion ! But, to proceed, the other children returned from the shore, and they too stood aside, amazed and grieved at the sudden destruction of their humble refuge, and at the absence of their two little sisters. At first they thought they were under the ruins, and creeping down on their knees they carefully removed every turf and stone, but found nothing except a few broken dishes. A consultation was now held and a search resolved upon. The mother, brothers and sisters set off in opposite directions, among the rocks, over hills, through moor and moss, searching every place, and calling aloud for them by name, but they could discover no trace of them. Night was now approaching and with it all hopes of finding them, till next day, were fast dying away. The mother was now returning 'home' (alas ! to what a *home*), the shades of night closed in, and still she had about three miles to travel. She made for the footpath, scrutinized every bush, and looked round every rock and hillock, hoping to find them. Sometimes she imagined that she saw her two lasses walking before her at some short distance, but it was an illusion caused by bushes just about their size. The moon now emerged from behind a cloud and spread its light on the path and surrounding district. A sharp frost set in, and ice began to form on the little pools. Passing near a rock and some bushes, where the children of the tenants used to meet when herding the cattle, she felt as if something beckoned her to search there ; this she did and found her two little children fast asleep, beside a favourite bush, the youngest with her head resting on the breast of the eldest ! Their own version of their mishap is this :

that when they saw the officers they creeped out and ran in the direction of Inverie to tell their mother; that they missed the footpath, then wandered about crying, and finally returned, they knew not how, to their favourite herding ground, and, being completely exhausted, fell asleep. The mother took the young one on her back, sent the other on before her, and soon joined her other children near the ruins of their old dwelling. They put a few sticks up to an old fence, placed a blanket over it, and slept on the bare ground that night. Macdugald soon returned from his distant journey, found his family shelterless, and again set about erecting some refuge for them from the wreck of the old buildings. Again, however, the local manager appeared with levellers, turned them all adrift, and in a few moments pulled down and destroyed all that he had built up. Matters continued in this way for a week or two until Macdugald's health became serious, and then a neighbouring farmer gave him and his family temporary shelter in an out-house; and for this act of disinterested humanity he has already received some most improper and threatening letters from the managers on the estate of Knoydart. It is very likely that in consequence of this interference Macdugald is again taking shelter among the rocks, or amid the wreck of his former residence.

John Mackinnon, a cottar, aged 44, with a wife and six children, had his house pulled down, and had no place to put his head in, consequently he and his family, for the first night or two, had to burrow among the rocks near the shore! When he thought that the factor and his party had left the district, he emerged from the rocks, surveyed the ruins of his former dwelling, saw his furniture and other effects exposed to the elements, and now scarcely worth the lifting. The demolition was so complete that he considered it utterly impossible to make any use of the ruins of the old house. The ruins of an old chapel, however, were near at hand, and parts of the walls were still standing; thither Mackinnon proceeded with his family, and having swept away some rubbish and removed some grass and nettles, they placed a few cabars up to one of the walls, spread some sails and blankets across, brought in some meadow hay, and laid it in a corner for a bed, stuck a piece of iron into the wall in another corner, on which they placed a crook, then kindled a fire, washed some potatoes, and put a pot on the fire and boiled them, and when these and a few fish roasted on the embers were ready, Mackinnon and his family had *one* good diet, being the first regular meal they tasted since the destruction of their house !

Mackinnon is a tall man, but poor and unhealthy-looking. His wife is a poor weak woman, evidently struggling with a diseased constitution and dreadful trials. The boys, Ronald and Archibald, were lying in ' bed '—(may I call a ' pickle hay on the bare ground a bed ?)—suffering from rheumatisms and cholic. The other children are apparently healthy enough as yet, but very ragged. There is no door to their wretched abode, consequently every breeze and gust that blow have free ingress to the inmates. A savage from Terra-del-Fuego, or a Red Indian from beyond the Rocky Mountains, would not exchange huts with these victims, nor humanity with their persecutors. Mackinnon's wife was pregnant when she was turned out of her house among the rocks. In about four days after she had a premature birth; and this and her exposure to the elements, and the want of proper shelter and nutritious diet, has brought on consumption, from which there is no chance whatever of her recovery.

There was something **very solemn** indeed in this scene.

Here, amid the ruins of the old sanctuary, where the swallows fluttered, where the ivy tried to screen the grey moss-covered stones, where nettles and grass grew up luxuriously, where the floor was damp, the walls sombre and uninviting, where there were no doors nor windows nor roof, and where the owl, the bat, and the fox used to take refuge, a Christian family was obliged to take shelter! One would think that as Mackinnon took refuge amid the ruins of this most singular place that he would be let alone, that he would not any longer be molested by man. But, alas! that was not to be. The manager of Knoydart and his minions appeared, and invaded this helpless family, even within the walls of the sanctuary. They pulled down the sticks and sails he set up within its ruins—put his wife and children out on the cold shore—threw his tables, stools, chairs, etc., over the walls—burnt up the hay on which they slept—put out the fire—and then left the district. Four times have these officers broken in upon poor Mackinnon in this way, destroying his place of shelter, and sent him and his family adrift on the cold coast of Knoydart. When I looked in upon these creatures last week I found them in utter consternation, having just learned that the officers would appear next day, and would again destroy the huts. The children looked at me as if I had been a wolf; they creeped behind their father, and stared wildly, dreading I was a law officer. The sight was most painful. The very idea that, in Christian Scotland, and in the 19th century, these tender infants should be subjected to such gross treatment reflects strongly upon our humanity and civilization. Had they been suffering from the ravages of famine, or pestilence, or war, I could understand it and account for it, but suffering to gratify the ambition of some unfeeling speculator in brute beasts, I think it most unwarranted, and deserving the em-

phatic condemnation of every Christian man. Had Mackinnon been in arrears of rent, which he was not, even this
would not justify the harsh, cruel, and inhuman conduct
pursued towards himself and his family. No language of
mine can describe the condition of this poor family, exaggeration is impossible. The ruins of an old chapel is the last
place in the world to which a poor Highlander would resort
with his wife and children unless he was driven to it by dire
necessity. Take another case :—

Elizabeth Gillies, a widow, aged 60 years.—This is a most
lamentable case. Neither age, sex, nor circumstance saved
this poor creature from the most wanton and cruel aggres-
sion. Her house was on the brow of a hill, near a stream
that formed the boundary between a large sheep farm and
the lands of the tenants of Knoydart. Widow Gillies was
warned to quit like the rest of the tenants, and was offered a
passage first to Australia and then to Canada, but she refused
to go, saying she could do nothing in Canada. The widow,
however, made no promises, and the factor went away. She
had then a nice young daughter staying with her, but, ere
the vessel that was to convey the Knoydart people away
arrived at Isle Ornsay, this young girl died, and poor
Widow Gillies was left alone. When the time for pulling
down the houses arrived, it was hoped that some mercy
would have been shown to this poor, bereaved widow, but
there was none. Widow Gillies was sitting inside her house
when the factor and officers arrived. They ordered her to
remove herself and effects instantly, as they were, they said,
to pull down the house ! She asked them where she would
remove to ; the factor would give no answer, but continued insisting on her leaving the house. This she at last
positively refused. Two men then took hold of her, and
tried to pull her out by force, but she sat down beside the

fire and would not move an inch. One of the assistants threw water on the fire and extinguished it, and then joined the other two in forcibly removing the poor widow from the house. At first she struggled hard, seized hold of every post or stone within her reach, taking a death grasp of each to keep possession. But the officers were too many and too cruel for her. They struck her over the fingers, and compelled her to let go her hold, and then all she could do was to greet and cry out murder! She was ultimately thrust out at the door, from where she creeped on her hands and feet to a dyke side, being quite exhausted and panting for breath, owing to her hard struggle with three powerful men. Whenever they got her outside, the work of destruction immediately commenced. Stools, chairs, tables, cupboard, spinning-wheel, bed, blankets, straw, dishes, pots, and chest, were thrown out in the gutter. They broke down the partitions, took down the crook from over the fire-place, destroyed the hen roosts, and then beat the hens out through the broad vent in the roof of the house. This done, they set to work on the walls outside with picks and iron levers. They pulled down the thatch, cut the couples, and in a few minutes the walls fell out, while the roof fell in with a dismal crash!

When the factor and his party were done with this house, they proceeded to another district, pulling down and destroying dwelling-places as they went along. The shades of night at last closed in, and here was the poor helpless widow sitting like a pelican, alone and cheerless. Allan Macdonald, a cottar, whose house was also pulled down, however, ran across the hill to see how the poor widow had been treated, and found her moaning beside the dyke. He led her to where his own children had taken shelter, treated her kindly, and did all he could to comfort her under the circumstances.

When I visited Knoydart I found the poor widow at work repairing her shed, and such a shed, and such a dwelling, I never before witnessed. The poor creature spoke remarkably well, and appeared to me to be a very sensible woman. I expressed my sympathy for her, and my disapprobation of the conduct of those who so unmercifully treated her. She said it was indeed most ungrateful on the part of the representatives of Glengarry to have treated her so cruelly—that her predecessors were, from time immemorial, on the Glengarry estates—that many of them died in defence of, or fighting for, the old cheftains—and that they had always been true and faithful subjects. I asked why she refused to go to Canada? 'For a very good reason,' she said, 'I am now old and not able to clear a way in the forests of Canada; and, besides, I am unfit for service; and, farther, I am averse to leave my native country, and rather than leave it, I would much prefer that my grave was opened beside my dear daughter, although I should be buried alive!' I do think she was sincere in what she said. Despair and anguish were marked in her countenance, and her attachment to her old habitation and its associations were so strong that I believe they can only be cut asunder by death! I left her in this miserable shed which she occupied, and I question much if there is another human residence like it in Europe. The wigwam of the wild Indian, or the cave of the Greenlander, are palaces in comparison with it; and even the meanest dog-kennel in England would be a thousand times more preferable as a place of residence. If this poor Highland woman will stand it out all winter in this abode it will be indeed a great wonder. The factor has issued an *ukase*, which aggravates all these cases of eviction with peculiar hardship ; he has warned all and sundry on the Knoydart estates from receiving or entertaining the evicted peasantry into their houses under pain of removal.

Allan Macdonald, aged 54, a widower, with four children, was similarly treated. Our informant says of him :—" When his late Majesty George IV. visited Scotland in 1823, and when Highland lairds sent up to Edinburgh specimens of the bone and sinew—human produce—of their properties, old Glengarry took care to give Allan Macdonald a polite invitation to this ' Royal exhibition '. Alas ! how matters have so sadly changed. Within the last 30 years *man* has fallen off dreadfully in the estimation of Highland proprietors. Commercially speaking, Allan Macdonald has now no value at all. Had he been a roe, a deer, a sheep, or a bullock, a Highland laird in speculating could estimate his 'real' worth to within a few shillings, but Allan is *only* a man. Then his children ; they are of no value, nor taken into account in the calculations of the sportsman. They cannot be shot at like hares, blackcocks, or grouse, nor yet can they be sent south as game to feed the London market." Another case is—

Archibald Macisaac's, crofter, aged 66 ; wife 54, with a family of ten children. Archibald's house, byre, barn, and stable, were levelled to the ground. The furniture of the house was thrown down the hill, and a general destruction then commenced. The roof, fixtures, and wood work were smashed to pieces, the walls razed to the very foundation, and all that was left for poor Archibald to look upon was a black dismal wreck. Twelve human beings were thus deprived of their home in less than half an hour. It was grossly illegal to have destroyed the barn, for, according even to the law of Scotland, the outgoing or removing tenant is entitled to the use of the barn until his crops are disposed of. But, of course, in a remote district, and among simple and primitive people like the inhabitants of Knoydart, the laws that concern them and define their rights are unknown to them.

Archibald had now to make the best shift he could. No mercy or favour could be expected from the factor. Having convened his children beside an old fence where he sat looking on when the destruction of his home was accomplished, he addressed them on the peculiar nature of the position in which they were placed, and the necessity of asking for wisdom from above to guide them in any future action. His wife and children wept, but the old man said, 'neither weeping nor reflection will now avail; we must prepare some shelter'. The children collected some cabars and turf, and in the hollow between two ditches, the old man constructed a rude shelter for the night, and having kindled a fire and gathered in his family, they all engaged in family worship and sung psalms as usual. Next morning they examined the ruins, picked up some broken pieces of furniture, dishes, etc., and then made another addition to their shelter in the ditch. Matters went on this way for about a week, when the local manager and his men came down upon them, and after much abuse for daring to take shelter on the lands of Knoydart, they destroyed the shelter and put old Archy and his people again out on the hill.

I found Archibald and his numerous family still at Knoydart and in a shelter beside the old ditch. Any residence more wretched, or more truly melancholy, I have never witnessed. A feal, or turf erection, about 3 feet high, 4 feet broad, and about 5 feet long, was at the end of the shelter, and this formed the sleeping place of the mother and her five daughters! They creep in and out on their knees, and their bed is just a layer of hay on the cold earth of the ditch!

There is surely monstrous cruelty in this treatment of British females, and the laws that sanction or tolerate such flagrant and gross abuses are a disgrace to the statute-book and to the country that permits it.   Macisaac and his family are, so far as I could learn, very decent, respectable, and well-behaved people, and can we not perceive a monstrous injustice in treating them worse than slaves because they refuse to allow themselves to be packed off to the Colonies just like so many bales of manufactured goods ?   Again :—

Donald Maceachan, a cottar at Arar, married, with a wife and five children.   This poor man, his wife, and children were fully twenty-three nights without any shelter but the broad and blue heavens.   They kindled a fire and prepared their food beside a rock, and then slept in the open air. Just imagine the condition of this poor mother, Donald's wife, nursing a delicate child, and subjected to merciless storms of wind and rain during a long October night.   One of these melancholy nights the blankets that covered them were frozen and white with frost.   The next is,

Charles Macdonald, aged 70 years, a widower, having no family.   This poor man was also 'keeled' for the Colonies, and, as he refused to go, his house or cabin was levelled to the ground.   What on earth could old Charles do in America ?   Was there any mercy or humanity in offering *him* a free passage across the Atlantic ?   In England, Charles would have been considered a proper object of parochial protection and relief, but in Scotland no such relief is afforded except to 'sick folks' and tender infants. There can be no question, however, that the factor looked forward to the period when Charles would become chargeable as a pauper, and, acting as a 'prudent man,' he resolved to get quit of him at once.   Three or four pounds would send the old man across the Atlantic, but if he remained in Knoydart, it would likely take four or five pounds to keep him each year that he lived. When the factor and his party arrived at Charles's door they knocked and demanded admission; the factor intimated his object, and ordered the old man to quit. 'As soon as I can,' said Charles, and, taking up his plaid and staff and adjusting his blue bonnet, he walked out, merely remarking to the factor that the man who could turn out an old, inoffensive High-lander of seventy, from such a place, and at such a season, could do a great deal more if the laws of the country permitted him. Charles took to the rocks, and from that day to this he has never gone near his old habitation. He has neither house nor home; but receives occasional supplies of food from his evicted neighbours, *and he sleeps on the hill!* Poor old man, who would not pity him—who would not share with him a crust or a covering—who?

Alexander Macdonald, aged 40 years, with a wife and family of four children, had his house pulled down. His wife was pregnant; still the levellers thrust her out, and then put the children out after her. The husband argued, re-monstrated, and protested, but it was all in vain; for in a few minutes all he had for his (to him once comfortable) home was a lot of rubbish, blackened rafters, and heaps of stones. The levellers laughed at him and at his protests, and when their work was over, moved away, leaving him to find refuge the best way he could. Alexander had, like the rest of his evicted brethren, to burrow among the rocks and in caves until he put up a temporary shelter amid the wreck of his old habitation, but from which he was repeatedly driven away. For three days Alexander Macdonald's wife lay sick beside a bush, where, owing to terror and exposure to cold, she had a miscarriage. She was then removed to the shelter of the walls of her former house, and for three days she lay so ill that her life was despaired of. These are facts as to which I challenge contradiction. I have not inserted them without the most satisfactory evidence of their accuracy.

Catherine Mackinnon, aged about 50 years, unmarried ; Peggy Mackinnon, aged about 48 years, unmarried ; and Catherine Macphee (a half-sister of the two Mackinnons), also unmarried; occupied one house. Catherine Mackinnon was for a long time sick, and she was confined to bed when the factor and his party came to beat down the house. At first they requested her to get up and walk out, but her sisters said she could not, as she was so unwell. They answered, ' Oh, she is scheming ; ' the sisters said she was not, that she had been ill for a considerable time, and the sick woman herself, who then feebly spoke, said she was quite unfit to be removed, but if God spared her and bestowed upon her better health that she would remove of her own accord. This would not suffice ; *they forced her out of bed, sick as she was, and left her beside a ditch from 10 a.m., to 5 p.m.*, when, afraid that she would die, as she was seriously unwell, they removed her to a house and provided her with cordials and warm clothing. Let the reader imagine the sufferings of this poor female, so ruthlessly torn from a bed of sickness and laid down beside a cold ditch and there left exposed for seven long hours, and then say if such conduct does not loudly call for the condemnation of every lover of human liberty and humanity. Peggy and her half-sister Macphee are still burrowing among the ruins of their old home. When I left Knoydart last week there were no hopes whatever of Catharine Mackinnon's recovery.

I challenge the factor to contradict one sentence in this short narrative of the poor females. The melancholy truth of it is too palpable, too well-known in the district to admit of even a tenable explanation. Nothing can palliate or excuse such gross inhumanity, and it is but right and proper that British Christians should be made aware of such unchristian conduct—such cruelty towards helpless fellow-creatures in sickness and distress. The last, at present, is

Duncan Robertson, aged 35 years, with wife aged 32 years, and a family of three children. Very poor ; the eldest boy is deformed and weak in mind and body, requiring almost the constant care of one of his parents. Robertson was warned out like the rest of the tenants, and decree of removal was obtained against him. At the levelling time the factor came up with his men before Robertson's door, and ordered the inmates out. Robertson pleaded for mercy on account of his sick and imbecile boy, but the factor appeared at first inexorable ; at last he sent in one of the officers to see the boy, who, on his return, said that the boy was really and truly an object of pity. The factor said he could not help it, that he must pull down. Some pieces of furniture were then thrown out, and the picks were fixed in the walls, when Robertson's wife ran out and implored delay, asking the factor, for heaven's sake, to come in and see her sick child. He replied, 'I am sure I am no doctor'. 'I know that,' she said, 'but God might have given you Christian feelings and bowels of compassion notwithstanding'. 'Bring him out here,' said the factor ; and the poor mother ran to the bed and brought out her sick boy in her arms. When the factor saw him, he admitted that he was an object of pity, but warned Robertson that he must quit Knoydart as soon as possible, or that his house would be pulled down about his ears. The levellers peep in once a-week to see if the boy is getting better, so that the house may be razed.

We could give additional particulars of the cruelties which

had to be endured by the poor wretches who remained—cruelties which would never be tolerated in any other civilized country than Britain, and which in Britain would secure instant and severe punishment if inflicted on a dog or a pig, but the record would only inflict further pain, and we have said enough.   In the words of our informant—"There is something melancholy in connection with the entire removal of a people from an inhabited and cultivated district—when a whole country-side is at one fell swoop cleared of its population to make room for sheep—when all the ties, affections, and associations that bind the inhabitants to their country and homes are struck at and cut asunder by one unflinching blow.   When the march of improvement and cultivation is checked; and when the country is transformed into a wilderness, and the land to perpetual barrenness, not only are the best feelings of our common humanity violated, but the decree is tantamount to interdicting the command of the Most High, who said to man—"Go, replenish the earth and subdue it".

Retribution has overtaken the evictors, and is it a wonder that the chiefs of Glengarry are now as little known, and own as little of their ancient domains in the Highlands as their devoted clansmen.   There is now scarcely one of the name of Macdonald in the wide district once inhabited by thousands.   It is a huge wilderness in which barely anything is met but wild animals and sheep, and the few keepers and shepherds necessary to take care of them.

STRATHGLASS.

It has been shown, under " Glengarry," that a chief's widow, during her son's minority, was responsible for the

Knoydart evictions in 1853. Another chief's widow, *Marsali Bhinneach*—Marjory, daughter of Sir Ludovick Grant of Dalvey, widow of Duncan Macdonnel of Glengarry, who died in 1788—gave the whole of Glencuaich as a sheep farm to one south country shepherd, and to make room for him she evicted over 500 people from their ancient homes. The late Edward Ellice stated before a Committee of the House of Commons, in 1873, that about the time of the rebellion in 1745, the population of Glengarry amounted to between 5000 and 6000. At the same time the glen turned out an able-bodied warrior in support of Prince Charles for every pound of rental paid to the proprietor. To-day it is questionable if the same district could turn out twenty men —certainly not that number of Macdonalds. The bad example of this heartless woman was unfortunately imitated afterwards by her daughter Elizabeth, who, in 1795, married William Chisholm of Chisholm, and to whose evil influence may be traced the great eviction which, in 1801, cleared Strathglass almost to a man of its ancient inhabitants. The Chisholm was delicate, and often in bad health, so that the management of the estate fell into the hands of his strong-minded and hard-hearted wife. In 1801, no less than 799 took ship at Fort-William and Isle Martin from Strathglass, the Aird, Glen-Urquhart, and the neighbouring districts, all for Pictou, Nova Scotia; while in the following year, 473 from the same district left Fort-William, for Upper Canada, and 128 for Pictou. 550 went aboard another ship at Knoydart, many of whom were from Strathglass. In 1803, four different batches of 120 souls each, by four different ships, left Strathglass, also for Pictou; while not a few went away with emigrants from other parts of the Highlands. During these three years we find that no less than 5390 were driven out of these Highland glens, and it will be seen that a very large portion of them were evicted from Strathglass by the daughter of the notorious *Marsali Bhinneach*. From among the living cargo of one of the vessels which sailed from Fort-William no less than fifty-three souls died, on the way out, of an epidemic ; and, on the arrival of the living portion of the cargo at Pictou, they were shut in on a narrow point of land, from whence they were not allowed to communicate with any of their friends who had gone before them, for fear of communicating the contagion.   Here they suffered indescribable hardships.

By a peculiar arrangement between the Chisholm who died in 1793, and his wife, a considerable portion of the people were saved for a time from the ruthless conduct of *Marsali Bhinneach's* daughter and her co-adjutors.   Alexander Chisholm married Elizabeth, daughter of a Dr. Wilson in Edinburgh.   He made provision for his wife in case of her outliving him, by which it was left optional with her to take a stated sum annually, or the rental of certain townships, or club farms.   Her husband died in 1793, when the estate reverted to his half-brother, William, and the widow, on the advice of her only child, Mary, who afterwards became Mrs. James Gooden of London, made choice of the joint farms, instead of the sum of money named in her marriage settlement ;   and though great efforts were made by *Marsali Bhinneach's* daughter and her friends, the widow, Mrs. Alexander Chisholm, kept the farms in her own hands, and took great pleasure in seeing a prosperous tenantry in these townships, while all their neighbours were heartlessly driven away.   Not one of her tenants was disturbed or interfered with in any way from the death of her husband, in February, 1793, until her own death in January, 1826, when, unfortunately for them, their farms all came into the hands of the young heir (whose sickly father died in

1817), and his cruel mother. For a few years the tenants were left in possession, but only waiting an opportunity to make a complete clearance of the whole Strath. Some had a few years of their leases to run on other parts of the property, and could not just then be expelled.

In 1830 every man who held land on the property was requested to meet his chief at the local inn of Cannich. They all obeyed, and were there at the appointed time, but no chief came to meet them. The factor soon turned up, however, and informed them that the laird had determined to enter into no negotiation or any new arrangements with them that day. They were all in good circumstances, without any arrears of rent, but were practically banished from their homes in the most inconsiderate and cruel manner, and it afterwards became known that their farms had been secretly let to sheep-farmers from the south, without the knowledge of the native population in possession.

Mr. Colin Chisholm, who was present at the meeting at Cannich, writes :—" I leave you to imagine the bitter grief and disappointment of men who attended with glowing hopes in the morning, but had to tell their families and dependants in the evening that they could see no alternative before them but the emigrant ship, and choose between the scorching prairies of Australia, and the icy regions of North America." It did not, however, come to that. The late Lord Lovat, hearing of the harsh proceedings, proposed to one of the large sheep-farmers on his neighbouring property to give up his farm, his lordship offering to give full value for his stock, so that he might divide it among those evicted from the Chisholm estate. This arrangement was amicably carried through, and at the next Whitsunday—1831—the evicted tenants from Strathglass came into possession of the large sheep-farm of Glenstrathfarrar, and paid over to the late tenant of the farm every farthing of the value set upon the stock by two of the leading valuators in the country; a fact which conclusively proved that the Strathglass tenants were quite capable of holding their own, and perfectly able to meet all claims that could be made upon them by their old proprietor and unnatural chief. They became very comfortable in their new homes; but about fifteen years after their eviction from Strathglass they were again removed to make room for deer. On this occasion the late Lord Lovat gave them similar holdings on other portions of his property, and the sons and grandsons of the evicted tenants of Strathglass are now, on the Lovat property, among the most respectable and comfortable middle-class farmers in the county.

The result of the Strathglass evictions was that only two of the ancient native stock remained in possession of an inch of land on the estate of Chisholm. When the present Chisholm came into possession he found, on his return from Canada, only that small remnant of his own name and clan to receive him. He brought back a few Chisholms from the Lovat property, and re-established on his old farm a tenant who had been evicted nineteen years before from the holding in which his father and grandfather died. The great-grandfather was killed at Culloden, having been shot while carrying his commander, young Chisholm, mortally wounded, from the field. The gratitude of that chief's successors had been shown by his ruthless eviction from the ancient home of his ancestors; but it is gratifying to find the present chief making some reparation by bringing back and liberally supporting the representatives of such a devoted follower of his forbears. The present Chisholm, who has the character of being a good landlord, is descended from a distant collateral branch of the family. The evicting

Chisholms, and their offspring have, however, every one of them, disappeared, and Mr. Colin Chisholm informs us that there is not a human being now in Strathglass of the descendants of the chief, or of the south country farmers, who were the chief instruments in evicting the native population.

To give the reader an idea of the class of men who occupied this district, it may be stated that of the descendants of those who lived in Glen Canaich, one of several smaller glens, at one time thickly populated in the Strath, but now a perfect wilderness—there lived in the present generation no less than three colonels, one major, three captains, three lieutenants, seven ensigns, one bishop, and fifteen priests.

Earlier in the history of Strathglass and towards the end of last century, an attempt was made by south country sheep-farmers to persuade Alexander Chisholm to follow the example of Glengarry, by clearing out the whole native population. Four southerners, among them Gillespie, who took the farm of Glencuaich, cleared by Glengarry, called upon the Chisholm, at Comar, and tried hard to convince him of the many advantages which would accrue to him by the eviction of his tenantry, and turning the largest and best portions of his estate into great sheep walks, for which they offered to pay him large rents. His daughter, Mary, already referred to as Mrs. James Gooden, was then in her teens. She heard the arguments used, and having mildly expressed her objection to the heartless proposal of the greedy southerners, she was ordered out of the room, crying bitterly. She, however, found her way to the kitchen, called all the servants together, and explained the cause of her trouble. The object of the guests at Comar was soon circulated through the Strath, and early the following morning over a thousand men met together in front of

Comar House, and demanded an interview with their chief. This was at once granted, and the whole body of the people remonstrated with him for entertaining, even for a moment, the cruel proceedings suggested by the strangers, whose conduct the frightened natives characterised as infinitely worse than that of the freebooting Lochaber men who, centuries before, came with their swords and other instruments of death to rob his ancestors of their patrimony, but who were defeated and driven out of the district by the ancestors of those whom it was now proposed to evict, out of their native Strath, to make room for the greedy freebooters of modern times and their sheep. The chief counselled quietness, and suggested that the action they had taken might be construed as an act of inhospitality to his guests, not characteristic, in any circumstances, of a Highland chief.

The sheep-farmers, who stood inside the open drawing-room window, heard all that had passed, and, seeing the unexpected turn events were taking, and the desperate resolve shown by the objects of their cruel purpose, they adopted the better part of valour, slipped quietly out by the back door, mounted their horses, galloped away as fast as their steeds could carry them, and crossed the river Glass among the hooting and derision of the assembled tenantry, heard until they crossed the hill which separates Strathglass from Corriemony. The result of the interview with their laird was a complete understanding between him and his tenants ; and the flying horsemen, looking behind them for the first time when they reached the top of the Maol-Bhuidhe, saw the assembled tenantry forming a procession in front of Comar House, with pipers at their head, and the Chisholm being carried, mounted shoulder-high, by his stalwart vassals, on their way to Invercannich. The pleasant outcome of the whole was that chief and clan expressed renewed confidence in each other, a determination to continue in future in the same happy relationship, and to maintain, each on his part, all—modern and ancient—bonds of fealty ever entered into by their respective ancestors.

This, in fact, turned out to be one of the happiest days that ever dawned on the glen. The people were left unmolested so long as this Chisholm survived—a fact which shows the wisdom of chief and people meeting face to face, and refusing to permit others—whether greedy outsiders or selfish factors—to come and foment mischief and misunderstanding between parties whose interests are so closely bound together, and who, if they met and discussed their differences, would seldom or ever have any disagreements of a serious character. Worse counsel prevailed after Alexander's death, and the result under the cruel daughter of the notorious *Marsali Bhinneach*, has been already described.

Reference has been made to the clearance of Glenstrathfarrar by the late Lord Lovat, but for the people removed from there and other portions of the Lovat property, he allotted lands in various other places on his estates, so that, although these changes were most injurious to his tenants, his lordship's proceedings can hardly be called evictions in the ordinary sense of the term. His predecessor, Archibald Fraser of Lovat, however, evicted, like the Chisholms, hundreds from the Lovat estates.

GUISACHAN.

The modern clearances which took place within the last quarter of a century in Guisachan, Strathglass, by Sir Dudley Marjoribanks, have been described in all their phases before a Committee of the House of Commons in 1873. The Inspector of Poor for the parish of Kilterlitz wrote a letter which was brought before the Committee, with a statement from another source that, "in 1855, there were 16 farmers on the estate; the number of cows they had was 62, and horses 24; the principal farmer had 2000 sheep, the next 1000, and the rest between them 1200, giving a total of 4200. Now (1873) there is but one farmer, and he leaves at Whitsunday; all these farmers lost the holdings on which they ever lived in competency; indeed it is well known that some of them were able to lay by some money. They have been sent to the four quarters of the globe, or to vegetate in Sir Dudley's dandy cottages at Tomich, made more for show than convenience, where they have to depend on his employment or charity. To prove that all this is true, take at random, the smith, the shoemaker, or the tailor, and say whether the poverty and starvation were then or now? For instance, under the old *regime*, the smith farmed a piece of land which supplied the wants of his family with meal and potatoes; he had two cows, a horse, and a score or two of sheep on the hill; he paid £7 of yearly rent; he now has nothing but the bare walls of his cottage and smithy, for which he pays £10. Of course he had his trade then as he has now. Will he live more comfortably now than he did then?" It was stated, at the same time, that when Sir Dudley Marjoribanks bought the property, there was a population of 255 souls upon it, and Sir Dudley, in his examination, though he threw some doubt upon that statement, was quite unable to refute it. The proprietor, on being asked, said that he did not evict any of the people. But Mr. Macombie having said, "Then the tenants went away of their own free will," Sir Dudley replied, "I must not say so quite. I told them that when they had found other places to go to, I wished to have their farms."

They were, in point of fact, evicted as much as any others of the ancient tenantry in the Highlands, though it is but fair to say that the same harsh cruelty was not applied in their case as in many of the others recorded in these pages. Those who had been allowed to remain in the new cottages, are without cow or sheep, or an inch of land, while those alive of those sent off are spread over the wide world, like those sent, as already described, from other places.

GLENELG.

IN 1849 more than 500 souls left Glenelg. These petitioned the proprietor, Mr. Baillie of Dochfour, to provide means of existence for them at home by means of reclamation and improvements in the district, or, failing this, to help them to emigrate. Mr. Baillie, after repeated communications, made choice of the latter alternative, and suggested that a local committee should be appointed to procure and supply him with information as to the number of families willing to emigrate, their circumstances, and the amount of aid necessary to enable them to do so. This was done, and it was intimated to the proprietor that a sum of £3000 would be required to land those willing to emigrate at Quebec. This sum included passage money, free-rations, a month's sustenance after the arrival of the party in Canada, and some clothing for the more destitute. Ultimately, the proprietor offered the sum of £2000, while the Highland Destitution Committee promised £500. A great deal of misunderstanding occurred before the *Liscard* finally sailed, in consequence of misrepresentations made as to the food to be supplied on board, while there were loud protests against sending the people away without any medical man in charge. Through the activity and generous sympathy of the late Mr. Stewart of Ensay, then tenant of

Ellanreach, on the Glenelg property, who took the side of the people, matters were soon rectified. A doctor was secured, and the people satisfied as to the rations to be served out to them during the passage, though these did not come up to one-half what was originally promised. On the whole, Mr. Baillie behaved liberally, but, considering the suitability of the beautiful valley of Glenelg for arable and food-producing purposes, it is to be regretted that he did not decide upon utilizing the labour of the natives in bringing the district into a state of cultivation, rather than have paid so much to banish them to a foreign land. That they would themselves have preferred this is beyond question.

Mr. Mulock, father of the author of "John Halifax, Gentleman," an Englishman who could not be charged with any preconceived prejudices or partiality for the Highlanders, travelled at this period through the whole North, and ultimately published an account of what he had seen. Regarding the Glenelg business, he says, as to their willingness to emigrate—"To suppose that numerous families would as a matter of choice sever themselves from their loved soil, abolish all the associations of local and patriotic sentiment, fling to the winds every endearing recollection connected with the sojourneying spot of vanished generations, and blot themselves, as it were, out of the book of 'home-borne happiness,' is an hypothesis too unnatural to be encouraged by any sober, well-regulated mind." To satisfy himself, he called forty to fifty heads of families together at Glenelg, who had signed an agreement to emigrate, but who did not find room in the *Liscard*, and were left behind, after selling off everything they possessed, and were consequently reduced to a state of starvation. "I asked," he says, "these poor perfidiously treated creatures if, notwithstanding all their hardships, they were willing emigrants from their native land. With one voice they assured me that nothing short of the impossibility of obtaining land or employment at home could drive them to seek the doubtful benefits of a foreign shore. So far from the emigration being, at Glenelg, or Lochalsh, or South Uist, a spontaneous movement springing out of the wishes of the tenantry, I aver it to be, on the contrary, the product of desperation, the calamitous light of hopeless oppression visiting their sad hearts." We have no hesitation in saying that this is not only true of those to whom Mr. Mulock specially refers, but to almost every soul who have left the Highlands for the last sixty years. Only those who know the people intimately, and the means adopted by factors, clergy, and others to produce an appearance of spontaneity on the part of the helpless tenantry, can understand the extent to which this statement is true. If a judicious system had been applied of cultivating excellent land, capable of producing food in abundance, in Glenelg, there was not another property in the Highlands on which it was less necessary to send the people away than in that beautiful and fertile valley.

GLENDESSERAY AND LOCHARKAIG.

GREAT numbers were evicted from the Cameron country of Lochaber, especially from Glendesseray and Locharkaig side. Indeed it is said that there were so few Camerons left in the district, that not a single tenant of the name attended the banquet given by the tenantry when the present Lochiel came into possession. The details of Cameron evictions would be found pretty much the same as those in other places, except that an attempt has been made in this case to hold the factor entirely and solely responsible for the removal of this noble people, so renowned in the martial history of the country. That is a question, however, which it is no part of our present purpose to discuss. What we wish to expose is the unrighteous system which allowed such cruel proceedings to take place here and elsewhere, by landlord or factor.

Principal Shairp of St. Andrews, and Professor of Poetry in the University of Oxford, has described the evictions from the country of the Camerons in a fine poem of seven cantos, entitled, "The Clearing of the Glens," published in Vol. II. of the *Celtic Magazine*, 1876-77. It would be impossible to describe them so completely as has been done in this excellent poem, and we shall therefore leave Principal Shairp to do so himself, by quoting, at some length, from his sixth and seventh cantos, though, to get the pathetic picture complete, the reader must peruse the whole poem.

In an introductory note, the Principal informs us that he attempts, in the poem, "to reproduce facts heard, and impressions received, during the wanderings of several successive summers among the scenes" which he describes. "Whatever view political economists may take of these events, it can hardly be denied that the form of human society, and the phase of human suffering, here attempted to be described, deserve at least some record. . . . Of the main outlines and leading events of the simple story, it may well be said, ' It's an over true tale '." After some beautiful and touching descriptions of the state, physically and socially, of the Cameron country, some years earlier, Angus Cameron, who had been away for seven years in the service of his country, returns, and is horror-stricken at seeing the desolation brought about during his absence, in Lochaber and the vicinity. As he comes in sight of his own native place, the poet describes the scene thus—

There far below, inlaid between
Steep mountain walls, lay calm and green
Glen Desseray, bright in morning sheen.
As down the rough track Angus trode
The path that led to his old abode,
Calm as of old the lone green glen
Lay stretched before him long miles ten ;
He looked, the braes as erst were fair,
But smoke none rose on the morning air ;
He listened, came no blithe cock-crowing
From wakening farms, no cattle lowing,
No voice of man, no cry of child,
Blent with the loneness of the wild ;
Only the wind thro' the bent and ferns,
Only the moan of the corrie-burns.
Can it be ? doth this silence tell
　　The same sad tale as yester-eve ?
My clansmen here who wont to dwell
　　Have they too ta'en their last long leave ?
Adown this glen too, hath there been
The besom of destruction keen
Sweeping it of its people clean ?
That anxious tremour in his breast
One half-hour onward set at rest ;
Where once his home had been, now stare
Two gables roofless, gaunt, and bare ;
Two gables, and a broken wall,
Are all now left of Sheniebhal.
The huts around of the old farm-toun,
　　Wherein the poorer tenants dwelt,
Moss-covered stone-heaps, crumbling down,
　　Into the wilderness slowly melt.
The slopes below, where had gardens been,
Lay thick with rushes darkly green,
The furrows on the braes above
Where erst the flax and the barley throve,
With ferns and heather covered o'er,
To Nature had gone back once more.
And there beneath, the meadow lay,
　　The long smooth reach of meadowy ground,
Where intertwining east away
　　In loop on loop the river wound :

There, where he heard a former day
The blithe, loud shouting, shinty play,
    Was silence now as the grave profound.

.   .   .   .

Then looking back with one wide ken,
Where stood the Farms, each side the glen—
Tome-na-hua, Cuil, Glac-fern,
Each he clearly could discern ;
Once groups of homes, wherein did dwell
The people he had known so well,
These stood blank skeletons, one and all,
Like his own home, Sheniebhal :
And he sighed as he gazed on the pathways untrodden,
"These be the homes of the men of Culloden !"
    "This desolation ! whence hath come ?
What power hath hushed this living glen,
Once blithe with happy sounds of men,
    Into a wilderness blank and dumb ?
Alas for them ! leal souls and true !
Kindred and clansmen whom I knew !
Their homes stand roofless on the brae,
And the hearts that loved them, where are they ?
Ah me ! what days with them I've seen
On the summer braes at the shielings green !
What nights of winter, dark and long,
Made brief and bright by the joy of song !
The men in peace so gentle and mild,
In battle onset lion-wild,
When the pibroch of Donald Dhu
    Sounded the summons of Lochiel,
From these homes to his standard flew,
    By him stood through woe and weal,
Against Clan-Chattan, age by age
Held his ancient heritage :
And when the Stuart cause was down,
And Lochiel rose for King and Crown,
Who like these same Cameron men
    Gave their gallant heart-blood pure
At Inverlochy, Killiecrankie,
    Preston-pans, Culloden Moor ?
And when red vengeance on the Gael

Fell bloody, did their fealty fail?
Did they not screen with lives of men
Their outlawed Prince in desert and den?
And when their chief fled far away,
Who were his sole support but they?
Alas for them! those faithful men!
    And this is all reward they have!
These unroofed homes, this emptied glen,
    A forlorn exile, then the grave."

That night, as October winds were tirling
    The birchen woods down Lochiel's long shore,
The wan, dead leaves on the rain-blast whirling,
    A low knock came to our cottage door.
"Lift the latch, bid him welcome," cried my sire,
    Straight a plaided stranger entered in,
And we saw by the light of the red peat fire,
    A long, lank form, and visage thin.
We children stared—as tho' a ghost
    Had crossed the door—on that face unknown;
But my father cried—"O loved and lost!
    That voice, my brother, is thine own."
Then each on the other's neck they fell,
    And long embraced, and wept aloud;
We children stood—I remember well—
    Our heads in wondering silence bowed.
But when our uncle raised his head,
    Gazing round the house, he said—
"I've travelled down Glendesseray bare,
    Looked on our desolate home to-day,
But those my heart most longed for, where?
    Father and mother, where are they?
For them has their own country found
No home, save underneath the ground."
    "Too truly has your heart divined,"
My father answered him, "for they
Came hither but not long to stay—
With the fall o' the year away they dwined,
Not loth another home to find,
    Where none could say them nay.

Above their heads to-night the sward
Is green in Kilmallie's old kirkyard."

In vain for him the board we strewed,
He little cared for rest or food—
On this alone intent—to know,
Whence had come the ruin and woe.
"Tell me, O tell me whence," he cried,
"Hath spread this desolation wide ;
What ministers of dark despair—
From neither pit or upper air—
On the poor country of the Gael,
Hath breathed this blasting blight and bale.
By lone Lochourn, too, I have been,
And Runieval in ruin seen :
I know that home is desolate—
Tell me the dweller's earthly fate."
" Ah, these are gone, with many more,"
My father said, " to a far-off shore,
By some great lake, whereof we know
Only the name— Ontario.
They tell us there are broad lands there,
Whereof whoever will may share,
Great forests—trees of giant stem—
Glen-mallie pines are naught to them.
But of all that we nothing know,
Save the great name, Ontario."
" But whence came all this ruin ?   Tell
From whom the cruel outrage fell,
On our poor people."   With a sigh
My father fain had put him by ;
" A tale so full of sorrow and wrong,
To-night to tell were all too long,
Weary and hungry thou need'st must be—
Sit down at the board we have spread for thee !"
I wot we had spread it of our best,
But for him our dainties had little zest ;
Nor would he eat or drink until,
Of that dark tale he had heard his fill.

" Since then it must be, I will try,
Rehearse that cruel history,"

My father said, " but why remount
Up to the first full-flowing fount,
Of misery? From whence it came,
That ruin, or with whom the blame,
These things I know not—only know
It fell with a crushing weight of woe,
And broke in twain those hearts for grief,
Who would have died for King and Chief.
Is inborn loyalty that could keep
Its troth to death, a thing so cheap—
Clan-love and honour, that would give
Their life-blood that the Chief might live—
So vile a growth, so little worth,
That men do well to sweep from earth,
Or trample under careless feet,
The truest hearts that ever beat.
As though they were of count no more
Than sea-weed on the wreck-strewn shore?"

Rememberest not how brightly burned
Our beacon-fires when the Chiefs returned?
When clansmen hailed Clanranald's lord,
   Glengarry, and our own Lochiel,
As fathers to their own restored—
   All wrongs to right, all wounds to heal?
They dreamed again 'neath Chiefs as kings,
   To live lives happy and secure?
They knew not that old form of things
   Had perished on Culloden Moor.
Like lairds or English squires—no more,
   As fathers of their people—they
Handed their kindly tenants o'er
   To factor's grinding sway,
And left their castles and lone glens,
To dwell as dainty citizens.
And 'mid the smiles of court and town,
Air their high names of old renown ;
While we with ceaseless toil and moil,
   Hard-struggling, scarce could win,
From drenching skies and niggard soil,
   Enough to keep life in.

Claymore and targe forever cast
　Behind them, foray and raid—
Their thoughts were changed, their days were passed
　'Mid mattock, plough, and spade.
Launched sudden on the industrial race
　'Gainst lowland thrift and trade,
If chance they sought the factor's face,
　For guidance, counsel, aid,
As well they might to the rocks have turned,
So rudely from his presence spurned,
Our people home with taunts were sent,
' Ye are idle, idle—rent, more rent '.

At length, poor souls, in their despair,
They looked around for help elsewhere.

.　　.　　.　　.　　.　　.　　.　　.　　.

Far down the loch I watched the sail,
　Round the last headland disappear,
But long the pibroch's moaning wail—
Knell of the broken-hearted Gael—
　Came back upon my ear,
Echoing to crag, and cave, and shore,
' We return no more—return no more '.

Three summers more went by—the third
Brought to our glen the warning word,
That from their homes at Martinmas,
The tenants, every man, must pass—
Must leave the glen their fathers held,
As clansmen, from an unknown eld,
To make room for some Sassenach loon
Who, from the Borders coming soon,
With flocks of long-woolled sheep would fill
The emptied country, glen, and hill.
Nor less dismayed Glenkinzie heard—
Glen-Pean, too—that startling word,
And all the lesser glens that hide
Down long Loch Arkaig, either side,
Then 'gan our men, in sore dismay,
Look each in other's face, and say—

"What have we done, that we should reap
　For all that's past, but this reward?
Is it that we have failed to keep
　All service due to our liege lord?
Is it because o'er seas abroad,
　We sent for years a second rent,
To succour our dear Chiefs outlawed,
　And pining lone in banishment?
Was it for this our beacons burned,
So brightly when Lochiel returned?"

But when November, bleak and wan,
　With moaning winds wound up the year,
Then rose the dim and dripping dawn,
　That saw our people disappear—
Saw thirty families close their door,
And leave the Glen for evermore.
Ah! then the grief, long inly pent,
From many a breaking heart found vent,
In one wild agony of lament;
Old men, and bairns of tender years,
Mingling their crying and their tears,
The wail of a forlorn leave-taking,
As though an hundred hearts were breaking,
And love and hope the world forsaking.
By afternoon our people crept
Past Achnacarry slow, and wept.
Lochiel was gentle and humane,
　As all his race before—
To see aught living suffer pain,
　It grieved his kind heart sore.
And he, the Chief, was by that day,
As our poor people wound their way
Down the Pass called 'The Darksome Mile,'
And when from out the deep defile,
The sounds of men and cattle brake,
He to the factor turned and spake—
"Whose lowing kine are these I hear?
What means this bleating in mine ear?"
But when the factor answered, "They
Are the people from Glendesseray,"

Lochiel, though mild, with anger burned,
And on the factor sternly turned—
"You told me they were abjects all,
Leading a squalid, hopeless life—
I never paupers knew withal,
Have store of sheep and kine so rife ;
Would that I ne'er thy face had known,
    Ere thus with all the past I broke,
And drove from homes that were their own,
    These leal and simple-hearted folk !
This deed, which you have made me do,
Until my dying day I'll rue."

Well might he rue it, he had driven,
    Forth from the homes to which they clave,
Without a home or hope but heaven,
Two hundred hearts that would have given
    Their lives his life to save.
Sad thoughts that night were with the Chief,
    But these the people could not know—
They only knew that no relief
    Came to their utter woe.
Our fate was fixed, the deed was done,
    Nor Chief nor factor could repeal ;—
We wandered on—that setting sun
    Sank o'er Loch-Linnhe and Lochiel,
As we that night, on cold shore bare,
Encamped beneath the frosty air.
To all who would were crofts assigned—
    Small, meagre crofts of moory lea—
Within this narrow marge confined,
    Between the mountains and the sea.
But all the strong, who would not brook
That day of ruin and rebuke—
Whose sturdy souls could not endure
To sink down 'mid the helpless poor,
They spurned the crofts, and launched away,
To seek new homes in Canada—
The flower of all the glens they bore,
Unwilling to that unknown shore,
Hearts warm with Highland love and lore,

There with home-yearnings sad to beat,
Such hearts as here no more we meet.

But we—our parents all too frail,
Too overdone with age to sail
On that far voyage—were constrained
To take the refuge that remained
Hard by, and on this croft to raise
A rooftree o'er their latest days.
    Not long they needed it—soon they found
A surer shelter, safely laid
    Within yon ancient kirkyard ground,
'Neath the old beech trees' shade.
While we, poor remnant, left behind,
Like the last leaves which autumn wind
Spares when it strips the forest bare—
    We still to poor Lochaber cling,
Content if ceaseless toil and care,
    Scant living from these rocks may wring,
Confined to this lean strip of shore,
The Mountains free to range no more,
All gone—our goats and bonny kye,
That were so bounteous to supply
Alike the children's wants and ours ;
We drudge through late and early hours,
And for our toiling hardly win,
Of fuel, food, and raiment thin,
Enough to keep this poor life in.
How different from the easeful wealth
    Of mountain-living, those old days,
When we drank freedom, joy, and health,
    High on Glendesseray braes !
But that dear Glen, as thou hast seen,
    To-day is silent as the grave,
No songs at the high shealings green,
    No voices in the valley, save
The bleating of the thousand sheep,
    Which o'er our fields and gardens feed,
That Lowland drover thence may reap,
    O'erflowing gain to glut his greed.
The floors on which we kneeled in prayer,

The hearths round which we wont to meet,
Lie roofless and forsaken—bare
  To Saxon shepherd's careless feet.
Enough of this! why linger o'er,
  Old homes gone back to wilderness?
A heavenly home lies on before—
  Thereto we'll forward press.

Not many days my father's roof
  That soldier-brother could retain ;
To wander to far lands aloof
  His heart was on the strain.
But while within our home he stayed,
  He turned him every day,
To where, in sombre beech trees' shade,
His parents both are lowly laid,
  'Neath mountain flag-stone grey,
The last time that he lingered there,
  Some moss he gathered from the grave,
The one memorial he could bear,
Where'er his wandering feet might fare,
  Beyond the western wave.
And then he left my father's door,
And bidding farewell evermore
To dwellers on this mountain shore,
He sets his face to that world afar,
On which descends the evening star.

   .   .   .   .   .   .

WESTER ROSS.

KINTAIL.

DURING the first years of the century a great many were cleared from Kintail by Seaforth at the instigation of his Kintail factor, Duncan Mor Macrae, and his father, who themselves added the land taken from the ancient tenantry to their own sheep farms, already far too extensive. In Glengarry, Canada, a few years ago, we met one man, 93 years of age, who was among the evicted. He was in excellent circumstances, his three sons having three valuable farms of their own, and considered wealthy in the district. In the same county there is a large colony of Kintail men, the descendants of those cleared from that district, all comfortable, many of them very well off, one of them being then member for his county in the Dominion Parliament. While this has been the case with many of the evicted from Kintail and their descendants in Canada, the grasping sheep farmer who was the original cause of their eviction from their native land, died ruined and penniless; and the Seaforths, not long after, had to sell the last inch of their ancient inheritance in Lochalsh and Kintail. Shortly after these Glenelchaig evictions, about fifiy families were banished in the same way and by the same people from the district of Letterfearn. This property has also changed hands since, and is now in possession of Sir Alexander Matheson, Baronet of Lochalsh. Letter of Lochalsh was cleared by Sir Hugh Innes, almost as soon as he came into possession by purchase of that portion of the ancient heritage of Seaforth and Kintail. The property has since passed into the hands of the Lillingstones.

COIGEACH.

The attempt to evict the Coigeach crofters must also be mentioned. Here the people made a stout resistance, the women disarming about twenty policemen and sheriff-officers, burning the summonses in a heap, throwing their batons into the sea, and ducking the representatives of the law in a neighbouring pool. The men formed the second line of defence, in case the women should receive any ill-treatment. They, however, never put a finger on the officers of the law, all of whom returned home without serving a single summons or evicting a single crofter. The proceedings of her subordinates fortunately came to the ears of the noble proprietrix, with the result that the Coigeach tenants are still where they were, and are to-day among the most comfortable crofters in the north of Scotland.

STRATHCONON.

From 1840 to 1848 Strathconon was almost entirely cleared of its ancient inhabitants to make room for sheep and deer, as in other places ; and also for the purposes of extensive forest plantations. The property was under trustees when the harsh proceedings were commenced by the factor, Mr. Rose, a notorious Dingwall solicitor. He began by taking away, first, the extensive hill-pasture, for generations held as club-farms by the townships, thus reducing the people from a position of comfort and independence; and secondly, as we saw done elsewhere, finally evicting them from the arable portion of the strath, though they were not a single penny in arrear of rent. Coirre-Bhuic and Scard-Roy were first cleared, and given, respectively, as sheep-farms to Mr. Brown, from Morayshire, and Colin Munro, from Dingwall. Mr. Balfour, when he came of age, cleared Coirre-Feola and Achadh-an-eas ; Carnach was similarly treated, while no less than twenty-seven families were evicted from Glen-Meine alone. Baile-a-Mhuilinn and Baile-na-Creige were cleared in 1844, no less than twenty-four families from these townships removing to the neighbourhood of Knock-farrel and Loch Ussie, above Dingwall, where they were provided with holdings by the late John Hay Mackenzie of Cromartie, father of the present Duchess of Sutherland, and where a few of themselves and many of their descendants are now in fairly comfortable circumstances. A great many more found shelter on various properties in the Black Isle—some at Drynie Park, Maol-Bui ; others at Kilcoy, Allangrange, Cromarty, and the Aird. It is computed that from four to five hundred souls were thus driven from Strathconon, and cast adrift on the world, including a large number of persons quite helpless, from old age, blindness, and other infirmities. The scenes were much the same as we have described in connection with other places. There is, however, one aspect of the harshness and cruelty of the fates to be recorded in the case of many of the Strathconon people, not applicable in many other cases, namely, that in most instances where they settled down and reclaimed land, they were afterwards re-evicted, and the lands brought into cultivation by themselves, taken from them, without any compensation whatever, and given at enhanced rents to large farmers.

This is specially true of those who settled down in the Black Isle, where they reclaimed a great deal of waste now making some of the best farms in that district. Next after Mr. Rose of Dingwall, the principal instrument in clearing Strathconon, was the late James Gillanders of Highfield, already so well and unfavourably known to the reader in connection with the evictions at Glencalvie, and elsewhere.

It may be remarked that the Strathconon evictions are worthy of note for the forcible illustration they furnish of how, by these arbitrary and unexpected removals, hardships and ruin have frequently been brought on families and communities who were at the time in contented and comfortable circumstances. At one time, and previous to the earlier evictions, perhaps no glen of its size in the Highlands had a larger population than Strathconon. The club farm system, once so common in the North, seems to have been peculiarly successful here. Hence a large proportion of the people were well to do, but when suddenly called upon to give up their hill pasture, and afterwards their arable land, and in the absence of other suitable places to settle in, the means they had very soon disappeared, and the trials and difficulties of new conditions had to be encountered. As a rule, in most of these Highland evictions, the evicted were lost sight of, they having either emigrated to foreign lands or become absorbed in the ever-increasing unemployed population of the large towns. In the case of Strathconon it was different, as has been already stated; many of the families evicted were allowed to settle on some of the wildest unreclaimed land in the Black Isle. Their subsequent history there, and the excellent agricultural condition into which they in after years brought their small holdings, is a standing refutation of the charge so often made against the Highland people, that they are lazy and incapable of properly cultivating the land.

THE BLACK ISLE.

Respecting the estates of Drynie and Kilcoy, a correspondent, who says, " I well remember my excessive grief when my father had to leave the farm which his forefathers had farmed for five generations," writes :—

"Within recent times all the tenants to the east of Drynie, as far as Craigiehow, were turned out, one by one, to make room for one large tenant, Mr. Robertson, who had no less than four centres for stackyards. A most prosperous tenantry were turned out to make room for him, and what is the end of it all! Mr. Robertson has come to grief as a farmer, and now holds a very humble position in the town of Inverness. Drumderfit used to be occupied by fifteen or sixteen tenants who were gradually, and from time to time, evicted, during the last fifty years. Balnakyle was tenanted by five very comfortable and respectable farmers, four of whom were turned out within the last thirty years; Balnaguie was occupied by three; Torr by six; and Croft-cruive by five; the once famous names of Drum-na-marg and Moreton are now extinct, as well as the old tenantry whose forefathers farmed these places for generations. The present farm of Kilcoy includes a number of holdings whose tenants were evicted to make room for one large farmer;" and this is equally true of many others in the district. Nothing can better illustrate the cruel manner in which the ancient tenantry of the country have been treated than these facts ; and special comment on the evictions from Strathconon and the Black Isle, after what has been said about others of a similar character would be superfluous.

THE ISLAND OF LEWS.

No one was evicted from the Island of Lews, in the strict sense of the term, but 2231 souls had to leave it between 1851 and 1863. To pay their passage money, their inland railway fares on arrival, and to provide them with clothing and other furnishings, the late Sir James Matheson paid a sum of £11,855. But notwithstanding all this expenditure, many of these poor people would have died from starvation on their arrival without the good offices of friends in Canada.

In 1841, before Mr. Matheson bought it, a cargo of emigrants from the Lews arrived at Quebec late in the autumn, accompanied by a Rev. Mr. Maclean, sent out to minister to their spiritual wants, but it appears that no provision had been made for the more pressing demands of a severe Canadian winter; and were it not for the Saint Andrew's Society of Montreal, every soul of them would have been starved to death that winter in a strange land. The necessities of the case, and how this patriotic Society saved their countrymen from a horrid death will be seen on perusal of the following minutes, extracted from the books of the Society, during the writer's recent tour in Canada :—
" A special meeting of the office-bearers was summoned on the 20th September, 1841, to take into consideration an application made by Mr. Morris, President of the Emigration Association of the district of St. Francis, for some pecuniary aid to a body of 229 destitute emigrants who had recently arrived from the Island of Lews (Scotland), and who were then supported chiefly by the contributions of the charitable inhabitants of the town of Sherbrooke and its neighbourhood. Mr. Morris' letter intimated that unless other assistance was received, it would be impossible for these emigrants to outlive the winter, as they were in a state

of utter destitution, and the inhabitants of the township could not support so large a number of persons from their own unaided resources. The meeting decided that the Constitution of the Society prohibited them from applying its funds to an object like the one presented—it did not appear to authorise the granting of relief from its funds except to cases of destitution in the city; but as this case appeared of an urgent nature, and one particularly calling for assistance, Messrs. Hew Ramsay and Neil M'Intosh were appointed to collect subscriptions on behalf of the emigrants. This committee acquitted itself with great diligence and success, having collected the handsome sum of £234 14s. 6d., the whole of which was, at different times, remitted to Mr. Morris, and expended by him in this charity. Letters were received from Mr. Morris, expressing the gratitude of the emigrants for this large and timely aid, which was principally the means of keeping them from starvation." The whole of these emigrants are now in easy circumstances.

Comment on the conduct of those in power, who sent out their poor tenantry totally unprovided for, is unnecessary. The idea of sending out a minister and nothing else, in such circumstances, makes one shudder to think of the uses which are sometimes made of the clergy, and how, in such cases, the Gospel they are supposed not only to preach but to practise, is only in many instances caricatured. The provisions sent by the Society had to be forwarded to where these starving emigrants were, a distance of 80 miles from Sherbrooke, on sledges, through a trackless and dense forest. The descendants of these people now form a happy and prosperous community at Lingwick and Winslow.

LECKMELM.

This small property, in the Parish of Lochbroom, changed
hands in 1879, Mr. A. C. Pirie, Paper Manufacturer,
Aberdeen, having purchased it for £19,000 from Colonel
Davidson, now of Tulloch. No sooner did it come into Mr.
Pirie's possession than a notice, dated 2nd November,
1879, in the following terms, was issued to all the
tenants :—

I am instructed by Mr. Pirie, proprietor of Leckmelm, to give you
notice that the present arrangements by which you hold the cottage,
byre, and other buildings, together with lands on that estate, will cease
from and after the term of Martinmas, 1880 ; and further, I am instructed
to intimate to you that at the said term of Martinmas, 1880, Mr. Pirie
purposes taking the whole arable and pasture lands, but that he is desirous of making arrangements whereby you may continue tenant of the
cottage upon terms and conditions yet to be settled upon. I have
further to inform you that unless you and the other tenants at once prevent your sheep and other stock from grazing or trespassing upon the
enclosures and hill and other lands now in the occupation or possession
of the said Mr. Pirie, he will not, upon any conditions, permit you to
remain in the cottage you now occupy, after the said term of Martinmas,
1880, but will clear all off the estate, and take down the cottages.

This notice affected twenty-three families, numbering about
one hundred souls. Sixteen tenants paid between them a
rent of £96 10s.—ranging from £3 to £12 each, per
annum. The stock allowed them was 72 head of cattle, 8
horses, and 320 sheep. The arable portion of Leckmelm
was about the best tilled and the most productive land in
possession of any crofters in the parish. It could all be
worked with the plough, now a very uncommon thing in the
Highlands ; for almost invariably land of that class is in the
hands of the proprietors themselves, when not let to sheep-
farmers or sportsmen. The intention of the new proprietor
was strictly carried out. At Martinmas, 1880, he took every

inch of land—arable and pastoral—into his own hands, and thus by one cruel stroke, reduced a comfortable tenantry from comparative affluence and independence to the position of mere cottars and day labourers, absolutely dependent for subsistence on his own will and the likes or dislikes of his subordinates, who may perhaps, for a short time, be in a position to supply the remnant that will remain, in their altered circumstances, with such common labour as trenching, draining, fencing, carrying stones, lime, and mortar, for the laird's mansion-house and outhouses. With the exception of one, all the tenants who remained are still permitted to live in their old cottages, but they are not permitted to keep a living thing about them—not even a hen. They are existing in a state of abject dependence on Mr. Pirie's will and that of his servants ; and in a constant state of terror that next they will even be turned out of their cottages. As regards work and the necessaries of life, they have been reduced to that of common navvies. In place of milk, butter, and cheese in fair abundance, they have now to be satisfied with sugar, treacle, or whatever else they can buy, to their porridge and potatoes, and their supply of meat, grown and fed hitherto by themselves, is gone for ever. Two, a man and his wife, if not more, have since been provided for by the Parochial authorities, and, no doubt, that will ultimately be the fate of many more of this once thriving and contented people.

An agitation against Mr. Pirie's conduct was raised at the time, and the advantage which he had taken of his position was universally condemned by the press (excepting the *Scotsman* of course), and by the general public voice of the country ; but conscious of his strength, and that the present law, made by the landlords in their own interest, was on his side, he relentlessly and persistently carried out his cruel purpose to the bitter end, and evicted from their lands and

hill grazings every soul upon his property ; but in the meantime allowed them to remain in their cottages, with the
exception of Donald Munro, to whose case reference will
be made hereafter, and two other persons whose houses were
pulled down, and themselves evicted.

When the notices of removal were received, the Rev.
John MacMillan, Free Church Minister of the Parish, called
public attention to Mr. Pirie's proceedings, in the Northern
newspapers, and soon the eye of the whole country was
directed to this modern evictor—a man, in other respects,
reputed considerate and even kind to those under him in
his business of paper manufacturing in Aberdeen. People,
in their simplicity, for years back, thought that evictions on
such a large scale, in the face of a more enlightened public
opinion, had become mere unpleasant recollections of a
barbarous past ; forgetting that the same laws which permitted the clearances of Sutherland and other portions of the
Scottish Highlands during the first half of the present
century were still in force, ready to be applied by any tyrant
who had the courage, for personal ends, to outrage the more
advanced and humane public opinion of the present
generation.

The noble conduct of the Rev. Mr. MacMillan, in connection with those evictions, deserves commemoration in a
work in which the name of his prototype in Sutherland, the
Rev. Mr. Sage, shows to such advantage during the infamous
clearances in that county, already described at length. At
the urgent request of many friends of the Highland crofters,
resident in Inverness, Mr. MacMillan agreed to lay the case
of his evicted parishioners before the public. Early in
December, 1880, he delivered an address in the Music Hall
to one of the largest and most enthusiastic meetings which
has ever been held within its walls, and we cannot do better

here than quote at considerable length from his instructive, eloquent, and rousing appeal on that occasion. Though his remarks do not seem to have influenced Mr. Pirie's conduct, or to have benefited his unfortunate subjects, the Inverness meeting was the real beginning in earnest of the present movement throughout the Highlands in favour of Land Reform, and the curtailment of landlord power over their unfortunate tenants. Mr. Pirie can thus claim to have done our poorer countrymen no small amount of good, though probably, quite contrary to his intentions, by his cruel and high-handed conduct in dealing with the ancient tenants of Leckmelm. He has set the heather on fire, and it is likely to continue burning until such proceedings as those for which he is responsible at Leckmelm will be finally made impossible in Scotland. Mr. MacMillan after informing his audience that Mr. Pirie "is now in a fair way of reaching a notoriety which he little dreamt of when he became owner of the Leckmelm estate," proceeds to tell how the harsh proceedings were gone about, and says :—

As the public are aware, Mr. Pirie's first step after becoming owner of the estate, was to inform the tenantry, by the hands of Mr. Manners, C.E., Inverness, that at Martinmas following they were to deliver their arable land and stock, consisting of sheep and cattle, into his hands, but that some of them, on conditions yet to be revealed, and on showing entire submission to the new *regime* of things, and, withal, a good certificate of character from his factotum, William Gould, might remain in their cottages to act as serfs or slaves on his farm. On this conditional promise they were to live in the best of hope for the future and all at the mercy of the absolute master of the situation, with a *summum jus* at his back to enable him to effect all the purposes of his heart. As a prologue to the drama which was to follow, and to give a sample of what they might expect in the sequel, two acts were presented, or properly speaking, one act in two parts. These were to prepare them for what was to come, reminding us of what we read somewhere in our youth, of a husband who on marrying his fair spouse wished to teach her prompt obedience to all his commands, whatever their character. His first lesson in this direction was one assuredly calculated to strike terror into her tender breast. It was the shooting on the spot of the horse which drew his carriage or conveyance, on showing some slight restiveness. The second lesson was of a similar nature ; we can easily imagine that his object was gained. Then, after coming home, he commanded his spouse to untie his boots and shoes and take them off, and to engage in the most servile acts. Of course prompt obedience was given to all these commands and his end was gained. His wife was obedient to him to the last degree. Of the wisdom and propriety of such a procedure in a husband towards his lawful wife, I shall not here and now wait to enquire, but one thing is plain to us all ; there was a species of earthly and carnal wisdom in it which was entirely overshadowed by its cruelty. Now this illustrates exactly how Mr. Pirie acted towards the people of Leckmelm. To strike terror into their hearts, first of all, two houses were pulled down, I might say about the ears of their respective occupants, without any warning whatever, except a verbal one of the shortest kind. The first was a deaf pauper woman, about middle life, living alone for years in a bothy of her own, altogether apart from the other houses, beside a purling stream, where she had at all seasons pure water to drink if her bread was at times somewhat scanty. After this most cruel eviction no provision was made for the helpless woman, but she was allowed to get shelter elsewhere or anywhere, as best she could. If any of you ever go the way of Leckmelm you can see a gamekeeper's house, the gentry of our land, close to the side of Iseabal Bheag's bothy, and a dog kennel quite in its neighbourhood, or, as I said in one of my letters, adorning it. This then is act the first of this drama. Act second comes next. Mrs. Campbell was a widow with two children; after the decease of her husband she tried to support herself and them by serving in gentlemen's families as a servant. Whether she was all the time in Tulloch's family I cannot say, but, at all events, it was from that family she returned to Leckmelm, in failing health, and on getting rather heavy for active service. Of course her father had died since she had left, and the house in which he lived and died, and in which in all likelihood he had reared his family, and in which she was born and bred, was now tenantless. It was empty, the land attached to it being in the hands of another person. Here Widow Campbell turned aside for a while until something else would in kind providence turn up. But behold during her sojourn from her native township, another king arose, who knew not Joseph, and the inexorable edict had gone forth to raze her habitation to the ground. Her house also was pulled down about her ears. This woman has since gone to America, the asylum of many an evicted family from hearth and home.   Such tragedies as I have mentioned roused some of us to remonstrate with the actors engaged in them, and to the best of our ability to expose their conduct, and, furthermore, we have brought them to the bar of public judgment to pass their verdict, which I hope before all is over will be one of condemnation and condign punishment.

Behold how great a matter a little fire kindleth.   Leckmelm and its inhabitants are a small matter, but it may be as the spark which sets on fire the vast prairie.   It may prove to be Janet Geddes's ghost again, which once caused an entire revolution in Scotland—a revolution which bears its mark and produces its fruits to this moment, and, I hope, for ever, while sun and season endure, while men and women remain on its soil.   And here I would say without pretending to be a prophet, that whatever becomes of Leckmelm and its interests, whose fate so far as I can apprehend is already sealed (I must say through the supineness of the country and the indifference of our representatives in Parliament), I confidently hope that a campaign has been inaugurated which shall not be abandoned until the cruel and ravaging foe is routed for ever off the field, and a yoke of iron which neither we nor our fathers were able to bear, will be wrenched and snapped asunder and removed from the necks of our peasantry never more to be replaced, until the civilisation of the 19th century will give place to the barbarism of the original Britons.

Having referred at some length to the worst classes of evictions throughout the Highlands in the past, and already described in this work, the Reverend Lecturer proceeded :—

But there is another way, a more gentle, politic, and insinuating way at work which depopulates our country quite as effectually as the whole-sale clearances of which we have been speaking and against which we protest, and to which we must draw your attention for a little.   There are many proprietors who get the name of being good and kind to their tenants, and who cannot be charged with evicting any of them save for misbehaviour—a deserving cause at all times—who are never-theless inch by inch secretly and stealthily laying waste the country and undermining the well-being of our people.   I have some of these gentlemen before my mind at this moment.   When they took possession of their estates all promised fair and well, but by-and-bye the fatal blow was struck, to dispossess the people of their sheep.   Mark that *first move* and resist it to the utmost.   As long as tenants have a hold of the hill pasture by sheep, and especially if it be what we term a com-monage or club farm, it is impossible to lay it waste in part.   But once you snap this tie asunder, you are henceforth at the mercy of the owner to do with you as he pleases. This then is how the business is transacted and in the most business-like fashion too. To be sure none are to be forcibly evicted from their holdings : that would be highly impolitic, because it would bring public condemnation on the sacred heads of the evictors, which some of them could in no way confront, for they have a character and a name to sustain, and also because they are more susceptible to the failings common to humanity. They are moving too in the choicest circles of society. It would not do that their names should be figuring in every newspaper in the land, as cruel and oppressive landlords, or that the Rev. this and the Rev. that should excommunicate them from society and stigmatise them as tyrants and despots. But all are not so sensitive as this of name and character, as we see abundantly demonstrated, because they have none to lose. You might expose them upon a gibbet before the gaze of an assembled universe and they would hardly blush, "they are harder than the nether mill stone". But the more sensitive do their work, all the same, after all, and it is done in this fashion. When a tenant dies, or removes otherwise, the order goes forth that his croft or lot is to be laid waste. It is not given to a neighbouring tenant, except in some instances, nor to a stranger, to occupy it. In this inch by inch clearance, the work of depopulation is effected in a few years, or in a generation at most, quite as effectually as by the more glaring and reprehensible method. This more secret and insinuating way of depopulating our native land should be as stoutly resisted as the more open and defiant one, the result it produces being the same.

Describing the character of the Highlanders, as shown by their conduct in our Highland regiments, and the impossibility of recruiting from them in future, if harsh evictions are not stopped, the reverend gentleman continued :—

Let me give you words more eloquent than mine on this point, which will show the infatuation of our Government in allowing her bravest soldiers to be driven to foreign lands and to be crushed and oppressed by the tyrant's rod. After having asked, What have these people done against the state, when they were so remorselessly driven from their native shores, year by year in batches of thousands ? What class have they wronged that they should suffer a penalty so dreadful ? this writer gives the answer :—"They have done no wrong. Yearly they have sent forth their thousands from their glens to follow the battle flag of Britain wherever it flew. It was a Highland *rearlorn* hope that followed the broken wreck of Cumberland's army after the disastrous day at Fontenoy when more British soldiers lay dead upon the field than fell at Waterloo itself. It was another Highland regiment that scaled the rock-face over the St. Lawrence, and first formed a line in the September dawn on the level sward of Abraham. It was a Highland line that broke the power of the Maharatta hordes and gave Wellington his maiden victory at Assaye. Thirty-four battalions marched from these glens to fight in America, Germany, and India ere the 18th century had run its course; and yet, while abroad over the earth, Highlanders were the first in assault and the last in retreat, their lowly homes in far away glens were being dragged down, and the wail of women and the cry of children went out on the same breeze that bore too upon its wings the scent of heather, the freshness of gorse blossom, and the myriad sweets that made the lowly life of Scotland's peasantry blest with health and happiness. These are crimes done in the dark hours of strife, and amid the blaze of man's passions, that sometimes make the blood run cold as we read them; but they are not so terrible in their red-handed vengeance as the cold malignity of a civilised law, which permits a brave and noble race to disappear by the operation of its legalised injustice. To convert the Highland glens into vast wastes untenanted by human beings; to drive forth to distant and inhospitable shores men whose forefathers had held their own among these hills, despite Roman legion, Saxon archer, or Norman chivalry, men whose sons died freely for England's honour through those wide dominions their bravery had won for her. Such was the work of laws formed in a cruel mockery of name by the Commons of England. Thus it was, that about the year 1808 the stream of Highland soldiery which had been gradually ebbing, gave symptoms of running completely dry. Recruits for Highland regiments could not be obtained for the simple reason that the Highlands had been depopulated. Six regiments which from the date of their foundation had worn the kilt and bonnet were ordered to lay aside there distinctive uniform and henceforth became merged into the ordinary line corps. From the mainland the work of destruction passed rapidly to the isles. These remote resting places of the Celt were quickly cleared, during the first ten years of the great war, Skye had given 4000 of its sons to the army. It has been computed that 1600 Skyemen stood in the ranks at Waterloo. To-day in Skye, far as the eye can reach nothing but a bare brown waste is to be seen, where still the mounds and ruined gables rise over the melancholy landscapes, sole vestiges of a soldier race for ever passed away."

Again the same writer in speaking of the strength of the

rank and file of Irishmen and Scotchmen who were engaged in the Russian war in the year 1854, says :—

"Victorious in every fight, the army perished miserably from want. Then came frantic efforts to replace that stout rank and file that lay beneath the mounds on Cathcart's Hill, and at Scutari, but it could not be done. Men were indeed got together, but they were as unlike the stuff that had gone, as the sapling is unlike the forest tree." "Has the nation," he asks, "ever realised the full meaning of the failure to carry the Redan on the 8th of September? 'The old soldiers behaved admirably and stood by their officers to the last, but the young,' writes an onlooker, 'were deficient in discipline and in confidence in their officers.' He might have added more : They were the sweepings of the large crowded cities. It is in moments such as this, that the cabin on the hillside, the shieling in the Highland glen, become towers of strength to the nation that possesses them. It is in moments such as this that between the peasant-born soldier and the man who first saw light in a crowded court, between the coster and the cottier there comes that gulf which measures the distance between victory and defeat. Alma and Inkerman on the one side, the Redan on the 18th June and 8th September on the other." *

The question which confronts us now is, Is there any remedy for all this? Can the work of depopulation in the Highlands be reversed? We believe there is a remedy and that in a great measure the evil which has been done can be reversed. It was the opinion of a few far-seeing men among us, when the mania for monster sheep farms began, that they would have their day and that again the hand of providence would take another turn for the better. This was especially the opinion of old Lachlan Mackenzie, Lochcarron, a household name in the Highlands, who raised his powerful voice against the system of depopulation which then began by preaching a series of sermons from the 5th chapter of Isaiah, 8th v., "Woe unto them that join house to house and lay field to field, till there be no place that they may be placed alone in the midst of the earth. In mine ears said the Lord of Hosts of a truth many houses shall be desolate even great and fair without inhabitant." He said that the system would be altered, or that the sheep would be destroyed in a way that was not expected in Scotland. He did not take upon himself to determine the times or the seasons of the great alteration which he predicted. But when one, in private conversation, mentioned to him that many thousands of sheep had been lost in a snow

* Major W. S. Butler, in *MacMillan's Magazine* for May, 1878.

storm, and took occasion to say that Mr. Lachlan's predictions were thus in the way of being fulfilled, he replied, that it was not in this way that he anticipated a change; he was not looking to present appearances—it was neither the snow of winter nor such heat as would dry the tongue of the raven that would bring deliverance from the system of oppression and grinding the face of the poor. But added he, if the people would be earnest and faithful in prayer, the deliverance will come sooner than it arrived to the children of Israel in Babylon. This was said in the year 1816, when the new leases were making great changes in Lochcarron.

These words which seem to have been delivered in a prophetic strain are now beginning to be fulfilled. It is felt on every side that monster farms are not the thing after all, and that smaller holdings are more profitable to the owner of the soil, as well as more beneficial to the nation at large. The hand of Him who guides the stars seems to fight against them in the seasons and in various ways; among others in the competition of foreign markets—in the increased quantities of preserved meat from America and Australia. From all these causes, it is evident that the days of unwieldy farms are numbered, and as for the deer forests, I hope they have received their death blow, as a certain member of Parliament remarked, in the Hares and Rabbits Bill.

Mr. MacMillan concluded by an eloquent appeal to his brother ministers of religion to rouse themselves and oppose their influence to the tyranny of the strong and powerful in their grinding and heartless conduct towards the poor and the weak; after which he received the unanimous thanks of one of the largest, as well as one of the most enthusiastic meetings ever held in the capital of the Highlands.

In January, 1882, news had reached Inverness that Murdo Munro, one of the most comfortable tenants on the Leckmelm property had been turned out, with his wife and young family in the snow; whereupon the writer started to enquire into the facts, and spent a whole day among the people. What he had seen proved to be as bad as any of the evictions of the past, except that it applied in this instance only to one family. Murdo Munro was too independent for the local managers, and to some extent led the people in their opposition to Mr. Pirie's proceedings : he was first persecuted and afterwards evicted in the most cruel fashion. Other reasons were afterwards given for the manner in which this poor man and his family were treated, but it has been shown conclusively, in a report published at the time, that these reasons were an after-thought.* From this report we shall quote a few extracts : —

So long as the laws of the land permit men like Mr. Pirie to drive from the soil, without compensation, the men who, by their labour and money, made their properties what they are, it must be admitted that he is acting within his legal rights, however much we may deplore the manner in which he has chosen to exercise them. We have to deal more with the system which allows him to act thus, than with the special reasons which he considers sufficient to justify his proceedings ; and if his conduct in Leckmelm will, as I trust it may, hasten on a change in our land legislation, the hardships endured by the luckless people who had the misfortune to come under his unfeeling yoke, and his ideas of moral right and wrong, will be more than counterbalanced by the benefits which will in consequence ultimately accrue to the people at large. This is why I, and, I believe, the public take such an interest in this question of the evictions at Leckmelm.

I have made the most careful and complete inquiry possible among Mr. Pirie's servants, the tenants, and the people of Ullapool. Mr. Pirie's local manager, after I had informed him of my object, and put him on his guard as to the use which I might make of his answers, informed me that he never had any fault to find with Munro, that he always found him quite civil, and that he had nothing to say against him. The tenants, without exception, spoke of him as a good neighbour. The people of Ullapool, without exception, so far as I could discover, after inquiries from the leading men in every section of the community, speak well of him, and condemn Mr. Pirie. Munro is universally spoken of as one of the best and most industrious workmen in the whole parish, and, by his industry and sobriety, he has been able to save a little money in Leckmelm, where he was able to keep a fairly good stock on his small farm, and worked steadily with a horse and cart. The stock handed over by him to Mr. Pirie consisted of 1 bull, 2 cows,

* See Pamphlet published at the time entitled *Report on the Leckmelm Evictions, by Alexander Mackenzie, F.S.A. Scot., Editor of the " Celtic Magazine," and Dean of Guild of Inverness.*

1 stirk, 1 Highland pony, and about 40 sheep, which represented a considerable saving. Several of the other tenants had a similar stock, and some of them had even more, all of which they had to dispense with under the new arràngements, and consequently lost the annual income in money and produce available therefrom. We all know that the sum received for this stock cannot last long, and cannot be advantageously invested in anything else. The people must now live on their small capital, instead of what it produced, so long as it lasts, after which they are sure to be helpless, and many of them become chargeable to the parish.

The system of petty tyranny which prevails at Leckmelm is scarcely credible. Contractors have been told not to employ Munro. For this I have the authority of some of the contractors themselves. Local employers of labour were requested not to employ any longer people who had gone to look on among the crowd, while Munro's family, goods, and furniture, were being turned out. Letters were received by others complaining of the same thing from higher quarters, and threatening ulterior consequences. Of all this I have the most complete evidence, but in the interests of those involved I shall mention no names, except in Court, where I challenge Mr. Pirie and his subordinates to the proof if they deny it.

.   .   .   .

The extract in the action of removal was signed only on the 24th of January last in Dingwall. On the following day the charge is dated, and two days after, on the 27th of January, the eviction is complete. When I visited the scene on Friday morning I found a substantially built cottage, and a stable at the end of it, unroofed to within three feet of the top on either side, and the whole surroundings a perfect scene of desolation ; the thatch, and part of the furniture, including portions of broken bedsteads, tubs, basins, teapots, and various other articles, strewn outside. The cross-beams, couples, and cabars were still there, a portion of the latter bought from Mr. Pirie's manager, and paid for within the last three years. The Sheriff-officers had placed a padlock on the door, but I made my way to the inside of the house through one of the windows from which the frame and glass had been removed. I found that the house, before the partitions had been removed, consisted of two good sized rooms and a closet, with a fireplace and chimney in each gable, the crook still hanging in one of them, the officer having apparently been unable to remove it after a considerable amount of wrenching. The kitchen window, containing eight panes of glass, was still whole, but the closet window, with four panes, had been smashed ; while the one in the "ben" end of the house had been removed. The cottage, as crofters' houses go, must have been fairly comfortable. Indeed, the cottages in Leckmelm are altogether superior to the usual run of crofters' houses on the West Coast, and the tenants are allowed to have been the most comfortable in all respects in the parish, before the land was taken from them. They are certainly not the poor, miserable creatures, badly housed, which Mr. Pirie and his friends led the public to believe within the last two years.

The barn, in which the wife and infant had to remain all night, had the upper part of both gables blown out by the recent storm, and the door was scarcely any protection from the weather. The potatoes, which had been thrown out in showers of snow, were still there, gathered, and a little earth put over them by the friendly neighbours.

The mother and children wept piteously during the eviction, and many of the neighbours, afraid to succour or shelter them, were visibly affected to tears ; and the whole scene was such that, if Mr. Pirie could have seen it, I feel sure that he would never consent to be held responsible for another. His humanity would soon drive his stern ideas of legal right out of his head, and we would hear no more of evictions at Leckmelm.

Those of the tenants who are still at Leckmelm are permitted to remain in their cottages as half-yearly tenants on payment of 12s. per annum, but liable to be removed at any moment that their absolute lord may take it into his head to evict them; or, what is much more precarious, when they may give the slightest offence to any of his meanest subordinates.

LOCHCARRON.

The following account was written in April, 1882, after a most careful enquiry on the spot :—So much whitewash has been distributed in our Northern newspapers of late by " Local Correspondents," in the interest of personal friends who are responsible for the Lochcarron evictions—the worst and most indefensible that have ever been attempted even in the Highlands—that we consider it a duty to state the actual facts. We are really sorry for those more immediately concerned, but our friendly feeling for them otherwise cannot be allowed to come between us and our plain duty. A few days before the famous "Battle of the Braes," in the Isle of Skye, we received information that summonses of ejectment were served on Mackenzie and Maclean, Lochcarron. The writer at once communicating with Mr. Dugald Stuart, the proprietor, intimating to him the statements received, and asking him if they were accurate, and if Mr. Stuart had anything to say in explanation of them. Mr. Stuart immediately replied, admitting the accuracy of the statements generally, but maintaining that he had good and valid reasons for carrying out the evictions, which he expressed himself anxious to explain to us on the following day, while passing through Inverness on his way South. Unfortunately, his letter reached us too late, and we were unable to see him. The only reason which he vouchsafed to give in his letter was to the following effect :—"Was it at all likely that he, a Highlander, born and brought up in the Highlands, the son of a Highlander, and married to a Highland lady, would be guilty of evicting any of his tenants without good cause?" We replied that, unfortunately, all these reasons could be urged by most of those who had in the past depopulated the country, but expressing a hope that, in his case, the facts stated by him would prove sufficient to restrain him from carrying out his determination to evict parents admittedly innocent of their sons' proceedings, even if those proceedings were unjustifiable. The day immediately preceding the "Battle of the Braes" we proceeded to Lochcarron to make enquiry on the spot, and the writer on his return from Skye a few days later, reported as follows to the Highland Land Law Reform Association :—

"Of all the cases of eviction which have hitherto come

under my notice I never heard of any so utterly unjustifiable as those now in course of being carried out by Mr. D. Stuart in Lochcarron. The circumstances which led up to these evictions are as follows :—In March, 1881, two young men, George Mackenzie and Donald Maclean, masons, entered into a contract with Mr. Stuart's ground-officer for the erection of a sheep fank, and a dispute afterwards arose as to the payment for the work. When the factor, Mr. Donald Macdonald, Tormore, was some time afterwards collecting the rents in the district, the contracters approached him and related their grievance against the ground-officer, who, while the men were in the room, came in and addressed them in libellous and defamatory language, for which they have since obtained substantial damages and expenses, in all amounting to £22 13s. 8d., in the Sheriff Court of the County. I have a certified copy of the whole proceedings in Court in my possession, and, without going into the merits, what I have just stated is the result, and Mr. Stuart and his ground-officer became furious.

" The contractors are two single men who live with their parents, the latter being crofters on Mr. Stuart's property, and as the real offenders—if such can be called men who have stood up for and succeeded in establishing their rights and their characters in Court—could not be got at, Mr. Stuart issued summonses of ejection against their parents— parents who, in one of the cases at least, strongly urged his son not to proceed against the ground-officer, pointing out to him that an eviction might possibly ensue, and that it was better even to suffer in character and purse than run the risk of eviction from his holding at the age of eighty. We have all heard of the doctrine of visiting the sins of the parents upon the children, but it has been left for Mr. Dugald Stuart of Lochcarron and his ground-officer, in the present generation—the highly-favoured nineteenth century—to reverse all this, and to punish the unoffending parents, for proceedings on the part of their children which the Sheriff of the County and all unprejudiced people who know the facts consider fully justifiable.

"Now, so far as I can discover, after careful enquiry among the men's neighbours and in the village of Lochcarron, nothing can be said against either of them. Their characters are in every respect above suspicion. The ground-officer, whom I have seen, admits all this, and makes no pretence that the eviction is for any other reason than the conduct of the young men in prosecuting and succeeding against himself in the Sheriff Court for defamation of character. Maclean paid rent for his present holding for the last 60 years, and never failed to pay it on the appointed day. His father, grandfather, and great-grandfather occupied the same place, and so did their ancestors before them. Indeed, his grandfather held one-half of the township, now occupied by more than a hundred people. The old man is in his 81st year, and bed-ridden—on his death-bed in fact—since the middle of January last, he having then had a paralytic stroke from which it is quite impossible he can ever recover. It was most pitiable to see the aged and frail human wreck as I saw him that day, and to have heard him talking of the cruelty and hard-heartedness of those who took advantage of the existing law to push him out of the home which he has occupied so long, while he is already on the brink of eternity. I quite agreed with him, and I have no hesitation in saying that if Mr. Stuart and his ground-officer only called to see the miserable old man, as I did, their hearts, however adamantine, would melt, and they would at once declare to him that he would be allowed to end his days and die in peace, under the roof which for generations had sheltered himself and his ancestors. The wife is over 70 years of age, and the frail old couple have no one to succour them but the son who has been the cause, by defending his own character, of their present misfortunes. Whatever Mr. Stuart and his ground-officer may do, or attempt to do, the old man will not, and cannot be evicted until he is carried to the churchyard ; and it would be far more gracious on their part to relent and allow the old man to die in peace.

"Mackenzie has paid rent for over 40 years, and his ancestors have done so for several generations before him. He is nearly sixty years of age, and is highly popular among his neighbours all of whom are intensely grieved at Mr. Stuart's cruel and hard-hearted conduct towards him and Maclean, and they still hope that he will not proceed to extremities.

"The whole case is a lamentable abuse of the existing law, and such as will do more to secure its abolition, when the facts are fully known, than all the other cases of eviction which have taken place in the Highlands during the present generation. There is no pretence that the case is anything else than a gross and cruel piece of retaliation against the innocent parents for conduct on the part of the sons which must have been very aggravating to this proprietor and his ground-officer, who appear to think themselves fully justified in perpetuating such acts of grossest cruelty and injustice— acts which indeed I dare not characterise as they deserve— but conduct which on the part of the young men has been fully justified and sustained by the courts of the country, and for which the son of a late Vice-Chancellor of England ought to have some respect."

This report was slightly noticed at the time in the local and Glasgow newspapers, and attention was thus directed to

Mr. Stuart's proceedings. His whole conduct appeared so cruelly tyrannical that most people expected him to relent before the day of eviction arrived. But not so: a sheriff-officer and his assistants from Dingwall duly arrived, and proceeded to turn Mackenzie's furniture out of the house. People congregated from all parts of the district, some of them coming more than twenty miles. The sheriff-officer sent for the Lochcarron policemen to aid him, but, notwithstanding, the law which admitted of such unmitigated cruelty and oppression was set at defiance; the sheriff-officers were deforced, and the furniture returned to the house by the sympathising crowd. What was to be done next? The Procurator-Fiscal for the county was Mr. Stuart's law agent in carrying out the evictions. How could he criminally prosecute for deforcement in these circumstances? The Crown authorities found themselves in a dilemma, and through the tyranny of the proprietor on the one hand, and the interference of the Procurator-Fiscal in civil business which has ended in public disturbance and deforcement of the Sheriff's officers, on the other, the Crown authorities found themselves helpless to vindicate the law. This is a pity; for all right thinking people have almost as little sympathy for law breakers, even when that law is unjust and cruel, as they have for those cruel landlords who, like Mr. Stuart of Lochcarron, bring the law and his own order into disrepute by the oppressive application of it against innocent people. The proper remedy is to have the law abolished, not to break it; and to bring this about such conduct as that of Mr. Stuart and his ground officer is more potent than all the Land Leagues and Reform Associations in the United Kingdom.*

Mr. William Mackenzie of the *Free Press*, who was on the

* *Celtic Magazine* for July, 1882.

ground, writes, next morning, after the deforcement of the sheriff-officers :—

" During the encounter the local police constable drew his baton, but he was peremptorily ordered to lay it down, and he did so. The officers then gave up the contest; and left the place about three in the morning. Yesterday, before they left, and in course of the evening, they were offered refreshments, but these they declined. The people are this evening in possession as before.

"When every article was restored to its place, the song and the dance were resumed, the native drink was freely quaffed —for ' freedom an' whisky gang thegither '—the steam was kept up throughout the greater part of yesterday, and Mackenzie's mantelpiece to-day is adorned with a long tier of empty bottles, standing there as monuments of the eventful night of the 29th-30th May, 1882.

> A chuirm sgaoilte chualas an ceòl
> Ard-shòlas an talla nan treun !

" While these things were going on in the quiet township of Slumbay, the Fiery Cross appears to have been despatched over the neighbouring parishes; and from Kintail, Lochalsh, Applecross, and even Gairloch, the Highlanders began to gather yesterday with the view of helping the Slumbay men, if occasion should arise. Few of these reached Slumbay, but they were in small detachments in the neighbourhood ready at any moment to come to the rescue on the appearance of any hostile force. After all the trains had come and gone for the day, and as neither policemen nor Sheriff's officers had appeared on the scene, these different groups retired to their respective places of abode. The Slumbay men, too, resolved to suspend their festivities. A procession was formed, and, being headed by the piper, they marched triumphantly through Slumbay and Jeantown, and escorted some of the strangers on their way to their homes, returning to Slumbay in course of the night."

As a contrast to Mr. Stuart's conduct we are glad to record the noble action of Mr. C. J. Murray, M.P. for Hastings, who has fortunately for the oppressed tenants on the Lochcarron property, just purchased the estate. He has made it a condition that Maclean and Mackenzie shall be allowed to remain; and a further public scandal has thus been avoided. This is a good beginning for the new proprietor, and we trust to see his action as widely circulated and commended as the tyrannical proceedings of his predecessor have been condemned.

It is also fair to state what we know on the very best authority, namely, that the factor on the estate, Mr. Donald Macdonald, Tormore, strongly urged upon Mr. Stuart not to evict these people, and that his own wife also implored and begged of him not to carry out his cruel and vindictive purpose. Where these agencies failed, it is gratifying to find that Mr. Murray has succeeded; and all parties—landlords and tenants—throughout the Highlands are to be congratulated on the result.

THE 78TH HIGHLANDERS.

IN connection with the evictions from the County of Ross, the following will appropriately come in at this stage. Referring to the glorious deeds of the 78th Highlanders in India, under General Havelock, the editor of the *Northern Ensign* writes:—All modern history, from the rebellion in 1715, to the Cawnpore massacre in 1857, teems with the record of Highland bravery and prowess. What say our Highland evicting lairds to these facts, and to the treatment of the Highlanders? What reward have these men received for saving their country, fighting its battles, conquering its enemies, turning the tide of revolt, rescuing women and children from the hands of Indian fiends, and establishing order, when disorder and bloody cruelty have held their murderous carnival? And we ask, in the name of men who have, ere now, we fondly hope, saved our gallant country-men and heroic countrywomen at Lucknow; in the name of those who fought in the trenches of Sebastopol, and proudly planted the British standard on the heights of the Alma, how are they, their fathers, brothers, and little ones treated? Is the mere shuttle-cocking of an irrepressible cry of admira-tion from mouth to mouth, and the setting to music of a song in their praise, all the return the race is to get for such noble acts? We can fancy the expression of admiration of High-land bravery at the Dunrobin dinner table, recently, when the dukes, earls, lairds, and other aristocratic notables en-joyed the princely hospitality of the Duke. We can imagine the mutual congratulations of the Highland lairds as they prided themselves on being proprietors of the soil which gave birth to the race of "Highland heroes". Alas, for the blush that would cover their faces if they would allow them-selves to reflect that, in their names, and by their authority, and at their expense, the fathers, mothers, brothers, wives, of the invincible "78th" have been remorselessly driven from their native soil; and that, at the very hour when Cawnpore was gallantly retaken, and the ruffian Nana Sahib was obliged to leave the bloody scene of his fiendish massacre, there were Highlanders, within a few miles of the princely Dunrobin, driven from their homes and left to starve and to die in the open field. Alas, for the blush that would reprint its scarlet dye on their proud faces as they thought in one county alone, since Waterloo was fought, more than 14,000 of this same "race of heroes" of whom Canning so proudly boasted, have been haunted out of their native homes ; and that where the pibroch and the bugle once evoked the martial spirit of thousands of brave hearts, razed and burning cottages have formed the tragic scenes of eviction and desolation ; and the abodes of a loyal and a liberty-loving people are made sacred to the rearing of sheep, and sanctified to the preservation of game ! Yes ; we echo back the cry, "Well done, brave Highlanders !" But to what purpose would it be carried on the wings of the wind to the once happy straths and glens of Sutherland ? Who, what, would echo back our acclaims of praise ? Perhaps a shepherd's or a gillie's child, playing amid the unbroken wilds, and innocent of seeing a human face but that of its own parents, would hear it ; or the cry might startle a herd of timid deer, or frighten a covey of partridges, or call forth a bleat from a herd of sheep ; but men, would not, could not, hear it. We must go to the backwoods of Canada, to Detroit, to Hamilton, to Woodstock, to Toronto, to Montreal ; we must stand by the waters of Lake Huron, or Lake Ontario, where the cry—"Well done, brave High-landers !" would call up a thousand brawny fellows, and draw down a tear on a thousand manly cheeks. Or we must go to the bare rocks that skirt the sea-coast of Suther-land, where the residuary population were generously treated to barren steeps and inhospitable shores, on which to keep up the breed of heroes, and fight for the men who dared—*dared*—to drive them from houses for which they fought, and from land, which was purchased with the blood of their fathers. But the cry, "Well done, brave High-landers," would evoke no effective response from the race. Need the reader wonder ? Wherefore should they fight ? To what purpose did their fathers climb the Peninsular heights, and gloriously write in blood the superiority of Britain, when their sons were rewarded by extirpation, or toleration to starve, in sight of fertile straths and glens devoted to beasts? These are words of truth and soberness. They are but repetitions in other forms of arguments, employed by us for years; and we shall continue to ring changes on them so long as our brave Highland people are subjected to treatment to which no other race would have submitted. We are no alarmists. But we tell Highland proprietors that were Britain some twenty years hence to have the misfortune to be plunged into such a crisis as the present, there will be few such men as the Highlanders of the 78th to fight her battles, and that the country will find when too late, if another policy towards the Highlanders is not adopted, that sheep and deer, ptarmigan and grouse, can do but little to save it in such a calamity.

The Rev. Dr. JOHN KENNEDY.

DR. JOHN KENNEDY, the highly, deservedly respected, and eminent minister of Dingwall, so long resident among the scenes which he describes, and so intimately acquainted with all classes of the people in his native County of Ross, informs us that it was at a time when the Highlanders became most distinguished as the most peaceable and virtuous peasantry in the world—"at the climax of their spiritual prosperity," in Ross-shire—"that the cruel work of eviction began to lay waste the hill-sides and the plains of the north. Swayed by the example of the godly among them, and away from the influences by which less sequestered localities were corrupted, the body of the people in the Highlands became distinguished as the most peaceable and virtuous peasantry in Britain. It was just then that they began to be driven off by ungodly oppressors, to clear their native soil for strangers, red deer, and sheep. With few exceptions, the owners of the soil began to act, as if they were also owners of the people, and, disposed to regard them as the vilest part of their estate, they treated them without respect to the requirements of righteousness or to the dictates of mercy. Without the inducement of gain, in the recklessness of cruelty, families by hundreds were driven across the sea, or gathered, as the sweepings of the hill-sides, into wretched hamlets on the shore. By wholesale evictions, wastes were formed for the red deer, that the gentry of the nineteenth century might indulge in the sports of the savages of three centuries before. Of many happy households sheep walks were cleared for strangers, who, fattening amidst the ruined homes of the banished, corrupted by their example the few natives who remained. Meanwhile their rulers, while deaf to the Highlanders' cry of oppression, were wasting their sinews and their blood on battle-fields, that, but for their prowess and their bravery, would have been the scene of their country's defeat." *

Mr. CHARLES INNES.

Mr. Charles Innes is a Tory of the bluest type. He is the Conservative agent for the county of Inverness, Sheriff-Clerk for the County of Ross; Secretary for the Northern Tory Newspaper and Printing Company; and general Organiser for the Tory landowners of the North of Scotland. Such a position gives peculiar interest to any

*The Days of the Fathers in Ross-shire, 1861, pp. 15-16.

opinions he may express on a question like this. In July, 1874, he had occasion to defend some of the Bernera crofters, in the Lews, who were tried on a charge of deforcing a sheriff-officer. A Report of the trial was afterwards published, in pamphlet form, containing the speech delivered by Mr. Innes on the occasion, and, it is understood, revised and edited by his own hand. The late Chamberlain of the Lews, it will be remembered, resolved to evict the tenants, since known as "the Bernera Rioters". The sheriff-officer who went to serve the notices of ejectment on them met with a reception which the Crown authorities in the person of the Chamberlain himself, who was also Procurator-Fiscal of the district, construed into the serious charge of deforcement, and the crofters were duly tried for that grave offence. Addressing the jury on their behalf, Mr. Innes eloquently declared that :—

" Love of Fatherland is a feeling which is implanted in the breasts of all men, and in none more so than those in whose veins Celtic blood flows. If, then, gentlemen, that sentiment and that feeling animates you—as I am sure it does—you can, when you think of it, readily understand that love of country not only may be, but is, as strongly felt by these poor men. You can understand what a wrench their heartstrings must receive when 'notice to quit' is served upon them without good cause. Their houses may be mere mud huts, but still they are their homes, and were the homes of their forefathers for many generations; and, however humble they are, there is, and ever will be, for them a venerated halo of fond and loving memories floating around them. So long as such men pay their rents with regularity; so long as they conduct themselves decently and with propriety; so long as they are wishful to remain in possession—I say that the man who summarily, without cause, and, in the face of an under-standing to the contrary, removes them, or attempts to remove them, from the soil on which they were reared, and which they cultivate, and turns them adrift on the cold world, IS NOT A FRIEND OF HIS COUNTRY."

The result was that the so-called " rioters" were dis-missed; their proposed eviction was brought under the notice of their humane proprietor, the late Sir James Matheson of the Lews, Baronet, and they are still in pos-session of their holdings; while the Chamberlain who tried to evict them was shortly after dismissed from his position as virtual king of the Island principality of the Lews, and soon after deprived of the office of Procurator-Fiscal for the district.

COUNTY OF PERTH.

ATHOL.

DONALD MACLEOD, referring to the evictions from this district, says :—"A Duke of Athol can, with propriety, claim the origin of the Highland clearances. Whatever merit the family of Sutherland may take to themselves for the fire and the faggot expulsion of the people from the glens of Sutherland, they cannot claim the merit of originality. The present [6th] Duke of Athol's grandfather cleared Glen Tilt, so far as I can learn, in 1784. This beautiful valley was occupied in the same way as other Highland valleys, each family possessing a piece of arable land, while the pasture was held in common. The people held a right and full liberty to fish in the Tilt, an excellent salmon river, and the pleasure and profits of the chase, with their chief ; but the then Duke acquired a great taste for deer. The people were, from time immemorial, accustomed to take their cattle, in the summer season, to a higher glen, which is watered by the river Tarf ; but the Duke appointed Glen Tarf for a deer-forest, and built a high dyke at the head of Glen Tilt. The people submitted to this encroachment on their ancient rights. The deer increased and did not pay much regard to the march ; they would jump over the dyke and destroy the people's crops ; the people complained, and his grace rejoiced ; and to gratify the raving propensities of these light-footed animals, he added another slice of some thousand acres of the people's land to the grazing ground of his favourite deer. Gradually the forest extended, and the marks of civilisation were effaced, till the last of the brave Glen Tilt men, who fought and often confronted and defeated the enemies of Scotland and her kings upon many a bloody battle-field were routed off, and bade a final farewell to the beautiful Glen Tilt, which they and their fathers had considered their own healthy and sweet home. An event occurred at this period, according to history, which afforded a pretext to the Duke for this heartless extirpation of the aborigines of Glen Tilt. Highland chieftains elsewhere were exhibiting their patriotism by raising regiments to serve in the American War, and the Duke of Athol could not be indifferent in such a cause. Great efforts were made to enlist the Glen Tilt people, who are still remembered in the district as a strong, athletic race. Perpetual possession of their lands, at their existing rents, was promised them, if they would raise a contingent force equal to a man from each family. Some consented, but the majority, with a praiseworthy resolution not to be dragged at the tail of a chief into a war of which they knew neither the beginning nor the end, refused. The Duke flew into a rage, and press-gangs were sent up the glen to carry off the young men by force. One of these companies seized a cripple tailor, who lived at the foot of Beneygloe, and afraid lest he might carry intelligence of their approach up the glen, they bound him, hand and foot, and left him lying on the cold hill-side, where he contracted disease from which he never recovered. By impressment and violence the regiment was at length raised; and when peace was proclaimed, instead of restoring the soldiers to their friends and their homes, the Duke, as if he had been a trafficker in slaves, was only prevented from selling them to the East Indian Company by the mutiny of the regiment. He afterwards pretended great offence at the Glen Tilt people for their obstinacy in refusing to enlist, and it may now be added—to be sold. Their conduct in this affair was given out as the reason why he cleared them out from the glen—an excuse which, in the present day, may increase our admiration of the people, but can never palliate the heartlessness of his conduct. His ireful policy, however, has taken full effect. The romantic Glen Tilt, with its fertile holms and verdant steeps, is little better than a desert. The very deer rarely visit it, and the wasted grass is burned like heather, at the beginning of the year, to make room for the new verdure. On the spot where I found the grass most luxuriant, I traced the seats of thirty cottages, and have no hesitation in saying, that under skill, the industrious habits, and the agricultural facilities, of the present day, the land, once occupied by the tenants of Glen Tilt, is capable of maintaining a thousand people and have a large proportion of sheep and cattle for exportation besides. In the meantime it serves no better purpose than the occasional playground of the Duke, to whom Pope's lines are most appropriate :—

> Proud Nimrod first the bloody chase began,
> A mighty hunter—and his prey was man.
> Our haughty Norman boasts the barbarous name,
> And makes his trembling slaves the royal game,
> The fields are ravished from industrious swains,
> From men their cities, and from gods their fanes.
> In vain kind seasons swell the beaming grain,
> Soft showers, distilled, and suns grow warm in vain ;
> The swain with tears, his prostrate labours yields,
> And, famished, dies amidst his ripening fields.
> What wonder then a beast or subject slain
> Were equal crimes in a despotic reign ?
> Both, doomed alike, for sportive tyrants bled ;
> But while the subject starved, the beast was fed.

" The Glens of Athol are intersected by smaller valleys, presenting various aspects, from the most fertile carse to the bleakest moorland. But man durst not be seen there. The image of God is forbidden unless it be stamped upon the Duke, his foresters, and gamekeepers, that the deer may not be disturbed."

In 1841 the Parish of Blair Athol had a population of 2231 ; in 1881 it was reduced to 1742, notwithstanding the great increase in Blair Athol and other rising villages.

———

RANNOCH.

Regarding the state of matters in this district a correspondent writes us as follows :—I am very glad to learn that you are soon to publish a new edition of your " Highland Clearances," with Macleod's " Gloomy Memories " included. You have done good work already in rousing the conscience of the public against the conduct of certain landlords in the Highlands, who long ere now should have been held up to public scorn and execration, as the best means of deterring others from pursuing a policy which has been so fatal to the best interests of our beloved land. . . . . And now, if I am not too late, I should like to direct your attention to a few authenticated facts connected with two districts in the Highlands that I am familiar with, and which facts you may utilise, though I shall merely give notes.

In 1851, the population of the district known as the Quod Sacra parish of Rannoch numbered altogether 1800 ; at last Census it was below 900. Even in 1851 it was not nearly what it was earlier. Why this constant decrease ?

Several no doubt left the district voluntarily; but the great bulk of those who left were evicted.

Take the Slios Mìn, north side of Loch Rannoch, first. Fifty years ago the farm of Ardlarich, near the west end, was tenanted by three farmers who were in good circumstances. These were turned out, to make room for one large farmer, who was rouped out last year, penniless; and the farm is now tenantless. The next place, further east, is the township of Killichoan, containing about thirty to forty houses, with small crofts attached to each. The crofters here are very comfortable and happy, and their houses and crofts are models of what industry, thrift, and good taste can effect. Further east is the farm of Liaran, now tenantless. Fifty years ago it was farmed by seven tenants who were turned out to make room for one man, and that at a lower rent than was paid by the former tenants. Further, in the same direction, there are Aulich, Craganour, and Annat, every one of them tenantless. These three farms, lately in the occupation of one tenant, and for which he paid a rental of £900, at one time maintained fifty to sixty families in comfort, all of whom have vanished, or were virtually banished from their native land.

It is only right to say that the present proprietor is not responsible for the eviction of any of the smaller tenants; the deed was done before he came into possession. On the contrary, he is very kind to his crofter tenantry, but unfortunately for him he inherits the fruits of a bad policy, which has been the ruin of the Rannoch estates.

Then take the Slios Garbh, south-side of Loch Rannoch. Beginning in the west-end, we have Georgetown, which, about fifty years ago, contained twenty-five or twenty-six houses, every one of which were knocked down by the late Laird of Struan, and the people evicted. The crofters of

Finnart were ejected in the same way. Next comes the township of Camghouran, a place pretty similar to Killichoan, but smaller. The people are very industrious, cleanly, and fairly comfortable, reflecting much credit upon themselves and the present proprietor. Next comes Dall, where there used to be a number of tenants, but now in the hands of the proprietor, an Englishman. The estate of Innerhaden, comes next. It used to be divided into ten lots—two held by the laird, and eight by as many tenants. The whole is now in the hands of one family. The rest of Bun-Rannoch includes the estates of Dalchosnie, Lassin-tullich, and Crossmount, where there used to be a large number of small tenants—most of them well-to-do—but now held by five.

Lastly, take the north side of the river Dubhag, which flows out from Loch Rannoch, and is erroneously called the Tummel. Kinloch, Druimchurn, and Druimchaisteil, always in the hands of three tenants, are now held by one. Druma-glass contains a number of small holdings, with good houses on many of them. Balmore, which always had six tenants in it, has now only one, the remaining portion of it being laid out in grass parks. Ballintuim, with a good house upon it, is tenantless. Auchitarsin, where there used to be twenty houses, is now reduced to four. The whole district from, and including, Kinloch to Auchitarsin belongs to General Sir Alastair Macdonald of Dalchosnie, Commander of Her Majesty's Forces in Scotland. His father, Sir John, during his life, took a great delight in having a numerous, thriving, and sturdy tenantry on the estates of Dalchosnie, Kinloch, Lochgarry, Dunalastair, and Morlaggan. On one occasion his tenant of Dalchosnie offered to take from Sir John on lease all the land on the north side of the river. "Ay man," said he, "You would take all that land, would you, and turn out all my people ! Who would I get, if my house took fire, to put it out ?"

The present proprietor has virtually turned out the great bulk of those that Sir John had loved so well. Though, it is said, he did not evict any man directly, he is alleged to have made their positions so hot for them that they had to leave. Sir John could have raised hundreds of Volunteers on his estates—men who would have died for the gallant old soldier. But how many could be now raised by his son? Not a dozen men ; though he goes about inspecting Volunteers, and praising the movement officially throughout the length and breadth of Scotland.

The author of the *New Statistical Account*, writing of the Parish of Fortingall, of which the district referred to by our correspondent forms a part, says : " At present [1838] no part of the parish is more populous than it was in 1790; whereas in several districts, the population has since decreased one half ; and the same will be found to have taken place, though not perhaps in so great a proportion, in most or all of the pastoral districts of the County ".

According to the Census of 1801 the population was   . 3875.
    ,,   ,,   ,, ,, 1811 ,,   ,,   ,,   . 3236.
    ,,   ,,   ,, ,, 1821 ,,   ,,   ,,   . 3189.
    ,,   ,,   ,, ,, 1831 ,,   ,,   ,,   . 3067.
In 1881 it was reduced to   .   .   .   .   .   . 1690.

Upwards of 120 families, the same writer says, " crossed the Atlantic from this parish, since the previous Account was drawn up [in 1791], besides many individuals of both sexes ; while many others have sought a livelihood in the Low Country, especially in the great towns of Edinburgh, Glasgow, Dundee, Perth, Crieff, and others. The system of uniting several farms together, and letting them to one individual has more than any other circumstance" produced this result.

———

BREADALBANE.

Mr. R. Alister, author of *Barriers to the National Prosperity of Scotland*, had a controversy with the Marquis of Breadalbane in 1853 about the eviction of his tenantry. In a letter dated July, of that year, Mr. Alister made a charge against his Lordship which, for obvious reasons, he never attempted to answer, as follows:—"Your Lordship states that in reality there has been no depopulation of the district. This, and other parts of your Lordship's letter, would certainly lead any who know nothing of the facts to suppose that there had been no clearings on the Breadalbane estates; whereas it is generally believed that your Lordship removed, since 1834, no less than 500 families! Some may think this a small matter; but I do not. I think it is a great calamity for a family to be thrown out, destitute of the means of life, without a roof over their heads, and cast upon the wide sea of an unfeeling world. In Glenqueich, near Amulree, some sixty families formerly lived, where there are now only four or five; and in America, there is a glen inhabited by its ousted tenants, and called Glenqueich still. Yet, forsooth, it is maintained there has been no depopulation here! The desolations here look like the ruins of Irish cabins, although the population of Glenqueich were always characterized as being remarkably thrifty, economical, and wealthy. On the Braes of Taymouth, at the back of Drummond Hill, and at Tullochyoule, some forty or fifty families formerly resided where there is not one now!

Glenorchy, by the returns of 1831, showed a population of 1806; in 1841, 831;—is there no depopulation there? Is it true that in Glenetive there were sixteen tenants a year or two ago, where there is not a single one now? Is it true, my Lord, that you purchased an island on the west coast, called Ling, where some twenty-five families lived at the beginning *of this year*, but who are now cleared off to make room for one tenant, for whom an extensive steading is now being erected! If my information be correct, I shall allow the public to draw their own conclusions; but, from every thing that I have heard, I believe that your Lordship has done more to exterminate the Scottish peasantry than any man now living; and perhaps you ought to be ranked next to the Marquis of Stafford in the uneviable clearing celebrities. If I have over-estimated the clearances at 500 families, please to correct me." As we have already said, his Lordship thought it prudent, and by far the best policy, not to make the attempt.

In another letter the same writer says:—" You must be aware that your late father raised 2300 men during the last war, and that 1600 of that number were from the Breadalbane estates. My statement is, that 150 could not *now* be raised. Your Lordship has most carefully evaded all allusion to this,—perhaps the worst charge of the whole. From your Lordship's silence I am surely justified in concluding that you may endeavour to evade the question, but you dare not attempt an open contradiction. I have often made inquiries of Highlanders on this point, and the number above stated was the *highest* estimate. Many who should know, state to me that your Lordship would not get *fifty* followers from the whole estates ; and another says:—" Why, he would not get half-a-dozen, and not one of them unless they could not possibly do otherwise ". This, then, is the position of the question; in 1793-4, there was such a numerous, hardy, and industrious population on the Breadalbane estates, that there could be spared of valorous defenders of their country in her hour of danger . 1600

Highest estimate now 150

   „   Banished 1450

     " *Per Contra*—Game of all sorts increased a hundred-fold."

In 1831, Glenorchy, of which his Lordship of Breadalbane was proprietor, the population, was 1806; in 1841 it was reduced to 831. Those best acquainted with the Breadalbane estates, assert that on the whole property, no less than 500 families, or about 2,500 souls, were driven into exile by the hard-hearted Marquis of that day.

It is, however, gratifying to know that the present Lord Breadalbane, who is descended from a different and remote branch of the family, is an excellent landlord, and takes an entirely different view of his duties and relationship to the tenants on his vast property.

COUNTY OF ARGYLL.

In many parts of Argyllshire the people have been weeded out none the less effectively, that the process generally was of a milder nature than that adopted in some of the places already described. By some means or other, however, the ancient tenantry have largely disappeared to make room for the sheep-farmer and the sportsman. Mr. Somerville, Lochgilphead, writing on this subject, says, "The watchword of all is exterminate, exterminate the native race. Through this monomania of landlords the cottier population is all but extinct; and the substantial yeoman is undergoing the same process of dissolution." He then proceeds:—
"About nine miles of country on the west side of Loch Awe, in Argyllshire, that formerly maintained 45 families, are now rented by one person as a sheep-farm; and in the island of Luing, same county, which formerly contained about 50 substantial farmers, besides cottiers, this number is now reduced to about six. The work of eviction commenced by giving, in many cases, to the ejected population, facilities and pecuniary aid for emigration; but now the people are turned adrift, penniless and shelterless, to seek a precarious subsistence on the sea-board, in the nearest hamlet or village, and in the cities, many of whom sink down helpless paupers on our poor-roll; and others, festering in our villages, form a formidable Arab population, who drink our

money contributed as parochial relief. This wholesale depopulation is perpetrated, too, in a spirit of invidiousness, harshness, cruelty, and injustice, and must eventuate in permanent injury to the moral, political, and social interests of the kingdom. . . . . The immediate effects of this new system are the dis-association of the people from the land, who are virtually denied the right to labour on God's creation. In L——, for instance, garden ground and small allotments of land are in great demand by families, and especially by the aged, whose labouring days are done, for the purpose of keeping cows, and by which they might be able to earn an honest, independent maintainence for their families, and whereby their children might be brought up to labour, instead of growing up vagabonds and thieves. But such, even in our centres of population, cannot be got ; the whole is let in large farms and turned into grazing. The few patches of bare pasture, formed by the delta of rivers, the detritus of rocks, and tidal deposits, are let for grazing at the exorbitant rent of £3 10s. each for a small Highland cow ; and the small space to be had for garden ground is equally extravagant. The consequence of these exorbitant rents and the want of agricultural facilities is a depressed, degraded, and pauperised population." These remarks are only too true, and applicable not only in Argyllshire, but throughout the Highlands generally.

A deputation from the Glasgow Highland Relief Board, consisting of Dr. Robert Macgregor, and Mr. Charles R. Baird, their Secretary, visited Mull, Ulva, Iona, Tiree, Coll, and part of Morvern in 1849, and they immediately afterwards issued a printed report, on the state of these places, from which a few extracts will prove instructive. They inform us that the population of

THE ISLAND OF MULL,

according to the Government Census in 1821, was 10,612; in 1841, 10,064. In 1871, we find it reduced to 6441, and by the Census of 1881, now before us, it is stated at 5624, or a fraction more than half the number that inhabited the Island in 1821.

TOBERMORY, we are told, "has been for some time the resort of the greater part of the small crofters and cottars, *ejected* from their holdings and houses on the surrounding estates, and thus there has been a great accumulation of distress"; and then we are told that " severe as the destitution has been in the rural districts, we think it has been still more so in Tobermory and other villages"—a telling comment on, and reply to, those who would now have us believe that the evictors of those days and of our own were acting the character of wise benefactors when they ejected the people from the inland and rural districts of the various counties to wretched villages, and rocky hamlets on the seashore.

ULVA.—The population of the Island of Ulva in 1849, was 360 souls. The reporters state that " a large portion " of it "has lately been converted into a sheep farm, and consequently a number of small crofters and cottars have been warned away" by Mr. Clark. " Some of these will find great difficulty in settling themselves anywhere, and all of them have little prospect of employment. . . . . Whatever may be the ultimate effect, to the landowners, of the conversion of a number of small crofts into large farms, we need scarcely say that this process is causing much poverty and misery among the crofters." How Mr. Clark carried out his intention of evicting the tenantry of Ulva may be seen from the fact that the population of 360 souls, in 1849, was reduced to 51 in 1881.

KILFINICHEN.—In this district we are told that, "The crofters and cottars having been warned off, 26 individuals emigrated to America at their own expense, and one at that of the Parochial Board; a good many removed to Kinloch, where they are now in great poverty, and those who remained were not allowed to cultivate any ground for crop or even garden stuffs. The stock and other effects of a number of crofters on Kinloch, last year (1848), and whose rents averaged from £5 to £15 per annum, having been sequestrated and sold, these parties are now reduced to a state of pauperism, having no employment or means of subsistence whatever." As to the cottars it is said that "the great mass of them are now in a very deplorable state". On the estate of

GRIBUN, Colonel Macdonald, of Inchkenneth, the proprietor, gave the people plenty of work, by which they were quite independent of relief from any quarter, and the character which he gives to the deputation of the people generally is most refreshing, when we compare it with the baseless charges usually made against them by the majority of his class. The reporters state that "Colonel Macdonald spoke in high terms of the honesty of the people and of their great patience and forbearance under their severe privations". It is gratifying to be able to record this simple act of justice, not only as the people's due, but specially to the credit of Colonel Macdonald's memory and goodness of heart.

BUNESSAN.—Respecting this district, belonging to the Duke of Argyll, our authority says :—" It will be recollected that the [Relief] Committee, some time ago, advanced £128 to assist in procuring provisions for a number of emigrants from the Duke of Argyll's estate, in the Ross of Mull and

Iona, in all 243 persons—125 adults and 118 children. When there, we made inquiry into the matter, and were informed [by those as it proved, quite ignorant of the facts] that the emigration had been productive of much good, as the parties who emigrated could not find the means of subsistence in this country, and had every *prospect* of doing so in Canada, where all of them had relations; and also because the land occupied by some of these emigrants had been given to increase the crofts of others. Since our return home, however, we have received the very melancholy and distressing intelligence, that many of these emigrants had been seized with cholera on their arrival in Canada; that not a few of them had fallen victims to it; and that the survivors had suffered great privations." Compare the "prospect," of much good, predicted for these poor creatures, with the sad reality of having been forced away to die a terrible death immediately on their arrival on a foreign shore!

Iona, at this time, contained a population of 500, reduced in 1881 to 243. It also is the property of the Duke of Argyll, as well as

The Island of Tiree, the population of which is given in the report as follows:—In 1755 it was 1509, increasing in 1777, to 1681; in 1801, to 2416; in 1821, to 4181; and in 1841, to 4687. In 1849, "after considerable emigrations," it was 3903; while in 1881, it is reduced to 2733. The deputation recommended emigration from Tiree, as imperatively necessary, but they "call especial attention to the necessity of emigration being conducted on proper principles, or, 'on a system calculated to promote the permanent benefit of those who emigrate, and of those who remain,' because we have reason to fear that not a few parties in these districts are anxious to get rid of the small crofters and cottars at all hazard, and without making sufficient provision for their future comfort and settlement elsewhere; and because we have seen the very distressing account of the privations and sufferings of the poor people who emigrated from Tiree and the Ross of Mull to Canada this year (1849), and would spare no pains to prevent a recurrence of such deplorable circumstances. As we were informed that the Duke of Argyll had expended nearly £1200 on account of the emigrants (in all 247 souls) from Tiree; as the Committee advanced £131 15s. to purchase provisions for them; and as funds were remitted to Montreal to carry them up the country, we sincerely trust that the account we have seen of their sufferings in Canada is somewhat over-charged, and that it is not at all events to be ascribed to want of due provision being made for them, ere they left this country, to carry them to their destination. Be this as it may, however, we trust that no emigration will in future be promoted by proprietors or others, which will not secure, as far as human effort can, *the benefit of those who emigrate*, as well as of those who are left at home. . . . Being aware of the poverty of the great majority of the inhabitants of this Island, and of the many difficulties with which they have to contend, we were agreeably surprised to find their dwellings remarkably neat and clean—very superior indeed, both externally and internally, to those of the other Islands; nay, more, such as would bear comparison with cottages in any part of the kingdom. The inhabitants too, we believe, are active and enterprising, and, if once put in a fair way of doing so, would soon raise themselves to comfort and independence." Very good indeed, Tiree!

THE ISLAND OF COLL, which is separated from Tiree by

a channel only two miles in width, had a population, in 1755, of 1193 ; in 1771, of 1200 ; in 1801, of 1162 ; in 1821, of 1264. In 1841, it reached 1409. At the time of the visit of the Deputation, from whose report we quote, the population of the Island was down to 1235 ; while in 1881, it had fallen to 643. The deputation report that during the destitution the work done by the Coll people "approximates, if it does exceed, the supplies given ;" they are "hard working and industrious. . . . . . . We saw considerable tracts of ground which we were assured might be reclaimed and cultivated with profit, and are satisfied that fishing is a resource capable of great improvement, and at which therefore, many of the people might be employed to advantage ; we are disposed to think that, by a little attention and prudent outlay of capital, the condition of the people here might ere long be greatly improved. The grand difficulty in the way, however, is the want of capital. Mr. Maclean, the principal proprietor, always acted most liberally when he had it in his power to do so, but, unfortunately he has no longer the ability, aud the other two proprietors are also under trust." Notwithstanding these possibilities the population has now been reduced to less than one half what it was only forty years ago.

WE shall now return to the mainland portion of County, and take a glance at the parish of

MORVERN.

THE population of this extensive Parish in 1755, was 1223 ; in 1795 it increased to 1764 ; in 1801 to 2000 ; in 1821 it was 1995 ; in 1831 it rose to 2137 ; and in 1841 it came down to 1781 ; in 1871 it was only 973 ; while in the Census Returns for 1881 we find it stated at 714, or less than one third of what it was fifty years ago.

The late Dr. Norman Macleod, after describing the happy state of things which existed in this parish before the clearances, says :—" But all this was changed when those tacksmen were swept away to make room for the large sheep farms, and when the remnants of the people flocked from their empty glens to occupy houses in wretched villages near the sea-shore, by way of becoming fishers—often where no fish could be caught. The result has been that 'the Parish' for example, which once had a population of 2,200 souls, and received only £11 per annum from public (Church) funds for the support of the poor, expends now [1863] under the poor law upwards of £600 annually, with a population diminished by one-half, [since diminished to one third] and with poverty increased in a greater ratio. . . . . Below these gentlemen tacksmen were those who paid a much lower rent, and who lived very comfortably, and shared hospitality with others, the gifts which God gave them. I remember a group of men, tenants in a large glen, which now has not a smoke in it, as the Highlanders say, throughout its length of twenty miles. They had the custom of entertaining in rotation every traveller who cast himself on their hospitality. The host on the occasion was bound to summon his neighbours to the homely feast. It was my good fortune to be a guest when they received the present minister of 'the Parish' while *en route* to visit some of his flock. We had a most sumptuous feast—oat-cakes, crisp and fresh from the fire ; cream, rich and thick, and more beautiful than nectar,—whatever that may be ; blue Highland cheese, finer than Stilton ; fat hens, slowly cooked on the fire in a pot of potatoes, without their

skins, and with fresh butter—'stored hens', as the superb
dish was called; and though last, not least, tender kid,
roasted as nicely as Charles Lamb's cracklin' pig. All was
served up with the utmost propriety, on a table covered
with a fine white cloth, and with all the requisites for a
comfortable dinner, including the champagne of elastic,
buoyant, and exciting mountain air. The manners and con-
versations of those men would have pleased the best-bred
gentleman. Every thing was so simple, modest, unassum-
ing, unaffected, yet so frank and cordial. The conversation
was such as might be heard at the table of any intelligent
man. Alas! there is not a vestige remaining of their homes.
I know not whither they are gone, but they have left no
representatives behind. The land in the glen is divided
between sheep, shepherds, and the shadows of the clouds."*

The Rev. Donald Macleod, editor of *Good Words*—describing the death of the late Dr. John Macleod, the "minister
of the Parish" referred to by Dr. Norman in the above
quotation, and for fifty years minister of Morvern—says, of
the noble patriarch:—" His later years were spent in pathetic
loneliness. He had seen his parish almost emptied of its people. Glen after glen had been turned into sheep-walks, and
the cottages in which generations of gallant Highlanders had
lived and died were unroofed, their torn walls and gables left
standing like mourners beside the grave, and the little plots
of garden or of cultivated enclosure allowed to merge into
the moorland pasture. He had seen every property in the
parish change hands, and though, on the whole, kindly and
pleasant proprietors came, in place of the old families, yet
they were strangers to the people, neither understanding
their language nor their ways. The consequence was that

Reminiscences of a Highland Parish—Good Words, 1863.

they perhaps scarcely realised the havoc produced by the changes they inaugurated. 'At one stroke of the pen,' he said to me, with a look of sadness and indignation, 'two hundred of the people were ordered off.—There was not one of these whom I did not know, and their fathers before them ; and finer men and women never left the Highlands.' He thus found himself the sole remaining link between the past and present—the one man above the rank of a peasant who remembered the old days and the traditions of the people. The sense of change was intensely saddened as he went through his parish and passed ruined houses here, there, and everywhere. 'There is not a smoke there now,' he used to say with pathos, of the glens which he had known tenanted by a manly and loyal peasantry, among whom lived song and story and the elevating influences of brave traditions. All are gone, and the place that once knew them, knows them no more ! The hill-side, which had once borne a happy people, and echoed the voices of joyous children, is now a silent sheep-walk. The supposed necessities of Political Economy have effected the exchange, but the day may come when the country may feel the loss of the loyal and brave race which has been driven away, and find a new meaning perhaps in the old question, 'Is not a man better than a sheep?' They who 'would have shed their blood like water' for Queen and country, are in other lands, Highland still, but expatriated for ever.—

> From the dim shieling on the misty island,
>   Mountains divide us and a world of seas,
> But still our hearts are true, our hearts are Highland,
>   And in our dreams we behold the Hebrides.
> Tall are these mountains, and these woods are grand,
>   But we are exiled from our father's land."*

* *Farewell to Fiunary*, by Donald Macleod, D.D., in *Good Words* for August, 1882.

GLENORCHY.

GLENORCHY, of which the Marquis of Breadalbane is sole proprietor, was, like many other places, ruthlessly cleared of its whole native population. The writer of the New Statistical Account of the Parish, in 1843, the Rev. Duncan Maclean, " Fior Ghaël " of the *Teachdaire*, informs us that the census taken by Dr. Webster in 1755, and by Dr. MacIntyre forty years later, in 1795, " differ exceedingly little," only to the number of sixty. The Marquis of the day, it is well known, was a good friend of his Reverence ; the feeling was naturally reciprocated, and one of the apparent results is that the reverend author abstained from giving, in his Account of the Parish, the population statistics of the Glenorchy district. It was, however, impossible to pass over that important portion of his duty altogether, and, apparently with reluctance, he makes the following sad admission :—" A great and rapid decrease has, however, taken place since [referring to the population in 1795]. This decrease is mainly attributable to the introduction of sheep, and the absorption of small into large tenements. The aboriginal population of the parish of Glenorchy (not of Inishail) has been nearly supplanted by adventurers from the neighbouring district of Breadalbane, who now occupy the far largest share of the parish. There are a few, and only a few, shoots from the stems that supplied the ancient population. Some clans, who were rather numerous and powerful, have disappeared altogether ; others, viz., the Downies, Macnabs, MacNicols, and Fletchers, have nearly ceased to exist. The Macgregors, at one time lords of the soil, have totally disappeared ; not one of the name is to be found among the population. The MacIntyres, at one time extremely numerous, are likewise greatly reduced."

By this nobleman's mania for evictions, the population of Glenorchy was reduced from 1806 in 1831, to 831 in 1841, or by nearly a thousand souls in the short space of ten years! It is, however, gratifying to find that it has since, under wiser management, very largely increased.

In spite of all this we have been seriously told that there has been no

DEPOPULATION OF THE COUNTY

In the rural districts. In this connection some very extra-ordinary public utterances were recently made by two gentlemen closely connected with the County of Argyll, questioning or attempting to explain away statements, made in the House of Commons by Mr. D. H. Macfarlane, M.P., to the effect that the rural population was, from various causes, fast disappearing from the Highlands. These utterances were —one by a no less distinguished person than the Duke of Argyll, who published his remarkable propositions in the *Times ;* the other by Mr. John Ramsay, M.P., the Islay distiller, who imposed his baseless statements on his brother members in the House of Commons. These oracles should have known better. They must clearly have taken no trouble whatever to ascertain the facts for themselves, or, having ascertained them, kept them back that the public might be misled on a question with which, it is obvious to all, the personal interests of both are largely mixed up.

Let us see how the assertions of these authorities agree with the actual facts. In 1831 the population of the County of Argyll was 100,973 ; in 1841 it was 97,371 ; in 1851 it was reduced to 88,567 ; and in 1881 it was down to 76,468. Of the latter number the Registrar-General classifies 30,387 as urban, or the population of " towns and villages," leaving us only 46,081 as the total rural population of the county of Argyll at the date of the last Census, in 1881.

It will be necessary to keep in mind that in 1831 the county could not be said to have had many "town and village" inhabitants—not more than from 12,000 to 15,000 at most. These resided chiefly in Campbelton, Inveraray, and Oban ; and if we deduct from the total population for that year, numbering 100,973, even the larger estimate, 15,000, of an urban or town population, we have still left, in 1831, an actual rural population of 85,973, or within a fraction of double the whole rural population of the county in 1881. In other words, the rural population of Argyll-shire is reduced in fifty years from 85,973 to 46,081, or nearly one-half.

The increase of the urban or town population is going on at a fairly rapid rate ; Campbeltown, Dunoon, Oban, Balla-chulish, Blairmore and Strone, Innellan, Lochgilphead, Tarbet, and Tighnabruaich, combined, having added no less than some 5,500 to the population of the county in the ten years from 1871 to 1881. These populous places will be found respectively in the parishes of Campbeltown, Lismore, and Appin, Dunoon and Kilmun, Glassary, Kilcalmonell and Kilbery, and in Kilfinan ; and this will at once account for the comparatively good figure which these parishes make in the tabulated statement in the Appendix. That table will show exactly in which parishes and at what rate depopulation progressed during the last fifty years. In many instances the population was larger prior to 1831 than at that date, but the years given will generally give the best idea of how the matter stood throughout that whole period. The state of the population given in 1831 was before the famine which occurred in 1836 ; while 1841 comes in between that of 1836 and 1846-47, during which period large numbers were sent away, or left for the Colonies. There was no famine between 1851 and 1881, a time during which the population was reduced from 88,567 to 76,468, notwithstanding the great increase which took place simultaneously in the "town and village" section of the people in the county, as well as throughout the country generally.

The Table in the appendix will be found, like its companions, of considerable interest and value, in the face of such absurd and groundless statements as those to which we have referred, coming as they do from such high authorities! We venture to think that these Tables will not only prove interesting, but valuable, at a time like this, in helping to remove the dust thrown for so many years past in the eyes of the public on this question of Highland depopulation by individuals personally interested in concealing the actual facts from those who have it in their power to put an effective check on the few unpatriotic proprietors in the North who are mainly responsible for clearing the country, by one means or another, for their own selfish ends.

THE TESTIMONY OF A LIVING WITNESS.

THE Rev. Dr. Maclauchlan, Edinburgh, wrote a series of articles in the *Witness*, during its palmy days under the editorship of Hugh Miller. These were afterwards published, in 1849, under the title of "The Depopulation System of the Highlands," in pamphlet form, by Johnston and Hunter. The rev. author visited all the places to which he refers, and all Highlanders are glad that he is still among us—perfectly able to maintain the accuracy of the following extracts from his pages. He says :—

A complete history of Highland clearances would, we doubt not, both interest and surprise the British public. Men talk of the Sutherland clearings as if they stood alone amidst the atrocities of the system ; but those who know fully the facts of the case can speak with as much truth of the Ross-shire clearings, the Inverness-shire clearings, the Perthshire clearings, and, to some extent, the Argyllshire clearings. The earliest of these was the great clearing on the Glengarry estate, towards, we believe, the latter end of the last century. The tradition among the Highlanders is (and some Gaelic poems composed at the time would go to confirm it), that the chief's lady had taken umbrage at the clan. Whatever the cause might have been, the offence was deep, and could only be expiated by the extirpation of the race. Summonses of ejection were served over the whole property, even on families the most closely connected with the chief; and if we now seek for the Highlanders of Glengarry, we must search on the banks of the St. Lawrence. To the westward of Glengarry lies the estate of Lochiel—a name to which the imperishable poetry of Campbell has attached much interest. It is the country of the brave clan Cameron, to whom, were there nothing to speak of but their conduct at Waterloo, Britain owes a debt. Many of our readers have passed along Loch Lochy, and they have likely had the mansion of Auchnacarry pointed out to them, and they have been told of the dark mile, surpassing, as some say, the Trossachs in romantic beauty ; but perhaps they were not aware that beyond lies the wide expanse of Loch Arkaig, whose banks have been the scene of a most extensive clearing. There was a day when three hundred able, active men could have been collected from the shores of this extensive inland loch ; but eviction has long ago rooted them out, and nothing is now to be seen but the ruins of their huts, with the occasional bothy of a shepherd, while their lands are held by one or two farmers from the borders. Crossing to the south of the great glen, we may begin with Glencoe. How much of its romantic interest does this glen owe to its desolation? Let us remember, however, that the desolation, in a large part of it, is the result of the extrusion of the inhabitants. Travel eastward, and the foot-prints of the destroyer cannot be lost sight of. Large tracks along the Spean and its tributaries are a wide waste. The southern bank of Loch Lochy is almost without inhabitants, though the symptoms of former occupancy are frequent. When we enter the country of the Frasers, the same spectacle presents itself—a desolate land. With the exception of the miserable village of Fort-Augustus the native population is almost extinguished, while those who do remain are left as if, by their squalid misery, to make darkness the more visible. Across the hills, in Stratherrick, the property of Lord Lovat, with the exception of a few large sheep farmers, and a very few tenants, is one wide waste. To the north of Loch Ness, the territory of the Grants, both Glenmoriston and the Earl of Seafield, presents a pleasing feature amidst the sea of desolation. But beyond this, again, let us trace the large rivers of the east coast to their sources. Trace the Beauly through all its upper reaches, and how many thousands upon thousands of acres, once peopled, are, as respects human beings, a wide wilderness! The lands of the Chisholm have been stripped of their population down to a mere fragment; the possessors of those of Lovat have not been behind with their share of the same sad doings. Let us cross to the Conon and its branches, and we will find that the chieftains of the Mackenzies have not been less active in extermination. Breadalbane and Rannoch, in Perthshire, have a similar tale to tell, vast masses of the population having been forcibly expelled. The upper portions of Athole have also suffered, while many of the valleys along the Spey and its tributaries are without an inhabitant, if we except a few shepherds. Sutherland, with all its atrocities, affords but a fraction of the atrocities that have been perpetrated in following out the ejectment system of the Highlands. In truth, of the habitable portion of the whole country but a small part is now really inhabited. We are unwilling to weary our readers by carrying them along the west coast from the Linnhe Loch, northwards; but if they inquire, they will find that the same system has been, in the case of most of the estates, relentlessly pursued. These are facts of which, we believe, the British public know little, but they are facts on which the changes should be rung until they have listened to them and seriously considered them. May it not be that part of the guilt is theirs, who might, yet did not, step forward to stop such cruel and unwise proceedings ?

Let us leave the past, however (he continues), and consider the present.   And it is a melancholy reflection that the year 1849 has added its long list to the roll of Highland ejectments.   While the law is banishing its tens for terms of seven or fourteen years, as the penalty of deep-dyed crimes, irresponsible and infatuated power is banishing its thousands for life for no crime whatever.   This year brings forward, as leader in the work of expatriation, the Duke of Argyll.   Is it possible that his vast possessions are over-densely peopled? " *Credat Judæus appelles.*"   And the Highland Destitution Committee co-operate.   We had understood that the large sums of money at their disposal had been given them for the purpose of relieving, and not of banishing, the destitute. Next we have Mr. Baillie of Glenelg, professedly at their own request, sending five hundred souls off to America.   Their native glen must have been made not a little uncomfortable for these poor people, ere they could have petitioned for so sore a favour.   Then we have Colonel Gordon expelling upwards of eighteen hundred souls from South Uist ; Lord Macdonald follows with a sentence of banishment against six or seven hundred of the people of North Uist, with a threat, as we learn, that three thousand are to driven from Skye next season; and Mr. Lillingston of Lochalsh, Maclean of Ardgour, and Lochiel, bring up the rear of the black catalogue, a large body of people having left the estates of the two latter, who, after a heart-rending scene of parting with their native land, are now on the wide sea on their way to Australia.   Thus, within the last three or four months considerably upwards of three thousand of the most moral and loyal of our people—people who, even in the most trying circumstances, never required a soldier, seldom a policeman, among them, to maintain the peace—are driven forcibly away to seek subsistence on a foreign soil.

Writing in 1850, on more "Recent Highland Evictions," the same author says :—The moral responsibility for these transactions lies in a measure with the nation, and not merely with the individuals immediately concerned in them. Some years ago the fearful scenes that attended the slave trade were depicted in colours that finally roused the national conscience, and the nation gave its loud, indignant, and effective testimony against them. The tearing of human beings, with hearts as warm, and affections as strong as dwell in the bosom of the white man, from their beloved homes and families— the packing them into the holds of over-crowded vessels, in the burning heat of the tropics—the stifling atmosphere, the clanking chain, the pestilence, the bodies of the dead corrupting in the midst of the living—presented a picture which deeply moved the national mind ; and there was felt to be guilt, deep-dyed guilt, and the nation relieved itself by abolishing the traffic. And is the nation free of guilt in this kind of white-slave traffic that is now going on—this tearing of men whether they will or not, from their country and kindred— this crowding them into often foul and unwholesome vessels with the accompanying deaths of hundreds whose eyes never rest on the land to which they are driven. Men may say that they have rights in the one case that they have not in the other. Then we say that they are rights into whose nature and fruits we would do well to enquire, lest it be found that the rude and lawless barbarism of Africa, and the high and boasted civilisation of Britain, land us in the same final results. . . . . It is to British legislation that the people of the Highlands owe the relative position in which they stand to their chiefs. There was a time when they were strangers to the feudal system which prevailed in the rest of the kingdom. Every man among them sat as free as his chief. But by degrees the power of the latter, assisted by Saxon legislation, encroached upon the liberty of the former. Highland chiefs became feudal lords—the people were robbed to increase their power—and now we are reaping the fruits of this in recent evictions.

At a meeting of the Inverness, Ross, and Nairn Club, in Edinburgh, in 1877, the venerable Doctor referred to the same sad subject amid applause and expressions of regret. We extract the following from a report of the meeting which appeared at the time in the *Inverness Courier*:—The current that ran against their language seemed to be rising against the people themselves. The cry seemed to be, " Do away with the people : this is the shorthand way of doing away with the language ". He reminded them of the saying of a Queen, that she would turn Scotland into a hunting field, and of the reply of a Duke of Argyll—" It is time for me to make my hounds ready," and said he did not know whether there was now an Argyll who would make the same reply, but there were other folks—less folks than Queens—who had gone pretty deep in the direction indicated by this Queen. He would not say it was not a desirable thing to see Highlanders scattered over the earth —they were greatly indebted to them in their cities and the colonies ; but he wished to preserve their Highland homes, from which the colonies and large cities derived their very best blood. Drive off the Highlander and destroy his home, and you destroy that which had produced some of the best and noblest men who filled important positions throughout the Empire. In the interests of great cities—as a citizen of Edinburgh—he desired to keep the Highlanders in their own country, and to make them as comfortable as they could. He only wished that some of the Highland proprietors could see their way to offer sections of the land for improvement by the people, who were quite as able to improve the land in their own country as to improve the great forests of Canada. He himself would rather to-morrow begin to cultivate an acre in any habitable part of the Highlands of Scotland than to begin to cultivate land such as that on which he had seen thousands of them working in the forests of Canada. What had all this to do with Celtic Literature? Dr. Maclauchlan replied that the whole interest which Celtic Literature had to him was connected with the Celtic people, and if they destroyed the Celtic people, his entire interest in their literature perished. They had been told the other day that this was sentiment, and that there were cases in which sentiment was not desirable. He agreed with this so far; but he believed that when sentiment was driven out of a Highlander the best part of him was driven out, for it ever had a strong place among mountain people. He himself had a warm patriotic feeling, and he grieved whenever he saw a ruined house in any of their mountain glens. And ruined homes and ruined villages he, alas! had seen—villages on fire—the hills red with burning homes. He never wished to see this sorry sight again. It was a sad, a lamentable sight, for he was convinced the country had not a nobler class of people than the Highland people, or a set of people better worth preserving.

Mr. ROBERT BROWN,

Sheriff-Substitute of the Western District of Inverness-shire, in 1806, wrote a pamphlet of 120 pp., now very scarce, entitled, "Strictures and Remarks on the Earl of Selkirk's 'Observations on the Present State of the Highlands of Scotland'". Sheriff Brown was a man of keen observation, and his work is a powerful argument against the forced depopulation of the country. Summing up the number who left from 1801 to 1803, he says:—"In the year 1801, a Mr. George Dennon, from Pictou, carried out two cargoes of emigrants from Fort-William to Pictou, consisting of about seven hundred souls. A vessel sailed the same season from Isle Martin with about one hundred passengers, it is believed, for the same place. No more vessels sailed that year; but, in 1802, eleven large ships sailed with emigrants to America. Of these, four were from Fort-William, one from Knoydart, one from Isle Martin, one from Uist, one from Greenock. Five of these were bound for Canada, four for Pictou, and one for Cape Breton. The only remaining vessel, which took in a cargo of people in Skye, sailed for Wilmington, in the United States. In the year 1803, exclusive of Lord Selkirk's transports, eleven cargoes of emigrants went from the North Highlands. Of these, four were from the Moray Firth, two from Ullapool, three from Stornoway, and two from Fort-William. The whole of these cargoes were bound for the British settlements, and most of them were discharged at Pictou."

Soon after, several other vessels sailed from the North-West Highlands with emigrants, the whole of whom were for the British Colonies. In addition to these, Lord Selkirk took out 250 from South Uist in 1802, and in 1803 he sent out to Prince Edward Island about 800 souls, in three different vessels, most of whom were from the Island of Skye, and the remainder from Ross-shire, North Argyll, the interior of the County of Inverness, and the Island of Uist. In 1804, 1805, and 1806, several cargoes of Highlanders left Mull, Skye, and other Western Islands, for Prince Edward Island and other North American Colonies. Altogether, not less than 10,000 souls left the West Highlands and Isles during the first six years of the present century, a fact which will now appear incredible.

SIR WALTER SCOTT

Writes :—" In too many instances the Highlands have been drained, not of their superfluity of population, but of the whole mass of the inhabitants, dispossessed by an unrelenting avarice, which will be one day, found to have been as short-sighted as it is unjust and selfish. Meantime, the Highlands may become the fairy ground for romance and poetry, or the subject of experiment for the professors of speculation, political and economical. But if the hour of need should come—and it may not, perhaps, be far distant —the pibroch may sound through the deserted region, but the summons will remain unanswered."

M. MICHELET,

The great Continental historian, writes :—" The Scottish Highlanders will ere long disappear from the face of the earth ; the mountains are daily depopulating ; the great estates have ruined the land of the Gael, as they did ancient Italy. The Highlander will ere long exist only in the romances of Walter Scott. The tartan and the claymore excite surprise in the streets of Edinburgh ; the Highlanders disappear—they emigrate—their national airs will ere long be lost, as the music of the Eolian harp when the winds are hushed."

MR. ALFRED RUSSEL WALLACE.

In his recent work on the Nationalisation of Land, Mr. Alfred Russel Wallace, in the chapter on " Landlordism in

Scotland," says to the English people :—The facts stated
in this chapter will possess, I feel sure, for many Englishmen,
an almost startling novelty; the tale of oppression and
cruelty they reveal reads like one of those hideous stories
peculiar to the dark ages, rather than a simple record
of events happening upon our own land and within the
memory of the present generation. For a parallel to this
monstrous power of the landowner, under which life and
property are entirely at his mercy, we must go back to
mediæval, or to the days when serfdom not having been
abolished, the Russian noble was armed with despotic
authority; while the more pitiful results of this landlord
tyranny, the wide devastation of cultivated lands, the heartless burning of houses, the reckless creation of pauperism
and misery, out of well-being and contentment, could only
be expected under the rule of Turkish Sultans or greedy and
cruel Pashas.   Yet these cruel deeds have been perpetrated
in one of the most beautiful portions of our native land.
They are not the work of uncultured barbarians or of
fanatic Moslems, but of so-called civilised and christian
men ; and—worst feature of all—they are not due to any
high-handed exercise of power beyond the law, but are
strictly legal, are in many cases the acts of members of the
Legislature itself, and, notwithstanding that they have been
repeatedly made known for at least sixty years past, no steps
have been taken, or are even proposed to be taken, by the
Legislature to prevent them for the future !   Surely it is
time that the people of England should declare that such
things shall no longer exist—that the rich shall no longer
have such legal power to oppress the poor—that the land
shall be free for all who are willing to pay a fair value for its
use—and, as this is not possible under landlordism, that
landlordism shall be abolished. . . . . The general

results of the system of modern landlordism in Scotland are not less painful than the hardship and misery brought upon individual sufferers. The earlier improvers, who drove the peasants from their sheltered valleys to the exposed sea-coast, in order to make room for sheep and sheep-farmers, pleaded erroneously the public benefit as the justification of their conduct. They maintained that more food and cloth-ing would be produced by the new system, and that the people themselves would have the advantage of the produce of the sea as well as that of the land for their support. The result, however, proved them to be mistaken, for thenceforth the cry of Highland destitution began to be heard, cul-minating at intervals into actual famines, like that of 1836-37, when £70,000 were distributed to keep the Highlanders from death by starvation, ... just as in Ireland, there was abundance of land capable of cultivation, but the people were driven to the coast and to the towns to make way for sheep, and cattle, and lowland farmers ; and when the barren and inhospitable tracts allotted to them became overcrowded, they were told to emigrate. As the Rev. J. Macleod says :—" By the clearances one part is depopulated and the other overpopulated ; the people are gathered into villages where there is no steady employment for them, where idleness has its baneful influence and lands them in penury and want ".

The actual effect of this system of eviction and emigration —of banishing the native of the soil and giving it to the stranger—is shown in the steady increase of poverty indicated by the amount spent for the relief of the poor having increased from less than £300,000 in 1846 to more than £900,000 now ; while in the same period the popula-tion has only increased from 2,770,000 to 3,627,000, so that pauperism has grown about nine times faster than popula-

tion! . . . . The fact that a whole population could
be driven from their homes like cattle at the will of a
landlord, and that the Government which taxed them, and
for whom they freely shed their blood on the battle-field,
neither would nor could protect them from cruel interference
with their personal liberty, is surely the most convincing
and most absolute demonstration of the incompatibility
of landlordism with the elementary rights of a free people.

As if, however, to prove this still more clearly, and to
show how absolutely incompatible with the well-being of the
Community is modern landlordism, the great lords of the
soil in Scotland have for the last twenty years or more, been
systematically laying waste enormous areas of land for purposes of sport, just as the Norman Conqueror laid waste the
area of the New Forest for similar purposes. At the present
time, more than two million acres of Scottish soil are devoted
to the preservation of deer alone—an area larger than the
entire Counties of Kent and Surrey combined. Glen Tilt
Forest includes 100,000 acres; the Black Mount is sixty
miles in circumference; and Ben Aulder Forest is fifteen
miles long by seven broad. On many of these forests there
is the finest pasture in Scotland, while the valleys would
support a considerable population of small farmers, yet all
this land is devoted to the sport of the wealthy, farms being
destroyed, houses pulled down, and men, sheep, and cattle
all banished to create a wilderness for the deer-stalkers!
At the same time the whole people of England are shut out
from many of the grandest and most interesting scenes of
their native land, gamekeepers and watchers forbidding the
tourist or naturalist to trespass on some of the wildest Scotch
mountains.

Now, when we remember that the right to a property in
these unenclosed mountains was most unjustly given to the

representatives of the Highland chiefs little more than a
century ago, and that they and their successors have grossly
abused their power ever since, it is surely time to assert
those fundamental maxims of jurisprudence which state
that—"No man can have a vested right in the misfortunes
and woes of his country," and that "the Sovereign ought
not to allow either communities or private individuals to
acquire large tracts of land in order to leave it uncultivated".
If the oft-repeated maxim that "property has its duties as
well as its rights" is not altogether a mockery, then we
maintain that in this case the *total* neglect of all the duties
devolving on the owners of these vast tracts of land affords
ample reason why the State should take possession of them
for the public benefit. A landlord government will, of
course, never do this till the people declare unmistakably
that it must be done. To such a government the rights of
property are *sacred*, while those of their fellow citizens are of
comparatively little moment; but we feel sure that when the
people fully know and understand the doings of the landlords of Scotland, the reckless destruction of homesteads,
and the silent sufferings of the brave Highlanders, they
will make their will known, and, when they do so, that *will*
must soon be embodied into law.

After quoting the opinion of the Rev. Dr. John Kennedy of
Dingwall, given at length at pp. 336-337, Mr. Wallace next
quotes from an article in the *Westminster Review*, in 1868.
"The Gaels," this writer says, "rooted from the dawn of
history on the slopes of the northern mountains, have been
thinned out and thrown away like young turnips too thickly
planted. Noble gentlemen and noble ladies have shown a
flintiness of heart and a meanness of detail in carrying out
their clearings upon which it is revolting to dwell; and after
all, are the evils of over-population cured? Does not the

desease still spring up under the very torture of the knife?
Are not the crofts slowly and silently taken at every opportunity out of the hands of the peasantry?   When a Highlander has to leave his hut there is now no resting place for
him save the cellars or attics of the closes of Glasgow, or
some other large centre of employment; it has been
noticed that the poor Gael is even more liable than the
Irishman to sink under the debasement in which he is then
immersed."   The same writer holds :—" No error could be
grosser than that of reviewing the chiefs as unlimited proprietors, not only of the land, but of the whole territory of
the mountain, lake, river, and sea-shore, held and won
during hundreds of years by the broad swords of the clansmen.   Could any Maclean admit, even in a dream, that his
chief could clear Mull of all the Macleans and replace them
with Campbells; or the Mackintosh people his lands with
Macdonalds, and drive away his own race, any more than
Louis Napoleon could evict all the population of France
and supply their place with English and German colonists?"
Yet this very power and right the English Government, in
its aristocratic selfishness, bestowed upon the chiefs, when,
after the great rebellion of 1745, it took away their privileges of war and criminal jurisdiction, and endeavoured to
assimilate them to the nobles and great landowners of England.   The rights of the clansmen were left entirely out of
consideration.*

* *Land Nationalisation, its Necessities and Aims ; being a comparison
of the System of Landlord and Tenant with that of occupying Ownership, in
their influence on the well-being of the people*, by Alfred Russel Wallace,
author of " The Malay Archipelago," " Island Life,".&c. London : Trübner
& Co., 1882.

MR. SAMUEL SMITH, M.P.

AT the Annual Meeting of the Federation of Celtic Societies, held in Liverpool, on the 2nd of January, 1883, a
Resolution dealing with Depopulation and Eviction in the
Highlands, was moved by Mr. D. H. Macfarlane, M.P.,
seconded by Mr. John Mackay, C.E., Hereford, and supported in a telling speech by Mr. Samuel Smith, M.P.,
recently returned as a supporter of the Gladstone Government for the City of Liverpool.   Such a statement from so
influential a quarter is, in present circumstances, of great
importance, and deserves all the permanency and circulation
which this work can give it.   The resolution, carried by
acclamation, by an audience largely composed of Englishmen, was as follows :—

*In view of the serious aspect recently assumed by events in
the Highlands of Scotland, and of the alarming decrease of the
rural population, as disclosed by the census returns of 1881,
the Federation of Celtic Societies is of opinion that such steps
ought to be immediately taken, as will deliver the Highland
crofters from the bondage in which they are at present held, increase the size of their holdings, relieve them from the fear of
arbitrary eviction, and define their rights to the soil upon
which they and their forefathers have lived from time immemorial.*

Mr. Smith, on rising to support this resolution, was received
with great enthusiasm, the audience rising to their feet, and
cheering lustily—as indeed they did throughout the delivery
of his able, eloquent, statesman-like, and sympathetic speech.
In the course of his remarks, he said :—

I am extremely happy to be with you to-night.   I have

come here more to be a learner than a teacher. I have so large a sympathy with the Highland population, and such a general knowledge of the wrongs they have suffered, that I felt I was in my right place amongst you to-night. I have been deeply interested in listening to the speeches that have been made. In the main, I can testify from a general knowledge of the history of Scotland, that what has been stated to-night is quite correct, and I am very glad that these facts are coming to be known throughout the country, and are forming the basis of a tide of popular opinion which I am sure will, sooner or later, rectify many of those wrongs in the Highlands. The fact is, the Highlanders may be said in some sense, to have suffered from the remarkable loyalty and peaceableness of their character. There is no part of the British Islands in which there is so little crime as in the Highlands of Scotland. There is no part of the British Islands where the people are naturally more loyal, more orderly, and more religious. From many points of view the Highlanders are one of the most valuable portions of the British population, and certainly it ought to be the policy of any government to preserve and develop such a population, instead of suffering them to be driven from our shores. The point that strikes me most in connection with the wrongs of the Highlands, is the turning of large tracts of country into deer forests. I have long felt that this was a use of the rights of proprietors which can only be called the greatest abuse. It is a use which the law has sanctioned, I think, very wrongfully, and the time has come when we must reconsider the whole basis of our law, and admit new principles into it, which will put an end to the depopulation of huge tracts of country for the purposes of deer. I largely agree with what several speakers have said about the very arbitrary and extreme rights our law has conceded to proprietors, and it ought to be well known to the English public, that these principles of law which have been pushed to such an unwarrantable degree in the Highlands, are modern principles unknown to the ancient Gaelic law. The ancient Gaelic law was identical with the ancient Irish law. It was of the tribal order, in which the clan was full proprietor with the chieftain. The Highlands were occupied from time immemorial by clans, bodies of men bound together by common ties of kindred, having the same name, presided over by an hereditary chief, and occupying a certain portion of soil in common. That existed until the battle of Culloden. After that the principles of English law was introduced. The old rights of the clansmen were confiscated, and superseded by a state of law totally unknown to them. In fact a very gross injustice was done, which has been going on these 130 years, and has led to the depopulation of large tracts of the Highlands, and to the loss by this country of a most valuable element of the population. Now, it has been strongly impressed upon my mind that those principles which we have conceded to Ireland—and I think justly conceded, for I believe Mr. Gladstone's Land Act was based on great and broad principles of justice—I think that the time has come when the same principles, perhaps modified by local circumstances, ought to be applied to the crofter population of the Highlands. I only regret, and I do so very deeply, that it is so very late in the day that we have begun to repair the errors of our forefathers. We have already lost a great portion of that loyal and brave population, and it seems very difficult indeed to recall them. Large tracts of the Highlands have been turned into wildernesses, and it seems at this time of day almost too late to bring back the native population. Were it possible to restore them, were there means to re-people the country with those hardy and loyal men who have been in the front of every British battle for the last 150 years, I for one should be very glad to consider them in order to see whether it was practicable or not. But there are many wrongs which, when once done, it is difficult to undo. Many of the people have sunk into the purlieus of the large towns, descended in the social scale, and lost the associations of their youth, and it would be difficult to replant them ; but we ought to do the best we can to retain what remains of that peasantry, and root them to the soil of their birth by wise and just laws. I do not suppose that any town population can fully understand the intense love of home that belongs to people among the mountains. All mountainous countries are patriotic in the highest possible degree. Whether it be Switzerland, the Tyrol, the Highlands of Scotland, or any other mountainous country, there is an intense love of country which exists nowhere else. That intense love of country is a great force in the State, a great power that ought not to be lightly thrown away. There is, as it were, an immense reserve which a Government can draw upon in a time of national crisis. There is no such intense love of country in town populations. I attribute, in some degree, that also to the strong tribal feeling, to the wonderful loyalty that the Highland soldiers have always shown to their leaders. There is also another point to be considered. A great portion of this Highland population has drifted away to our large towns. It has not always emigrated. Those who have emigrated have done the best, I think ; they have improved their condition by going to foreign countries—America and Canada. The Canadian settlements have been on the whole prosperous. I do not say, in the least degree, I object to a healthy emigration. I hold for this densely-populated country a continuous stream of healthy emigration is necessary to keep us in a proper state, and whether in Ireland or in the Highlands of Scotland the population is congested—wherever there is an immense number of small cottiers dwelling together—a healthy emigration is not to be deplored. But I object to clear whole districts of a country to make room for deer. And, as it has been well said by one of the speakers, these wholesale clearances have in no way improved the condition of the people they leave behind. If they had improved the condition of those behind, one could have looked upon them in a somewhat different light. I think we may even take broader grounds in looking at this question. The whole tendency of English law for many years past has been to deplete the rural districts. It is a fact that we have to look in the face, and a fact that we have to deplore, that the rural population of the British Islands has been steadily decreasing for many years past. Now, I think it is a matter of national policy to keep up the rural population of the country. The rural population, I venture to say, is the backbone of any country. The rural populations are much hardier; they live in a much simpler way; they are capable of undergoing greater fatigue and toil than town populations. A rural population which drifts into a town often falls into a much lower state than they occupied in their country homes. They are not fitted to contend with the temptations of large towns, and oftentimes fall victims to the vices and habits of the low quarters of our towns. If a Gaelic population were drifted into Edinburgh or Glasgow, it would be found, as in the case of the Irish population who have come into our large English towns, that a considerable part would fall into habits they would not have contracted if they had remained in their native place. The associations of youth and the public

opinion of our native home is one of the most powerful
means of supporting people in the paths of virtue and rectitude. Break up these associations, separate people from
the friends of their youth, let them become mere units
amongst the masses, with poor and degraded people about
them, and you will find that, for the most part, they will
sink morally as well as socially. I think that it ought to be
the policy of any government to do whatever it can by wise
legislation to maintain the rural population, to encourage its
growth—at all events, to do what it can to prevent its
gradual extinction. I hold that the proprietorship of land
ought to be made subject to just laws, and that land ought
not to be treated as goods and chattels. I object to the
principle which our law at present recognises that, if a man
by the accident of birth happens to own a county in Scotland, he may drive out every human being in it, and put in
deer. I hold that no principles of justice can sanction such
rights as these. I look upon it as a gross abuse that a man
who owns a large track of country should drain it of the last
sixpence he can get, and then spend it perhaps at the gaming
tables of Paris, Baden-Baden, and such places. I hold very
strongly that property has its duties as well as its rights—
that proprietors should live during the greater part of the
year amongst their tenantry, that they should identify themselves with the people and cultivate a family feeling amongst
them, and be the friends of the weak and helpless. Where
proprietors perform these duties, and recognise the position
in which they stand, there are no men who are more popular,
or to whom is accorded more freely the first position in the
county in which they live ; but where, as I am sorry to say
it is so in too many cases, they entirely neglect those duties,
live for pure selfishness, and totally ignore the interests of
the tenants, they gradually lose all hold upon their attach-

ment; and I am afraid that has taken place already in too many cases in the Highlands. It is a very difficult thing, as we have found in Ireland, to define rights which existed some 200 years ago—rights which have no existence in the statute book, and which are only traditional; to restore such rights now by means of law, you must all admit, is an extremely difficult thing. But in the case of the small crofters it may be necessary. I don't think that with regard to the sheep farms it is necessary. In such cases the relations between landlord and tenant are purely commercial, and the large farmer can protect himself as well as the landlord. It is with regard to the small tenantry that I am speaking. I only desire to keep the rural population fixed upon the soil, and, in order to do so, to concede to them something like fixity of tenure. There are no people more valuable to the country than the Highlanders, and it is to the interest of the State to maintain that people. I hope that this agitation will be conducted constitutionally, and that all Highlanders will use their influence to prevent anything being done that will stain the character of that people with a dark blot. I think it is only a question of time, when these rights will be conceded. The county franchise must be soon extended, and when it is we will have a different class of representatives, not only in Scotland, but in England, who will be very much more alive to the interests of the labouring classes. This cannot be deferred for more than two or three years, and in the meantime your object should be to enlighten the people upon the subject, and to call upon the Government to appoint a Royal Commission to thoroughly and exhaustively analyse the subject, and prepare the way for a parliamentary measure which would do a great deal to satisfy our Highland brethren.*

* From the *Liverpool Mercury* of 3rd January, 1883.

M. DE LAVALEYE.

THE following remarks by the celebrated French economist, M. de Lavaleye, will prove interesting. There is no
greater living authority on land tenure than this writer,
and being a foreigner, his opinions are not open—as the
opinions of our own countrymen may be—to the suspicion
of political bias or partizanship on a question which is of
universal interest all over the world. Referring to land
tenure in this country, he says :—

The dispossession of the old proprietors, transformed
by time into new tenants, was effected on a larger scale by
the "clearing of estates". When a lord of the manor, for
his own profit, wanted to turn the small holdings into large
farms, or into pasturage, the small cultivators were of no
use. The proprietors adopted a simple means of getting rid
of them ; and, by destroying their dwellings, forced them
into exile. The classical land of this system is Ireland, or
more particularly the Highlands of Scotland.

It is now clearly established that in Scotland, just as in
Ireland, the soil was once the property of the clan or sept.
The chiefs of the clan had certain rights over the communal
domain ; but they were even further from being proprietors
than was Louis XIV. from being proprietor of the territory
of France. By successive encroachments, however, they
transformed their authority of suzerain into a right of private
ownership, without even recognising in their old co-proprie-
tors a right of hereditary possession. In a similar way the
Zemindars and Talugdars in India were, by the Act of the
British Government, transformed into absolute proprietors.
Until modern days the chiefs of the clan were interested in
retaining a large number of vassals, as their power, and often
their security, were only guaranteed by their arms. But

when order was established, and the chiefs—or lords, as they now were—began to reside in the towns, and required large revenues rather than numerous retainers, they endeavoured to introduce large farms and pasturage.

We may follow the first phases of this revolution, which commences after the last rising under the Pretender, in the works of James Anderson and James Stuart. The latter tells us that in his time—in the last third of the 18th century —the Highlands of Scotland still presented a miniature picture of the Europe of four hundred years ago. "The rent" (so he misnames the tribute paid to the chief of the clan) "of these lands is very little in comparison with their extent, but if it is regarded relatively to the number of mouths which the farm supports, it will be seen that land in the Scotch Highlands supports perhaps twice as many persons as land of the same value in a fertile province." When, in the last 30 years of the 18th century, they began to expel the Gaels, they at the same time forbade them to emigrate to a foreign country, so as to compel them by these means to congregate in Glasgow and other manufacturing towns. In his observations on Smith's *Wealth of Nations*, published in 1814, David Buchanan gives us an idea of the progress made by the clearing of estates. "In the Highlands," he says, "the landed proprietor, without regard to the hereditary tenants" (he wrongly applies this term to the clansmen who were joint proprietors of the soil), "offers the land to the highest bidder, who, if he wishes to improve the cultivation, is anxious for nothing but the introduction of a new system. The soil, dotted with small peasant proprietors, was formerly well populated in proportion to its natural fertility. The new system of improved agriculture and increased rents demands the greatest net profit with the least possible outlay, and with this object the cultivators are got rid of as being of no further use. Thus cast from their native soil, they go to seek their living in the manufacturing towns." George Ensor, in a work published in 1818, says :—" They (the landed proprietors of Scotland) dispossessed families as they would grub up coppice-wood, and they treated the villages and their people as Indians harassed with wild beasts do in their vengeance a jungle with tigers. . . . Is it credible, that in the 19th century, in this missionary age, in this Christian era, man shall be bartered for a fleece or a carcase of mutton—nay, held cheaper ? . . . Why, how much worse is it than the intention of the Moguls, who, when they had broken into the northern provinces of China, proposed in Council to exterminate the inhabitants, and convert the land into pasture ! This proposal many Highland proprietors have effected in their own country against their own countrymen."

M. de Sismondi has rendered celebrated on the Continent the famous clearing executed between 1814 and 1820 by the Duchess of Sutherland. More than three thousand families were driven out ; and 800,000 acres of land, which formerly belonged to the clan, were transformed into seignorial domain. Men were driven out to make room for sheep. The sheep are now replaced by deer, and the pastures converted into deer forests, which are treeless solitudes. The *Economist* of June 2, 1866, said on this subject :—" Feudal instincts have as full career now as in the times when the Conquerer destroyed thirty-six villages to make the New Forest. Two millions of acres, comprising most fertile land, have been changed into desert. The natural herbage in Glen Tilt was known as the most succulent in Perth ; the deer forest of Ben Aulder was the best natural meadow of Badenoch; the forest of Black Mount was the best pasturage in Scotland for black-woolled sheep. The soil thus sacrificed for the pleasures of the chase extends over an area larger than the county of Perth. The land in the new Ben Aulder forest supported 15,000 sheep; and this is but the thirtieth part of the territory sacrificed, and thus rendered as unproductive as if it were buried in the depths of the sea."

The destruction of small property is still going on, no longer, however, by encroachment, but by purchase. Whenever land comes into the market it is bought by some rich capitalist, because the expenses of legal inquiry are too great for a small investment. Thus, large properties are consolidated, and fall, so to speak, into mortmain, in consequence of the law of primogeniture and entails. In the 15th century, according to Chancellor Fortescue, England was quoted throughout Europe for its number of proprietors and the comfort of its inhabitants. In 1688, Gregory King estimates that there were 180,000 proprietors, exclusive of 16,560 proprietors of noble rank. In 1786, there were 250,000 proprietors of England. According to the "Domesday Book" of 1876 there were 170,000 rural proprietors in England owning above an acre, 21,000 in Ireland, and 8000 in Scotland. A fifth of the entire country is in the hands of 523 persons. "Are you aware," said Mr. Bright, in a speech delivered at Birmingham, August 27, 1866, "that one-half of the soil of Scotland belongs to ten or twelve persons? Are you aware of the fact that the monopoly of landed property is continually increasing and becoming more and more exclusive?"

In England, then, as at Rome, large property has swallowed up small property, in consequence of a continuous evolution unchecked from the beginning to the end of the nation's history; and the social order seems to be threatened just as in the Roman Empire.

An ardent desire for a more equal division of the produce of labour inflames the labouring classes, and passes
from land to land.   In England, it arouses agitation among
the industrial classes, and is beginning to invade the rural
districts.   It obviously menaces landed property, as constituted in this country.   The labourers who till the soil will
claim their share in it; and, if they fail to obtain it here, will
cross the sea in search of it.   To retain a hold on them they
must be given a vote; and there is fresh danger in increasing
the number of electors while that of proprietors diminishes,
and maintaining laws which render inequality greater and
more striking, while ideas of equality are assuming more
formidable sway.   To make the possession of the soil a
closed monopoly and to augment the political powers of the
class who are rigidly excluded, is at once to provoke
levelling measures and to facilitate them.   Accordingly we
find that England is the country where the scheme of the
nationalisation of the land finds most adherents, and is most
widely proclaimed.   The country which is furthest from the
primitive organisations of property, is likewise the one where
the social order seems most menaced.

HARDSHIPS ENDURED BY THE FIRST HIGH-
LAND EMIGRANTS TO NOVA SCOTIA.

THE reader is already acquainted with the misery endured
by those evicted from Barra and South Uist by Colonel
Gordon, after their arrival in Canada.   This was no isolated
case.   We shall here give a few instances of the unspeakable
suffering of those pioneers who left so early as 1773, in the

ship *Hector*, for Pictou, Nova Scotia, gathered from trust-worthy sources during the author's late visit to that country. The *Hector* was owned by two men, Pagan and Witherspoon, who bought three shares of land in Pictou, and they engaged a Mr. John Ross as their agent, to accompany the vessel to Scotland, to bring out as many colonists as they could induce, by misrepresentation and falsehoods, to leave their homes. They offered a free passage, a farm, and a year's free provisions to their dupes. On his arrival in Scotland, Ross drew a glowing picture of the land and other manifold advantages of the country to which he was enticing the people. The Highlanders knew nothing of the difficulties awaiting them in a land covered over with a dense unbroken forest; and, tempted by the prospect of owning splendid farms of their own, they were imposed upon by his promise, and many of them agreed to accompany him across the Atlantic and embraced his proposals. Calling first at Greenock, three families and five single young men joined the vessel at that port. She then sailed to Lochbroom, in Ross-shire, where she received 33 families and 25 single men, the whole of her passengers numbering about 200 souls. This band, in the beginning of July, 1773, bade a final farewell to their native land, not a soul on board having ever crossed the Atlantic except a single sailor and John Ross, the agent. As they were leaving, a piper came on board who had not paid his passage; the captain ordered him ashore, but the strains of the national instrument affected those on board so much that they pleaded to have him allowed to accompany them, and offered to share their own rations with him in exchange for his music during the passage. Their request was granted, and his performances aided in no small degree to cheer the noble band of pioneers in their long voyage of eleven weeks, in a miserable hulk, across the Atlantic. The pilgrim band kept up their spirits as best they could by song, pipe-music, dancing, wrestling, and other amusements, through the long and painful voyage. The ship was so rotten that the passengers could pick the wood out of her sides with their fingers. They met with a severe gale off the Newfoundland coast, and were driven back by it so far that it took them about fourteen days to get back to the point at which the storm met them. The accommodation was wretched, small-pox and dysentery broke out among the passengers. Eighteen of the children died, and were committed to the deep amidst such anguish and heart-rending agony as only a Highlander can understand. Their stock of provisions became almost exhausted, the water became scarce and bad; the remnant of provisions left consisted mainly of salt meat, which, from the scarcity of water, added greatly to their sufferings. The oatcake carried by them became mouldy, so that much of it had been thrown away before they dreamt of having such a long passage; but, fortunately for them, one of the passengers, Hugh MacLeod, more prudent than the others, gathered up the despised scraps into a bag, and during the last few days of the voyage his fellows were too glad to join him in devouring this refuse to keep souls and bodies together.

At last the *Hector* dropped anchor in the harbour, opposite where the town of Pictou now stands. Though the Highland dress was then proscribed at home, this emigrant band carried theirs along with them, and, in celebration of their arrival, many of the younger men donned their national dress—to which a few of them were able to add the *Sgian Dubh* and the claymore—while the piper blew up his pipes with might and main, its thrilling tones, for the first time, startling the denizens of the endless forest, and its echoes resounding through the wild solitude.

Scottish immigrants are admitted upon all hands to have given its backbone of moral and religious strength to the Province, and to those brought over from the Highlands in this vessel is due the honour of being in the forefront—the pioneers and vanguard.

But how different was the reality to the expectations of these poor creatures, led by the plausibility of the emigration agent, to expect free estates on their arrival. The whole scene, as far as the eye could see, was a dense forest. They crowded on the deck to take stock of their future home, and their hearts sank within them. They were landed without the provisions promised, without shelter of any kind, and were only able by the aid of those few before them, to erect camps of the rudest and most primitive description, to shelter their wives and their children from the elements. Their feelings of disappointment were most bitter, when they compared the actual facts with the free farms and the comfort promised them by the lying emigration agent. Many of them sat down in the forest and wept bitterly; hardly any provisions were possessed by the few who were before them, and what there was among them was soon devoured; making all—old and new comers—almost destitute. It was now too late to raise any crops that year. To make matters worse they were sent some three miles into the forest, so that they could not even take advantage with the same ease of any fish that might be caught in the harbour. The whole thing appeared an utter mockery. To unskilled men the work of clearing seemed hopeless; they were naturally afraid of the Red Indian and of the wild beasts of the forest; without roads or paths, they were frightened to move for fear of getting lost in the unbroken forest. Can we wonder that, in such circumstances, they refused to settle on the company's lands? though, in consequence, when provisions arrived, the agents refused to give them any.   Ross and the company quarrelled, and he ultimately left the new comers to their fate.   The few of them who had a little money bought what provisions they could from the agents, while others, less fortunate, exchanged their clothes for food ; but the greater number had neither money nor clothes to spend or exchange, and they were all soon left quite destitute. Thus driven to extremity, they determined to have the provisions retained by the agents, right or wrong, and two of them went to claim them.   They were positively refused, but they determined to take what they could by force. They seized the agents, tied them, tooks their guns from them, which they hid at a distance ; told them that they must have the food for their families, but that they were quite willing and determined to pay for them if ever they were able to do so.   They then carefully weighed or measured the various articles, took account of what each man received and left, except one, the latter, a powerful and determined fellow, who was left behind to release the two agents.   This he did, after allowing sufficient time for his friends to get to a safe distance, when he informed the prisoners where they could find their guns.   Intelligence was sent to Halifax that the Highlanders were in rebellion, from whence orders were sent to a Captain Archibald in Truro, to march his company of militia to suppress and pacify them ; but to his honour be it said, he, point blank, refused, and sent word that he would do no such thing.   "I know the Highlanders," he said, "and if they are fairly treated there will be no trouble with them."   Finally, orders were given to supply them with provisions, and Mr. Paterson, one of the agents, used afterwards to say that the Highlanders who arrived in poverty, and who had been so badly treated, had paid him every farthing with which he had trusted them.

It would be tedious to describe the sufferings which they afterwards endured. Many of them left. Others, fathers, mothers, and children, bound themselves away, as virtual slaves, in other settlements, for mere subsistence. Those who remained lived in small huts, covered only with the bark or branches of trees to shelter them from the bitter winter cold, of the severity of which they had no previous conception. They had to walk some eighty miles, through a trackless forest, in deep snow to Truro, to obtain a few bushels of potatoes, or a little flour in exchange for their labour, dragging these back all the way again on their backs, and endless cases of great suffering from actual want occurred. The remembrance of these terrible days sank deep into the minds of that generation, and long after, even to this day, the narration of the scenes and cruel hardships through which they had to pass beguiled, and now beguiles many a winter's night as they sit by their now comfortable firesides.

In the following spring they set to work. They cleared some of the forest, and planted a larger crop. They learned to hunt the moose, a kind of large deer. They began to cut timber, and sent a cargo of it from Pictou—the first of a trade very profitably and extensively carried on ever since. The population had, however, grown less than it was before their arrival; for in this year it amounted only to 78 persons. One of the modes of laying up a supply of food for the winter was to dig up a large quantity of clams or large oysters, pile them in large heaps on the sea shore, and then cover them over with sand, though they were often, in winter, obliged to cut through ice more than a foot thick to get at them. This will give a fair idea of the hardships experienced by the earlier emigrants to these Colonies.

In Prince Edward Island, however, a colony from Lockerbie, in Dumfrieshire, who came out in 1774, seemed to have fared even worse. They commenced operations on the Island with fair prospects of success, when a plague of locusts, or field mice, broke out, and consumed everything, even the potatoes in the ground; and for eighteen months the settlers experienced all the miseries of a famine, having for several months only what lobsters or shell-fish they could gather from the sea-shore. The winter brought them to such a state of weakness that they were unable to convey food a reasonable distance even when they had means to buy it.

In this pitiful position they heard that the Pictou people were making progress that year, and that they had even some provisions to spare. They sent one of their number to make enquiry. An American settler, when he came to Pictou, brought a few slaves with him, and at this time he had just been to Truro to sell one of them, and brought home some provisions with the proceeds of the sale of his negro. The messenger from Prince Edward Island was putting up at this man's house. He was a bit of a humorist, and continued cheerful in spite of all his troubles. On his return to the Island, the people congregated to hear the news. "What kind of place is Pictou?" enquired one. "Oh, an awful place. Why, I was staying with a man who was just eating the last of his nigger"; and the poor creatures were reduced to such a point themselves that they actually believed the people of Pictou to be in such a condition as to oblige them to live on the flesh of their coloured servants. They were told, however, that matters were not quite so bad as that, and fifteen families left for the earlier settlement, where, for a time, they fared but very little better, but afterwards became prosperous and happy. A few of their children, and thousands of their grandchildren, are now living in comfort and plenty.

But who can think of these early hardships and cruel existences without condemning—even hating—the memories of the harsh and heartless Highland and Scottish lairds, who made existence at home even almost as miserable for those noble fellows, and who then drove them in thousands out of their native land, not caring one iota whether they sank in the Atlantic, or were starved to death on a strange and uncongenial soil? Retributive justice demands that posterity should execrate the memories of the authors of such misery and horrid cruelty. It may seem uncharitable to write thus of the dead; but it is impossible to forget their inhuman conduct, though, no thanks to them—cruel tigers in human form—it has turned out for the better, for the descendants of those who were banished to what was then infinitely worse than transportation for the worst crimes. Such criminals were looked after and cared for; but those poor fellows, driven out of their homes by the Highland lairds, and sent across there, were left to starve, helpless, and uncared for. Their descendants are now a prosperous and thriving people, and retribution is at hand. The descendants of the evicted from Sutherland, Ross, Inverness-shires, and elsewhere, to Canada, are producing enormous quantities of food, and millions of cattle, to pour them into this country. What will be the consequence? The sheep-farmer—the primary and original cause of the evictions—will be the first to suffer. The price of stock in Scotland must inevitably fall. Rents must follow, and the joint authors of the original iniquity will, as a class, then suffer the natural and just penalty of their past misconduct.

AN IRISH COMPANION PICTURE.

WE have read with warm sympathy and interest Mr. A. M. Sullivan's Chapter, entitled "Lochaber no more," in his brilliant and intensely interesting work, *New Ireland.* Mr. Sullivan has always exhibited a friendly side to the Highlanders of Scotland, and we desire to acknowledge this kindly sympathy in the only way which has yet presented itself, by calling attention on this side, among Highlanders especially, to this remarkable work, and, at the same time, quote from it, to give the reader an idea of the brutality meted out by Irish landlords to their countrymen in the past, in connection with this infamous mania for driving the people away from their native soil. Mr. Sullivan introduces his chapter on Irish evictions thus :—A Highland friend whose people were swept away by the great Sutherland clearances, describing to me some of the scenes in that great dispersion, often dwelt with emotion on the spectacle of the evicted clansmen marching through the glens on their way to exile, their pipes playing as a last farewell, "Lochaber no more "!

> Lochaber no more ! Lochaber no more !
> We'll maybe return to Lochaber no more !

I sympathised with his story; I shared all his feelings. I had seen my own countrymen march in like sorrowful procession on their way to an emigrant ship. Not alone in one district, however, but all over the island, were such scenes to be witnessed in Ireland, from 1847 to 1857. Within that decade of years nearly one million of people were cleared off the island by eviction, or emigration.

The picture which Mr. Sullivan presents as to the attachment of his countrymen to their native soil, and the unspeakable cruelties involved in a simple eviction are equally true in the case of the Highlanders. He says:—As a rule, his farm has been to him and his forefathers for generations a fixed and cherished home. Every bush and brake, every shrub and tree, every meadow-path or grassy knoll, has some association for him which is, as it were, a part of his existence. Whatever there is on or above the surface of the earth in the shape of house or office, or steading, of fence or road, of gate or stiles, has been created by the tenant's hand. Under this humble thatch roof he first drew breath, and has grown to manhood. Hither he brought the fair young girl he won as a wife. Here have his little children been born. This farm-plot is his whole dominion, his world, his all; he is verily a part of it, like the ash or the oak, that has sprung from its soil. Removal in his case is a tearing up by the roots, where transplantation is death. The attachment of the Irish peasant to his farm is something almost impossible to be comprehended by those who have not spent their lives amongst the class, and seen from day to day the depth and force and intensity of these home feelings.

An Irish eviction, therefore, it may well be supposed, is a scene to try the sternest nature. I know sheriffs and sub-sheriffs who have protested to me that, odious and distressing as were the duties they had to perform at an execution on the public scaffold, far more painful to their feelings were those which fell to their lot in carrying out an eviction, where, as in the case of these "clearances," the houses had to be levelled. The anger of the elements affords no warrant for respite or reprieve. In hail or thunder, rain or snow, out the inmate must go. The bed-ridden grandsire, the infant in the cradle, the sick, the aged, and the dying, must alike be thrust forth, though other roof or home the world has naught for them, and the stormy sky must be their canopy during the night at hand. This is no fancy picture. It is but a brief and simple outline sketch of realities witnessed all over Ireland in the ten years that followed the famine. I recall the words of an eye-witness, describing one of these scenes: "Seven hundred human beings," says the Most Rev. Dr. Nulty, Catholic Bishop of Meath, "were driven from their homes on this one day. There was not a shilling of rent due on the estate at the time, except by one man. The sheriffs' assistants employed on the occasion to extinguish the hearths and demolish the homes of those honest, industrious men, worked away with a will at their awful calling until evening fell. At length an incident occurred that varied the monotony of the grim and ghastly ruin which they were spreading all around. They stopped suddenly and recoiled, panic-stricken with terror, from two dwellings which they were directed to destroy with the rest. They had just learned that typhus fever held these houses in its grasp, and had already brought death to some of their inmates. They therefore supplicated the agent to spare these houses a little longer; but he was inexorable, and insisted that they should come down. He ordered a large winnowing sheet to be secured over the beds in which the fever-victims lay—fortunately, they happened to be delirious at the time—aud then directed the houses to be unroofed cautiously and slowly. I administered the last Sacrament of the Church to four of these fever-victims next day, and save the above-mentioned winnowing sheet, there was not then a roof nearer to me than the canopy of heaven. The scene of that eviction day I must remember all my life long. The wailing of women, the screams, the terror, the consternation of children, the speechless agony of men, wrung tears of grief from all who saw them. I saw the officers and men of a large police force who were obliged to attend on the occasion cry like children. The heavy rains that usually attend the autumnal equinoxes descended in cold copious torrents throughout the night, and at once revealed to the houseless sufferers the awful realities of their condition. I visited them next morning, and rode from place to place administering to them all the comfort and consolation I could. The landed proprietors in a circle all round, and for many miles in every direction, warned their tenantry against admitting them to even a single night's shelter. Many of these poor people were unable to emigrate. After battling in vain with privation and pestilence, they at last graduated from the workhouse to the tomb, and in little more than three years nearly a fourth of them lay quietly in their grave."

The picture is most painful, but the evicted must be followed yet a little further to complete it. The author, after giving a vivid description of the *mode* of eviction which had almost become a science in his native land, continues:—
The Irish exodus had one awful concomitant, which in the Irish memory of that time, fills nearly as large a space as the famine itself. The people, flying from fever-tainted hovel and workhouse, carried the plague with them on board. Each vessel became a floating charnel-house. Day by day the American public was thrilled by the ghastly tale of ships arriving off the harbours reeking with typhus and cholera; the track they had followed across the ocean strewn with the corpses flung overboard on the way. Speaking in the House of Commons on the 11th of February, 1848, [the late] Mr. Labouchere referred to one year's havoc on board the ships sailing to Canada and New Brunswick alone in the following words :—

Out of 106,000 emigrants who during the last twelve months crossed the Atlantic for Canada and New Brunswick, 6100 perished on the voyage, 4100 on their arrival, 5200 in the hospitals, and 1900 in the towns to which they repaired. The total mortality was not less than 17 per cent. of the total number emigrating to those places ; the number of deaths being 17,300.

In all the great ports of America and Canada, huge quarantine hospitals had to be hastily erected. Into these every day newly arriving plague-ships poured what survived of their human freight, for whom room was as rapidly made in those wards by the havoc of death. Whole families disappeared between land and land, as sailors say. Frequently the adults were swept away, the children alone surviving. It was impossible in every case to ascertain the names of the sufferers, and often all clue to identification was lost. The public authorities, or the nobly humane organisations that had established those lazar-houses, found themselves towards the close of their labours in charge of hundreds of orphan children, of whom name and parentage alike were now impossible to be traced. About eight years ago I was waited upon in Dublin by one of these waifs, now a man of considerable wealth and honourable position. He had come across the Atlantic in pursuit of a purpose to which he is devoting years of his life—an endeavour to obtain some clue to his family, who perished in one of the great shore hospitals in 1849. Piously he treasures a few pieces of a red-painted emigrant box, which he believes belonged to his father. Eagerly he travels from place to place in Clare, and Kerry, and Galway, to see if he may dig from the tomb of that terrible past the secret lost to him, I fear, for ever !

"From Grosse Island, the great charnel-house of victimised humanity," says the Official Report of the Montreal Emigrant Society for 1847, "up to Port Sarnia, and along the borders of our magnificent river ; upon the shores of Lakes Ontario and Erie—wherever the tide of emigration has extended, are to be found the final resting places of the sons and daughters of Erin; one unbroken chain of graves, where repose fathers and mothers, sisters and brothers, in one commingled heap, without a tear bedewing the soil or a stone marking the spot. Twenty thousand and upwards have thus gone down to their graves."*

LAND LEGISLATION IN THE FIFTEENTH CENTURY.

A REMARKABLE CONTRAST: 1482 v. 1882.

THE following passage will be found in Bacon's History of Henry VII :—

"Inclosures at that time began to be more frequent, whereby arable land, which could not be manured without people and families, was turned into pasture, which was easily rid by a few herdsmen; and tenancies for years, lives, and at will, whereupon much of the yeomanry lived, were turned into demesnes. This bred a decay of people, and by consequence a decay of towns, churches, by this, and the like. The King likewise knew full well and in nowise forgot, that there ensued withal upon this a decay and diminution of subsidies and taxes; for the more gentlemen even the lower books of subsidies. In remedying of this inconvenience, the King's wisdom was admirable, and the parliament's at that time. Inclosures they would not forbid, for that had been to forbid the improvement of the patrimony

* New Ireland: Political Sketches and Personal Reminiscences of Thirty Years of Irish Public Life, by A. M. Sullivan.

of the Kingdom; nor tillage they would not compel, for that was to strive with nature and utility; but they took a course to take away depopulating inclosures and depopulating pasturage, and yet not by that name, or by any imperious express prohibition, but by consequence. The ordinance was, 'That all houses of husbandry that were used with twenty acres of ground or upwards, should be maintained and kept for ever'."

In the preambles to several acts of parliament about that date, references are found which are singularly appropriate to the present state of things in the Highlands of Scotland. In 4th Henry VII. c. 16, it is laid down that:—

"Forasmuch as it is to the King our Sovereign lord's great surety and also to the surety of this realm of England, that the Isle of Wight, in the county of Southampton, be well inhabited with English people for the defence as well of his antient enemies of the realm of France as of other parties, the which isle is lately decayed of people by reason that many towns and villages have been beaten down, and the fields ditched and made pastures for beasts and cattles; and also many dwelling places, ferms and fermholds, have of late times been used to be taken in one man's hold and hands, that of old time were wont to be in many persons holds and hands, and many several households kept in them, and thereby much people multiplied, and the same isle well inhabited, the which now by the occasion aforesaid is desolate and not inhabited, but occupied with beasts and cattles. The enactment is, that none shall take more ferms than one in the Isle of Wight exceeding ten merks rent."

Another preamble not less remarkable is that of 25 Henry VIII. chap. 13. It is as follows:—

"Forasmuch as divers and sundry persons of the King's subjects of this realm, to whom God of His goodness hath disposed great plenty and abundance of moveable substance, now of late within few years have daily studied, practised, and invented ways and means how they might accumulate and gather together into few hands, as well great multitude of farms as great plenty of cattle, and in especial sheep, putting such lands as they can get, to pasture, and not to tillage, whereby they have not only pulled down churches and towns, and enchanced the old rates of the rents of the possessions of this realm, or else brought it to such excessive fines that no poor man is able to meddle with it, but also have raised and enchanced the prices of all manner of corn, cattle, wool, pigs, geese, hens, chickens, eggs, and such other, almost double above the prices which have been accustomed ; by reason whereof a marvellous multitude and number of the people of this realm be not able to provide meat, drink, and clothes, necessary for themselves, their wives, and children, but be so discouraged with misery and poverty that they fall daily to theft, robbery, and other inconveniences, or pitifully die for hunger and cold ; and as it is thought by the King's most humble and loving subjects, that one of the greatest occasions that moveth and provoketh those greedy and covetous people so to accumulate and keep in their hands such great portions and parts of the grounds and lands of this realm from the occupying of the poor husbandmen, and so to use it in pasture and not in tillage, is only the great profit that cometh of sheep, which now be come to a few persons hands of this realm, in respect of the whole number of the King's subjects, that some have four-and-twenty thousand, some twenty thousand, some ten thousand, some six thousand, some five thousand, and some more, and some less ; by the which a good sheep for victual that was accustomed to be sold for two shillings fourpence, or three shillings at the most, is now sold for six shillings or five shillings, or four shillings at the least; and a stone of clothing wool, that in some shires in this realm was accustomed to be sold for eighteen-pence or twenty-pence, is now sold for four shillings, or three shillings fourpence at the least; and in some countries where it hath been sold for two shillings fourpence or two shillings eightpence, or three shillings at the most, it is now sold for five shillings, or four shillings eightpence at least, and so raised in every part of this realm; which things, thus used, be principally to the high displeasure of Almighty God, to the decay of the hospitality of this realm, to the diminishing of the King's people, and to the let of the cloth making, whereby many poor people have been accustomed to be set on work; and in conclusion, if remedy be not found, it may turn to the utter destruction and desolation of this realm, which God defend."

Hume, in his History of England, remarks that "during a century and a half after this period, there was a continual renewal of laws against depopulation, whence we may infer that none of them were ever executed. The natural course of improvement at last provided a remedy."—*Vol. III., p. 425, ed. 1763.*

Of the popular clamours on the subject, a curious specimen occurs in some lines preserved in Lewis's *History of the English Translations of the Bible* :—

> "Before that sheepe so much dyd rayne,
>   Where is one plough there was then twayne ;
>   Of corne and victual right greate plentye,
>   And for one pennve egges twentye.
>   I truste to God it will be redressed,
>   That men by sheepe be not subpressed.
>   Sheepe have eaten men full many a yere,
>   Now let men eate sheepe and make good cheere.

> Those that have many sheepe in store
> They may repente it more and more ;
> Seynge the greate extreme necessitee,
> And yet they shewe no more charitee."

Is this not, in many respects, curiously appropriate to our own day ?

THE ISLE OF SKYE IN 1882.

THE BRAES CROFTERS AND LORD MACDONALD.

No evictions have yet taken place in consequence of the social revolution which has, during this year, directed the attention of the world to the position of landlord and tenant in the Isle of Skye. Matters have, however, reached such a pass, that in a work like this considerable space must be devoted to what has already occurred. The writer went over the ground, and he has carefully considered the whole question. The following statement was published by him, on his return from the Island, in the *Celtic Magazine* for May last, and he has not hitherto found it necessary to modify a single sentence of what he then wrote, though he has watched all the proceedings which have since occurred— including the evidence given at the trial of the Braes crofters—with great care. Indeed, it has been admitted by those more immediately concerned on the landlords' side, that his account was exceedingly moderate in tone, carefully couched in temperate language, and accurately stated in all its details. It is as follows :—

That we were, and still are, on the verge of a social revolution in Skye is beyond question, and those who have any influence with the people as well as those lairds and factors who have the interests of the population virtually in their keeping, will incur a very grave responsibility at a critical time like this, unless the utmost care is taken to keep the action of the aggrieved tenants within the law, and on the other hand grant to the people, in a friendly and judicious spirit, material concessions in response to grievances regarding any hardships which can be proved to exist.

It is quite true that, though innumerable grievances unquestionably do exist, no single one by itself is of sufficient magnitude to make a deep impression on the public mind, or upon any mere superficial enquirer. It is the constant accumulation of numberless petty annoyances, all in the same direction, that exasperate the people. The whole tendency, and, it is feared, the real object of the general treatment of the crofter is to crush his spirit, and keep him enslaved within the grasp of his landlord and factor. Indeed, one of the latter freely admitted to us that his object in sometimes serving large numbers of notices of removal, which he had not the slightest intention of carrying into effect, was that he might " have the whip-hand over them ". This practice can only be intended to keep the people in a constant state of terror and insecurity, and it has hitherto succeeded only too well.

The most material grievance, however, as well as the most exasperating, is the gradual but certain encroachment made on the present holdings. The pasture is taken from the crofters piecemeal; their crofts are in many cases subdivided to make room for those gradually evicted from other places—in a way to avoid public attention—to make room for sheep or deer, or both. The people see that they are being gradually but surely driven to the sea, and that if they do not resist in time they will ultimately, and at no distant date, be driven into it, or altogether expelled from their native land. A little more pressure in this direction, and no amount of argument or advice will keep the people from taking the law into their own hands and resisting it by force. The time for argument has already gone. The powers that be has hitherto refused to listen to the voice of reason, and the consequence is that scarcely any one can now be found on either side who will wait to argue whether or not a change is necessary. It is admitted on all hands that a change, and a very material change, must take place at no distant date, and the only question at present being considered in the West at least, is, What is to be the nature of the change? This is what we have now been brought face to face to, and, however difficult the problem may be —and it is surrounded with endless difficulties on all sides —the change must come; and it is admitted all round that the day when it shall take place has been brought much nearer by the inconsiderate action and unbending spirit of those at present in power in the Isle of Skye. This is now seen and admitted by themselves. In short, a great blunder has been committed. This opinion is almost universal in the Island, and it will be a crime against owners of land, against the interests of society, and against common sense, if the blunder is not at once rectified by the good sense of those who have it in their power to do so. The error will soon be forgotten if rectified with as little delay as possible; and the class of men who are willing to sacrifice their own ideas of self-importance to confer a great boon upon society is so limited, that we appeal with no slight confidence to Lord Macdonald's factor to retrace his steps, and arrange a settlement with his people in the Braes; and thus assuredly raise himself to a higher position in public estimation than he has ever yet occupied, with all his power; and at the same time become an example for good to others. He can do all this with the less difficulty, seeing that not a single one of the grievances of the Braes tenants were originated since he became factor on the Macdonald estates, and that the only thing with which he can fairly be charged in connection with them was a too imperious disinclination to listen to the people's claims, and that he had not fully and sufficiently early enquired into the justice of them. On his prudence very much depends at present the amicable settlement of a great question, or at least the shape which the present agitation for the settlement of the relations of landlord and tenant in the Highlands will ultimately take.

We believe that the sad consequences of the recent proceedings against the Braes tenants is deplored by himself as much as by any in the Isle of Skye, where the feeling of regret and shame is universal among the people, from the highest to the lowest, irrespective of position or party.

There is a very strong feeling that the law must be maintained; but the opinion is very generally expressed that the people ought not on this occasion, and in the present state of the public mind, to have been brought into contact with the criminal authorities; and that by a little judicious reasoning this could have been very easily avoided. We quite agree that the law must not only be respected, but firmly vindicated, when occasion demands it; but at the same time the owners of land who press hard upon their poor tenants are living in a fool's paradise if they expect that harsh laws, harshly administered, will be allowed to stand much longer on the statute-book if such as the recent proceedings at the Braes are to be repeated elsewhere throughout the country. Just now the facts of history deserve careful study, and we trust that the lessons they teach will not be thrown away on those more immediately concerned in maintaining their present position in connection with the land.

An attempt has been made to show that the Braes tenants have no real grievances; and our own opinion before we went to examine them on the spot was, and it is so still, that they are, from a legal standpoint, in a far worse position to assert their claims than the tenants of Glendale, Dr. Nicol Martin's, and other proprietors on the Island. We are now satisfied, however, that they have very considerable grievances from a moral standpoint, and no one will dispute that grievances of that kind are generally as important, and often more substantial and exasperating than those which can be enforced in a court of law.

The Braes tenants maintain that in two instances considerable portions of their lands have been taken from them without any reduction of rent, and their contentions are capable of legal proof.

I. There is no doubt at all that they had the grazings of Benlee—the original cause of the present dispute—down to 1865, when it was taken from them and let to a sheep farmer as a separate holding. It can be proved that Lord Macdonald paid them rent for a small portion of it, which he took into his own hands for the site of a forester's house and garden. It can also be proved that it was not a "common" in the ordinary acceptation of that term, though it is called so in a map made by a surveyor, named Blackadder, who, in 1810, divided the crofts from the run-rig system into ordinary lots, while the grazings of Benlee continued to be held *in common* as before. The Uist people, and others from the West, paid a rent for the use of it to the Braes tenants when resting their droves on their way to the Southern markets.

II. The townships are, or were, divided into seven crofts, occupied by as many tenants, and an eighth, called the shepherd's croft, which that necessary adjunct to a common or club farm received in return for his services. The shepherd's croft has been since withdrawn, and let direct by the factor to an eighth tenant, and that without any reduction of rent to the other seven crofters in each township, while they have now to bear the burden of paying their shepherd from their own resources. This is a virtual raising of the rents, without any equivalent, by more than $13\frac{1}{2}$ per cent., altogether apart from the appropriation of Benlee.

These grievances took shape long before the present factor came into power, and he himself has stated that it was only since the present agitation began that he became even acquainted with the complaint regarding the shepherds' crofts. For townships to have such a croft is quite common in the Island, and the practice is well known and understood.

It has been stated that the rents are now not higher than they were in 1810, but, apart from the fact that Benlee and the eighth croft have since been taken away, why compare the present with 1810, a time at which, in consequence of the wars of the period, and the high price obtained for kelp, rents and produce of every kind were very high. The rental of Lord Macdonald's Skye property, we understand, was £8000, while in 1830, it fell to £5000, but no corresponding reduction was made in the Braes. The tenants maintain that they have repeatedly claimed Benlee, and that the late factor told them if they had been firm when the previous lease expired, they would have got it, though whether with or without rent was not stated. This is admitted, though different views were held by each as to the payment of rent —the tenants expecting they were to get it in terms of their request, without any payment, while the factor says that he meant them to get it on payment of the then rent. In any case it is impossible that they can now obtain a decent livelihood without additional pasture for their stock, for they have been obliged to allow a great portion of their arable land to run into waste, to graze their cattle upon it. They are willing to pay some rent for Benlee, and it is to be hoped, in all the circumstances, that the factor will meet them in a liberal spirit (as he can, without difficulty, get the lands from the present tenant at Whitsunday next),* and thus avoid further heart-burnings and estrangements between the landlord and his tenants.   That they have moral claims of a very substantial character cannot be disputed, and the mere fact that the lands have been taken from them so long back as 1865, can scarcely be pleaded as a reason why this state of matters should be continued.   It has indeed been suggested, with some amount of apparent justice, whether in all the circumstances the people have not a moral claim to a return of the value of Benlee for the period during which it has been out of their possession, seeing that they still have the arable portions and part of the grazings of their original holdings.

GLENDALE.

We visited this property, some 30 to 35 miles from Portree, and 7 to 12 miles from Dunvegan, accompanied by the special commissioners for the *Aberdeen Daily Free Press*, the *Dundee Advertiser*, and the *Glasgow Citizen*.   The whole surroundings of Glendale at once indicate a more than average comfortable tenantry, indeed, the most prosperous, to outward appearance, that we have seen in the North-West Highlands.   The estate is owned by the Trustees of the late Sir John Macpherson Macleod.   The people are remarkably intelligent and well informed, and their grievances place those of the Braes men entirely in the shade.   The following account of them and their position generally, largely from Mr. William Mackenzie's account in

---

* This was written in April, 1882.

the *Free Press*, and taken down in the presence of the writer, may be accepted as a true statement of their case :—

While the people are thoroughly firm in their demands, it would be a mistake to call their attitude and actions a "no rent" agitation. They are all alive to their obligation to pay rent to the landlord, and where rent is witheld that is done, not in defiance of the landlord's rights, but as the best, and perhaps the only, means they can devise to induce the landlord to consider the claims and grievances of the people. The estate managed by the trustees of the late John Macpherson Macleod consists of about a dozen townships. According to the current valuation roll, lands, etc., of the annual value of £400 9s. are in the occupancy of the trustees. Dr. Martin pays £133 for Waterstein, and the shooting tenant pays £140. The ground officer pays some £30 for lands at Colbost, while the rest of the estate is occupied by crofters, who among them pay a rent of about £700. The extent of the estate is about 35,000 acres. Ten years ago the rent was £1257, while now it is £1397 odds, shewing a net increase on the decade of £139 16s. 1d. or slightly over 11 per cent.

The tenants complain that the different townships were deprived of rights anciently possessed by them ; that some townships were by degrees cleared of the crofters to enable the laird or the factor to increase his stock of sheep, and that such of these people as did not leave the estate were crowded into other townships, individual tenants in these townships being required to give a portion of their holdings to make room for these new comers. They also complain of the arrogant and dictatorial manner in which the factor deals with them. So the Glendale crofters, wearied for years with what they have regarded as oppression, have now risen as one man, resolved to unfold before the public gaze those matters of which they complain, and to demand of their territorial superiors to restore to them lands which at one time were occupied by themselves and their ancestors, to lessen, if not to remove, what they regard as the severity of the factor's yoke, and generally to place them in that position of independence and security to which they consider they are fairly and justly entitled. The functions performed by the factor of Glendale are exceedingly varied in their character. He is, they say, as a rule, sole judge of any little dispute that may arise between the crofters. He decides these disputes according to his own notions of right or wrong, and if anyone is dissatisfied—a not uncommon occurrence even among litigants before the Supreme Courts —the dissatisfied one dare not carry the matter to the regularly constituted tribunals of the land. To impugn the judgment of the factor by such conduct might entail more serious consequences than any one would be disposed to incur, and, further, the extraordinary and mistaken notion appears to have prevailed that if any one brought a case before the Sheriff Court the factor's letter would be there before him to nonsuit him. This factorial mode of administrating the law is probably a vestige that still lingers in isolated districts of the ancient heritable jurisdiction of Scotland ; and it is only right to state that Glendale is not the only place in the Highlands where the laird or the factor have been wont to administer the law. Among the privileges which the Glendale people formerly possessed was the right to collect and get the salvage for timber drifted from wrecks to the shore. Of this privilege it was resolved to deprive them, as may be seen from the following written notice which was posted up at the local post-office, the most public part of the district :—

Notice.—Whereas parties are in the habit of trespassing on the lands of Glendale, Lowergill, Ramasaig, and Waterstein, in searching and carrying away drift timber, notice is hereby given that the shepherds and herds on these lands have instructions to give up the names of any persons found hereafter on any part of said lands, as also anyone found carrying away timber from the shore by boats or otherwise, that they may be dealt with according to law.—Factor's Office, Tormore, 4th January, 1882.

The lands over which they were thus forbidden to walk, consist mainly of sheep grazing, in the occupation of the trustees, and managed for them by the factor. The people were also forbidden to keep dogs.

These notices, it is stated, had the desired effect; trespassing ceased, and the crofter, with a sad heart, destroyed his canine friend. Grievances multiplying in this way, it was resolved by some leader in the district to convene a public meeting of the crofters to consider the situation. The notice calling the meeting together, was in these terms :—

We, the tenants on the estate of Glendale, do hereby warn each other to meet at Glendale Church on the 7th day of February, on or about one P.M., of 1882, for the purpose of stating our respective grievances publicly, in order to communicate the same to our superiors, when the ground-officer is requested to attend.

Such a revolutionary movement as this, the people actually daring to meet together to consider their relations with the laird, and make demands, was not to be lightly entered upon, and it need not be wondered at if some of them at first wanted the moral courage to come up to the occasion. If any one showed symptoms of weakness in this way he was encouraged, and on the appointed day the clansmen met and deliberated on the situation. At that meeting their grievances received full expression. It was in particular pointed out that the township of Ramasaig, which fifteen years ago was occupied by 22 separate crofters, is now reduced to two, the land taken from or given up by the other twenty families having been put under sheep by the factor. The people, who presumably were less valuable than the sheep, in some cases left the country altogether, while those that remained were provided with half crofts on another part of the estate.

For instance, a crofter who perhaps had a ten pound croft, say, at Milivaig was requested to give up the one-half of it to a crofter removed from Ramasaig, a corresponding reduction being made in the rent. In this way, while the sheep stocks under the charge of the factor were increasing, the status of the crofters was gradually diminishing, and the necessity for their depending more and more on other industries than the cultivation of their croft was increasing. To illustrate this all the more forcibly, we may state that the crofters at Ramasaig had eight milk cows and their followers, and about forty sheep on each whole croft—altogether over a hundred head of cattle and from 300 to 400 sheep. Lowerkell was similarly cleared. At the meeting of the crofters, to which I have alluded, it was resolved that, as a body, they should adopt a united course of action. They were all similarly situated. Each man and each township had a grievance, and no individual was to be called upon to make a separate claim. Each township or combination of townships was to make one demand, and if any punishment should follow on such an act of temerity, it should not be allowed to fall on any one person, but on the united body as a whole. To guard against any backsliding, and to prevent any weakling or chicken-hearted leaguer (if any should exist) from falling out of the ranks, they, one and all, subscribed their names in a book, pledging themselves as a matter of honour to adhere in a body to the resolution thus arrived at. The scheme having thus been

formulated, each township or combination proceeded to get
up petitions embodying their respective cases, and sending
them to the trustees, Professor Macpherson, of Edinburgh,
and his brother.

The tenants of Skinidin claim two islands, opposite their
crofts, in Loch Dunvegan. Apart from this, they complain
that they do not get the quantity of seaweed to which they
were entitled. This may appear to some a small matter,
but to the cultivator of a croft it is a matter of great importance, for seaware is the only manure which he can conveniently get, excepting, of course, the manure produced by his
cows. The quantity of ware promised to the Skinidin
crofters was one ton each, but the one-half of it, they say,
was taken from them some time ago, and given to the
"wealthy men" and favourites of the place. The result is
that they have to cross to the opposite side of Loch Dunvegan and buy sea-ware there at 31s. 6d. per ton. This is
not only an outlay of money, which the poor crofters can ill
afford to incur, but it also entails great labour, which is
attended with no inconsiderable danger to life. The crofters
accordingly demand the quantity of ware to which, they say,
they are entitled.

The Colbost tenants, to the number of twenty-five, also
sent in a petition, in which they complained of high rents,
and stated that owing to incessant tilling the land is becoming exhausted, and ceasing to yield that crop which they
might fairly expect. In 1848, they say they got Colbost
with its old rights at its old rent with the sanction of the
proprietor. The local factor, Norman Macraild, subsequently deprived them of these privileges, while the rents
were being constantly increased. They accordingly demand
that their old privileges should be restored, and the rents

reduced to the old standard, otherwise they will not be able to meet their engagements.

We shall next take the petition of the Harmaravirein crofters. The place is occupied by John Campbell, who pays £9 15s. 4d.; John Maclean, £5 3s. 4d.; John Mackay, £6 2s. 8d.; and Donald Nicolson, £4 12s. The petition, which was in the following terms, deserves record :—

We, the crofters of Harmaravirein, do humbly show by this petition that we agree with our fellow-petitioners in Glendale as to their requests. We do, by the same petition, respectfully ask redress for grievances laid upon us by a despotic factor, Donald Macdonald, Tormore, who thirteen years ago for the first time took from us part of our land, against our will, and gave it to others, whom he drove from another quarter of the estate of Glendale, to extend his own boundaries, and acted similarly two years ago, when he dispersed the Ramasaig tenancy. We, your humble petitioners, believe that none of the grievances mentioned were known to our late good and famous proprietor, being an absentee, in whom we might place our confidence had he been present to hear and grant our request. As an instance of his goodwill to his subjects, the benefits he bestowed on the people of St. Kilda are manifest to the kingdom of Great Britain. We, your petitioners, pray our new proprietors to consider our case, and grant that the tenantry be reinstated in the places which have been cleared of their inhabitants by him in Tormore.

The petition of the Upper and Lower Milivaig and Borrodale crofters set forth that, notwithstanding their going north and south all over the country to earn their bread, they are still declining into poverty. The crofts too are getting exhausted through constant tilling. Before 1845 they say there were only 16 families in the two Milivaigs and one in Borrodale. There are now 5 in Borrodale, 19 in Upper Milivaig, and 20 in Lower Milivaig, averaging six souls in each family. The rent before 1845 for the two Milivaigs was £40. At the date mentioned, Macleod of Macleod, who was then proprietor, divided each of the two Milivaigs into 16 crofts.

They prayed that they might get the lands of Waterstein now tenanted by Dr. Martin.   The petition concluded:—

Further, we would beg, along with our fellow-petitioners in Glendale, that the tenantry who have been turned out of Lowerkell, Ramasaig, and Hamara by our ill-ruling factor be reinstated.

The tenants of Holmesdale and Liepbein, 29 in number, stated in their petition, that 48 years ago the place was let to ten tenants at about £60, and afterwards re-let to 25 tenants at about £85, besides a sum of £3 2s. 6d. for providing peats for the proprietor.   The rents, they say, have nearly doubled since then, and the inhabitants increased, the present number being nearly 200, occupying 33 dwellings.   There was much overcrowding, there being as many as 15 persons upon crofts of four acres.   The petition contained the following estimate of factors:—" Unless poor crofters are to be protected by the proprietor of the estate, we need not expect anything better than suppression from factors who are constantly watching and causing the downfall of their fellow-beings, in order to turn their small portion of the soil into sheep-walks."   These tenants prayed that the evicted townships of Lowerkell, Ramasaig, and Hamara, should be restored to the tenants, and thus to afford relief to the overcrowded townships.   The crofters of Glasvein said they had no hill pasture for sheep, and no peat moss to get their fuel from.   When some of the present crofters, they say, came into possession of their crofts, the township of Glasvein was allotted to seven tenants, each paying an average rent of £5, whereas now the township is in the possession of 12 crofters, paying each an average rent of £4 or so.   They accordingly sought to have this matter remedied.

It may be stated that most of the tenants of Glendale

appear to be all hard-working, industrious men, and their houses are better, on the whole, than any crofter district that that we have yet visited in Skye. The soil is more fertile, well drained, and comparatively well cultivated. The men seem to be thoroughly intelligent, and some of them not only read newspapers, but have very decided opinions in regard to some of them. One of these, the *Scotsman*, we heard them designating as "The United Liar". But newspaper reading—that is Liberal newspaper reading—is not encouraged in Glendale. One man whom we met informed us that a crofter in Glendale was accused of reading too many newspapers, a circumstance which the factor strongly suspected accounted for the heinous crime of the crofter being a Liberal. At one time there were some small shops in Glendale, but these would appear to have practically vanished. Some years ago the factor set up a meal store himself, and the crofters, we are informed, were given to understand that shopkeepers would have to pay a rent of £2 each for these so-called shops, in addition to their rents. No one, however, appears to have ever been asked to pay this, but the shops ceased to exist!

Perhaps the most indefensible custom of all was to compel the incoming tenant to pay up the arrears, however large a sum, of his predecessor. This appeared so incredible that no one present felt justified in publishing it; but on our consulting the factor personally, he not only admitted but actually defended the practice as a kind of fair enough premium or "goodwill" for the concern, and said it was quite a common practice in the Isle of Skye. We would describe it in very different terms, but that is unnecessary. It only wants to be stated to be condemned by all honest men as an outrage on public morality.

As we left the district the crofters were in great glee at the prospect of a visit from the trustees to arrange matters with them. They are hopeful that important concessions may be made to them, and if these hopes should not be realised, they appear to be animated with an unflinching determination to stand by one another, and, shoulder to shoulder, agitate for the redress of what they firmly maintain to be great and serious grievances.

Dr. Martin's Estate.

We have left ourselves but little space to speak of the condition of affairs on the estate of Dr. Martin. This estate is one which is of great interest to Highlanders. Borreraig, one of the townships in revolt, was anciently held rent free by the MacCrimmons, the hereditary pipers of Macleod of Dunvegan. The principal grievance complained of by the crofters may be briefly stated. The crofters are required to sell to the laird all the fish they catch at a uniform rate of sixpence for ling and fourpence for cod, and we have actually been informed of a case where some one was accused at a semi-public meeting of interfering in a sort of clandestine way with the doctor's privileges by buying the fish at higher prices. The crofters were also required to sell their cattle to the doctor's bailiff at his own price. A man spoke of his having some time ago sold a stirk to a foreign drover, and was after all required to break his bargain with the outsider and hand over the animal to the bailiff. This bailiff was, however, dismissed last Whitsunday, a fact stated in defence by Dr. Martin's friends. Tenants are also required to give eight days' free labour each year to the laird, failing which to pay a penalty of 2s. 6d. per day ; and while thus working, we were informed that if any one by accident broke any of the tools he used, he was required to pay for the damage. The breaking of a shearing-hook subjected the man who did it to pay 2s. 6d. for it. We are aware that the friends of the laird maintain that the labour thus contributed by the people is in reality not for labour, but an equivalent for a portion of the rent. This is a very plausible excuse, but it will not bear examination. If it is regarded as a part of the rent, rates should be paid upon it, and the "annual value" or rent returned to the county valuator each year should be the amount actually paid in money plus the value of the eight days' labour. Thus, either the labour is free, or there is an unjust and inequitable burden thrown on the other crofters in the parish who do not perform such labour, as, of course, the labour given by Dr. Martin's tenants is not rated. The tenants have now struck against performing this work, and Dr. Martin's work was done this year on ordinary day labour.

The people also complain that the hill land was taken from the tenants of Galtrigill, and the hill grounds of Borreraig, the neighbouring township, thrown open to them. This was a very material curtailment of the subjects let, but further, sums of from 10s. to 30s. were added to the rent of each holding. No crofter on the estate has a sheep or a horse, and they are obliged to buy wool for their clothing from a distance, as Dr. Martin, they say, will not sell them any. The tenants paid their rents at Martinmas last, but they have given notice that unless their demands are conceded they will not pay the rent due at Martinmas next. The leading points of their petition are that the rents be reduced, the old land-marks restored, and the hill grounds as of old given to them. This petition the tenants sent to Dr. Martin some time ago, but he has not made any reply. The tenants do not appear to be very hopeful that

he will make any concession, but they are evidently determined to walk in the same paths as their neighbours on the
estate of Sir John Macpherson Macleod, and they are in
great hopes that the friends of the Gael in the large towns
of the south will manfully aid them in their battle against
landlordism. This statement will enable the reader to form
his own opinion on the question which has produced such a
feeling of insecurity and terror in the minds of both crofter
and proprietor for the last two years in the Isle of Skye,
indeed throughout the whole Highlands.

Burning the Summonses in the Braes.

We shall next give a short account of what followed upon
the refusal of these proprietors to give favourable consideration to the claims of their crofting tenantry. A correspondent of the *Free Press*, early in April last, described what
had occurred—after the tenants had refused to pay any rent
until their grievances were considered—in the following
terms :—

The quarrel between Lord Macdonald and his tenants of
Balmeanach, Peinichorrain, and Gedintaillear, in the Braes
of Portree, is developing into portentous importance. His
lordship, it appears, has made up his mind to put the law in
force against them, and not on any account to yield to their
demands ; and on Friday a sheriff-officer and assistant,
accompanied by his lordship's ground-officer from Portree,
proceeded to serve summonses of removing, and small debt
summonses for rent upon about a score of the refractory
ones. The tenants, however, for some time past, since they
took up their present attitude, have been posting regular
sentinels on watch to give warning of any stranger's approach,
and when the officer and his party were at the Bealach near

the schoolhouse, two youngsters who were on duty thereabout gave the signal, and, immediately, it was transmitted far and near with the result of bringing together from all quarters from their spring work a gathering of about 150 or 200 men, women, and children, who rushed to meet the officer before he had got near the intended scene of his operation, viz., the townships of Peinichorrain, Balmeanach, and Gedintaillear, and, surrounding him, demanded his business. Upon understanding it, and being shown the summonses, the documents were immediately taken from him and burnt before his eyes, and thereupon he was coolly requested to go to his master for more of them. The officer, who is well known among them, with good tact, humoured them, and so escaped with a sound skin, so that no violence was used ; but it appears the temper of the people was such that had he been less conciliatory, or had he attempted to resist the people, the consequence would have been inevitably very serious for him. When they were gathering from the sea-shore, where many of them were cutting sea-ware with reaping-hooks, their leaders judiciously shouted out to leave their hooks behind, which was done, so that the risk of using such ugly arms in the event of a *melée* was avoided. The officer spoke lightly before proceeding to the place of the resistance he was likely to meet, and thought there would really be none, as he knew the people so well and they knew him, many of them being his relations, but his impressions now of the real state of the people's minds is said to be very different, and he believes there would be no use attempting any legal steps again by the employment of the officers of civil law. The same paper in a later issue says :—

We have received the following narrative of the manner in which the summonses were burned on Friday last :—The people met the officer on the road, about a mile from the scene of his intended labours. They were clamorous and angry, of course. He told them his mission, and that he would give them the summonses on the spot if they liked. They said, " Thoir dhuinn iad," (Give them to us) and he did so. The officer was then asked to light a fire. He did so ; and a fish liver being placed upon it, that oily material was soon in a blaze. The officer was then peremptorily ordered to consign the summonses to the flames, which he did ! The summonses were of course straightway consumed to ashes. The interchange of compliments between the officers of the law and the people were, as might be ex- pected, of a fiery character. The chief officer was graciously and considerately informed that his conduct—as he had only acted in the performance of a public official duty—was excusable ; but with his assistant, or concurrent, it was different. He was there for pay, and he would not go home without it. Certain domestic utensils, fully charged, were suddenly brought on the scene, and their contents were showered on the unlucky assistant, who immediately disappeared, followed by a howling crowd of boys.

MARCH OF THE DISMAL BRIGADE.

The summonses were never served, and the County Au- thorities after full consideration determined to arrest and punish the ringleaders for deforcing the officers of the law. Sheriff Ivory obtained a body of police from Glasgow, and with these, twelve from the mainland of the County of In- verness, and the Skye portion of the force, he, with the leading county officials invaded the Isle of Skye during the night of the 17th of April. After consulting with the local

authorities in Portree, an early start was made for the Braes
to surprise and arrest the ringleaders. The secret was well
kept, but two newspaper correspondents were fortunate
enough to get an inkling of the proceedings, namely, Mr.
Mackinnon Ramsay, of the *Citizen*, who followed the invading force from Glasgow, and Mr. Alexander Gow, a
special correspondent of the *Dundee Advertiser*, who had
gone to Portree a few days before the Battle of the Braes.
These gentlemen accompanied the county officials, saw the
whole proceedings, and sent a full description of the desperate and humiliating scrimmage to their respective papers.
We give below Mr. Gow's graphic account, every particular
of which we found corroborated by the leading county
officials on our arrival in Portree the same evening. After
describing the state of feeling, and the acts on the part of
the crofters which led up to direct contact with the criminal
authorities, Mr. Gow proceeds :—

Here we were, then—two Sheriffs, two Fiscals, a Captain
of police, forty-seven members of the Glasgow police force,
and a number of the county constabulary, as well as a
couple of newspaper representatives from Dundee and Glasgow, and a gentleman representing a well-known Glasgow
drapery house—fairly started on an eight-mile tramp to the
Land League camp at Braes, in weather that for sheer brutal
ferocity had not been experienced in Skye for a very long
time. In the cold grey dawn the procession wore a sombre
aspect. It looked for all the world like a Highland funeral.
It was quite on the cards, indeed, that the return journey
might partake of the nature of a funeral procession. There
could be no doubt that every one was fully impressed with
the gravity of the mission on which we were proceeding.
It is literal truth to say that no member of the company
expected to return without receiving knocks, if not some-

thing more serious. We were perfectly aware that the crofters had made preparations for giving us a warm reception. In front, some distance ahead of the main body, walked the sheriff-officer, a policeman, and another person occupying for the time being some official position. Then came the police detachment, and the Sheriffs and the Fiscals brought up the rear—the three unofficial persons already mentioned forming what may be termed the rearguard. In this manner we proceeded without incident for four miles, when the Sheriff and his friends left the vehicle and sent it back. About half-past six o'clock we reached the boundary of the disaffected district nearest Portree. Hitherto scarcely a single soul was observed along the route, and some surprise was expressed by those in charge. At the schoolhouse, however, it was expected that a portion of the colony would be encountered, but the place was untenanted. On another mile, and signs of life appeared among the hillocks. Presently our ears were saluted with whistling and cheering, and this was interpreted as a sign that it was time to close the ranks. Gedentailler township was passed without any demonstrations of hostility. At the south end of this township there is an ugly looking pass, which seemed to cause some anxiety to the officers in charge. No wonder, as there could not be a finer position for an attack on a hostile body of men. On the west, a steep rocky brae rises sheer from the road to the height of about 400 or 500 feet. On the other side, a terrific precipice descends to the sea. We passed through it in safety, however, but Inspector Cameron, of the Skye police, had reason to believe that the return passage would be disputed.

Arrived at the boundary of Balmeanach, we found a collection of men, women, and children, numbering well on to 100. They cheered as we mounted the knoll, and the women saluted the policemen with volleys of sarcasms about their voyage from Glasgow. A halt was then called, and a parley ensued between the local inspector and what appeared to be the leader of the townships. What is passing between the two it is difficult for an outsider to understand, and while the conversation is in progress it is worth while to look about. At the base of the steep cliff on which we stood, and extending to the seashore, lay the hamlet of Balmeanach. There might be about a score of houses dotted over this plain. From each of these the owners were running hillward with all speed. It was evident they had been taken by surprise. Men, women, and children rushed forward, in all stages of attire, most of the females with their hair down and streaming loosely in the breeze. Every soul carried a weapon of some kind or another, but in most cases these were laid down when the detachment was approached. While we were watching the crowds scrambling up the declivity, scores of persons had gathered from other districts, and they now completely surrounded the procession. The confusion that prevailed baffles description. The women, with infuriated looks and bedraggled dress—for it was still raining heavily—were shouting at the pitch of their voices, uttering the most fearful imprecations, hurling forth the most terrible vows of vengeance against the enemy. Martin was of course the object of greatest abuse. He was cursed in his own person and in that of his children, if he should have any, one female shrieking curses with especial vehemence. The authorities proceeded at once to perform their disagreeable task, and in the course of twenty minutes the five suspected persons were apprehended. A scene utterly indescribable followed. The women, with the most violent gestures and imprecations, declared that the police should be attacked. Stones began to be thrown, and so serious an aspect did matters assume that the police drew their batons and charged. This was the signal for a general attack. Huge boulders darkened the horizon as they sped from the hands of infuriated men and women. Large sticks and flails were brandished and brought down with crushing force upon the police—the poor prisoners coming in for their share of the blows. One difficult point had to be captured, and as the expedition approached this dangerous position, it was seen to be strongly occupied with men and women, armed with stones and boulders. A halt was called and the situation discussed. Finally it was agreed to attempt to force a way through a narrow gully. By this time a crowd had gathered in the rear of the party. A rush was made for the pass, and from the heights a fearful fusilade of stones descended. The advance was checked. The party could neither advance nor recede. For two minutes the expedition stood exposed to the merciless shower of missiles. Many were struck, and a number more or less injured. The situation was highly dangerous. Raising a yell that might have been heard at a distance of two miles, the crofters, maddened by the apprehension of some of the oldest men in the township, rushed on the police, each person armed with huge stones, which, on approaching near enough, they discharged with a vigour that nothing could resist. The women were by far the most troublesome assailants. Thinking apparently that the constables would offer them no resistance, they approached to within a few yards' distance, and poured a fearful volley into the compact mass. The police charged, but the crowd gave way scarcely a yard. Returning again, Captain Donald gave orders to drive back the howling mob, at the same time advising the Sheriffs and the constables in charge of the prisoners to move rapidly forward. This second charge was more effective, as the attacking force was

driven back about a hundred yards. The isolated constables now, however, found their position very dangerous.
The crofters rallied and hemmed them in, and a rush had
to be made to catch up the main body in safety. At this
point several members of the constabulary received serious
buffetings, and had they not regained their comrades, some
of their number would in all probability have been mortally
wounded. Meanwhile the crowd increased in strength.

The time within which summonses of ejectment could
be legally served having expired, the crofters had for a
day or two relaxed their vigilance, and not expecting the
constables so early in the morning, they had no time
to gather their full strength. But the "Fiery Cross" had
in five minutes passed through the whole township from
every point. Hundreds of determined looking persons
could be observed converging on the procession, and
matters began to assume a serious aspect. With great
oaths, the men demanded where were the Peinichorrain men.
This township was the most distant, and the men had not
yet had time to come up. But they were coming. Cheers
and yells were raised. "The rock! the rock!" suddenly
shouted some one. "The rock! the rock!" was taken
up, and roared out from a hundred throats. The strength
of the position was realised by the crofters; so also it
was by the constables. The latter were ordered to run at
the double. The people saw the move, and the screaming
and yelling became fiercer than ever. The detachment
reached the opening of the gulley. Would they manage
to run through? Yes! No! On went the blue coats, but
their progress was soon checked. It was simply insane to
attempt the passage. Stones were coming down like hail,
while huge boulders where hurled down before which
nothing could stand. These bounded over the road and

descended the precipice with a noise like thunder. An order was given to dislodge a number of the most determined assailants, but the attempt proved futile. They could not be dislodged. Here and there a constable might be seen actually bending under the pressure of a well-directed rounder, losing his footing, and rolling down the hill, followed by scores of missiles. This state of matters could not continue. The chief officials were securing their share of attention. Captain Donald is hit in the knee with a stone as large as a matured turnip. A rush must be made for the pass, or there seems a possibility that Sheriff Ivory himself will be deforced. Once more the order was given to double. On, on, the procession went—Sheriffs and Fiscals forgetting their dignity, and taking to their heels. The scene was the most exciting that either the spectators or those who passed through the fire ever experienced, or are likely ever to see again. By keeping up the rush, the party got through the defile, and emerged triumphantly on the Portree side, not however, without severe injuries. If the south end township had turned out, the pass would, I believe, never have been forced, and some would in all probability have lost their lives.

The crofters seemed to have become more infuriated by the loss of their position, and rushing along the shoulder of the hill prepared to attack once more. This was the final struggle. In other attacks the police used truncheons freely. But at this point they retaliated with both truncheons and stones. The consequences were very serious indeed. Scores of bloody faces could be seen on the slope of the hill. One woman, named Mary Nicolson, was fearfully cut in the head, and fainted on the road. When she was found, blood was pouring down her neck and ears. Another woman, Mrs. Finlayson, was badly gashed on the cheek with some missile. Mrs. Nicolson, whose husband, James Nicolson, was one of the prisoners, had her head badly laid open, but whether with a truncheon or stone is not known. Another woman, well advanced in years, was hustled in the scrimmage on the hill, and, losing her balance, rolled down a considerable distance, her example being followed by a stout policeman, the two ultimately coming into violent collision. The poor old person was badly bruised, and turned sick and faint. Of the men a considerable number sustained severe bruises, but so far as I could ascertain none of them were disabled. About a dozen of the police were injured more or less seriously. One of the Glasgow men had his nose almost cut through with a stone, and was terribly gashed about the brow. Captain Donald, as already stated, was struck on the knee, and his leg swelled up badly after the return to Portree. Neither the Sheriffs nor the Fiscals were injured, but it is understood that they all received hits in the encounter on the hill.

After the serious scrimmage at Gedintailler, no further demonstrations of hostility were made, and the procession went on, without further adventure, to Portree. Rain fell without intermission during the entire journey out and home, and all arrived at their destination completely exhausted. On arrival in town the police were loudly hooted and hissed as they passed through the square to the jail, and subsequently when they marched from the Court-house to the Royal Hotel. The prisoners were lodged in the prison. There names are :—Alexander Finlayson, aged between 60 and 70 years ; Malcolm Finlayson, a son of the above, and living in the same house (the latter is married); Peter Macdonald has a wife and eight of a family ; Donald Nicolson, 66 years of age, and is married ; and James Nicolson, whose wife was one of the women seriously injured.

Unless appearances are totally misleading, the work which they were obliged to accomplish was most repugnant to Sheriff Ivory, Sheriff Spiers, Mr. James Anderson, Procurator-Fiscal for the County, and Mr. MacLennan; and the hope may be expressed that they will never again be called upon to undertake similar duties.

The "Battle of the Braes" has been capitally hit off in the following parody, published in the *Daily Mail* of the 26th of April last :—

CHARGE OF THE SKYE BRIGADE.

Half a league, half a league !
　Four a-breast—onward !
All in the valley of Braes
　Marched the half-hundred.
"Forward, Police Brigade !
In front of me," bold Ivory said ;
Into the valley of Braes
　Charged the half-hundred.

"Forward, Police Brigade !
Charge each auld wife and maid !"
E'en though the Bobbies knew
　Some one had blundered !
Their's not to make reply ;
Their's not to reason why ;
Their's but to do or die ;
Into the valley of Braes
　Charged the half-hundred.

"Chuckies" to right of them,
"Divots" to left of them,
Women in front of them,
　Volleyed and thundered !
Stormed at with stone and shell,
Boldly they charged, they tell,
Down on the Island Host !
Into the mouth of—well !
　Charged the half-hundred.

Flourished their batons bare,
Not in the empty air—
Clubbing the lasses there,
Charging the Cailleachs, while
   All Scotland wondered !
Plunged in the mist and smoke,
Right thro' the line they broke ;—
Cailleach and maiden
Reeled from the baton stroke,
   Shattered and sundered ;
Then they marched back—intact—
   All the half-hundred.

Missiles to right of them,
Brickbats to left of them,
Old wives behind them
   Volleyed and floundered.
Stormed at with stone and shell—
Whilst only Ivory fell—
They that had fought so well
Broke thro' the Island Host,
Back from the mouth of—well !
All that was left of them—
   All the half-hundred !

When can their glory fade ?
O, the wild charge they made !
   All Scotland wondered !
Honour the charge they made !
Honour the Skye Brigade !
   Donald's half-hundred !

          ALFRED TENNYSON, JUNIOR.

TRIAL OF THE BRAES CROFTERS.

WHEN the "Battle of the Braes" had been fought and won, and the gallant Sheriff with his brave contingent of blue-coats covered with the mud of the Braes and the glory of their masterly retreat before the old men and women of Gedintailler had retired to their quarters in Portree, the friends of the prisoners began to think of their defence when they came before the Law Courts for trial.

A few hours after the Police Brigade returned to Portree, Dean of Guild Mackenzie, Inverness, editor of the *Celtic Magazine*, who had gone, as representative of the Highland Land Law Reform Association, to report upon the alleged grievances of the crofters in Skye, arrived ln Portree. Him the friends of the prisoners consulted, with the result that he dispatched a telegram to Mr. Kenneth Macdonald, Town Clerk of Inverness, asking him to undertake the defence. Curiously enough a number of sympathisers in Glasgow, who had formed themselves into a defence committee, met about the same time, and they also, through their secretary, Mr. Hugh Macleod, Writer, Glasgow, telegraphed to know if Mr. Macdonald would defend the prisoners. Both telegrams were delivered about the same time and to each an affirmative reply was immediately sent.

At this time nothing definite was known of the charge preferred against the prisoners, and it was not until the 26th of April, 1882, a week after the arrest, and when they could no longer be legally detained without having a copy of the charge delivered to them, that the prisoners were committed for trial and allowed to see an adviser. Such is the humanity of the Criminal Law of Scotland. During the week which a prisoner can thus be legally kept in close confinement, he will not be permitted to see friend or adviser of any kind, but he may be brought day after day before the Sheriff and subjected to examination by a skilful lawyer whose main if not sole object is to get from him admissions which will tend to prove his guilt, and every word he utters during this time is taken down for the purpose of being used against him at his trial.

After the prisoners were committed for trial, they were visited by their agent, with the editor of the *Celtic Magazine* as interpreter, and in course of conversation, and in reply to questions, the prisoners expressed a desire to get home to proceed with the spring work on their crofts. By this time the sympathy with the prisoners among the outside public, not merely in the Highlands but in the large cities of the south, had extended through all classes of society. Many who were in entire sympathy with them in their personal grievances thought that they saw in the proceedings taken against them, and in the outrages perpetrated in Skye in the name of law, a means of creating a public opinion which would compel the Legislature to take up the question of land tenure in the Highlands. It was the desire of this party that the accused should be allowed to remain in prison until their trial came on, in order that the public sympathy which their apprehension and imprisonment evoked should have time to take definite form. If the calculations of these sympathisers should turn out accurate, the infliction of a slight hardship upon these men would result in permanent good to themselves and the whole class to which they belonged. The desires of the men themselves, however, of their friends in Inverness, and the interest of their families, naturally guided Mr. Macdonald's proceedings, and he presented a petition to the Sheriff to fix bail. The bail was fixed by Sheriff Blair at £20 sterling for each prisoner —£100 in all—and immediately it became known that persons were wanted, to sign the bond, gentlemen offered themselves, the required subscriptions were obtained, and the five prisoners were liberated that night. The gentlemen who signed the bond were: Mr. John Macdonald, merchant, Exchange; Dean of Guild Mackenzie; Councillor Duncan Macdonald; Councillor W. G. Stuart; Mr. Wm. Gunn, Castle Street; Mr. T. B. Snowie, gunmaker; Mr. Donald Campbell, draper; and Mr. Duncan MacBeath, Duncraig Street—all of Inverness. On the following day the accused left Inverness for Skye by the 9 A.M. train, accompanied to the station by several of their friends, including the Reverend and venerable Dr. George Mackay.

The following account of the reception of the liberated men on their return to Portree is taken from the *Aberdeen Daily Free Press*, whose special correspondent, Mr. William Mackenzie, was on the spot :—

The five men from the prison of Inverness arrived at Portree this evening, and were received with unbounded enthusiasm. Early in the day a telegram was received intimating that they had left Inverness in the morning, and that the venerable pastor of the North Church, the Rev. Dr. Mackay, gave them there a friendly farewell. Mairi Nighean Iain Bhain, to whose poetic effusions on the men of the Braes and Benlee, I have formerly alluded, went by the steamer from Portree in the morning to meet them at Strome Ferry. She was accompanied by Colin the piper, and on the homeward journey the men were inspired with the songs of the poetess, the music of the Highland war-pipe, and a scarcely less potent stimulant, the famous Talisker. It was known far and wide that the men were to come to-night, and their fellow-crofters in the Braes resolved to give them a hearty reception. The Braes men accordingly began to straggle into the town in the afternoon, and groups of them might be seen along the street eagerly discussing the situation. Endeavours were made to induce the "suspects" to leave the steamer at Raasay and row afterwards to the Braes. This would, of course, deprive their friends of any chance to give them an ovation at Portree, and lead outsiders to suppose that the Portree people regarded the matter with indifference. The liberated men were, however, warned against being caught in the snare which was laid for them, and they came straight on to Portree. The steamer did not arrive till about eight o'clock, but whenever she reached the quay the assembled multitude raised a deafening cheer, again and again renewed, which completely drowned Colin's pipes. As soon as the steamer was brought alongside the quay, Colin stepped out, playing "Gabhaidh sinn an rathad mor". He was followed by the poetess, and after her the five liberated men. Each man, as he stepped on the quay, was embraced by the males, and hugged and kissed by the females, amid volumes of queries as to their condition since they left, and congratulations on their return. These friendly greetings were not allowed to be of any duration, for each man was hoisted and carried shoulder-high in triumph through the streets of Portree. The Braes men themselves mustered in full force, and in the procession they were joined by numerous sympathisers in the district and the village of Portree. The crowd, headed by the piper and the poetess, proceeded along the principal thoroughfare to the Portree Hotel. Bonnets were carried on the tops of walking sticks, and held up above the heads of the people, amid cries of "Still higher yet my bonnet," while the women of Portree waved their white hand-kerchiefs and shouted Gaelic exclamations of joy as the "lads wi' the bonnets o' blue" were carried along in triumph. On reaching the Portree Hotel a number of them, including the "suspects," went in, and Mr. MacInnes, the popular tenant of that excellent and well-conducted establishment, treated the "suspects" to refreshments. Who should happen to turn up unexpectedly at the hotel but the factor, accompanied by some of his friends, and when that individual emerged from the door of the hotel, he was received with a volume of groans. The Braes men left the hotel without any delay and marched to their homes in a body, shouting and cheering as they proceeded on their way. A carriage was sent after them to convey the five men from Inverness to their respective places of abode.

In the meantime an intimation had been conveyed to the Prisoners' Agent by Mr. James Anderson, Procurator-Fiscal of Inverness, that he had been ordered by the Crown Agent to have the prisoners tried summarily before the Sheriff for the crimes of deforcement and assault. This was, so far as known, the first time in Scottish Legal History that so serious a crime, so seriously treated by the authorities at the outset, had been ordered for summary trial. There was something suspicious in the order, and although the letter of it was adhered to, it is probable that but for the protests made on behalf of the prisoners, both in and out of Parliament, the true meaning of the order would have been made evident at the trial. On receiving intimation of the order, Mr. Macdonald wrote to the Lord-Advocate for Scotland, requesting that he should instruct the trial to proceed before a jury. To that letter the following reply was received :—

WHITEHALL, April 29, 1882.

SIR,

I am directed by the Lord-Advocate to acknowledge receipt of your letter of 27th current, and to say in reply that he sees no reason for re-calling the order for trial of the Skye crofters charged with assault and deforcement before the Sheriff summarily, and that the order will therefore be carried out.

I am,
Sir,
Your obedient servant,
D. CRAWFORD.

KENNETH MACDONALD, Esq.

Mr. Macdonald, immediately on receiving the reply, addressed the following letter to the Lord-Advocate :—

INVERNESS, 1st May, 1882.

MY LORD,

I have received from your Secretary a letter stating that you "see no reason for recalling the order for trial of the Skye crofters charged with assault and deforcement before the Sheriff summarily, and that the order will therefore be carried out". I thought when I first wrote you that the request for a jury trial was so fair and reasonable that I did not require to adduce any reason in support of it, and that it lay with you, if you refused it, to give a reason for the refusal. Since, however, you do not seem to take this view of the matter, you will permit me to state some of the reasons which I think ought to induce you to grant the request of the prisoners.

The crime with which the men are charged is said to have been com-mitted in the Skye district of this county. In that district there is a Court which has hitherto, so far as I can ascertain, tried *all* summary cases arising in the district. And yet without any reason assigned, the present case has been ordered for trial at Inverness. Had the case been sent for a jury trial it would have been the usual, and indeed, necessary, course to try the case here, but it is a thing hitherto unheard of that a summary trial from one of the outlying districts of the county should be taken here. With a complete machinery for conducting summary trials in the District Court, the prisoners are entitled to some explanation of the reason why they are put to the expense of bringing their witnesses and themselves from Skye to Inverness, when, in the ordinary course of things, they ought to go no further from home than Portree. It may be answered that as the resident Sheriff at Portree was engaged in the apprehension of the prisoners, he ought not to try the case. That is perfectly true. The prisoners quite agree that it would be improper to have the case tried by Mr. Spiers, but they are not responsible for what he has done, and ought not to suffer for it. If Sheriff Spiers has disqualified himself from trying the case, that affords no reason for punishing the persons to be tried. All that would be required to be done would be to have the trial conducted in Portree by Sheriff Blair, who would, according to your order, conduct it in Inverness.

What I have said is sufficient to show that your order is an exceptional one, and the prisoners, and, I believe, the public also, will expect you to justify it. Had these prisoners stood alone, their poverty would have prevented them bringing a single witness from Skye to establish their innocence, and your order would have meant a simple denial of justice.

But, further, the crime with which these men are charged is that of deforcement of an officer of the Sheriff of Inverness, and your order is that the Sheriff, whose servant is said to have been deforced, shall be the sole judge of whether the crime was committed or not. It is not my wish to draw historical parallels, but the circumstances will, no doubt, suggest to your lordship a series of trials which took place in Scotland nearly ninety years ago, when Muir and his fellow-reformers were convicted of sedition. It is not for me to suggest, and I do not suggest, that any of our local judges would deal unfairly with the prisoners, but I ask what is your reason for refusing them a trial by jury. It is to *you* they look in the first instance, and it is *your* reasons for pursuing an exceptional course with men who have already been harshly dealt with that the public will canvass.

I presume the object of the proceedings which have already been adopted with regard to these men, and of the trial which is to follow, is to inspire them and their fellows with a proper respect for the law. If this is so, let them have no excuse for saying they have not got fair play. If their crime was so important as to call for the exceptional measures taken for their apprehension, it is surely too important to be disposed of by a Court whose duties are usually confined to mere matters of police. The belief of the prisoners is that the object of your order is to secure their conviction at all hazards irrespective of their guilt or innocence, and this belief is shared by a growing number of the outside public. It is for you to dispel this misapprehension if it is one.

In such circumstances as I have described a summary trial would be little else than a farce ; and you will never inspire the Highland crofters or their friends with respect for the law if you persist in enacting such a farce in its name. I trust, therefore, you will reconsider your resolution, and yet order the trial of the prisoners in a manner which will inspire them with confidence in the administration of the law of their country.

I am,

Your obedient servant,

KENNETH MACDONALD.

The Honourable the LORD-ADVOCATE for Scotland,
    Home Office, Whitehall, London, S.W.

On the same evening that the letter was written Mr. Fraser-Mackintosh (M.P. for the Inverness Burghs), in the House of Commons, asked the Lord-Advocate whether he would order that the Skye crofters now committed for trial should, instead of being tried summarily, have the privilege of being tried by a jury of their countrymen, and that the presiding judge should be one disconnected with the exceptional proceedings attendant on their recent apprehension ?

Mr. Dick Peddie had also the following question to ask the Lord-Advocate—Whether it is the case that instructions have been given that the five crofters recently arrested in Skye, and now released on bail, be tried summarily; whether they have applied through their agent to be tried by jury : and whether he intended to comply with their application ?

The Lord-Advocate, in reply, said he saw no reason for recalling the order for the trial before a summary magistrate.

After due consideration with his learned friend, the Solicitor-General for Scotland, this decision had been arrived at when the case was before them during the Easter recess. The people of Skye were generally peaceful, and having reason to believe that they were misled by bad advice, or they would not have resisted officers of the law in the execution of a legal warrant, he, with his learned colleague, thought that the offence would not be repeated if it was made clear to the people as rapidly as possible that the law will be vindicated. The charges preferred were of the least grave class that could be preferred on behalf of the Crown, and summary trial proceedings afforded little delay. The maximum sentence that could be inflicted was sixty days, and of course a lighter sentence would be passed if in the discretion of the magistrate it met the justice of the case. As to the last part of the question, it was intended that the trial should proceed before the Sheriff of Inverness who had not hitherto taken part in measures which unfortunately became necessary to vindicate the authority of the law in Skye.

The refusal of a Jury trial was final so far as the Crown was concerned. Curious as it may seem, an accused person in Scotland has no right to demand a trial by his peers. Our forefathers were not so careful of their liberties in this respect, or not so powerful to enforce them as our neighbours over the border. They took care centuries ago to secure this right; we have not secured it yet.

What might have occurred in this particular case but for the fear of public indignation it is hard to say. Tyranny has a peculiar fascination for weak men. Lord-Advocate Balfour, a good lawyer, but a weak politician, the holder of an office which was long since stripped of most of its power, and which immediately before his accession to it was so emasculated that his predecessor declined to sacrifice his self-respect by continuing to hold it,—desired to do one official act which had an appearance of strength about it without the reality. He had brought contempt upon the administration of the law by sanctioning or suggesting the sending of a large body of police from Glasgow to Skye to arrest a few old men of peaceful habits and general good character, whose worst weapon, it has been proved, was a lump of wet turf, and when the whole country was indulging in a roar of laughter over the ignominious retreat of the invading army of policemen before the women of the Braes, and the ridiculous ending of a performance which was intended to represent the dignity of the Law, he, the person primarily responsible for the mistake which had been committed, would naturally desire to cover his blunder by securing a conviction against the few harmless cottars whom the policemen in their blind panic had first laid hands on.

If ever there was a case which ought to be tried by a Jury this was one. At no time is the right of Jury trial more valuable than when the opinions of the public, and the acts of the Crown, as represented by its officials, run counter to each other, and when these acts are in any way connected with the offence to be tried. At no time ought the right to be more readily conceded. Here, however, it was determinedly denied. To Mr. Macdonald's second letter no answer was ever given. We believe none was expected. Except in the answer given to the questions of Mr. Fraser-Mackintosh and Mr. Dick Peddie in the House of Commons, at least twenty-four hours before Mr. Macdonald's letter reached him, the Lord-Advocate did not attempt either to explain or defend his conduct. In point of fact, complete explanation or defence was impossible. All that time the Crown officers must have known what was not known to the prisoners' advisers at the time, that there was no evidence against the prisoners upon which any sane Jury would convict. But the Lord-Advocate seems never to have forgotten that the officialism of the County of Inverness had involved itself in the mess, and in a summary trial officialism might be left to vindicate its own dignity. This would also vindicate the dignity of the law, and the wisdom of its administrators—at least so they thought. This theory was universally accepted outside official circles as the reason for the resolution to try summarily, and but for the protests made by outsiders, and particularly a number of Scottish Members of Parliament to secure a fair trial for the prisoners, most people believed that the trial would have been even a greater farce than it turned out to be, but with a far different ending.

The efforts of the Scottish Members to obtain a Jury trial did not end with the questions in the House of Commons. Efforts were made privately by some of these gentlemen to save the Administration of Justice in Scotland from being sullied, but without result, and when all their efforts failed, the members who had taken most interest in the matter, published the following protest in the *Times* of 10th May, 1882, from which it was quoted by almost every newspaper in the Kingdom :—

The circumstances of the arrest, by a large body of police brought from Glasgow, of half-a-dozen Skye crofters, accused of deforcing a sheriff's officer who went among them to serve writs, and the attempt at a rescue which attended it, must be fresh in the minds of your readers. We need not say that the case has excited great public interest in Scotland. It is most important, therefore, in order to secure any moral effect, that the trial should be conducted under such circumstances as will place the verdict above all suspicion. This, we regret to say, is not to be done, and already many persons who sympathise with the men, and desire that their case shall be fairly heard, openly accuse the Executive of resorting to unworthy means to obtain a conviction. For ourselves, we may at once state our perfect belief in the sincerity of the Lord Advocate in his profession of a desire, while vindicating the law, to provide for the accused that form of trial which will protect them from an unnecessarily heavy punishment. But punishment pre-supposes guilt, while what the accused contend is that they are not guilty. What they claim is that they shall first have their guilt established in the ordinary way, and if found guilty they are willing to take their chance of that punishment their conduct may seem to deserve.

Now, persons accused of crimes committed in Skye have hitherto been invariably tried in one of two ways. If the cases are considered so trivial as to be dealt with summarily, they are tried by a sheriff-substitute sitting at Portree. This course secures to the accused the important advantage that evidence for his defence is procurable at a *minimum* of expense and inconvenience. If the case is of a grave character, it is tried by a jury at Inverness. This, of course, involves much more inconvenience and expense to the defence, but it secures the services of a jury, a tribunal which, for the purpose of deciding on matters of fact, is admittedly superior to a Judge, however impartial, sitting alone. But in the case of the Skye crofters the trial is to be at Inverness, without a jury. The defence thus incurs all the inconvenience and expense usually attendant on a jury trial, and obtains none of the advantages in the way of a tribunal the best qualified to pronounce on the question of the guilt or innocence of the accused. It is stated that Portree is in such an excited state that it is unadvisable that the trial should take place there, and that, therefore, it has to be removed to Inverness. There is not the smallest reason, however, why, being held at Inverness, it should not be held in the usual manner. The accused dispute the facts alleged by the prosecution. Their agent has asked for a jury to decide on the question of fact. A jury trial is the invariable mode of disposing of Skye cases tried at Inverness ; but a jury trial, though in this case specially demanded, has been refused. The reason given for its refusal is that the Crown authorities having originally intended that the trial should be a summary one at Portree, though it has now been deemed advisable to remove it to Inverness, they see no reason to change the form of trial on that account. The reply is that at Portree there would have been nothing unusual in a summary trial, and trial at Portree would have secured material advantages to the accused. At Inverness the summary trial of a Skye case is unprecedented, and the expense to the accused as heavy as would be that of a jury trial.

But the Lord Advocate has explained that if the cases had been tried by jury the sentences might have been much heavier than those to which they would be exposed on summary conviction. That is true, but it is equally true that the judge might have awarded sentences as light as he deemed proper. In the interests of justice it is desirable that the punishment should be commensurate with the offence. There is no reason why a judge sitting with a jury on circuit or in the Sheriff Court should not award the slightest possible sentence. That is what the agent for accused thinks, and, knowing their case, he is willing to take his chance of the heavier sentence if they are found guilty and are thought to deserve it.

On the point of guilt or innocence, however, he prefers the verdict of a jury to the decision of a judge, and that has been refused. In criminal cases in Scotland a bare majority of the jury convicts, and if the case is not strong enough to convince eight men out of fifteen, the prisoners are surely entitled to the benefit of the doubt. That is all that has been asked, and that, despite the strongest representations, has been refused. To us its refusal in this particular case, on grounds of public policy, seems particularly regretable, and we beg through your columns publicly to protest against it.

> CHARLES CAMERON.
> C. FRASER-MACKINTOSH.
> P. STEWART MACLIVER.
> JAMES COWAN.
> FRANK HENDERSON.
> J. DICK PEDDIE.
> JAMES W. BARCLAY.

House of Commons, May 9, 1882.

Commenting on this protest the *Pall Mall Gazette* of 10th May, said :—

It is hard to see what answer there can be to the protest on behalf of the Skye crofters raised in the *Times* this morning by seven Scotch members. Skye cases have hitherto always been disposed of either summarily at Portree or by trial before a jury at Inverness. If the accused had not the satisfaction of submitting his case to a jury, he was, at least, relieved from the expense of being tried at a distance from home. But in the present instance it is proposed to try the crofters at Inverness, but without a jury. Why should the crofters be subjected to the disadvantage of both methods of trial without the benefit of either ?

Whether if published earlier this Protest would have had any effect it is hard to say. Probably not. As it was, it only appeared in the *Times* the day before that fixed for the trial. By that time the arrangements were complete. Some days before then Mr. Macdonald, the accused's agent, finding that the trial was to proceed summarily, had gone to Skye and precognosced a large number of witnesses, several of whom were cited for the defence. On the morning the Protest appeared in the *Times* the accused and the witnesses for the prosecution and defence left Portree for Inverness, the trial having been fixed for the 11th of May, 1882.

On that day the accused took their place at the Bar of the Sheriff Court in the Castle of Inverness. The hour of commencement was noon, and by that time the Court-house was crowded. Sheriff Blair, the presiding judge, was accompanied on the bench by Sheriff Shaw, late of Lochmaddy. Besides numerous members of the Faculty, there were around the bar—Mr. Alex. Macdonald, factor, Portree; Mr. Macleod, secretary of the Skye Vigilance Committee, Glasgow; Dean of Guild Mackenzie; Bailie Smith; Mr. Alex. Macdonald Maclellan; Mr. MacHugh; Mr. Cameron of the *Standard*, and several others.

The indictment set forth that Alexander Finlayson, tenant or crofter; Donald Nicolson, tenant or crofter; James Nicolson, now or lately residing with the said Donald Nicolson; Malcolm Finlayson, son of, and now or lately residing with, the said Alexander Finlayson; and Peter Macdonald, son of, and now or lately residing with, Donald Macdonald, tenant or crofter, all residing at Balmeanach, had all and each, or one or more of them, been guilty of the crime of *deforcing an officer of the law in the execution of his duty ; or of the crime of violently resisting and obstructing an officer of the law in the execution of his duty, or persons employed by and assisting an officer of the law in the execution of his duty ; and also of the crime of* assault, or of one or other of these crimes, actor or actors or art and part, in so far as Angus Martin, now or lately residing at Lisigarry, near Portree, in the parish

Portree aforesaid, having been as a sheriff-officer of the County of Inverness, on or about the 7th day of April, 1882, instructed by Alexander Macdonald, solicitor in Portree aforesaid, as agent for the Right Honourable Ronald Archibald Macdonald, Lord Macdonald, of Armadale Castle, Skye, to go to Balmeanach, Penachorain, and Gedentailor, three of the townships in the district of Braes, in the parish of Portree aforesaid, to serve actions of removing, which, with the warrants thereon, he delivered to the said Angus Martin for that purpose, raised in the Sheriff Court of Inverness, Elgin, and Nairn at Portree, at the instance of the said Right Honourable Ronald Archibald Macdonald, Lord Macdonald, upon the tenants in the said townships . . . and also to serve small debt summonses for debt . . . and the said Angus Martin having upon the said 7th day of April, 1882, or about that time, proceeded towards, or in the direction of the said three townships of Balmeanach, Penachorain, and Gedentailor, in order to serve the said actions and small debt summonses, accompanied by Ewen Robertson, now or lately residing at Lisigary aforesaid, as his concurrent and assistant, and by Norman Beaton, ground-officer on the estates of the said Lord Macdonald, and now or lately residing at Shullisheddar, in the parish of Portree aforesaid, the said Alex. Finlayson, Donald Nicolson, James Nicolson, Malcolm Finlayson, and Peter Macdonald, did all and each, or one or more of them, assisted by a crowd of people to the number of 150 or thereby, whose names are to the complainer unknown, actors or actor, or art and part, at or near Gedentailor aforesaid [and at a part thereof three hundred yards or thereby on the south of the schoolhouse, known by the name of MacDermid's Institution, on the lands of Olach in the parish of Portree aforesaid, and now or lately occupied by Kenneth MacLean, teacher there], wickedly and feloniously attack and assault the said Angus Martin, *well knowing him to be an officer of the law, and in the execution of his duty as such, and that he held the said actions and small debt summonses and warrants for service*, and the said Ewen Robertson, *well knowing him to be the assistant and concurrent and witness of the said Angus Martin* and the said Norman Beaton, and did knock them, or one or more of them to the ground, and did by force at or near Gedentailor aforesaid, forcibly seize hold of, and destroy the service copies of the actions and small debt summonses before mentioned, and did also upon the lands of Upper Olach, being another township in the said district of Braes, and in the parish of Portree aforesaid [and at a part of said lands occupied by Donald Macpherson, crofter, there, forty yards or thereby on the south of the said schoolhouse], forcibly seize hold of and burn, or cause, or procure to be burned, the principal copies of the said actions and small debt summonses and warrants thereon, and did further upon the said township of Gedentailor, and upon the said township of Upper Olach, and upon the high road leading from these townships to Portree aforesaid [and on that part of said road lying between Gedentailor aforesaid and the said Schoolhouse], throw stones and clods of earth and peat at the said Angus Martin, Ewen Robertson, and Norman Beaton, by which they, or one or more of them were struck to the hurt and injury of their persons ; *and by all which or part thereof the said Angus Martin, and the said Ewen Robertson were deforced and by force, prevented from executing and discharging their duty and from serving the said actions and small debt summonses.*

Mr. James Anderson, Procurator-Fiscal for the county, conducted the prosecution, and Mr. Kenneth Macdonald, solicitor, and Town Clerk of Inverness, appeared for the prisoners.

The Procurator-Fiscal asked that certain amendments should be made on the complaint with the object of more specifically defining the places at which the acts charged against the prisoners were alleged to have been committed. The amendments were not objected to and were allowed. The lines introduced are those within [ ] in the preceding copy of the libel.

Immediately after the amendments had been made, Mr. Macdonald said that, before the complaint was gone into, he had to state objections to the relevancy of the indictment and also to the competency of the Court to try the case. He objected to the competency of the Court on the ground that the crime charged was of such a serious nature that it ought to be tried by a jury ; and he objected to the competency of the complaint on the ground that the punishment attached by law to the crime charged in the indictment is beyond that which could be imposed in that court. The charge in this case was that of deforcing an officer of the law in the execution of his duty, and that was said to have been done by the prisoners in concert with a crowd of 150 people; so that the deforcement ran into the other serious charge of mobbing and rioting, the most serious kind of deforcement known to the law. This was the first time, he believed, in the legal history of Scotland that a charge of such a serious nature had been tried in a Summary Court. The accused had been brought to that Court; they objected to being brought there. The public prosecutor had no right to dictate what was the competent Court for the trial of a case; it was for his lordship to say whether the Court was competent or incompetent. The public prosecutor had refused to go to a higher Court; he had refused to give these men the benefit of trial by jury; and it was now for his lordship to say whether these men were to have that benefit. It had been said that the reason for bringing the trial in the Summary Court was the fact that the maximum sentence was so small, but his lordship had the same power in the Jury Court as he had in the Summary Court.

The Sheriff said there was no question whatever in regard to the power of a judge sitting in the Jury Court to inflict the minimum punishment in a case of deforcement; and he instanced a case of that kind, tried by Lord Young at the Inverness Circuit Court, in which the sentence was a fine of 40s., with the alternative of one month's imprisonment.

Mr. Macdonald quoted the acts of the Scottish Parliament of 1581 (C. 118), 1587, (C. 85), and 1591 (C. 152), which regulated the punishment which by statute followed on conviction, to show the serious nature of the charge against the prisoners, and argued that as the libel concluded generally for "the pains of law" and these pains were statutory and such as were beyond the power of a Court of summary jurisdiction to inflict, the Court was incompetent to dispose of the cause.   He also quoted from Hume and Alison to show that the High Court had frequently suspended sentences pronounced in a Summary Court when the crime charged was too serious for such a mode of trial.   He maintained that before 1864 there never was a case of such magnitude tried before a Summary Court, and if not before 1864 there was nothing in the Act of that date which would entitle them to try it.

The Sheriff said that this was an offence at common law as well as under the statute.   They were proceeding at common law, and the pains and penalties which the prosecutor asked should be inflicted, were the pains and penalties applicable under the Summary Procedure Acts.

Mr. Macdonald held that the punishment was statutory, even though the offence was charged at common law.

The Sheriff said the punishment was statutory if the prosecution was under the statute ; but if the prosecution was at common law, it was not necessary for the Court to take the statutory penalty.

Mr. Macdonald contended that when his lordship was asked generally, as in this complaint, to inflict the pains of law upon defenders, that carried them back to the statute law.

The Sheriff—That carries you back to the statute under which you are proceeding; and the statute under which you are proceeding is the Summary Procedure Acts.

Mr. Macdonald—If that is your lordship's view, there is no use in any further pressing my contention.

The Sheriff said that was the view he was inclined to take. He might mention that he had been aware that some objection of this sort might be taken, and he had given the point careful consideration.   Personally he should have preferred that the case had been tried by jury, on the ground that it would have relieved him of a considerable deal of personal responsibility ; but it was not what he desired, but what was really the law on the point. It was quite true, and it had been the opinion of most distinguished lawyers in this country, that there was no point less fixed than as to when a trial was to be by jury or not. In the present case, even should he have been of opinion—which he was not—that the nature of the offence as detailed in the complaint before him was unfit for summary trial, he did not think he could interfere with the discretion of the public prosecutor in trying under the Summary Procedure Acts, as the penalty craved did not extend beyond the limits set forth in these Acts.

Mr. Macdonald then stated that he objected to the relevancy of the indictment. The libel amounted to this—that Angus Martin, who lived at Portree, proceeded on a certain day towards, or in the direction of, certain townships ; and that on the way there, at a certain place, he was met by certain people, and had his warrants taken from him. The question for his lordship was whether that amounted to deforcement. The act charged in the indictment, Mr. Macdonald contended, might be theft, or mobbing and rioting, or assault, but it was not deforcement. To be deforced, an officer must be assaulted, and be in bodily fear while in the execution of his duty ; but in the libel it was not mentioned that Martin ever made an attempt to execute the warrants he carried. There was nothing to show that the officers had got near to the residences of any of the persons upon whom they meant to serve the summonses— nothing even to show that even on the road they were near to any of the men against whom they held summonses. He quoted from Hume, Alison, and Macdonald's works on Criminal Law to show that an officer could only be deforced while he was actually in the execution of his duty as an officer, or *in actu proximo* to its execution. There was nothing in the libel to show that the officers in this case were in the execution of their duty, or on the point of executing it, or even near any of the places where their duty fell to be executed, indeed, the presumption was, from the terms of the libel—and this presumption was strengthened by the amendments just made by the Public Prosecutor—that they had not reached the place when they were met by the people.

As to the alternative charge of violently resisting and obstructing an officer of the law in the execution of his duty, that was simply an unsuccessful attempt at deforcement, and would only be committed in circumstances which, had the resistance been successful, would have amounted to deforcement. In short, here also the officer must be executing, or on the point of executing, his duty, otherwise the crime would not be committed. If, therefore, the libel was irrelevant as regarded the charge of deforcement it was necessarily so as regards the less serious charge of obstructing also.

The Procurator-Fiscal, in reply, quoted from Alison and Macdonald to show that it was unquestionably deforcement if when a messenger had come near to the debtor's house he was met by a host of people who drove him off on notice or suspicion of his purpose. In this case the officer was in the immediate neighbourhood of the place where he intended to serve his warrants, as stated in the libel ; and therefore the act charged amounted to deforcement.

The Sheriff, after full consideration, said—The objection taken to the complaint is one of very great importance, and if sustained detracts very materially from the gravity of the offence with which they are charged. The offence of deforcement, as Mr. Hume says, is not to the individual, but to the officer and the law, which is violated in his person ; and it lies in the hindrance of these formal and solemn proceedings, which took place under regular written authority, which it belongs only to an officer of the law to perform. It therefore appears to me to be indispensable that the complaint should bear that the officer said to be deforced was at or near the premises of the parties against whom the writs were issued; or that the officer had assumed that official character and entered on his commission, being in the near and immediate preparation with proceeding to the first formalities in the execution of that commission. This complaint does not, in my opinion, contain those essentials ; and therefore, to the extent that I have now stated, the objection must be sustained.

The Procurator-Fiscal—In these circumstances, there is no case of deforcement, and I propose now to proceed with the case as one of assault.

The Sheriff—Of course the offence, though not deforcement, may be assault and battery, aggravated certainly by the station of the officer.

Mr. Macdonald—All that there is in the complaint regarding assault is the phrase, "as also of the crime of assault". There is not a single word about aggravation. I hope there will be no attempt to prove aggravation when there is no aggravation libelled.

The Sheriff—The offence now to be tried is that of assault. Assault, as we know, may be of various degrees. It may be of such a character as would be met by the minimum sentence, and it may be a serious assault. I used the word "aggravated" in the popular rather than the technical sense. The case to be tried was not an assault with an aggravation, but an assault which might or might not be of a serious character.

The effect of this judgment was that the charge of deforcement was struck out of the libel and the words printed in italics were held as deleted.

The prisoners were then asked to plead to the charge of assault, and Mr. Macdonald stated that their plea was "Not Guilty".

THE SHERIFF-OFFICER AT THE BRAES.

Angus Martin, sheriff-officer, Portree, was the first witness called. Examined by Mr. Anderson, he said—A few days before the 7th April last I received instructions to go to the Braes for the purpose of serving summonses. I went on the 7th April to the Braes, which is about eight miles from Portree. It is on the estate of Lord Macdonald. The summonses I had were for removal, and I had also some small debt summonses for arrears of rent. I left Portree about twelve o'clock, accompanied by Ewen Robertson, and Norman Beaton. As we were going towards the Braes, my attention was directed to two little boys, who came out on the road and looked at us. They ran away, but returned a second time with small flags in their hands. Then they ran towards the townships of Balmeanach, Peinachorrain, and Gedintailler. When I went to Gedintailler I saw two young men with flags. They were bawling out and waving the flags, the boys were also waving their flags. When I got to Gedintailler a great number of persons came out.

The Sheriff—Were there two flags? Witness—Yes.

The Sheriff—After the waving a great many people came? Witness —Yes. A crowd came from the townships.

The Sheriff—How many would there be? Witness—I should say there would be from 150 to 200, including women and children. (Laughter.)

Mr. Anderson—When you say women and children do you also include men? Yes.

Did they surround you? Yes, sir, they did.

The Sheriff—They came towards you and surrounded you? Yes, my lord. I had not then gone off the public road.

Mr. Anderson—Did they ask you anything?—They called out to me to return. I had the summonses in my pocket, and I took them out and told them my name was Angus Martin, and that I was a sheriff-officer from the Sheriff. When I took out the summonses they rushed forward and snatched the summonses out of my hand. This was done by Donald Nicolson.

Mr. Macdonald—I think we might stop this line of examination now.

Mr. Anderson—On what principle?

Mr. Macdonald—The charge is one of assault merely, and the evidence with which it was intended to support the charge of deforcement is now being led for the purpose as I take it of proving an aggravation which is not libelled.

The Sheriff overruled the objection.

Mr. Anderson—Were the crowd quiet at that time?—No. They were very excited.

What was done with the summonses?—They tried to tear them up and threw them on the ground.

Did any person come up to you then?—Yes, Alex. Finlayson, who had a staff in his hand. He told us that unless we turned back we would lose our lives, meaning myself and the ground-officer.

Did he dare you to proceed further?—Yes. He was also brandishing the stick. Stones were thrown by the crowd, and the whole five prisoners were amongst the crowd. I cannot say who threw the stones. My concurrent was taken hold of by Donald Nicolson, who said, "Get away you b——". He had a hold of Robertson about the back, and Robertson was afterwards thrown to the ground. Nicolson said (evidently referring to the summonses), "Lift them now, and take them away, you——". I do not know who it was among the crowd who threw Robertson on the ground. The women were very busy at that time. (Laughter.) I saw James Nicolson when my concurrent was on the ground. He rushed forward with his two hands closed, and asked who was that? On being told, he said, "Kill the b——". I can't say what Robertson did then, as I did not like to turn my back. I wished to keep my front to them. (Laughter.) I think he ran towards Portree. He was followed by a large crowd. The crowd continued to threaten me. I spoke to them, and tried to pacify them as best I could, though I was very shaky. (Laughter.) I proceeded towards Portree, but the crowd followed, and continued to threaten me. Stones were thrown by the crowd from Gedintailler until I reached the school-house at Olach, when I got rid of them.

Mr. Anderson—Did they say anything about you not coming back there again?—Yes. They told me not to come back, because I might be killed, and said if it had been any other officer he would have been killed.

Mr. Anderson—Did Malcolm Finlayson do anything?—He came to me in a great hurry and said the people wished to speak to me; and I said I would be very glad. He asked me, If I had any summonses, and I told him I had the principals and copies. He snatched them out of my hand, and after trying to tear them threw them on the ground. The crowd were about me at this time, and one of the prisoners, Peter Macdonald, said something about burning the summonses. He said, addressing me, "unless you burn these you will not go home alive". There were murmurs among the crowd and I was asked to burn the summonses. They tried to burn the summonses themselves first, and tried to light them at a burning peat, but were unsuccessful. When I was threatened with my life, I asked for a piece of paper, and one of the crowd handed me a bit of the torn summons. I blew the burning peat as hard as I could to make it burn and I lighted the piece paper at the burning peat, and handed it to some one in the crowd, crying "go ahead". I was induced to do this, because I was afraid of my life, as I had been told before I went up that I would be killed. Nothing else induced me to burn the summonses.

Mr. Anderson—You were afraid of your life?—Yes; I was, and I was very glad to get away. (Laughter.)

Between the place where the summonses were torn and where they were destroyed was there much stone-throwing?—Yes, stones and clods, but I was not struck with them.

Did you see your assistants struck?—Well, I did not like to look back—(Laughter)—but I think they must have been getting some of them.

When you got home you reported the matter to the Fiscal?—Yes.

Cross-examined by Mr. Kenneth Macdonald—What do you do?—I am a sheriff-officer and auctioneer.

Are you also a clerk in the office of Lord Macdonald's factor?—I am.

Mr. Macdonald—Anything else?—I am sanitary inspector, clerk to the Local Authority, and clerk to the Road Trustees.

Do you hold many other offices?—I am a crofter. (Laughter.)

In which capacity did you go to the Braes?—I went in my capacity as sheriff-officer. I called in to Mr. Macdonald, the factor's office, that morning to tell that I was going away for a time. I did not get the summonses against these people signed as the Factor's clerk. They were handed to me by the Sheriff-Clerk. I was instructed to get them from him by Mr. Macdonald, and I proceeded to the Braes to serve them.   I was quite sober then, as sober as I am now, and I think I am sober.   Donald Nicolson snatched the summonses from me.

Mr. Macdonald—Will you swear to that ?—Yes.

Who saw him ?—Lots of people, besides my concurrent and the ground-officer.   He tore some of them and did not hand them back to me.   I turned my back shortly afterwards, but by that time the papers were lying on the ground.

Did Nicolson ask you for the summonses ? —No.

How did he come to get them from you ?—I did not give them to him.

How did he come to have them then ?—I took them out of my pocket and said I would give the summonses to them as I saw some of the persons for whom they were in the crowd.

Was the bundle tied up ?—There was an elastic band about it.

Did you hand the summonses to anyone ?—They were snatched out of my hand by Nicolson.

Do you swear that he did not hand them back ?—No.   I swear that, so far as I can remember.

You must remember that ?

The Sheriff—Have you any doubt about it ?—No, my lord.

Mr. Macdonald—What became of the summonses ?—I don't know. They were lying on the road.

You were not struck by a stone ?—No.

Or by anything else ?—One of the women, I think, struck me with some soft stuff on the head.

One of the women ?—I think so.

Was that Mrs. Flora Nicolson ?   Witness—Which Mrs. Nicolson ?

Mr. Macdonald—You know Mrs. Nicolson ?—There are so many Mrs. Nicolsons.

Do you know Widow Nicolson, to whom you made the statement about the widows of Gedintailler ?—I know two widows of that name.

Do you remember a widow you made remarks about before that ?— There are so many of them I can't remember.

Do you know Widow Nicolson of Gedintailler to whom you made a statement about the widows of Gedintailler ?—I know more than one Widow Nicolson in Gedintailler, but I don't know their first names.

The Sheriff—Did you see any of these widows ?—Yes, I saw Widow Nicolson, Balmeanach.

By Mr. Macdonald—Did she strike you ?—No, Sir.

Did she call upon the widows of Gedintailler to come round Martin to get their character ?—No, I am not sure.

Did you make a statement about the widows of Gedintailler in Portree before that?—I do not think it. I would always be speaking to them about rents.

Did you make a statement about the character of the widows?—No, no.

Were you rebuked by Norman Beaton about the filthiness of your language about these women?—Filthy language! I do not remember. I was not checked by Norman Beaton or any other.

The Sheriff objected to this, but Mr. Macdonald said he wished to show that the whole of the disturbance arose out of an attack made by Martin a short time before, on the character of the ladies who formed the major part of the crowd.

Mr. Macdonald—Did Widow Nicolson strike you?—No.

Did any one strike you?—No, but it was a narrow shave.

Did any one threaten to strike you?—Yes, Donald Finlayson with a stick.

And you did not attempt to proceed further?—No, not I.

Did you make any attempt to regain the doubles of your summonses? I just let them go.

I suppose you were glad to get rid of them?—Oh no, not in that way.

How far had you gone back towards Portree before you were again overtaken by the crowd?—Well, I think it would be about three-quarters of a mile. Malcolm Finlayson came up to me then, and I took the summonses out of my pocket. He snatched them from me, although I had a good hold of them. He did not return them, and I heard nobody tell him to return them to me.

You said some one tried to burn the summonses and failed?—Yes.

And then you said "I have a good breath," did you not?—I was hearing murmurs in the crowd that they would make me burn them, so I took a piece of paper and set fire to a bit of one of the summonses.

What did you say then?—I handed it to some one in the crowd, and immediately there was a great clapping of hands.

Now, did you not set fire to the summonses?—No, I set fire to a bit of one of them with a piece of paper which I lighted at a burning peat.

Did you not bend down and set fire to them?—No, I am quite certain I did not.

Did you not, Martin, in setting fire to these summonses say, "Now, keep back, boys, and give it air?"—I did not set fire to the summonses, but after they set fire to them there was a great cheering.

Did you call on the crowd to keep back and give it (the fire) air ?—
I may have said stand back, but not to give it air.

Now, why did you say that ?—In order to please them.

Did you make a speech after that ?—Yes, for their kindness. I
thanked them because they had not struck me, and as I wanted to get
rid of their company.

Did anbody say—"Angus, boy, you need not fear ?"—Yes. That
was at the first stage of the proceedings, when I said don't kill me.

Did you say you were not afraid of anything ?—I said I was there
independent of factor or anybody else.

Did you say you were not afraid of anybody ?—Well, I might have
said so.

Was that true ?—No, it was not. (Laughter).

Did you say that all the people of the Braes would not hurt you ?—
Very likely.

And that was not true ?—Well, I saw it was not true at that stage.
(Laughter).

Did you tell any more lies that day ?—Well, I do not remember. It
is not my profession to tell lies.

You seem to practice it occasionally. (Laughter).

You asked for a smoke ?—Yes.

Why did you ask for that ?—I was not a smoker, but I asked for it
to please them.

How long did you smoke ?—For five or six minutes.

In answer to further questions, witness said that when leaving he
shook hands with a number of the men in the crowd. He denied
having advised the crowd, in his speech, to be smart and hard about
Ben-Lee, and that they would get it. He had no whisky that day, and
denied emphatically that he had lately been dismissed for drunkenness.
He reported the case to the Fiscal when he went home.

Mr. Macdonald—Is this the first criminal charge against the Braes
tenants ?—No.

There was a charge of intimidation, but it broke down ?—Yes.

Did you go to the Braes with the intention of serving these summonses ?—Yes, and I thought I was safe in serving summonses in any part
of Skye up to that time,

Is it not the case that you were sent to the Braes with the view of
getting up a charge of deforcement against these people ?—It was not, sir.

EVIDENCE OF EWEN ROBERTSON, PORTREE.

Ewen Robertson, who spoke through Mr. Whyte as interpreter,

said—I am a labourer, residing at Portree. On the 7th April last, I went as witness with Angus Martin to the Braes with summonses. The ground officer, Norman Beaton, was also with us. When we came to Gedintailler we saw two boys, and they had flags in their hands on the point of a stick. They ran ahead of us. They were waving the flags, and ran away to a knoll on the low side of Gedintailler. When we went on we saw a man, and he came down where we were. A number of people collected, but I do not know how many. The crowd surrounded us. I knew the people, but did not see but Donald and James Nicolson. The crowd knocked me down three times. I was pushed down on the road. The crowd was much excited. I was hurt every time they knocked me down. I went off when I got on my feet. I heard them saying to us that they would kill us. I heard James Nicolson saying so. I did not hear Donald. After throwing the summonses down, Donald seized me by the back of the neck. Donald plucked the summonses from Martin and tore them, and then seized me. He did not throw me down, but caught me by the back of the neck and told me to lift the pieces, and I said there was no use of them. He told me where the summonses were. I was frightened at that stage, "and it was not little". The crowd were excited, and I took myself away, and was followed by about a dozen youths throwing mud at me. I do not know who knocked me down, but I was thrown down three times. They also threw a pail of water at me, but I don't know who did. When I ran away a great deal of stones and earth were thrown at me. Some of them struck me, but I was avoiding them as well as I could. It was only a few youths who followed me. The youths were among the crowd first.

You did not go back again?—Oh, indeed, I would not go. I did not see the summonses burned, and was frightened for my life.

By Mr. Macdonald—What is your occupation?—Anything I can do if I get payment for it.

Are you in the habit of accompanying Martin?—Yes, and his father before him for forty years, and others of the same kind before him, and nothing ever happened to me.

This profession I take it is not very highly respected in the Island of Skye?—I never heard anything about it. Before that time everything went on quietly, and we did our message and got the best in the house before we went away.

Did you see anything happen to Martin?—No; I did not. I went away.

When you were asked in Portree to submit to precognition on behalf of the Prisoners, what was your reply the first time?—I said who asked that of me.

Did you refuse to answer any question when I asked you?—I said I had been already examined, and until I would go before the judge I would not answer more questions.

You came the following day and gave information. What led to the change in your opinion?—Yes; I did that when I heard who it was.

Did I not tell you the first night who it was?—Oh, yes, you did. (Laughter).

What brought about the change?—I did not wish to be examined.

Did Martin tell you not to answer any questions?—He did not.

Did you see Martin that night?—Yes.

Where?—On the street at Portree.

At the hotel door?—Yes.

Waiting for you?—I do not know whether he was or not.

Did he tell you to refuse to answer questions?—No! he did not indeed.

How did Donald Nicolson come to get hold of the summonses?—He just came over from where he was and took them from him.

How long had Martin the summonses in his hand before Nicolson got them?—No time; and he said he had come to deliver the summonses with the Sheriff's warrant.

Did he take them out of his pocket?—Yes.

How long was that before Nicolson got them?—I cannot say what time. I had no watch.

Did Martin offer the men the summonses?—I did not hear him. The people would not take them from him.

Then he did offer them?—He did not offer them at that time.

Why had he the summonses in his hand?—There were some there for whom the summonses were.

My question was, why had Martin the summonses in his hand?—Oh, God! How could I know what they were in his hand for.

Did he offer them?—He did not require to offer them.

How long were you beside Martin at this time?—I was not long when I was thrust away by the people.

Did you know all the people?—I did not know them all.

Had they anything on their heads?—The women had handkerchiefs on their heads, but I do not know was it to protect them from the sun or hide them.

Why did you not lift up the summonses?—Why should I lift them when they were in pieces.

Who tore them ?—Nicolson did.

Did you see him ?—I will swear that.

Did you see the destruction of the other summonses ?

Witness (before interpretation)—No.

Mr. Macdonald—This witness had good English a week ago. (Laughter).

Did you see any person touch Martin ?—No, I did not see them.

Or Beaton ?—No, I do not, but they might have killed him for all I know.

You ran home ?—I ran back as fast as I could.

Did any of them touch you ?—I am not aware of any of them touching me.

EVIDENCE OF NORMAN BEATON.

Norman Beaton, ground-officer, said—I reside at Shullisheddar. I accompanied the sheriff-officer on 17th April last. I went to point out the places. He had summonses to serve at Penachorrain, Balmeanach, and Gedintailler. On coming near Gedintailler we saw two boys, and they ran away. We afterwards saw a man with a flag waving it. They came and asked where we were going, and Martin said he was going to serve summonses on them. He took the summonses out of his pocket. Alexander Finlayson said he would not allow them to go on. He said lifting his staff, "You won't go any further". He said, "Surely you all know me, I came here by order of the Sheriff". Donald Nicolson took the summonses out of Martin's hands and threw them on the road, but I could not say who tore them. I saw them in bits on the road. The people were gathering. There was about 150 altogether—men, women, and children and girls. I saw them all in the crowd. Martin I and returned back towards Portree. Robertson turned first, and after he left I saw him knocked down in the road. The crowd followed us when we turned back to Portree, and some of them were throwing stones and clods at us, near Gedintailler on the road. Not many of them struck me. Near Murchison's schoolhouse, about three-quarters of a mile from the place where the summonses were destroyed, the crowd followed us, and amongst them were James Nicolson, Peter Macdonald, and Malcolm Finlayson. They were very much excited, and using threats. They ran after us, and asked if we had any more summonses. Martin said he had the principal summonses to bring them back to Portree. He took them out of his pocket and showed them, and Malcolm Finlayson snatched them out of his hand

and threw them in the road. They were not torn, and I could not say if they were afterwards torn. I saw peat lying beside them; it was alive. Martin stood on the road, and I stood nearer Portree. I saw smoke, but could not say if the summonses were burning. I was alarmed but not hurt, and afraid to go on.

Cross-examined by Mr. Macdonald—In what capacity did you go with Martin to the Braes ?—I think I went as ground-officer—as Lord Macdonald's servant.

You did not go as Martin's concurrent ?—I was sent there by Lord Macdonald's factor, by whom I was employed. Martin was not to pay me.

Were the crowd principally women and children ?—Yes, and men.

Were they principally women and children ?—No answer. Were there more women and children than there were men ? I believe there were more men. To make three shares of them, I believe there were more men. More than one third were men.

You said that Robertson was knocked down by some women and men ?—Yes.

He had gone away from the crowd at that time ?—Yes.

When Martin came up first with the summonses, how was it he happened to take them out of his pocket ?—They asked him where he was going, and what brought him there, and he took the summonses out of his pocket. He told them it was for that purpose he came. He kept the summonses in his hand.

Close to his body ?—He held them out a little. He said, " Here they are ". Donald Nicolson then took them. He was not very close to them, just past him a yard or two.

Was not this what took place ? Did not Nicolson put out his hand and take them ?—He was not so close as that.—Was Martin offering them at the time ?

The Procurator-Fiscal—Martin did'nt say that. You are putting words in the witness's mouth he never used.

Mr. Macdonald—If I put a question, it is not the part of the Procurator-Fiscal to instruct his own witness what to say in answer to it.

Cross-examination continued—What were Martin's words ?—He said, " Here they are ". I swear he did not say, " Here they are to you ". I will swear to that.

Were they pointed in the direction of Nicolson ?—They were pointed in the way of the crowd as well as Nicolson. He was along with the crowd.

And he took the summonses ?—Yes.

Did he offer them back to Martin?—I did not see that. I was close to Martin all the time and I did not see that. I was very close behind.

Might they have been offered to Martin without you seeing it?—They could not, and I did not see them offered. He tore the summonses. I could not see Nicolson put them on the ground.

Were they torn then?—No, they were not torn when he put them on the ground.

How long after you first saw them on the ground did you see them torn?—I could not say. It was some little time.

Did you see them in anybody's hand between the time you saw them on the ground untorn and when you saw them torn?—No.

The whole crowd was walking over them. I cannot say if that would account for the tearing of them. The band which bound the summonses was off when I saw them on the road. It was torn off about the time they were dropped upon the road. Nicolson took the band off and threw it upon the road. By the time I went down to the school-house, I was struck with stones and clods by some women—not by men—in the crowd.

Did you hear anything said by Mrs. Nicolson there as to the character of the women of Gedintailler?—I did not.

Did not you hear her say, "Now, come, women of Gedintailler, and hear your character from Angus Martin?"—I did. I heard her also say that he should burn the summonses. I heard her say that he was saying some words to her in Portree about the character of the women of Gedintailler. She told words to me herself at that time.

At what time?—At Olach. Not in the presence of Martin. It was said to me near Murchison's school-house. Martin was not there at the time.

She complained of the language Martin had used?—I cannot remember what words he had used. It occurred after the meeting of the Disaster Committee in Portree. I did not hear anything about the language till she told me there that day.

Is it not a fact that you and Lachlan Ross checked him for the language in Portree?—I can't remember of it. Was it filthy language? —Yes, very filthy.

And she referred to it this day at Gedintailler?—Yes.

After you got down to near Murchison's school-house the principal summonses were produced by Martin?—Yes. He was asked if he had any more of them, and he took them out of his pocket. He caught them in his hand and told me to bring them back to Portree. He did not offer them to Malcolm Finlayson. He said, "I have them here, and I have to take them back to Portree ". I did not hear him ask for a match. I heard some one in the crowd ask for a match to burn them. I did not see any weapons in their hands.

No sticks or anything of that sort ?—No.

I heard Martin asking for a smoke from some of the crowd who were about. I think he got a smoke. I believe Martin was afraid.

And yet he asked for a smoke ?—Yes.

How long did he stand smoking ?—I could not say. I saw him on the road and some of the crowd speaking to him. It was about that time Mrs. Nicolson came, and there were some women with her.

She wanted Martin to repeat what he had said at Portree ?—I could not say.

Did you hear Martin make a speech ?—No, sir.

Did you observe her speaking to the crowd—can you tell us what was said ?—No. I could not say how many he shook hands with. There was not many about that time. I was struck in Gedintailler with stones and clods by the women. They did not hurt me. I was struck at Olach with stones and clods again, but they did not hurt me. Some women were throwing them.

Did one of the men wipe off the mark of a clod on Martin's clothes with the sleeve of his coat ?—I saw that done to Martin. A woman before that had taken a handful of turf and rubbed it on his jacket.

Did one of the men come and wipe it off with his sleeve ?—One of the men of the crowd came and wiped off the mark with his coat.

Mr. Macdonald here turned to consult his notes, and witness, who was apparently getting rather uneasy, hurriedly left the box. Mr. Macdonald, without turning fully round, put the question, "Did Martin make a speech," but getting no answer he found to his surprise that the box was empty, and the witness escaping rapidly by the door of the Court-room. He was recalled amidst much laughter, and, having answered a few questions, was allowed to go.

ESTATE MANAGEMENT IN SKYE.

EVIDENCE OF MR. MACDONALD, FACTOR FOR LORD MACDONALD.

Alexander Macdonald, factor, examined—I am a solicitor at Portree, and act as factor for Lord Macdonald. In the middle of April, I instructed summonses against Donald Nicolson, Balmeanach ; Alex. Finlayson, do. ; Samuel Nicolson, do. ; John Nicolson, do. ; James Matheson, Widow C. Matheson, Widow C. Nicolson, Widow Mackinnon, John Stuart, and Donald Macwilliam. I instructed Martin to go and serve the summonses, and he proceeded to do so.

Cross-examined by Mr. Macdonald—Is Martin your clerk?—Yes, and has been so for a long time.

How long has he been so?—I think he entered my office first, at the very beginning, and then he went to Glasgow, and came back, and has been with me for the last eight or ten years.

From the beginning of what?—Of his career.

How many years will that be?—I cannot tell you, Mr. Macdonald.

He was in your office before he became sheriff-officer?—Yes.

Is he your clerk still?—Yes.

Was he absent for a time recently?—Well, I think he was.

What was that for?—I cannot tell you. I was away (a pause). Let me see (another pause). I think I was away in the south somewhere, and when I came home (a pause)——

Mr. K. Macdonald—Oh, don't be afraid—(laughter).

Witness—I am not afraid at all. I beg to assure you——

Mr. Macdonald—Well, go on then.

Witness—I was absent from the office lately, and, during my absence from home, I understand he was absent.

The Sheriff—What was the cause of the absence?

Witness—I don't know. He was absent when I returned. I think he was absent for a fortnight, or nine or ten days.

Did you enquire what was the cause of his absence?—No, I did not enquire particularly.

The Sheriff—Did you not enquire at all?—Yes.

By Mr. Macdonald—And what was the result of your enquiries?— I heard a suspicion cast on him by some people that he was rather unsteady, but I do not think it is true at all.

Did you dismiss him?—No, certainly not.

You took him back whenever he came?—I forget the circumstances. I was not prepared to speak to this. I took him back.

And made little enquiry?—I asked of his mother and wife, but I don't remember much about it,

Martin is your clerk and a sheriff-officer. Does he hold other offices? —He is clerk to the Road Trustees and collector of rates for the parish of Snizort, about five miles from Portree, and collector of poor rates for Bracadale, nine miles away. I do not recollect if he is collector for any other parish.

How many proprietors are you factor for besides Lord Macdonald?

—Macleod of Macleod, Mr. Macallister of Strathaird, Mr. Macdonald of Skaebost, and Major Fraser of Kilmuir.

I suppose that is the greater part of Skye?—Yes, decidedly.

And in addition to this you are also a landed proprietor yourself?—Well, I believe I am.   (Laughter).

You are also a solicitor and bank-agent?—Yes.

And I believe you are agent for Captain Macdonald of Waternish?—Oh, I have a number of appointments besides these, and lots of clients.

And your influence extends all over the Isle of Skye?—I do not know about my influence, but I hold the positions mentioned.

You are distributor of stamps?—Yes.

And Clerk of the Peace for the Skye district?—Yes, Depute under Mr. Andrew Macdonald.   (Laughter).

Any other offices?—I may have some, but I do not remember any more.   I do not see what right you have to ask these questions.   Do you mean to assess my income?   I will tell the Assessor of Taxes when he asks me, but you have no right to inquire.

You are also a coal-merchant?—I am not aware, Mr. Macdonald. (Laughter).

And how many School Boards and Parochial Boards are you a member of?—Several.

The Sheriff—I don't want to interrupt you, but what has this to do with the case?

Mr. K. Macdonald—To show that this gentleman is the King of Skye —the uncrowned King of the Island—(laughter)—an absolute monarch who punishes a murmur by transportation to the mainland.   There are some other offices which you hold in Skye?   Witness—Yes.

Mr. Macdonald—In point of fact, you and Martin hold between you pretty much all the valuable offices in Skye except that of parish minister?—(great laughter).   Witness (warmly)—Not all, sir; not at all—(laughter).

Did the people of the Braes petition you about Benlee?—They lodged a document, but I do not call it a petition.   I call it a demand or ultimatum.   The witness read the document, which was to the effect that the petitioners "demand" the grazings of Benlee, otherwise they would not pay their rents.

Mr. K. Macdonald—These people of the Braes are not very well educated?   Witness—Some of them are.

What did you do with that petition when you got it?—I kept it.

Did you send it to Lord Macdonald?—No, but I wrote to Lord Macdonald about it.

Did you make any inquiry on the spot as to the grievances of these people?—I understood what they meant by the petition itself.

Did you make any inquiry to ascertain if their grievances could be substantiated?—Yes, I made inquiries of a number of people.

Did you go to the place to make the inquiries?—No, I do not require to do that, as I know the place perfectly well.

Is the statement which they made true or not?—I believe that the demand for the exclusive possession of Benlee is not a well founded claim.

The Sheriff—That is irrelevant; we need not go into that matter.

Mr. Anderson was of the same opinion, but would not object.

Mr. K. Macdonald—If your lordship wishes me to stop, I will do so. I am probably outside of the immediate issue now, but I am led on by the hope that if an explanation is now made of the position taken up by Lord Macdonald and his factor in relation to the demands of the prisoners and their neighbours in Skye, an arrangement may be come to which will prevent a recurrence of the events which have led to the present trial.

The Sheriff—If any opposition was taken by the prosecution, I would stop this course of examination at once.

Mr. Anderson—I do not object, my lord.

The Sheriff—I do not see what bearing it has on the case.

Mr. K. Macdonald—Did these people refuse to pay their rents until the grievances complained of were inquired into and redressed?—Until they got Benlee. I sent them circulars and letters, copies of which are produced.

You state in the printed letter that they have each 6½ acres arable land, with a right to keep 5 cows, 20 sheep, and 1 horse?—Yes.

Did you ascertain the accuracy of that statement before you made it? —I have only acted as factor for two and a-half years, and that statement regarding the townships was given to me shortly after I entered, and I think it is quite correct.

Are you not aware now that, if these tenants would put all these cattle and sheep on the ground, they would die from starvation?—I am not aware of anything of the sort, sir, but we are quite prepared to look into that. The request was never civilly made.

Did a deputation of these people come to you in November last?— There was a deputation of their sons, but there were no tenants except one.

An old man of 85?—I do not think he was 85. I told them the tenants must come themselves, and not their sons. I saw this man

Nicolson, but I do not think Nicolson came into my office, though I met him on the street.

Was there a man Angus Stewart there?—Well, I don't remember.

Was not Angus Stewart, a tenant of Lord Macdonald for the last 65 years, their principal speaker?—You refer to a different occasion.

When was that?—When they came arm-in-arm and shoulder-to-shoulder with a piper at their head. (Laughter).

Is it not the case that they were met by this piper, who plays for money in Portree?—On the first occasion there was no piper, but on the second occasion they came with this piper, and would scarcely listen to me. They never came quietly to me. (Laughter). The time they came with a piper they entered the rent collection room and would scarcely listen to me. I called over their names to see I had nobody but tenants to deal with.

What was the object of this, Mr. Macdonald?—I told you before that it was to ascertain that I had nobody but tenants to deal with.

No intimidation in it?—I do not believe the men were ever afraid of me, nor that they are so yet. (Laughter). I do not see why they should be so unless they were doing wrong.

Did you prefer a criminal charge against some of these men before this charge was made?—Two widows——

Mr. Kenneth Macdonald—Never mind the widows.

Witness (excitedly)—You have asked me a question, and I must answer it.

The Sheriff—Did you make a criminal charge against these people? Witness—I cannot answer no or yes, but two widows came to me weeping, saying they had been intimidated by a number of men in the Braes for paying their rents, and I went with these two widows to the Fiscal.

Mr. K. Macdonald—Was there a charge of intimidation made to the Fiscal?

The Sheriff—He says the two old ladies——

Mr. K. Macdonald—They are widows, my lord, but not old. (Laughter.)

The Sheriff—The question is a simple one. Did you or did you not? Witness—They made a charge of intimidation.

Mr. K. Macdonald—But the charge fell through?—Not so far as I know.

When did you hear the last of it?—I do not know if I have heard the last of it yet. (Laughter.)

Did you hear that Crown Counsel had órdered no further proceedings to be taken on that charge ?—Yes.

Was it after that you caused the summonses of removing to be prepared ?—Yes, but the one thing has no connection with the other. There may have been a coincidence of time, but there was no relation between the two cases. The summonses were for ejectment for non-payment of rent.

Was it not the fact that Martin arranged to be deforced before he left Portree ?—Certainly not ; he did not expect it. (Laughter.)

The Sheriff—Is Martin a native of the Braes ?—No ; he is a native of Portree. His people belong to Kilmuir.

Mr. K. Macdonald—Is it your practice to issue summonses of removing that you have no intention to enforce ?—No, of course I do not enforce them if the cause for which they were issued has been removed.

Question repeated ?—No, but they may not be followed out, because if the rent be paid there is nothing more about it.

Then you intend to evict these people ?—Certainly, if they do not pay their rent, or show good reason why they should not.

Had you Lord Macdonald's authority for evicting these people ?—I did not want to evict them, nor do I intend to evict them if they pay their rent.

Mr. Macdonald—Kindly answer my question. Had you Lord Macdonald's authority for what you did ?—I cannot give you a more direct answer. I believe I said something to Lord Macdonald that it would be necessary to do something to the ringleaders. I did not ask for any instructions to evict, but said it would be necessary to warn them out for not paying their rents.

Had you Lord Macdonald's authority for evicting these people ?—I did not require his authority for that.

The Sheriff—Were your instructions special or general ?—I had no special instructions, as I did not ask for them.

Mr. Anderson—When you got the petition, Mr. Macdonald, did you write to say that they would get the hill according to the value of the present day, and expressed your wish to have it valued by an experienced person, and sent to Lord Macdonald for his consideration ?

Witness—Yes, but I got no answer from them.

Did you also offer them Benlee ?—I offered them Benlee if they would pay for it, and would give a lease of it to any tacksman who would come forward.

The Sheriff—That will do.

Witness—(sharply)—Are you done, Mr. Macdonald ? (Laughter.)

Mr. K. Macdonald—Oh, yes.

PRISONERS' DECLARATIONS.

The prisoners' declarations were then read. They are as follows :—

Donald Nicolson, Balmeanach, sixty-six 'years of age, declared—I know Angus Martin, Portree, and I know that he is a sheriff-officer. I also know, but only by sight, Ewen Robertson, residing at Lisigarry, Portree. I also know Norman Beaton, ground-officer, Portree. I saw the three of them at Braes about a fortnight ago. They were on the township of Gedintailler, and there was a crowd about them. We were hearing that they were going up with summonses of removing. I was in the crowd, and I saw papers in Martin's hand. I could not tell what they were.

Did you take the papers out of his hands ?—He knows himself. There were plenty of witnesses if they saw me do so. I did not catch hold of Ewen Robertson or touch any one there ; neither did I throw anything, nor was I swearing. I asked Robertson to lift up the papers which were at the time scattered on the road.

James Nicolson, son-in-law, residing with the above Donald Nicolson, is 30 years of age. He knew Martin to be a sheriff-officer, and he also knew Robertson and Beaton. He saw the three of them at Gedintailler on the occasion in question. The Declaration continued— There was a crowd about them when I saw them. I joined the crowd. I knew that it was with summonses of removing they had come. When I joined the crowd I did not cry out to kill Martin. I have no recollection of saying, or hearing said, that even with the support of the Volunteers no one would dare to come to Braes to put us out. I saw Martin having papers. I did not know what the papers were, but I thought they were the summonses. I saw Martin handing out the papers, and some one taking them out of his hand, and I afterwards saw them on the road torn. I did not see Ewen Robertson down on the ground. I saw a crowd of boys and girls after him along the road. They were saying that I was cursing and swearing, but I was not, and I did not put a hand on any one that day or on the papers which the sheriff-officer had. I did not think there was any harm in anything I saw done.

Peter Macdonald, Balmeanach, aged 48, and married, said he heard that Martin was a sheriff-officer. He saw Martin and Beaton at the Braes, but not Robertson. He was not present when Martin arrived. The Declaration continued—We were thinking it was with the summonses of removing he (Martin) came. There was a crowd gathered about him when he arrived of about 150 women and children. I did not see papers with him until I saw them on the road at Olach. I saw them before they were burnt. The crowd called out—that is, the women called out—that Martin and his assistants would require to burn them themselves. I did not say to Martin that he would be made to burn them himself. It was at Olach that I joined the crowd. I have nothing further to say but that Martin burned the papers himself. The place Olach above alluded to is about half a-mile from Gedentailler, in the direction of Portree.

Alexander Finlayson, Balmeanach, 70 years of age, declared that he did not know until Martin arrived that he had come to the Braes to serve the summonses. He was not present when Martin arrived, and he saw him first among a number of men, women, and children at Gedentailler. He did not know that Robertson was helping Martin. The Declaration continued—I told him to return and burn them. At this time there was some torn papers scattered about the road, and it was to these papers I referred. The papers were torn and on the ground before I joined the crowd. I did not know that these papers were summonses of removing, but some of the people were saying that they were. I did not know that Martin was going with summonses to us that day, but we were hearing a rumour that we were to be warned. I did not dare Martin to proceed further with his summonses that day. I had a staff in my hand. I was not flourishing it. I did not hear Martin say that he had the Sheriff's warrant for serving the summonses that day. I thought we ought to get justice concerning the matter in dispute, which was the hill pasture of Benlee, which we ever had. When had you the pasture?—We had it ever in connection with our town-ships. It was taken from us about sixteen years ago by bad rulers. We have not possessed it for the last seventeen years. It was let to another tenant. I and my father before me, and my grandfather, great-grandfather, and great-great-grandfather, have been living in the township of Balmeanach, and the hill of Benlee was all that time connected with our township.

Alex. Finlayson, son of and residing with the said Alex. Finlayson, Balmeanach, is married, and about thirty years of age. He saw Martin at the Braes on the day in question. The Declaration continued—I did not know then that Martin was a sheriff-officer. I only knew that he was the factor's clerk when I saw him at the Braes on that occasion. Martin had a bunch of papers. I did not know what the papers were, but he told us they were summonses, some of removing and some of rent. I did not take these papers out of Martin's hands, but after seeing them in his hands, I saw them torn and scattered on the road. I saw some of the papers which Martin had burnt at Olach that day, but these were different papers from those I saw scattered on the road at Gedentailler. It was I who took the papers which were burnt at Olach out of Martin's hand. He stretched out his hand holding these papers, and I took them out of his hands. Somebody said I should not take them, and I offered them back to him, but he would not take them, and I let them fall on the road. At this time there were a good many people about Martin, and some of them cried out to burn the papers, but I am not sure whether I said this or not. Martin then asked for a match, but there was no match to be found. A lighted peat, however, was produced, and Martin set fire to one of the summonses, and then the whole caught fire and were burned. The crowd did not very much force Martin to burn the summonses. They told him to burn them, and he did so. The crowd did not call bad names to Martin, but he told the people he would be put out of his situation by the factor if he had not come to give them the summonses that day. They did not say anything worse than his name to him. I told him to move on, as I was afraid the scholars and women would come and hurt him. He then asked us to see him safe over the burn, and we did so.

THE EVIDENCE FOR THE DEFENCE.

Mr. Donald Macdonald, Tormore, examined by Mr. K. Macdonald—You were factor for Lord Macdonald until about two years and a-half ago?—Some time about that.

You know the Braes?—I do.

When you were factor did the tenants of the Braes townships complain to you about the want of the hill of Ben-Lee?—They may have done. I have no distinct recollection about their making any specific charge.

You know the story about the shepherd's house being built, about which some of the crofters complained?—Yes.

What did you do?—Well, the complaint was that the tenant of Ben-lee was building a house on a portion of what they considered their land.

The Sheriff—All this occurred two or three years ago, Mr. Macdonald?—Yes.

The Sheriff asked Mr. K. Macdonald if he meant to justify the action of the prisoners by this evidence? He did not see that it had any relevancy.

Mr. K. Macdonald—It has a bearing on what followed.

Mr. K. Macdonald (to witness)—There was a lease of Benlee which expires at Whitsunday 1882. Is not that so?—I believe it does.

And the people wished to get the land back at that term ?—There was some indication that way.

Did you make them any promise ?—I made no promise.

Did you hold out any hope ?—No ; certainly no distinct hope.

Then, was it from you they got their information ?—I don't remember, but it is quite possible.

Did you renew the lease during your factorship ? I believe I did.

For a further period ?—Yes. And without informing them ? I don't remember, but it is quite possible.

In answer to Mr. Anderson, Mr. Macdonald said Benlee had not been in the possession of the crofters for the past 16 or 17 years.

The Sheriff.—Benlee is advertised to let now.

Mr. K. Macdonald—Yes, in the *Courier* of to-day.

Mr. A. Macdonald, factor—And the tenants may have it if they like to pay rent for it.

EVIDENCE OF CROFTERS.

John Finlayson, a tenant of the Braes, said, in reply to Mr. Macdonald—I was at the Braes when Martin arrived, and saw him with the papers in his hands. He handed them over to Donald Nicolson, who took them and threw them back to Martin, who turned his back, and I think refused to take them back. Some one in the crowd said to Nicolson that he had no right to the papers, and he then dropped them on the ground, and the children trod upon them. No one struck Martin, or even threatened to strike him. I heard some one saying to Martin, "Be not afraid, no one will touch you". Robertson at this time had gone homewards, the children following him. Martin also followed, but after he had gone some distance he stopped, and asked for a light. He got an ember of a peat, with which he set a paper (a paper about the size of a summons) on fire, and put some more with it. He said, "Stand back and don't smother it," and added, "There it is for you, boys". He appeared to be laughing, and did not seem to be afraid. He afterwards had a smoke and chatted with the people. He made a speech before leaving, in which he said, "Be hardy and active ; you will not see me again, and you will get Benlee". He also said he did not blame them for what they had done, and said if he had been in their place he would have done the same thing. He shook hands with a number of people before leaving. I did not see any person strike Martin.

By Mr. Anderson—I joined the crowd when they began. I went there just because I followed the rest.

You saw some boys with flags on the watch ?—There were.

And what were these boys to do ?—They were to give us notice.

Of what ?—About the force that was being sent to us.

Was that a sheriff-officer you expected ?—We did not know that it was a sheriff-officer.

Did you expect Martin ?—No.

Did you expect summonses ?—Yes, I expected a summons.

Now, was it for persons coming with summonses that you placed the boys on the watch ?—Yes.

And it was arranged that as soon as a boy saw them he was to give warning ?—Yes.

And you were to collect then ?—Yes.

Mr. Macdonald objected to this line of examination, as being really an attempt to prove the charge of Deforcement which the Prosecutor had not been able to libel relevantly. The Sheriff however allowed it.

Was it said that he would not be allowed to serve a summons ?—I did not hear that.

What were you going to do when you met the persons comiug with the summonses ?—To return them.

That is to return him to Portree?—I do not know where. (Laughter.)

I suppose you know that you were to turn him off the Braes ?—Yes, we were going to turn him off the Braes.

Are you any relation of Finlaysons in the box ?—I am a brother of Malcolm's and a son of Alexander Finlayson.

Did you see any stones thrown ?—No.

Nor clods of earth ?—No.

Nor peats ?—No.

Did you see Robertson on the ground ?—Yes.

Did you see him lying on the ground ?—No.

Did you see anybody touch him ?—No.

What became of him ?—I saw him going away, and the children were cheering him home. (Laughter.)

Were they throwing anything after him?—I did not see, I was far from him. Witness saw only two of the prisoners, Malcolm Finlayson and Patrick Macdonald following Martin to the second crowd, near Murchison's schoolhouse.

Alexander Finlayson, Peinachorrain, was at Gedentailler on the day when Martin came with the papers. He knew that Martin was the factor's clerk, but did not know that he was a sheriff-officer. The papers were lying on the road when he saw them first, and Martin was laughing and talking, and did not appear to be frightened. He generally corroborated the previous witness regarding the burning of the papers, and said he did not see any stones thrown at Martin. In answer to Mr. Anderson, he said he was a son of Alexander Finlayson, one of the prisoners, and brother of Malcolm Finlayson, another of the prisoners. Martin did not seem to be in the least afraid.

James Mathieson, on being asked to take the oath in English, declined. He said—Oh no. All the speaking in this case has been done in Gaelic, and I am not going to interpret Gaelic into English. (Laughter.) The oath having been administered in Gaelic, he said he resided at Balmeanach, and was at Gedentailler on the 17th April when Martin came to serve the summonses. When the people came up Martin held out some papers in his hands. He held them out in the direction of Donald Nicolson, and said, "There they are, take them". I don't know whether he said this to Nicolson or to the rest of the people. Nicolson, however, took them. He did not snatch them from Martin, and Martin did not endeavour to keep them from him. In answer to other questions, witness said Martin did not appear to be frightened, and had no occasion to be so.

What occurred near Murchison's schoolhouse?—I saw him with more papers there. When I arrived he had them in his hand as at first. He was offering them to anyone who would receive them. I don't know where Robertson was. He went along before them. I don't know if they were following him at that time, but they were before that, and some children.

Was Martin quite sober at that time?—Well, I don't know. I would think him like a man that would have a little.

Did you hear Martin ask for a match?—Yes. He said, Was there no one there had a match? They replied that they had a burning ember for lighting his pipe. After this Martin asked where it was. They said, It was here. I was standing at the side of the road, and I saw him go over by the papers. I saw him point to them and say, "Lads, there is a fire, stand back and don't choke it". I saw the papers on fire after that. I saw him drink at the well. He was inclined to bend at the well, but they told him there was a pail. He asked, Have any of you a pipe till I smoke? Alexander Nicolson went to give him his pipe, but it was broken. Nicolson then went to get another man's, and after cleaning it so (here the witness made a movement as if wiping a pipe clean) he handed it to Martin, and Martin smoked it. He (Martin) was in the very middle of the crowd smoking it.

Was he talking to them and smoking?—Yes, smoking and talking. I did not see any appearance of fright about him. There was no occasion for his being frightened.

Did you hear Murdo Nicolson say anything to him?—I heard some one say, I am not very certain if it was Angus Nicolson, but I heard some one say, "No one here will do anything to him".

What did he say to that?—He said, "Oh, I had no fear. I know that the Braes people will not do anything to me." He was shaking hands with the people before he went away. He was shaking hands and thanking them for dealing so gently with him. He told them to be active after this, as it was now they had it to do. I don't know what he meant by that. I did not hear him say he was a sheriff-officer, or that he came from the Sheriff. I know he is the factor's clerk in Portree. I thought the "bailie" sent him there that day. I saw the widows standing up as if they were speaking to him. One of them, Widow Nicolson, seemed to be angry. I did not hear Martin say anything to her at the time. She was done speaking to him before I came. I don't know what they were talking about, but people were telling me afterwards. I did not see anyone touching Martin other than to shake him by the hand.

John Nicolson, Gedintailler, gave corroborative evidence. He saw no one putting a hand on Martin, and said Martin seemed quite pleased, and put the papers on the top of the fire.

John Nicolson, Peinachorrain, also gave evidence regarding the proceedings at Martin's visit. He saw no stones thrown. In cross-examination by Mr. Anderson, he admitted that clods had been thrown by the school children, but if Martin was frightened it was only at seeing so many women. (Laughter.)

John Maclean, Balmeanach, described the scene at the schoolhouse where the papers were burnt. He said Martin stepped into the centre of the crowd, and getting a fire-brand blew it until he had lighted the papers. He then set them on the ground, and said, "Men of the Braes, I am obliged to you for your kindness". He appeared quite hearty, and shook hands with the people. There was no reason for Martin fearing anything. He added, I was in the factor's office in November last as one of the deputation. Our names were taken down at that time, and we were charged with impertinence. The factor was sending us letters after that threatening us.

This brought the evidence to a close.

Mr. Anderson did not address the court, but simply asked a conviction for assault.

Mr. Macdonald began by showing the effect upon the indictment, of the judgment sustaining his objection to the relevancy of the charge of deforcement, and the minor charge of obstructing an officer of the law in the performance of his duty; and he read what was left of the indictment, to show that all that remained was a charge of simple assault against the prisoners. He went on to say:—When I first addressed your Lordship to-day, I attempted to show that the case as it then stood was too important for trial in this court. It has now been reduced to such slender proportions that the wonder is it was ever brought into any court. It has been attempted, by leading irrelevant evidence, to give the case a fictitious importance, but the prosecutor has been flogging a dead horse. A common assault such as is now charged would never have justified the measures taken to apprehend the men now in the dock. Would the public have looked on in silent wonder if they had been told that the army of policemen sent to Skye had been sent there to apprehend a few men—most of them old men—whose only crime was that they looked on while a few respectable women threw dirt at a man who had slandered them. I rather think they would then do what those of them who have not to pay for it will do now—they would laugh outright. I really feel some difficulty in discussing seriously the very small mouse which this mountain in labour has brought forth. The charge is assault. What is the evidence in support of it? It is certainly not the sort of evidence usually led in cases of assault. We heard of a sheriff-officer being sent from Portree to serve writs at a place nine or ten miles away, of his seeing boys with flags and afterwards being met by a crowd of people, of his papers being burnt by himself, and of his making a speech thanking the people for their kindness to him, and encouraging them to persevere in their demands; but very little, and that unreliable, of an assault by anybody, nothing of an assault by the men

at the bar.   In fact the public prosecutor never anticipated
having to prove a charge of assault, and had no evidence to
support it.   The turn the case took when the Court held
his main charges irrelevantly stated had taken him by surprise, and he ought then to have thrown up the whole case.
He had not done that.   He had led evidence which showed
that the prisoners had done certain things which might or
might not be criminal, but which certainly did not constitute
the crime with which they now stood charged, nor, for that
matter, any of the crimes with which the indictment, as it
originally stood, sought to charge them.   The prosecutor
had not stated the grounds upon which he asked for a conviction on the charge of assault,—there were none to state.
The only hope he could have was that the Court would
convict them of a crime of which they were not guilty,
because the evidence showed that they came near committing another and a totally different offence with which they
could not be charged.   If this was the hope of the prosecutor, he hoped it would be disappointed, and that these
men would not be convicted of a crime of which they were
not guilty simply because some victims were required to
shield officials from the charge of playing a huge practical
joke at the expense of the public.   I shall now, with your
Lordship's permission, go over the evidence shortly, and I
think I shall be able to show that there is no evidence—no
reliable evidence—that any one of the accused committed
an assault, while there is a considerable amount of reliable
evidence to show that not only was no assault committed,
but that Martin and the ground-officer were on the best of
terms with the prisoners while they were together—terms so
friendly that the idea of an assault having been committed
during the interview is utterly precluded.   As to Robertson,
he was clearly not a popular favourite, and he retreated

towards Portree at an early stage, followed by some children. If he was assaulted at that time, the prisoners were no parties to it. Robertson was, however, the only person who was said in evidence to have been touched by one of the accused; but the evidence on that point came from so suspicious a source, and was, as would be shown immediately, so strongly contradicted, that I have no hesitation in asking your Lordship to disbelieve it. Mr. Macdonald then proceeded to review the evidence for the purpose of showing that Martin, Robertson, and Beaton had contradicted each other in important particulars in their account of what had taken place, and that the story told by the witnesses for the defence was consistent throughout, and entirely inconsistent with those of Martin and his associates. Martin, he said, had to account to his master, the factor, for his failure to serve the summonses, if, indeed, it was not intended before he went that he should fail; and this was the story he told on his return. The enlightened management of Lord Macdonald's estates in Skye by his omnipotent and unapproachable factor had brought about a state of matters which the usual machinery of the factor's office—summonses of removing and occasional evictions, supplemented by threats of undefined pains and penalties—was unable to deal with. An attempt even to get up a criminal prosecution had failed. What more natural, then, than to get up a sensational charge which would bring a large force to the rescue of the powerless factor without expense to his employer. I do not say this is the explanation of what took place, but it is a possible interpretation of the evidence, and it would go a long way to account for the peculiar "coincidence," as Mr. Macdonald calls it, that while the criminal authorities intimated the abandonment of the first criminal charge on 1st April, the attempt to serve the summons of removing was made on the 7th of the same month. Be that, however, as it may, the evidence which, by the forbearance of the Court, I was permitted to lead, showed that the present unhappy state of matters among Lord Macdonald's tenants was entirely attributable to mismanagement on the part of successive factors. Before 1865 those people were comfortable and contented. They had their patches of arable land near the sea and the hill grazings beyond. The grazings were on Benlee, of which so much has been heard. The rent for both lands was paid in one sum, and was fixed on the basis of the number of cattle, sheep, and horses each tenant was able to keep. In 1865, however, a factor deprived them of the hill while their rents remained the same. They were pushed down towards the sea-shore, and there, under the shadow of their mountain, and a few inches above highwater mark, on what was at no very distant date a sea-beach, they eked out a precarious living from their patches of mixed rock and sand, dignified with the name of arable land. For years these people went on uncomplainingly, while year by year they became poorer. Their horses first went,—in 1865 every man had a horse—most of them several; now there is not a horse for every three tenants. Then the little stocks of sheep and cattle gradually dwindled down, while all the time their owners were paying rents for the grazing of three or four times the number of sheep and cattle the grazings left to them would feed. At last the inevitable came—the people saw starvation or pauperism staring them in the face, and they made a humble appeal for redress. To whom? To Lord Macdonald? No! To his factor, and the factor made fair promises—at least so say the people. He told them, they say, that the hill was let on lease, but the lease would expire in 1882, when they would get it. How does he keep his promise? Several years before 1882, he, without saying anything to the crofters who were patiently enduring poverty and hardship waiting for the fulfilment of his promise, let the hill on a new lease, and then leaving this little complication for his successor to settle, he resigned his factorship. The successor was Mr. Alexander Macdonald. It was Mr. Macdonald's misfortune that in his time the crofters found out how they had been deceived, and that, not taking the trouble to understand their grievances, he threatened them when he ought to exhibit at least the appearance of sympathy, and to attempt to conciliate them. To the crofters Martin was simply the factor's clerk, Beaton the factor's underling, and with the factor and all his belongings they resolved to have nothing to do. To Lord Macdonald they must appeal. They believed that he had never authorised the harsh measures adopted towards them, and the evidence led to-day shows that their belief was well founded. Lord Macdonald, in whose name these proceedings were carried on, never authorised them, was never even consulted about them. Proceedings which had for their ostensible object the eviction of the inhabitants of three townships,— several hundred people in all,—were not important enough forsooth to lead the factor to consult his master. The people knew well that less than thirty years before similar proceedings had been carried out to their bitter end in the name of their landlord's father without his authority, and they knew that to the day of his death that Lord Macdonald bitterly regretted these proceedings. Well might they believe that this Lord Macdonald would not lightly consent to their wholesale eviction and expatriation. They knew, and he knew, that the strong arm of *their* ancestors was the only title deed by which *his* ancestors held their land, and that but for the sturdy clansmen of the Isles, Lord Macdonald would not now hold an acre of land in Skye. It was not, therefore, the

law in the person of its officers, it was not even their landlord, these men resisted, it was the factor—the man who was
in their eyes the impersonation of all the injustice and hardship to which they had been subjected, and I ask was there
not some justification for their resistance? This being the
position taken up by the accused and their neighbours, was
it probable that they would degrade themselves and their
cause by assaulting a person in Martin's position? I think
not. Further, was Martin's own story consistent with the
theory of an assault? Would a man who had just been
assaulted, and who was in mortal terror, as Martin says he
was, find himself so sound in wind as Martin admits he was.
When a lighted peat was procured to burn the summonses,
some of the men in the crowd tried to blow it into a flame
but failed. Martin, however, notwithstanding his terror
found himself, as he admits, "in better breath" than his
alleged assailants, and succeeded in blowing the peat into a
flame when they had failed to do so. (Laughter.) Though
terror-stricken and in mortal fear he managed somehow to
enjoy a smoke quietly. When he wanted a drink of water
he was not afraid to go off the road to a well, and to go on
his knees and dip his head into it. It never occurred to him
that this dangerous crowd finding his head in the water might
keep it there. He gauged the crowd correctly enough as his
conduct showed. He stood among them, chatted with them,
drunk out of their pails, borrowed and smoked one of their
pipes, and on parting made them a speech. That was the
evidence of the prosecution, as well as of the defence. The
Prosecutor did not make an attempt, after hearing the
evidence, to argue that Martin had been assaulted. To do
so in the face of such evidence would be an outrage on
common sense. Mr. Macdonald concluded by asking for a
verdict of not guilty. (Applause.)

THE PRISONERS FOUND GUILTY—THE SENTENCE.

The Sheriff said—The charge now is one of assault against these men combinedly or against one or other of them, "actor or art and part," so that if the prosecution has proved that one of them assaulted one or other of the men said to be assaulted, and that the other prisoners aided and abetted them in that assault, that, I take it, would be sufficient to enable me to find the whole of them guilty as libelled. Throwing aside all that is really unnecessary, the simple question for me to determine is this—Did these men "or one or other of them" do something to one or other of the three men, Martin, Beaton, and Robertson, which in the eye of the law is assault? Now, it is quite true that there are certain discrepancies in the evidence which has been adduced. There is no doubt whatever that the witnesses for the defence do not support the evidence for the prosecution; but the evidence for the defence confirms to a very great extent the statements that are made by the principal witnesses for the prosecution. And part of the evidence of the defence is really of a mere negative character. Certain of the witnesses —the first three—say that they were not present at the beginning of this disturbance. They came to the ground after the papers were taken out of Martin's pocket. Now, Martin says that when he came to the place he had the papers in his pocket, and they were only taken out of it when he was asked for them. I may mention, before proceeding further, that I see no reason whatever to doubt Martin's statement. Martin gave his evidence fairly, and in a way which convinced me at least that he really was telling the truth, and I do not think there was anything in his cross-examination which tended to render Martin's evidence untrustworthy. Now Martin says that Donald Nicolson took a leading part in this affair, and he stated that Donald Nicolson caught hold of Ewen Robertson by the back of the neck "and called out to me in language which was not very polite," but it had reference to things which had taken place before then. Robertson tells us more particularly how Donald acted after the summonses had been plucked from Martin. He laid hold of him by the neck and so on. Now, I take it that this is an assault within the four corners of this complaint. It will not do for any one to say that because five or six witnesses did not see this that the affair did not take place. There is the direct evidence of two witnesses which is a great deal better than the indirect evidence or negative testimony of a score. Therefore, if Robertson's and Martin's evidence were true, Donald Nicolson was guilty of an assault. Now, if Donald Nicolson was guilty of an assault, the question will then come to be, what part did the others take in regard to this? Donald Nicolson, according to Martin, came forward and took the papers from him. The next person who comes on the scene is Alex. Finlayson, and the proceedings that he adopts are certainly of a most threatening character. There is no doubt whatever that he had a stick in his hand, and the testimony given by Robertson and others is that he comes forward and threatens them, flourishing his stick and daring them to proceed further. And then he proceeds to tell us of the throwing of stones, in which Finlayson took an active part, and in this way he became "art and part" with Nicolson in the assault upon these men. I therefore take it that when you have Nicolson behaving as he had done, and Finlayson being there with him, and taking the part he did, that Finlayson is guilty of the assault as a party—as one acting art and part with Nicolson. Then the next persons who come before us are James Nicolson and the other two.

These three men are not said to have done anything except to be accessories along with these people. Peter Macdonald, indeed, after a time, comes to make himself conspicuous by telling Martin that unless he burns his papers, Martin would not get home alive; but there is no evidence of Macdonald doing anything in particular beyond threatening Martin and the others. Malcolm Finlayson appears afterwards near the schoolhouse, and all three form part of the threatening crowd. It appears to me, however, that Peter Macdonald, Malcolm Finlayson, and James Nicolson did not take that conspicuous part which Donald Nicolson and Alexander Finlayson took. And, therefore, although the case against each and all of these prisoners has been proved, I think there is a distinction between the conduct of Donald Nicolson, and Alexander Finlayson, and the others. These two are really the persons who committed the assault, and a distinction must be made between them and the others. The judgment of the Court is that Donald Nicolson and Alexander Finlayson be each fined £2 10s., or, failing payment, one month's imprisonment; and the other three prisoners, Peter Macdonald, Malcolm Finlayson, and James Nicolson, be each fined 20s., or fourteen days' imprisonment.

LIBERATION OF THE PRISONERS.

The result was received with some surprise, though not with dissatisfaction. As the Sheriff summed up strongly against two of the prisoners it was anticipated that the full penalty in their case, at least, would be inflicted, and that on the other three prisoners the sentence would have been more severe than that pronounced. The leniency of the judgment, therefore, was satisfactory to the audience. Dean of Guild Mackenzie at once passed a cheque for the full amount of the fines to Mr. Anderson, but the agent for the prisoners (Mr. Macdonald) intimated that it was paid under protest in order to enable him to lodge an appeal if this should afterwards be resolved upon. *

The prisoners, who had been confined between two policemen throughout the day, were then liberated. As they emerged from the Castle, they were met by a large crowd, who greeted them with cheers and calls for a speech. They, however, were allowed to proceed to their hotel without any further demonstration.

The men and the witnesses were lodged, and provided with a liberal supply of all the creature comforts, in the Glenalbyn Hotel, where they were visited by many of those in Inverness who sympathised with their position. Next morning they left by train and steamer for Portree, their fares having been paid, and provision made for anything they might require on the journey. On their arrival the same evening in the Capital of Skye they were met by their friends and the people of Portree, who greeted them with great enthusiasm, and many of whom convoyed them the greater part of their way to the Braes.

THE AUTUMN CAMPAIGN.

NOTHING of importance occurred for months after the trial, until the crofters appear to have allowed their sheep to take possession of Benlee, and, it is alleged, refused to take them back to their own ground.

Early in October, Lord Macdonald's Edinburgh agents

* A cheque for the whole amount of the fines was shortly afterwards received from Mr. Norman Macleod, Bookseller, Bank Street, Edinburgh, on behalf of a few Highlanders in that city, who were quite willing to subscribe much more had it been found necessary. The whole of the other expenses of the Trial was paid by the Federation of Celtic Societies.

sent to the Braes crofters registered letters requesting them to withdraw their stock from Benlee without delay. These letters were, in the ordinary course, sent to the district post-office. Delivery of two or three was accepted, but on their contents becoming known the rest of the crofters resolved to have nothing to do with them, and refused to take delivery. A copy of one of these letters appeared at the time in the *Aberdeen Free Press.* The burden of its contents was a request to the crofters to pay up their arrears and remove their stock from Benlee, otherwise proceedings would be taken against them. The rents had not been paid, the stock was still on Benlee, and the threat by Lord Macdonald's agents was immediately followed up ; the Court of Session granted notes of suspension and interdict against the crofters with regard to the grazings of Benlee. Mr. Alexander Mac-donald, Messenger-at-arms, Inverness, proceeded from Inverness with the Court of Session writs in his possession. On Saturday morning, the 2nd of September, he left Portree for the Braes to serve the writs, accompanied by Lord Macdonald's ground-officer. Gedentailler is the township nearest to Portree, and on arriving there the officer of Court proceeded to serve the documents on the different crofters. He appears to have got on smoothly enough there, but word seems to have been sent to Balmeanach, the largest of the three townships, that the officer and his companions were approaching. Thereupon the women and children of Balmeanach gathered in large numbers, covering their heads with handkerchiefs to disguise themselves as well as they could. They proceeded towards Gedentailler, and met the officers on the way. There the second Battle of the Braes began. Stones and clods were flying freely, the officers thought it expedient to beat a retreat, and the writs were not served in the township of Balmeanach, or Peinachorrain.

Mr. William Mackenzie, the special correspondent of the *Aberdeen Free Press*, to whom we are indebted for the narrative of these proceedings, visited the Braes on the following Tuesday, while the sheriff-officers were still in Portree, waiting for further instructions from the authorities at Inverness. He writes on Tuesday evening :—

The serving of writs at Gedentailler was evidently managed with great rapidity, for the work was done before the people realised their position. The people of the other townships got hurried word of what was going on, and they mustered and drove the officers away before they reached Balmeanach. The whole of the people are now in a state of great anxiety, and every stranger visiting the district is watched. The children, indeed, run away weeping and crying "Tha iad a' tighinn, tha iad a' tighinn" (They are coming, they are coming), on the approach of any suspected person. An impression was abroad last night that the officers were again to proceed to the Braes to-day, and, accordingly, the women and children, in large numbers, gathered and formed themselves into two divisions—the one being detailed to watch and protect Peinachorrain—(the farthest south of the townships), in case of the officers coming on them from Sligachan, and the other to defend Balmeanach, the middle township, in case of their coming from Portree. They occupied their respective positions for a considerable time during the day, but ultimately as the "foe" did not appear, they retired to their homes, leaving sentries on duty, to warn them of the approach of danger. These sentinels soon saw me, and gave the alarm, and in a very short time I was surrounded by a large crowd of women and children, and a few men. Each Amazon as she came up looked anything but friendly; but as I came to be known I received a cordial welcome. The old men who were present regarded the conduct of the proprietor towards them as harsh ; but they thought that the Court of Session writs should be peaceably accepted. The Amazons, however, thought otherwise, and they expressed in no qualified terms their intention to resist.

Those who suffered in spring are looked upon as heroes and martyrs, and some feel themselves driven to such a state of desperation and exasperation that they are well nigh indifferent as to what may happen. "Whatever becomes of us," they say, "we cannot he worse off than we are." The application of force may crush them individually, but in the present frame of mind of these people, force will be no more a remedy in the Braes than in Ireland ; and I am satisfied that any attempt at evicting them, or selling them out, without some attempt at an amicable settlement, will be attended with some rough work.

The officers were re-called to Inverness on the 11th of September, having remained in the Island for nine days without again attempting to serve the writs.

The same correspondent, in one of a series of able articles, writes, under date of 11th October, regarding a rumour which was then current in well-informed circles, to the following effect:—"During the week of the Argyle-shire gathering, when the gentry and nobility of the west were promoting social intercourse in Oban, an informal meeting of proprietors was there held in private, to consider the present position and future prospects of land ownership in the Highlands. The Skye question naturally formed a leading topic of discussion, and the opinion was expressed that Lord Macdonald, in the interests of his class, ought to have gone long ago to the Braes and to have endeavoured to settle the dispute between himself and the crofters ; and it was felt that so long as the question remained in its present aspect it will naturally be kept before the country, and the popular mind will be imbibing doctrines with regard to the land which may probably end in restricting the liberties in dealing with landed estates now enjoyed by their owners." The Northern Meeting at Inverness took place on 21st and 22nd September (in the following week), and many of the gentlemen present at the Argyleshire Meeting attended the meeting in the Highland capital. Lord Macdonald was also present. Whether his lordship had any interview with those gentlemen I know not, but on Saturday, 23rd of September, he left Inverness, and on Monday, the 25th, he visited the Braes. The conference was fruitless. The tenants, who had hitherto demanded Benlee free of rent, now, in order to put an end to the present turmoil, offered to give about £40. Lord Macdonald, who receives £128 from the present tenant, agreed to accept £100. Possibly another interview might lead to a compromise between parties—the tenants offering more and the landlord agreeing to accept less. But whether there will be another interview or not is a matter that must lie with the proprietor, for in their present frame of mind the tenants are not likely to seek an interview at the stage which the case has now reached.

Now, with regard to the threatened military invasion. That it was the intention of the authorities at one time to send one or two companies of soldiers to Skye is not denied; aud that these companies were to go from Fort-George. This would undoubtedly be very distasteful work to Highland soldiers, but if *ordered* they would have no alternative but to obey. That they were warned to be in readiness for "active service" in the Braes is certain; but I have good reasons for stating that military opinion at the Fort was decidedly against any such task being assigned to Highland soldiers, and that such remonstrances as could be made consistent with military discipline were sent to the superior authorities. The reasons for this are obvious. The country is now divided into regimental districts, and Skye is one of the recruiting districts for the Highland regiments which have their depôts at Fort-George. The belief among Highland officers is that if a company of Highland soldiers were sent to Skye on such an errand there would be no more recruits from that island for at least half a century. That this opinion is a sound one will be readily admitted by any one acquainted with the Highland character.

It was ultimately resolved to make another attempt, with a larger force of police, to serve the writs on the tenants of Balmeanach and Peinachorrain, on Tuesday the 24th of October. The special correspondent of the *Inverness Courier*, who accompanied the expedition, describes the proceedings thus :—

At half-past eight this morning, in weather as pleasant as one could desire, there drove from Portree for the Braes two. waggonettes containing Mr. A. Macdonald, messenger-at-arms, Inverness (who was to serve the writs); his concurrent; his guide, the ground-officer on Lord Macdonald's estates ; Mr. Aitchison, superintendent of the County Police ; Mr. Macdonald, inspector, Portree ; and a body of nine police constables. Some newspaper correspondents followed in a third conveyance. All along the route there was manifested the most intense interest—I may say excitement. Soon after leaving Portree we met two pleasant old men—crofters at Balmeanach—who had not heard that the officers were coming, but who, when asked as to what kind of reception they might expect, shook their heads, and indicated that their reception would be somewhat warm, but decidedly unpleasant. One of them told us that the officers had spoken to him as he came along, he having been pointed out as one of the crofters in question by Mr. Beaton. They asked him to accept the "paper," but he would have nothing to do with it ; he did not understand that it was anything else than a paper the reception of which would end in his being reduced to misery and want. Then, as we proceeded, we met people who told us that a reception was quite prepared at the Braes for the officers, and for the police. Here, and at several other points, information which we received in Portree last night was confirmed, information, namely, that the crofters had been advised that officers were approaching them, had been counselled to receive the papers, and that they had been on the watch all night. We passed on and on through a country which plainly had at one time been thickly peopled, but which is now a scene solitary to an extent that is painful to contemplate. At a little township near the Braes, women stopped their work at the peats to look at the passing carriages. A little further on the officers and policemen left their waggonettes, and walked to Gedintailler—a distance of over two miles—on foot. We adopted the same course.

The high green hill which, at the very entrance to the township of Gedintailler, rises right up from the roadside, was soon before us—a little over a mile ahead. We could see that there were groups of people on the height, and a couple of crofters belonging to a place immediately on the Portree side of Gedintailler, and who joined us here—going forward to see the fun—said that sixty people had been on the watch there ever since the dawn of day, and that they carried flags with which they were to wave to the whole community signals of approaching strangers. As soon as we approached the borders of Gedintailler, it was plainly seen that the officers, who were now a third of a mile ahead of us, were engaged in a task of a most delicate and difficult nature. A band of young men, and stout lads, and girls, occupied a height, from which, with stones, they could command the passage by the road underneath. Here we learned that the people whose writs were served successfully on the 2nd September last had driven their cattle off, thinking that the officers had come to seize them. Further on, we could see that the officers and the policemen were marching along a road, on each side of which were gathered here and there small knots of men, women, and children. As the officers and police force advanced, these knots of people retreated before them—all, however, to concentrate at a point just within the march that separates the township of Gedintailler from the township of Balmeanach. The people were angry and excited. Some carried sticks. Others doubtless were quite prepared to use the stones that lay everywhere about. Many wore an aspect of determination which was ominous in the extreme. It was clear that a whole country-side was up in arms against the messenger-at-arms, the police, and the writs. One young fellow, in answer to a question by myself, spoke in a tone and with a look which were the opposite of encouraging; and only changed his behaviour when he heard that I had come from a newspaper. This much must be said of everyone else; they were kind and courteous to those who were not connected with the officials who came to visit them; they seem well disposed too so long as you did not propose to take Benlee from them; in appearance and demeanour altogether there was nothing when they were away from the officers, but what is creditable. They, however, hate the writs, and all connected with them; and they entertain a bitter aversion to the very word "police"—an aversion deeply rooted in the minds of the youngest—because presumably of the recollection of the visit which was made to them in April last. But extreme excitement is perfectly compatible with this courtesy towards those who they know are not connected with the writs. If I were asked to describe the Braes to-day, I should say the whole community resembled a barrel of gunpowder that only required the lighted match to produce an explosion.

The officers and the police were stopped at the entrance to the township of Balmeanach—quite near the first house in the township—by a body of men, women, and children, variously estimated at from 140 to 160 individuals.

The scene, while officers and crowd were face to face with each other, was one both striking and picturesque. While officers and people discussed in Gaelic we wandered around to see what was to be seen, and hear what of English was to be heard. There they were, a great crowd engaged in loud and angry talk, varied now and again by strange cries and shouts from the women; and the very gathering and the noise and the excitement lent additional interest to the more distant scenes, which were already striking in solitude and grandeur. The girls, who were attending to the cattle on the green hill-sides, gathered in little knots to hear what was going on. The children who played on the roadside, or watched on the green turf infants of tender years, whose mothers were confronting the officers, seemed to have a perfect idea of what was taking place. At the beach, far down below the roadway, there lay a little boat in which three fishermen were engaged in shaking out of the nets some herrings which the night before they had got in Loch-Eynart. They, too, had to be apprised of what was going on. Occasionally one of the crew would land, ascend the steep brae, and look on the crowd. But while he was in the boat a knot of young women far up above the beach, would report the movements.

The interview between the people and the officers continued near an hour and a-half. The conversation was carried on in Gaelic. It would appear that every advice given to the crofters to receive the writs was lost upon them; they apparently did not know what the papers were, what they meant, or what the receiving of them would result in beyond the taking from them of Benlee. It is said they had been advised to receive the writs by two ministers and others; and in the afternoon we were shown the following telegram which had been handed in at Inverness at 4.52 P.M., Monday, and which had been received in Portree at 5 P.M. :—

"*From Dean of Guild Mackenzie, Inverness.*

"*To Mr. Neil Buchanan, or any of the Braes Crofters, near Portree.*

"Sheriff-officers, with body of County Police, left to-day with writs for Braes crofters. Be wise. Receive summonses peaceably. Trust to support of public opinion afterwards."

But the unfortunate crofters declined the counsel thus given. They regard Benlee as belonging to their holdings, and Benlee, and nothing but Benlee they would have.

There were heads of families in the crowd, and these were pointed out to the messenger-at-arms by the ground-officer. The messenger-at-arms then endeavoured to effect the service of the writs, but his efforts were of no avail. The officer tried them over and over again, but in vain. At length, he said he would go to the houses, and lodge the papers there. He endeavoured to go, but women rushed to intercept him, carrying stones and sticks, and all indicating that the proposed action on the part of the officers would not be allowed. At this stage, Beaton, the ground-officer, declined to go further to point out the houses, the enterprise threatening to be accompanied with danger. Shortly thereafter Mr. Macdonald said, "Very well, good-bye, ladies and gentlemen". Some women replied, "Good morning and a half to you, sir". The officers and the police force—the "dismal brigade," as they were once happily termed—turned their backs on the Braes, marched to the spot where the waggonettes were awaiting them, and returned to Portree, bearing with them the undelivered writs of the Court of Session.

During the interview with the officers, some of the women were weeping, and even at a distance from the crowd could be heard exclamations in Gaelic about the number of helpless widows and orphans that were in the Braes. Some called out that the curses of the orphans and widows would follow all these things. One woman said she would not like to see any one suffer greatly, but if those over them continued these actions much longer she did not know what she might wish them. Once a man was heard to say that the officers seemed to have come in a friendly way; but he was replied to with a chorus of voices that they came in no friendly way, that they were come to ruin poor people, and that they would not be allowed to go further. The police came in for a considerable share of the angry expressions of the women. One person reminded the police that there were people there who yet suffered from wounds they received in April. Actions and expressions were frequently greeted with cries on the part of the crowd, which were very far from encouraging to the officers. Occasionally, however, there were signs of good humour; but these were few, and disappeared as soon as the officers tried to go to the dwelling-houses. Altogether, as will have been clearly seen, the atmosphere was troubled in the extreme. A single injudicious act on the part of the messenger or police would unquestionably have produced an explosion of feeling which would have compelled the legal force to retreat with greater haste and with less dignity than that with which they did actually retire. At one point a row seemed imminent, but it was prevented by the officers and the police exercising prudence as the better virtue.

Judging from the appearance and the demeanour of the people to-day, my own opinion is that, if these writs are to be served by force, they must be served by men protected by the military. This, too, is the opinion of many people in Portree. The truth is, these frequent visits of officers and men in driblets to serve papers, which the crofters associate with impending misery, and possibly, eviction, are irritating and distressing the people. As it is, the people have become exasperated ; and it will be absolutely cruel, considering their ignorance of legal forms, their extreme poverty, and their attachment to the soil, to serve the writs by any other force than one which, by previously overawing them, will preclude the possibility of inflicting personal wounds on either man or woman. The appearance of the military may possibly overawe them, if they be sent in sufficient force ; but a police force will only still more exasperate them, and lead to a repetition of the painful scenes of April last.

The tone and spirit of this communication was altogether different to anything that had hitherto appeared in the *Courier.* It began to dawn upon the landlords that there must be something in the complaints of the people, after all, when this newspaper published such an account of the Braes and its unfortunate inhabitants. The change in its views produced a sensation, and pressure was immediately brought to bear upon Lord Macdonald by some of the Highland lairds to bring about a settlement with his people, if at all possible; but hitherto, so long as he expected a military force to crush them, without avail.

The urgent appeals made by the County authorities to the Home Office for a military force completely failed. It is well known in certain circles that Sir William Harcourt would not even listen to the proposal, and that he openly ridiculed the idea of sending Her Majesty's soldiers to settle a paltry dispute between a landlord and a few of his crofters, which, by the exercise of a little sound judgment and ordinary prudence, could be arranged by sensible men in a few minutes. In consequence of this attitude on the part of the Crown authorities further pressure was brought to bear upon Lord Macdonald to come to terms with the Braes crofters, and it is well known in well-informed circles that under this pressure he finally agreed to enter into negotiation, in the event of proposals to that effect emanating from the crofters themselves or from any of their friends. After a good deal of private correspondence in influential circles on both sides, negotiations were arranged, as we shall see hereafter, which ultimately ended in a settlement satisfactory in the circumstances to all concerned.

The special correspondence in the *Courier* had an effect also in other quarters than that of the landowners. Immediately on its perusal a patriotic Highland gentleman of means, who resides in the Channel Islands during the winter months, telegraphed on the 28th of October, as follows, to the writer of these pages :—

"*To Alexander Mackenzie, Esq., Dean of Guild of Inverness, from Malcolm Mackenzie, Vue du Lac, Guernsey.*

"Tender by telegraph to Lord Macdonald's agent all arrears of rent due by Braes crofters, and to stay proceedings. I write by post and send securities for one thousand pounds on Monday."

These instructions were carried out, and the following reply was received in due course :—

5 Thistle Street, Edinburgh, 30th Oct., 1882.

Sir,—We have received your telegram of to-day stating that you are authorised by a Mr. Malcolm Mackenzie, Guernsey, to tender payment of the last two years' arrears of rent due to Lord Macdonald by the Braes crofters, on condition that all proceedings against them are stopped, and that you will be prepared to deposit securities for one thousand pounds to-morrow.

Although we know nothing of the gentleman you mention, we will communicate your telegram to Lord Macdonald. At the same time, we must observe, that you seem to be labouring under a misapprehension as to the matter at issue between his lordship and the crofters, the proceedings against whom were raised for the purpose of preventing trespass, and not for recovering arrears of rent.—We are, &c.,

(Signed)   JOHN C. BRODIE & SONS.

To Dean of Guild Mackenzie, *Celtic Magazine* Office, Inverness.

To the above letter the writer replied as follows :—

Celtic Magazine Office, Inverness, Nov. 1, 1882.

Sirs,—I am in receipt of your favour of Monday acknowledging my telegram on behalf of Malcolm Mackenzie, Esq., Guernsey, offering to pay arrears of Braes crofters on terms stated therein.

I was fully aware of the *nature* of the proceedings against the crofters, though possibly Mr. Mackenzie was not, and I simply carried out my instructions. I think, however, that, if Lord Macdonald desires to settle amicably with the people, this proposal, if it does nothing else, will give him an opportunity of doing so without any sacrifice of his position beyond showing a willingness to discuss the matter with a view to settle it in a way that will extricate all parties from a difficult position.

Mr. Mackenzie has now, through me, deposited securities amounting to over £1000 in bank here, and I shall be glad to hear from you when you shall have heard from his lordship.—I am, Sirs, your obedient servant,

A. MACKENZIE.

Messrs. John C. Brodie & Sons, W.S.

Lord Macdonald's agents having published their letter, as above, in the *Inverness Courier* of 2nd November, Dean of Guild Mackenzie wrote them another letter in the course of which he said :—

Referrring to the second paragraph of my letter of yesterday, permit me to express my opinion that a favourable opportunity has now arrived to compromise the question in dispute advantageously to both parties, and if I can in any way aid in that object, nothing will give me greater satisfaction.   I have had no communication either direct or indirect with the Braes people since the recent trial, except the telegram which has appeared in the papers ; but if a desire is expressed for an amicable arrangement, I shall be glad to visit them and do what I can to bring such about.   I believe if a proposal were made to appoint an independent valuator connected with the West, and one in whom the people might fairly place confidence as to his knowledge of the country and the climate, the question might be settled in a few days.   This valuator should value the crofts and Benlee together, and name one sum for the whole.   Though I have no authority for making this proposal, I believe it could be carried out to the satisfaction of all concerned, and it would extricate the authorities and Lord Macdonald from a most unenviable position.

To these letters no reply was received.

Mr. Malcolm Mackenzie followed up his telegram of 28th October with a letter, of the same date, at once published in almost all the newspapers in Scotland, in the course of which he said :—

On reading in the *Inverness Courier* an account of the proceedings of Tuesday last against the Braes crofters, I thought that something might be done to take everybody out of a difficulty, and wired you the following message :—" Tender by telegraph to Lord Macdonald's agent all arrears of rent due by Braes crofters, and to stay proceedings.   I write by post, and send securities for one thousand pounds on Monday."

I trust that Lord Macdonald will be advised to accept payment of arrears, and to leave the people of the Braes in peace until the Government of the country can overtake measures to judge between him and them.   It will be a heavy responsibility and a disgrace to call soldiers to Skye at the present time.   Her Majesty has more important work to do with her soldiers than to place them at the service of the Court of Session in vindication of an unconstitutional law which is not based on principles of justice, and which has, by the progress of events and the evolution of time, become inoperative. The Court of Session looks for precedents. Where are these precedents for the reign of Queen Victoria?

Our dual system is no longer possible. Lord Macdonald does not know what to do. Nobody knows what to do. There is an absence of law and justice. In Scotland the administrator of justice is the robber who deprives the people of their natural and indefeasible right to the soil and of the labour which they have incorporated with it. Is that not a terrible contingency for any country to be in? It is peculiarly disgraceful that it should be so in respect of the Highland race, who successfully defended their country, their lands, and liberties, against Romans and Normans. What have we come to? Are they going to send for the Highland Brigade from Egypt to slaughter the people of Skye?

We call for Mr. Gladstone. What can poor Mr. Gladstone do, with time against him, society in a state of revolt, a demoralised House of Commons, a recalcitrant House of Lords, and the Court of Session at its wit's ends? Let us pray that he may be able to act as a *governor* on this rickety steam-engine of society which, under high pressure, and by reason of great friction, is in danger of tearing itself to pieces. In the meantime, and until the machine is put in some sort of order, by Rules of Procedure and alteration of the law, it is every man's duty to keep her Majesty's peace and prevent bloodshed; and as you appear to me, sir, to be doing yours, like a good Seaforth Highlander, or Ross-shire Buff, allow me to subscribe myself, very faithfully and loyally yours.

The following letters explain themselves:—

TO THE EDITOR OF THE INVERNESS COURIER.

Celtic Magazine Office, 2 Ness Bank, Inverness, 8th November, 1882.

Sir,—I have just received the enclosed letter from Mr. Malcolm Mackenzie, Guernsey. Please publish it in the *Courier*, as you have already published the reply to my telegram from Lord Macdonald's agents.

Permit me, at the same time, to state that the sum of £1000, in actual cash, has now been placed by Mr. Mackenzie at my disposal in the Caledonian Bank, and, in the event of his offer being entertained by

Lord Macdonald, that I shall be ready at any moment to implement Mr. Mackenzie's offer.—I am, &c.,

ALEXANDER MACKENZIE.

Guernsey, 4th November, 1882.

Alexander Mackenzie, Esq., Dean of Guild, Inverness.

Dear Sir,—1 am in receipt of your letter of the 1st, enclosing the reply of Lord Macdonald's solicitors to your telegram tendering them payment of two years' rent due by the Braes crofters.

From Lord Macdonald's dignified position, he might be thought entitled to ask me for an introduction before accepting any assistance on behalf of his tenants ; but acting as I was, on the spur of the moment, to prevent bloodshed, and possibly to avert an act of civil war, I did not think that in these hard-money days his solicitors would raise any objections on the ground of my being unknown to them, especially as I made the Dean of Guild of Inverness the medium of my communication.

As the days of chivalry are gone, and as clan ties and feelings of patriotism and humanity are no longer of binding obligation, I could not imagine that a firm of solicitors would stand on so much ceremony.

Whatever misapprehension Lord Macdonald's advisers are labouring under, I can assure them that I am labouring under none as to the real issues between him and his crofters. It would, doubtless, suit them to have the case tried on a false issue of trespass before a Court which must be bound by former decisions and prevailing canons as to the rights of Highland landlords. The plea of the poor people is that Lord Macdonald is the trespasser, in depriving them of their mountain grazings, without consent or compensation, and thereby reducing them to abject poverty. What can they do ? It would raise the whole question of constitutional right, and, as I have said, the Court is bound by former decisions that the landlord has the right to resume possession, and to evict and *banish* the peasantry after having first reduced them to the last nettle of subsistence. A sentence of banishment used to be regarded as a punishment only next to death, but in the phraseology of landlords it is now an "improvement".

In the days of "bloody" George of our own ilk, the Court of Session knew better how to apply the "boot" and the thumb-screw than constitutional law. Even later, such ruffians as old Braxfield recognised no right in the people, and according to their dog Latin, they found that the landlord was the only person who had a *persona standi*. It might, indeed, be an interesting question for more enlightened and better men to discuss, whether the Crown of Scotland conferred on the chieftains by their charters the right of wholesale clearances and forcible banishment of the people from their native country ; and when their military service was commuted into rent charges, if it extended to the landlord the right to make it so oppressive that they could not live without appealing to the public bounty for charity. But I fear it is now too late to expect the High Court of Scotland to remedy the evil, and that we must look to some other Court for redress.

It is in the hope that such a Court of equity may be established for Scotland as regards land and the well-being of the people, that I ventured to offer my assistance, and I thought that Lord Macdonald and his advisers would be glad to make it the means of getting out of a difficulty, and quashing a case that has become a public scandal, instead of standing on ceremony.—I am, sir, faithfully yours,

(Signed)   MAL. MACKENZIE.

No further reply was received from Lord Macdonald or his agents to Mr. Mackenzie's munificent offer, the accepting of it being understood by them as equivalent to giving up the grazings in question to the people, without any rent whatever, the only proceedings then current against them being the Note of Suspension and Interdict to remove and keep their stock off Benlee. They quite understood that, if these proceedings were withdrawn, as conditioned in Mr. Mackenzie's offer, the Braes Crofters would have the grazings in dispute on their own terms, until some settlement was arrived at between them and Lord Macdonald; and rather than agree to this, his Lordship, if the crown authorities had been pliant enough, would have chosen to see them slaughtered by a military force. Better counsels have fortunately prevailed, and his Lordship was saved by others from making his name for ever infamous among the Highlanders, especially among his own clansmen, and this although it was only through the strong arms and trusty blades of their forbears that his ancestors were able to leave him an inch of his vast estates !

While strong efforts were being made in private to induce his Lordship to yield, the following letter, refusing the expected military force, was received from the Lord Advocate by the Sheriff of the County :—

Whitehall, 3rd November, 1882.

Sir,—I received on the 28th ulto. the Report of the Procurator-Fiscal at Portree, relative to the occurrences which took place at Braes on the 24th, and the precognitions referred to in the Report reached me on the 30th. These documents have been carefully considered, along with the previous papers, and I have now to communicate to you the view entertained by the Government on the subject to which they relate.

It is clear that Lord Macdonald is entitled to have adequate protection for the Messengers-at-Arms whom he may employ for the purpose of serving writs upon the crofters at Braes, and the question to be determined is, by whom should that protecting force be provided, and should it consist of police or soldiers?

The duty of preserving the peace and executing the law within the County rests upon the County Authorities, who are by statute authorised to provide and maintain a police force for these purposes. The number of the force must necessarily depend upon the condition of the county, and the nature of the services which require to be performed in it. Recourse should not be had to military aid unless in cases of sudden riot or extraordinary emergency, to deal adequately with which police cannot be obtained, and soldiers should not be employed upon police duty which is likely to be of a continuing character. From the various reports which have been received, it appears that one or more places in the Island of Skye are in a disturbed condition, though actual riot or violence is not anticipated unless on the occasion of the service of writs, or the apprehension of offenders, and it further appears, that any force employed in protecting the officers performing such duties would probably be required not once only, but in connection with services falling to be made throughout the successive stages of the process of Suspension and Interdict, and of the Petition for Breach of Interdict, by which it would, in all likelihood, be followed. It further seems to be the view of the Authorities in Skye that the force would require to remain in the Island for a considerable time. These considerations have led the Government to the conclusion that they ought not to sanction the employment of a military force under existing circumstances, but that the County Authorities should provide or obtain the services of such a force of police as they may consider necessary for preserving the peace and executing the law within the county. It is not for the Government to prescribe or even to suggest the particular mode in which the County Authorities should fulfil this duty, whether by adding to their own police force, or by temporarily obtaining the services of police from other Counties or Burghs, but I am authorised by Sir William Harcourt to say, that if they should resolve to make an addition to the number of their own police, he will be ready to grant his consent, in terms of section 5 of the Police (Scotland) Act of 1857, to whatever addition they may consider requisite.—I am, Sir, Your obedient Servant,

(Signed)   J. B. BALFOUR.

To William Ivory, Esq., Sheriff of Inverness.

This letter was a bitter pill for the County Authorities, who naturally desired to escape the serious responsibility of serving the writs in Skye by the small police force at their disposal. The Police Committee held a meeting on the 13th of November to consider the document, and to decide what was necessary to be done in the altered circumstances. After serious deliberation Mackintosh of Mackintosh moved :

"That while protesting against the assumption that under existing circumstances the county was bound, without the special aid asked for from the Government, to execute the Supreme Court's warrants within the disturbed districts ; and while disclaiming all responsibility for any consequences which may result from the action which is now forced upon them, the Committee ageee to make a strenuous effort to execute the Court's warrants, and with that view they resolve that the police authorities of Scotland be immediately communicated with, asking them to furnish the largest number of constables they can possibly spare on a given date, and to place this force at the disposal of the executive of the county;" which motion was seconded by Mr. Davidson of Cantray, and unanimously agreed to.

Lord Lovat then moved "That the Committee recommend to the Commissioners of Supply to increase the present force by 50 constables;" which motion was seconded by Mr. Davidson, and unanimously agreed to.

It was also agreed to recommend that a meeting of Commissioners be held on Monday following to consider and dispose of this recommendation.

The meeting of Commissioners of Supply was duly held on the following Monday, when the subjoined interesting Report, dated Edinburgh, 18th November, was submitted by Sheriff Ivory :—

1. The second deforcement at the Braes took place on 2nd September, 1882. A full account of that and the previous deforcement is given in my report to the Home Secretary, and appending which is sent herewith.

2. On 6th September an order was issued by Crown Counsel, after consultation with the Lord Advocate, to serve on upwards of fifty crofters at Braes notes of suspension and interdict prohibiting them from trespassing on Benlee, which was then, and had been for seventeen years previous, occupied by another tenant, at a rent of £130.

3. That order was given to the Procurator-Fiscal of the Skye district, who was directed to judge of the amount of the police force that would be required, and to ask the police authorities to furnish it, the particular mode in which the writs were to be served being distinctly specified in Crown Counsel's order.

4. The above order was on the 7th September communicated by the Procurator-Fiscal (Skye District) to the Clerk of the Police Committee, the former intimating at the same time that he and Sheriff Spiers considered 100 police necessary, and that they should be supported by troops. The order was thereafter communicated to me as Chairman of the Police Committee, whereupon I at once put myself in communication with the Lord Advocate, and asked for instructions.

5. The Lord Advocate thereafter requested the Procurator-Fiscal of Inverness-shire and myself to go to Edinburgh, and consult with him there. We went, and on the 16th September, after a long and anxious consultation (in the course of which I strongly advocated an expedition with a Government steamer and marines), it was finally resolved that, as the calling in of strange police had caused a serious riot on a previous occasion, and would be likely on the next occasion to cause much more disturbance and bloodshed than a military force, it was the best course to prevent a serious riot and perhaps loss of life, to call in the aid of the military, and I was requested by the Lord Advocate to make the necessary requisition to the military authorities.

6. On 21st September I intimated to the Home Secretary that, after consultation with the Lord Advocate, I intended to make a requisition for troops, and sent him at the same time, through the Lord Advocate,

a full report in regard to the disturbed state of Skye, and the previous deforcements and assault on 50 Glasgow police and myself at Braes.

7. The requisition for troops was made by me on 23rd September, and on my informing the Lord Advocate of the fact, his lordship wrote me on 25th September that he did not see that the county authorities had then any alternative but to request military aid.

8. On 30th September the Home Secretary wrote me deprecating the use of military, unless it was absolutely necessary, and suggesting that if the expedition had not started I should again consult with the Lord Advocate on the subject.

9. On 30th September, and again on 1st October, I pressed on the Lord Advocate my decided opinion that (failing the Government furnishes a steamer and marines) it was absolutely necessary to make use of the military.

10. Shortly after this Lord Macdonald visited the Braes, and in consequence the Lord Advocate directed me to suspend the requisition for the military; and on 12th October, I intimated this order to Colonel Preston.

11. On 17th October, the Lord Advocate wrote me that the Braes arrangement was at an end; that the position of matters had altered since the requisition for the military was made; and that, in his lordship's opinion, a further attempt should be made to ascertain, by the test of experience, whether a military force was absolutely essential.

12. That further attempt was made on 23rd October and failed. A full report of the expedition was afterwards communicated to the Lord Advocate.

13. Considerable misapprehension exists in regard to this expedition. The Lord Advocate was of opinion that, from what passed during the negotiations between Lord Macdonald and his crofters, the latter had indicated a more peaceable frame of mind, and that there was no ground for assuming that they would forcibly resist a well-conducted service. The Police Sub-committee and I entertained doubts as to the propriety of sending such a small force of police to the Braes, as in the present excited state of the people they might suffer severe injury. These doubts were intimated to the Lord Advocate and Home Secretary, but at the same time, in deference to the views of the former, the expedition was carried out. In giving their consent to this expedition, the Sub-committee stated that they ' were decidedly of opinion that if the messenger should be deforced on this occasion it will be absolutely necessary that a military or naval force should immediately thereafter be sent with the messenger to insure service and the vindication of the law. The com-

mittee were strongly of opinion that a gun-boat and naval force would be preferable, and that the boat should remain for some time in the district.

Sheriff Ivory here relates, in paragraphs 14, 15, and 16, the resolution of the Police Committee to apply to counties and burghs in Scotland for a special police force, and to permanently increase the force of the county by 50 men (see excerpt from their minute already given). He proceeds—

17. These resolutions on the part of the Police Committee are in my opinion highly creditable to them, and I sincerely trust that they will be unanimously approved of and adopted by the Commissioners of Supply. For, while the latter have no doubt great reason to complain of the great delay that has already occurred in consequence of the manner in which the Government has acted, and of the delay that in all probability must still take place, if the Government adhere to their resolution to refuse military aid, and while I think the Commissioners ought to protest against the present attempt of the Government to throw on the county authorities the whole responsibility of serving writs, apprehending offenders, executing the law, and preserving the peace of the county, without naval or military aid, in the present disturbed state of Skye, and to disclaim all responsibility for the consequences, should serious bloodshed or loss of life ensue—I am of opinion that the conduct of the Government in the matter renders it all the more necessary for the county authorities to do their utmost in the meantime to preserve the peace, and vindicate the authority of the law in Skye.

18. For my own part I regret exceedingly the delay that has already occurred, and that will in all probability still occur, before the law is duly vindicated in Skye. Such delay will be most prejudicial, in my opinion, to the best interests of the island. Had I foreseen the course which matters have unfortunately taken, I should at once have recommended the county authorities—when application was made to them for a sufficient force to serve the writs—to do then what they propose to do now—viz., to apply to Glasgow and other police authorities for a larger force of police to ensure the due service of the writs. But this course appeared to me objectionable in many respects. In particular, nothing gave such great offence to the crofters and their friends as the sending on the last occasion a large force of strange police to Skye, and I am credibly informed, and believe that if such a force was sent again, a serious riot, and probably bloodshed would ensue. Further, it appeared to me far from a judicious course to apply to Glasgow and other burgh and county authorities for police, thereby necessitating innumer-

able discussions regarding the rights of crofters before the Police Com-
mittees of Scotland, while at the same time it was very doubtful
whether these authorities could or would supply the necessary force.
On the other hand, I was assured by many persons who were much
interested in Skye, and who knew the people well, that if a force was
sent by Government—whether naval or marine—the people would see
that the Government were determined to vindicate the law in Skye—
that in that case in all probability no resistance would be offered, and
the writs would not only be served in peace and quietness, but in all
likelihood the people would in future refrain from trespassing on ground
to which they had no right or committing breaches of interdict, or
otherwise setting the law at defiance. On these grounds when I failed
to get the use of a Government steamer and marines, I willingly accepted the other alternative of making a requisition for military aid.
It must be kept in view, however, that the suggestion for military aid
came neither from the county authorities nor from myself. It was
originally insisted on by the Procurator-Fiscal of Skye (acting as the
hand of the Lord Advocate in the matter) as necessary to enable him
to fulfil the order of the Crown Counsel to serve the writs at Braes ; it
was afterwards adopted by the Lord Advocate, after long and anxious
consultation with the parties on whose judgment his lordship thought
proper to rely—as the best course to be followed in all the circumstances;
and while the formal requisition was made—as it could only formally
be made by me as Sheriff of the county—in point of fact the requisition for military aid, which has now after two months' delay been
refused by her Majesty's Government, was truly made at the request,
and for the purpose of carrying out the views of the Lord Advocate,
who at the time represented her Majesty's Government in Scotland.

(Signed) W. IVORY.

The following excerpt from the Minutes of the Police
Committee Meeting, held on the 18th of September was
also read :—

The Committee, having reference to the Procurator-Fiscal's letter, as
to the nature and extent of the force necessary to be employed, and to
the reports made to them at the time of the previous disturbances at the
Braes, were of opinion that no force of police at their disposal will be
adequate to the duty the county authorities are now called upon to perform, and that with the view not only of securing the service of the
writs, and the apprehension of the accused parties, but of duly impressing

the people of Skye with the resolution of the authorities to maintain the law, a military or naval force should accompany the authorities in their endeavour to enforce the law, to be employed as a protection and aid to the civil officers, in the event of their being overpowered; and the Sheriff was requested to make requisition to that effect in the proper quarter.

It was agreed that the county police force should be placed at the Sheriff's disposal, but they do not think it advisable again to apply for police from Glasgow. Especially, seeing that a strong feeling of irritation was excited in Skye against them on the former occasion, the moral effect would be less than were the military employed, and also because difficulties may be anticipated with the Glasgow Town Council in procuring the necessary force.

After considerable discussion and some opposition, it was resolved to increase the police force of the county from 44 to 94 men; at an estimated cost of over £3000 per annum. It was also agreed

"To make a strenuous effort to execute the Court's warrants, and with that view they resolve that the police authorities of Scotland be immediately communicated with, asking them to furnish the largest number of constables they can possibly spare on a given date, and to place this force at the disposal of the executive of the county."

The police authorities of Scotland had been applied to, and the response was of so discouraging a character that the proposed police force has not yet been sent to Skye, and it is most unlikely that it ever shall be. A few counties agreed to send small detachments, which resolution some of them afterwards rescinded. All the burghs point blank refused to send any. This indicated an ominous state of adverse feeling throughout the country regarding the proposed action of the Inverness County Authorities, and they became paralyzed in consequence. The Commissioners of Police for the Burgh of Inverness, on the motion of the present writer, refused the application of the County Authorities (on the evening of the day on which the Commissioners of Supply resolved to ask for it), by a majority of 14 to 5, the minority, it has been pointed out, consisting of three factors—Culloden's, Sir Alexander Mathieson's, and Flichity's, with Lord Lovat's Law Agent, and the local architect of Mackintosh and Sir John Ramsden.

What was to be done next? Neither military nor police could be had to serve Lord Macdonald's writs ; the county authorities were virtually powerless, and various efforts were made to secure a settlement. They had in fact to fall back on the friends of the crofters, one of whom, a gentleman in Skye, was communicated with by his Lordship's agents, urging him to use his good offices to get the crofters to let his Lordship drop easy, by getting proposals of settlement to emanate from them. The result was a visit by the factor, Mr. Alexander Macdonald, to the Braes, on the 27th of November last ; a long conference with the tenants, and a final settlement, the people agreeing to pay a rent of £74 15s. a year for the now celebrated Benlee, for which the late tenant, Mr. John Mackay, had been paying £128 per annum, and he, who was joint-petitioner with Lord Macdonald, in the Note of Suspension and Interdict, in the Court of Session, having given his consent, the case was withdrawn in the month of December, and peace, which, with a little prudence, and the exercise of the smallest modicum of common-sense, need never to have been broken, now reigns supreme in the Braes.

It should be mentioned that the Braes crofters told their friends from the beginning that, although they considered themselves entitled to Benlee without any rent, still they were willing to pay a fair sum for it, if Lord Macdonald or his factor would only listen to their grievances or condescend to discuss with them, with the view of arriving at any reasonable compromise, such as that which has now been agreed upon, apparently to the satisfaction of all concerned.

The Glendale Crofters in the Court of Session.

It appears that the Glendale crofters have permitted their stock to remain on the farm of Waterstein, notwithstanding an interdict procured against them, in absence, in the Court of Session, and they are now further charged with an assault on one of the shepherds. Unlike the Braes tenants, they are apparently not only quite willing to receive any number of writs, but they are at the same time most courteous to the officers of the law, who have had occasion to visit them repeatedly in the performance of their official duties. On the last occasion they, with the greatest consideration, ferried Mr. MacTavish, the sheriff officer, across the loch from one district to another with the unserved portion of the writs, for those on the opposite side, in his possession.

The following report of what took place in the Court of Session will explain how the matter stands with them, as we go to press —

Petition and Complaint.—Macleod's Trustees v. Mackinnon and Others,—Glendale Crofters.

This petition and complaint was presented by the Trustees of the late Sir John Macpherson MacLeod, of Duirinish, K.C.S.I., and the petitioners complain of various breaches of interdict against five of the crofters on the estate of Duirinish and Glendale, in the island of Skye, which estate is in the hands of the petitioners as trustees. The case was before the Court on the 11th of January, when

Mr. Murray, for the petitioners, appeared and said—In this case no answers have been lodged, and I have to ask your lordships to pronounce an order ordaining the respondents to appear at the bar. In the special circumstances of this case I shall ask your lordships to allow us to send the order by registered letter.

The Lord-President—What is the order you ask for?

Mr. Murray—The order I ask for is to ordain the respondents to appear at the bar.

Lord Mure—How many respondents are there?

Mr. Murray—There are five of them.

The Lord-President—Have you any precedent for that mode of sending an order, Mr. Murray?

Mr. Murray—No, my lord : there is no authority. I think the matter is entirely in your lordships' hands. The matter is not regulated by any express enactment. The Act of Sederunt that deals with it is 28, which simply says that the procedure shall be, so far as possible, the same as the procedure in a petition and complaint against the freeholders. Your lordships see that this is really simply intimating an order of Court, and one great reason for this, without directing your attention to any other special circumstances, is the very large expense that is incurred by service in such a remote part. The service in this case practically costs £40. Now, there have already been three services. There was first the original service of interdict; and then there was the service of interim interdict; and then, lastly, there was the service of the petition and complaint.

The Lord-President—Is there any messenger-at-arms?

Mr. Murray—There is nobody nearer than Glasgow or Inverness.

Lord Mure—What do you say the expense was?

Mr. Murray—£40 on each occasion. £30 of fee, and £10 of expenses.

The Lord-President—Is there a Sheriff Court officer in Skye?

Lord Mure—There is a Sheriff-Substitute at Skye if there is not a sheriff officer.

After a consultation the Lord-President stated that their

lordships would dispose of the matter in the course of the day.

When the case again came up in the afternoon, the Lord-President said their lordships did not see their way to grant the request to serve the order by registered letter, and they would just have to serve it in the ordinary way. They would make an order for the respondents to appear personally at the bar, but he thought probably they had better make it so many days after service. He supposed it was a matter of no consequence whether they authorised it to be done by a sheriff officer rather than a messenger-at-arms.

Mr. Murray said it would be better if they had the option of employing either the one or the other. He would not like to be tied down to a sheriff officer.

The Court, therefore, in respect of no answer and no appearance for the respondents, made an order for them to appear personally at the bar on the 1st day of February next, provided this order was served on them ten days before that date, and authorised either a sheriff officer or messenger-at-arms to serve the order.

The Sheriff-Officer, in due course, proceeded to Skye, to serve the Order of the Court, but on arriving in Glendale he was met by a large crowd of men, women, and children, who refused to receive the writs. As we go to press with these lines, a warrant has been granted for the apprehension of four of the men on the charge of deforcement, but what the result may be it is difficult to predict. Application has again been made to the Crown authorities for a military force for the apprehension of the accused, without which it is admitted on all hands, no apprehensions can possibly be made.

Alluding to our present Land Laws, St. Michael, addressing the Preacher, in a recently published extreme, but, in many respects, true and powerful poem, says :—

> Can Law be Law when based on Wrong ?
> Can Law be Law when for the strong ?
> Can Law be Law when landlords stand
> Rack-renting mankind off the land ?
> By 'Law' a landlord can become
> The ghost of every Crofter's home ;
> By 'Law' their little cots can be
> Dark dens of dirt and misery ;
> By 'Law' the tax upon their toil
> Is squandered on an alien soil ;
> By 'Law' their daughters, sons, and wives,
> Are doomed to slavish drudgery's lives ;
> By 'Law' Eviction's dreadful crimes
> Are possible in Christian times ;
> By 'Law' a spendthrift lord's intents
> Are met by drawing higher rents ;
> By 'Law' all food-producing glens
> Are changed from farms to cattle pens :
> This is your 'Law' whereby a few
> Are shielded in the deeds they do.*

* *St. Michael and the Preacher, a Tale of Skye.* By the Rev. Donald MacSiller, Minister of the [New] Gospel, Portree. Inverness: Law, Justice, and Co.

APPENDIX.

THE figures given in the following tables will show at what rate the population increased or decreased in the different Parishes, in whole or in part, within the counties named, during the periods between 1831, 1841, 1851, and 1881, and, in the case of the County of Sutherland, during each decennial period since 1801. The total population of each County for each decade is as follows :—

PERTH.—This County had a total population, in 1801, of 126,366; in 1811, of 135,093; in 1821, of 139,050; in 1831, of 142,166; in 1841, of 137,457; in 1851, of 138,660; in 1861, of 133,500; in 1871, of 127,768; and in 1881, of 129,007. The present total population will thus be found more than 6,000 less than it was 70 years ago; 10,000 less than it was 60 years ago ; and more than 13,000 less than it was 50 years ago. The town and village population increased in the last decade—from 1871 to 1881—by 14,420. The total rural population in 1881 was 57,016, against 78,364 in 1831, making a decrease in the rural inhabitants of the County in 50 years of 21,348 souls, or considerably more than one-third of the present rural population of the County. A few parishes, in the more Southern, non-Highland, portions of this County are not given in the Table applicable to it in this Appendix.

ARGYLL.—This County had a population in 1801, of of 71,859; in 1811, of 85,859; in 1821, of 97,316; in 1831, of 100,973; in 1841, of 97,371; in 1851, of 89,298; in 1861, of 79,724; in 1871, of 75,679; and in 1881, of 76,468. The present total population will thus be found 9,117 less than it was 70 years ago; 20,848 less than it was 60 years ago; and 24,505 less than it was 50 years ago. The town and village population increased, between 1871 and 1881, from 25,713 to 30,387; while during the same decennial period, the rural population decreased from 49,966 to 46,081, or by nearly 4,000 souls. The rural population of the County in 1881 was 46,081. Thus, while the town population more than doubled since 1831, the rural population decreased by more than one-half. There could not have been 15,000 of a town population in 1831, as suggested at page 362, and therefore the decrease in the rural population is necessarily greater than is there stated.

INVERNESS.—This County had a population in 1801, of 74,292; in 1811, of 78,336; in 1821, of 90,157; in 1831, of 94,797; in 1841, of 97,799; in 1851, of 96,500; in 1861, of 88,261; in 1871, of 88,015; and in 1881, of 90,454. The present total population of the County will thus be found only 297 more than it was 60 years ago; 4,343 less than it was 50 years ago; and 7,345 less than it was 40 years ago, notwithstanding that the population of the Town of Inverness alone increased during the last 50 years, from 9,663, in 1831, to 17,385, in 1881, or 7,922 souls. The village population also increased considerably during the same period. From 4,624 in 1871, it increased to 5,714 in 1881, while, during the same decade, the rural population shows a decrease from 68,881, in 1871, to 67,355, in 1881, or 1,526 souls. The town and village population of the County in 1881, was 23,099. Of this number there could not have been more than 12,000 in 1841, making the rural population at that date nearly 86,000, as against 67,355, in 1881, or a reduction of considerably more than one-fourth, of the present rural population of the County, in forty years.

ROSS AND CROMARTY.—The population of these Counties, combined, in 1801, was 55,343. In 1811, they had a population of 60,853; in 1821, of 68,828; in 1831, of 74,820; in 1841, of 78,685; in 1851, of 82,707; in 1861, of 81,406; in 1871, of 80,955; and in 1881, of 78,547. These figures show an increase of 3,727 on the population of 1831, or of fifty years ago, while they show a decrease of 238 on that of 1841, and a reduction of 4,160 on that of 1851. The population of the towns and villages appear to have remained stationary, except in the villages of Alness and Invergordon, on the mainland. The latter accounts for the increase which appears in the Table, in the population of the parishes of Roskeen and Fearn. The same remarks hold true of the town and parish of Stornoway, in the Lews. The rural population of Ross and Cromarty decreased from 53,223 in 1871, to 49,882 in 1881; or 3,341 during the last ten years.

SUTHERLAND.—This County had a population in 1801, of 23,117; in 1811, of 23,629; in 1821, of 23,840; in 1831, of 25,518; in 1841, of 24,782; in 1851, of 25,793; in 1861, of 25,246; in 1871, of 24,317; and in 1881, of 23,370. It will be seen that the population of the whole County was, in 1881, only 253 souls more than it was in 1801, and that it was decreasing at the rate of nearly 1000 each decade since 1851. The County may be said to be entirely rural, if we except the wretched villages of Bonar, Dornoch, Helmsdale, Embo, and Portskerra, with those of Golspie, and Brora, which are in a slightly less wretched condition from their contiguity to Dunrobin Castle. These, among them, had a village population of 4,674, in 1881, as against 4,779, in 1871. Most of these villages have arisen since the Clearances, which took place in the beginning of the century, and the result of which, in the parishes more particularly affected, may be traced in the tabulated statement for the County, which is carried back to 1801, for this purpose.

CAITHNESS.—This County had a population, in 1801, of 22,609; in 1811, of 23,419; in 1821, of 30,238; in 1831, of 34,529; in 1841, of 36,343; in 1851, of 38,709; in 1861, of 41,111; in 1871, of 39,992; and in 1881, of 38,865. In 1811, the population of the town of Wick was only 994; in 1881, it was 1,860. The population of Pultneytown, Louisburgh, and Bankhead, in 1811, was only 755; in 1881, it numbered 6,193; total in 1811—1749; total in 1881—8,053. The fishing villages of Broadhaven, Staxigoe, Papigoe, and others, have also added considerably to the population of the Parish. The same remarks also hold true of the parish of Olrig, which includes the modern village of Castletown, containing a population of 932, mainly slate quarriers, in 1881. The town of Thurso had a population of only 2,429, in 1831; in 1881, it increased to 4,055. From these figures it is clear that the rural population of the County, which, in 1881, only numbered 24,309, is rapidly decreasing. Since 1871, it fell from 25,763 to 24,309, or 1,454 in one decade.

Population in 1831, 1841, 1851, *and* 1881, *of all the Parishes in whole or in part in the* COUNTY OF PERTHSHIRE.

	1831.	1841.	1851.	1881.
Aberdalgie	434	360	343	297
Aberfoyle	660	543	514	465
Abernethy	1915	1920	2026	1714
Abernyte	254	280	275	275
Arngask	712	750	685	547
Auchterarder	3182	3434	4160	3648
Auchtergeven	3417	3366	3232	2195
Balquhidder	1049	871	874	627
Bendochy	780	783	773	715
Blackford	1897	1782	2012	1595
Blair-Athol	2495	2231	2084	1742
Blairgowrie	2644	3471	2497	5162
Callander	1909	1665	1716	2167
Caputh	2303	2317	2037	2096
Cargill	1628	1642	1629	1348
Cluny	944	763	723	582
Collace	730	702	581	409
Culross	1484	1444	1487	1130
Comrie	2622	2471	2463	1858
Dron	464	441	394	335
Dull	4590	3811	3342	2565
Dunbarney	1162	1104	1066	756
Dunkeld	2032	1752	1662	791
Dunning	2045	2128	2206	1639
Errol	2992	2832	2796	2421
Findo-Gask	428	436	405	364
Forgandenny	913	796	828	617
Forteviot	624	638	638	618
Fortingall	3067	2740	2486	1690
Fossoway and Tulliebole	1576	1724	1621	1267
Fowlis-Wester	1681	1609	1483	412
Glendevon	620	157	128	147
Inchture	878	769	745	650
Kenmore	3126	2539	2257	1508
Killin	2002	1702	1608	1277

	1831.	1841.	1851.	1881.
Kilmadock	3752	4055	3659	3012
Kilspindie	760	709	684	693
Kincardine	2455	2232	1993	1351
Kinclaven	890	880	881	588
Kinfauns	732	720	650	583
Kinnaird	461	458	370	260
Kinnoull	2957	2879	3134	3461
Kirkmichael	1568	1412	1280	849
Lethendy and Kinloch	708	662	556	404
Little Dunkeld	2867	2718	2155	2175
Logierait	3138	2959	2875	2323
Longforgan	1638	1660	1787	1854
Madderty	713	634	593	527
Meigle	873	728	686	696
Methven	2714	2446	2454	1910
Moneydie	300	315	321	233
Monzie	1195	1261	1199	753
Monievaird and Strowan	926	853	790	700
Moulin	2022	2019	2022	2066
Muckhart	617	706	685	601
Muthill	3297	3067	2972	1702
Redgorton	1866	1929	2047	1452
Rhynd	400	402	338	297
St. Madoes	327	327	288	316
St. Martins	1135	1071	983	741
Scone	2268	2422	2381	2402
Tibbermore	1223	1661	1495	1883
Trinity-Gask	620	620	597	396
Tulliallan	3550	3196	3043	2207
Weem	1209	890	740	474

Population in 1831, 1841, 1851, *and* 1881, *of all the Parishes in whole or in part in the* COUNTY OF ARGYLL.

	1831.	1841.	1851.	1881.
Ardchattan and Muckairn	2420	2264	2313	2005
Ardnamurchan	5669	5581	5446	4105
Campbelton	9472	9539	9381	9755
Craignish	892	970	873	451
Dunoon and Kilmun	2416	2853	4518	8002
Gigha and Cara	534	550	547	382
Glassary	4054	5369	4711	4348
Glenorchy and Inishail	1806	831	1450	1705
Inveraray	2233	2277	2229	946
Inverchaolain	596	699	474	407
Jura and Colonsay	2205	2291	1901	1343
Kilbrandon and Kilchattan	2833	2602	2375	1767
Kilcalmonell and Kilberry	3488	2460	2859	2304
Kilchoman	4822	4505	4142	2547
Kilchrenan and Dalavich	1096	894	776	504
Kildalton	3065	3315	3310	2271
Kilfinan	2004	1816	1695	2153
Kilfinichen and Kilviceuen	3819	4102	3054	1982
Killarrow and Kilmeny	7105	7341	4882	2756
Killean and Kilchenzie	2866	2401	2219	1368
Kilmallie	4210	5397	5235	4157
Kilmartin	1475	1213	1144	811
Kilmodan	648	578	500	323
Kilmore and Kilbride	2836	4327	3131	5142
Kilninian and Kilmore	4830	4322	3954	2540
Kilninver and Kilmelford	1072	970	714	405
Knapdale, North	2583	2170	1666	927
Knapdale, South	2137	1537	2178	2536
Lismore and Appin	4365	4193	4097	3433
Lochgoilhead and Kilmorich	1196	1100	834	870
Morvern	2036	1781	1547	828
Saddell and Skipness	2152	1798	1504	1163
Small Isles	1015	993	916	550
Southend	2120	1598	1406	955
Strachur and Stralachan	1083	1086	915	932
Tiree and Coll	5769	6096	4818	3376
Torosay	1889	1616	1361	1102

Population in 1831, 1841, 1851, *and* 1881, *of all the Parishes in whole or in part in the* COUNTY OF INVERNESS.

	1831.	1841.	1851.	1881.
Abernethy	2092	1920	1871	1530
Alvie	1092	972	914	707
Ardersier	1268	1475	1241	*2086
Ardnamurchan	5669	5581	5446	4105
Boleskine and Abertarff	1829	1876	2006	1448
Cawdor	1187	1150	1202	1070
Cromdale	3234	3561	3990	3642
Croy	1664	1684	1770	1709
Daviot and Dunlichity	1641	1681	1857	1252
Dores	1736	1745	1650	1148
Duthil	1920	1759	1788	1664
Glenelg	2874	2729	2470	1601
Inverness	14324	15418	16496	21725
Kilmallie	4210	5397	5235	4157
Kilmonivaig	2869	2791	2583	1928
Kilmorack (including Beauly)	2709	2694	3007	2618
Kiltarlity	2715	2896	2965	2134
Kingussie and Insh	2080	2047	2201	1987
Kirkhill	1715	1829	1730	1480
Laggan	1196	1201	1223	917
Moy and Dalarossie	1098	967	1018	822
Petty	1836	1749	1784	1531
Urquhart and Glenmoriston	2942	3104	3280	2438
Urray	2768	2716	2621	2478
Insular—				
Barra	2097	2363	1873	2161
Bracadale	1769	1824	1597	929
Duirinish	4765	4983	5330	4319
Harris	3900	4429	4250	4814
Kilmuir	3415	3629	3177	2562
North Uist	4603	4428	3918	4264
Portree	3441	3574	3557	3191
Sleat	2756	2706	2531	2060
Small Isles	1015	993	916	550
Snizort	3487	3220	3101	2120
South Uist	6890	7333	6173	6078
Strath	2962	3150	3243	2616

* Including 948 military and militia in Fort-George in 1881.

Population in 1831, 1841, 1851, and 1881, of all the Parishes in whole or in part in the COUNTIES OF ROSS AND CROMARTY.

	1831.	1841.	1851.	1881.
Alness	1437	1269	1240	1033
Applecross	2892	2861	2709	2239
Avoch	1956	1931	2029	1691
Contin	2023	1770	1562	1422
Cromarty	2900	2662	2727	2009
Dingwall	1159	2100	2364	2220
Edderton	1023	975	890	431
Fearn	1695	1914	2122	2135
Fodderty ..	2232	2437	2342	2047
Gairloch	4445	4880	5186	4594
Glenshiel	715	745	573	424
Killearnan	1479	1643	1794	1059
Kilmuir-Easter	1556	1486	1437	1146
Kiltearn	1605	1436	1538	1182
Kincardine	1887	2108	1896	1472
Kintail	1240	1186	1009	688
Knockbain	2139	2565	3005	1866
Lochalsh	2433	2597	2299	2050
Lochbroom	4615	4799	4813	4191
Lochcarron	2136	1960	1612	1456
Logie-Easter	934	1015	965	827
Nigg	1404	1426	1457	1000
Resolis or Kirkmichael	1470	1549	1551	1424
Rosemarkie	1799	1719	1776	1357
Rosskeen	2916	3222	3699	3773
Tain	3078	3128	3754	3009
Tarbat	1809	1826	2151	1878
Urquhart and Logie-Wester	2864	2997	3153	2525
Urray	2768	2716	2621	2474
Insular—				
Barvas	3011	3850	4189	5325
Lochs	3067	3653	4256	6284
Stornoway	5491	6218	8057	10389
Uig	3041	3316	3209	3489

Population in 1801, 1811, 1821, 1831, 1841, 1851, 1871, *and* 1881, *of all the Parishes in whole or in part in the* COUNTY OF SUTHERLAND.

	1801.	1811.	1821.	1831.	1841.	1851.	1871.	1881.
Assynt......	2419	2479	2803	3161	3178	2989	3006	2781
Clyne.......	1643	1639	1874	1711	1765	1933	1733	1812
Creich......	1974	1969	2354	2562	2852	2714	2524	2223
Dornoch ...	2362	2681	3100	3380	2714	2981	2764	2525
Durness....	1208	1155	1004	1153	1109	1152	1049	987
Eddrachillis	1253	1147	1229	1965	1699	1576	1530	1525
Farr.........	2408	2408	1994	2073	2217	2403	2019	1930
Golspie.....	1616	1391	1049	1149	1214	1529	1804	1556
Kildonan..	1440	1574	565	257	256	*2288	1916	1942
Lairg........	1209	1354	1094	1045	913	1162	978	1355
Loth	1374	1330	2008	2234	2526	*640	583	584
Reay........	2406	2317	2758	2881	2811	2506	2331	2191
Rogart	2022	2148	1986	1805	1501	1535	1341	1227
Tongue.....	1348	1493	1736	2030	2041	2018	2051	1929

* The lands of Helmsdale and others previously in the Parish of Loth were, about this time, added to Kildonan, which accounts for this large increase. It also accounts for the decrease in Loth.

Population in 1831, 1841, 1851, *and* 1881, *of all the Parishes in whole or in part in the* COUNTY OF CAITHNESS.

	1831.	1841.	1851.	1881.
Bower..........................	1615	1689	1658	1608
Canisbay	2364	2306	2437	2626
Dunnet	1906	1880	1868	1607
Halkirk........................	2847	2963	2918	2705
Latheron	7030	7637	8224	6675
Olrig	1146	1584	1873	2002
Reay	2881	2811	2506	2191
Thurso........................	4679	4881	5096	6217
Watten........................	1234	1966	1351	1406
Wick..........................	9850	10393	11851	12822

MURDER MOST ROYAL

By the same author in PAN Books

The Lucrezia Borgia Series

MADONNA OF THE SEVEN HILLS
LIGHT ON LUCREZIA

The Tudor Series

THE SIXTH WIFE
ST THOMAS'S EVE
THE SPANISH BRIDEGROOM
THE THISTLE AND THE ROSE
GAY LORD ROBERT

The Mary Queen of Scots Series

ROYAL ROAD TO FOTHERINGAY
THE CAPTIVE QUEEN OF SCOTS

The Charles II Trilogy

THE WANDERING PRINCE
A HEALTH UNTO HIS MAJESTY
HERE LIES OUR SOVEREIGN LORD

Also

DAUGHTER OF SATAN
THE GOLDSMITH'S WIFE
EVERGREEN GALLANT

The Tudor Series

MURDER MOST ROYAL

JEAN PLAIDY

UNABRIDGED

PAN BOOKS LTD : LONDON

First published 1949 by Robert Hale Ltd.
This edition published 1966 by Pan Books Ltd.,
33 Tothill Street, London, S.W.1

ISBN O 330 20154 9

2nd Printing 1967
3rd Printing 1968
4th Printing 1968
5th Printing 1969
6th Printing 1971

PRINTED AND BOUND IN ENGLAND BY
HAZELL WATSON AND VINEY LTD
AYLESBURY, BUCKS

Defiled is my name, full sore
   Through cruel spite and false report,
That I may say for evermore,
   Farewell to joy, adieu comfort.

For wrongfully ye judge of me;
   Unto my fame a mortal wound,
Say what ye list, it may not be,
   Ye seek for that shall not be found.

Written by Anne Boleyn in the Tower of London

Contents

THE KING'S PLEASURE

IN THE SEWING-ROOM at Hever, Simonette bent over her work and, as she sat there, her back to the mullioned window through which streamed the hot afternoon sunshine – for it was the month of August and the sewing-room was in the front of the castle, overlooking the moat – a little girl of some seven years peeped round the door, smiled and advanced towards her. This was a very lovely little girl, tall for her age, beautifully proportioned and slender; her hair was dark, long and silky smooth, her skin warm and olive, her most arresting feature her large, long-lashed eyes. She was a precocious little girl, the most brilliant little girl it had ever been Simonette's good fortune to teach; she spoke Simonette's language almost as well as Simonette herself; she sang prettily and played most excellently those musical instruments which her father would have her taught.

Perhaps, Simonette had often thought, on first consideration it might appear that there was something altogether too perfect about this child. But no, no! There was never one less perfect than little Anne. See her stamp her foot when she wanted something really badly and was determined at all costs to get it; see her playing shuttlecock with the little Wyatt girl! She would play to win; she would have her will. Quick to anger, she was ever ready to speak her mind, reckless of punishment; she was strong-willed as a boy, adventurous as a boy, as ready to explore those dark dungeons that lay below the castle as her brother George or young Tom Wyatt. No, no one could say she was perfect; she was just herself, and of all the Boleyn children Simonette loved her best.

From whom, Simonette wondered, do these little Boleyns acquire their charm? From Sir Thomas, their father, who with the inheritance from his merchant ancestors had bought Blickling in Norfolk and Hever in Kent, as well as an aristocratic wife to go with them? But no! One could not say it came from Sir Thomas; for he was a mean man, a grasping man, a man who was determined to make a place for himself no matter at what cost to others. There was no warmth in his heart, and these young Boleyns were what Simonette would call warm little people. Reckless they might be; ambitious one could well believe they would be; but every one of them – Mary, George and Anne – were loving people; one could touch their hearts easily; they gave love, and so received it. And that, thought Simonette, is perhaps the secret of charm. Perhaps then from their lady mother? Well . . . perhaps a little. Though her ladyship had been a very pretty woman her charm was a fragile thing compared with that of her three children. Mary, the eldest, was very pretty, but one as French as Simonette must tremble more for Mary than for George and Anne. Mary at eleven was a woman already; vivacious and shallow as a pleasant little brook that babbled incessantly because it liked people to pause and say: 'How pretty!' Unwise and lightsome, that was Mary. One trembled to think of the little baggage already installed in a foreign court where the morals – if one could believe all one heard – left much to be desired by a prim French governess. And handsome George, who had always a clever retort on his lips, and wrote amusing poetry about himself and his sisters – and doubtless rude poetry about Simonette – he had his share of the Boleyn charm. Brilliant were the two youngest; they recognized each other's brilliance and loved each other well. How often had Simonette seen them, both here at Hever and at Blickling, heads close together, whispering, sharing a secret! And their cousins, the Wyatt children, were often with them, for the Wyatts were neighbours here in Kent as they were in Norfolk. Thomas, George and Anne; they were the three friends. Margaret and Mary Wyatt with Mary Boleyn were outside that friendship; not that they cared greatly, Mary Boleyn at any rate, for she could always amuse herself planning what she would do when she was old enough to go to court.

Anne came forward now and stood before her governess,

her demure pose – hands behind her back – belying the sparkle in her lovely eyes. The pose was graceful as well as demure, for grace was as natural to Anne as breathing. She was unconsciously graceful, and this habit of standing thus had grown out of a desire to hide her hands, for on the little finger of her left one there grew the beginning of a sixth nail. It was not unsightly; it would scarcely be noticed if the glance were cursory; but she was a dainty child, and this difference in her – it could hardly be called a deformity – was most distasteful to her. Being herself, she had infused into this habit a charm which was apparent when she stood with others of her age; one thought then how awkwardly they stood, their hands hanging at their sides.

'Simonette,' she said in Simonette's native French, 'I have wonderful news! It is a letter from my father. I am to go to France.'

The sewing-room seemed suddenly unbearably quiet to Simonette; outside she heard the breeze stir the willows that dripped into the moat; the tapestry slipped from her fingers. Anne picked it up and put it on the governess's lap. Sensitive and imaginative, she knew that she had broken the news too rashly; she was at once contrite, and flung her arms round Simonette's brown neck.

'Simonette! Simonette! To leave you will be the one thing to spoil this news for me.'

There were real tears in her eyes, but they were for the hurt she had given Simonette, not for the inevitable parting; for she could not hide the excitement shining through her tears. Hever was dull without George and Thomas who were both away continuing their education. Simonette was a darling; Mother was a darling; but it is possible for people to be darlings and at the same time be very, very dull; and Anne could not endure dullness.

'Simonette!' she said. 'Perhaps it will be for a very short time.' She added, as though this should prove some consolation to the stricken Simonette: 'I am to go with the King's sister!'

Seven is so young! Even a precocious seven. This little

one at the court of France! Sir Thomas was indeed an ambitious man. What did he care for these tender young things who, because they were of an unusual brilliance, needed special care! This is the end, thought Simonette. Ah, well! And who am I to undertake the education of Sir Thomas Boleyn's daughter for more than the very early years of her life!

'My father has written, Simonette. . . . He said I must prepare at once . . .'

How her eyes sparkled! She who had always loved the stories of kings and queens was now to take part in one herself; a very small part, it was true, for surely the youngest attendant of the princess *must* be a very small part; Simonette did not doubt that she would play it with zest. No longer would she come to Simonette with her eager questions, no longer listen to the story of the King's romance with the Spanish princess. Simonette had told that story often enough. 'She came over to England, the poor little princess, and she married Prince Arthur and he died, and she married his brother, Prince Henry . . . King Henry.' 'Simonette, have you ever seen the King?' 'I saw him at the time of his marriage. Ah, there was a time! Big and handsome, and fair of skin, rosy like a girl, red of hair and red of beard; the handsomest prince you could find if you searched the whole world.' 'And the Spanish princess, Simonette?' Simonette would wrinkle her brows; as a good Frenchwoman she did not love the Spaniards. 'She was well enough. She sat in a litter of cloth of gold, borne by two white horses. Her hair fell almost to her feet.' Simonette added grudgingly: 'It was beautiful hair. But he was a boy prince; she was six years older.' Simonette's mouth would come close to Anne's ear: 'There are those who say it is not well that a man should marry the wife of his brother.' 'But this is not a man, Simonette. This is a king!'

Two years ago George and Thomas would sit in the window seats and talk like men about the war with France. Simonette did not speak of it; greatly she had feared that she, for the sins of her country, might be turned from the castle. And the following year there had been more war, this time with the treacherous Scots; of this Anne loved to talk, for at the battle of Flodden Field it was her grandfather the Duke of Norfolk and her two uncles, Thomas and Edmund, who had saved England for the King. The two wars were now satisfactorily concluded, but wars have reverberating consequences; they shake even the lives of those who believe themselves remote. The echoes extended from Paris and Greenwich to the quiet of a Kentish castle.

'I am to go in the train of the King's sister who is to marry the King of France, Simonette. They say he is very, very old and . . .' Anne shivered. 'I should not care to marry a very old man.'

'Nonsense!' said Simonette, rising and throwing aside her tapestry. 'If he is an old man, he is also a king. Think of that!'

Anne thought of it, her eyes glistening, her hands clasped behind her back. What a mistake it is, thought Simonette, if one is a governess, to love too well those who come within one's care.

'Come now,' she said. 'We must write a letter to your father. We must express our pleasure in this great honour.'

Anne was running towards the door in her eagerness to speed up events, to bring about more quickly the exciting journey. Then she thought sadly once more of Simonette . . . dear, good, kind, but so dull Simonette. So she halted and went back and slipped one hand into that of her governess.

*　　*　　*

In their apartments at Dover Castle the maids of honour giggled and whispered together. The youngest of them, whom they patronized shamefully – more because of her youth than because she lacked their noble lineage – listened eagerly to everything that was said.

How gorgeous they were, these young ladies, and how different in their own apartments from the sedate creatures they became when they attended state functions! Anne had thought them too lovely to be real, when she had stood with them at the formal solemnization of the royal marriage at Greenwich, where the Duke of Longueville had acted as proxy for the King of France. Then her feet had grown weary with so much standing, and her eyes had ached with the dazzle, and in spite of all the excitement she had thought longingly of Simonette's strong arms picking her up and carrying her to bed. Here in the apartment the ladies threw aside their brilliant clothes and walked about without any, discussing each other and the lords and esquires with a frankness astonishing – but at the same time very interesting – to a little girl of seven.

The King was at Dover, for he had accompanied his favourite sister to the coast; and here in the castle they had tarried a whole month, for outside the waves rose high against the cliffs, and the wind shrieked about the castle walls, rattling its windows and doors and bellowing down the great chimneys as if it mocked the plans of kings. Challengingly the wind and the waves tossed up the broken parts of ships along that coast, to show what happened to those who would ignore the sea's angry mood. There was nothing to be done but wait; and in the castle the time was whiled away with masques, balls and banquets, for the King must be amused.

Anne had had several glimpses of him – a mountain of a man with fair, glowing skin and bright hair; when he spoke, his voice, which matched his frame, bellowed forth, and his laughter shook him; his jewel-trimmed clothes were part of his dazzling personality; men went in fear of him, for his anger came sudden as his laughter; and his little mouth, ready enough to smile at a jest which pleased him, could as readily become the most cruel in the world.

Here in the apartment the ladies talked constantly of the King, of his Queen, and – to them all just now the most fascinating of the royal family group – of Mary Tudor, whom they were accompanying across the Channel to Louis of France.

'Would it not be strange,' said Lady Anne Grey, 'if my lady ran off with Suffolk!'

'Strange indeed!' answered her sister Elizabeth. 'I would

14

not care to be in her shoes, nor in my Lord Suffolk's, if she were to do that. Imagine the King's anger!'

Little Anne shivered, imagining it. She might be young, but she was old enough to sense the uneasy atmosphere that filled the castle. The waiting had been too long, and Mary Tudor – the loveliest creature, thought Anne, she had ever set eyes on – was wild as the storm that raged outside, and about as dependable as the English climate. Eighteen she was, and greatly loved by the King; she possessed the same auburn coloured hair, fair skin, blue eyes; the same zest for living. The resemblance between them was remarkable, and the King, it was said, was moved to great tenderness by her. Wilful and passionate, there were two ingredients in her nature which mixed together to make an inflammable brew; one was her ambition, which made her eager to share the throne of France; the other was her passionate love for handsome Charles Brandon; and as her moods were as inconstant as April weather, there was danger in the air. To be queen to a senile king, or duchess to a handsome duke? Mary could not make up her mind which she wanted, and with her maids she discussed her feelings with passion, fretful uncertainty and Tudor frankness.

'It is well,' she had said to little Anne, for the child's grace and precocity amused her, 'that I do not have to make up my mind myself, for I trow I should not know which way to turn.' And she would deck herself with a gift of jewels from the King of France and demand that Anne should admire her radiant beauty. 'Shall I not make a beautiful Queen of France, little Boleyn?' Then she would wipe her eyes. 'You cannot know . . . how could you, how handsome he is, my Charles! You are but a child; you know nothing of the love of men. Oh, that I had him here beside me! I swear I would force him to take me here and now, and then perhaps the old King of France would not be so eager for me, eh, Anne?' She wept and laughed alternately; a difficult mistress.

How different the castle of Dover from that of Hever! How one realized, listening to this talk, of which one understood but half, that one was a child in worldly matters. What matter if one did speak French as well as the Ladies Anne and Elizabeth Grey! What was a knowledge of French when one was in almost complete ignorance of the ways of the world? One must learn by listening.

'The King, my dear, was mightily affected by the lady in scarlet. Did you not see?'

'And who was she?'

Lady Elizabeth put her fingers to her lips and laughed cunningly.

'What of the Queen?' asked little Anne Boleyn; which set the ladies laughing.

'The Queen, my child, is an old woman. She is twenty-nine years old.'

'Twenty-nine!' cried Anne, and tried to picture herself at that great age, but she found this impossible. 'She is indeed an old woman.'

'And looks older than she is.'

'The King – he too is old,' said Anne.

'You are very young, Anne Boleyn, and you know nothing . . . nothing at all. The King is twenty-three years old, and that is a very good age for a man to be.'

'It seems a very great age,' said little Anne, and set them mocking her. She hated to be mocked, and reproved herself for not holding her tongue; she must be silent and listen; that was the way to learn. The ladies twittered together, whispering secrets which Anne must not hear. 'Hush! She is but a child! She knows nothing . . .' But after awhile they grew tired of whispering.

'They say he has long since grown tired of her . . .'

'No son yet . . . no child of the marriage!'

'I have heard it whispered that she, having been the wife of his brother . . .'

'Hush! Do you want your head off your shoulders?'

It was interesting, every minute of it. The little girl was silent, missing nothing.

As she lay in her bed, sleeping quietly, a figure bent over

her, shaking her roughly. She opened startled eyes to find Lady Elizabeth Grey bending over her.

'Wake up, Anne Boleyn! Wake up!'

Anne fought away sleep which was reluctant to leave her.

'The weather has changed,' said Lady Elizabeth, her teeth chattering with cold and excitement. 'The weather has changed; we are leaving for France at once.'

*　　*　　*

It had been comforting to know her father was with her. Her grandfather was there also – her mother's father, that was, the Duke of Norfolk – and with them sailed too her uncle, Surrey.

It was just getting light when they set off, being not quite four o'clock in the morning. The sea was calmer than Anne had seen it since her arrival at Dover. Mary was gay, fresh from the fond farewell kiss of her brother.

'I will have the little Boleyn to sit near me,' she had said. 'Her quaintness amuses me.'

The boat rocked, and Anne shivered and thought, my father is sailing with us . . . and my uncle and my grandfather. But she was glad she was with Mary Tudor and not with any of these men, for she knew them little, and what time would such important people have to bestow on a seven-year-old girl, the least important in the entire retinue!

'How would you feel, Anne,' asked Mary, 'if you were setting out to a husband you had never seen in the flesh?'

'I think I should be very frightened,' said Anne, 'but I should like to be a queen.'

'Marry and you would! You are a bright little girl, are you not? You would like to be a queen! Do you think the old man will dote on me?'

'I think he will not be able to help himself.'

Mary kissed her.

'They say the French ladies are very beautiful. We shall see. Oh, Charles, Charles, if you were only King of France! But what am I, little Anne? Nothing but a clause in a treaty, a pawn in the game which His Grace, my brother, and the French King, my husband, play together. . . . How the boat rocks!'

'The wind is rising again,' said Anne.

'My faith! You are right, and I like it not.'

Anne was frightened. Never had she known the like of this. The ship rocked and rolled as though it was out of control; the waves broke over it and crashed down on it. Anne lay below, wrapped in a cloak, fearing death and longing for it.

But when the sickness passed a little, and the sea still roared and it seemed that this inadequate craft would be overturned and all its crew and passengers sucked down to the bottom of the ocean, Anne began to cry because she now no longer wished to die. It is sad to die when one is but seven and the world is proving to be a colourful pageant in which one is destined to play a part, however insignificant. She thought longingly of the quiet of Hever, of the great avenues at Blickling, murmuring: 'I shall never see them again. My poor mother will be filled with sorrow . . . George too; my father perhaps . . . if he survives, and Mary will hear of this and cry for me. Poor Simonette will weep for me and be even more unhappy than she was when she said goodbye.' Then Anne was afraid for her wickedness. 'I lied to Simonette about the piece of tapestry. It did not hurt anyone that I should lie? But it was a lie, and I did not confess it. It was wrong to pull up the trap-door in the ballroom and show Margaret the dungeons, for Margaret was frightened; it was wrong to take her there and pretend to leave her. . . . Oh, dear, if I need not die now, I will be so good. I fear I have been very wicked and shall burn in hell.'

Death was certain; she heard voices whispering that they had lost the rest of the convoy. Oh, to be so young, to be so full of sin, and to die!

But later, when the sickness had passed completely, her spirits revived, for she was by nature adventurous. It was something to have lived through this; even when the boat was run aground in Boulogne harbour, and Anne and the ladies were taken off into small waiting boats, her exhilaration persisted. The wind caught at her long black hair and flung it round her face, as though it were angry that the sea had not taken her and kept her for ever; the salt spray dashed against her cheeks. She was exhausted and weary.

But a few days later, dressed in crimson velvet, she rode in the procession, on a white palfrey, towards Abbeville.

'How crimson becomes the little Boleyn!' whispered the ladies one to another; and were faintly jealous even though she were but a child.

* * *

When Anne came to the French court, it had not yet become the most scintillating and the gayest court in Europe; which reputation it was to acquire under François. Louis, the reigning king, was noted for his meanness; he would rather be called mean, he had said, than burden his people with taxes. He indulged in few excesses; he drank in moderation; he ate in moderation; he had a quiet and unimaginative mind; there was nothing brilliant about Louis; he was the essence of mediocrity. His motto was France first and France above all. His court still retained a good deal of that austerity, so alien to the temperament of its people, which had been forced on it during the life of his late queen; and his daughters, the little crippled Claude and young Renée were like their mother. It was small wonder that the court was all eagerness to fall under the spell of gorgeous François, the heir-apparent. François traced his descent to the Duke of Orleans as did Louis, and though François was in the direct line of succession, he would only attain the throne if Louis had no son to follow him; and with his mother and sister, François impatiently and with exasperation awaited the death of the King who, in their opinion, had lived too long. Imagine their consternation at this marriage with a young girl! Their impatience turned to anger, their exasperation to fear.

Louise of Savoy, the mother of François, was a dark,

swarthy woman, energetic in her ambition for her son – her Caesar, as she called him – passionate in her devotion to his interests. They were a strange family, this mother and her son and daughter; their devotion to each other had something of a frenzy in it; they stood together, a trinity of passionate devotion. Louise consulted the stars, seeking good omens for her son; Marguerite, Duchess of Alençon, one of the most intellectual women of her day, trembled at the threat to her brother's accession to the throne; François himself, the youngest of the trio, twenty years old, swarthy of skin with his hooked nose and sensuous mouth, already a rake, taking, as it was said, his sex as he took his meals, was as devoted a member of the trinity as the other two. At fifteen years of age he had begun his amorous adventures; he was lavishly generous, of ready wit, a poet of some ability, an intellectual, and never a hypocrite. With him one love affair followed another, and he liked to see those around him indulging in similar pleasures. 'Toujours l'amour!' cried François. 'Hands off love!' Only fools were not happy, and what happiness was there to compare with the delight of satisfied love? Only the foolish did not use this gift which the kindliest gods had bestowed on mankind. Only blockheads prided themselves on their virtue. Another name for virginity was stupidity!

Louise looked on with admiration at her Caesar; Marguerite of Alençon said of her stupid husband: 'Oh, why is he not like my brother!' And the court of France, tired of the niggardly Louis and the influence of the Queen whom they had called 'the vestal', awaited eagerly that day when François should ascend the throne.

And now the old King had married a young wife who looked as if she could bear many children; Louise of Savoy raged against the Kings of France and England. Marguerite grew pale, fearing that her beloved brother would be cheated of his inheritance. François said: 'Oh, but how she is charming, this little Mary Tudor!' and he looked with distaste on his affianced bride, the little limping Claude.

Anne Boleyn was very sorry for Claude. How sad it was to be ill-favoured, to look on while he who was to be your husband flitted from one beautiful lady to another like a gorgeous dragonfly in a garden of flowers! How important it was to be beautiful! She went on learning, by listening, her eyes wide to miss nothing.

Mary, the new French Queen, was wild as a young colt, and much more beautiful. Indiscreetly she talked to her attendants, mostly French now, for almost her entire retinue of English ladies had been sent home. The King had dismissed them; they made a fence about her, he said, and if she wanted advice, to whom should she go but to her husband? She had kept little Anne Boleyn, though. The King had turned his sallow face, on which death was already beginning to set its cold fingers, towards the little girl and shrugged his shoulders. A little girl of such tender years could not worry him. So Anne had stayed.

'He is old,' Mary murmured, 'and he is all impatience for me. Oh, it can be amusing . . . he can scarcely wait. . . .' And she went off into peals of laughter, reconstructing with actions her own coy reluctance and the King's impatience.

'Look at the little Boleyn! What long ears she has! Wait till you are grown up, my child . . . then you will not have to learn by listening when you think you are not observed. I trow those beautiful black eyes will gain for you an opportunity to experience the strange ways of men for yourself.'

And Anne asked herself: 'Will it happen so? Shall I be affianced and married?' And she was a little afraid, and then glad to be only seven, for when you are seven marriage is a long way off.

'*Monsieur mon beau-fils*, he is very handsome, is he not?' demanded Mary. And she laughed, with secrets in her eyes.

Yes, indeed, thought Anne, François was handsome. He was elegant and charming, and he quoted poetry to the ladies as he walked in the gardens of the palace. Once he met Anne herself in the gardens, and he stopped her and she was afraid; and he, besides being elegant and charming, was very clever, so that he understood her fear which, she was wise enough to see, amused him vastly. He picked her up and held her close to him, so that she could see the dark, coarse hair on his face and the bags already visible beneath his dark, flashing eyes; and she trembled for fear he should do to her that which it was whispered he would do to any who pleased him for a passing moment.

He laughed his deep and tender laugh, and as he laughed the young Queen came along the path, and François put Anne down that he might bow to the Queen.

'*Monsieur mon beau-fils . . .*' she said, laughing.

'*Madame . . . la reine . . .*'

Their eyes flashed sparks of merriment one to the other; and little Anne Boleyn, having no part in this sport that amused them so deeply, could slip away.

I am indeed fortunate to learn so much, thought Anne. She had grown a long way from that child who had played at Hever and stitched at a piece of tapestry with Simonette. She knew much; she learned to interpret the smiles of people, to understand what they meant, not so much from the words they used as from their inflection. She knew that Mary was trying to force François into a love affair with her, and that François, realizing the folly of this, was yet unable to resist it. Mary was a particularly enticing flower full of golden pollen, but around her was a great spider's web, and he hovered, longing for her, yet fearing to be caught. Louise and her daughter watched Mary for the dreaded signs of pregnancy, which for them would mean the death of hope for Caesar.

'Ah, little Boleyn,' said Mary, 'if I could but have a child! If I could come to you and say "I am *enceinte*", I would dance for joy; I would snap my fingers at that grim old Louise, I would laugh in the face of that clever Marguerite. But what is the good! That old man, what can he do for me! He tries though . . . he tries very hard . . . and so do I!'

She laughed at the thought of their efforts. There was

always laughter round Mary Tudor. All around the court those words were whispered – '*Enceinte!* Is the Queen *enceinte?* If only . . . the Queen is *enceinte!*'

Louise questioned the ladies around the Queen; she even questioned little Anne. The angry, frustrated woman buried her head in her hands and raged; she visited her astrologer; she studied her charts. 'The stars have said my son will sit on the throne of France. That old man . . . he is too old, and too cold . . .'

'He behaves like a young and hot one,' said Marguerite. 'He is a dying fire . . .'

'A dying fire has its last flicker of warmth, my mother!'

Mary loved to tease them, feigning sickness. 'I declare I cannot get up this morning. I do not know what it can be, except that I may have eaten too heartily last evening . . .' Her wicked eyes sparkling; her sensuous lips pouting.

'The Queen is sick this morning . . . she looked blooming last night. Can it be . . .?'

Mary threw off her clothes and pranced before her mirror.

'Anne, tell me, am I not fattening? Here . . . and here. Anne, I shall slap you unless you say I am!' And she would laugh hysterically and then cry a little. 'Anne Boleyn, did you never see my Lord of Suffolk? How my body yearns for that man!' Ambition was strong in Mary. 'I would be mother to a king of France, Anne. Ah, if only my beautiful *beau-fils* were King of France! Do you doubt, little Boleyn, that he would have had me with child ere this? What do I want from life? I do not know, Ann . . . . Now, if I had never known Charles . . .' And she grew soft, thinking of Charles Brandon, and the King would come and see her softness, and it would amuse her maliciously to pretend the softness was for him. The poor old King was completely infatuated by the giddy creature; he would give her presents, beautiful jewels one at a time, so that she could express her gratitude for each one. The court tittered, laughing at the old man. 'That one will have his money's worth!' It was a situation to set a French court, coming faster and faster under the influence of François, rocking with laughter.

Wildly, Mary coquetted with the willing François. If she cannot get a child from the King, whispered the court, why not from François? She would not lose from such a bargain; only poor François would do that. What satisfaction could there be in seeing yourself robbed of a throne by your own offspring? Very little, for the child could not be acknowledged as his. Oh, it was very amusing, and the French were fond of those who amused them. And that it should be Mary Tudor from that gloomy island across the Channel, made it more amusing still. Ah, these English, they were unaccountable. Imagine it! An English princess to give them the best farce in history! François was cautious; François was reckless. His ardour cooled; his passion flared. There was none, he was sure, whom he could enjoy as heartily as the saucy, hot-blooded little Tudor. There were those who felt it their duty to warn him. 'Do you not see the web stretched out to catch you?' François saw, and reluctantly gave up the chase.

On the first day of January, as Anne was coming from the Queen's apartment, she met Louise – a distraught Louise, her black hair disordered, her eyes wild.

Anne hesitated, and was roughly thrust aside.

'Out of my way, child! Have you not heard the news? The King is dead.'

Now the excitement of the court was tuned to a lower key, though it had increased rather than abated. Louise and her daughter were overjoyed at the death of the King, but their happiness in the event was overshadowed by their fear. What of the Queen's condition? They could scarcely wait to know; they trembled; they were suspicious. What did this one know? What had that one overheard? Intrigue . . . and, at the heart of it, mischievous Mary Tudor.

The period of mourning set in, and the Queen's young body was seen to broaden with the passing of the days. Louise endured agonies; François lost his gaiety. Only the Queen, demure and seductive, enjoyed herself. In her apartments Louise pored over charts; more and more men

24

learned in the study of the stars, came to her. Is the Queen *enceinte*? She begged, she implored to be told this was not so, for how could she bear it if it were! During those days of suspense she brooded on the past; her brief married life, her widowhood; the birth of her clever Marguerite, and then that day at Cognac nearly twenty-one years ago when she had come straight from the agony of childbirth to find her Caesar in her arms. She thought of her husband, the profligate philanderer who had died when François was not quite two years old, and whom she had mourned wholeheartedly and then had given over her life to her children, superintending the education of both of them herself, delighting in their capacity for learning, their intellectual powers which surely set them apart from all others; they were both of them so worthy of greatness – a brilliant pair, her world, or at least Caesar was; and where that king of men was concerned, was not Marguerite in complete accord with her mother? He should be King of France, for he was meant to be King of France since there was never one who deserved the honour more than he, the most handsome, the most courteous, the most virile, the most learned François. And now this fear! This cheating of her beautiful son by a baggage from England! A Tudor! Who were the Tudors? They did not care to look far back into their history, one supposed!

'My Caesar *shall* be King!' determined Louise. And, unable to bear the suspense any longer, she went along to the Queen's apartments and, making many artful enquiries as to her health, she perceived that Her Majesty was not quite as large about the middle as she had been yesterday. So she – for, after all, she was Louise of Savoy, a power in France even in the days of her old enemy and rival, Anne of Brittany – shook the naughty Queen until the padding fell from the creature's clothes. And . . . oh, joy! Oh, blessed astrologers who had assured her that her son would have the throne! There was the wicked girl as straight and slender as a virgin.

So Mary left the court of France, and in Paris, secretly and in great haste, she married her Charles Brandon; and the court of France tittered indulgently until it began to laugh immoderately, for it was whispered that Brandon, not daring to tell his King of his unsanctioned marriage with the Queen of France and the sister of the King of England, had written his apologia to Wolsey, begging the great Cardinal to break the news gently to the King.

François triumphantly mounted the throne and married Claude, while Louise basked in the exquisite pleasure of ambition fulfilled; she was now Madame of the French court.

Little Anne stayed on to serve with Claude. The Duchesse d'Alençon had taken quite a fancy to the child, for her beauty and grace and for her intelligence; she was not yet eight years old, but she had much worldly wisdom; she knew that crippled Claude was submissive, ignored by her husband, and that it was the King's sister who was virtually Queen of France. Anne would see brother and sister wandering in the palace grounds, their arms about each other, talking of affairs of state; for Marguerite was outstanding in a court where intellect was given the respect it deserved, and she could advise and help her brother; or Marguerite would read her latest writing to the King, and the King would show a poem he had written; he called her his pet, his darling, *ma mignonne*. She wanted nothing but to be his slave; she had declared she would be willing to follow her brother as his washerwoman, and for him she would cast to the wind her ashes and her bones.

The shadow of Anne of Brittany was banished from the court, and the King amused himself, and the court grew truly Gallic, and gayer than any in Europe. It was elegant; it was distinctive; its gallantry was of the highest order; its wit flowed readily. It was the most scintillating of courts, the most intellectual of courts, and Marguerite of Alençon, the passionately devoted slave and sister to the King, was queen of it.

It was in this court that Anne Boleyn cast off her childishness and came to premature womanhood, and with the passing of the years and the nourishing of that friendship which she enjoyed with the strange and fascinating Marguerite, she herself became one of the brightest of its brilliant lights.

* * *

Between the towns of Guisnes and Ardres was laid a brilliant pageant. A warm June sun showed the palace of Guisnes in all its glittering glory. A fairy-tale castle this, though a temporary one; and one on which many men had worked since February, to the great expense of the English people. It was meant to symbolize the power and riches of Henry of England. At its gates and windows had been set up sham men-at-arms, their faces made formidable enough to terrify those who looked too close; *they* represented the armed might of the little island across the Channel, not perhaps particularly significant in the eyes of Europe until the crafty statesman, that wily Wolsey, had got his hands on the helm of its ship of state. The hangings of cloth of gold, the gold images, the chairs decorated with pommels of gold, all the furnishings and hangings ornamented wherever possible with the crimson Tudor rose – these represented the wealth of England. The great fountain in the courtyard, from which flowed wine – claret, white wine, red wine – and over which presided the great stone Bacchus round whose head was written in Tudor gold *'Faictes bonne chere qui vouldra'* – this was to signify Tudor hospitality.

The people of England, who would never see this lavish display and who had contributed quite a large amount of money towards it, might murmur; those lords who had been commanded by their King to set out on this most opulent and most expensive expedition in history might think uneasily of return to their estates, impoverished by the need to pay for their participation in it; but the King thought of none of these things. He was going to meet his rival, Francis; he was going to prove to Francis that he was the better king, which was a matter of opinion; he was going to show himself to be a better man, which some might think doubtful; he was going to show he was a richer

27

king, which, thanks to his cautious father, was a fact; and that he was a power in Europe, of which there could no longer be a doubt. He could smile expansively at this glittering palace which he had erected as fitting to be the temporary resting place of his august self; he could smile complacently because in spite of its size it could not accommodate his entire retinue, so that all around the palace were the brightly coloured tents of his less noble followers. He could congratulate himself that Francis's lodging at Ardres was less magnificent than his; and these matters filled the King of England with a satisfaction which was immense.

In the pavilion which was the French King's lodging, Queen Claude prepared herself for her meeting with Queen Katharine. Her ladies, too, prepared themselves; and among these was one whose beauty set her aside from all others. She was now in her fourteenth year, a lovely, slender girl who wore her dark hair in silken ringlets, and on whose head was an aureole made of plaited gauze, the colour of gold. The blue of her garments was wonderfully becoming to her dark beauty; her vest was of blue velvet spattered with silver stars; her surcoat of watered silk was lined with miniver and the sleeves of the surcoat were of her own designing; they were wide and long, and hung below her hands, hiding them, for she was more sensitive about her hands than she had been at Blickling and Hever. Over this costume she wore a blue velvet cape trimmed with points, and from the end of each of these points hung little golden bells; her shoes were covered in the same blue velvet as her vest, and diamond stars twinkled on her insteps. She was one of the very fashionable ladies in the smart court of France, and even now the ladies of the court were striving to copy those long hanging sleeves, so that what had been a ruse to hide a deformity was becoming a fashion. She was the gayest of the young ladies. Who would not be gay, sought after as she was? She was quick of speech, ready of wit; in the dance she excelled all others; her voice was a delight; she played the virginals competently; she composed a little. She was worldly wise, and yet there was about her a certain youthful innocence.

François himself had cast covetous eyes upon her, but Anne was no fool. She laughed scornfully at those women who were content to hold the King's attention for a day. Marguerite was her friend, and Marguerite had imbued her with a new, advanced way of thinking, the kernel of which was equality of the sexes. 'We are equal with men,' Marguerite had said, 'when we allow ourselves to be.' And Anne determined to allow herself to be. So cleverly and with astonishing diplomacy she held off François, and he, amused and without a trace of malice, gracefully accepted defeat.

Now Anne was in her element; there was nothing she enjoyed more than a round of gaiety, and here was gaiety such as even she had never encountered before. She was proud of her English birth, and eagerly she drank in the news of English splendour. 'My lord Cardinal seemed as a king,' she heard, and there followed an account of his retinue, the gorgeousness of his apparel, the display of his wealth. 'And he is but the servant of his master! The splendour of the King of England it would be difficult to describe.' Anne saw him now and then – the great red King; he had changed a good deal since she had last seen him, at Dover. He was more corpulent, coarser; perhaps without his dazzling garments he would not be such a handsome man. His face was ruddier, his cheeks more pouchy; his voice, though, bellowed as before. What a contrast he presented with the dark and subtle François! And Anne was not the only one who guessed that these two had little love for each other in spite of the gushing outward displays of affection.

During the days that followed the meeting of the Kings, Anne danced and ate and flirted with the rest. Today the French court were guests of the English; pageants, sports, jousting, a masked ball and a banquet. Tomorrow the French court would entertain the English. Everything must be lavish; the French court must outshine the English, and then again the English must be grander still. Never mind the cost to nations groaning under taxations; never mind if the two Kings, beneath the show of jovial good fellowship, are sworn enemies! Never mind! This is the most brilliant and lavish display in history; and if it is also the most vulgar, the most recklessly stupid, what of that! The Kings must amuse themselves.

*   *   *

Mary Boleyn had come to attend Queen Katharine at Guisnes. She was eighteen then – a pretty, plumpish voluptuous creature. It was years since she had seen her young sister, and it was therefore interesting to meet her in the pavilion at Ardres. Mary had returned to England from the Continent with her reputation in shreds; and her face, her manner, her eager little body suggested that rumour had not been without some foundation. She looked what she was – a lightly loving little animal, full of desire, sensuous, ready for adventure, helpless to avert it, saying with her eyes 'This is good; why fret about tomorrow?'

Anne read these things in her sister's face, and was disturbed by them, for it hurt Anne's dignity to have to acknowledge this wanton as her sister. The Boleyns were no noble family; they were not a particularly wealthy family. Anne was half French in outlook; impulsive, by nature she was also practical. The sisters were as unlike as two sisters could be. Anne set a high price upon herself; Mary, no price at all. The French court opened one's eyes to worldly matters when one was very young; the French shrugged philosophical shoulders; *l'amour* was charming – indeed what was there more charming? But the French court taught one elegance and dignity too. And here was Mary, Anne's sister, with her dress cut too low and her bosom pressed upwards provocatively; and in her open mouth and her soft doe's eyes there was the plea of the female animal, begging to be taken. Mary was pretty; Anne was beautiful. Anne was clever, and Mary was a fool.

How she fluttered about the ladies' apartments, examining her sister's belongings, her little blue velvet brodiquins, her clothes! Those wonderful sleeves! Trust Anne to turn a disadvantage into an asset! I will have those sleeves on my new gown, thought Mary; they give an added grace to the figure – but is that because grace comes naturally to her? Mary could not but admire her. Simple Anne Boleyn looked elegant as a duchess, proud as a queen.

'I should not have known you!' cried Mary.

'Nor I you.'

Anne was avid for news of England.

'Tell me of the court of England.'

Mary grimaced. 'The Queen . . . oh, the Queen is very dull. You are indeed fortunate not to be with Queen Katharine. We must sit and stitch, and there is mass eight times a day. We kneel so much, I declare my knees are worn out with it!'

'Is the King so devoted to virtue?'

'Not as the Queen, the saints be praised! He is devoted to other matters. But for the King, I would rather be home at Hever than be at court; but where the King is there is always good sport. He is heartily sick of her, and deeply enamoured of Elizabeth Blount; there was a son born to them some little while since. The King is delighted . . . and furious.'

'Delighted with the son and furious with the Queen because it is not hers?' inquired Anne.

'That is surely the case. One daughter has the Queen to show for all those years of marriage; and when he gets a son, it is from Elizabeth Blount. The Queen is disappointed; she turns more and more to her devotions. Pity us . . . who are not so devoted and must pray with her and listen to the most mournful music that was ever made. The King is such a beautiful prince, and she such a plain princess.'

Anne thought of Claude then – submissive and uncomplaining – not a young woman enjoying being alive, but just a machine for turning out children. I would not be Claude, she thought, even for the throne of France. I would not be Katharine, ugly and unwanted Katharine of the many miscarriages. No! I would be as myself . . . or Marguerite.

31

'What news of our family?' asked Anne.

'Little but what you must surely know. Life is not unpleasant for us. I heard a sorry story, though, of our uncle, Edmund Howard, who is very, very poor and is having a family very rapidly; all he has is his house at Lambeth, and in that he breeds children to go hungry with him and his lady.'

'His reward for helping to save England at Flodden!' said Anne.

'There is talk that he would wish to go on a voyage of discovery, and so doing earn a little money for his family.'

'Is it not depressing to hear such news of members of our family!'

Mary looked askance at her sister; the haughtiness had given place to compassion; anger filled the dark eyes because of the ingratitude of a king and a country towards a hero of Flodden Field.

'You hold your head like a queen,' said Mary. 'Grand ideas have been put into your head since you have been living at the French court.'

'I would rather carry it like a queen than a harlot!' flashed Anne.

'Marry and you would! But who said you should carry it like a harlot?'

'No one says it. It is I who say I would prefer not to.'

'The Queen,' said Mary, 'is against this pageantry. She does not love the French. She remonstrated with the King; I wonder she dared, knowing his temper.'

Mary prattled lightly; she took to examining the apartment still further, testing the material of her sister's gown; she asked questions about the French court, but did not listen to the answers. It was late when she left her sister. She would be reprimanded perhaps; it would not be the first time Mary had been reprimanded for staying out late.

But for a sister! thought Mary, amused by her recollections.

* * *

In a corridor of the gorgeous palace at Guisnes, Mary came suddenly upon a most brilliantly clad personage, and hurrying as she was, she had almost run full tilt into him before she could pull herself up. She saw the coat of russet velvet trimmed with triangles of pearls; the buttons of the coat were diamonds. Mary's eyes opened wide in dismay as confusedly she dropped onto her knee.

He paused to look at her. His small bright eyes peered out from the puffy red flesh around them.

'How now! How now!' he said, and then 'Get up!' His voice was coarse and deep, and it was that perhaps and his brusque manner of speech which had earned him the adjective 'bluff'.

The little eyes travelled hastily all over Mary Boleyn, then rested on the provocative bosom, exposed rather more than fashion demanded, on the parted lips and the soft, sweet eyes.

'I have seen you at Greenwich . . . Boleyn's girl! Is that so?'

'Yes . . . if it please Your Grace.'

'It pleases me,' he said. The girl was trembling. He liked his subjects to tremble, and if her lips were a little dumb, her eyes paid him the homage he liked best to receive from pretty subjects in quiet corridors where, for once in a while, he found himself unattended.

'You're a pretty wench,' he said.

'Your Majesty is gracious . . .'

'Ah!' he said, laughing and rumbling beneath the russet velvet. 'And ready to be more gracious still when it's a pretty wench like yourself.'

There was no delicacy about Henry; if anything he was less elegant, more coarse, during this stay in France. Was he going to ape these prancing French gallants! He thought not. He liked a girl, and a girl liked him; no finesse necessary. He put a fat hand, sparkling with rings, on her shoulder. Any reluctance Mary might have felt – but, being Mary, she would of course have felt little – melted at his touch. Her admiration for him was in her eyes; her face had the strained set look of a desire that is rising

33

and will overwhelm all else. To her he was the perfect man, because, being the King, he possessed the strongest ingredient of sexual domination – Power. He was the most powerful man in England, perhaps the most powerful in France as well. He was the most handsome prince in Christendom, or perhaps his clothes were more handsome than those worn by any others, and Mary's lust for him, as his for her, was too potent and too obvious to be veiled.

Henry said 'Why, girl . . .' And his voice slurred and faded out as he kissed her, and his hands touched the soft bosom which so clearly asked to be touched. Mary's lips clung to his flesh, and her hands clung to his russet velvet. Henry kissed her neck and her breasts, and his hands felt her thighs beneath the velvet of her gown. This attraction, instantaneous and mutual, was honey-sweet to them both. A king such as he was could take when and where he would in the ordinary course of events; but this coarse, crude man was a complex man, a man who did not fully know himself; a deeply sentimental man. He had great power, but because of this power of his which he loved to wield, he wanted constant reassurance. When a man's head can be taken off his shoulders for a whim, and when a woman's life can hang on one's word, one has to accept the uncertainty that goes with this power; one is surrounded by sycophants and those who feign love because they dare show nothing else. And in the life of a king such as Henry there could only be rare moments when he might feel himself a man first, a king second; he treasured such moments. There was that in Mary Boleyn which told him she desired him – Henry the man, divested of his diamond-spattered clothes; and that man she wanted urgently. He had seen her often enough sitting with his pious Queen, her eyes downcast, stitching away at some woman's work. He had liked her mildly; she was a pretty piece enough; he had let his eyes dwell lightly on her and thought of her, naked in bed, as he thought of them all; nothing more than that. He liked her family; Thomas was a good servant; George a bright boy; and Mary . . . well, Mary was just what he needed at this moment.

34

Yesterday the King of France had thrown him in a wrestling match, being more skilled than he in a game which demanded quickness of action rather than bullock strength such as his. He had smarted from the indignity. And again, while he had breakfasted, the King of France had walked unheralded into his apartment and sat awhile informally; they had laughed and joked together, and Francis had called him Brother, and something else besides. Even now while the sex call sounded insistently in his ears, it rankled sorely, for Francis had called him 'My prisoner!' It was meant to be a term of friendship, a little joke between two good friends. And so taken aback had Henry been that he had no answer ready; the more he thought of it, the more ominous it sounded; it was no remark for one king to make to another, when they both knew that under their displays of friendship they were enemies. He needed homage after that; he always got it when he wanted it; but this which Mary Boleyn offered him was different; homage to himself, not to his crown. Francis disconcerted him and he wanted to assure himself that he was as good a man as the French King. Francis shocked him; Francis had no shame; he glorified love, worshipped it shamelessly. Henry's affairs were never entirely blatant; he regarded them as sins to be confessed and forgiven; he was a pious man. He shied away from the thought of confession; one did not think of it before the act. And here was little Mary Boleyn ready to tell him that he was the perfect man as well as the perfect king. She was as pretty a girl as he would find in the two courts. French women! Prancing, tittering, elegant ladies! Not for him! Give him a good English bedfellow! And here was one ready enough. She was weak at the knees for him; her little hands fluttering for him, pretending to hold him off, while what they meant really was 'Please . . . now . . . no waiting.'

He bit her ear, and whispered into it: 'You like me then, sweetheart?'

She was pale with desire now. She was what he wanted.

In an excess of pleasure, the King slapped her buttocks jovially and drew her towards his privy chamber.

This was the way, the way to wash the taste of this scented French gallantry out of his mouth! There was a couch in this chamber. Here! Now! No matter the hour, no matter the place.

She opened her eyes, stared at the couch in feigned surprise, tried to simulate fear; which made him slap his thigh with mirth. They all wanted to be forced . . . every one of them. Well, let them; it was a feminine trait that didn't displease him. She murmured: 'If it please Your Grace, I am late and . . .'

'It does please Our Grace. It pleases us mightily. Come hither to me, little Mary. I would know if the rest of you tastes as sweet as your lips.'

She was laughing and eager, no longer feigning feminine modesty when she could not be anything but natural. The King was amused and delighted; not since he had set foot on this hated soil had he been so delighted.

He laughed and was refreshed and eased of his humiliation. He'd take this girl the English way – no French fripperies for him! He would say what he meant and she could too.

He said: 'Why, Mary, you're sweet all over. And where did you hide yourself, Mary? I'm not sure you have not earned a punishment, Mary, for keeping this from your King so long; we might say it was treason, that we might!'

He laughed, mightily pleased, as he always was, with his own pleasantries; and she was overawed and passive, then responsive and pretending to be afraid she had been over-presumptuous to have so enjoyed the King. This was what he wanted, and he was grateful enough to those of his subjects who pleased him. In an exuberance of good spirits he slapped her buttocks — no velvet to cover them now — and she laughed, and her saucy eyes promised much for other times to come.

'You please me, Mary,' he said, and in a rush of crude tenderness added: 'You shall not suffer for this day.'

When he left her and when she was scrambling into her

clothes, she still trembled from the violence of the experience.

In the Queen's apartment she was scolded for her lateness; demurely, with eyes cast down, she accepted the reprimand.

* * *

Coming from Mary Boleyn, the King met the Cardinal.

Ah, thought the Cardinal, noting the flushed face of his royal master, and guessing something of what had happened, who now?

The King laid his hand on the Cardinal's shoulder, and they walked together along the corridor, talking of the entertainment they would give the French tonight, for matters of state could not be discussed in the palace of Guisnes; these affairs must wait for Greenwich or York House; impossible to talk of important matters, surrounded by enemies.

This exuberance, thought the Cardinal, means one thing – success in sport. And as sport the Cardinal would include the gratification of the royal senses. Good! said the Cardinal to himself; this has put that disastrous matter of the wrestling from his thoughts.

The Cardinal was on the whole a contented man – as contented, that is, as a man of ambition can ever be. He was proud of his sumptuous houses, his rich possessions; it was a good deal to be, next the King, the richest man in England. But that which he loved more than riches, he also had; and to those who have known obscurity, power is a more intoxicating draught than riches. Men might secretly call him 'Butcher's cur', but they trembled before his might, for he was greater than the King. He led the King, and if he managed this only because the King did not know he was led, that was of little account. Very pleasant it was to reflect that his genius for statecraft, his diplomacy, had put the kingdom into the exalted position it held today. This King was a good king, because the goodness of a king depends upon his choice of ministers.

There could be no doubt that Henry was a good king, for he had chosen Thomas Wolsey.

It pleased the statesman therefore to see the King happy with a woman, doubtless about to launch himself on yet another absorbing love affair, for then the fat, bejewelled hands, occupied in caressing a woman's body, could be kept from seeking a place on the helm of the ship of state. The King must be amused; the King must be humoured; when he would organize this most ridiculous pageant, this greatest farce in history, there was none that dare deny him his pleasures. Buckingham, the fool, had tried; and Buckingham should tread carefully, for, being so closely related to the King, his head were scarcely safe on his shoulders, be he the most docile of subjects. Francis was not to be trusted. He would make treaties one week, and discard them the next. But how could one snatch the helm from those podgy hands, once the King had decided they must have a place on it? How indeed! Diplomacy for ever! thought the Cardinal. Keep the King amused. It was good to see the King finding pleasure in a woman, for well the Cardinal knew that Elizabeth Blount, who had served her purpose most excellently, was beginning to tire His Majesty.

They parted affectionately at the King's apartments, both smiling, well pleased with life and with each other.

*   *   *

The Queen was retiring. She had dismissed her women when the King came in. Her still beautiful auburn hair hung about her shoulders; her face was pale, thin and much lined, and there were deep shadows under her eyes.

The King looked at her distastefully. With Mary Boleyn still in his thoughts, he recalled the cold submissiveness to duty of this Spanish woman through the years of their marriage. She had been a good wife, people would say; but she would have been as good a wife to his brother Arthur had he lived. Being a good wife was just another of the virtues that irritated him. And what had his marriage with her been but years of hope that never brought him

38

his desires? The Queen is with child; prepare to sing a Te Deum. Prepare to let the bells of London ring. And then . . . miscarriage after miscarriage; five of them in four years. A stillborn daughter, a son who lived but two months, a stillborn son, one who died at birth and another prematurely born. And then . . . a daughter!

He had begun to be afraid. Rumours spread quickly through a country, and it is not always possible to prevent their reaching the kingly ear. Why cannot the King have a son? murmured his people. The King grew fearful. I am a very religious man, he thought. The fault cannot be mine. Six times I hear mass each day, and in times of pestilence or war or bad harvest, eight times a day. I confess my sins with regularity; the fault cannot be mine.

But he was superstitious. He had married his brother's widow. It had been sworn that the marriage had never been consummated. Had it though? The fault could not be his. How could God deny the dearest wish of such a religious man as Henry VIII of England! The King looked round for a scapegoat, and because her body was shapeless with much fruitless child-bearing, and because he never had liked her pious Spanish ways for more than a week or two, because he was beginning to dislike her heartily, he blamed the Queen. Resentfully he thought of those nights when he had lain with her. When he prayed for male issue he reminded his God of this. There were women in his court who had beckoned him with their charms, who had aroused his ready desire; and for duty's sake he had lain with the Queen, and only during her pregnancies had he gone where he would. What virtue . . . to go unrewarded! God was just; therefore there was some reason why he had been denied a son. There it was . . . in that woman on whom he had squandered his manhood without reward.

He knew, when Elizabeth Blount bore his son, that the fault could not lie with him. He had been in an ecstacy of delight when that boy had been born. His virility vindicated, the guilt of Katharine assured, his dislike had become tinged with hatred on that day.

But on this evening his dislike for the Queen was mellowed by the pleasure he had had in Mary Boleyn; he smiled that remote smile which long experience had taught the Queen was born of satisfied lust. His gorgeous clothing was just a little disarranged; the veins stood out more than usual on the great forehead.

He had thrown himself into a chair, and was sitting, his knees wide apart, the glazed smile on his face, making plans which included Mary Boleyn.

The Queen would say a special prayer for him tonight. Meanwhile she asked herself that question which had been in the Cardinal's mind – 'Who now?'

*　　*　　*

*'Venus était blonde, l'on m'a dit.
L'on voit bien qu'elle est brunette.'*

So sang François to the lady who excited him most in his wife's retinue of ladies. Unfortunately for François, she was the cleverest as well as the most desirable.

'Ah!' said François. 'You are the wise one, *Mademoiselle* Bouillain. You have learned that the fruit which hangs just out of reach is the most desired.'

'Your Majesty well knows my mind,' explained Anne. 'What should I be? A king's mistress. The days of glory for such are very short; we have evidence of that all around us.'

'Might it not depend on the mistress, *Mademoiselle* Bouillain?'

She shrugged her shoulders in the way which was so much more charming than the gesture of the French ladies, because it was only half French.

'I do not care to take the risk,' she said.

Then he laughed and sang to her, and asked that she should sing to him. This she did gladly, for her voice was good and she was susceptible to admiration and eager to draw it to herself at every opportunity. Contact with the Duchesse d'Alençon had made her value herself highly, and though she was as fond of amorous adventures as any, she knew exactly at what moment to retire. She was enjoying every moment of her life at the court of France. There was so much to amuse her that life could never be dull. Light-hearted flirtations, listening to the scandal of the court, reading with Marguerite, and getting a glimmer of the new religion that had begun to spring up in Europe, since a German monk named Martin Luther had nailed a set of theses on a church door at Wittenberg. Yes, life was colourful and amusing, stimulating mind and body. Though the news that came from England was not so good; disaster had set in after the return from the palace of Guisnes. Poverty had swept over the country; the harvest was bad, and people were dying of the plague in the streets of London. The King was less popular than he had been before his love of vulgar show and pageantry had led him to that folly which men in England now called 'The Field of the Cloth of Gold.'

There was not very exhilarating news from her family. Uncle Edmund Howard had yet another child, and that a daughter. Catherine, they called her. Anne's ready sympathy went out to poor little Catherine Howard, born into the poverty of that rambling old house at Lambeth. Then Mary had married – hardly brilliantly – a certain William Carey. Anne would have liked to hear of a better match for her sister; but both she and George, right from Hever days, had known Mary was a fool.

And now war clouds were looming up afresh, and this time there was fear of a conflict between France and England. At the same time there was talk of a marriage for Anne which was being arranged in England to settle some dispute one branch of her family was having with another.

So Anne left France most reluctantly, and sailed for England. At home they said she was most Frenchified; she was imperious, witty, lovely to look at, and her clothes caused comment from all who beheld them.

She was just sixteen years old.

* * *

Anne's grandfather, the old Duke of Norfolk, was not at home when Anne, in the company of her mother, visited

the Norfolk's house at Lambeth. The Duchess was a somewhat lazy, empty-headed woman who enjoyed listening to
the ambitious adventures of the younger members of her
family, and she had learned that her granddaughter, Anne,
had returned from France, a charming creature. Nothing
therefore would satisfy the Duchess but that this visit
should be paid, and during it she found an especial delight
in sitting in the grounds of her lovely home on the river's
edge, dozing and indulging in light conversation with the
girl whom she herself would now be ready to admit was
the most interesting member of the family. And, thought
the vain old lady, the chit has a look of me about her; moreover, I declare at her age I looked very like her. What
honours, she wondered, were in store for Anne Boleyn, for
the marriage with the Butlers was not being brought at
any great speed to a satisfactory conclusion; and how sad
if this bright child must bury herself in the wilds of that
dreary, troublesome, uncivilized Ireland! But – and the
Duchess sighed deeply – what were women but petty
counters to be bartered by men in the settlement of their
problems? Thomas Boleyn was too ambitious. Marry! An
the girl were mine, to court she should go, and a plague on
the Butlers.

She watched Anne feeding the peacocks; a figure of grace
in scarlet and grey, she was not one whit less gorgeous than
those arrogant, elegant birds. She's Howard, mused the
Duchess with pride. *All* Howard! Not a trace of Boleyn
there.

'Come and sit beside me, my dear,' she said. 'I would talk
to you.'

Anne came and sat on the wooden seat which overlooked
the river; she gazed along its bank at the stately gabled
houses whose beautiful gardens sloped down to the water,
placing their owners within comfortable distance of the
quickest and least dangerous means of transport. Her gaze
went quickly towards those domes and spires that seemed
to pierce the blue and smokeless sky. She could see the
heavy arches of London Bridge and the ramparts of the
Tower of London – that great, impressive fortress whose

towers, strong and formidable, stood like sentinels guarding the city.

Agnes, Duchess of Norfolk, saw the girl's eager expression, and guessed her thoughts. She tapped her arm.

'Tell me of the court of France, my child. I'll warrant you found much to amuse you there.'

As Anne talked, the Duchess lay back, listening, now and then stifling a yawn, for she had eaten a big dinner and, interested as she was, she was overcome by drowsiness.

'Why, bless us!' she said. 'When you went away, your father was of little import; now you return to find him a gentleman of much consequence – Treasurer of the Household now, if you please!'

'It does please,' laughed Anne.

'They tell me,' said Agnes, 'that the office is worth a thousand pounds a year! And what else? Steward of Tonbridge. . . .' She began enumerating the titles on her fingers. 'Master of the Hunt. Constable of the Castle. Chamberlain of Tonbridge. Receiver and Bailiff of Bradsted, and the Keeper of the Manor of Penshurst. And now it is whispered that he is to be appointed Keeper of the Parks at Thundersley, to say nothing of Essex and Westwood. Never was so much honour done a man in so short a time!'

'My father,' said Anne, 'is a man of much ability.'

'And good fortune,' said Agnes slyly, eyeing the girl mischievously, thinking – Can it be that she does not know why these honours are heaped on her father, and she fresh from the wicked court of France? 'And your father is lucky in his children,' commented Agnes mischievously.

The girl turned puzzled eyes on her grandmother. The old lady chuckled, thinking – She makes a pretty pose of ignorance, I'll swear!

Anne said, her expression changing: 'I would it were as well with every member of our family.' And her eyes went towards a house less than half a mile away along the river's bank.

'Ah!' sighed the Duchess. '*There* is a man who served his country well, and yet . . . She shrugged her shoulders. '*His* children are too young to be of any use to him.'

43

'I hear there is a new baby,' said Anne. 'Do they not visit you?'

'My dear, Lord Edmund is afraid to leave his house for fear he should be arrested. He has many debts, poor man, and he's as proud as Lucifer. Ah, yes . . . a new baby. Why, little Catherine is but a baby yet.'

'Grandmother, I should like to see the baby.'

The Duchess yawned. It had ever been her habit to push unpleasant thoughts aside, and the branch of her family which they were now discussing distressed her. What she enjoyed hearing was of the success of Sir Thomas and the adventures of his flighty daughter. She could nod over them, simper over them, remember her own youth and relive it as she drowsed in her pleasant seat overlooking the river. Still, she would like the Edmund Howards to see this lovely girl in her pretty clothes. The Duchess had a mischievous turn of mind. The little Howards had a distinguished soldier for a father, and they might starve; the Boleyn children had a father who might be a clever enough diplomatist, but, having descended from merchants, was no proud Howard; still, he had a most attractive daughter. There were never two men less alike than Lord Edmund Howard and Sir Thomas Boleyn. And to His Majesty, thought the Duchess, smiling into a lace handkerchief, a sword grown rusty is of less use than a lovely, willing girl.

'Run to the house and get cloaks,' she said. 'We will step along to see them. A walk will do me good and mayhap throw off this flatulence which, I declare, attacks me after every meal these days.'

'You eat too heartily, Grandmother.'

'Off with you, impudent child!'

Anne ran off. It does me good to look at her, thought her grandmother. And what when the King claps eyes on *her*, eh, Thomas Boleyn? Though it occurs to me that she might not be to his taste. I declare were I a man I'd want to spank the haughtiness out of her before I took her to bed. And the King would not be one to brook such ways. Ah, if you go to court, Anne Boleyn, you will have to lose your French dignity – if you hope to do as well as your saucy sister.

44

Though you'll not go to court; you'll go to Ireland. The Ormond title and the Ormond wealth must be kept in the family to satisfy grasping Thomas, and he was ever a man to throw his family to the wolves.

The Duchess rose, and Anne, who had come running up, put a cloak about her shoulders; they walked slowly through the gardens and along the river's edge.

The Lambeth house of the Edmund Howards was a roomy place, cold and draughty. Lady Edmund was a delicate creature on whom too frequent child-bearing and her husband's poverty were having a dire effect. She and her husband received their visitors in the great panelled hall, and wine was brought for them to drink. Lord Edmund's dignity was great, and it touched Anne deeply to see his efforts to hide his poverty.

'My dear Jocosa,' said the Duchess to her daughter-in-law, 'I have brought my granddaughter along to see you. She has recently returned from France, as you know. Tell your aunt and uncle all about it, child.'

'Uncle Edmund would doubtless find my adventuring tame telling,' said Anne.

'Ah!' said Lord Edmund. 'I remember you well, niece. Dover Castle, eh? And the crossing! Marry, I thought I should never see your face again when your ship was missed by the rest of us. I remember saying to Surrey: "Why, our niece is there, and she but a baby!"'

Anne sipped her wine, chatting awhile with Lord Edmund of the court of France, of old Louis, of gay François, and of Mary Tudor who had longed to be Queen of France and Duchess of Suffolk, and had achieved both ambitions.

The old Duchess tapped her stick imperiously, not caring to be left to Jocosa and her domesticity. 'Anne was interested in the children,' she said. 'I trow she will be disappointed if she is not allowed to catch a glimpse of them.'

'You must come to the nursery,' said Jocosa. 'Though I doubt that the older ones will be there at this hour. The babies love visitors.'

In the nursery at the top of the house, there was more evidence of the poverty of this branch of the Howard family. Little Catherine was shabbily dressed; Mary, the baby, was wrapped in a piece of darned flannel. There was an old nurse who, Anne guessed, doubtless worked without her wages for very love of the family. Her face shone with pride in the children, with affection for her mistress; but she was inclined to be resentful towards Anne and her grandmother. Had I known, thought Anne, I could have put on a simpler gown.

'Here is the new baby, Madam,' said the nurse, and put the flannel bundle into Anne's arms. Its little face was puckered and red; a very ugly little baby, but it was amusing and affecting to see the nurse hovering over it as though it were very, very precious.

A little hand was stroking the silk of Anne's surcoat. Anne looked down and saw a large-eyed, very pretty little girl who could not have been very much more than a year old.

'This is the next youngest,' said Jocosa.

'Little Catherine!' said the Duchess, and stooping picked her up. 'Now, Catherine Howard, what have you to say to Anne Boleyn?'

Catherine could say nothing; she could only stare at the lovely lady in the gorgeous, bright clothes. The jewels at her throat and on her fingers dazzled Catherine. She wriggled in the Duchess's arms in an effort to get closer to Anne, who, always susceptible to admiration, even from babies, handed the flannel bundle back to the nurse.

'Would you like me to hold you, cousin Catherine?' she asked, and Catherine smiled delightedly.

'She does not speak,' said the Duchess.

'I fear she is not as advanced as the others,' said Catherine's mother.

'Indeed not!' said the Duchess severely. 'I remember well this girl here as a baby. I never knew one so bright – except perhaps her brother George. Now, Mary . . . she was more like Catherine here.'

At the mention of Mary's name Jocosa stiffened, but the

old Duchess went on, her eyes sparkling: 'Mary was a taking little creature, though she might be backward with her talk. She knew though how to ask for what she wanted, without words . . . and I'll warrant she still does!'

Anne and Catherine smiled at each other.

'There!' said the Duchess. 'She is wishing she had a child of her own. Confess it, Anne!'

'One such as this, yes!' laughed Anne.

Catherine tried to pluck out the beautiful eyes.

'She admires you vastly!' said Jocosa.

Anne went to a chair and sat down, holding Catherine on her lap, while her grandmother drew Jocosa into a corner and chatted with her of the proposed match for Anne, of the advancement of Sir Thomas and George Boleyn, of Mary and the King.

Catherine's little hands explored the lovely dress, the glittering jewels; and the child laughed happily as she did so.

'They make a pretty picture,' said the Duchess. 'I think I am proud of my granddaughters, Anne Boleyn and Catherine Howard. They are such pretty creatures, both of them.'

Catherine's fingers had curled about a jewelled tablet which hung by a silken cord from Anne's waist; it was a valuable trinket.

'Would you like to have it for your own, little Catherine?' whispered Anne, and detached it. They can doubtless sell it, she thought. It is not much, but it is something. I can see it would be useless to offer help openly to Uncle Edmund.

When they said farewell, Catherine shed tears.

'Why, look what the child has!' cried the Duchess. 'It is yours, is it not, Anne? Catherine Howard, Catherine Howard, are you a little thief then?'

'It is a gift,' said Anne hastily. 'She liked it, and I have another.'

*   *   *

It was pleasant to be back at Hever after such a long absence. How quiet were the Kentish woods, how solitary the green meadows! She had hoped to see the Wyatts, but they were not in residence at Allington Castle just now; and it was a quiet life she led, reading, sewing, playing and singing with her mother. She was content to enjoy these lazy days, for she had little desire to marry the young man whom it had been ordained she should. She accepted the marriage as a matter of course, as she had known from childhood that when she reached a certain age a match would be made for her. This was it; but how pleasant to pass these days at quiet Hever, wandering through the grounds which she would always love because of those childhood memories they held for her.

Mary paid a visit to Hever; splendidly dressed – Anne considered her over-dressed – she was very gay and lively. Her laughter rang through the castle, shattering its peace. Mary admired her sister, and was too good-natured not to admit it wholeheartedly. 'You should do well at court, sister Anne,' she told her. 'You would create much excitement, I trow. And those clothes! I have never seen the like; and who but you could wear them with effect!'

They lay under the old apple trees in the orchard together; Mary, lazy and plump, carefully placing a kerchief over her bosom to prevent the sun from spoiling its whiteness.

'I think now and then,' said Mary, 'of my visit to you . . . Do you remember Ardres?'

'Yes,' said Anne, 'I remember perfectly.'

'And how you disapproved of me then? Did you not? Confess it.'

'Did I show it then?'

'Indeed you did, Madam! You looked down your haughty nose at me and disapproved right heartily. You cannot say you disapprove now, I trow.'

'I think you have changed very little,' said Anne.

Mary giggled. '*You* may have disapproved that night Anne, but there was one who did not!'

'The tastes of all are naturally not alike.'

'There was one who approved most heartily – and he of no small import either!'

48

'I perceive,' said Anne, laughing, 'that you yearn to tell me of your love affairs.'

'And you are not interested?'

'Not very. I am sure you have had many, and that they are all monotonously similar.'

'Indeed! And what if I were to tell His Majesty of that!'

'Do you then pour your girlish confidences into the royal ear?'

'I do now and then, Anne, when I think they may amuse His Grace.'

'What is this?' said Anne, raising herself to look more closely at her sister.

'I was about to tell you. Did I not say that though you might disapprove of me, there was one who does not? Listen, sister. The night I left you to return to the Guisnes Palace I met him; he spoke to me, and we found we liked each other.'

Anne's face flushed, then paled; she was understanding many things – the chatter of her grandmother, the glances of her Aunt Jocosa, the nurse's rather self-righteous indignation. One of the heroes of Flodden may starve, but the family of Boleyn shall flourish, for the King likes well one of its daughters.

'How long?' asked Anne shortly.

'From then to now. He is eager for me still. There never was such a man! Anne, I could tell you . . .'

'I beg that you will not.'

Mary shrugged her shoulders and rolled over on the grass like an amorous cat.

'And William, your husband?' said Anne.

'Poor William! I am very fond of him.'

'I understand. The marriage was arranged, and he was given a place at court so that you might be always there awaiting the King's pleasure, and to place a very flimsy cover of propriety over your immorality.'

Mary was almost choked with laughter.

'Your expressions amuse me, Anne. I declare, I shall tell the King; he will be vastly amused. And you fresh from the court of France!'

'I am beginning to wish I were still there. And our father . . .'

'Is mightily pleased with the arrangements. A fool he would be otherwise, and none could say our father is a fool.'

'So all these honours that have been heaped upon him . . .'

'. . . are due to the fact that your wicked sister has pleased the King!'

'It makes me sick.'

'You have a poor stomach, sister. But you are indeed young, for all your air of worldly wisdom and for all your elegance and grace. Why, bless you, Anne, life is not all the wearing of fine clothes.'

'No? Indeed it would seem that for you it is more a matter of putting them off!'

'You have a witty tongue, Anne. I cannot compete with it. You would do well at court, would you but put aside your prudery. Prudery the King cannot endure; he has enough of that from his Queen.'

'She knows of you and . . .'

'It is impossible to keep secrets at court, Anne.'

'Poor lady!'

'But were it not I, 'twould be another, the King being as he is.'

'The King being a lecher!' said Anne fiercely.

'That is treason!' cried Mary in mock horror. 'Ah! It is easy for you to talk. As for me, I could never say no to such a man."

'You could never say no to any man!'

'Despise me if you will. The King does not, and our father is mightily pleased with his daughter Mary.'

Now the secret was out; now she understood the sly glances of servants, her father's looks of approbation as his eyes rested on his elder daughter. There was no one to whom Anne could speak of her perturbation until George came home.

He was eighteen years old, a delight to the eye, very like Anne in appearance, full of exuberant animal spirits; a poet and coming diplomat, and he already had the air of both. His eyes burned with his enthusiasm for life; and Anne was happy when he took her hands, for she had been afraid that the years of separation might divide them and that she would lose for ever the beloved brother of her childhood. But in a few short hours those fears were set aside; he was the same George, she the same Anne. Their friendship, she knew, could not lose from the years, only gain from them. Their minds were of similar calibre; alert, intellectual, they were quick to be amused, quick to anger, reckless of themselves. They had therefore a perfect understanding of each other, and, being troubled, it was natural that she should go to him.

She said as they walked together through the Kentish lanes, for she had felt the need to leave the castle so that she might have no fear of being overheard: 'I have learned of Mary and the King.'

'That does not surprise me,' said George. 'It is common knowledge.'

'It shocked me deeply, George.'

He smiled at her. 'It should not.'

'But *our* sister! It is degrading.'

'She would degrade herself sooner or later, so why should it not be in that quarter from which the greatest advantages may accrue?'

'Our father delights in this situation, George, and our mother is complaisant.'

'My sweet sister, you are but sixteen. Ah, you look wonderfully worldly wise, but you are not yet grown up. You are very like the little girl who sat in the window seats at Blickling, and dreamed of knightly deeds. Life is not romantic, Anne, and men are not frequently honourable knights. Life is a battle or a game which each of us fights or plays with all the skill at his command. Do not condemn Mary because her way would not be yours.'

'The King will tire of her.'

'Assuredly.'

'And cast her off!'

'It is Mary's nature to be happy, Anne. Do not fear. She will find other lovers when she is ejected from the royal bed.

51

She has poor Will Carey, and she has been in favour for the best part of three years and her family have not suffered for it yet. Know, my sweet sister, that to be mistress of the King is an honour; it is only the mistress of a poor man who degrades herself.'

His handsome face was momentarily set in melancholy lines, but almost immediately he was laughing merrily.

'George,' she said, 'I cannot like it.'

'What! Not like to see your father become a power in the land! Not like to see your brother make his way at court!'

'I would rather they had done these things by their own considerable abilities.'

'Bless you!' said George. 'There are more favours won this way than by the sweat of the brow. Dismiss the matter from your mind. The Boleyns' fortunes are in the ascendant. Who knows whither the King's favour may lead – and all due to our own plump little Mary! Who would have believed it possible!'

'I like it not,' she repeated.

Then he took her hands and kissed them lightly, wishing to soothe her troubled mind.

'Fear not, little sister.'

Now he had her smiling with him – laughing at the incongruity of this situation. Mary – the one who was not as bright as the rest – was leading the Boleyns to fame and fortune.

* * *

It seemed almost unbearably quiet after Mary and George had gone. Anne could not speak of Mary's relationship with the King to her mother, and it irked her frank nature perpetually to have to steer the conversation away from a delicate topic. She was glad when her father returned to the court, for his obvious delight in his good fortune angered Anne. Her father thought her a sullen girl, for she was not one, feeling displeased, to care about hiding her displeasure. Mary was his favourite daughter; Mary was a sensible girl; and Anne could not help feeling that he would be relieved when the arrangements for the

Butler marriage were completed. She spent the days with her mother, or wandered often alone in the lanes and gardens.

Sir Thomas returned to Hever in a frenzy of excitement. The King would be passing through Kent, and it was probable that he would spend a night at Hever. Sir Thomas very quickly roused the household to his pitch of excitement. He went to the kitchen and gave orders himself; he had flowers set in the ballroom and replaced by fresh ones twice a day; he grumbled incessantly about the inconvenience of an old castle like Hever, and wished fervently that he had a modern house in which to entertain the King.

'The house is surely of little importance,' said Anne caustically, 'as long as Mary remains attractive to the King!'

'Be silent, girl!' thundered Sir Thomas. 'Do you realize that this is the greatest of honours?'

'Surely not the greatest!' murmured Anne, and was silenced by a pleading look from her mother who greatly feared discord; and, loving her mother while deploring her attitude in the case of Mary and the King, Anne desisted.

The King's having given no date for his visit, Sir Thomas fumed and fretted for several days, scarcely leaving the castle for fear he should not be on the spot to welcome his royal master.

One afternoon Anne took a basket to the rose garden that she might cut some of the best blooms for her mother. It was a hot afternoon, and she was informally dressed in her favourite scarlet; as the day was so warm she had taken off the caul from her head and shaken out her long, silky ringlets. She had sat on a seat in the rose garden for an hour or more, half dozing, when she decided it was time she gathered the flowers and returned to the house; and as she stood by a tree of red roses she was aware of a footfall close by, and turning saw what she immediately thought of as 'a Personage' coming through the gap in the conifers which was the entrance to this garden. She felt the blood rush to her face, for she knew him at once. The jewels in his clothes were caught and held by the sun, so that it seemed as if he were on fire; his face was ruddy, his beard seemed golden, and his presence seemed to fill the garden. She could not but think of Mary's meeting with him in the palace of Guisnes, and her resentment towards him flared up within her, even as she realized it would be sheer folly to show him that resentment. She sought therefore to compose her features and, with admirable calm – for she had decided now that her safest plan was to feign ignorance of his identity – she went on snipping the roses.

Henry was close. She turned as though in surprise to find herself not alone, gave him the conventional bow of acknowledgment which she would have given to one of her father's ordinary acquaintances, and said boldly: 'Good day, sir.'

The King was taken aback. Then inwardly he chuckled, thinking – She has no notion who I am! He studied her with the utmost appreciation. Her informal dress was more becoming, he thought, than those elaborate creations worn by some ladies at a court function. Her beautiful hair was like a black silk cloak about her shoulders. He took in each detail of her appearance and thought that he had never seen one whose beauty delighted him more.

She turned her head and snipped off a rose.

'My father is expecting the King to ride this way. I presume you to be one of his gentlemen!'

Masquerade had ever greatly appealed to Henry. There was nothing he enjoyed as much as to appear disguised at some ball or banquet, and after much badinage with his subjects and at exactly the appropriate moment, to make the dramatic announcement – 'I am your King!' And how could this game be more delightfully played out than in a rose garden on a summer's afternoon with, surely, the loveliest maiden in his kingdom! .

He took a step closer to her.

'Had I known,' he said, 'that I should come face to face with such beauty, depend upon it, I should have whipped up my horse.'

'Would you not have had to await the King's pleasure?'

'Aye!' He slapped his gorgeous thigh. 'That I should!'

She, who knew so well how to play the coquette, now did so with a will, for in this rôle she could appease that resentment in herself which threatened to make her very angry as she contemplated this lover of her sister Mary. Let him come close, and she – in assumed ignorance of his rank – would freeze him with a look. She snipped off a rose and gave it to him.

'You may have it if you care to.'

He said: 'I do care. I shall keep it for ever.'

'Bah!' she answered him contemptuously. 'Mere court gallantry!'

'You like not our court gallants?'

Her mocking eyes swept his padded, jewelled figure.

'They are somewhat clumsy when compared with those of the French court.'

'You are lately come from France?'

'I am. A match has been arranged for me with my cousin.'

'Would to God I were the cousin! Tell me . . .' He came yet closer, noting the smooth skin, the silky lashes, the proud tilt of the head and its graceful carriage on the tiny neck. 'Was that less clumsy?'

'Nay!' she said, showing white teeth. 'Not so! It was completely without subtlety; I saw it coming.'

Henry found that, somewhat disconcerting as this was, he was enjoying it. The girl had a merry wit, and he liked it; she was stimulating as a glass of champagne. And I swear I never clapped eyes on a lovelier wench! he told himself. The airs she gives herself! It would seem I were the subject – she the Queen!

She said: 'The garden is pretty, is it not? To me this is one of the most pleasant spots at Hever.'

They walked around it; she showed him the flowers, picked a branch of lavender and held it to her nose; then she rolled it in her hands and smelt its pleasant fragrance there.

Henry said: 'You tell me you have recently come from the court of France. How did you like it there?'

'It was indeed pleasant.'

'And you are sorry to return?'

55

'I think that may be, for so long have I been there that is seems as home to me.'

'I like not to hear that.'

She shrugged her shoulders. 'They say I am as French as I am English.'

'The French,' he said, the red of his face suddenly tinged with purple that matched his coat, 'are a perfidious set of rascals.'

'Sir!' she said reproachfully and, drawing her skirts about her, she walked from him and sat on the wooden seat near the pond. She looked at him coldly as he hurried towards her.

'How now!' he said, thinking he had had enough of the game.

He sat down beside her, pressing his thigh against hers, which caused her immediate withdrawal from him. 'Perfidious!' she said slowly. 'Rascals! And when I have said I am half French!'

'Ah!' he said. 'I should not use such words to you. You have the face of an angel!'

She was off the seat, as though distrusting his proximity. She threw herself onto the grass near the pond and looked into still waters at her own reflection, a graceful feminine Narcissus, her hair touching the water.

'No!' she said imperiously, as he would have risen: 'You stay there, and mayhap I will tarry awhile and talk to you.'

He did not understand himself. The joke should have been done with ere this. It was time to explain, to have her on her knees craving forgiveness for her forwardness. He would raise her and say: 'We cannot forgive such disrespectful treatment of your sovereign. We demand a kiss in payment for your sins!' But he was unsure; there was that in her which he had never before discovered in a woman. She looked haughty enough to refuse a kiss to a king. No, no! he thought. Play this little game awhile.

She said: 'The French are an interesting people. I was fortunate there. My friend was *Madame la Duchesse*

D'Alençon, and I count myself indeed happy to have such a friend.'

'I have heard tales of her,' he said.

'Her fame travels. Tell me, have you read Boccaccio?'

The King leaned forward. Had he read Boccaccio! Indeed he had, and vastly had the fellow's writing pleased him.

'And you?' he asked.

She nodded, and they smiled at each other in the understanding of a pleasure shared.

'We would read it together, the Duchess and I. Tell me, which of the stories did you prefer?'

Finding himself plunged deep into a discussion of the literature of his day, Henry forgot he was a king, and an amorous king at that. There was in this man, in addition to the coarse, crude, insatiable sensualist, a scholar of some attainment. Usually the sensualist was the stronger, ever ready to stifle the other, but there was about this girl sitting by the pond a purity that commanded his respect, and he found he could sit back in his seat and delight in her as he would in a beautiful picture or piece of statuary, while he could marvel at her unwomanly intellect. Literature, music and art could have held a strong position in his life, had he not in his youth been such a healthy animal. Had he but let his enthusiasm for them grow in proportion to that which he bestowed on tennis, on jousting, on the hunting of game and of women, his mind would assuredly have developed as nobly as his body. An elastic mind would have served him better than his strong muscles; but the jungle animal in him had been strong, and urgent desires tempered by a narrow religious outlook had done much to suppress the finer man, and from the mating of the animal and the zealot was born that monster of cruelty, his conscience. But that was to come; the monster was as yet in its infancy, and pleasant it was to talk of things of the mind with an enchanting companion. She was full of wit, and Marguerite of Alençon talked through her young lips. She had been allowed to peep into the *Heptameron* –

that odd book which, under the influence of Boccaccio, Marguerite was writing.

From literature she passed to the pastimes of the French court. She told of the masques, less splendid perhaps than those he indulged in with such pleasure, but more subtle and amusing. Wit was to the French court what bright colours and sparkling jewels were to the English. She told of a play which she had helped Marguerite to write, quoting lines from it which set him laughing with appreciative merriment. He was moved to tell her of his own compositions, reciting some verses of his. She listened, her head on one side, critical.

She shook her head: 'The last line is not so good. Now this would have been better . . .' And so would it! Momentarily he was angered, for those at court had declared there never were such verses written as those penned by his hand. From long practice he could pretend, even to himself, that his anger came from a different cause than that from which it really sprang. Now it grew – he assured himself – not from her slighting remarks on his poetry, but from the righteous indignation he must feel when he considered that this girl, though scarcely out of her childhood, had been exposed to the wickedness of the French court. Where he himself was concerned he had no sense of the ridiculous; he could, in all seriousness, put aside the knowledge that even at this moment he was planning her seduction, and burn with indignation that others – rakes and libertines with fancy French manners – might have had similar intentions. Such a girl, he told himself, smarting under the slights which she, reared in that foreign court, had been able to deliver so aptly, should never have been sent to France.

He said with dignity: 'It grieves me to think of the dangers to which you have been exposed at that licentious court presided over by a monarch who . . .' His voice failed him, for he pictured a dark, clever face, a sly smile and lips which had referred to him as 'My prisoner.'

She laughed lightly. 'The King of France is truly of an amorous nature, but never would I be a king's mistress!'

It seemed to him that this clever girl then answered a question which he had yet to ask. He felt worsted, and angry to be so.

He said severely: 'There are some who would not think it an indignity to be a king's mistress, but an honour.'

'Doubtless there are those who sell themselves cheaply.'

'Cheaply!' he all but roared. 'Come! It is not kingly to be niggardly with those that please.'

'I do not mean in worldly goods. To sell one's dignity and honour for momentary power and perhaps riches – that is to sell cheaply those things which are beyond price. Now I must go into the house.' She stood up, throwing back her hair. He stood too, feeling deflated and unkingly.

Silently he walked with her from the rose garden. Now was the time to disclose his identity, for it could not much longer be kept secret.

'You have not asked my name,' he said.

'Nor you mine.'

'You are the daughter of Sir Thomas Boleyn, I have gathered.'

'Indeed, that was clever of you!' she mocked. 'I am Anne Boleyn.'

'You still do not ask my name. Have you no curiosity to know it?'

'I shall doubtless learn in good time.'

'My name is Henry.'

'It is a good English name.'

'And have you noticed nothing yet?'

She turned innocent eyes upon him. 'What is there that I should have noticed?'

'It is the same as the King's.' He saw the mockery in her eyes now. He blurted out: 'By God! You knew all the time!'

'Having once seen the King's Grace, how could one of his subjects ever forget him?'

He was uncertain now whether to be amused or angry; in vain did he try to remember all she had said to him and he to her. 'Methinks you are a saucy wench!' he said.

'I hope my sauciness has pleased my mighty King.'

He looked at her sternly, for though her words were respectful, her manner was not.

'Too much sauce,' he said, 'is apt to spoil a dish.'

'And too little, to destroy it!' she said, casting down her eyes. 'I had thought that Your Majesty, being a famous epicure, would have preferred a well-flavoured one.'

He gave a snort of laughter and put out a hand which he would have laid on her shoulders, but without giving him a glance she moved daintily away, so that he could not know whether by accident or design.

He said: 'We shall look to see you at court with your sister.'

He was unprepared for the effect of those words; her cheeks were scarlet as her dress, and her eyes lost all their merriment. Her father was coming across the lawn towards them; she bowed low and turning from him ran across the grass and into the castle.

'You have a beautiful daughter there, Thomas!' exclaimed the King. And Thomas, obsequious, smiling, humbly conducted Henry into Hever Castle.

The sight of the table in the great dining-hall brought a glister of pride into Sir Thomas's eyes. On it were laid out in most lavish array great joints of beef, mutton and venison, hare and seasoned peacocks; there were vegetables and fruit, and great pies and pastries. Sir Thomas's harrying of his cooks and scullions had been well worth while, and he felt that the great kitchens of Hever had done him justice. The King eyed this display with an approval which might have been more marked, had not his thoughts been inclined to dwell more upon Sir Thomas's daughter than on his table.

They took their seats, the King in the place of honour at the right hand of his host, the small company he had brought with him ranged about the table. There was one face for which the King looked in vain; Sir Thomas, ever eager to anticipate the smallest wish of his sovereign, saw the King's searching look and understood it; he called a serving-maid to him and whispered sharply to her to go at once to his daughter and bid her to the table without a second's delay. The maid returned with the disconcerting message that Sir Thomas's daughter suffered from a headache and would not come to the table that day. The King, watching this little by-play with the greatest interest, heard every word.

'Go back at once,' said Sir Thomas, 'and tell the lady I command her presence here at once!'

'Stay!' interceded Henry, his voice startling Sir Thomas by its unusual softness. 'Allow me to deal with the matter, good Thomas. Come hither, girl.'

The poor little serving-maid dropped a frightened curtsey and feared she would not be able to understand the King's commands, so overawed was she by his notice.

'Tell the lady from us,' said Henry, 'that we are indeed sorry for the headache. Tell her it doubtless comes from lingering too daringly in the rays of the sun. Tell her we excuse her and wish her good speed in her recovery.'

He did not see Anne again, for she kept to her room. Next morning he left Hever. He looked up at its windows, wondering which might be hers, telling himself that no girl, however haughty, however self-possessed, would be able to prevent herself from taking one glimpse at her King. But there was no sign of a face at any window. Disconsolate, bemused, the King rode away from Hever.

* * *

The great Cardinal, he who was Lord Chancellor of the realm, rode through the crowds. Before him and behind went his gentlemen attendants, for the great man never rode abroad but that he must impress the people with his greatness. He sat his mule with a dignity which would have become a king. What though his body were weak, his digestion poor, that he was very far from robust and suffered many ailments! His mind was the keenest, the most able, the most profound in the kingdom; and thus, first through the King's father, and more effectively through his gracious son, had Thomas Wolsey come to his high office. His success, he knew well, lay with his understanding of the King – that fine robustious animal – and when he was but almoner to his gracious lord he had used that knowledge and so distinguished himself. There had been those counsellors who might urge the King to leave his pleasure and devote more time to affairs of state. Not so Thomas Wolsey! Let the King leave tiresome matters to his most dutiful servant. Let the King pursue his pleasures. Leave the wearisome matters to his most obedient – and what was all-important – to his most able Wolsey! How well the King loved those who did his will! This King, this immense man – in whom all emotions matched his huge body – hated fiercely and could love well. And he had loved Wolsey, in whose hands he could so safely place those matters that were important to his kingdom but so monotonously dull to his royal mind. And never was a man more content than Wolsey that this should be so. He, arrogant, imperious as his master, had had the indignity to be born the son of a poor man of Ipswich, and by his own fine brain had replaced indignity with honour. The Ipswich merchant's son was the best loved friend of the English King, and how doubly dear were those luxuries and those extravagances with which he, who had once suffered from obscurity, now surrounded himself! If he were over-lavish, he forgave himself; he had to wash the taste of Ipswich from his mouth.

As he rode on his ceremonious way, the people watched him. To his nose he held what might appear to be an orange, and what was really a guard against disease; for all the natural matter had been taken from the orange and in its place was stuffed part of a sponge containing vinegar and such concoctions as would preserve a great man from the pestilence which floated in the London air. Perhaps the people murmured against him; there were those who gave him sullen looks. Is this a man of God? they asked each other. This Wolsey – no higher born than you or I – who surrounds himself with elegance and luxury at the expense of the hard-pressed people! This gourmet, who must get special dispensation from the Pope that he need not follow the Lenten observances! They say he never forgives a slight. They say his hands are as red as his robes.

What of brave Buckingham! A marvel it is that the head-less ghost of the Duke does not haunt his murderer!

If Wolsey could have spoken to them of Buckingham, he could have told them that a man, who will at any cost hold the King's favour, must often steep his hands in blood. Buckingham had been a fool. Buckingham had insulted Wolsey, and Wolsey had brought a charge against him of treasonable sorcery. Buckingham went to the block, not for his treasonable sorcery; he died because he had committed the unforgivable sin of being too nearly related to the King. He stood too close to the throne, and the Tudors had not been in possession of it long enough to be able to regard such an offence lightly. Thus it was one kept the favour of kings; by learning their unuttered desires and anticipating their wishes; thus one remained the power behind the throne, one's eyes alert, one's ears trained to catch the faintest inflection of the royal voice, fearful lest the mighty puppet might become the master.

In the presence-chamber Wolsey awaited audience of the King. He came, fresh from his Kentish journey, flushed with health, his eyes beaming with pleasure as they rested on his best-loved statesman.

'I would speak with Your Majesty on one or two matters,' said the Chancellor-Cardinal when he had congratulated the King on his healthy appearance.

'Matters of state! Matters of state, eh? Let us look into these matters, good Thomas.'

Wolsey spread papers on the table, and the royal signature was appended to them. The King listened, though his manner was a little absent.

'You are a good man, Thomas,' he said, 'and we love you well.'

'Your Majesty's regard is my most treasured possession.'

The King laughed heartily, but his voice was a trifle acid when he spoke. 'Then the King is pleased, for to be the most treasured of all your possessions, my rich friend, is indeed to be of great price!'

Wolsey felt the faintest twinge of uneasiness, until he saw in his sovereign's face a look he knew well. There was a glaze over the bright little eyes, the cruel mouth had softened, and when the King spoke, his voice was gentle.

'Wolsey, I have been discoursing with a young lady who has the wit of an angel, and is worthy to wear a crown.'

Wolsey, alert, suppressed his smile with the desire to rub his hands together in his glee.

'It is sufficient if Your Majesty finds her worthy of your love,' he whispered.

The King pulled at his beard.

'Nay, Thomas, I fear she would never condescend that way.'

'Sire, great princes, if they choose to play the lover, have that in their power to mollify a heart of steel.'

The King shook his great head in melancholy fashion, seeing her bending over the pond, seeing her proud young head on the small neck, hearing her sweet voice: 'I would never be a king's mistress!'

'Your Majesty has been saddened by this lady,' said Wolsey solicitously.

'I fear so, Wolsey.'

'This must not be!' Wolsey's heart was merry. There was nothing he desired so much at this time as to see his master immersed in a passionate love affair. It was necessary at this moment to keep the fat, jewelled finger out of the French pie.

'Nay, my master, my dear lord, your chancellor forbids such sadness.' He put his head closer to the flushed face. 'Could we not bring the lady to court, and find a place for her among the Queen's ladies?'

The King placed an affectionate arm about Wolsey's shoulders.

'If Your Majesty will but whisper the name of the lady . . .'

'It is Boleyn's daughter . . . Anne.'

Now Wolsey had great difficulty in restraining his mirth. Boleyn's daughter! Anne! Off with the elder daughter! On with the younger!

'My lord King, she shall come to the court. I shall give a banquet at Hampton Court – a masque it shall be! I shall

64

ask my Gracious Liege to honour me with his mighty presence. The lady shall be there!'

The King smiled, well pleased. A prince, had said this wise man, has that power to mollify a heart of steel. Good Wolsey! Dear Thomas! Dear friend and most able statesman!

'Methinks, Thomas,' said the King with tears in his eyes, 'that I love thee well.'

Wolsey fell on his knees and kissed the ruby on the forefinger of the fat hand. And I do love this man, thought the King; for he was one to whom it was not necessary to state crude facts. The lady would be brought to court, and it would appear that she came not through the King's wish. That was what he wanted, and not a word had he said of it; yet Wolsey had known. And well knew the King that Wolsey would arrange this matter with expedience and tact.

* * *

Life at the English court offered amusement in plenty, and the coming of one as vivacious and striking as Anne Boleyn could not pass unnoticed. The ladies received her with some interest and much envy, the gentlemen with marked appreciation. There were two ways of life at court; on the one hand there was the gay merry-making of the King's faction, on the other the piety of the Queen. As Queen's attendant, Anne's actions were restricted; but at the jousts and balls, where the Queen's side must mingle with the King's, she attracted a good deal of attention for none excelled her at the dance, and whether it was harpsichord, virginals or flute she played there were always those to crowd about her; when she sang, men grew sentimental, for there was that in her rich young voice to move men to tears.

The King was acutely aware of her while feigning not to notice her. He would have her believe that he had been not entirely pleased by her disrespectful manners at Hever, and that he still remembered the levity of her conversation with pained displeasure.

Anne laughed to herself, thinking – Well he likes a masquerade, when he arranges it; well he likes a joke against others! Is he angry at my appointment to attend the Queen? How I hope he does not banish me to Hever!

Life had become so interesting. As lady-in-waiting to the Queen, she was allowed a woman attendant and a spaniel of her own; she was pleased with the woman and delighted with the spaniel. The three of them shared a breakfast of beef and bread, which they washed down with a gallon of ale between them. Other meals were taken with the rest of the ladies in the great chamber, and at all these meals ale and wine were served in plenty; meat was usually the fare – beef, mutton, poultry, rabbits, peacocks, hares, pigeons – except on fast days when, in place of the meats, there would be a goodly supply of salmon or flounders, salted eels, whiting, or plaice and gurnet. But it was not the abundance of food that delighted Anne; it was the gaiety of the company. And if she had feared to be dismissed from the court in those first days, no sooner had she set eyes on Henry, Lord Percy, eldest son of the Earl of Northumberland, than she was terrified of that happening.

These two young people met about the court, though not as often as they could have wished, for whilst Anne, as maid of honour to Queen Katharine, was attached to the court, Percy was a protégé of the Cardinal. It pleased Wolsey to have in his retinue of attendants various high-born young men, and so great was his place in the kingdom that this honour was sought by the noblest families in the realm. Young Percy must therefore attend the Cardinal daily, accompany him to court, and consider himself greatly honoured by the patronage of this low-born man.

Lord Percy was a handsome young man of delicate features and of courteous manners; and as soon as he saw the Queen's newest lady-in-waiting he was captivated by her personal charms. And Anne, seeing this handsome boy, was filled with such a tenderness towards him, which she had experienced for none hitherto, that whenever she knew the Cardinal to be in audience with the King she would look for the young nobleman. Whenever he came to the palace he was alert for a glimpse of her. They were both young; he was very shy; and so, oddly enough, was she, where he was concerned.

One day she was sitting at a window overlooking a court-yard when into this courtyard there came my lord Cardinal and his attendants; and among these latter was Henry, Lord Percy. His eyes flew to the window, saw Anne, and emboldened by the distance which separated them, flashed her a message which she construed as 'Wait there, and while the Cardinal is closeted with the King I will return. I have so long yearned to hold speech with you!'

She waited, her heart beating fast as she pretended to stitch a piece of tapestry; waiting, waiting, feeling a sick fear within her lest the King might not wish to see the Cardinal, and the young man might thus be unable to escape.

He came running across the courtyard, and she knew by his haste and his enraptured expression that his fear had been as hers.

'I feared to find you gone!' he said breathlessly.

'I feared you would not come,' she answered.

'I look for you always.'

'I for you.'

They smiled, beautiful both of them in the joyful discovery of loving and being loved.

Anne was thinking that were he to ask her, she, who had laughed at Mary for marrying Will Carey, would gladly marry him though he might be nothing more than the Cardinal's Fool.

'I know not your name,' said Percy, 'but your face is the fairest I ever saw.'

'It is Anne Boleyn.'

'You are daughter to Sir Thomas?'

She nodded, blushing, thinking Mary would be in his mind, and a fear came to her that her sister's disgrace might discredit herself in his eyes. But he was too far gone in love to find her anything but perfect.

'I am recently come to court,' she said.

'That I know! You could not have been here a day but that I should have found you.'

She said: 'What would your master say an he found you lingering beneath this window?'

'I know not, nor care I!'

'Were you caught, might there not be those who would prevent you from coming again? Already you may have been missed.'

He was alarmed. To be prevented from enjoying the further bliss of such meetings was intolerable.

'I go now,' he said. 'Tomorrow . . . you will be here at this hour?'

'You will find me here.'

'Tomorrow,' he said, and they smiled at each other.

Next day she saw him, and the next. There were many meetings, and for each of those two young lovers the day was good when they met, and bad when they did not. She learned of his exalted rank, and she could say with honesty that this mattered to her not at all, except of course that her ambitious father could raise no objection to a match with the house of Northumberland.

One day her lover came to her and pleasure was written large on his face.

'The Cardinal is to give a ball at his house at Hampton. All the ladies of the court will be invited!'

'You will be there?'

'You too!' he replied.

'We shall be masked.'

'I shall find you.'

'And then . . . ?' she said.

His eyes held the answer to that question.

Anne had dreamed of such happiness, though of late her observation of those about her had led her to conclude that it was rarely known. But to her it had come; she would treasure it, preserve it, keep it for ever. She could scarcely wait for that day when Thomas Wolsey would entertain the court at his great house at Hampton on the Thames.

* * *

The King was uneasy. The Cardinal had thought to help him when he had had Anne appointed a maid of honour to the Queen; but had he? Never, for the sake of a woman, had the King been so perplexed. He must see her every day, for how could he deny his eyes a sight of the most charming creature they had ever rested on! Yet he dared not speak with her. And why? For this reason; no sooner had the girl set foot in the Queen's apartments than that old enemy, his conscience, must rear its ugly head to leer at him.

'Henry,' said the conscience, 'this girl's sister, Mary Boleyn, has shared your bed full many a night, and well you know the edict of the Pope. Well you know that association with one sister gives you an affinity with the other. Therein lies sin!'

'That I know well,' answered Henry the King. 'But as there was no marriage . . .'

Such reasoning could not satisfy the conscience; it was the same – marriage ceremony or no marriage ceremony – and well he knew it.

'But there was never one like this girl; never was I so drawn to a woman; never before have I felt myself weak as I would be with her. Were she my mistress, I verily believe I should be willing to dispense with all others, and would not that be a good thing, for in the eyes of Holy Church, is it not better for a man to have one mistress than many? Then, would not the Queen be happier? One mistress is forgivable; her distress comes from there being so many.'

He was a man of many superstitions, of deep religious convictions. The God of his belief was a king like himself, though a more powerful being since, in place of the axe, he was able to wield a more terrifying weapon whose blade was supernatural phenomena. Vindictive was the King's god, susceptible to flattery, violent in love, more violent in hate – a jealous god, a god who spied, who recorded slights and insults, and whose mind worked in the same simple way as that of Henry of England. Before this god Henry trembled as men trembled before Henry. Hence the conscience, the uneasiness, his jealous watchfulness of Anne

Boleyn, and his reluctance to make his preference known.

In vain he tried to soothe his senses. All women are much alike in darkness. Mary is very like her sister. Mary is sweet and willing; and there are others as willing.

He tried to placate his conscience. 'I shall not look at the girl; I will remember there is an affinity between us.'

So those days, which were a blissful heaven to Anne and another Henry, were purgatory to Henry the King, racked alternately by conscience and desire.

*   *   *

She was clad in scarlet, and her vest was cloth of gold. She wore what had become known at court as the Boleyn sleeves, but they did not divulge her identity, for many wore the Boleyn sleeves since she had shown the charm of this particular fashion. Her hair was hidden by her gold cap, and only the beautiful eyes showing through her mask might proclaim her as Anne Boleyn.

He found her effortlessly, because she had described to him in detail the costume she would wear.

'I should have known you though you had not told me. I should always know you.'

'Then, sir,' she answered pertly, 'I would I had put you to the test!'

'I heard the music on the barges as they came along the river,' he said, 'and I do not think I have ever been so happy in my life.'

He was a slender figure in a coat of purple velvet embroidered in gold thread and pearls. Anne thought there was no one more handsome in this great ballroom, though the King, in his scarlet coat on which emeralds flashed, and in his bonnet dazzling rich with rubies and diamonds, was a truly magnificent sight.

The lovers clasped hands, and from a recess watched the gay company.

'There goes the King!'

'Who thinks,' said Anne, laughing, 'to disguise himself with a mask!'

'None dare disillusion him, or 'twould spoil the fun. It seems as though he searches for someone.'

'His latest sweetheart, doubtless!' said Anne scornfully.

Percy laid his hand on her lips.

'You speak too freely, Anne.'

'That was ever a fault of mine. But do you doubt that is the case?'

'I doubt it not – and you have no faults! Let us steal away from these crowds. I know a room where we can be alone. There is much I would say to you.'

'Take me there then. Though I should be most severely reprimanded if the Queen should hear that one of her ladies hides herself in lonely apartments in the house.'

'You can trust me. I would die rather than allow any hurt to come to you.'

'That I know well. I like not these crowds, and would hear what it is that you have to say to me.'

They went up a staircase and along a corridor. There were three small steps leading into a little antechamber; its one window showed the river glistening in moonlight.

Anne went to that window and looked across the gardens to the water.

'There was surely never such a perfect night!' she exclaimed.

He put his arms about her, and they looked at each other, marvelling at what they saw.

'Anne! Make it the most perfect night there ever was, by promising to marry me.'

'If it takes that to make this night perfect,' she answered softly, 'then now it is so.'

He took her hands and kissed them, too young and mild of nature to trust entirely the violence of his emotion.

'You are the most beautiful of all the court ladies, Anne.'

'You think that because you love me.'

'I think it because it is so.'

'Then I am happy to be so for you.'

'Did you ever dream of such happiness, Anne?'

'Yes, often . . . but scarce dared hope it would be mine.'

'Think of those people below us, Anne. How one pities them! For what can they know of happiness like this!'

She laughed suddenly, thinking of the King, pacing the floor, trying to disguise the fact that he was the King, looking about him for his newest sweetheart. Her thoughts went swiftly to Mary.

'My sister . . .' she began.

'What of your sister! Of what moment could she be to us!'

'None!' she cried, and taking his hand, kissed it. 'None, do we but refuse to let her.'

'Then we refuse, Anne.'

'How I love you!' she told him. 'And to think I might have let them marry me to my cousin of Ormond!'

'They would marry me to Shrewsbury's daughter!'

A faint fear stirred her then. She remembered that he was the heir of the Earl of Northumberland; it was meet that he should marry into the Shrewsbury family, not humble Anne Boleyn.

'Oh, Henry,' she said, 'what if they should try to marry you to the Lady Mary?'

'They shall marry me to none but Anne Boleyn!'

It was not difficult, up here in the little moonlight chamber, to defy the world; but they dare not tarry too long. All the company must be present when the masks were removed, or absent themselves on pain of the King's displeasure.

In the ballroom the festive air was tinged with melancholy. The Cardinal was perturbed, for the King clearly showed his annoyance. A masked ball was not such a good idea as it had at first seemed, for the King had been unable to find her whom he sought.

The masks were removed, the ball over, and the royal party lodged in the two hundred and forty gorgeous bedrooms which it was the Cardinal's delight to keep ready for his guests.

The news might seem a rumour just at first, but before many days had passed the fact was established that Henry Lord Percy, eldest son and heir to the noble Earl of North umberland, was so far gone in love with sparkling Anne Boleyn that he had determined to marry her.

And so the news came to the ear of the King.

* * *

The King was purple with fury. He sent for him to whom he always turned in time of trouble. The Cardinal came hastily, knowing that to rely on the favour of a king is to build one's hopes on a quiet but not extinct volcano. Over the Cardinal flowed the molten lava of Henry's anger.

'By Christ!' cried the King. 'Here is a merry state of affairs! I would take the fool and burn him at the stake, were he not such a young fool. How dare he think to contract himself without our consent!'

'Your Majesty, I fear I am in ignorance . . .'

'Young Percy!' roared His Majesty. 'Fool! Dolt that he is! He has, an it please you, decided he will marry Anne Boleyn!'

Inwardly the Cardinal could smile. This was a mere outbreak of royal jealousy. I will deal with this, thought the Cardinal, and deplored that his wit, his diplomacy must be squandered to mend a lover's troubles.

'Impertinent young fool!' soothed the Cardinal. 'As he is one of my young men, Your Majesty must allow me to deal with him. I will castigate him. I will make him aware of his youthful . . . nay, criminal folly, since he has offended Your Majesty. He is indeed a dolt to think Northumberland can mate with the daughter of a knight!'

Through the King's anger beamed his gratitude to Wolsey. Dear Thomas, who made the way easy! That was the reason, he told his conscience – Northumberland cannot mate with a mere knight's daughter!

' 'Twere an affront to us!' growled mollified Henry. 'We gave our consent to the match with Shrewsbury's girl.'

'And a fitting match indeed!' murmured the Cardinal.

'A deal more fitting than that he should marry Boleyn's girl. My dear Wolsey, I should hold myself responsible to Shrewsbury and his poor child if anything went amiss. . . .'

'Your Grace was ever full of conscience. You must not blame your royal self for the follies of your subjects.'

'I do, Thomas . . . I do! After all, 'twas I who brought the wench to court.'

Wolsey murmured: 'Your Majesty . . .? Why, I thought 'twas I who talked to Boleyn of his younger daughter. . . .'

'No matter!' said the King, his eyes beaming with affection. 'I thought I mentioned the girl to you. No matter!'

'I spoke to Boleyn, Your Grace, I remember well.'

The King's hand patted the red-clad shoulder.

'I know this matter can be trusted to you.'

'Your Majesty knows well that I shall settle it most expeditiously.'

'They shall both be banished the court. I will not be flouted by these young people!'

Wolsey bowed.

'The Shrewsbury marriage can be hastened,' said the King.

Greatly daring, Wolsey asked: 'And the girl, Your Majesty? There was talk of a marriage . . . the Ormond estates were the issue . . . Perhaps Your Majesty does not remember.'

The brows contracted; the little eyes seemed swallowed up in puffy flesh. The King's voice cracked out impatiently: 'That matter is not settled. I like not these Irish. Suffice it that we banish the girl.'

'Your Majesty may trust me to deal with the matter in accordance with your royal wishes.'

'And, Thomas . . . let the rebuke come from you. I would not have these young people know that I have their welfare so much at heart; methinks they already have too high a conceit of themselves.'

After Wolsey retired, the King continued to pace up and down. Let her return to Hever. She should be punished for daring to fall in love with that paltry boy. How was she in love? Tender? It was difficult to imagine that. Eager? Ah! Eager with a wretched boy! Haughty enough she had been with her lord the King! To test that eagerness he would have given the brightest jewel in his crown, but she would refuse her favours like a queen. And in a brief acquaintance, she had twice offended him; let her see that even she could not do that with impunity!

So she should be exiled to Hever, whither he would ride one day. She should be humble; he would be stern . . . just at first.

He threw himself into a chair, legs apart, hands on knees, thinking of a reconciliation in the rose garden at Hever.

His anger had passed away.

*　　*　　*

Immediately on his return to his house at Westminster, Wolsey sent for Lord Percy.

The young man came promptly, and there in the presence of several of his higher servants Wolsey began to upbraid him, marvelling, he said, at his folly in thinking he might enter into an engagement with a foolish girl at the court. Did the young fool not realize that on his father's death he would inherit and enjoy one of the noblest earldoms in the kingdom? How then could he marry without the consent of his father? Did Percy think, he thundered, that either his father or the King would consent to his matching himself with such a one? Moreover, continued the Cardinal, working himself up to a fine frenzy of indignation such as struck terror into the heart of the boy, he would have Percy know that the King had at great trouble prepared a suitable match for Anne Boleyn. Would he flout the King's pleasure!

Lord Percy was no more timid than most, but he knew the ways of the court well enough to quail before the meaning he read into Wolsey's words. Men had been committed to the Tower for refusing to obey the King's command, and Wolsey clearly had the King behind him in this matter. Committed to the Tower! Though the dread Cardinal did not speak the words, Percy knew they were there ready to be pronounced at any moment. Men went to the Tower and were heard of no more. Dread happenings there were in the underground chambers of the Tower of

London. Men were incarcerated, and never heard of again. And Percy had offended the King!

'Sir,' he said, trembling, 'I knew not the King's pleasure, and am sorry for it. I consider I am of good years, and thought myself able to provide me a convenient wife as my fancy should please me, not doubting that my lord and father would have been well content. Though she be but a simple maid and her father a knight, yet she is descended of noble parentage, for her mother is of high Norfolk blood and her father descended from the Earl of Ormond. I most humbly beseech Your Grace's favour therein, and also to entreat the King's Majesty on my behalf for his princely favour in this matter which I cannot forsake.'

The Cardinal turned to his servants, appealing to them to observe the wilful folly of this boy. Sadly he reproached Percy for knowing the King's pleasure and not readily submitting to it.

'I have gone too far in this matter,' said Percy.

'Dost think,' cried Wolsey, 'that the King and I know not what we have to do in weighty matters such as this!'

He left the boy, remarking as he went that he should not seek out the girl, or he would have to face the wrath of the King.

The Earl arrived, coming in haste from the north since the command was the King's, and hastened to Wolsey's house. A cold man with an eye to his own advantage, the Earl listened gravely, touched his neck uneasily as though he felt the sharp blade of an axe there – for heads had been severed for less than this – hardened his face, and said that he would set the matter to rights.

He went to his son and railed at him, cursing his pride, his licentiousness, but chiefly the fact that he had incurred the King's displeasure. So he would bring his father to the block and forfeit the family estate, would he! He was a waster, useless, idle. . . . He would return to his home immediately and proceed with the marriage to the Lady Mary Talbot, to which he was committed.

Percy, threatened by his father, dreading the wrath of

the King, greatly fearing the mighty Cardinal, and not being possessed of the same reckless courage as his partner in romance, was overpowered by this storm he and Anne had aroused. He could not stand out against them. Wretchedly, broken-heartedly he gave in, and left the court with his father.

He was, however, able to leave a message for Anne with a kinsman of hers, in which he begged that she would remember her promise from which none but God could loose her.

And the Cardinal, passing through the palace courtyard with his retinue, saw a dark-eyed girl with a pale, tragic face at one of the windows.

Ah! thought the Cardinal, turning his mind from matters of state. The cause of all the trouble!

The black eyes blazed into sudden hatred as they rested on him, for there had been those who had overheard Wolsey's slighting remarks about herself and hastened to inform her. Wolsey she blamed, and Wolsey only, for the ruin of her life.

Insolently she stared at him, her lips moving as though she cursed him.

The Cardinal smiled. Does she think to frighten me? A foolish girl! And I the first man in the kingdom! I would reprove her, but for the indignity of noting one so lacking in significance!

The next time he passed through the courtyard, he did not see Anne Boleyn. She had been banished to Hever.

* * *

At home in Hever Castle, a fierce anger took possession of her. She had waited for a further message from her lover. There was no message. He will come, she had told herself. They would ride away together, mayhap disguised as country folk, and they would care nothing for the anger of the Cardinal.

She would awake in the night, thinking she heard a tap on her window; walking in the grounds, she would feel her heart hammering at the sound of crackling bracken. She longed for him, thinking constantly of that night in the little chamber at Hampton Court, which they had said should be a perfect night and which by promising each other marriage they had made so; she thought of how sorry they had been for those who were dancing below, knowing nothing of the enchantment they were experiencing.

She would be ready when he came for her. Where would they go? Anywhere! For what did place matter! Life should be a glorious adventure. Taking her own courage for granted, why should she doubt his?

He did not come, and she brooded. She grew bitter, wondering why he did not come. She thought angrily of the wicked Cardinal whose spite had ruined her chances of happiness. Fiercely she hated him. 'This foolish girl . . .' he had said. 'This Anne Boleyn, who is but the daughter of a knight, to wed with one of the noblest families in the kingdom!'

She would show my lord Cardinal whether she was a foolish girl or not! Oh, the hypocrite! The man of God! He who kept house as a king and was vindictive as a devil and hated by the people!

When she and Percy went off together, the Cardinal should see whether she was a foolish girl!

And still her lover did not come.

'I cannot bear this long separation!' cried the passionate girl. 'Perhaps he thinks to wait awhile until his father is dead, for they say he is a sick man. But I do not wish to wait!'

She was melancholy, for the summer was passing and it was sad to see the leaves fluttering down.

The King rode out to Hever. In her room she heard the bustle his presence in the castle must inevitably cause. She locked her door and refused to go down. If Wolsey had ruined her happiness, the King – doubtless at the wicked man's instigation – had humiliated her by banishing her from the court. Unhappy as she was, she cared for nothing – neither her father's anger nor the King's.

Her mother came and stood outside the door to plead with her.

'The King has asked for you, Anne. You must come ... quickly.'

'I will not! I will not!' cried Anne. 'I was banished, was I not? Had he wished to see me, he should not have sent me from the court.'

'I dare not go back and say you refuse to come.'

'I care not!' sobbed Anne, throwing herself on her bed and laughing and weeping simultaneously, for she was beside herself with a grief that she found herself unable to control.

Her father came to her door, but his threats were as vain as her mother's pleas.

'Would you bring disgrace on us!' stormed Sir Thomas. 'Have you not done enough!'

'Disgrace!' she cried furiously. 'Yes, if it is a disgrace to love and wish to marry, I have disgraced you. It is an honour to be mistress of the King. Mary has brought you honour! An I would not come for my mother, assuredly I will not come for you!'

'The King commands your presence!'

'You may do what you will,' she said stubbornly. 'He may do what he will. I care for nothing ... now.' And she burst into fresh weeping.

Sir Thomas – diplomatic over a family crisis as on a foreign mission – explained that his daughter was sadly indisposed; and the King, marvelling at his feelings for this wilful girl, replied: 'Disturb her not then.'

The King left Hever, and Anne returned to that life which had no meaning – waiting, longing, hoping, fearing.

One cold day, when the first touch of winter was in the air and a fresh wind was bringing down the last of the leaves from the trees in the park, Sir Thomas brought home the news.

He looked at Anne expressionlessly and said: 'Lord Percy has married the Lady Mary Talbot. This is an end of your affair.'

She went to her room and stayed there all that day. She

did not eat; she did not sleep; she spoke to none; and on the second day she fell into a fit of weeping, upbraiding the Cardinal, and with him her lover. 'They could have done what they would with me,' she told herself bitterly. 'I would never have given in!'

Drearily the days passed. She grew pale and listless, so that her mother feared for her life and communicated her fears to her husband.

Sir Thomas hinted that if she would return to court, such action would not be frowned on.

'That assuredly I will not do!' she said, and so ill was she that none dared reason with her.

She called to mind then the happiness of her life in France, and it seemed to her that her only hope of tearing her misery from her heart lay in getting away from England. She thought of one whom she would ever admire – the witty, sparkling, Duchess of Alençon; was there some hope, with that spritely lady, of renewing her interest in life?

Love she had experienced, and found it bitter; she wanted no more such experience.

'With Marguerite I could forget,' she said; and, fearing for her health, Sir Thomas decided to humour her wishes; so once more Anne left Hever for the court of France.

THE HOUSE at Lambeth was wrapped in deepest gloom. In the great bed which Jocosa had shared with Lord Edmund Howard since the night of her marriage, she now lay dying. She was very tired, poor lady, for her married life had been a wearying business. It seemed that no sooner had one small Howard left her womb than another was growing there; and poverty, in such circumstances, had been humiliating.

Death softened bitter feelings. What did it matter now, that her distinguished husband had been so neglected! Why, she wondered vaguely, were people afraid of death? It was so easy to die, so difficult to live.

'Hush! Hush!' said a voice. 'You must not disturb your mother now. Do you not see she is sleeping peacefully?'

Then came to Jocosa's ears the sound of a little girl's sobbing. Jocosa tried to move the coverlet to attract attention. That was little Catherine crying, because, young as she was, she was old enough to understand the meaning of hushed voices, the air of gloom, old enough to smell the odour of death.

Jocosa knew suddenly why people were afraid of death. The fear was for those they left behind.

'My children . . .' she murmured, and tried to start up from her bed.

'Hush, my lady,' said a voice. 'You must rest, my dear.'

'My children,' she breathed, but her lips were parched, too stiff for the words to come through.

She thought of Catherine, the prettiest of her daughters, yet somehow the most helpless. Gentle, loving little Catherine, so eager to please that she let others override her. Some extra sense told the mother that her daughter Catherine would sorely miss a mother's care.

With a mighty effort she spoke. 'Catherine. . . . Daughter. . . .'

'She said my name!' cried Catherine. 'She is asking for me.'

'C ... Catherine ...'

'I am here,' said Catherine.

Jocosa lifted the baby fingers to her parched lips. Perhaps, she thought, she will acquire a stepmother. Stepmothers are not always kind; they have their own children whom they would advance beyond those of the woman they have replaced, and a living wife has power a dead one lacks. Perhaps her Aunt Norfolk would take this little Catherine; perhaps her Grandmother Norfolk. No, not the Norfolks, a hard race! Catherine, who was soft and young and tender, should not go to them. Jocosa thought of her own childhood at Hollingbourne, in the lovely old house of her father, Sir Richard Culpepper. Now her brother John was installed there; he had a son of his own who would be playing in her nursery. She remembered happy days spent there, and in her death-drugged thoughts it was Catherine who seemed to be there, not herself. It was soothing to the dying mother to see her daughter Catherine in her own nursery, but the pleasure passed and she was again conscious of the big, bare room at Lambeth.

'Edmund ...' she said.

Catherine turned her tearful eyes to the nurse.

'She speaks my father's name.'

'Yes, my lady?' asked the nurse, bending over the bed.

'Edmund ...'

'Go to your father and tell him your mother would speak to him.'

He stood by the bedside – poor, kind, bitter Edmund, whose life with her had been blighted by that pest, poverty. Now he was sorry for the sharp words he had spoken to her, for poverty had ever haunted him, waylaid him, leered at him, goaded him, warping his natural kindness, wrecking that peace he longed to share with his family.

'Jocosa ...' There was such tenderness in his voice when he said her name that she thought momentarily that this was their wedding night, and he her lover; but she heard then the rattle in her throat and was conscious of her body's burning heat, and thus remembered that this was not the prologue but the epilogue to her life with Edmund, and that Catherine – gentlest of her children – was in some danger, which she sensed but did not comprehend.

'Edmund . . . Catherine . . .'

He lifted the child in his arms and held her nearer the bed.

'Jocosa, here is Catherine.'

'My lord . . . let her go . . . let Catherine go . . .'

His head bent closer, and with a great effort the words came out.

'My brother John . . . at Hollingbourne . . . in Kent. Let Catherine . . . go to my brother John.'

Lord Edmund said: 'Rest peacefully, Jocosa. It shall be as you wish.'

She sank back, smiling, for it was to be, since none dared disregard a promise made to a dying woman.

The effort had tired her; she knew not where she lay, but she believed it must be at Hollingbourne in Kent, so peaceful was she. The weary beating of her heart was slowing down. 'Catherine is safe,' it said. 'Catherine is . . . safe.'

* * *

At Hollingbourne, whither Catherine had been brought at her father's command, life was different from that lived in the house at Lambeth. The first thing that struck Catherine was the plenteous supply of good plain country fare. There was a simplicity at Hollingbourne which had been entirely lacking at Lambeth; and Sir John, in his country retreat, was lord of the neighbourhood, whereas Lord Edmund, living his impecunious life among those of equally noble birth, had seemed of little importance. Catherine looked upon her big Uncle John as something like a god.

The nurseries were composed of several airy rooms at the top of the house, and from these it was possible to look over the pleasant Kentish country undisturbed by the sombre grandeur of the great city on whose outskirts the Lambeth house had sat. Catherine had often looked at the forts of the great Tower of London, and there was that in them to frighten the little girl. Servants were not over-careful; and though there were some who had nothing but adulation to give to Lord Edmund and his wife, poverty proved to be a leveller, and there were others who had but little respect for one who feared to be arrested at any moment for debt, even though he be a noble lord; and these servants were careless of what was said before the little Howards. There was a certain Doll Tappit who had for lover one who was a warder at the Tower, and fine stories he could tell her of the bloodcurdling shrieks which came from the torture chambers, of the noble gentlemen who had displeased the King and who were left to starve in the rat-infested dungeons. Therefore Catherine was glad to see green and pleasant hills against the skyline, and leafy woods in place of the great stone towers.

There was comfort at Hollingbourne, such as there had never been at Lambeth.

She was taken to the nurseries, and there put into the charge of an old nurse who had known her mother; and there she was introduced to her cousin Thomas and his tutor.

Shyly she studied Thomas. He, with his charming face in which his bold and lively eyes flashed and danced with merriment, was her senior by a year or so, and she was much in awe of him; but, finding the cousin who was to share his nursery to be but a girl – and such a little girl – he was inclined to be contemptuous.

She was lonely that first day. It was true she was given food; and the nurse went through her scanty wardrobe, clicking her tongue over this worn garment and that one, which should have been handed to a servant long ago.

'Tut-tut!' exclaimed the nurse. 'And how have you been brought up, I should wonder!' Blaming little Catherine Howard for her father's poverty; wondering what the world was coming to, when such beggars must be received in the noble house of Culpepper.

Catherine was by nature easy-going, gay and optimistic;

never saying – This is bad; always – This might be worse. She had lost her mother whom she had loved beyond all else in the world, and she was heartbroken; but she could not but enjoy the milk that was given her to drink; she could not but be glad that she was removed from Lambeth. Her sisters and brothers she missed, but being one of the younger ones, in games always the unimportant and unpleasant rôles were given to her; and if there were not enough parts to go round, it was Catherine who was left out. The afternoon of her first day at Hollingbourne was spent with the nurse who, tutting and clicking her tongue, cut up garments discarded by my lady, to make clothes for Catherine Howard. She stood still and was fitted; was pushed and made to turn about; and she thought the clothes that would soon be hers were splendid indeed.

Through the window she saw Thomas ride by on his chestnut mare, and she ran to the window and knelt on the window seat to watch him; and he, looking up, for he suspected she might be there, waved to her graciously, which filled Catherine with delight, for she had decided, as soon as he had looked down his haughty nose at her, that he was the most handsome person she had ever seen.

She had a bedroom to herself – a little panelled room with latticed windows – which adjoined the main nursery. At Lambeth she had shared her room with several members of her family.

Even on that first day she loved Hollingbourne, but at that time it was chiefly because her mother had talked to her of it so affectionately.

But on the first night, when she lay in the little room all by herself, with the moon shining through the window and throwing ghostly shadows, she began to sense the solitude all about her and her quick love for Hollingbourne was replaced by fear. There was no sound from barges going down the river to Greenwich or up it to Richmond and Hampton Court; there was only silence broken now and then by the weird hooting of an owl. The strange room seemed menacing in this half-light, and suddenly she longed for the room at Lambeth with the noisy brothers and sisters; she thought of her mother, for Catherine Howard had had that sweet companionship which so many in her station might never know, since there was no court life to take Jocosa from her family, and her preoccupations were not with the cut of a pair of sleeves but with her children; that, poverty had given Catherine, but cruel life had let it be appreciated only to snatch it away. So in her quiet room at Hollingbourne, Catherine shed bitter tears into her pillow, longing for her mother's soft caress and the sound of her gentle voice.

'You have no mother now,' they had said, 'so you must be a brave girl.'

But I'm not brave, thought Catherine, and immediately remembered how her eldest brother had jeered at her because she, who was so afraid of ghosts, would listen to and even encourage Doll Tappit to tell tales of them.

Doll Tappit's lover, Walter the warder, had once seen a ghost. Doll Tappit told the story to Nurse as she sat feeding the baby; Catherine had sat, round-eyed, listening.

'Now you know well how 'tis Walter's task to walk the Tower twice a night. Now Walter, as you know, is nigh on six foot tall, near as tall as His Majesty the King, and not a man to be easily affrighted. It was a moonlit night. Walter said the clouds kept hurrying across the moon as though there was terrible sights they wanted to hide from her. There is terrible sights, Nurse, in the Tower of London! Walter, he's heard some terrible groaning there, he's heard chains clanking, he's heard screams and shrieking. But afore this night he never *see* anything . . . And there he was on the green, right there by the scaffold, when . . . clear as I see you now, Nurse . . . the Duke stood before him; his head was lying in a pool of blood on the ground beside him, and the blood ran down all over his Grace's fine clothes!'

'What then?' asked Nurse, inclined to be sceptical. 'What would my lord Duke of Buckingham have to say to Walter the warder?'

'He said nothing. He was just there . . . just for a minute he was there. Then he was gone.'

'They say,' said Nurse, 'that the pantler there is very hospitable with a glass of metheglin . . .'

'Walter never takes it!'

'I'll warrant he did that night.'

'And when the ghost had gone, Walter stooped down where it was . . .'

'Where what was?'

'The head . . . all dripping blood. And though the head was gone, the blood was still there. Walter touched it; he showed me the stain on his coat.'

Nurse might snort her contempt, but Catherine shivered; and there were occasions when she would dream of the headless duke, coming towards her, and his head making stains on the nursery floor.

And here at Hollingbourne there were no brothers and sisters to help her disbelief in ghosts. Ghosts came when people were alone, for all the stories Catherine had ever heard of ghosts were of people who were alone when they saw them. Ghosts had an aversion to crowds of human beings, so that, all through her life, being surrounded by brothers and sisters, Catherine had felt safe; but not since she had come to Hollingbourne.

As these thoughts set Catherine shivering, outside her window she heard a faint noise, a gentle rustling of the creeper; it was as though hands pulled at it. She listened fearfully, and then it came again.

She was sitting up in bed, staring at the window. Again there came that rustle; and with it she could hear the deep gasps of one who struggles for breath.

She shut her eyes; she covered her head with the clothes; then, peeping out and seeing a face at her window, she screamed. A voice said: 'Hush!' very sternly, and Catherine thought she would die from relief, for the voice was the voice of her handsome young cousin, Thomas Culpepper.

He scrambled through the window.

'Why, 'tis Catherine Howard! I trust I did not startle you, Cousin?'

'I . . . thought you . . . to be a . . . ghost!'

That made him rock with merriment.

'I had forgotten this was your room, Cousin,' he lied, for well he had known it and had climbed in this way in order to impress her with his daring. 'I have been out on wild adventures.' He grimaced at a jagged tear in his breeches.

'Wild adventures . . . !'

'I do bold things by night, Cousin.'

Her big eyes were round with wonder, admiring him, and Thomas Culpepper, basking in such admiration that he could find nowhere but in this simple girl cousin, felt mightily pleased that Catherine Howard had come to Hollingbourne.

'Tell me of them,' she said.

He put his fingers to his lips.

'It is better not to speak so loudly, Cousin. In this house they believe me to be but a boy. When I am out, I am a man.'

'Is it witchcraft?' asked Catherine eagerly, for often had she heard Doll Tappit speak of witchcraft.

He was silent on that point, silent and mysterious; but before he would talk to her, he would have her get off her bed to see the height of the wall which he had climbed with naught to help him but the creeper.

She got out, and naked tiptoed to the window. She was greatly impressed.

'It was a wonderful thing to do, Cousin Thomas,' she said.

He smiled, well pleased, thinking her prettier in her very white skin than in the ugly clothes she had worn on her arrival.

'I do many wonderful things,' he told her. 'You will be cold, naked thus,' he said. 'Get back into your bed.'

'Yes,' she said, shivering, half with cold and half with excitement. 'I am cold.'

She leapt gracefully into bed, and pulled the clothes up to her chin. He sat on the bed, admiring the mud on his shoes and the unkempt appearance of his clothes.

'Do tell me,' she said, her knees at her chin, her eyes sparkling.

'I fear it is not for little girls' ears.'

'I am not such a little girl. It is only because you are big that it seems so.'

'Ah!' he mused, well pleased to consider it in that way. 'That may well be so; perhaps you are not so small. I have been having adventures, Cousin; I have been out trapping hares and shooting game!'

Her mouth was a round O of wonder.

'Did you catch many?'

'Hundreds, Cousin! More than a little girl like you could count.'

'I could count hundreds!' she protested.

'It would have taken you days to count these. Do you know that, had I been caught, I could have been hanged at Tyburn?'

'Yes,' said Catherine, who could have told him more gruesome stories of Tyburn than he could tell her, for he had never known Doll Tappit.

'But,' said Thomas, 'I expect Sir John, my father, would not have allowed that to happen. And then again 'twas scarcely poaching, as it happened on my father's land which will be one day mine, so now, Cousin Catherine, you see what adventures I have!'

'You are very brave,' said Catherine.

'Perhaps a little. I have been helping a man whose acquaintance I made. He is a very interesting man, Cousin; a poacher. So I for fun, and he for profit, poach on my father's land.'

'Were he caught, he would hang by the neck.'

'I should intercede for him with my father.'

'I would that I were brave as you are!'

'Bah! You are just a girl . . . and frightened that you might see a ghost.'

'I am not now. It is only when I am alone.'

'Will you be afraid when I have gone?'

'Very much afraid,' she said.

He surveyed her in kingly fashion. She was such a little girl, and she paid such pleasant tribute to his masculine superiority. Yes, assuredly he was glad his cousin had come to Hollingbourne.

'I shall be here to protect you,' he said.

'Oh, will you? Cousin Thomas, I know not how to thank you.'

'You surely do not think I could be afraid of a ghost!'

'I know it to be impossible.'

'Then you are safe, Catherine.'

'But if, when I am alone . . .'

'Listen!' He put his head close to hers conspiratorially. 'There' – he pointed over his shoulder – 'is my room. Only one wall dividing me from you, little Cousin. I am ever alert for danger, and very lightly do I sleep. Now listen very attentively, Catherine. Should a ghost come, all you must do is tap on this wall, and depend upon it you will have me here before you can bat an eyelid. I shall sleep with my sword close at hand.'

'Oh, Thomas! You have a sword too?'

'It is my father's, but as good as mine because one day it will be so.'

'Oh, Thomas!' Sweet was her adulation to the little braggart.

'None dare harm you when I am by,' he assured her. 'Dead or living will have to deal with me.'

'You would make yourself my knight then, Thomas,' she said softly.

'You could not have a braver . . .'

'Oh, I know it. I do not think I shall cry very much now.'

'Why should you cry?'

'For my mother, who is dead.'

'No, Catherine, you need not cry; for in place of your mother you have your brave cousin, Thomas Culpepper.'

'Shall I then tap on the wall if . . .?'

He wrinkled his brows. 'For tonight, yes. Tomorrow we shall find a stick for you . . . a good, stout stick I think; that will make a good banging on the wall, and you could, in an emergency, hit the ghost should it be necessary before I arrive.'

'Oh, no, I could not! I should die of fear. Besides, might a ghost not do terrible things to one who made so bold as to hit it?'

'That may be so. The safest plan, my cousin, is to wait for me.'

'I do not know how to thank you.'

'Thank me by putting your trust in me.'

He stood back from the bed, bowing deeply.

'Good night, Cousin.'

'Good night, dear, *brave* Thomas.'

He went, and she hugged her pillow in an ecstasy of delight. Never had one of her own age been so kind to her; never had she felt of such consequence.

As for ghosts, what of them! What harm could they do to Catherine Howard, with Thomas Culpepper only the other side of her bedroom wall, ready to fly to her rescue!

*   *   *

There was delight in the hours spent at Hollingbourne. Far away in a hazy and unhappy past were the Lambeth days; and the sweetest thing she had known was the ripening of her friendship with her cousin Thomas. Catherine, whose nature was an excessively affectionate one, asked nothing more than that she should be allowed to love him. Her affection he most graciously accepted, and returned it in some smaller measure. It was a happy friendship, and he grew more fond of her than his dignity would allow him to make known; she, so sweet already, though so young, so clingingly feminine, touched something in his manhood. He found great pleasure in protecting her, and thus love grew between them. He taught her to ride, to climb trees, to share his adventures, though he never took her out at night; nor did he himself adventure much this way after her coming, wishing to be at hand lest in the lonely hours of evening she might need his help.

Her education was neglected. Sir John did not believe overmuch in the education of girls; and who was she but a dependant, though the child of his sister! She was a girl, and doubtless a match would be made for her; and bearing such a name as Howard, that match could be made without the unnecessary adornment of a good education. Consider the case of his kinsman, Thomas Boleyn. He had been, so Sir John had heard, at great pains to educate his two younger children who, in the family, had acquired the reputation of possessing some brilliance. Even the girl had been educated, and what had education done for her? There was some talk of a disaster at court; the girl had aspired to marry herself to a very highly born nobleman – doubtless due to her education. And had her education helped her? Not at all! Banishment and disgrace had been her lot. Let girls remain docile; let them cultivate charming manners; let them learn how to dress themselves prettily and submit to their husbands. That was all a girl needed from life. And did she want to construe Latin verse to do these things; did she want to give voice to her frivolous thoughts in six different languages! No, the education of young Catherine Howard was well taken care of.

Thomas tried to teach his cousin a little, but he quickly gave up the idea. She had no aptitude for it; rather she preferred to listen to the tales of his imaginary adventures, to sing and dance and play musical instruments. She was a frivolous little creature, and having been born into poverty, well pleased to have stepped out of it, happy to have for her friend surely the most handsome and the dearest cousin in the world. What more could she want?

And so the days passed pleasantly – riding with Thomas, listening to Thomas's stories, admiring him, playing games in which he took the glorious part of knight and rescuer, she the rôle of helpless lady and rescued; now and then taking a lesson at the virginals, which was not like a lesson at all because she had been born with a love of music; she had singing lessons too which she loved, for her voice was pretty and promised to be good. But life could not go on in this even tenor for ever. A young man such as Thomas Culpepper could not be left to the care of a private tutor indefinitely.

He came to the music room one day while Catherine sat over the virginals with her teacher, and threw himself into a window seat and watched her as she played. Her auburn hair fell about her flushed face; she was very young, but there was always in Catherine Howard, even when a baby, a certain womanliness. Now she was aware of Thomas there, she was playing with especial pains to please him. That, thought Thomas, was so typical of her; she would always care deeply about pleasing those she loved. He was going to miss her very much; he found that watching her brought a foolish lump into his throat, and he contemplated running from the room for fear his sentimental tears should betray him. It was really but a short time ago that she had come to Hollingbourne, and yet she had made a marked difference to his life. Strange it was that that should be so; she was meek and self-effacing, and yet her very wish to please made her important to him; and he, who had longed for this childish stage of his education to be completed, was now sorry that it was over.

The teacher had stood up; the lesson was ended.

Catherine turned a flushed face to her cousin.

'Thomas, do you think I have improved?'

'Indeed yes,' he said, realizing that he had hardly heard what she had played. 'Catherine,' he said quickly, 'let us ride together. There is something I would say to you.'

They galloped round the paddock, he leading, she trying to catch up but never succeeding – which made her so enchanting. She was the perfect female, for ever stressing her subservience to the male, soft and helpless, meek, her eyes ever ready to fill with tears at a rebuke.

He pulled up his horse, but did not dismount; he dared not, because he felt so ridiculously near tears himself. He must therefore be ready to whip up his horse if this inclination became a real danger.

'Catherine,' he said, his voice hardly steady, 'I have bad news. . . .'

He glanced at her face, at the hazel eyes wide now with fear, at the little round mouth which quivered.

'Oh, sweet little Cousin,' he said, 'it is not so bad. I shall come back; I shall come back very soon.'

'You are going away then, Thomas?'

The world was suddenly dark; tears came to her eyes and brimmed over. He looked away, and sought refuge in hardening his voice.

'Come, Catherine, do not be so foolish. You surely did not imagine that my father's son could spend all his days tucked away here in the country!'

'No . . . no.'

'Well then! Dry your eyes. No handkerchief? How like you, Catherine!' He threw her his. 'You may keep that,' he said, 'and think of me when I am gone.'

She took the handkerchief as though already it were a sacred thing.

He went on, his voice shaking: 'And you must give me one of yours, Catherine, that I may keep it.'

She wiped her eyes.

He said tenderly: "It is only for a little while, Catherine.'

Now she was smiling.

'I should have known,' she said. 'Of course you will go away.'

'When I return we shall have very many pleasant days together, Catherine.'

'Yes, Thomas.' Being Catherine, she could think of the reunion rather than the parting, even now.

He slipped off his horse, and she immediately did likewise; he held out his hands, and she put hers into them.

'Catherine, do you ever think of when we are grown up . . . really grown up, not just pretending to be?'

'I do not know, Thomas. I think perhaps I may have.'

'When we are grown up, Catherine, we shall marry . . . both of us. Catherine, I may marry *you* when I am of age.'

'Thomas! Would you?'

'I might,' he said.

She was pretty, with the smile breaking through her tears.

'Yes,' he said, 'I think mayhap I will. And now, Catherine, you will not mind so much that I must go away, for you must know, we are both young in actual fact. Were we not, I would marry you now and take you with me.'

They were still holding hands, smiling at each other; he, flushed with pleasure at his beneficence in offering her such a glorious prospect as marriage with him; she, overwhelmed by the honour he did her.

He said: 'When people are affianced, Catherine, they kiss. I am going to kiss you now.'

He kissed her on either cheek and then her soft baby mouth. Catherine wished he would go on kissing her, but he did not, not over-much liking the operation and considering it a necessary but rather humiliating formality; besides, he feared that there might be those to witness this and do what he dreaded most that people would do, laugh at him.

'That,' he said, 'is settled. Let us ride.'

* * *

Catherine had been so long at Hollingbourne that she came to regard it as her home. Thomas came home occasionally, and there was nothing he liked better than to talk of the wild adventures he had had; and never had he known a better audience than his young cousin. She was so credulous, so ready to admire. They both looked forward to these re-unions, and although they spoke not of their marriage which they had long ago in the paddock decided should one day take place, they neither of them forgot nor wished to repudiate the promises. Thomas was not the type of boy to think over-much of girls except when they could be fitted into an adventure where, by their very helplessness and physical inferiority, they could help to glorify the resourcefulness and strength of the male. Thomas was a normal, healthy boy whose thoughts had turned but fleetingly to sex; Catherine, though younger, was conscious of sex, and had been since she was a baby; she enjoyed Thomas's company most when he held her hand or lifted her over a brook or rescued her from some imaginary evil fate. When the game was a pretence of stealing jewels, and she must pretend to be a man, the adventure lost its complete joy for her. She remembered still the quick, shame-faced kisses he had given her in the paddock, and she would have loved to have made plans for their marriage, to kiss now and then. She dared not tell Thomas this, and little did he guess that she was all but a woman while he was yet a child.

So passed the pleasant days until that sad afternoon when a serving-maid came to her, as she sat in the wide window seat of the main nursery, to tell her that her uncle and aunt would have speech with her, and she was to go at once to her uncle's chamber.

As soon as Catherine reached that room she knew that something was amiss, for both her uncle and her aunt looked very grave.

'My dear niece,' said Sir John, who frequently spoke for both, 'come hither to me. I have news for you.'

Catherine went to him and stood before him, her knees trembling, while she prayed: 'Please, God, let Thomas be safe and well.'

'Now that your grandfather, Lord Thomas the Duke, is no more,' said Sir John in the solemn voice he used when speaking of the dead, 'your grandmother feels that she would like much to have you with her. You know your father has married again. . . .' His face stiffened. He was a righteous man; there was nothing soft in his nature; it seemed to him perfectly reasonable that, his sister's husband having married a new wife, his own responsibility for his sister's child should automatically cease.

'Go . . . from here . . . ?' stammered Catherine.

'To your grandmother in Norfolk.'

'Oh . . . but I . . . do not wish . . . Here, I have been . . . so happy. . . .'

Her aunt put an arm about her shoulders and kissed her cheek.

'You must understand, Catherine, your staying here is not in our hands. Your father has married again . . . he wishes that you should go to your grandmother.'

Catherine looked from one to the other, her eyes bright with tears which overflowed, for she could never control her emotion.

Her aunt and uncle waited for her to dry her eyes and listen to them.

Then Sir John said: 'You must prepare yourself for a long journey, so that you will be ready when your grandmother sends for you. Now you may go.'

Catherine stumbled from the room, thinking, When he

comes next time, I shall not be here! And how shall I ever see him . . . he in Kent and I in Norfolk?

In the nursery the news was received with great interest.

'Well may *you* cry!' she was told. 'Why, when you are at your grandmother's house you will feel very haughty towards us poor folk. I have heard from one who served the Duchess that she keeps great state both at Horsham and Lambeth. The next we shall hear of you is that you are going to court!'

'I do not care to go to court!' cried Catherine.

'Ah!' she was told. 'All you care for is your cousin Thomas!'

Then Catherine thought, is it so far from here to Norfolk? Not so far but that *he* could come to me. He will come; and then in a few years we shall be married. The time will pass quickly. . . .

She remembered her grandmother – plumpish, inclined to poke her with a stick, lazy Grandmother who sat about and laughed to herself and made remarks which set her wheezing and chuckling, such as 'You have pretty eyes, Catherine Howard. Keep them; they will serve you well!' Grandmother, with sly eyes and chins that wobbled, and an inside that gurgled since she took such delight in the table.

Catherine waited for the arrival of those who would take her to her grandmother, and with the passage of the days her fears diminished; she lived in a pleasant dream in which Thomas came to Horsham and spent his holidays there instead of at Hollingbourne; and Catherine, being the granddaughter of such a fine lady as the Dowager Duchess of Norfolk, wore beautiful clothes and jewels in her hair. Thomas said: 'You are more beautiful in Norfolk than you were in Kent!' And he kissed her, and Catherine kissed him; there was much kissing and embracing at Horsham. 'Let us elope,' said Thomas. Thus pleasantly passed the last days at Hollingbourne, and when the time came for her departure to Norfolk, she did not greatly mind, for she had planned such a happy future for herself and Thomas.

*   *   *

The house at Horsham was indeed grand. It was built round the great hall; it had its ballroom, its many bedrooms, numerous small chambers and unpredictable corridors; from its mullioned windows there were views of gracious parklands; there was comfort in its padded window seats; there was luxury in its elegant furniture. One could lose oneself with ease in this house, and so many servants and attendants waited on her grandmother that in the first weeks she spent there, Catherine was constantly meeting strangers.

On her arrival she was taken to her grandmother whom she found in her bed, not yet having risen though the afternoon was advancing.

'Ah!' said the Dowager Duchess. 'So here you are, little Catherine Howard! Let me look at you. Have you fulfilled the promise of your babyhood that you would be a very pretty girl?'

Catherine must climb onto the bed and kiss one of the plump hands, and be inspected.

'Marry!' said the Duchess. 'You are a big girl for your years! Well, well, there is time yet before we must find a husband for you.' Catherine would have told her of her contract with Thomas Culpepper, but the Duchess was not listening. 'How neat you look! That is my Lady Culpepper, I'll swear. Catherine Howard and such neatness appear to me as though they do not belong one to the other. Give me a kiss, child, and you must go away. Jenny!' she called, and a maid appeared suddenly from a closet. 'Call Mistress Isabel to me. I would talk with her of my granddaughter.' She turned to Catherine. 'Now, Granddaughter, tell me, what did you learn at Hollingbourne?'

'I learned to play the virginals and to sing.'

'Ah! That is well. We must look to your education. I will not have you forget that, though your father is a poor man, you are a Howard. Ah! Here is Mistress Isabel.'

A tall, pale young woman came into the room. She had small eyes and a thin mouth; her eyes darted at once to Catherine Howard, sitting on the bed.

'This is my little granddaughter, Isabel. You knew of her coming.'

'Your Grace mentioned it to me.'

'Well, the child has arrived. Take her, Isabel . . . and see that she lacks nothing.'

Isabel curtseyed, and the Duchess gave Catherine a little push to indicate that she was to get off the bed and follow Isabel. Together they left the Duchess's apartment.

Isabel led the way upstairs and along corridors, occasionally turning, as though to make sure that Catherine followed. Catherine began to feel afraid, for this old house was full of shadows, and in unexpected places were doors and sudden passages; all her old fear of ghosts came back to her, and her longing for Thomas brought tears to her eyes. What if they should put her in a bedroom by herself, remote from other rooms! If Hollingbourne might have contained a ghost, this house assuredly would! Isabel, looking over her shoulder at her, alone stopped her from bursting into tears, for there was something about Isabel which frightened Catherine more than she cared to admit to herself.

Isabel had thrown open a door, and they were in a large room which contained many beds; this dormitory was richly furnished, as was every room in this house, but it was an untidy room; across its chairs and beds were flung various garments; shoes and hose littered the floor. There was perfume in the air.

'This room,' said Isabel, 'is where Her Grace's ladies sleep; she has told me that temporarily you are to share it with us.'

Relief flooded Catherine's heart; there was now nothing to fear; her pale face became animated, flushed with pleasure.

'That pleases you?' asked Isabel.

Catherine said it did, adding: 'I like not solitude.'

Another girl had come into the room, big bosomed, wide hipped and saucy of eye.

'Isabel . . .'

Isabel held up a warning hand.

'Her Grace's granddaughter has arrived.'

'Oh . . . the little girl?'

The girl came forward, saw Catherine, and bowed.

'Her Grace has said,' began Isabel, 'that she is to share our room.'

The girl sat down upon a bed, drew her skirts up to her knees, and lifted her eyes to the ornate ceiling.

'It delights her, does it not . . . Catherine?'

'Yes,' said Catherine.

The girl, whose name it seemed was Nan, threw a troubled glance at Isabel, which Catherine intercepted but did not understand.

Nan said: 'You are very pretty, Catherine.'

Catherine smiled.

'But very young,' said Isabel.

'Marry!' said Nan, crossing shapely legs and looking down at them in an excess of admiration. 'We must all be young at some time, must we not?'

Catherine smiled again, liking Nan's friendly ways better than the quiet ones of Isabel.

'And you will soon grow up,' said Nan.

'I hope to,' said Catherine.

'Indeed you do!' Nan giggled, and rose from the bed. From a cabinet she took a box of sweetmeats, ate one herself and gave one to Isabel and one to Catherine.

Isabel examined Catherine's clothes, lifting her skirts and feeling the material between thumb and finger.

'She has lately come from her uncle, Sir John Culpepper of Hollingbourne in Kent.'

'Did they keep grand style in Kent?' asked Nan, munching.

'Not such as in this house.'

'Then you are right glad to be here where you will find life amusing?'

'Life was very good at Hollingbourne.'

'Isabel,' laughed Nan, 'the child looks full of knowledge. . . . I believe you had a lover there, Catherine Howard!'

Catherine blushed scarlet.

'She did! She did! I swear she did!'

Isabel dropped Catherine's skirt, and exchanged a glance with Nan. Questions trembled on their lips, but these questions went unasked, for at that moment the door opened and a young man put his head round the door.

'Nan!' he said.

Nan waved her hand to dismiss him, but he ignored the signal, and came into the room.

Catherine considered this a peculiar state of affairs, for at Hollingbourne gentlemen did not enter the private apartments of ladies thus unceremoniously.

'A new arrival!' said the young man.

'Get you gone!' said Isabel. 'She is not for you. She is Catherine Howard, Her Grace's own granddaughter.'

The young man was handsomely dressed. He bowed low to Catherine, and would have taken her hand to kiss it, had not Isabel snatched her up and put her from him. Nan pouted on the bed, and the young man said: 'How is my fair Nan this day?' But Nan turned her face to the wall and would not speak to him; then the young man sat on the bed and put his arms round Nan, so that his left hand was on her right breast, and his right hand on her left breast; and he kissed her neck hard, so that there was a red mark there. Then she arose and slapped him lightly on the face, laughing the while, and she leaped across the bed, he after her and so gave chase, till Isabel shooed him from the room.

Catherine witnessed this scene with much astonishment, thinking Isabel to be very angry indeed, expecting her to castigate the laughing Nan; but she did nothing but smile, when, after the young man had left, Nan threw herself onto the bed laughing.

Nan sat up suddenly and, now that the youth was no longer there to claim her interest, once more bestowed it on Catherine Howard.

'You had a lover at Hollingbourne, Catherine Howard! Did you not see how her cheeks were on fire, Isabel, and still are, I'll warrant! I believe you to be a sly wench, Catherine Howard.

Isabel put her hands on Catherine's shoulders.

'Tell us about him, Catherine.'

Catherine said: 'It was my cousin, Thomas Culpepper.'

'He who is son of Sir John?'

Catherine nodded. 'We shall marry when that is possible.'

'Tell us of Thomas Culpepper, Catherine. Is he tall? Is he handsome?'

'He is both tall and handsome.'

'Tell me, did he kiss you well and heartily?'

'But once,' said Catherine. 'And that in the paddock when he talked of marriage.'

'And he kissed you,' said Nan. 'What else?'

'Hush!' said Isabel. 'What if she should tell Her Grace of the way you have talked!'

'Her Grace is too lazy to care what her ladies may say or do.'

'You will be dismissed the house one day,' said Isabel. 'Caution!'

'So your cousin kissed you, Catherine, and promised he would marry you. Dost not know that when a man talks of marriage it is the time to be wary?'

Catherine did not understand; she was aware of a certain fear, and yet a vivid interest in this unusual conversation.

'Enough of this,' said Isabel, and Nan went to her bed and lay down, reaching for the sweetmeats.

'Your bed,' said Isabel, 'shall be this one. Are you a good sleeper?'

'Yes,' said Catherine; for indeed the only occasions when she could not sleep were those when she was afraid of ghosts, and if she were to sleep in a room so full of beds, each of which would contain a young lady, she need have no fear of gruesome company, and she could say with truth that she would sleep well.

Isabel looked at her clothes, asked many questions about Lambeth and Hollingbourne; and while Catherine was answering her, several ladies came in, and some gave her sweetmeats, some kissed her. Catherine thought them all pretty young ladies; their clothes were bright, and they wore gay ribands in their hair; and many times during that afternoon and evening a young man would put his head round the door and be waved away with the words 'The Duchess's granddaughter, Catherine Howard, is come to share our apartment.' The young men bowed and were as kind to Catherine as the ladies were; and often one of the ladies would go outside and speak with them, and Catherine would hear muffled laughter. It was very gay and pleasant, and even Isabel, who at first had appeared to be a little stern, seemed to change and laugh with the rest.

Catherine had food and drink with the ladies and their kindness persisted through the evening. At length she went to bed, Isabel escorting her and drawing the curtains around her bed. She was very soon asleep for the excitement of the day had tired her.

She awoke startled and wondered where she was. She remembered and was immediately aware of whispering voices. She lay listening for some time, thinking the ladies must just be retiring, but the voices went on and Catherine, in astonishment, recognized some of them as belonging to men. She stood up and peeped through the curtains. There was no light in the room but sufficient moonlight to show her the most unexpected sight.

The room seemed to be full of young men and women; some sitting on the beds, some reclining on them, but all of them in affectionate poses. They were eating and drinking, and stroking and kissing each other. They smacked their lips over the dainties, and now and then one of the girls would make an exclamation of surprise and feigned indignation, or another would laugh softly; they spoke in whispers. The clouds, hurrying across the face of the moon which looked in at the windows, made the scene alternately light and darker; and the wind which was driving the clouds whined now and then, mingling its voice with those of the girls and young men.

Catherine watched, wide-eyed and sleepless for some time. She saw the youth who had aroused Nan's displeasure now kissing her bare shoulders, taking down the straps of her dress and burying his face in her bosom. Catherine watched and wondered until her eyes grew weary and her lids pressed down on them. She lay down and slept.

She awakened to find it was daylight and Isabel was drawing her bed curtains. The room was now occupied by girls only, who ran about naked and chattering, looking for their clothes which seemed to be scattered about the floor.

Isabel was looking down at Catherine slyly.

'I trust you slept well?' she asked.

Catherine said she had.

'But not through the entire night?'

Catherine could not meet Isabel's piercing eyes, for she was afraid that the girl should know she had looked on that scene, since something told her it was not meant that she should.

Isabel sat down heavily on the bed, and caught Catherine's shoulder.

'You were awake part of last night,' she said. 'Dost think I did not see thee, spying through the curtains, listening, taking all in?'

'I did not mean to spy,' said Catherine. 'I was awakened, and the moon showed me things.'

'What things, Catherine Howard?'

'Young gentlemen, sitting about the room with the ladies.'

'What else?'

Isabel looked wicked now. Catherine began to shiver, thinking perhaps it would have been better had she spent the night in a lonely chamber. For it was daylight now, and it was only at night that Catherine had great fear of ghosts.

'What else?' repeated Isabel. 'What else, Catherine Howard?'

'I saw that they did eat . . .'

The grip on Catherine's shoulder increased.

'What else?'

'Well . . . I know not what else, but that they did kiss and seem affectionate.'

'What shall you *do*, Catherine Howard?'

'What shall I do? But I know not what you mean, Mistress Isabel. What would you desire me to do?'

'Shall you then tell aught of what you have seen . . . to Her Grace, your grandmother?'

Catherine's teeth chattered, for what they did must surely be wrong since it was done at her grandmother's displeasure.

Isabel released Catherine's shoulder and called to the others. There was silence while she spoke.

'Catherine Howard,' she said spitefully, 'while feigning

sleep last night, was wide awake, watching what was done in this chamber. She will go to Her Grace the Duchess and tell her of our little entertainment.'

There was a crowd of girls round the bed, who looked down on Catherine, while fear and anger were displayed in every face.

'There was naught I did that was wrong,' said one girl, almost in tears.

'Be silent!' commanded Isabel. 'Should what happens here of nights get to Her Grace's ears, you will all be sent home in dire disgrace.'

Nan knelt down by the bed, her pretty face pleading. 'Thou dost not look like a teller of tales.'

'Indeed I am not!' cried Catherine. 'I but awakened, and being awake what could I do but see . . .'

'She will, I am sure, hold her counsel. Wilt thou not, little Catherine?' whispered Nan.

'If she does not,' said Isabel, 'it will be the worse for her. What if we should tell Her Grace of what you did, Catherine Howard, in the paddock with your cousin, Thomas Culpepper!'

'What . . . I . . . did!' gasped Catherine. 'But I did nothing wrong. Thomas would not. He is noble . . . he would do no wrong.'

'He kissed her and he promised her marriage,' said Isabel.

All the ladies put their mouths into round O's, and looked terribly shocked.

'She calls that naught! The little wanton!'

Catherine thought: Did we sin then? Was that why Thomas was ashamed and never kissed me again?

Isabel jerked off the clothes, so that she lay naked before them; she stooped and slapped Catherine's thigh.

'Thou darest not talk!' said Nan, laughing. 'Why 'twould go harder with thee than with us. A Howard! Her Grace's own granddaughter! Doubtless he would be hanged, drawn and quartered for what he did to you!'

'Oh, no!' cried Catherine, sitting up. 'We did no wrong.'

The girls were all laughing and chattering like magpies.

Isabel put her face close to Catherine's: 'You have heard!

Say nothing of what you have seen or may see in this chamber, and your lover will be safe.'

Nan said: ' 'Tis simple, darling. Say naught of our sins, and we say naught of thine!'

Catherine was weeping with relief.

'I swear I shall say nothing.'

'Then that is well,' said Isabel.

Nan brought a sweetmeat to her, and popped it into her mouth.

'There! Is not that good? They were given to me last night by a very charming gentleman. Mayhap one day some fine gentleman will bring sweetmeats to you, Catherine Howard!'

Nan put her arms about the little girl, and gave her two hearty kisses, and Catherine, munching, wondered why she had been so frightened. There was nothing to fear; all that was necessary was to say nothing.

* * *

The days passed as speedily as they had at Hollingbourne, and a good deal more excitingly. There were no lessons at Horsham. There was nothing to do during the long, lazy days but enjoy them. Catherine would carry notes from ladies to gentlemen; she was popular with them all, but especially with the young gentlemen. Once one said to her: 'I have awaited this, and 'tis double sweet to me when brought by pretty Catherine!' They gave her sweetmeats too and other dainties. She played a little, played the flute and the virginals; she sang; they liked well to hear her sing, for her voice was indeed pretty. Occasionally the old Duchess would send for her to have a talk with her, and would murmur: 'What a little tomboy you are, Catherine Howard! I declare you are an untidy chit; I would you had the grace of your cousin, Anne Boleyn. . . . Though much good her grace did her!'

Catherine loved to hear of her cousin, for she remembered seeing her now and then at Lambeth before she went to Hollingbourne. When she heard her name she thought of beauty and colour, and sparkling jewels and sweet smiles; she hoped that one day she would meet her cousin again. The Duchess often talked of her, and Catherine knew by the softening of her voice that she liked her well, even though, when she spoke of her disgrace and banishment from court, her eyes would glint slyly as though she enjoyed contemplating her granddaughter's downfall.

'A Boleyn not good enough for a Percy, eh! Marry, and there's something in that! But Anne is part Howard, and a Howard is a match for a Percy at any hour of the day or night! And I would be the first to tell Northumberland so, were I to come face to face with him. As for the young man, a plague on him! They tell me his Lady Mary hates him and he hates her; so much good that marriage did to either of them! Aye! I'll warrant he does not find it so easy to forget my granddaughter. Ah, Catherine Howard, there was a girl. I vow I never saw such beauty . . . such grace. And what did it do for her? There she goes . . . To France! And what has become of the Ormond marriage? She will be growing on into her teens now . . . I hope she will come back soon. Catherine Howard, Catherine Howard, your hair is in need of attention. And your dress, my child! I tell you, you will never have the grace of Anne Boleyn.'

It was not possible to tell the Duchess that one could not hope to have the grace of one's cousin who had been educated most carefully and had learned the ways of life at the French court; who had been plenteously supplied with the clothes she might need in order that Sir Thomas Boleyn's daughter might do her father credit in whatever circles she moved. One could not explain that the brilliant Anne had a natural gift for choosing the most becoming clothes, and knew how to wear them. The Duchess should have known these things.

But she rocked in her chair and dozed, and was hardly aware of Catherine's standing there before her. 'Marry! And the dangers that girl was exposed to! The French court! There were adventures for her, I'll warrant, but she keeps her secrets well. Ah! How fortunate it is, Catherine, that I have taken you under *my* wing!'

And while the Duchess snored in her bedroom, her ladies

held many midnight feasts in their apartments. Catherine was one of them now, they assured themselves. Catherine could be trusted. It was no matter whether she slept or not; she was little but a baby and there were those times when she would fall asleep suddenly. She was popular; they would throw sweetmeats onto her bed. Sometimes she was kissed and fondled.

'Is she not a pretty little girl!'

'She is indeed, and you will keep your eyes off her, young sir, or I shall be most dismayed.'

Laughter, slapping, teasing. . . . It was fun, they said; and with them Catherine said: 'It is fun!'

Sometimes they lay on the tops of the beds with their arms about each other; sometimes they lay under the clothes, with the curtains drawn.

Catherine was accustomed to this strange behaviour by now, and hardly noticed it. They were all very kind to her, even Isabel. She was happier with them than she was when attending her grandmother, sitting at her feet or rubbing her back where it itched. Sometimes she must massage the old lady's legs, for she had strange pains in them and massage helped to soothe the pain. The old lady would wheeze and rattle, and say something must be done about Catherine's education, since her granddaughter, a Howard, could not be allowed to run wild all the day through. The Duchess would talk of members of her family; her stepsons and her numerous stepdaughters who had married wealthy knights because the Howard fortunes needed bolstering up. 'So Howards married with Wyatts and Bryans and Boleyns,' mused the Duchess. 'And mark you, Catherine Howard, the children of these marriages are goodly and wise. Tom Wyatt is a lovely boy . . .' The Duchess smiled kindly, having a special liking for lovely boys. 'And so is George Boleyn . . . and Mary and Anne are pleasant creatures. . . .'

'Ah!' said the Duchess one day. 'I hear your cousin, Anne, is back in England and at court.'

'I should like well to see her,' said Catherine.

'Rub harder, child! There! Clumsy chit! You scratched me. Ah! Back at court, and a beauty more lovely than when she went away . . .' The Duchess wheezed, and was so overcome with laughter that Catherine feared she would choke. 'They say the King is deeply affected by her,' said the Duchess happily. 'They say too that she is leading him a merry dance!'

*　　*　　*

When the Duchess had said that the King was deeply affected by Anne Boleyn, she had spoken the truth. Anne had left the court of France and returned to that of England, and no sooner had she made her spectacular appearance than once more she caught the King's eye. The few years that had elapsed had made a great change in Anne; she was not one whit less beautiful than she had been when Henry had seen her in the garden at Hever; indeed she was more so; she had developed a poise which before would have sat oddly on one so young. If she had been bright then, now she was brilliant; her beauty had matured and gained in maturity; the black eyes still sparkled and flashed; her tongue was more ready with its wit, she herself more accomplished. She had been engaged in helping Marguerite to fête François, so recently released from captivity, a François who had left his youth behind in a Madrid prison in which he had nearly died and would have done so but for his sister's loving haste across France and into Spain to nurse him. But François had made his peace treaty with his old enemy, Charles V, although he did repudiate it immediately, and it was the loving delight of his sister and his mother to compensate him for the months of hardship. Anne Boleyn had been a useful addition to the court; she could sing and dance, write lyrics, poetry, music; could always be relied upon to entertain and amuse. But her father, on the Continent with an embassy, had occasion to return to England, and doubtless feeling that a girl of nineteen must not fritter away her years indefinitely, had brought her back to the court of her native land. So Anne had returned to find the entire family settled at the palace. George, now Viscount Rochford, was married, and his wife, who had been Jane Parker and granddaughter to Lord Morley and Monteagle, was still one of the Queen's ladies. Meeting George's wife had been one of the less pleasant surprises on Anne's return, since she saw that George was not very happy in this marriage with a wife who was frivolous and stupid and was not accepted into the brilliant set of poets and intellectuals – most of them cousins of the Boleyns – in which George naturally took a prominent place. This was depressing. Anne, still smarting from the Percy affair – though none might guess it – would have wished for her brother that married happiness which she herself had missed. Mary, strangely enough, seemed happy with William Carey; they had one boy – who, it was whispered, was the King's – and none would guess that their union was not everything that might be desired. Anne wondered then if she and George asked too much of life.

There was no sign of melancholy about Anne. She could not but feel a certain glee – though she reproached herself for this – when she heard that Percy and his Mary were the most wretched couple in the country. She blamed Percy for his weakness; it was whispered that the Lady Mary was a shrew, who never forgave him, being contracted to her, for daring to fall in love with Anne Boleyn and make a scandal of the affair. Very well, thought Anne, let Percy suffer as she had! How many times during the last years had she in her thoughts reproached him for his infidelity! Perhaps he realized now that the easy way is not always the best way. She held her head higher, calling her lost lover weak, wishing fervently that he had been more like Thomas Wyatt who had pursued her ever since her return to court, wondering if she were not a little in love – or ready to fall in love – with her cousin Thomas, surely the most handsome, the most reckless, the most passionate man about the court. There was no doubt as to his feelings for her; it was both in his eyes and in his verses; and he was reckless enough not to care who knew it.

There was one other who watched her as she went about the court; Anne knew this, though others might not, for though he was by no means a subtle man, he had managed so far to keep this passion, which he felt for one of his wife's ladies-in-waiting, very secret.

Anne did not care to think too much of this man. She did not care to feel those little eyes upon her. His manner was correct enough, yet now there were those who were beginning to notice something. She had seen people whispering together, smiling slyly. Now the King is done with the elder sister, is it to be the younger? What is it about these Boleyns? Thomas is advanced as rapidly as my lord Cardinal ever was; George has posts that should have gone to a grey-haired man; Mary . . . of course we understand how it was with Mary; and now, is it to be the same story with Anne?

No! Anne told herself fiercely. Never!

If Thomas Wyatt had not a wife already, she thought, how pleasant it would be to listen to his excellent verses, which were chiefly about herself. She could picture the great hall at Allington Castle decked out for the Christmas festivities, herself and Thomas taking chief parts in some entertainment they had written for the amusement of their friends. But that could not be.

Her position at court had become complicated. She was thinking of a conversation she had had with the King, when he, who doubtless had seen her walking in the palace grounds, had come down to her unattended and had said, his eyes burning in his heated face, that he would have speech with her.

He had asked her to walk with him to a little summer-house he knew of where they could be secret. She had felt limp with terror, had steeled herself, had realized full well that in the coming interview she would have need of all her wits; she must flatter him and refuse him; she must soothe him, pacify him, and pray that he might turn his desirous eyes upon someone more willing.

She had entered the summer-house, feeling the colour in her cheeks, but her fear made her hold her head the higher; her very determination helped to calm her. He had stood looking at her as he leaned against the doors, a mighty man, his padded clothes, glittering and colourful, adding to his great stature. He would have her accept a costly gift of jewels; he told her that he had favoured her from the moment he had seen her in her father's garden, that never had he set eyes on one who pleased him more; in truth he loved her. He spoke with confidence, for at that time he had believed it was but necessary to explain his feelings towards her to effect her most willing surrender. Thus it had been on other occasions; why should this be different?

She had knelt before him, and he would have raised her, saying lightly and gallantly: No, she must not kneel; it was he who should kneel to her, for by God, he was never more sure of his feelings towards any in his life before.

She had replied: 'I think, most noble and worthy King, that Your Majesty speaks these words in mirth to prove me, without intent of degrading your noble self. Therefore, to ease you of the labour of asking me any such question hereafter, I beseech Your Highness most earnestly to desist and take this my answer, which I speak from the depth of my soul, in good part. Most noble King! I will rather lose my life than my virtue, which will be the greatest and best part of the dowry I shall bring my husband.'

It was bold; it was clever; it was characteristic of Anne. She had known full well that something of this nature would happen, and she had therefore prepared herself with what she would say when it did. She was no Percy to be browbeaten, she was a subject and Henry was King, well she knew that; but this matter of love was not a matter for a king and subject – it was for a man and woman; and Anne was not one to forget her rights as a woman, tactful and cautious as the subject in her might feel it necessary to be.

The King was taken aback, but not seriously; she was so beautiful, kneeling before him, that he was ready to forgive her for putting off her surrender. She wanted to hold him off; very well, he was ever a hunter who liked a run before the kill. He bade her cease to kneel, and said, his eyes devouring her since already in his mind he was possessing her, that he would continue to hope.

But her head shot up at that, the colour flaming in her cheeks.

'I understand not, most mighty King, how you should retain such hope,' she said. 'Your wife I cannot be, both in respect of mine own unworthiness and also because you have a Queen already.' And then there came the most disturbing sentence of all: 'Your mistress I will not be!'

Henry left her; he paced his room. He had desired her deeply when she had been a girl of sixteen, but his conscience had got between him and desire; he had made no protest when she had wrenched open the cage door and flown away. Now here she was back again, more desirable, a lovely woman where there had been a delightful girl. This time, he had thought, she shall not escape. He believed he had but to say so and it would be so. He had stifled the warnings of his conscience and now he had to face the refusal of the woman. It could not be; in a long and amorous life it had never been so. He was the King; she the humblest of his Queen's ladies. No, no! This was coquetry; she wished to keep him waiting, that he might burn the fiercer. If he could believe that was all, how happy he would be!

For his desire for Anne Boleyn astonished him. Desire he knew well; how speedily it came, how quickly it could be gratified. One's passion flamed for one particular person; there was a sweet interlude when passion was slaked and still asked to be slaked; then . . . the end. It was the inevitable pattern. And here was one who said with a ring of determination in her voice: 'Your mistress I will not be!' He was angry with her; had she forgotten he was the King? She had spoken to him as though he were a gentleman of the court . . . any gentleman. Thus had she spoken to him in her father's garden at Hever. The King grew purple with fury against her; then he softened, for it was useless to rail against that which enslaved him; it was her pride, it was her dignity which would make the surrender more sweet.

The King saw himself in his mirror. A fine figure of a man . . . if the size of him was considered. The suit he was wearing had cost three thousand pounds, and that not counting all the jewels that adorned it. But she was not the one to say yes to a suit of clothes; it would be the man inside it. He would smile at himself; he could slap his thigh; he was sure enough of eventual success with her.

He too had changed since those days when he allowed his

conscience to come between him and this Anne Boleyn. The change was subtle, but definite enough. The conscience was still the dominating feature in his life. There it was, more than life size. The change was this: The conscience no longer ruled him; he ruled the conscience. He soothed it and placated it, and put his own construction on events before he let the conscience get at them. There was Mary Boleyn; he had done with Mary; he had decided that when Anne returned. He would cease to think of Mary. Oh, yes, yes, he knew there were those who might say there was an affinity between him and Anne, but in the course of many years of amorous adventures had this never happened before? Was there no man at court who had loved two sisters, perhaps unwittingly? Mayhap he himself had! For – and on this point Henry could be very stern – court morals being as they were, who could be sure who was closely related to whom? Suppose these sisters had had a different father! There! Was not the affinity reduced by one half? One could never know the secret of families. What if even the one mother did not give birth to the two daughters! One could never be sure; there had been strange stories of changeling children. This matter was not really worth wasting another moment's thought on. What if he were to eschew Anne on account of this edict, and make a match for her, only to discover then that she was not Mary's sister after all! Would it not be more sinful to take another man's wife? And this desire of his for this unusual girl could but be slaked one way, well he knew. Better to take her on chance that she might be Mary Boleyn's sister. He would forget such folly!

There was another matter too, about which his conscience perturbed him deeply and had done so for some time, in effect ever since he had heard that Katharine could bear no more children. Very deeply was he perturbed on this matter; so deeply that he had spoken of it to his most trusted friends. For all the years he had been married to Katharine there was but one daughter of the union. What could this mean? Why was it that Katharine's sons died one after the other? Why was it that only one of their offspring – and this a girl – had been allowed to live? There was some deep meaning in this, and Henry thought he had found it. There was assuredly some blight upon his union with Katharine, and what had he done, in the eyes of a righteous God, to deserve this? He knew not . . . except it be by marrying his brother's wife. Was it not written in the book of Leviticus that should a man marry his brother's wife their union should be childless? He had broken off all marital relations with Katharine when the doctors had told him she would never have any more children. Ah! Well he remembered that day; pacing up and down his room in a cold fury. No son for Henry Tudor! A daughter! And why? Why? Then his mind had worked fast and furiously on this matter of a divorce. Exciting possibility it had seemed. Divorces – forbidden by Holy Church on principle – could be obtained for political reasons from the Pope, who was ever ready to please those in high places. I must have an heir! Henry told his conscience. What would happen, should I die and not leave an heir? There is mine and Katharine's daughter, Mary; but a woman on the throne of England! No! I must have a male heir! Women are not made to rule great countries; posterity will reproach me, an I leave not an heir.

There in his mirror looked back the great man. He saw the huge head, the powerful, glittering shoulders; and *this* man could not produce a son for England! A short while ago he had had his son by Elizabeth Blount brought to him, and had created him Duke of Richmond, a title which he himself had carried in his youth; that he had done in order to discomfort Katharine. I could have a son, he implied. See! Here *is* my son. It is you who have failed! And all the tears she shed in secret, and all her prayers, availed her little. She had nothing to give him but a daughter, for – and when he thought of this, the purple veins stood out on Henry's forehead – she had lied. She had sworn that her marriage with Arthur had never been consummated; she had tricked him, deceived him; this pale, passionless Spanish woman had tricked him into marriage, had placed in jeopardy the Tudor dynasty. Henry was filled with self-righteous anger, for he wanted a divorce and he wanted it for the noblest of reasons . . . not for himself, but for the house of Tudor; not to establish his manhood and virility in the eyes of his people, not to banish an ageing, unattractive wife . . . not for these things, but because he, who had previously not hesitated to plunge his people into useless war, feared civil war for them; because he feared he lived in sin with one who had never been his wife, having already lived with his brother. This, his conscience – now so beautifully controlled – told Henry. And all these noble thoughts were tinged rose-colour by a beautiful girl who was obstinately haughty, whose cruel lips said : 'I will never be your mistress!' But it was not necessary for his conscience to dwell upon that matter as yet, for a king does not raise a humble lady-in-waiting to be his queen, however desirable she may be. No, no! No thought of that had entered his head . . . not seriously, of course. The girl was there, and it pleased him to think of her in his arms, for such reflections were but natural and manly; and how she was to be got into that position was of small consequence, being a purely personal matter, whereas this great question of divorce was surely an affair of state.

So was his mind active in these matters, and so did he view the reluctance of her whom he desired above all others with a kindly tolerance, like a good hunter contented to stalk awhile, and though the stalking might be arduous, that would be of little account when the great achievement would be his.

Thus was there some truth in the remarks of the Duchess of Norfolk when she had said to her granddaughter, Catherine Howard, that Anne Boleyn was leading the King a merry dance.

*   *   *

In their apartments at the palace Jane Boleyn was quarrelling with her husband. He sat there in the window seat, handsome enough to plague her, indifferent enough to infuriate her. He was writing on a scrap of paper, and he was smiling as he composed the lyrics that doubtless his clever sister would set to music, that they might be sung before the King.

'Be silent, Jane,' he said lightly, and it was his very lightness that maddened her, for well she knew that he did not care sufficiently for her even to lose his temper. He was tapping with his foot, smiling, well pleased with his work.

'What matters it,' she demanded bitterly, 'whether I speak or am silent? You do not heed which I do.'

'As ever,' said George, 'you speak without thought. Were that so, why should I beg you for silence?'

She shrugged her shoulders impatiently.

'Words! Words! You would always have them at your disposal. I hate you. I wish I had never married you!'

'Sentiments, my dear Jane, which it may interest you to know are reciprocated by your most unwilling husband.'

She went over to him, and sat on the window seat.

'George . . .' she began tearfully.

He sighed. 'Since your feelings towards me are so violent, my dear, would it not be wiser if you removed yourself from this seat, or better still from this room? Should you prefer it, of course, I will be the one to go. But you know full well that you followed me hither.'

As he spoke his voice became weary; the pen in his hand moved as though it were bidding him stop this stupid bickering and get on with what was of real moment to him. His foot began to tap.

Angrily she took the quill from him and threw it to the floor.

He sat very still, looking at it, not at her. If she could have roused him to anger, she would have been less angry with him; it was his indifference – it always had been – that galled her.

'I hate you!' she said again.

'Repetition detracts from, rather than adds to vehemence,' he said in his most lightsome tone. 'Venom is best expressed briefly; over-statement was ever suspect, dear Jane.'

'*Dear* Jane!' she panted. 'When have I ever been dear to you?'

'There you ask a question which gallantry might bid me answer one way, truth another.'

He was cruel, and he meant to be cruel; he knew how to hurt her most; he had discovered her to be jealous, possessive and vindictive, and having no love for her he cared nothing for the jealousy, while the possessiveness irked him, and her vindictiveness left him cold; he was careless of himself and reckless as to what harm might come to him.

Her parents had thought it advantageous to link their daughter's fortunes with those of the Boleyns, which were rising rapidly under the warming rays of royal favour; so she had married, and once married had fallen victim to the Boleyn charm, to that ease of manner, to that dignity, to that cleverness. But what hope had Jane of gaining George's love? What did she know of the things for which he cared so deeply? He thought her stupid, colourless, illiterate. Why, she wondered, could he not be content to make merry, to laugh at the frivolous matters which pleased her; why could he not enjoy a happy married life with her, have children? But he did not want her, and foolishly she thought that by quarrelling, by forcing him to notice her, she might attract him; instead of which she alienated him, wearied him, bored him. They were strange people, thought Jane, these two younger Boleyns; amazingly alike, both possessing in a large degree the power of attracting not only those who were of the same genre as themselves, but those who were completely opposite. Jane believed them both to be cold people; she hated Anne; indeed she had never been so wretched in her life until the return of her sister-in-law; she hated her, not because Anne had been unpleasant to her, for indeed Jane must admit that Anne had in the first instance made efforts to be most sisterly; but she hated Anne because of the influence she had over her brother, because he could give her who was merely his young sister much affection and admiration, while for Jane, his wife who adored him, he had nothing but contempt.

So now she tried to goad him, longed for him to take her by the shoulders and shake her, that he might lay hands on her if only in anger. Perhaps he knew this, for he was diabolically clever and understood most uncomfortably the workings of minds less clever than his own. Therefore he sat, arms folded, looking at the pen stuck in the polished floor, bored by Jane, weary of the many scenes she created, and heartlessly careless of her feelings.

'George. . . .'

He raised weary eyebrows in acknowledgment.

'I . . . I am so unhappy!'

He said, with the faintest hint of softness in his voice: 'I am sorry for that.'

She moved closer; he remained impassive.

'George, what are you writing?'

'Just an airy trifle,' he said.

'Are you very annoyed that I interrupted?'

'I am not annoyed,' he replied.

'That pleases me, George. I do not mean to interrupt. Shall I get your pen?'

He laughed and, getting up, fetched it himself with a smile at her. Any sign of quiet reason on her part always pleased him; she struggled with her tears, trying to keep the momentary approval she had won.

'I *am* sorry, George.'

'It is of no matter,' he said. 'I'll warrant also that I should be the one to be sorry.'

'No, George, it is I who am unreasonable. Tell me, is that for the King's masque?'

'It is,' he said, and turned to her, wanting to explain what he, with Wyatt, Surrey and Anne, was doing. But he knew that to be useless; she would pretend to be interested; she would try very hard to concentrate, then she would say something that was maddeningly stupid, and he would realize that she had not been considering what he was saying, and was merely trying to lure him to an amorous interlude. He had little amorous inclination towards her; he found her singularly unattractive and never more so than when she tried to attract him.

She came closer still, leaning her head forward to look at the paper. She began to read.

'It is very clever, George.'

'Nonsense!' said George. 'It is very bad and needs a deal of polishing.'

'Will it be sung?'

'Yes, Anne will write the music.'

Anne! The very mention of that name destroyed her good resolutions.

'Anne, of course!' she said with a sneer.

She saw his eyes flash; she wanted to control herself, but she had heard the tender inflection of his voice when he said his sister's name.

'Why not Anne?' he asked.

'Why not Anne?' she mimicked. 'I'll warrant the greatest musician in the kingdom would never write music such as Anne's . . . in your eyes!'

He did not answer that.

'The King's own music,' she said, 'you would doubtless consider inferior to Anne's!'

That made him laugh.

'Jane, you little fool, one would indeed be a poor musician if one was not more talented in that direction than His Majesty!'

'Such things as you say, George Boleyn, were enough to take a man's head off his shoulders.'

'Reported in the right quarter, doubtless. What do you propose, sweet wife? To report in the appropriate quarter?'

'I swear I will one day!'

He laughed again. 'That would not surprise me, Jane. You are a little fool, and I think out of your vindictive jealousy might conceivably send your husband to the scaffold.'

'And he would richly deserve it!'

'Doubtless! Doubtless! Do not all men who go to the scaffold deserve their fate? They have spoken their minds, expressed an opinion, or have been too nearly related to the King . . . all treasonable matters, my dear Jane.'

For this recklessness she loved him. How she would have liked to be as he was, to have snapped her fingers at life and enjoyed it as he did!

'You are a fool, George. It is well for you that you have a wife such as I!'

'Well indeed, Jane!'

'Mayhap,' she cried, 'you would rather I *looked* like your

sister Anne, *dressed* like your sister Anne, wrote as she wrote.... Then I might find approval in your sight!'

'You never could look like Anne.'

She flashed back: 'It is not given to all of us to be perfect!'

'Anne is far from that.'

'What! Sacrilege! In your eyes she is perfect, if ever any woman was in man's eyes.'

'My dear Jane, Anne is charming, rather because of her imperfections than because of her good qualities.'

'I'll warrant you rage against Fate that you could not marry your sister!'

'I never was engaged in such a foolish discussion in all my life.'

She began to cry.

'Jane,' he said, and put a hand on her shoulder. She threw herself against him, forcing the tears into her eyes, for they alone seemed to have the power to move him. And as they sat thus, there was the sound of footsteps in the corridor, and these footsteps were followed by a knock on the door.

George sat up, putting Jane from him.

'Enter!' he called.

They trooped in, laughing and noisy.

Handsome Thomas Wyatt was a little ahead of the others, singing a ballad. Jane disliked Thomas Wyatt; indeed she loathed them all. They were all of the same calibre, the most important set at court these days, favourites of the King every one of them, and all connected by the skein of kinship. Brilliant of course they were; the songsters of the court. One-eyed Francis Bryan, Thomas Wyatt, George Boleyn, all of them recently returned from France and Italy, and eager now to transform the somewhat heavy atmosphere of the English court into a more brilliant copy of other courts they had known. These gay young men were anxious to oust the duller element, the old set. No soldiers nor grim counsellors to the King these; they were the poets of their generation; they wished to entertain the King, to make him laugh, to give him pleasure. There was nothing the King asked more; and as this gay crowd circulated round none other than the lady who interested him so deeply, they were greatly favoured by His Majesty.

Jane's scowl deepened, for with these young men was Anne herself.

Anne threw a careless smile at Jane, and went to her brother.

'Let us see what thou hast done,' she said, and snatched the paper from him and began reading aloud; and then suddenly she stopped reading and set a tune to the words, singing them, while the others stood round her. Her feet tapped, as her brother's had done, and Wyatt, who was bold as well as handsome, sat down between her and George on the window seat, and his eyes stayed on Anne's face as though they could not tear themselves away.

Jane moved away from them, but that was of no account for they had all forgotten Jane's presence. She was outside the magic circle; she was not one of them. Angrily she watched them, but chiefly she watched Anne. Anne, with the hanging sleeves to hide the sixth nail; Anne, with a special ornament at her throat to hide what she considered to be an unbecoming mole on her neck. And now all the ladies at the court were wearing such ornaments. Jane put her hand to her throat and touched her own. Why, why was life made easy for Anne? Why did everyone applaud what she did? Why did George love her better than he loved his wife? Why was clever, brilliant and handsome Thomas Wyatt in love with her?

Jane went on asking herself these questions as she had done over and over again; bitter jealousy ate deeper and deeper into her heart.

*　　*　　*

Wyatt saw her sitting by the pond in the enclosed garden, a piece of embroidery in her hands. He went to her swiftly. He was deeply and passionately in love.

She lifted her face to smile at him, liking well his handsome face, his quick wit.

'Why, Thomas . . .'

'Why, Anne . . .'

He threw himself down beside her.

'Anne, do you not find it good to escape from the weary ceremony of the court now and then?'

'Indeed I do.'

Her eyes were wistful, catching his mood. They were both thinking of Hever and Allington in quiet Kent.

'I would I were there,' he said, for such was the accord between them that they sometimes read the other's thoughts.

'The gardens at Hever will be beautiful now.'

'And at Allington, Anne.'

'Yes,' she said, 'at Allington also.'

He moved closer.

'Anne, what if we were to leave the court . . . together? What if we were to go to Allington and stay there . . . ?'

'You to talk thus,' she said, 'and you married to a wife!'

'Ah!' His voice was melancholy. 'Anne, dost remember childhood days at Hever?'

'Well,' she answered. 'You locked me in the dungeons once, and I declare I all but died of fright. A cruel boy you were, Thomas.'

'I! Cruel . . . and to you! Never! I swear I was ever tender. Anne, why did we not know then that happiness for you and me lay in the one place?'

'I suppose, Thomas, that when we are young we are so unwise. It is experience that teaches us the great lessons of life. How sad that, in gaining experience, we so often lose what we would most cherish!'

He would have taken her hand, but she held him off.

'Methinks we should return,' she said.

'Now . . . when we are beginning to understand each other!'

'You, having married a wife . . .' she began.

'And therein being most unhappy,' he interrupted; but she would have none of his interruptions.

'You are in no position to speak in this wise, Thomas.'

'Anne, must we then say a long farewell to happiness?'

'If happiness would lie in marriage between us two, then we must.'

'You would condemn me to a life of melancholy.'

'You condemned yourself to that, not I!'

'I was very young.'

'You were, I mind well, a most precocious boy.'

He smiled back sadly over his youth. A boy of great precocity, they had sent him to Cambridge when he was twelve,
and at seventeen had married him to Elizabeth Brooke, who
was considered a good match for him, being daughter of
Lord Cobham.

'Why,' he said, 'do our parents, thinking to do well for us,
marry us to their choice which may well not be our own?
Why is the right sort of marriage so often the unhappy one?'

Anne said: 'You are spineless, all of you!' And her eyes
flashed as her thoughts went to Percy. Percy she had loved
and lost, for Percy was but a leaf wafted by the winds. The
wicked Cardinal whom she hated now as she had ever done,
had said, 'It shall not be!' And meekly Percy had acquiesced.
Now he would complain that life had denied him happiness,
forgetting he had not made any great effort to attain it. And
Wyatt, whom she could so easily love, complained in much
the same manner. They obeyed their parents; they married,
not where they listed, but entered into any match that was
found for them; then they bitterly complained!

'I would never be forced!' she said. 'I would choose my
way, and, God help me, whatever I might encounter I would
not complain.'

'Ah! Why did I not know then that my happiness was
with Anne Boleyn!'

She softened. 'But how should you know it . . . and you but
seventeen, and I even less?'

'And,' he said, 'most willing to engage yourself to Percy!'

'That!' She flushed, remembering afresh the insults of the
Cardinal. 'That . . . Ah! That failed just as your marriage
has failed, Thomas, though differently. Perchance I am glad
it failed, for I never could abide a chicken-livered man!'

Now he was suddenly gay, throwing aside his melancholy;
he would read to her some verses he had written, for they
were of her and for her, and it was meet that she should hear
them first.

So she closed her eyes and listened and thrilled to his

poetry, and was sad thinking of how she might have loved him. And there in the pond garden it occurred to her that life had shown her little kindness in her love for men. Percy she had lost after a brief glimpse into a happy future they were to have shared; Wyatt she had lost before ever she could hope to have him.

What did the future hold for her? she wondered. Was she going on in this melancholy way, loving but living alone? It was unsatisfactory.

Thomas finished reading and put the poem into his pocket, his face flushed with appreciation for his work. He has his poetry, she mused, and what have I? Yes, the rest of us write a little; it is to us a pleasant recreation, it means not to us what it does to Wyatt. He has that, and it is much. But what have I?

Wyatt leaned forward; he said earnestly: 'I shall remember this day for ever, for in it you all but said you loved me!'

'There are times,' she said, 'when I fear that love is not for me.'

'Ah, Anne! You are gloomy today. Whom should love be for, if not for those who are most worthy to receive it! Be of good cheer, Anne! Life is not all sadness. Who knows but that one day you and I may be together!'

She shook her head. 'I have a melancholy feeling, Thomas.'

'Bah! You and melancholy mate not well together.' He leaped to his feet and held out his hands to her; she put hers in his, and he helped her to rise. He refused to release her hands; his lips were close to hers. She felt herself drawn towards him, but it seemed to her that her sister was between them . . . Mary, lightsome, wanton, laughing, leering. She drew away coldly. He released her hands at once, and they fell to her side; but his had touched a jewelled tablet she wore and which hung from her pocket on a golden chain. He took it and held it up, laughing. 'A memento, Anne, of this afternoon when you all but said you loved me!'

'Give it back!' she demanded.

'Not I! I shall keep it for ever, and when I feel most melancholy I shall take it out and look at it, and remember that on the afternoon I stole it you all but said you loved me.'

'This is foolishness,' she said. 'I do not wish to lose that tablet.'

'Alas then, Anne! For lost it you have. It is a pleasing trinket – it fills me with hope. When I feel most sad I shall look at it, for then I shall tell myself I have something to live for.'

'Thomas, I beg of you . . .'

She would have snatched it, but he had stepped backwards and now was laughing.

'Never will I give it up, Anne. You would have to steal it back.'

She moved towards him. He ran, she after him; and running across the enclosed pond garden, trying to retrieve that which he had stolen was poignantly reminiscent of happy childhood days at Allington and Hever.

*   *   *

The Cardinal rode through the crowds, passing ceremoniously over London Bridge and out of the capital on his way to France, whither he had been bidden to go by the King. Great numbers of his attendants went before him and followed after him; there were gentlemen in black velvet with gold chains about their necks, and with them their servants in their tawny livery. The Cardinal himself rode on a mule whose trappings were of crimson velvet, and his stirrups were of copper and gold. Before him were borne his two crosses of silver, two pillars of silver, the Great Seal of England, his Cardinal's hat.

The people regarded him sullenly, for it was now whispered, even beyond the court, of that which had come to be known as the King's Secret Matter; and the people blamed the Cardinal, whispering that he had put these ideas into the King's head. Whither went he now, but to France? Mayhap he would find a new wife to replace the King's lawful one, their own beloved Queen Katharine. They found new loyalty towards their quiet Queen, for they pictured her as a poor, wronged woman, and the London crowd was a sentimental crowd ever ready to support the wronged.

In the crowd was whispered the little ditty which malicious Skelton had written, and which the public had taken up, liking its simple implication, liking its cutting allusions to a Cardinal who kept state like a king.

> *'Why come ye not to court*
> *To which court?*
> *To the King's court*
> *Or to Hampton Court!'*

He was well hated, as only the successful man can be hated by the unsuccessful. That he had risen from humble circumstances made the hatred stronger. *'We* are as good as this man!' 'With his luck, there might *I* have gone!' So whispered the people, and the Cardinal knew of their whisperings and was grieved; for indeed many things grieved this man as he passed through London on his way to Sir Richard Wiltshire's house in Dartford wherein he would spend the first night of his journey to the coast.

The Cardinal was brooding on the secret matter of the King's. It was for him to smooth the way for his master, to get him what he desired at the earliest possible moment; and he who had piloted his state ship past many dangerous rocks was now dismayed. Well he could agree with His Majesty that the marriages of kings and queens depend for their success on the male issue, and what had his King and Queen to show for years of marriage but one daughter! The Cardinal's true religion was statecraft; thus most frequently he chose to forget that as Cardinal he owed allegiance to the Church. When he had first been aware of the King's passion for Mistress Anne Boleyn, many fêtes had he given at his great houses, that the King and this lady might meet. Adultery was a sin in the eyes of Holy Church; not so in the liberal mind of Thomas Wolsey. The adultery of the King was as necessary as the jousts and tourneys he himself arranged for His Majesty's diversion. And though he was ever ready to give the King opportunities for meeting this lady, he gave but slight thought to the amorous adventures of His Majesty. This affair seemed to him but one of many; to absorb, to offer satiety; that was inevitable. And then . . . the next. So when this idea of divorce had been passed to him by the King, glorious possibilities of advancing England's interests through an advantageous marriage began to take hold of the Cardinal's mind.

Should England decide to ally herself with France against the Emperor Charles, what better foundation for such an alliance could there be than marriage! Already he had put out feelers for Francis's widowed sister, Marguerite of Alençon, but her brother, uncertain of Henry who still had an undivorced wife – and she none other than the aunt of the Emperor Charles himself – had dallied over negotiations, and married his sister to the King of Navarre. There was, however, Renee of France, sister to the late Queen Claude, and Wolsey's heart glowed at the prospect of such a marriage. Had not Claude borne Francis many children? Why, therefore, should Renee not bear Henry many sons? And to make the bargain complete, why not contract the King's daughter Mary to Francis's son, the Duke of Orleans? Of these matters had Wolsey spoken to the King, and craftily the King appeared to consider them, and whilst considering them he was thinking of none but Anne Boleyn, so did he yearn towards her; and so had her reluctance inflamed his passion that already he was toying with the idea of throwing away Wolsey's plans for a marriage which would be good for England; he was planning to defy his subjects' disapproval, to throw tradition to the wind, to satisfy his desires only and marry Anne Boleyn. He knew his Chancellor; wily, crafty, diplomatic; let Wolsey consider this divorce to be a state affair, and all his genius for statecraft would go into bringing it about; let him think it was but to satisfy his master's overwhelming desire for a humble gentlewoman of his court – who persistently and obstinately refused to become his mistress – and could Wolsey's genius then be counted on to work as well? The King thought not; so he listened to Wolsey's plans with feigned interest and approval, but unknown to the Cardinal, he despatched his own secretary as messenger to the Pope, for he wished to appease his conscience regarding a certain matter which worried him a little. This was his love affair with Mary Boleyn, which he feared must create an affinity between himself and Anne, though he had determined it should be of small consequence should his secretary fail to obtain the Pope's consent to remove the impediment.

Riding on to Dartford, the Cardinal was busily thinking. There was within him a deep apprehension, for he was aware that this matter of the divorce was to be a delicate one and one less suited to his genius, which loved best to involve itself in the intricacies of diplomacy and was perhaps less qualified to deal with petty domesticities. Of Anne Boleyn he thought little. To him the King's affair with this foolish girl was a matter quite separate from the divorce, and unworthy of much thought. It appeared to him that Anne was a light o' love, a younger version of her sister Mary, a comely creature much prone to giving herself airs. He smiled on her, for, while not attaching over-much importance to the King's favourites whose influence had ever been transient, it was well not to anger them. Vaguely he remembered some affair with Percy; the Cardinal smiled faintly at that. Could it be then that the King had remained faithful so long?

He fixed his eyes on his Cardinal's hat being borne before him, and that symbol of his power, the Great Seal of England; and his mind was busy and much disturbed, recent events having complicated the matter of divorce. He thought of the three men of consequence in Europe – Henry, Charles and Francis. Francis – even enfeebled as he was just now – had the enviable rôle of looker-on, sly and secret, waiting to see advantage and leap on it; Henry and Charles must take more active parts in the drama, for Henry's wife was Charles's aunt, and it was unlikely that Charles would stand calmly by to see Henry humiliate Spain through such a near relation. Between these two the Pope, a vacillating man, was most sorely perplexed; he dared not offend Henry; he dared not offend Charles. He had granted a divorce to Henry's sister Margaret on the flimsiest of grounds, but that had proved simple; there was no mighty potentate to be offended by such a divorce. Henry, ranting, fuming, urgently wanting what, it seemed to him, others conspired to keep from him, was a dangerous man; and to whom should he look to gratify his whims but Wolsey? And on whom would he vent his wrath, were his desires frustrated?

This sorry situation had been vastly aggravated by a recent event in Europe; the most unexpected, horrible and sacriligious event the Cardinal could conceive, and the most disastrous to the divorce. This was the sack of Rome by the Duke of Bourbon's forces in the name of the Empire.

Over the last few years Wolsey had juggled dexterously in Europe; and now, riding on to Dartford, he must wonder whether out of his cunning had not grown this most difficult situation. For long Wolsey had known of the discord which existed between Francis and one of the most powerful nobles of France, the mighty Duke of Bourbon. This nobleman, to safeguard his life, had fled his country, and being a very proud and high-spirited gentleman was little inclined to rest in exile all his life; indeed for years before his flight he had been in treasonable communication with the Emperor Charles, France's hereditary enemy, and when he left his country he went to Charles with plans for making war on the French King.

Now it had occurred to Wolsey that if the Duke could be supplied secretly with money he could raise an army from his numerous supporters and thus be, as it were, a general under the King of England while none need know that the King of England had a hand in this war. Therefore would England be in secret alliance with Spain against France. Henry had felt the conception of such an idea to be sheer genius, for the weakening of France and the reconquering of that country had ever been a dream of his. A secret ambassador had been sent to Emperor Charles, and the King and Wolsey with their council laughed complacently at their own astuteness. Francis, however, discovered this and sent a secret messenger to make terms with England, with the result that Bourbon's small army – desperate and exhausted – awaited in vain the promised help from England. Wolsey had calculated without the daring of the Duke and the laxity of the French forces, without Francis's poor generalship which alternately hesitated and then was over-bold. At Pavia the French King's forces were beaten, and the King taken prisoner; and among his documents was found the secret treaty under the Great Seal of England. Thus was Francis a prisoner in the hands of the Emperor, and thus was English double-dealing exposed. Francis was to languish and come near to death in a Madrid prison; and Charles would not be over-eager to link himself with England again. So that the master-stroke which was to have put England in the enviable position of being on the winning side – whichever it was to be – had failed.

That had happened two years ago; yet it was still unpleasant to contemplate, as was Wolsey's failure, in spite of bribery, to be elected Pope. And now had come the greatest blow; Bourbon had turned his attentions to the city of Rome itself. True, this had cost the hasty Duke his life, but his men went on with his devilish scheme, and the city was ransacked, laid waste by fire and pillage, its priests desecrated, its virgins raped; and the sacred city was the scene of one of the most terrible massacres in history. But most shocking of all was the fact that the Pope, who was to grant Henry's divorce, was a prisoner at Castle Angell – prisoner of the Emperor Charles, the nephew of that lady who was to be most deeply wronged by the divorce.

Small wonder that the Cardinal's head ached, but even as it ached it buzzed with plans, for it had ever been this man's genius to turn every position in which he found himself to his own advantage; and now an idea had come to him that should make him more famous, make his master love him more. A short while ago it had seemed to him that a vast cloud was beginning to veil the sun of his glory, as yet so vapourish that the sun was but slightly obscured and blazed hotly through. He trusted in the sun's fierce rays to disperse that cloud; and so it should be. The Pope was a prisoner; why not set up a Deputy-Pope while he was thus imprisoned? And who more fitted for the office than Cardinal Wolsey? And would not such a deputy feel kindly disposed towards his master's plea for a divorce?

On rode the Cardinal, renewed and refreshed, until he came to Canterbury; and there he was the leader of a mighty procession that went into the Abbey; and, gorgeously attired, wearing his Cardinal's hat, he prayed for the captive Pope and wept for him, while his mind was busy with the plans for reigning in Clement's stead, granting the divorce, and marrying his master to a French princess.

And so passed the Cardinal on to France where he was received royally by the Regent, Louise of Savoy – who reigned during the absence of her son François – and by the King's gifted sister, Marguerite of Navarre. He assured them of his master's friendship with their country; he arranged the marriage of the King's daughter to the Duke of Orleans; and he hinted at the King's divorce and his marriage with Renee. He was entertained lavishly, well assured of French friendship.

But among the people of France the Cardinal was no more popular than he was in England; and although he came with offers of friendship, and though he brought English gold with him, the humble people of France did not trust him and made his journey through their land an uncomfortable one. He was robbed in many places where he rested, and one morning when he arose from his bed, he went to his window and there saw that on the leaning stone some mischievous person had engraved a cardinal's hat, and over it a gallows.

* * *

The whole court whispered of nothing else but the King's Secret Matter. Anne heard it; Katharine heard it. The Queen was afraid. Great pains she took with her toilet, hoping thereby to please the King, that there might yet be a hope of defying the doctors and producing an heir. Katharine was melancholy; she prayed more fervently; she fretted.

Anne heard it and was sorry for the Queen, for though she was as different from Anne as one woman could be from another, a gloomy woman, rarely heard to laugh, yet had Anne a deep respect for such piety as her mistress's while feeling herself unable to emulate it.

But Anne was busy with thoughts of her own affairs. Wyatt was plaguing her, making wild and impossible suggestions; and she feared she thought too much and too often of Wyatt. There came to her little scraps of paper with his handwriting, and in the poems inscribed on these he expressed his passion for her, the unhappiness of his marriage, the hope he might have, would she but give it, of the future. There had been those who had said that Anne was half French; in character this was so. She was frivolous, sentimental, excessively fond of admiration; but mingling with these attributes was something essentially practical. Had Wyatt been unmarried, ready would she have been to listen to him; and now, admitting this to herself – at the same time giving him no hope that his plans would ever reach fruition – she found it impossible to refuse his attentions entirely. She looked for him; she was ever ready to dally with him. With her cousin, Surrey, and her brother to ensure the proprieties, she was often to be found with Wyatt. They were the gayest and most brilliant quartet at the court; their cousinship was a bond between them. Life was pleasant for Anne with such friends as these, and she was enjoying it as a butterfly flutters in the sunshine even when the first cool of evening is setting in.

Preparing herself for the banquet which was to be given at the palace of Greenwich in honour of the departing French ambassadors, Anne thought of Wyatt. This banquet was to be the most gorgeous of its kind as a gesture of friendship towards the new allies. At Hampton these gentlemen had been entertained most lavishly by my lord Cardinal, who had recently returned from France, and so magnificent a feast had the Cardinal prepared for them that the King, jealous that one of his subjects could provide such a feast fit only for a king's palace, would have Wolsey's hospitality paled to insignificance by his own.

George, Anne, Surrey, Bryan and Wyatt had organized a most lavish carnival for the entertainment of these French gentlemen. They were delighted with their work, sure of the King's pleasure. Such events were ever a delight to Anne; she revelled in them, for she knew that, with her own special gifts she excelled every other woman present, and this was intoxicating to Anne, dispersing that melancholy which she had experienced periodically since she had lost Percy and which was returning more frequently, perhaps on account of Wyatt.

Anne's dress was of scarlet and cloth of gold; there were diamonds at her throat and on her vest. She discarded her head-dress, deciding it made her look too much like the others; she would wear her beautiful hair flowing and informal.

She was, as she had grown accustomed to be, the shining light of the court. Men's eyes turned to watch her; there was Henry Norris, the groom of the stole, Thomas Wyatt, smouldering and passionate, the King, his eyes glittering. To Norris she was indifferent; of Thomas Wyatt she was deeply aware; the King she feared a little; but admiration, no matter whence it came, was sweet. George smiled at her with approval; Jane watched her with envy, but there was little to disturb in that, as all the women were envious; though perhaps with Jane the envy was tinged with hatred. But what did Anne care for her brother's foolish wife! Poor George! she thought. Better to be alone than linked with such a one. It could be good to be alone, to feel so many eyes upon her, watching, admiring, desiring; to feel that power over these watching men which their need of her must give her.

About her, at the banquet, the laughter was louder, the fun more riotous. The King would join the group which surrounded her, because he liked to be with gay young people; and all the time his eyes burned to contemplate her who was the centre of this laughing group.

The Queen sat, pale and almost ugly. She was a sad and frightened woman who could not help thinking continually of the suggested divorce; and this feast in itself was a humiliation to her, since she, a Spaniard, could find little joy in friendship with the French!

The King's distaste for his Queen was apparent; and those courtiers who were young and loved gaiety, scarcely paid her the homage due to her; they preferred to gather round Anne Boleyn, because to be there was to be near the King, joining in his fun and laughter.

Now, from his place at the head of the table, the King was

watching Wyatt. Wine had made the poet over-bold and he would not move from Anne's side though he was fully aware of Henry's watching eyes. There was hardly anyone at the table who was ignorant of the King's passion, and there was an atmosphere of tension in the hall, while everyone waited for the King to act.

Then the King spoke. There was a song he wished the company to hear. It was of his own composing. All assumed great eagerness to hear the song.

The musicians were called. With them came one of the finest singers in the court. There was a moment's complete silence, for no one dared move while the King's song was about to be sung. The King sat forward and his eyes never left Anne's face until the song was finished and the applause broke out.

> *'The eagle's force subdues each bird that flies:*
> *What metal can resist the flaming fire?*
> *Doth not the sun dazzle the clearest eyes*
> *And melt the ice, and make the frost retire?*
> *The hardest stones are pierced through with tools,*
> *The wisest are with princes made but fools.'*

There could be no doubt of the meaning of these arrogant words; there could be no doubt for whom they were written. Anne was freshly aware of the splendour of this palace of Greenwich, of the power it represented. The words kept ringing in her ears. He was telling her that he was weary of waiting; princes, such as he was, did not wait over-long.

This evening had lost its joy for her now; she was afraid. Wyatt had heard those words and realized their implication; George had heard them, and his eyes smiled into hers reassuringly. She wanted to run to her brother, she wanted to say: 'Let us go home; let us go back to being children. I am afraid of the glitter of this court. His eyes watch me now. Brother, help me! Take me home!' George knew her thoughts. She saw the reckless tilt of his head, and imitated it, feeling better, returning his smile. George was reassuring. 'Never fear, Anne!' he seemed to convey. 'We are the Boleyns!'

The company was applauding. Great poetry, was the verdict. Anne looked to him who, some said, was the literary genius of the court, Sir Thomas More; his *Utopia* she had just read with much pleasure. Sir Thomas was gazing at his large and rather ugly hands; he did not, she noticed, join in the effusive praise of the others. Was it the poetry or the sentiments, of which Sir Thomas did not approve?

The King's song was the prelude of the evening's entertainment, and Anne with her friends would have a big part in this. She thrust aside her fears; she played that night with a fervour she had rarely expressed before in any of these masquerades and plays which the quartet contrived. Into her fear of the King there crept an element which she could not have defined. What was it? The desire to make him admire her more? The company were over-courteous to her; even her old enemy, Wolsey, whom she had never ceased to hate, had a very friendly smile! The King's favourites were to be favoured by all, and when you had known yourself to be slighted on account of your humble birth ... when such a man as Wolsey had humiliated you ... yes, there was pleasure mingling with the fear of this night.

She was like a brilliant flame in her scarlet and gold. All eyes were upon her. For months to come they would talk of this night, on which Anne had been the moon to all these pale stars.

The evening was to end with a dance, and in this each gentleman would choose his partner. The King should take the Queen's hand and lead the dance, whilst the others fell in behind them. The Queen sat heavy in her chair, brooding and disconsolate. The King did not give her a look. There was a moment of breathless silence while he strode over to Anne Boleyn, and thus, choosing her, made public his preference.

His hand held hers firmly; his was warm and strong; she felt he would crush her fingers.

They danced, His eyes burned bright as the jewels on his clothes. Different this from the passion of Wyatt; fiercer, prouder, not sad but angry passion.

He would have speech with her away from these people, he

said. She replied that she feared the Queen's disapproval should she leave the ballroom.

He said: 'Do you not fear mine if you stay!'

'Sir,' she said, 'the Queen is my mistress. '

'And a hard one, eh?'

'A very kind one, Sir, and one whose displeasure I should not care to incur.'

He said angrily: 'Mistress, you try our patience sorely. Did you like our song?'

'It rhymed well,' she said, for now she sat with him she could see that his anger was not to be feared; he would not hurt her, since mingling with his passion there was a tenderness, and this tenderness which she observed, while it subdued her fear, filled her with a strange and exalted feeling.

'What mean you?' he cried, and he leaned closer, and though he would know himself to be observed he could not keep away.

'Your Majesty's rhyme I liked well; the sentiments expressed, not so well.'

'Enough of this folly!' he said. 'You know I love you well.'

'I beg your Majesty . . .'

'You may beg anything you wish an you say you love me.'

She repeated the old argument. 'Your Majesty, there can be no question of love between us . . . I would never be your mistress.'

'Anne,' he said earnestly, pleadingly, 'should you but give yourself to me body and soul there should be no other in my heart I swear. I would cast off all others that are in competition with you, for there is none that ever have delighted me as you do.'

She stood up, trembling; she could see he would refuse to go on taking no for an answer, and she was afraid.

She said: 'The Queen watches us, Your Majesty. I fear her anger.'

He arose, and they joined the dancers.

'Think not,' he said, 'that this matter can rest here.'

'I crave Your Majesty's indulgences. I see no way that it can end that will satisfy us both.'

'Tell me, he said, 'do you like me?'

'I hope I am a loving subject to Your Majesty...'

'I doubt not that you could be a very loving one, Anne, if you gave your mind to it; and I pray you will give your mind to it. For long have I loved you, and for long have I had little satisfaction in others for my thoughts of you.'

'I am unworthy of Your Majesty's regard.'

She thought: Words! These tiresome words! I am frightened. Oh, Percy, why did you leave me! Thomas, if you loved me when you were a child, why did you let them marry you to a wife!

The King towered over her, massive and glittering in his power. He breathed heavily; his face was scarlet; desire in his eyes, desire in his mouth.

She thought: Tomorrow I shall return secretly to Hever.

*　　*　　*

The Queen was sulky. She dismissed her maids and went into that chamber wherein was the huge royal bed which she still shared with Henry, but the sharing of which was a mere formality. She lay at one extreme edge; he at the other.

She said: 'It is useless to pretend you sleep.'

He said: 'I had no intention of pretending, Madam.'

'It would seem to be your greatest pleasure to humiliate me.'

'How so?' he said.

'It is invariably someone; tonight it was the girl Boleyn. It was your kingly duty to have chosen me.'

'Chosen you, Madam!' he snorted. 'That would I never have done; not now, nor years ago, an the choice were mine!'

She began to weep and to murmur prayers; she prayed for self-control for herself and for him. She prayed that he might soften towards her, and that she might defy the doctors who had prophesied that he would never get a male heir from her.

He lay listening to her but paying little attention, being much accustomed to her prayers, thinking of a girl's slender body in scarlet and gold, a girl with flowing hair and a clever, pointed face, and the loveliest dark eyes in the court. Anne, he thought, you witch! I vow you hold off to provoke me.... Pleasant thoughts. She was holding off to plague him. But enough, girl. How many years since I saw you in your father's garden, and wanted you then! What do you want, girl? Ask for it; you shall have it, but love me, love me, for indeed I love you truly.

The Queen had stopped praying.

'They give themselves such airs, these women you elevate with your desires.'

'Come,' he said, gratified, for did not she give herself airs, and was it then because of his preference for her? 'It is natural, is it not, that those noticed by the King should give themselves airs?'

'There are so many,' she said faintly.

Ah! he thought, there would be but one, Anne, and you that one!

The Queen repeated: 'I would fain Your Majesty controlled himself.'

Oh, her incessant chatter wearied him. He wished to be left alone with his dreams of her whose presence enchanted him.

He said cruelly: 'Madam, you yourself are little inducement to a man to forsake his mistresses.'

She quivered; he felt that, though the width of the vast bed separated them.

'I am no longer young,' she said. 'Am I to blame because our children died?' He was silent; she was trembling violently now. 'I have heard the whispering that goes on in the court. I have heard of this they call The King's Secret Matter.'

Now she had dragged his mind from the sensuous dream which soothed his body. So the whispering had reached her ears, had it! Well, assuredly it must reach them some time; but he would rather the matter had been put before her in a more dignified manner.

She said appealingly: 'Henry, you do not deny it?'

He heaved his great body up in the bed. 'Katharine,' he

said, 'you know well that for myself I would not replace you; but a king's life does not belong to him but to his kingdom. And Katharine, serious doubts have arisen in my mind, not lately but for some time past; and well would I have suppressed them had my conscience let me. I would have you know, Katharine, that when our daughter's marriage with the Duke of Orleans was proposed, the French ambassador raised the question of her legitimacy.'

'Legitimacy!' cried Katharine, raising herself. 'What meant he? My lord, I hope you reproved him most sternly!'

'Ah! That I did! And sorely grieved was I.' The King felt happier now; he was no longer the erring husband being reproved by his too faithful wife; he was the King, who put his country first, before all personal claims; and in this matter, he could tell himself, the man must take second place to the King. He could, lying in this bed with a woman whose pious ways, whose shapeless body had long since ceased to move him except with repugnance, assure himself that the need to remain married to her was removed.

He had married Katharine because there had been England's need to form a deep friendship with Spain, because England had then been weak, and across a narrow strip of channel lay mighty France, a perennial enemy. In those days of early marriage it had been a hope of Henry's to conquer France once more; with Calais still in English hands, this had not seemed an impossibility; he had hoped that with the Emperor's help this might be effected, but since the undignified affair at Pavia, Charles was hardly likely to link himself with English allies; thus was the need for friendship with Spain removed; Wolsey's schemes had been called to a halt; the new allies were the French. Therefore, what could be better for England than to dissolve the Spanish marriage! And in its place . . . But no matter, dissolve the Spanish marriage since it could no longer help England.

These were minor matters compared with the great issue which disturbed his conscience. God bless the Bishop of Tarbes, that ambassador who had the tact at this moment to question the legitimacy of the Princess Mary.

' 'Twere a matter to make a war with France,' said Katharine hotly. 'My daughter ... a bastard! *Your* daughter ...'

'These matters are not for women's wits,' said the King. 'Wars are not made on such flimsy pretexts.'

'Flimsy!' she cried, her voice sharp with fear. Katharine was no fool; to the suppers given in her apartments there came the most learned of men, the more serious courtiers, men such as Sir Thomas More; she was more fastidious than the English ladies, and she had never tried to learn the English ways. She did not enjoy the blood sports so beloved by her husband. At first he had protested when she had told him that Spanish ladies did not follow the hawk and hound. But that was years ago; he thought it well now that she did not attend sporting displays, since he had no wish for her company. But there was that in her which must make him respect her, her calm dignity, her religious faith; and even now, when this great catastrophe threatened her, she had not shown publicly – apart from her melancholy which was natural to her – that she knew what was afoot. But she was tenacious; she would fight, he knew, if not for herself for her daughter. Her piety would tell her that she fought for Henry as well as for herself, that divorce was wrong in the eyes of the Church, and she would fight with all her quiet persistence against it.

'Katharine,' said the King, 'dost thou remember thy Bible?' He began to quote a passage from Leviticus wherein it was said that for a man to take his brother's wife was an unclean thing, for thus had he uncovered his brother's nakedness; they should therefore be childless. He repeated the last sentence.

'Thou knowest I was never truly thy brother's wife.'

'It is a matter which perplexes me greatly.'

'You would say you believe me not?'

'I know not what to say. Your hopes of an heir have been blighted; it looks like Providence. Is it natural that our sons should die one after the other? Is it natural that our efforts should be frustrated?'

'Not all,' she said plaintively.

'A daughter!' he retorted contemptuously.

'She is a worthy girl. . . .'

'Bah! A girl! What good are women on the throne of England! She is no answer to our prayers, Katharine. Sons have been denied to us. . . . The fault does not lie in me. . . .'

Tears were in the Queen's eyes. She would hate this man if most of her natural instincts had not been suppressed by piety; she knew not now whether she hated or loved; she only knew she must do what was right according to her religion. She must not hate the King; she must not hate her husband; for therein was mortal sin. So all through the years when he had slighted her, humiliated her, shown utter carelessness of the hurt his lack of faith might cause her, she had assured herself that she loved him. Small wonder that he found her colourless; small wonder that now he compared this woman of forty-one with a laughing, wilful girl of nineteen years! He was thirty-five; surely a good age for a man – his prime. But he must be watchful of the years, being a king who had so far failed to give his kingdom an heir.

A short while ago he had brought his illegitimate son to court, and heaped honours upon him to the deep humiliation of the Queen, whose fears were then chiefly for her daughter. This huge man cared nothing for her, little for her daughter; he only cared that he should get what he wanted, and that the world should think that in procuring his own needs he did it not for his own, but for duty's sake.

When he said that the fault was not with him, he meant she had lied when she declared herself a virgin; he meant that she had lived with his brother as his wife. She began to weep as she prayed for strength to fight this powerful man and his evil intentions to displace her daughter from the throne with a bastard he might beget through one whom he would call his wife.

'Search your soul!' he said now, his voice trembling with righteousness. 'Search your soul, Katharine, for the truth. Does the blame for this disaster to our kingdom lie with you or with me? I have a clear conscience. Ah, Katharine, can you say you have the same?'

'That I can,' she said, 'and will!'

He could have struck her, but he calmed himself and said

in melancholy fashion: 'Nothing would have made me take this step, but that my conscience troubled me.'

She lay down and was silent; he lay down too; and in a very short while he had forgotten Katharine and was thinking of her who, he had determined, should be his.

* * *

Anne arrived at Hever with the words of the King's song still in her thoughts. She found it difficult to analyse her feelings, for to be the object of so much attention from one as powerful as the King was to reflect that power; and to Anne, bold and eager for life, power, though perhaps not the most cherished gift life could bestow, was not to be despised.

She wondered what he would say when the news of her departure reached him. Would he be angry? Would he decide that it was beneath his dignity to pursue such an unappreciative female? Would he banish her from court? She fervently hoped not that, for she needed gaiety as she never had before. She could suppress her melancholy in feverish plans for the joust, and moreover her friends were at court – George and Thomas, Surrey and Francis Bryan; with them she could laugh and frivol; and indeed talk most seriously too, for they were all – perhaps with the exception of Surrey – interested in the new religion of which she had learned a good deal from Marguerite, now the Queen of Navarre. They leaned towards that religion, all of them, perhaps because they were young and eager to try anything that was different from the old way, liking it by virtue of its very novelty.

She had not been at Hever more than a day, when the King arrived. If she had any doubt of his intense feeling for her, she need have no doubt any longer. He was inclined to be angry, but at the sight of her his anger melted; he was humble, which was somehow touching in one in whom humility was such a rare virtue; he was eager and passionate, anxious that she should have no doubt of the nature of his feelings for her.

They walked in that garden which had been the scene of

their first encounter; and that was at his wish, for he was a sentimental man when it pleased him to be so.

'I have seriously thought of this matter of love between us,' he told her. 'I would have you know that I understand your feelings. I must know – so stricken am I in my love for you – what your feelings to me are, and what they would be if I no longer had a wife.'

She was startled. Dazzling possibilities had presented themselves. Herself a Queen! The intoxicating glory of power! The joy of snapping her fingers at the Cardinal! Queen of England... !

'My lord ...' she stammered. 'I fear I am stupid. I understand not ...'

He put a hand on her arm, and she felt his fingers burning there; they crept up to her forearm, and she faced him, saw the intensity of his desire for her, and thrilled to it because, though he might not be a man she loved, he was King of England, and she felt his power, and she felt his need of her, and while he was in such urgent need it was she who held the power, for the King of England would be soft in her hands.

She cast down her eyes, fearful lest he should read her thoughts. He said she was fairer than any lady he had ever seen, and that he yearned to possess her, body and soul.

'Body and soul!' he repeated, his voice soft and humble, his eyes on her small neck, her slender body; and his voice slurred suddenly with desire as, in his mind, he took her, just as he had when he had lain beside the Queen and conjured up pictures of her so vividly that it had seemed she was there with him.

She was thinking of Percy and of Wyatt, and it seemed to her that these two mingled together and were one, representing love; and before her beckoned this strong, powerful, bejewelled man who represented ambition.

He was kissing her hand with swift, devouring kisses; there was a ring on her forefinger which she wore always; he kissed this ring, and asked that he might have it as a token, but she clenched her hands and shook her head. There was a large diamond on his finger that he would give to her, he said; and these two rings would be symbols of the love between them.

'For now I shall soon be free,' he said, 'to take a wife.'

She lifted her eyes incredulously to his face. 'Your Majesty cannot mean he would take me!'

He said passionately: 'I will take none other!'

Then it was true; he was offering her marriage. He would lift her up to that lofty eminence on which now sat Queen Katharine, the daughter of a King and Queen. She, humble Anne Boleyn, was to be placed there . . . and higher, for Katharine might be Queen, but she had never had the King's regard. It was too brilliant to be contemplated. It dazzled. It gave her a headache. She could not think clearly, and it seemed as though she saw Wyatt smiling at her, now mocking, now melancholy. It was too big a problem for a girl who was but nineteen and who, longing to be loved, had been grievously disappointed in her lovers.

'Come, Anne!' he said. 'I swear you like me.'

'It is too much for me to contemplate. . . . I need . . .'

'You need me to make up your mind for you!' he said, and there and then he had her in his arms, his lips hard and hot against her own. She felt his impatience, and sought to keep her wits. Already she knew something of this man; a man of deep needs, ever impatient of their immediate gratification; now he was saying to her: 'I've promised marriage. Why wait longer? Here! Now! Show your gratitude to your King and your trust in him, and believe that he will keep his promise!'

The Secret Matter . . . would it be granted? And if so . . . what would her old enemy, Wolsey, have to say of such a marriage? There would be powerful people at court who would exert all their might to prevent it. No, she might be falling in love with the thought of herself as Queen, but she was not in love with the King.

She said, with that haughty dignity which while it exasperated him never failed to subdue him: 'Sire, the honour you do me is so great that I would fain . . .'

With a rough edge to his voice he interrupted: 'Enough of such talk, sweetheart! Let us not talk as King and subject, but as man and woman.' One hand was at her throat. She felt his body hot against her own. With both hands she held him off.

'As yet,' she said coldly, 'I am unsure.'

The veins stood out on his forehead.

'Unsure!' he roared. 'Your King has said he loves you ... aye, and will marry you, and you are unsure!'

'Your Majesty suggested we should talk as man and woman, not as King and subject.'

She had freed herself and was running towards the hedge of fir-trees which enclosed this garden; he ran after her, and she allowed herself to be caught at the hedge. He held both her hands tightly in his.

'Anne!' he said. 'Anne! Dost seek to plague me?'

She answered earnestly: 'I never felt less like plaguing anyone, and why should I plague Your Majesty who has done me this great honour! You have offered me your love, which is to me the greatest honour, you being my King and I but a humble girl; but it was Your Majesty's command that I should cease to think of you as King..'

He interrupted: 'You twist my words, Anne. You clever little minx, you do!' And, forcing her against the hedge, he put his hands on her shoulders and kissed her lips; then those hands sought to pull apart her dress.

She wriggled free.

He said sternly: 'I would have you regard me now as your King. I would have you be my obedient, loving little subject.'

She was breathless with fear. She said, greatly daring: 'You could never win my love that way! I beg of you, release me.'

He did so, and she stood apart from him, her eyes flashing, her heart beating madly; for she greatly feared that he would force on her that which till now she had so cleverly avoided. But suddenly she saw her advantage, for there he stood before her, not an angry King but a humble man who, besides desiring her, loved her; and thus she knew that it was not for him to say what should be, but for herself to decide. Such knowledge was sweet; it calmed her sorely troubled mind, and calm she was indeed mistress of the situation. Here he was, this great bull of a man, for the first time in his life in love, and therefore inexperienced in this great emotion which swept over him, governing his actions, forcing him to take orders instead of giving them; forcing him to supplicate instead of demanding.

'Sweetheart . . .' he began hoarsely; but she lifted a hand.

'Your rough treatment has grieved me.'

'But my love for you . . .'

She looked at the red marks his hands had made on her shoulder, where he had torn the neck of her gown.

'It frightens me,' she said, looking not the least frightened, but mistress of herself and of him. 'It makes me uncertain . . .'

'Have no uncertainty of me, darling! When I first met you I went back and said to Wolsey: "I have been discoursing with one who is worthy to wear a crown!"'

'And what said my lord Cardinal? He laughed in your face I dare swear!'

'Dost think he would dare!'

'There are many things my lord Cardinal might dare that others would not. He is an arrogant, ill-bred creature!'

'You wrong him, sweetheart . . . nor do we wish to speak of him. I beg of you, consider this matter in all seriousness, for I swear there is none that can make me happy but yourself.'

'But Your Majesty could not make me your Queen! I have said your mistress I would never be.'

Now he was eager, for his mind, which had weighed this point since she began to torment him, was now firmly made up.

'I swear,' he said, 'I would never take another queen but that she was Anne Boleyn. Give me the ring, sweetheart, and take you this so that I may have peace in my mind.'

These were sweet words to her, but still she wavered. Love first; power second. Ah, she thought, could I but love this man!

'Your Grace must understand my need to think this matter over well.'

'Think it over, Anne? I ask you to be my Queen!'

'We do not discuss kings and queens,' she reproved him, and the reproof enchanted him. 'This is a matter between a man and a woman. Would you then wish me to be your Queen and not to be wholly sure that I loved you more than a subject loves a king?'

This was disarming. Where was there a woman who could hesitate over such a matter! Where was one like her! In wit, in beauty, he had known she had no equal; but in virtue too she stood alone. She was priceless, for nothing he could give would buy her. He must win her love.

He was enchanted. This was delightful – for how could he doubt that she would love him! There was none who excelled as he did at the jousts; always he won – or almost always. His songs were admired more than Wyatt's or Surrey's even; and had he not earned the title of Defender of The Faith by his book against Luther! Could More have written such a book? No! He was a king among men in all senses of the words. Take away the throne tomorrow and he would still be king. In love . . . ah! He had but to look at a woman, and she was ripe for him. So it had always been . . . except with Anne Boleyn. But she stood apart from others; she was different; that was why she should be his Queen.

'I would have time to think on this matter,' she said, and her words rang with sincerity, for this man's kisses had aroused in her a desire for those of another man, and she was torn between love and ambition. If Wyatt had not had a wife, if it was a dignified love he could have given her, she would not have hesitated; but it was the King who offered dignity, and he offered power and state; nor was Wyatt such a humble lover as this man, for all his power, could be; and, lacking humility herself, she liked it in others.

'I stay here till I have your answer,' said the King. 'I swear I will not leave Hever till I wear your ring on my finger and you mine on yours.'

'Give me till tomorrow morning,' she said.

'Thus shall it be, sweetheart. Deal kindly with me in your thoughts.'

'How could I do aught else, when from you I and mine have had naught but kindness!'

He was pleased at that. What had he not done for these Boleyns! Aye, and would do more still. He would make old Thomas's daughter a queen. Then he wondered, did she mean to refer to Mary? Quick of speech was his love; sharp of wits; was she perhaps a little jealous of her sister Mary?

He said soberly: 'There shall be none in competition with you, sweetheart.'

And she answered disconcertingly: 'There would need to be none, for I could not believe in the love of a man who amused himself with mistresses.' Then she was all smiles and sweetness. 'Sire, forgive my forwardness. Since you tell me you are a man who loves me, I forget you are the King.'

He was enraptured; she would come to him not for what the coming would mean to her in honour; she would come to him as the man.

That evening was a pleasant one. After the meal in the great dining-hall she played to him and sang a little.

He kissed her hands fervently on retiring.

'Tomorrow,' he said, 'I must have that ring.'

'Tomorrow,' she answered, 'you shall know whether or not you shall have it.'

He said, his eyes on her lips: 'Dost think of me under this roof knowing you so near and refusing me?'

'Perhaps it will not always be so,' she said.

'I will dream you are already Queen of England. I will dream that you are in my arms.'

She was afraid of such talk; she bade him a hasty good night, repeating her promise that he should hear her decision in the morning. She went to her chamber and locked her door.

Anne passed a night that was tortured with doubts. To be Queen of England! The thought haunted her, dominated her. Love, she had lost – the love she had dreamed of. Ambition beckoned. Surely she was meant to be a queen, she on whom the Fates had bestowed great gifts. She saw her ladies about her, robing her in the garments of state; she saw herself stately and gracious, imperious. Ah! she thought, there are so many people I can help. And her thoughts went to a house in Lambeth and a little girl tugging at her skirts.

That would be indeed gratifying, to lift her poor friends and members of her family out of poverty; to know that they spoke of her lovingly and with respect. . . . We owe this to the Queen – the Queen, but a humble girl whose most unusual gifts, whose wit and beauty so enslaved the King that he would make her his Queen. And then . . . there were some who had laughed at her, her enemies who had said: 'Ah! There goes Anne Boleyn; there she goes, the way of her sister!' How pleasant to snap the fingers at them, to make them bow to her!

Her eyes glittered with excitement. The soft girl who had loved Percy, who was inclined to love Wyatt, had disappeared, and in her place was a calculating woman. Ambition was wrestling desperately with love; and ambition was winning.

I do not dislike the King, she thought – for how could one dislike a man who had the good taste to admire one so wholeheartedly.

And the Queen? Ah! Something else to join the fight against ambition. The poor Queen, who was gentle enough, though melancholy, she a queen to be wronged. Oh, but the glitter of queenship! And Anne Boleyn was more fit to occupy a throne than Katharine of Aragon, for queenship is innate; it is not to be bestowed on those who have nothing but their relationship to other kings and queens.

Thomas, Thomas! Why are you not a king, to arrange a divorce, to take a new queen!

Would you be faithful, Thomas? Are any men? And if not, is love the great possession to be prized above all else? Thomas and his wife! George and Jane! The King and the Queen! Look around the court; where has love lasted? Is it not overrated? And ambition . . . Wolsey! How high he had come! From a butcher's shop, some said, to Westminster Hall. From tutor's cold attic to Hampton Court! Ambition beckoned. Cardinals may be knocked down from their proud perches, but it would need a queen to knock them down; and who could displace a queen of the King's choice!

A queen! A queen! Queen Anne!

While Henry, restless, dreamed of her taking off those

elegant clothes, of caressing the shapely limbs, she, wakeful, pictured herself riding in a litter of cloth of gold, while on either side crowds of people bared their heads to the Queen of England.

The next day Henry, after extracting a promise from her that she would return to court at once, rode away from Hever wearing her ring on his finger.

* * *

The Cardinal wept; the Cardinal implored; all his rare gifts were used in order to dissuade the King. But Henry was more determined on this than he had ever been on any matter. As wax in the hands of the crafty Wolsey he had been malleable indeed; but Wolsey had to learn that he had been so because, being clever enough to recognize the powers of Wolsey, he had been pleased to let him have his way. Now he desired the divorce, he desired marriage with Anne Boleyn as he had never desired anything except the throne, and he would fight for these with all the tenacity of the obstinate man he was; and being able to assure himself that he was in the right he could do so with unbounded energy. The divorce was right, for dynastic reasons; Anne was right for him, for she was young and healthy and would bear him many sons. An English Queen for the English throne! That was all he asked.

In vain did Wolsey point out what the reaction in France must surely be. Had he not almost affianced Henry to Renee? And the people of England? Had His Grace, the King, considered their feelings in the matter? There was murmuring against the divorce throughout the capital. Henry did what he ever did when crossed; he lost his temper, and in his mind were sown the first seeds of suspicion towards his old friend and counsellor. Wolsey had no illusions; well he knew his royal master. He must now work with all his zest and genius for the divorce; he must use all his energies to put on the throne one whom he knew to be his enemy, whom he had discovered to be more than a feckless woman seeking admiration and gaiety, whom he knew to be interested in the new religion, to be involved in a powerful party comprising her uncle of Norfolk, her father, her brother, Wyatt and the rest; this he must do, or displease the King. He could see no reward for himself in this. To please the King he must put Anne Boleyn on the throne, and to put Anne Boleyn on the throne was to advance one who would assuredly have the King under her influence, and who was undoubtedly – if not eager to destroy him – eager to remove him from that high place to which years of work had brought him.

But he was Wolsey the diplomat, so he wrote to the Pope extolling the virtues of Anne Boleyn.

Anne herself had returned to court a changed person. Now she must accept the adulation of all; there were those who, disliking her hitherto, now eagerly sought her favour; she was made to feel that she was the most important person at court, for even the King treated her with deference.

She was nineteen – a girl, in spite of an aura of sophistication. Power was sweet, and if she was a little imperious it was because of remembered slights when she had been considered not good enough for Percy – she who was to be Queen of England. If she was a little hard, it was because life had been unkind to her, first with Percy, then with Wyatt. If she were inclined to be overfond of admiration and seek it where it was unwise to do so, was not her great beauty responsible? She was accomplished and talented, and it was but human that she should wish to use these gifts. Very noble it might seem for Queen Katharine to dress herself in sober attire; she was ageing and shapeless, and never, even in her youth, had she been beautiful. Anne's body was perfectly proportioned, her face animated and charming; it was as natural for her to adorn herself as it was for Wyatt to write verses, or for the King in his youth to tire out many horses in one day at the hunt. People care about doing things which they do well, and had Katharine possessed the face and figure of Anne, doubtless she would have spent more time at her mirror and a little less with her chaplain. And if Anne offended some a little at this point, she was but nineteen, which is not very old; and she was gay by nature and eager to live an exciting, exhilarating and stimulating life.

Her pity for the Queen was diminished when that lady, professing friendship for her, would have her play cards every evening to keep her from the King, and that playing she might show that slight deformity on her left hand. Ah! These pious ones! thought Anne. Are they as good as they would seem? How often do they use their piety to hurt a sinner like myself!

She was over-generous perhaps, eager to share her good fortune with others, and one of the keenest joys she derived from her newly won power was the delight of being able to help the needy. Nor did she forget her uncle, Edmund Howard, but besought the King that something might be done for him. The King, becoming more devoted with each day and caring not who should know it, promised to give the Comptrollership of Calais to her uncle. This was pleasant news to her; and she enjoyed many similar pleasures.

But she, seeming over-gay, not for one moment relaxed in the cautious game she must continue to play with the King; for the divorce was long in coming, and the King's desire was hard to check; for ever must she be on her guard with him, since it was a difficult game with a dangerous opponent.

Nor did she forget it, for with her quickness of mind very speedily did she come to know her royal lover; and there were times in this gay and outwardly butterfly existence when fears beset her.

Wyatt, reckless and bold, hovered about her, and though she knew it was unwise to allow his constant attendance, she was very loth to dismiss him from her companionship. Well she had kept her secret, and Wyatt did not yet know of the talk of marriage which had taken place between her and the King. Wyatt himself was similar to Anne in character, so that the relationship between them often seemed closer than that of first cousin. He was reckoned the handsomest man at court; he was certainly the most charming. Impulsive as Anne herself, he would slip unthinking into a dangerous situation.

There was such an occasion when he was playing bowls with the King. The Duke of Suffolk and Sir Francis Bryan completed the quartet. There was a dispute over the game, which any but Wyatt would have let pass; not so Wyatt; he played to win, as did the King, and he would not allow even Henry to take what was not his. Henry was sure he had beaten Wyatt in casting the bowl. Wyatt immediately replied: 'Sire, by your leave, it is not so.'

The King turned his gaze upon this young man whom he could not help but like for his charm, his gaiety and his wit; his little eyes travelled over Wyatt's slim body, and he remembered that he had seen him but that morning hovering about Anne. Wyatt was handsome, there was no denying that. Wyatt wrote excellent verses. The King also wrote verses. He was a little piqued by Wyatt's fluency. And Anne? He had heard it whispered, before it was known that such whispers would madden him, that Wyatt was in love with Anne.

He was suddenly angry with Wyatt. He had dared to raise a dispute over a game. He had dared write better verses than Henry. He had dared to cast his eyes on Anne Boleyn, and was young enough, handsome enough, plausible enough to turn any girl's head.

Significantly, and speaking in the parables he so loved to use, Henry made a great show of pointing with his little finger on which was the ring Anne had given him. Wyatt saw the ring, recognized it and was nonplussed; and that again added fuel to Henry's anger. How dared Wyatt know so well a ring which had been Anne's! How often, wondered Henry, had he lifted her hand to his lips!

'Wyatt!' said the King; and smiling complacently and significantly: 'I tell thee it is mine!'

Wyatt, debonair, careless of consequences, looked for a moment at the ring and with a nonchalant air brought from his pocket the chain on which hung the tablet he had taken from Anne. He said with equal significance to that used by the King: 'And if it may please Your Majesty to give me leave to measure the cast with this, I have good hopes yet it will be mine!'

Gracefully he stooped to measure, while Henry, bursting with jealous fury, stood by.

'Ah!' cried Wyatt boldly. 'Your Majesty will see that I am right. The game is mine!'

Henry, his face purple with fury, shouted at Wyatt: 'It may be so, but then I am deceived!' He left the players staring after him.

'Wyatt,' said Bryan, 'you were ever a reckless fool! Why did you make such a pother about a paltry game?'

But Wyatt's eyes had lost their look of triumph; he shrugged his shoulders. He knew that he had lost, and guessed the ring Anne had given the King to be a symbol.

Henry stormed into the room where Anne was sitting with some of the ladies. The ladies rose at his entrance, curtseyed timidly, and were quick to obey the signal he gave for their departure.

'Your Majesty is angry,' said Anne, alarmed.

'Mistress Anne Boleyn,' said the King, 'I would know what there is betwixt thee and Wyatt.'

'I understand not,' she said haughtily. 'What should there be?'

'That to make him boast of his success with you.'

'Then he boasts emptily.'

He said: 'I would have proof of that.'

She shrugged her shoulders. 'You mean that you doubt my words.'

She was as quick to anger as he was, and she had great power over him because, though he was deeply in love with her, she was but in love with the power he could give her, and she was as yet uncertain that this honour was what she asked of life. That was the secret of her power over him. She wavered, swaying away from him, and he, bewitched and enflamed with the strong sexual passion which coloured his whole existence, was completely at her mercy.

He said: 'Anne, I know well that you would speak the truth. But tell me now with good speed, sweetheart, that there is naught between you and Wyatt.'

'You would blame me,' she said haughtily, 'since he writes his verse to me?'

'Nay, sweetheart. I would blame you for nothing. Tell me

now that I have naught to fear from this man, and restore my happiness.'

'You have naught to fear from him.'

'He had a jewelled tablet of yours.'

'I remember it. He took it one day; he would not return it, and I, valuing it but little, did not press the matter.'

He sat heavily beside her on the window seat, and put an arm about her.

'You have greatly pleased me, sweetheart. You must excuse my jealousy.'

'I do excuse it,' she said.

'Then all is well.' He kissed her hand hungrily, his eyes asking for much that his lips dared not. He had angered her; he could not risk doing so again, for he sensed the uncertainty in her. Thus he marvelled at his infatuation for this girl; as did the court. He had never loved like this; nay, he had never loved before. He was thirty-six, an old thirty-six in some ways, for he lived heartily; this was the last flare-up of youth, and the glow lighted everything about him in fantastic colours. He was the middle-aged man in love with youth; he felt inexpressibly tender towards her; he was obsessed by her; he chafed against the delay of the divorce.

After this affair of the bowls, Anne knew she was committed. Wyatt's glance was sardonic now; Wyatt was resigned. She had chosen the power and the glory; his rival had tempted her with the bait of marriage.

> '*And wilt thou leave me thus*, he wrote,
> *That hath loved thee so long*
> *In wealth and woe among:*
> *And is thy heart so strong*
> *As for to leave me thus?*'

Her heart must be strong; she must cultivate ambition; she must tread warily, since in that court of glittering men and women she now began to find her enemies, and if their malice was cloaked in soft words, they were none-the-less against her. The Cardinal, watchful and wary; the Duke of Suffolk and his wife – that Mary with whom she had gone to France – who now saw her throwing a shadow over the prospects of their descendants' claim to the throne; Chapuys, the Spaniard who was more of a spy for his master, the Emperor Charles, than his ambassador; Katharine, the Queen whom she would displace; Mary, the princess who would be branded as illegitimate. All these there were in high places to fight against her. There was a more dangerous enemy still – the people of London. Discontent was rampant in the city; the harvest had been a poor one, and the sober merchants felt that an alliance with France was folly, since it merely changed old friends for new ones who had previously shown they were not to be trusted. There was famine throughout the country, and though the King might lend to the city corn from his own granaries, still the people murmured. The cloth merchants fretted, for the trouble with Spain meant losing the great Flanders market. The County of Kent petitioned the King, in view of their poverty, to repay a loan made to him two years before. The Archbishop of Canterbury did what he could to soothe these people, but they remained restive.

For these troubles did the people of England blame Wolsey. During the prosperous years the King received the homage of his subjects; he had been taken to their hearts during the period of his coronation when he, a magnificent figure of an Englishman, fair and tall and skilled in sport, had ridden among them – such a contrast to his ugly, mean old father. During the dark years, however, they blamed Wolsey; for Wolsey had committed the sin of being of the people and rising above them. The whispers went round: 'Which court? Hampton Court or the King's court?' This was the twilight hour of Wolsey's brilliant day. And the starving and wretched gazed at a bright and beautiful girl, reclining in her barge or riding out with friends from court; more gaily dressed than the other ladies, she sparkled with rich jewels, presents from the King – a sight to raise the wrath of a starving people. 'We'll have none of Nan Bullen!' they murmured together. 'The King's whore shall not be our Queen. Queen Katharine for ever!'

From the choked gutters there arose evil smells; decaying matter lay about for weeks; rats, tame as cats, walked the cobbles; overhanging gables, almost touching across narrow streets, shut out the sun and air, held in the vileness. And in those filthy streets men and women were taken suddenly sick; many died in the streets, the sweat pouring from their bodies; and all men knew that the dreaded sweating sickness had returned to England. Thus did the most sorely afflicted people of London wonder at this evil which had fallen upon them; thus did they murmur against her who by her witch's fascination had turned the King from his pious ways. The sick and suffering of London whispered her name; the rebellious people of Kent talked of her; in the weaving counties her name was spoken with distaste. Everywhere there was murmuring against the devil's instrument, Wolsey, and her who had led the King into evil ways and brought down the justice of heaven upon their country. Even at Horsham, where the news of the sweating sickness had not yet reached, they talked of Anne Boleyn. The old Duchess chuckled in great enjoyment of the matter.

'Come here, Catherine Howard. Rub my back. I declare I must be full of lice or suffering from the itch! Rub harder, child. Ah! Fine doings at the court, I hear. The King is bewitched, it seems, by your cousin, Anne Boleyn, and I am not greatly surprised to hear it. I said, when she came visiting me at Lambeth: "Ah! There is a girl the King would like!" though I will say I added that he might feel inclined to spank the haughtiness out of her before carrying her off to bed. Don't scratch, child! Gently . . . gently. Now I wonder if . . .' The Duchess giggled. 'You must not look so interested, child, and I should not talk to you of such matters. Why, of course . . . As if he would not . . . From what I know of His Majesty . . . Though there are those that say . . . It is never wise to give in . . . and yet what can a poor girl do . . . and look how Mary kept him dancing attendance all those years! There is something about the Boleyns, and of course it comes from the Howards . . . though I swear I see little of it in you, child. Why, look at your gown! Is that a rent? You should make Isabel look after you better. And what do you do of nights when you should be sleeping?

I declare I heard such a noise from your apartment that I was of good mind to come and lay about the lot of you . . .'

It was merely the Duchess's talk; she would never stir from her bed. But Catherine decided she must tell the others.

'And your cousin, I hear, is to do something for your father, Catherine Howard. Oh, what it is to have friends at court! Why, you are dreaming there . . . Rub harder! Or leave that . . . you may do my legs now.'

Catherine was dreaming of the beautiful cousin who had come to the house at Lambeth. She knew what it meant to be a king's favourite, for Catherine had a mixed knowledge; she knew of the attraction between men and women, and the methods in which such attraction was shown; of books she knew little, as the Duchess, always meaning to have her taught, was somehow ever forgetful of this necessity. The cousin had given her a jewelled tablet, and she had it still; she treasured it.

'One day,' said the Duchess, 'I shall go to Lambeth that I may be near my granddaughter who is almost a queen.'

'She is not really your granddaughter,' said Catherine. 'You were her grandfather's second wife.'

The Duchess cuffed the girl's ears for that. 'What! And you would deny my relationship to the queen-to-be! She who is all but Queen has never shown me such disrespect. Now do my legs, child, and no more impertinence!'

Catherine thought – Nor are you my real grandmother either! And she was glad, for it seemed sacrilege that this somewhat frowsy old woman – Duchess of Norfolk though she might be – should be too closely connected with glorious Anne.

When Catherine was in the room which she still shared with the ladies-in-waiting, she took out the jewelled tablet and looked at it. It was impossible in the dormitory to have secrets, and several of them wanted to know what she had.

'It is nothing,' said Catherine.

'Ah!' said Nan. 'I know! It is a gift from your lover.'

'It is not!' declared Catherine. 'And I have no lover.'

'You should say so with shame! A fine big girl like you!' said a tall, lewd-looking girl, even bolder than the rest.

'I'll swear it is from her lover,' said Nan. 'Why, look! It has an initial on it – A. Now who is A? Think hard, all of you.'

Catherine could not bear their guessings, and she blurted out: 'I will tell you then. I have had it since I was a very little baby. It was given to me by my cousin, Anne Boleyn.'

'Anne Boleyn!' screamed Nan. 'Why, of course, our Catherine is first cousin to the King's mistress!' Nan leaped off the bed and made a mock bow to Catherine. The others followed her example, and Catherine thrust away the tablet, wishing she had not shown it.

Now they were all talking of the King and her cousin Anne, and what they said made Catherine's cheeks flush scarlet. She could not bear that they should talk of her cousin in this way, as though she were one of *them*.

The incorrigible Nan and the lewd-faced girl were shouting at each other.

'We will stage a little play . . . for tonight . . . You may take the part of the King. I shall be Anne Boleyn!'

They were rocking with laughter. 'I shall do this. You shall do that . . . I'll warrant we'll bring Her Grace up with our laughter . . .'

'We must be careful . . .'

'If she discovered . . .'

'Bah! What would she do?'

'She would send us home in disgrace.'

'She is too lazy . . .'

'What else? What else?'

'Little Catherine Howard shall be lady of the bed-chamber!'

'Ha! That is good. She being first cousin to the lady . . . Well, Catherine Howard, we have brought you up in the right way, have we not? We have trained you to wait on your lady cousin, even in the most delicate circumstances, with understanding and . . .'

'Tact!' screamed Nan. 'And discretion!'

'She'll probably get a place at court!'

'And Catherine Howard, unless you take us with you, we shall tell all we know about you and . . .'

'I have done nothing!' said Catherine hastily. 'There is nothing you could say against me.'

'Ah! Have you forgotten Thomas Culpepper so soon then?'

'I tell you there was nothing . . .'

'Catherine Howard! Have you forgotten the paddock and what he did there . . .'

'It was nothing . . . nothing!'

Nan said firmly: 'Those who excuse themselves, accuse themselves. Did you know that, Catherine?'

'I swear . . .' cried Catherine. And then, in an excess of boldness: 'If you do not stop saying these things about Thomas, I will go and tell my grandmother what happens in this room at night.'

Isabel, who had been silent amidst the noise of the others, caught her by her wrist.

'You would not dare . . .'

'Don't forget,' cried Nan, 'we should have something to say of *you*!'

'There is nothing you could say. I have done nothing but look on . . .'

'And enjoyed looking on! Now, Catherine Howard, I saw a young gentleman kiss you last evening.'

'It was not my wish, and that I told him.'

'Oh, well,' said Nan, 'it was not my wish that such and such happened to me, and I told him; but it happened all the same.'

Catherine moved to the door. Isabel was beside her.

'Catherine, take no heed of these foolish girls.'

There were tears in Catherine's eyes.

'I will not hear them say such things of my cousin.'

'Heed them not, the foolish ones! They mean it not.'

'I will not endure it.'

'And you think to stop it by telling your grandmother?'

'Yes,' said Catherine, 'for if she knew what happened here, she would dismiss them all.'

'I should not tell, Catherine. You have been here many nights yourself; she might not hold you guiltless. Catherine, listen to me. They shall say nothing of your cousin again; I will stop them. But first you must promise me that you will not let a word of what happens here get to your grandmother's ears through you.'

'It is wrong of them to taunt me.'

'Indeed it is wrong,' said Isabel, 'and it must not be. Trust me to deal with them. They are but foolish girls. Now promise you will not tell your grandmother.'

'I will not tell unless they taunt me to it.'

'Then rest assured they shall not.'

Catherine ran from the room, and Isabel turned to the girls who had listened open-eyed to this dialogue.

'You fools!' said Isabel. 'You ask for trouble. It is well enough to be reckless when there is amusement to be had, but just to taunt a baby . . . What do you achieve but the fear of discovery?'

'She would not dare to tell,' said Nan.

'Would she not! She has been turning over in her baby mind whether she ought not to tell ever since she came here. Doubtless the saintly Thomas warned her it was wrong to tell tales.'

'She dared not tell,' insisted another girl.

'Why not, you fool? She is innocent. What has she done but be a looker-on? We should be ruined, all of us, were this known to Her Grace.'

'Her Grace cares nothing but for eating, sleeping, drinking, scratching and gossip!'

'There are others who would care. And while she is innocent, there is danger of her telling. Now if she were involved . . .'

'We shall have to find a lover for her,' said Nan.

'A fine big girl such as she is!' said the lewd-faced girl who had promised to take the part of Henry.

The girls screamed together light-heartedly. Only Isabel, aloof from their foolish chatter, considered this.

*　　　*　　　*

The King sat alone and disconsolate in his private apartments. He was filled with apprehension. Through the South-eastern corner of England raged that dread disease, the sweating sickness. In the streets of London men took it whilst walking; many died within a few hours. People looked suspiciously one at the other. Why does this come upon us to add to our miseries! Poverty we have; famine; and now the sweat! Eyes were turned to the palaces, threatening eyes; voices murmured: 'Our King has turned his lawful wife from his bed, that he might put there a witch. Our King has quarrelled with the holy Pope. . . .'

Wolsey had warned him, as had others of his council: 'It would be well to send Mistress Anne Boleyn back to her father's castle until the sickness passes, for the people are murmuring against her. It might be well if Your Majesty appeared in public with the Queen.'

Angry as the King had been, he realized there was wisdom in their words.

'Sweetheart,' he said, 'the people are murmuring against us. This matter of divorce, which they cannot understand, is at the heart of it. You must go to Hever for awhile.'

She, with the recklessness of youth, would have snapped her fingers at the people. 'Ridiculous,' she said, 'to associate this sickness with the divorce! I do not want to leave the court. It is humiliating to be sent away in this discourteous manner.'

Was ever a man so plagued, and he a king! To his face she had laughed at his fears, despising his weakness in bowing to his ministers and his conscience. She would have defied the devil, he knew. He had forced himself to be firm, begging her to see that it was because he longed for her so desperately that he wished this matter of the divorce concluded with the minimum of trouble. Ever since she had gone he had been writing letters to her, passionate letters in which he bared his soul, in which he clearly told her more than it was wise to tell her. 'Oh,' he wrote, 'Oh, that you were in my arms!' He was not subtle with the pen; he wrote from the heart. He loved her; he wanted her with him. He told her these things, and so did he, the King of England, place himself at the mercy of a girl of nineteen.

He believed, with his people, that the sweat was a visitation from Heaven. It had come on other occasions; there had been one epidemic just before his accession to the throne. Ominous this! Was God saying he was not pleased that the Tudors should be the heirs of England? Again it had come in 1517, at about the time when Martin Luther was denouncing Rome. Was it God's intention to support the German, and did He thus show disapproval of those who followed Rome? He had heard his father's speaking of its breaking out after Bosworth . . . and now, here it was again when Henry was thinking of divorce. Assuredly it was alarming to contemplate these things!

So he prayed a good deal; he heard mass many times a day. He prayed aloud and in his thoughts. 'Thou knowest it was not for my carnal desires that I would make Anne my wife. There is none I would have for wife but Katharine, were I sure that she *was* my wife, that I was not sinning in continuing to let her share my bed. Thou knowest that!' he pleaded. 'Thou hast taken William Carey, O Lord. Ah! He was a complaisant husband to Mary, and mayhap this is his punishment. For myself, I have sinned in this matter and in others, as Thou knowest, but always I have confessed. I have repented . . . And if I took William's wife, I gave him a place at court beyond his deserts, for, as Thou knowest, he was a man of small ability.'

All his prayers and all his thoughts were tinged with his desire for Anne. 'There is a woman who will give sons to me and to England! That is why I would elevate her to the throne.' It was reassuring to be able to say 'England needs my sons!' rather than 'I want Anne.'

Henry was working on his treatise, in which he was pointing out the illegality of his marriage, and which he would despatch to the Pope. He was proud of it; for its profound and wise arguments; its clarity; its plausibility; its literary worth. He had shown what he had done to Sir Thomas More; had eagerly awaited the man's compliments; but More had merely said that he could not judge it since he knew so little of such matters. Ah! thought Henry. Professional jealousy, eh! And he had scowled at More, feeling suddenly a ridiculous envy of the man, for there was in More an agreeable humour, deep learning, wit, charm and a serenity of mind which showed in his countenance. Henry had been entertained at More's riverside house; had walked in the pleasant garden and watched More's children feed his peacocks; had seen this man in the heart of his family, deeply loved and reverenced by them; he had watched his friendship with men like the learned Erasmus, the impecunious Hans Holbein who, poor as he might be, knew well how to wield a brush. And being there, he the King – though he could not complain that they gave him not his rightful homage – had been outside that magic family circle, though Erasmus and Holbein had obviously been welcomed into it.

A wild jealousy had filled his heart for this man More who was known for his boldness in stating his opinions, for his readiness to crack a joke, for his love of literature and art, and for his practical virtue. Henry could have hated this man, had the man allowed him to, but ever susceptible to charm in men as well as women, he had fallen a victim to the charm of Sir Thomas More; and so he found, struggling in his breast, a love for this man, and even when More refused to praise his treatise, and even though he knew More was amongst those who did not approve of the divorce, he must continue to respect the man and seek his friendship. How many of his people, like More, did not approve of the divorce! Henry grew hot with righteous indignation and the desire to make them see this matter in the true light.

He had written a moralizing letter to his sister Margaret of Scotland, accusing her of immorality in divorcing her husband on the plea that her marriage had not been legal, thus making her daughter illegitimate. He burned with indignation at his niece's plight while he – at that very time – was planning to place his daughter Mary in a similar position. He did this in all seriousness, for his thoughts were governed by his muddled moral principles. He saw himself as noble, the perfect king; when the people murmured against Anne, it was because they did not understand! He was ready to sacrifice himself to his country. He did not see himself as he was, but as he wished himself to be; and, surrounded by those who continually sought his favour, he could not know that others did not see him as he wished to be seen.

One night during this most unsatisfactory state of affairs occasioned by Anne's absence, an express messenger brought disquieting news.

'From Hever!' roared the King. 'What from Hever?'

And he hoped for a letter, for she had not answered his in spite of his entreaties, a letter in which she was more humble, in which she expressed a more submissive mood of sweet reasonableness. It was not however a letter, but the alarming news that Anne and her father had taken the sickness, though mildly. The King was filled with panic. The most precious body in his kingdom was in danger. Carey had died. Not Anne! he prayed. Not Anne!

He grew practical; grieving that his first physician was not at hand, he immediately despatched his second, Doctor Butts, to Hever. Desperately anxious, he awaited news.

He paced his room, forgetting his superstitious fears, forgetting to remind God that it was just because she was healthy and could give England sons that he proposed marrying her; he thought only of the empty life without her.

He sat down and poured out his heart to her in his direct and simple manner.

'The most displeasing news that could occur came to me suddenly at night. On three accounts I must lament it. One, to hear of the illness of my mistress whom I esteem more than all the world, and whose health I desire as I do mine own: I would willingly bear half of what you suffer to cure you. The second, from the fear that I shall have to endure thy wearisome absence much longer, which has hitherto given me all the vexation that was possible. The third, because my physician (in whom I have most confidence) is absent at the very time when he could have given me the greatest pleasure. But I hope, by him and his means, to obtain one of my chief joys on earth; that is the cure of my mistress. Yet from the want of him I send you my second (Doctor Butts) and hope he will soon make you well. I shall then love him more than ever. I beseech you to be guided by his advice in your illness. By your doing this, I hope soon to see you again. Which will be to me a greater comfort than all the precious jewels in the world.

166

'Written by the hand of that secretary who is, and for ever will be, your loyal and most assured servant. H.R.'

And having written and despatched this, he must pace his apartment in such anxiety as he had never known, and marvel that there could be such a thing as love, all joy and sorrow, to assail even the hearts of princes.

*   *   *

The Queen was jubilant. Was this God's way of answering her prayers? She rejoiced with her daughter, because Anne Boleyn lay ill of the sweating sickness at Hever.

'Oh,' cried the Queen to her young daughter, 'this is the vengeance of the Lord. This is a judgment on the girl's wickedness.'

Twelve-year-old Mary listened wide-eyed, thinking her mother a saint.

'My father . . .' said the girl, 'loves he this woman?'

Her mother stroked her hair. Loving her dearly, she had until now superintended her education, kept her with her, imbued her with her own ideas of life.

'He thinks to do so, daughter. He is a lusty man, and thus it is with men. It is no true fault of his; she is to blame.'

'I have seen her about the court,' said Mary, her eyes narrowed, picturing Anne as she had seen her. That was how witches looked, thought Mary; they had flowing hair and huge dark eyes, and willowy bodies which they loved to swathe in scarlet; witches looked like Anne Boleyn!

'She should be burned at the stake, Mother!' said Mary.

'Hush!' said her mother. 'It is not meet to talk thus. Pray for her, Mary. Pity her, for mayhap at this moment she burns in hell.'

Mary's eyes were glistening; she hoped so. She had a vivid picture of flames the colour of the witch's gown licking her white limbs; in her imagination she could hear the most melodious voice at court, imploring in vain to be freed from hideous torment.

Mary understood much. This woman would marry her father; through her it would be said that Mary's mother was no wife, and that she, Mary, was a bastard. Mary knew the meaning of that; she would no longer be the Princess Mary; she would no longer receive the homage of her father's subjects; she would never be Queen of England.

Mary prayed each night that her father would tire of Anne, that he would banish her from the court, that he would grow to hate her, commit her to the Tower where she would be put in a dark dungeon to be starved and eaten by rats, that she might be put in chains, that her body might be grievously racked for every tear she had caused to fall from the eyes of Mary's saintly mother.

Mary had something of her father in her as well as of her mother; her mother's fanaticism perhaps, but her father's cruelty and determination.

Once her mother had said: 'Mary, what if your father should make her his Queen?'

Mary had answered proudly: 'There could be but one Queen of England, Mother.'

Katharine's heart had rejoiced, for deeply, tenderly, she loved her daughter. While they were together there could not be complete despair. But all their wishes, all their prayers, were without effect.

When the news came to Henry that Anne had recovered, he embraced the messenger, called for wine to refresh him, fell on his knees and thanked God.

'Ha!' said he to Wolsey. 'This is a sign! I am right to marry the lady; she will give me many lusty sons.'

Poor Katharine! She could but weep silently; and then her bitterness was lost in fear, for her daughter had taken the sickness.

Anne convalesced at Hever. At court she was spoken of continually. Du Bellay, the witty French ambassador, joked in his light way. He wagered the sickness of the lady had spoiled her beauty in some measure; he was certain that during her absence some other one would find a way to the King's susceptible heart. Chapuys, the Spanish ambassador, laughed with him, and gleefully wrote to his master of the 'concubine's' sickness. Blithely he prophesied an end of this – in Spain's eyes – monstrous matter of the divorce.

But Henry did not wait for her convalescence to end. How could he wait much longer! He had waited enough already. Privately he would ride from Greenwich or from Eltham to Hever Castle, and Anne, from the castle grounds, hearing his bugle call on a nearby hill, would go out to meet him. They would walk the gallery together, or sit in the oak-panelled chamber while he told her how the matter of the divorce progressed; he would talk of his love, would demand in fierce anger – or meek supplication – why now she could not make him the happiest of men.

And when the pestilence had passed over and she returned to court, Du Bellay reported to his government: 'I believe the King to be so infatuated with her that God alone can abate his madness.'

*   *   *

Thomas Wolsey, knowing sickness of heart, feigned sickness of body. He knew his master; sentimental as a girl, and soft as wax in the fiery hands of Anne Boleyn.

Wolsey saw his decline now, as clearly as he had so often seen the sun set; for him though, there would be no rising again after the coming of night.

He did not complain; he was too wise for that. Well he knew that he had made his mistake, and where. He had humiliated her who had now the King's ear. And she was no soft, weak woman; she was strong and fierce, a good friend and a bad enemy. Oh! he thought, There is a night crow that possesses the royal ear and misrepresents all my actions.

He must not complain. He remembered the days of his own youth. He could look back to the humble life when he was tutor to the sons of Lord Marquess Dorset. Then there had been a certain knight, one Sir Amyas Pawlet, who had dared to humiliate young Wolsey; and had young Wolsey forgotten? He had not! Sir Amyas Pawlet grew to wish he had considered awhile before heaping indignities upon a humble tutor. So it was with Mistress Anne Boleyn and Thomas Wolsey. He could go to her; he could say: 'I would explain to you. It was not I who wished to hurt you. It was not I who would have prevented your marriage with Percy.

It was my lord King. I was but his servant in this matter.' It might well be that she, who was noted for her generous impulses, would forgive him; it might be that she would not continue to plan against him. It might be . . . but she was not his only enemy. Her uncle, Norfolk, was with her in this matter; the Duke of Suffolk, also; and that Percy of Northumberland who had loved her and still brooded on his loss. These powerful men had had enough of Wolsey's rule.

He was very weary; defeated by this divorce, feigning sickness that he might appeal to the sentiment of the King, that he might make him sorry for his old friend; hiding himself away until Campeggio whom the Pope was sending from Rome was due to arrive. This was Wolsey in decline.

Foolishly he had acted over this matter of Eleanor Carey. He was in disgrace with the King over that matter, and he had received such a rebuke as he had never had before, and one which told him clearly that the King was no longer his to command. The night crow and her band of vultures watched him, waiting for his death. Yet stupidly and proudly he had acted over the Eleanor Carey affair; she was the sister-in-law of Anne, and with characteristic generosity, when the woman had asked Anne to make her Abbess of Wilton – which place had fallen vacant – Anne had promised she should have her wish. And he, Wolsey, had arrogantly refused Eleanor Carey and given the place to another. Thus was Mistress Anne's anger once more raised against him; how bitterly had she complained of his action to the King! Wolsey had explained that Eleanor was unfit for the post, having had two illegitimate children by a priest. Knowing that, Henry, whose attitude towards others was rigorously moral, must see the point of this refusal. Gently and with many apologies for the humiliation she had suffered in the matter, the King explained this to Anne. 'I would not,' wrote Henry to his sweetheart, 'for all the gold in the world clog your conscience and mine to make her a ruler of a house . . .'

Anne, who was by nature honest, had no great respect for her lover's conscience; she was impatient, and showed it; she insisted that Wolsey's arrogance should not be allowed to pass. And Henry, fearing to lose her, ready to give her anything she wished, wrote sternly to Wolsey; and that letter showed Wolsey more clearly than anything that had gone before that he was slipping dangerously, and he knew no way of gaining a more steady foothold on the road of royal favour.

Now at last he understood that she who had the King's ear was indeed a rival to be feared. And he was caught between Rome and Henry; he had no plans; he could see only disaster coming out of this affair. So he feigned sickness to give himself time to prepare a plan, and sick at heart, he felt defeat closing in on him.

* * *

The legate had arrived from Rome, and old gouty Campeggio was ready to try the case of the King and Queen. Crowds collected in the streets; when Queen Katharine rode out, she was loudly cheered, and so likewise was her daughter Mary. Katharine, pale and wan from worry, Mary, pale from her illness, were martyrs in the eyes of the people of London; and the King begged Anne not to go abroad for fear the mob might do her some injury.

Anne was wretched, longing now to turn from this thorny road of ambition; not a moment's real peace had she known since she had started to tread it. The King was continually trying to force her surrender, and she was weary with the fight she must put up against him. And when Henry told her she must once more go back to Hever, as the trial was about to begin, she was filled with anger.

Henry said humbly: 'Sweetheart, your absence will be hard to bear, but my one thought is to win our case. With you here . . .'

Her lips curled scornfully, for did she not know that he would plead his lack of interest in a woman other than his wife? Did she not know that he would tell the Cardinals of his most scrupulous conscience?

She was wilful and cared not; she was foolish, she knew, for did she not want the divorce? She was hysterical with fear sometimes, wishing fervently that she was to marry someone who was more agreeable to her, seeing pitfalls yawning at the feet of a queen.

'An I go back,' she said unreasonably, 'I shall not return. I will not be sent back and forth like a shuttlecock!'

He pleaded with her. 'Darling, be reasonable! Dost not wish this business done with? Only when the divorce is complete can I make you my Queen.'

She went back to Hever, having grown suddenly sick of the palace, since from her window she saw the angry knots of people and heard their sullen murmurs. 'Nan Bullen! The King's whore ... We want no Nan Bullen!'

Oh, it was shameful, shameful! 'Oh, Percy!' she cried. 'Why did you let them do this to us?' And she hated the Cardinal afresh, having convinced herself that it was he who, in his subtle, clever way, had turned the people against her. At Hever her father treated her with great respect – more respect than he had shown to Mary; Anne was not to be the King's mistress, but his wife, his Queen. Lord Rochford could not believe in all that good fortune; he would advise her, but scornfully she rejected his advice.

Two months passed, during which letters came from the King reproaching her for not writing to him, assuring her that she was his entirely beloved; and at length telling her it would now be safe for her to return to court.

The King entreated her; she repeated her refusals to all the King's entreaties.

Her father came to her. 'Your folly is beyond my understanding!' said Lord Rochford. 'The King asks that you will return to court! And you will not!'

'I have said I will not be rushed back and forth in this uncourtly way.'

'You talk like a fool, girl! Dost not realize what issues are at stake?'

'I am tired of it all. When I consented to marry the King, I thought 'twould be but a simple matter.'

'When you consented. . . !' Lord Rochford could scarcely believe his ears. She spoke as though she were conferring a favour on His Majesty. Lord Rochford was perturbed. What if the King should grow weary at this arrogance of his foolish daughter!

'I command you to go!' he roared; which made her laugh at him. Oh, how much simpler to manage had been his daughter Mary! He would have sent Anne to her room, would have said she was to be locked in there, but how could one behave so to the future Queen of England!

Lord Rochford knew a little of this daughter. Wilful and unpredictable, stubborn, reckless of punishment, she had been from babyhood; he knew she wavered even yet. Ere long she would be telling the King she no longer wished to marry him.

'I command you go!' he cried.

'You may command all you care to!' And at random she added: 'I shall not go until a very fine lodging is found for me.'

Lord Rochford told the King, and Henry, with that pertinacity of purpose which he ever displayed when he wanted something urgently, called in Wolsey; and Wolsey, seeking to reinstate himself, suggested Suffolk House in place of Durham House which the King had previously placed at her disposal.

'For, my lord King, my own York House is next to Suffolk House, and would it not be a matter of great convenience to you, if, while the lady is at Suffolk House, Your Highness lived at York House?'

'Thomas, it is a plan worthy of you!' The fat hand rested on the red-clad shoulder. The small eyes smiled into those of his Cardinal; the King was remembering that he had ever loved this man.

*　　*　　*

Anne came to Suffolk House. Its grandeur overawed even her, for it was the setting for a queen. There would be her ladies-in-waiting, her trainbearer, her chaplain; she would hold levees, and dispense patronage to church and state.

'It is as if I were a queen!' she told Henry who was there to greet her.

'You are a queen,' he answered passionately.

173

Now she understood. The fight was over. He who had waited so long had decided to wait no longer.

They would eat together informally at Suffolk House, he told her. Dear old Wolsey had lent him York House, next door, that he might be close and could visit her unceremoniously. Did she not think she had judged the poor old fellow too harshly?

There was about the King an air of excitement this day. She understood it, and he knew she understood it.

'Mayhap we judge him too hardly,' she agreed.

'Darling, I would have you know that you must lack nothing. Everything that you would have as my Queen – which I trust soon to make you – shall be yours.' He put burning hands on her shoulders. 'You have but to ask for what you desire, sweetheart.'

'That I know,' she said.

Alone in her room, she looked at herself in her mirror. Her heart was beating fast. 'And what have you to fear, Anne Boleyn?' she whispered to her reflection. 'Is it because after tonight there can be no turning back, that you tremble? Why should you fear? You are beautiful. There may be ladies at court with more perfect features, but there is none so intoxicatingly lovely, so ravishingly attractive as Anne Boleyn! What have you to fear from this? Nothing! What have you to gain? You have made up your mind that you will be Queen of England. There is nothing to fear.'

Her eyes burned in her pale face; her beautiful lips were firm. She put on a gown of black velvet, and her flesh glowed as lustrous as the pearls that decorated it.

She went out to him, and he received her with breathless wonder. She was animated now, warmed by his admiration, his passionate devotion.

He led her to a table where they were waited upon discreetly; and this *tête à tête* meal, which he had planned with much thought, was to him complete happiness. Gone was her wilfulness now; she was softer; he was sure of her surrender; he had waited so long, he had lived through this so often in his dreams; but nothing he had imagined, he was sure, could be as wonderful as the reality.

He tried to explain his feelings for her, tried to tell her of how she had changed him, how he longed for her, how she was different from any other woman, how thoughts of her coloured his life; how, until she came, he had never known love. Nor had he, and Henry in love was an attractive person; humility was an ill-fitting garment that sat oddly on those great shoulders, but not less charming because it did not fit. He was tender instead of coarse, modest instead of arrogant; and she warmed towards him. She drank more freely than was her custom: she had confidence in herself and the future.

Henry said, when they rose from the table: 'Tonight I think I am to be the happiest man on Earth!' Apprehensively he waited for her answer, but she gave no answer, and when he would have spoken again he found his voice was lost to him; he had no voice, he had no pride; he had nothing but his great need of her.

She lay naked in her bed, and seeing her thus he was speechless, nerveless, fearful of his own emotion; until his passion rushed forth and he kissed her white body in something approaching a frenzy.

She thought: I have nothing to fear. If he was eager before, he will be doubly eager now. And, as she lay crushed by his great weight, feeling his joy, his ecstasy, she laughed inwardly and gladly, because now she knew there was to be no more wavering and she, being herself, would pursue this thing to the end.

His words were incoherent, but they were of love, of great love and desire and passion and pleasure.

'There was never one such as thee, my Anne! Never, never I swear . . . Anne . . . Queen Anne . . . My Queen. . . .'

He lay beside her, this great man, his face serene and completely happy, so she knew how he must have looked when a very small boy; his face was purged of all that coarseness against which her fastidiousness had turned in disgust; and she felt she must begin to love him, that she almost did love him, so that on impulse she leaned over to him and kissed him. He seized her then, laughing, and told her again that she was beautiful, that she excelled his thoughts of her.

'And many times have I taken you, my Queen, in my thoughts. Dost remember the garden at Hever? Dost remember thy haughtiness? Why, Anne! Why I did not take thee there and then I do not know. Never have I wanted any as I wanted thee, Anne, my Queen, my little white Queen!'

She could laugh, thinking – Soon he will be free, and I shall be truly Queen . . . and after this he will never be able to do without me.

'Aye, and I wonder I was so soft with you, my entirely beloved, save that I loved you, save that I could not hurt you. Now you love me truly . . . not as your King, you said, but as a man. . . . You love me as I love you, and you find pleasure in this, as I do. . . .'

And so he would work himself to a fresh frenzy of passion; so he would stroke and caress her, lips on her body, his hands at her hair and her throat and her breasts.

'There was never love like this!' said Henry of England to Anne Boleyn.

HAPPIEST OF WOMEN

AT HORSHAM there was preparation for the Christmas festivities; excitement was high in the ladies' dormitory. There should be a special Yuletide feast, they said, a good deal more exciting than that one which would be held in the great hall to be enjoyed by all; the ladies were busy getting together gifts for their lovers, speculating as to what they would receive.

'Poor little Catherine Howard!' they said, laughing. 'She has no lover!'

'What of the gallant Thomas? Alas, Catherine! He soon forgot thee.'

Catherine thought guiltily that, though she would never forget him, she had thought of him less during the last months; she wondered if he ever thought of her; if he did, he evidently did not think it necessary to let her know.

'It is unwise,' said Isabel, 'to think of those who think not of us.'

In the Duchess's rooms, where Catherine often sat with her grandmother, the old lady fretted about the monotony of life in the country.

'I would we were at Lambeth. Fine doings I hear there are at court.'

'Yes,' answered Catherine, rubbing her grandmother's back. 'My cousin is a most important lady now.'

'That I swear she is! Ah! I wonder what Lord Henry Algernon Percy . . . I beg his pardon, the Earl of Northumberland . . . has to say now! He was too high and mighty to marry her, was he? "Very well," says Anne, "I'll take the King instead." Ha! Ha! And I declare nothing delights me more than to hear the haughty young man is being made wretched by his wife; for so does anyone deserve who thinks himself too fine for my granddaughter.'

'The granddaughter of your husband,' Catherine reminded her once more; and was cuffed for her words.

'How I should like to see her at Suffolk House! I hear that she holds daily levees, as though she is already Queen. She dispenses charity, which is the Queen's task. There are those who storm against her, for, Catherine, my child, there will always be the jealous ones. Ah! How I should love to see my granddaughter reigning at Greenwich! I hear the Queen was most discomfited, and that last Christmas Anne held her revels apart from those of Katharine – which either shocked or delighted all. Imagine *her* revels! Imagine poor Katharine's! Herself, my granddaughter, the centre of attraction, with George and Wyatt and Surrey and Bryan with her; and who could stand up against them, eh? And the King so far gone in love, dear man, that everything she asks must be hers. Ah! How I should love to be there to see it! And Wolsey, that old schemer, trembling in his shoes, I dare swear. And so he should . . . trying to keep our sovereign lord from marrying her who should be his Queen – for if ever woman was born to be a queen, that woman was my granddaughter Anne! '

'I should love to see her too,' said Catherine wistfully. 'Grandmother, when will you go to court?'

'Very soon. I make my plans now. Why, I have only to let her know my desires, and she would send for me. She was ever my favourite granddaughter, and it has always seemed to me that I was a favourite of hers. Bless her! God bless Queen Anne Boleyn!'

'God bless her!' said Catherine.

Her grandmother regarded the girl through narrowed eyes.

'I declare I never saw one so lacking in dignity. I would hear you play to me awhile, Catherine. Music is the only thing for which you seem to have the least aptitude. Go over and play me a tune.'

Catherine eagerly went to the virginals; she hated the ministrations to her grandmother, and regretted that they must be an accompaniment to her racy conversation which she always enjoyed.

The Duchess, her foot tapping, was only half listening, for her thoughts were far away, at Greenwich, at Eltham, at Windsor, at Suffolk House, at York House. She saw her beautiful granddaughter, queening it in all these places; she saw the King, humble in his love; the colour, the music, the gorgeous clothes, the masques; the terror of that man Wolsey whom she had ever hated; and Anne, the loveliest woman in the kingdom, queen of the court.

To be there! To be favoured of her who was most favoured of the King! 'My granddaughter, the Queen.' To see her now and then, lovely, vital; to think of her, loved passionately by the King; mayhap to be on the best of terms oneself with His Majesty, for he would be kind to those beloved of his beloved; and Anne had always had a regard for her scandal-loving, lazy old grandmother – even if she were only the wife of her grandfather!

'I shall go to Lambeth!' said the Duchess. And little Catherine there should have a place at court, she thought. . . . Attendant to her cousin, the Queen? Why not? As soon as this wearisome divorce was done with, she would go to Lambeth. And surely it would not be long now; it had been dragging on for more than two years; and now that the King's eyes were being opened to that Wolsey's wickedness, surely it could not be long.

Yes, little Catherine should have a place at court. But how very unfitted she was for that high honour! Anne, my child, you were at the French court at her age, a little lady delighting all who beheld you, I swear, with your grace and your charm and your delicious clothes and the way you wore them. Ah, Catherine Howard! You will never be an Anne Boleyn; one could not hope for that. Look at the child! Sitting humped over the virginals.

And yet she was not unattractive; she already had the air of a woman; her little body had that budding look which meant that Catherine might well flower early. But she had about her a neglected look, and it was that which made the Duchess angry. What right had Catherine Howard to look neglected! She lived in the great establishment of the Duchess; she was in the charge of the Duchess's ladies. Something should be done about the child, thought the Duchess, and knowing herself to blame – had she not often taken herself to task about the girl's education, promised herself that it should be attended to and then forgotten all about it? – she felt suddenly angry with Catherine, and rising from her chair, went over and slapped the girl at the side of her head.

Catherine stopped playing and looked up in surprise; she was not greatly disturbed by the blow, as the Duchess often cuffed her and there was no great strength in her flabby muscles.

'Disgraceful!' stormed the old lady.

Catherine did not understand. Playing musical instruments was one of the few things she did really well; she did not know that the Duchess, her thoughts far away at Suffolk House where another granddaughter was a queen in all but name, had not heard what she played; she thought that her playing was at fault, for how should she realize that the Duchess was comparing her with Anne and wondering how this child could possibly go to court uneducated as she was.

'Catherine Howard,' said the Duchess, trying to convince herself that she was in no way to blame for the years of neglect, 'you are a disgrace to this house! What do you think Queen Anne would say if I asked for a place at court for you – which she of course would find, since I asked it – and then I presented you to her . . . her cousin? Look at your hair! You are bursting forth from your clothes, and your manners are a disgrace! I declare I will give you such a beating as you never had, you untidy, ignorant little chit! And worse, it seems to me that were you less lazy, you might be quite a pretty girl. Now we shall begin your education in earnest; we are done with this dreaming away of the days. You will work, Catherine Howard, and if you do not, you shall answer to me. Did you hear that?'

'I did hear, Grandmother.'

The Duchess rang a bell, and a serving maid appeared.

'Go bring to me at once young Henry Manox.'

The maid complied, and in a very short time a young man with hair growing low upon his brow but a certain handsome swagger in his walk and an elegance about his person, combined with a pair of very bold black eyes to make him an attractive creature, appeared and bowed low before the Duchess.

'Manox, here is my granddaughter. I fear she needs much tuition. Now I would you sat down at the virginals and played awhile.'

He flashed a smile at Catherine which seemed to suggest that they were going to be friends. Catherine, ever ready to respond to friendship, returned the smile, and he sat down and played most excellently, so that Catherine, loving music as she did, was delighted and clapped her hands when he ended.

'There. child!' said the Duchess. 'That is how I would have you play. Manox, you shall teach my granddaughter. You may give her a lesson now.'

Manox stood up and bowed. He came to Catherine, bowed again, took her hand and led her to the virginals.

The Duchess watched them; she liked to watch young people; there was something, she decided, so delightful about them; their movements were graceful. Particularly she liked young men, having always had a fondness for them from the cradle. She remembered her own youth; there had been a delightful music master. Nothing wrong about that of course; she had been aware of her dignity at a very early age. Still it had been pleasant to be taught by one who had charm; and he had grown quite fond of her, although always she had kept him at a distance.

There they sat, those two children – for after all he was little more than a child compared with her old age – and they seemed more attractive than they had separately. If Catherine were not so young, thought the Duchess, I should have to watch Manox; I believe he has quite a naughty reputation and is fond of adventuring with the young ladies.

Watching her granddaughter take a lesson, the Duchess thought – From now on I shall superintend the child's education myself. After all, to be cousin to the Queen means a good deal. When her opportunity comes, she must be ready to take it.

Then, feeling virtuous, grandmotherly devotion rising within her, she told herself that even though Catherine was such a child, she would not allow her to be alone with one of Manox's reputation; the lessons should always take place in this room and she herself would be there.

For the thousandth time the Duchess assured herself that it was fortunate indeed that little Catherine Howard should have come under her care; after all, the cousin of a Queen needs to be very tenderly nurtured, for who can say what honours may await her?

*　　*　　*

Anne was being dressed for the banquet. Her ladies fluttered about her, flattering her. Was she happy? she asked herself, as her thoughts went back over the past year which had seen her rise to the height of glory, and which yet had been full of misgivings and apprehensions, even fears.

She had changed; none knew this better than herself; she had grown hard, calculating; she was not the same girl who had loved Percy so deeply and defiantly; she was less ready with sympathy, finding hatreds springing up in her, and with them a new, surprising quality which had not been there before – vindictiveness.

She laughed when she saw Percy. He was changed from that rather delicate, beautiful young man whom she had loved; he was still delicate, suffering from some undefined disease; and such unhappiness was apparent in his face that should have made her weep for him. But she did not weep; instead she was filled with bitter laughter, thinking: You fool! You brought this on yourself. You spoiled your life – and mine with it – and now you must suffer for your folly, and I shall benefit from it!

But did she benefit? She was beginning to understand her royal lover well; she could command him; her beauty and her wit, being unsurpassed in his court, must make him their slave. But how long does a man, who is more polygamous than most, remain faithful? That was a question that would perplex her now and then. Already there was a change in his attitude towards her. Oh, he was deeply in love, eager to please, anxious that every little wish she expressed should be granted. But who was it now who must curse the delay,

Anne or Henry? Henry desired the divorce; he wanted very much to remove Katharine from the throne and put Anne on it, but he was less eager than Anne. Anne was his mistress; he could wait to make her his wife. It was Anne who must rail against delay, who must fret, who must deplore her lost virtue, who must ask herself, Will the Pope ever agree to the divorce?

Sometimes her thoughts would make her frantic. She had yielded in spite of her protestations that she would never yield. She had yielded on the King's promise to make her Queen; her sister Mary had exacted no promise. Where was the difference between Anne and Mary, since Mary had yielded for lust, and Anne for a crown! Anne had a picture of herself returning home to Hever defeated, or perhaps married to one as ineffectual as the late William Carey.

Henry had given Thomas Wyatt the post of High Marshal of Calais, which would take him out of England a good deal. Anne liked to dwell on that facet of Henry's character; he loved some of his friends, and Wyatt was one of them. He did not commit Wyatt to the Tower – which would have been easy enough – but sent him away . . . Oh, yes, Henry could feel sentimental where one he had really loved was concerned, and Henry did love Thomas. Who could help loving Thomas? asked Anne, and wept a little.

Anne tried now to think clearly and honestly of that last year. Had it been a good year? It had . . . of course it had! How could she say that she had not enjoyed it . . . she had enjoyed it vastly! Proud, haughty, as she was, how pleasant it must be to have such deference shown to her. Aware of her beauty, how could she help but wish to adorn it! Such as Queen Katharine might call that vanity; is pride in a most unusual possession, then, vanity? Must she not enjoy the revels when she herself was acclaimed the shining light, the star, the most beautiful, the most accomplished of women, greatly loved by the King?

She had her enemies, the Cardinal the chief among them. Her Uncle Norfolk was outwardly her friend, but she could never like and trust him, and she believed him now to be annoyed because the King had not chosen to favour his daughter, the Lady Mary Howard, who was of so much nobler birth than Anne Boleyn. Suffolk! There was another enemy, and Suffolk was a dangerous, cruel man. Her thoughts went back to windy days and nights in Dover Castle, when Mary Tudor talked of the magnificence of a certain Charles Brandon. And this was he, this florid, cruel-eyed, relentless and ambitious man! An astute man, he had married the King's sister and placed himself very near the throne, and because a strange fate had placed Anne even nearer, he had become her enemy. These thoughts were frightening.

How happy she had been, dancing with the King at Greenwich last Christmas, laughing in the faces of those who would criticize her for holding her revels at Greenwich in defiance of the Queen; hating the Queen, who so obstinately refused to go into a nunnery and to admit she had consummated her marriage with Arthur! She had danced wildly, had made brilliantly witty remarks about the Queen and the Princess, had flaunted her supremacy over them – and afterwards hated herself for this, though admitting the hatred to none but the bright-eyed reflection which looked back at her so reproachfully from the mirror.

The Princess hated her and took no pains to hide the fact; and had not hesitated to whisper to those who had been ready to carry such talk to the ears of Anne, of what she would do to Anne Boleyn, were she Queen.

'I would commit her to the Tower, where I would torture her; we should see if she would be so beautiful after the tormentors had done with her! I should turn the rack myself. We should see if she could make such witty remarks to the rats who came to The Pit to gnaw her bones and bite her to death. But I would not leave her to die that way; I would burn her alive. She is all but a witch, and I hear that she has those about her who are of the new faith. Aye! I would pile the faggots at her feet and watch her burn, and before she had burnt, I would remove her that she might burn and burn again, tasting on Earth that which she will assuredly meet in hell.'

The eyes of the Princess, already burning with fanatical

fervour, rested on Anne with loathing, and Anne laughed in the face of the foolish girl and feigned indifference to her, but those eyes haunted her when she was awake and when she slept. But even as she professed scorn and hatred for the girl, Anne well understood what her coming must have meant to Mary, who had enjoyed the privileges of being her father's daughter, Princess Mary and heiress of England. Now the King sought to make her but a bastard, of less importance than the Duke of Richmond who was at least a boy.

As she lay in the King's arms, Anne would talk of the Princess.

'I will not be treated thus by her! I swear it. There is not room for both of us at court.'

Henry soothed her while he put up a fight for Mary. His sentimental streak was evident when he thought of his daughter; he was not without affection for her and, while longing for a son, he had become – before the prospect of displacing Katharine had come to him, and Anne declared she would never be his mistress – reconciled to her.

Anne said: 'I shall go back to Hever. I will not stay to be insulted thus.'

'I shall not allow you to go to Hever, sweetheart. Your place is here with me.'

'Nevertheless,' said Anne coldly, 'to Hever I shall go!'

The fear that she would leave him was a constant threat to Henry, and he could not bear that she should be out of his sight; she could command him by threatening to leave him.

When Mary fell into disgrace with her father, there were those who, sorry for the young girl, accused Anne of acute vindictiveness. It was the same with Wolsey. It was true that she did not forget the slights she had received from him, and that she pursued him relentlessly, determined that he should fall from that high place on which he had lodged himself. Perhaps it was forgotten by those who accused her that Anne was fighting a desperate battle. Behind all the riches and power, all the admiration and kingly affection which was showered upon her, Anne was aware of that low murmur of the people, of the malicious schemes of her enemies who even now were seeking to ruin her. Prominent among these enemies were Wolsey and Princess Mary. What therefore could Anne do but fight these people, and if she at this time held the most effective weapons, she merely used them as both Wolsey and Mary would have done, had they the luck to hold them.

But her triumphs were bitter to her. She loved admiration; she loved approval, and she wanted no enemies. Wolsey and she, though they flattered each other and feigned friendship, knew that both could not hold the high positions they aspired to; one must go. Anne fought as tenaciously as Wolsey had ever fought, and because Wolsey's star was setting and Anne's was rising, she was winning. There were many little pointers to indicate this strife between them, and perhaps one of the most significant – Anne was thinking – was the confiscation of a book of hers which had found its way into the possession of her equerry, young George Zouch. Anne, it was beginning to be known – and this knowledge could not please the Cardinal – was interested in the new religion which was becoming a matter of some importance on the Continent, and one of the reformers had presented her with Tindal's translation of the holy scriptures.

Anne had read it, discussed it with her brother and some of her friends, found it of great interest and passed it on to one of the favourite ladies of her retinue, for Mistress Gaynsford was an intelligent girl, and Anne thought the book might be of interest to her. However, Mistress Gaynsford was loved by George Zouch who, one day when he had come upon her quietly reading, to tease her snatched the book and refused to return it; instead he took it with him to the King's chapel, where, during the service, he opened the book and becoming absorbed in its contents attracted the attention of the dean who, demanding to see it and finding it to be a prohibited one, lost no time in conveying it to Cardinal Wolsey. Mistress Gaynsford was terrified at the course of events, and went trembling to Anne, who, ever ready to complain against the Cardinal, told the King that he had confiscated her book and demanded its immediate return. The book was brought back to Anne at once.

'What book is this that causes so much pother?' Henry wanted to know.

'You must read it,' Anne answered and added: 'I insist!'

Henry promised and did; the Cardinal was disconcerted to learn that His Majesty was as interested as young George Zouch had been. This was a deeply significant defeat for Wolsey.

This year, reflected Anne as the coif was fixed upon her hair and her reflection looked back at her, had been a sorry one for the Cardinal. The trial had gone wrong. Shall we ever get this divorce, wondered Anne. The Pope was adamant; the people murmured: 'Nan Bullen shall not be our Queen!'

Henry would say little of what had happened at Blackfriars Hall, but Anne knew something of that fiasco; of Katharine's coming into the court and kneeling at the feet of the King, asking for justice. Anne could picture it – the solemn state, the May sunshine filtering through the windows, the King impatient with the whole proceedings, grey-faced Wolsey praying that the King might turn from the folly of his desire to marry Anne Boleyn, gouty old Campeggio procrastinating, having no intention of giving a verdict. The King had made a long speech about his scrupulous conscience and how – Anne's lips curled with scorn – he did not ask for the divorce out of his carnal desires, how the Queen pleased him as much as any woman, but his conscience . . . his conscience . . . his most scrupulous conscience . . .

And the trial had dragged on through the summer months, until Henry, urged on by herself, demanded a decision. Then had Campeggio been forced to make a statement, then had he been forced to show his intention – which was, of course, not to grant the divorce at all. He must, he had said – to Henry's extreme wrath – consult with his master, the Pope. Then had Suffolk decided to declare open war on the Cardinal, for he had stood up and shouted: 'It was never merry in England whilst we had cardinals among us!' And the King strode forth from the court in an access of rage, cursing the Pope, cursing the delay, cursing Campeggio and with him Wolsey, whom he was almost ready to regard as Campeggio's confederate. Anne's thoughts went to two men who, though obscure before, had this year leaped into prominence – the two Thomases, Cromwell and Cranmer. Anne thought warmly of them both, for from these two did she and Henry hope for much. Cranmer had distinguished himself because of his novel views, particularly on this subject of the divorce. He was tactful and discreet, clever and intellectual. As don, tutor, priest and Cambridge man, he was interested in Lutherism. He had suggested that Henry should appeal to the English ecclesiastical courts instead of to Rome on this matter of the divorce; he voiced this opinion constantly, until it had been brought to Henry's notice.

Henry, eager to escape from the meshes of Rome, was ready to welcome anyone who could wield a knife to cut him free. He liked what he heard of Cranmer. 'By God!' he cried. 'That man hath the right sow by the ear!'

Cranmer was sent for. Henry was crafty, clever enough when he gave his mind to a matter; and never had he given as much thought to anything as he had to this matter of the divorce. Wolsey, he knew, was attached to Rome, for Rome had its sticky threads about the Cardinal as a spider has about the fly in its web. The King was crying out for new men to take the place of Wolsey. There could never be another Wolsey; of that he was sure; but might there not be many who together could carry the great burdens which Wolsey had carried alone? When Cranmer had talked with Henry a few times, Henry saw great possibilities in the man. He was obedient, he was docile, he was loyal; he was going to be of inestimable value to a Henry who had lost his Wolsey to the Roman web.

Anne's thoughts went to that other Thomas – Cromwell. Cromwell was of the people, just as Wolsey had been, but with a difference. Cromwell bore the marks of his origins and could not escape from them; Wolsey, the intellectual, had escaped, though there were those who said that he showed the marks of his upbringing in his great love of splendour, in his vulgar displays of wealth. (But, thought Anne, laughing to herself, had not the King even greater delight in flamboyant display!) Cromwell, however – thickset, impervious to insult, with his fish-like eyes and his ugly hands – could not hide his origins and made but little attempt to do so. He was serving Wolsey well, deploring the lack of fight he was showing. Cromwell was not over-nice; Henry knew this and, while seeing in him enormous possibilities, had never taken to him. 'I love not that man!' said Henry to Anne. 'By God! He has a touch of the sewer about him. He sickens me! He is a knave!'

There was a peculiar side to Henry's nature which grew out of an almost childish love and admiration for certain people, which made him seek to defend them even while he planned their destruction. He had had that affection for Wolsey, Wolsey the wit, in his gorgeous homes, in his fine clothes; he had liked Wolsey as a man. This man Cromwell he could never like, useful as he was; more useful as he promised to be. Cromwell was blind to humiliation; he worked hard and took insults; he was clever; he helped Wolsey, advised him to favour Anne's friends, placated Norfolk, and so secured a seat in parliament. Would there always be those to spring up and replace others when the King needed them? What if she herself lost the King's favour! It was simpler to replace a mistress than a Wolsey ...

Pretty Anne Saville, Anne's favourite attendant, whispered that she was preoccupied tonight. Anne answered that indeed she was, and had been thinking back over the past year.

Anne Saville patted Anne's beautiful hair lovingly.

'It has been a great and glorious year for your ladyship.'

'Has it?' said Anne, her face so serious that the other Anne looked at her in sudden alarm.

'Assuredly,' said the girl. 'Many honours have come your ladyship's way, and the King grows more in love with you with the passing of each day.'

Anne took her namesake's hand and pressed it for awhile, for she was very fond of this girl.

'And you grow more beautiful with each day,' said Anne Saville earnestly. 'There is no lady in the court who would not give ten years of her life to change places with you.'

In the mirror the coif glittered like a golden crown. Anne trembled a little; in the great hall she would be gayer than any, but up here away from the throng she often trembled, contemplating the night before her, and afraid to think further than that.

Anne was ready; she would go down. She would take one last look at herself – The Lady Anne Rochford now, for recently her father had been made Earl of Wiltshire, George became Lord Rochford, and she herself was no longer plain Anne Boleyn. The Boleyns had come far, she thought, and was reminded of George, laughing-eyed and only sad when one caught him in repose.

When she thought of George she would feel recklessness stealing over her, and the determination to live dangerously rather than live without adventure.

Thoughts of George were pleasant. She realized with a pang that of all her friends who now, with the King at their head, swore they would die for her, there was only one she could really trust. There was her father, her Uncle Norfolk, the man who would be her husband . . . but on those occasions when Fear came and stood menacingly before her, it was of her brother she must think. 'There is really none but George!'

'Thank God for George!' she said to herself, and dismissed gloomy thoughts.

In the great hall the King was waiting to greet her. He was magnificent in his favourite russet, padded and sparkling, larger than any man there, ruddy from the day's hunting, flushed already and flushing more as his eyes rested on Anne.

He said: 'It seems long since I kissed you!'

''Tis several hours, I'll swear!' she answered.

'There is none like you, Anne.'

He would show his great love for her tonight, for of late she had complained bitterly of the lack of courtesy shown her by the Queen and Princess.

He had said: 'By God! I'll put an end to their obstinacy. They shall bow the knee to you, sweetheart, or learn our displeasure!' The Princess should be separated from her mother, and they should both be banished from court; he had said last night that he was weary of them both; weary of the pious obstinacy of the Queen, who stuck to her lies and refused to make matters easy by going into a nunnery; weary of the rebellious daughter who refused to behave herself and think herself fortunate – she, who was no more than a bastard, though a royal one – in receiving her father's affection. 'I tell thee, Anne,' he had said, his lips on her hair, 'I am weary of these women.'

She had answered: 'Need I say I am too?' And she had thought, They would see me burn in hell; nor do I blame them for that, for what good have I done them! But what I cannot endure is their attitude of righteousness. They burn with desire for revenge, and they pray that justice shall be dealt me; they pray to God to put me in torment. Hearty sinful vengeance I can forgive; but when it is hidden under a cloak of piety and called justice . . . never! Never! And so will I fight against these two, and will not do a thing to make their lot easier. I am a sinner; and so are they; nor do sins become whiter when cloaked in piety.

But this she did not tell her lover, for was he not inclined to use that very cloak of piety to cover his sins? When he confessed what he had done this night, last night, would he not say: 'It is for England; I must have a son!' Little eyes, greedy with lust; hot straying hands; the urgent desire to possess her again and again. And this, not that she might give the King pleasure, but that she should give England a son!

Was it surprising that sometimes in the early hours of the morning, when he lay beside her breathing heavily in sleep, his hand laid lightly on her body, smiling as he slept the smile of remembrance, murmuring her name in his sleep – was it surprising that then she would think of her brother's handsome face, and murmur to herself: 'Oh, George, take me home! Take me to Blickling, not to Hever, for at Hever I should see the rose garden and think of him. But take me to Blickling where we were together when we were very young . . . and where I never dreamed of being Queen of England.'

But she could not go back now. She must go on and on. I want to go on! I want to go on! What is love? It is ethereal, so that you cannot hold it; it is transient, so that you cannot keep it. But a queen is always a queen. Her sons are kings. I want to be a queen; of course I want to be a queen! It is only in moments of deepest depression that I am afraid.

Nor was she afraid this night as he, regardless of all these watching ladies and gentlemen, pressed his great body close to hers and showed that he was impatient for the night.

Tonight he wished to show her how greatly he loved her; that he wished all these people to pay homage to this beautiful girl who had pleased him, who continued to please him, and whom, because of an evil Fate in the shape of a weak Pope, an obstinate Queen, and a pair of scheming Cardinals, he could not yet make his Queen.

He would have her take precedence over the two most noble ladies present, the Duchess of Norfolk and his own sister of Suffolk.

These ladies resented this, Anne knew, and suddenly a mood of recklessness came over her. What did she care! What mattered it, indeed. She had the King's love and none of her enemies dared oppose her openly.

The King's sister? She was ageing now; different indeed from the giddy girl who had led poor Louis such a dance, who had alternated between her desire to bear a king of France and marry Brandon; there was nothing left to her but ambition; and ambition for what? Her daughter Frances Brandon? Mary of Suffolk wanted her daughter on the throne. And now here was Anne Boleyn, young and full of life, only waiting for the divorce to bear the King many sons and so set a greater distance between Frances Brandon and the throne of England.

And the Duchess of Norfolk? She was jealous, as was her husband, on account of the King's having chosen Anne instead of their daughter the Lady Mary Howard. She was angry because of Anne's friendship with the old Dowager Duchess of Norfolk.

What do I care? What have I to fear!

Nothing! For the King was looking at her with deep longing; nor could he bear that she should not be with him. She only had to threaten to leave him, and she could have both of these arrogant ladies banished from court.

So she was bold and defiant, and flaunted her supremacy in the faces of all those who resented her. Lady Anne Rochford, beloved of the King, leader of the revels, now taking precedence over the highest in the land as though she were already Queen.

She had seen the Countess Chateau-briant and the Duchess D'Estampes treated as princesses by poor little Claude at the court of Francis. So should she be treated by these haughty Duchesses of Norfolk and Suffolk; yes, and by Katharine of Aragon and her daughter Mary!

But of course there was a great difference between the French ladies and the Lady Anne Rochford. They were merely the mistresses of the King of France; the Lady Anne Rochford was to be Queen of England!

*　　*　　*

In her chair the Dowager Duchess of Norfolk dozed; her foot tapped automatically, but she was not watching the pair at the virginals. She was thinking of the court and the King's passion for that gorgeous lady, her dear granddaughter. Ah! And scheming Thomas now has his Earldom and all that goes with it; and well pleased he is, I'll swear, for money means more to Thomas than aught else. And she is the Lady Anne Rochford, if you please, and George on very pleasant terms with the King . . . though not with his own sly little wife! Poor George! A pity there can't be a divorce. Why not a princess wife for your brother, eh, Queen Anne? Eh? Of course you are Queen! But she'll look after George . . . those two would stick together no matter what befell. Ah, how I wish she would send for me! I trow she would if she knew how eager I am to be gone . . . What if I sent a messenger . . . Ah! The court, the masques . . .

though indeed I am a little old for such pleasures. Charming, if she came to visit me at Lambeth ... We would sit in the gardens, and I would make her talk to me of the King ... My granddaughter, the Queen of England! My granddaughter ... Queen Anne ...

She was asleep, and Henry Manox, sensing this, threw a sly glance over his shoulder at her.

'There!' said Catherine. 'Was that better?'

He said, moving nearer to Catherine: 'That was perfect!'

She flushed with pleasure, and he noticed the delicate skin and the long, fair lashes, and the charming strand of auburn hair that fell across her brow. Her youth was very appealing; he had never made love to one so young before; and yet, in spite of her youth, already she showed signs of an early ripening.

'Never,' he whispered, 'have I enjoyed teaching anyone as I have enjoyed our lessons!'

The Duchess snored softly.

Catherine laughed, and he joined in the laugh; he leaned forward suddenly and kissed the tip of her nose. Catherine felt a pleasurable thrill; it was exciting because it had to be done while the Duchess slept; and he was handsome, she thought, with his dark, bold eyes; and it was flattering to be admired by one so much older than herself; it was gratifying to be treated as though one were charming, after the reproaches her grandmother had showered upon her.

'I am glad I am a good pupil.'

'You are a very good pupil!' he said. 'Right glad I am that it is my happy lot to teach you.'

'Her Grace, my grandmother, thinks me very stupid.'

'Then it is Her Grace, your grandmother, who is stupid!'

Catherine hunched her shoulders, laughing.

'I take it, sir, that you do not then think me stupid.'

'Indeed not; but young, very young, and there is much you have to learn yet.'

The Duchess awoke with a start, and Catherine began to play.

'That was better,' said the Duchess, 'was it not, Manox?'

'Indeed, Your Grace, it was!'

'And you think your pupil is improving?'

'Vastly, Madam!'

'So thought I. Now you may go, Catherine. Manox, you may stay awhile and talk with me.'

Catherine went, and he stayed and talked awhile; they talked of music, for they had nothing in common but music. But the Duchess did not mind of what her young men talked as long as they talked and entertained her. It was their youth she liked; it was their flattery. And as Manox talked to her, she drifted back to the days of her own youth, and then forward again to the court as it was today, ruled by her loveliest of granddaughters.

'Methinks I shall go to Lambeth,' she announced, and dismissed Manox.

Catherine went to the apartment, where she found Isabel.

'How went the lesson?' asked Isabel.

'Very well.'

'How you love your music!' said Isabel. 'You look as if you had just left a lover, not a lesson.'

Their talk was continually of lovers; Catherine did not notice this, as it seemed natural enough to her. To have lovers was not only natural but the most exciting possibility; it was all part of the glorious business of growing up, and now Catherine longed to be grown-up.

She still thought of Thomas Culpepper, but she could only with difficulty remember what he looked like. She still dreamed that he rode out to Horsham and told her they were to elope together, but his face, which for so long had been blurred in her mind, now began to take on the shape of Henry Manox. She looked forward to her lessons; the most exciting moment of her days was when she went down to the Duchess's room and found him there; she was always terrified that he would not be there, that her grandmother had decided to find her a new teacher; she looked forward with gleeful anticipation to those spasmodic snores of the Duchess which set both her and Manox giggling, and made his eyes become more bold.

As he sat very close to her, his long musician's fingers would come to rest on her knee, tapping lightly that she might keep in time. The Duchess nodded; her head shook; then she would awake startled and look round her defiantly, as though to deny the obvious fact that she had dozed.

There was one day, some weeks after the first lesson, which was a perfect day, with spring in the sunshine filtering through the window, in the songs of the birds in the trees outside it, in Catherine's heart and in Manox's eyes.

He whispered: 'Catherine! I think of you constantly.'

'Have I improved so much then?'

'Not of your music, but of you, Catherine . . . of you.'

'I wonder why you should think constantly of me.'

'Because you are very sweet.'

'Am I?' said Catherine.

'And not such a child as you would seem!'

'No,' said Catherine. 'Sometimes I think I am very grown-up.'

He laid his delicate hands on the faint outline of her breasts.

'Yes, Catherine, I think so too. It is very sweet to be grown-up, Catherine. When you are a woman you will wonder how you could ever have borne your childhood.'

'Yes,' said Catherine, 'I believe that. I have had some unhappy times in my childhood; my mother died, and then I went to Hollingbourne, and just when I was beginning to love my life there, that was over.'

'Do not look so sad, sweet Catherine! Tell me, you are not sad, are you?'

'Not now,' she said.

He kissed her cheek.

He said: 'I would like to kiss your lips.'

He did this, and she was astonished by the kiss, which was different from those Thomas had given her. Catherine was stirred; she kissed him.

'I have never been so happy!' he said.

They were both too absorbed in each other to listen for the Duchess's snores and heavy breathing; she awoke suddenly, and hearing no music, looked towards them.

'Chatter, chatter, chatter!' she said. 'I declare! Is this a music lesson!'

Catherine began to play, stumbling badly.

The Duchess yawned; her foot began to tap; in five minutes she was asleep again.

'Do you think she saw us kiss?' whispered Catherine.

'Indeed I do not!' said Manox, and he meant that, for he well knew that if she had he would have been immediately turned out, possibly dismissed from the house; and Mistress Catherine would have received a sound beating.

Catherine shivered ecstatically.

'I am terrified that she might, and will stop the lessons.'

'You would care greatly about that?'

Catherine turned candid eyes upon him. 'I should care very much!' she said. She was vulnerable because her mind was that of a child, though her body was becoming that of a woman; and the one being so advanced, the other somewhat backward, it was her body which was in command of Catherine. She liked the proximity of this man; she liked his kisses. She told him so in many ways; and he, being without scruples, found the situation too novel and too exciting not to be exploited.

He was rash in his excitement, taking her in his arms before the sleeping Duchess and kissing her lips. Catherine lifted her face eagerly, as a flower will turn towards the sun.

The Duchess was sleeping, when there was a faint tap on the door and Isabel entered. The lesson had extended beyond its appointed time, and she, eager to see the teacher and pupil together, had an excuse ready for intruding. Isabel stood on the threshold, taking in the scene – the sleeping Duchess, the young man, his face very pale, his eyes very bright; Catherine, hair in some disorder, her eyes wide, her lips parted, and with a red mark on her chin. Where he has kissed her, the knave! thought Isabel.

The Duchess awoke with a start.

'Come in! Come in!' she called, seeing Isabel at the door.

Isabel approached and spoke to the Duchess. Catherine rose, and so did Manox.

'You may go, Catherine,' said the Duchess. 'Manox! Stay awhile. I would speak to you.'

Catherine went, eager to be alone, to remember everything he had said, how he had looked; to wonder how she was going to live through the hours until the next lesson on the morrow.

When Isabel was dismissed, she waited for Manox to come out.

He bowed low, smiling when he saw her, thinking that he had made an impression on her, for his surface charm and his reputation had made him irresistible to quite a number of ladies. He smiled at Isabel's pale face and compared it with Catherine's round childish one. He was more excited by Catherine than he had been since his first affair; for this adventuring with the little girl was a new experience, and though it was bound to be slow, and needed tact and patience, he found it more intriguing than any normal affair could be.

Isabel said: 'I have never seen you at our entertainments.'

He smiled and said that he had heard of the young ladies' revels, and it was a matter of great regret that he had never attended one.

She said: 'You must come . . . I will tell you when. You know it is a secret!'

'Never fear that I should drop a hint to Her Grace.'

'It is innocent entertainment,' said Isabel anxiously.

'I could not doubt it!'

'We frolic a little; we feast; there is nothing wrong. It is just amusing.'

'That I have heard.'

'I will let you know then.'

'You are the kindest of ladies.'

He bowed courteously, and went on his way, thinking of Catherine.

* * *

Through the gardens at Hampton Court Anne walked with Henry. He was excited, his head teeming with plans, for the Cardinal's palace was now his. He had demanded of a humiliated Wolsey wherefore a subject should have such a palace; and with a return of that wit which had been the very planks on which he had built his mighty career, the

Cardinal, knowing himself lost and hoping by gifts to reinstate himself a little in the heart of the King, replied that a subject might build such a palace only to show what a noble gift a subject might make to his King.

Henry had been delighted by that reply; he had all but embraced his old friend, and his eyes had glistened to think of Hampton Court. Henry had inherited his father's acquisitive nature, and the thought of riches must ever make him lick his lips with pleasure.

'Darling,' he said to Anne, 'we must to Hampton Court, for there are many alterations I would make. I will make a palace of Hampton Court, and you shall help in this.'

The royal barge had carried them up the river; there was no ceremony on this occasion. Perhaps the King was not eager for it; perhaps he felt a little shame in accepting this magnificent gift from his old friend. All the way up the river he laughed with Anne at the incongruity of a subject's daring to possess such a place.

'He was another king . . . or would be!' said Anne. 'You were most lenient with him.'

' 'Twas ever a fault of mine, sweetheart, to be over-lenient with those I love.'

She raised her beautifully arched eyebrows, and surveyed him mockingly.

'I fancy it is so with myself.'

He slapped his thigh – a habit of his – and laughed at her; she delighted him now as ever. He grew sentimental, contemplating her. He had loved her long, nor did his passion for her abate. To be in love was a pleasant thing; he glowed with self-sacrifice, thinking: She shall have the grandest apartments that can be built! I myself will plan them.

He told her of his ideas for the alterations.

'Work shall be started for my Queen's apartments before aught else. The hangings shall be of tissue of gold, sweetheart. I myself will design the walls.' He thought of great lovers' knots with the initials H and A intwined. He told her of this; sentimental and soft, his voice was slurred with affection. 'Intwined, darling! As our lives shall be and have been ever since we met. For I would have the world know that naught shall come between us two.'

Unceremoniously they left the barge. The gardens were beautiful – but a cardinal's gardens, said Henry, not a king's!

'Dost know I have a special fondness for gardens?' he asked. 'And dost know why?'

She thought it strange and oddly perturbing that he could remind her of his faithfulness to her here in this domain which he had taken – for the gift was enforced – from one to whom he owed greater loyalty. But how like Henry! Here in the shadow of Wolsey's cherished Hampton Court, he must tell himself that he was a loyal friend, because he had been disloyal to its owner.

'Red and white roses,' said the King, and he touched her cheek. 'We will have this like your father's garden at Hever, eh? We will have a pond, and you shall sit on its edge and talk to me, and watch your own reflection. I'll warrant you will be somewhat kinder to me than you were at Hever, eh?'

'It would not surprise me,' she laughed.

He talked with enthusiasm of his plans. He visualized beds of roses – red and white to symbolize the union of the houses of York and Lancaster, to remind all who beheld them that the Tudors represented peace; he would enclose those beds with wooden railings painted in his livery colours of white and green; he would set up posts and pillars which should be decorated with heraldic designs. There would be about the place a constant reminder to all, including himself, that he was a faithful man; that when he loved, he loved deeply and long. H and A! Those initials should be displayed in every possible spot.

'Come along in, sweetheart,' he said. 'I would choose your apartments. They shall be the most lavish that were ever seen.'

They went up the staircase, across a large room. It was Anne who turned to the right and descended a few steps into the panelled rooms which had been Wolsey's own. Henry had not wished to go into those rooms, but when he saw their splendid furnishings, their rich hangings, the magnificent plate, the window seats padded with red window carpets, the twisted gold work on the ceilings, he was loth to leave them. He had seen this splendour many times before; but then it had been Wolsey's, now it was his.

Anne pointed to the damask carpets which lay about the floors, and reminded the King of how, it was whispered, Wolsey had come by these.

Henry was less ready to defend his old favourite than usual. He recounted the story of the Venetian bribe, and his mouth was a thin line, though previously he had laughed at it, condoned it.

They went through the lavishly furnished bedrooms, admired the counterpanes of satin and damask, the cushions of velvet and satin and cloth of gold.

'Good sweetheart,' said Henry, 'I think your apartment shall be here, for I declare it to be the finest part of Hampton Court. The rooms shall be enlarged; I will have new ceilings; everything here shall be of the best. It shall be accomplished as soon as possible.'

'It will take many years,' said Anne, and added: 'So therefore it is just possible that the divorce may be done with by then, if it ever is!'

He put an arm about her shoulders.

'How now, darling! We have waited long, and are impatient, but methinks we shall not wait much longer. Cranmer is a man of ideas . . . and that knave, Cromwell, too! My plans for your apartments may take a year or two completely to carry out, but never fear, long ere their accomplishment you shall be Queen of England!'

They sat awhile on the window seat, for the day was warm. He talked enthusiastically of the changes he would make. She listened but listlessly; Hampton Court held memories of a certain moonlit night, when she and Percy had looked from one of those windows and talked of the happiness they would make for each other.

She wondered if she would ever occupy these rooms which he planned for her. Wolsey had once made plans in this house.

'Our initials intwined, sweetheart,' said the King. 'Come! You shiver. Let us on.'

*   *   *

In his house at Westminster, Wolsey awaited the arrival of Norfolk and Suffolk. His day was over, and Wolsey knew it; this was the end of his brightness; he would live the rest of his life in the darkness of obscurity, if he were lucky; but was it not a proven fact that when great men fell from favour their heads were not long in coming to the block? Those who lived gloriously must often die violently. Wolsey was sick, of mind and body; there was a pain in his solar plexus, a pain in his throat; and this was what men called heartbreak. And the most heartbreaking moment of his career was when he had arrived at Grafton with Campeggio, to find that there was no place for him at the court. For his fellow cardinal there were lodgings prepared in accordance with his state, but for Thomas Wolsey, once beloved of the King, there was no bed on which to rest his weary body. Then did he know to what depths of disfavour he had sunk. But for young Henry Norris, he knew not what he would have done; already had he suffered enough humiliation to break the heart of a proud man.

Norris, groom of the stole, a young handsome person with compassion in his pleasant eyes, had offered his own apartment to the travel-stained old man; such moments were pleasant in a wretched day. And yet, next day when he and Campeggio had had audience with the King, had not His Majesty softened to him, his little eyes troubled, his little mouth pursed with remembrance? Henry would never hate his old friend when he stood face to face with him; there were too many memories they shared; between them they had given birth to too many successful schemes for all to be forgotten. It is the careless, watching, speculating eyes which hurt a fallen man. He knew those callous courtiers laid wagers on the King's conduct towards his old favourite. Wolsey had seen the disappointment in their faces when Henry let his old affection triumph; and Lady Anne's dark eyes had glittered angrily, for she believed that the resuscitation of Wolsey's dying influence meant the strangulation of her own. Her beautiful face had hardened, though she had smiled graciously enough on the Cardinal; and Wolsey, returning her smile, had felt fear grip his heart once more, for what hope had he with such an enemy!

It had come to his ears, by way of those who had waited on her and the King when they dined, that she had been deeply offended by Henry's show of affection for the Cardinal; and she, bold and confident in her power over the King, did not hesitate to reprove him. 'Is it not a marvellous thing,' so he had heard she said, 'to consider what debt and danger the Cardinal hath brought you in with your subjects?' The King was puzzled. 'How so, sweetheart?' Then she referred to that loan which the Cardinal had raised from his subjects for the King's use. And she laughed and added: 'If my lord Norfolk, my lord Suffolk, my lord my father, or any other noble person within your realm had done much less than he, they should have lost their heads ere this.' To which the King answered: 'I perceive ye are not the Cardinal's friend.' 'I have no cause!' she retorted. 'Nor more any other that love Your Grace, if ye consider well his doings!'

No more had been heard at the table, but Wolsey knew full well how gratifying it would be for the King to imagine her hatred for the Cardinal had grown out of her love for the King. She was an adversary to beware of. He had no chance of seeing the King again, for the Lady Anne had gone off riding with him next morning, and had so contrived it that His Majesty did not return until the cardinals had left. What poison did this woman pour into his master's ears by day and night? But being Wolsey he must know it was himself whom he must blame; he it was who had taken that false step. He was too astute not to realize that had he been in Lady Anne's place he would have acted as she did now. Imagination had helped to lift him, therefore it was easy to see himself in her position. He could even pity her, for her road was a more dangerous one than his, and those who depend for prosperity upon a prince's favour – and such a prince – must consider each step before they take it, if they wish to survive. He had failed with the divorce, and looking back, that seemed inevitable, for as Cardinal he owed allegiance to Rome, and the King was straining to break those chains which bound him to the Holy See. He, who was shrewd, diplomatic, had failed. She was haughty, imperious, impulsive; what fate awaited her? Where she was concerned he had been foolish; he had lacked imagination. A man does not blame himself when enemies are made by his greatness; it is only when they are made by his folly that he does this. Perhaps humiliation was easier to bear, knowing he had brought it on himself.

His usher, Cavendish, came in to tell him that the Dukes of Norfolk and Suffolk had arrived. The Cardinal received them ceremoniously – the cold-eyed Norfolk, the cruel-eyed Suffolk, both rejoicing in his downfall.

'It is the King's pleasure,' said Suffolk, 'that you should hand over the Great Seal into our hands, and that you depart simply unto Esher.'

Esher! To a house near splendid Hampton Court which was his through the Bishopric of Winchester. He summoned all his dignity.

'And what commission have you, my lords, to give me such commandment?'

They said they came from the King, that they had received the commission from his royal mouth.

'Then that is not sufficient,' said Wolsey, 'for the Great Seal of England was delivered me by the King's own person, to enjoy during my life. I have the King's letters to show it.'

The Dukes were angered by this reply, but seeing the King's letters, all they could do was return to Henry.

Wolsey knew he but put off the evil day. The Great Seal, the symbol of his greatness, remained in his hands for but one more day; on the morrow the Dukes returned from Windsor with letters from the King, and there was nothing more that Wolsey could do but deliver up the seal.

The ex-chancellor was filled with deep foreboding and set his servants to make inventories of all the rich possessions in his house; these goods he would give to the King, for if his master could not be touched by affection it might well be that he could by rich gifts; many times had Wolsey noted that the little eyes glinted with envy when they rested on these things. When a man is in danger of drowning, thought Wolsey, he throws off all his fine apparel that he may swim more easily. What are possessions, compared with life itself!

He took his barge at his privy stairs, having ordered horses to be awaiting him at Putney; and the river, he saw, was crowded with craft, for news had travelled quickly and there were those who find the spectacle of a fallen man pleasurable indeed. He saw their grins; he heard their jeers; he sensed the speculation, the disappointment that he was not going straightway to the Tower.

Riding through Putney town, he saw Norris coming towards him, and his heart was lightened, since he had come to look upon Norris as a friend. And so it proved, for the King's peace of mind had been profoundly disturbed by the story which Norfolk and Suffolk had told him of the giving up of the seal. The King could not forget that he had once loved Wolsey; he was haunted by a pale, sick face under a cardinal's hat; and he remembered how this man had been his friend and counsellor; and though he knew that he had done with Wolsey, he wanted to reassure his conscience that it was not he who had destroyed his old friend, but others. Therefore, to appease that conscience, he sent Norris to Putney with a gold ring which Wolsey would recognize by the rich stone it contained, as they had previously used this ring for a token. He was to be of good cheer, Norris told him, for he stood as high as ever in the King's favour.

Wolsey's spirits soared; his body gained strength; the old fighting spirit came back to him. He was not defeated. He embraced Norris, feeling great affection for this young man, and took a little chain of gold from his neck to give to him; on this chain there hung a tiny cross. 'I desire you to take this small reward from my hand,' he said, and Norris was deeply moved.

Then did the Cardinal look about his retinue; and saw one who had been close to him, and in whom he delighted, for the man's wit and humour were of the subtlest, and many times had he brought mirth into the Cardinal's heaviest hours.

'Take my Fool, Norris,' he said. 'Take him to my lord the King, for well I know His Majesty will like well the gift. Fool!' he called. 'Here, Fool!'

The man came, his eyes wide with fear and with love for his master; and seeing this, the Cardinal leaned forward and said almost tenderly: 'Thou shalt have a place at court, Fool.'

But the Fool knelt down in the mire and wept bitterly. Wolsey was much moved that his servant should show such love, since to be Fool to the King, instead of to a man who is sinking in disgrace, was surely a great step forward.

'Thou art indeed a fool!' said Wolsey. 'Dost not know what I am offering thee?'

All foolery was gone from those droll features; only tears were in the humorous eyes now.

'I will not leave you, master.'

'Didst not hear I have given thee to His Majesty?'

'I will not serve His Majesty. My lord, I have but one master.'

With tears in his eyes the Cardinal called six yeomen to remove the man; and struggling, full of rage and sorrow, went the Fool.

Then on rode Wolsey, and when he reached his destination to find himself in that barren house in which there were not even beds nor dishes, plates nor cups, his heart was warmed that in this world there were those to love a man who is fallen from his greatness.

* * *

Lady Anne Rochford sat in her apartment, turning the leaves of a book. She had found this book in her chamber, and even as she picked it up she knew that someone had put it there that she might find it. As she looked at this book, the colour rose from her neck to her forehead, and she was filled with anger. She sat for a long time, staring at the open page, wondering who had put it there, how many of her attendants had seen it.

The book was a book of prophecies; there were many in the country, she knew, who would regard such prophecies as miraculous; it was alarming therefore to find herself appearing very prominently in them.

She called Anne Saville to her, adopting a haughty mien, which was never difficult with her.

'Nan!' she called. 'Come here! Come here at once!'

Anne Saville came and, seeing the book in her mistress's hand, grew immediately pale.

'You have seen this book?' asked Anne.

'I should have removed it ere your ladyship set eyes on it.'

Anne laughed.

'You should have done no such thing, for this book makes me laugh so much that it cannot fail to give me pleasure.'

She turned the pages, smiling, her fingers steady.

'Look, Nan! This figure represents me . . . and here is the King. And here is Katharine. This must be so, since our initials are on them. Nan, tell me, I do not look like that! Look, Nan, do not turn away. Here I am with my head cut off!'

Anne Saville was seized with violent trembling.

'If I thought that true, I would not have him were he an emperor!' she said.

Anne snapped her fingers scornfully, 'I am resolved to have him, Nan.'

Anne Saville could not take her eyes from the headless figure on the page.

'The book is a foolish book, a bauble. I am resolved that my issue shall be royal, Nan . . .' She added: '. . . whatever may become of me!'

'Then your ladyship is very brave.'

'Nan! Nan! What a little fool you are! To believe a foolish book!'

If Anne Saville was very quiet all that day as though her thoughts troubled her, Lady Anne Rochford was especially gay, though she did not regard the book as lightly as she would have those about her suppose. She did not wish to give her enemies the satisfaction of knowing that she was disturbed. For one thing was certain in her mind – she was surrounded by her enemies who would undermine her security in every possible way; and this little matter of the book was but one of those ways. An enemy had put the book where she might see it, hoping thereby to sow fear in her mind. What a hideous idea! To cut off her head!

She was nervous; her dreams were disturbed by that picture in the book. She watched those about her suspiciously, seeking her enemies. The Queen, the Princess, the Duke and Duchess of Suffolk, the Cardinal . . . all of the most important in the land. Who else? Who had brought the book into her chamber?

Those about her would be watching everything she did; listening to everything she said. She felt very frightened. Once she awoke trembling in a cold sweat; she had dreamed that Wolsey was standing before her, holding an axe, and the blade was turned towards her. The King lay beside her, and terrified, she awoke him.

'I had an evil dream . . .'

'Dreams are nothing, sweetheart.'

She would not let him dismiss her dream so. She would insist that he put his arms about her, assure her of his undying love for her.

'For without your love, I should die,' she told him. He kissed her tenderly and soothed her.

'As I should, without yours.'

'Nothing could hurt you,' she said.

'Nothing could hurt you, sweetheart, since I am here to take care of you.'

'There are many who are jealous of your love for me, who seek to destroy me.' She blurted out the story of her finding the book.

'The knave who printed it shall hang, darling. We'll have his head on London Bridge. Thus shall people see what happens to those who would frighten my sweetheart.'

'This you say, but will you do it, when you suffer those who hate me, to enjoy your favour?'

'Never should any who hated you receive my favour!'

'I know of one.'

'Oh, darling, he is an old, sick man. He wishes you no ill. . . .'

'No!' she cried fiercely. 'Has he not fought against us consistently! Has he not spoken against us to the Pope! I know of those who will confirm this.'

She was trembling in his arms, for she felt his reluctance to discuss the Cardinal.

'I fear for us both,' she said. 'How can I help but fear for you too, when I love you! I have heard much of his wickedness. There is his Venetian physician, who has been to me. . . .'

'What!' cried the King.

'But no more! You think so highly of him that you will see him my enemy, and leave him to go unpunished. He is in York, you say. Let him rest there! He is banished from Westminster; that is enough. So in York he may pursue his wickedness and set the people against me, since he is of more importance to you than I am.'

'Anne, Anne, thou talkest wildly. Who could be of more importance to me than thou?'

'Your late chancellor, my lord Cardinal Wolsey!' she retorted. She was seized with a wild frenzy, and drew his face close to hers and kissed him, and spoke to him incoherently of her love and devotion, which touched him deeply; and out of his tenderness for her grew passion such as he had rarely experienced before, and he longed to give her all that she asked, to prove his love for her and to keep her loving him thus.

He said: 'Sweetheart, you talk with wildness!'

'Yes,' she said, 'I talk with wildness; it is only your beloved Cardinal who talks with good sense. I can see that I must not stay here. I will go away. I have lost those assets which were dearer to me than aught else – my virtue, my honour. I shall leave you. This is the last night I shall lie in your arms, for I see that I am ruined, that you cannot love me.'

Henry could always be moved to terror when she talked of leaving him; before he had given her Suffolk House, she had so often gone back and forth to Hever. The thought of losing her was more than he could endure; he was ready to offer her Wolsey if that was the price she asked.

He said: 'Dost think I should allow thee to leave me, Anne?'

She laughed softly. 'You might force me to stay; you could force me to share your bed!' Again she laughed. 'You are big and strong, and I am but weak. You are a king and I am a poor woman who from love of you has given you her honour and her virtue. . . . Yes, doubtless you could force me to stay, but though you should do this, you would but keep my body; my love, though it has destroyed me, would be lost to you.'

'You shall not talk thus! I have never known happiness such as I have enjoyed with you. Your virtue . . . your honour! My God, you talk foolishly, darling! Shall you not be my Queen?'

'You have said so these many years. I grow weary of waiting. You surround yourself with those who hinder you rather than help. I have proof that the Cardinal is one of these.'

'What proof?' he demanded.

'Did I not tell you of the physician? He knows that Wolsey wrote to the Pope, asking him to excommunicate you, an you did not dismiss me and take back Katharine.'

'By God! And I will not believe it.'

She put her arms about his neck, and with one hand stroked his hair.

'Darling, see the physician, discover for yourself. . . .'

'That will I do!' he assured her.

Then she slept more peacefully, but in the morning her fears were as strong as ever. When the physician confirmed Wolsey's perfidy, when her cousin, Francis Bryan, brought her papers which proved that Wolsey had been in communication with the Pope, had asked for the divorce to be delayed; when she took these in triumph to the King and saw the veins stand out on his forehead with anger against the Cardinal, still she found peace of mind elusive. She remembered the softness of the King towards this man; she remembered how, when he had lain ill at Esher, he had sent Butts, his physician – the man he had sent to her at Hever – to attend his old friend. She remembered how he had summoned Butts, recently returned from Esher, and had asked after Wolsey's health; and when Butts had said he feared the old man would die unless he received some token of the King's regard, then had the King sent him a ruby ring, and – greater humiliation – he had turned to her and bidden her send a token too. Such was the King's regard for this man; such was his reluctance to destroy him.

But she would not let her enemy live; and in this she had behind her many noblemen, at whose head were the powerful Dukes of Norfolk and Suffolk, men such as would not let the grass grow under their feet in the matter. George had talked with her of Wolsey. 'There will be no peace for us, Anne, while that man lives. For, if ever you had an enemy, that man is he!' She trusted George completely. He had said: 'You can do this, Anne. You have but to command the King. Hesitate not, for well you know that had Wolsey the power to destroy you, he would not hesitate.'

'That I do know,' she answered, and was suddenly sad. 'George,' she went on, 'would it not be wonderful if we could go home and live quietly, hated by none!'

'I would not wish to live quietly, sister,' said George. 'Nor would you. Come! Could you turn back now, would you?' She searched her mind and knew that he was right. 'You were meant to be Queen of England, Anne. You have all the attributes.'

'I feel that, but I could wish there were not so much hating to be done!'

But she went on hating furiously; this was a battle between herself and Wolsey, and it was one she was determined to win. Norfolk watched; Suffolk watched; they were waiting for their opportunity.

There was a new charge against the Cardinal. He had been guilty of asserting and maintaining papal jurisdiction in England. Henry must accept the evidence; he must appease Anne; he must satisfy his ministers. Wolsey was to be arrested at Cawood Castle in York, whither he had retired these last months.

'The Earl of Northumberland should be sent to arrest him,' said Anne, her eyes gleaming.

This was to be. She went to her apartment, dismissed her ladies, and flung herself upon her bed overcome by paroxysms of laughter and tears. She felt herself to be, not the woman who aspired to the throne of England, but a girl in love who through this man had lost her lover.

Now he would see! Now he should know! 'That foolish girl!' he had said. 'Her father but a knight, and yours one of the noblest houses in the land. . . .'

Her father was an earl now; and she all but Queen of England.

Oh, you wise Cardinal! How I should love to see your face when Percy comes for you! You will know then that you were not so wise in seeking to destroy Anne Boleyn.

*　　*　　*

As the Cardinal sat at dinner in the dining-hall at Cawood Castle, his gentleman usher came to him and said: 'My lord, His Grace, the Earl of Northumberland is in the castle!'

Wolsey was astounded.

'This cannot be. Were I to have the honour of a visit from such a nobleman, he would surely have warned me. Show him in to me that I may greet him.'

The Earl was brought into the dining-hall. He had changed a good deal since Wolsey had last seen him, and Wolsey scarcely recognized him as the delicate, handsome boy whom he had had occasion to reprimand at the King's command because he had dared to fall in love with the King's favourite.

Wolsey reproached Northumberland: 'My lord Earl, you should have let me know, that I might have done you the honour due to you!'

Northumberland was quiet; he had come to receive no honour, he said. His eyes burned oddly in his pallid face. Wolsey remembered stories he had heard of his unhappy marriage with Shrewsbury's daughter. A man should not allow a marriage to affect him so strongly; there were other things in life. A man in Northumberland's position had much; was he not reigning lord of one of the noblest houses in the land! Bah! thought Wolsey enviously, an I were earl . . .

He had an affection for this young man, remembering him well when he had served under him. A docile boy, a charming boy. He had been grieved when he had to send him away.

'It is well to meet again,' said Wolsey. 'For old times' sake.'

'For old times' sake!' said Northumberland, and he spoke as a man speaks in his sleep.

'I mind thee well,' said Wolsey. 'Thou wert a bright, impetuous boy.'

'I mind thee well,' said Northumberland.

With malice in his heart, he surveyed the broken old man. So were the mighty fallen from their high places! This man had done that for which he would never forgive him, for he had taken from him Anne Boleyn whom in six long years of wretched marriage he had never forgotten; nor had he any intention of forgiving Wolsey. Anne should have been his, and he Anne's. They had loved; they had made vows; and this man, who dared now to remind him of the old times, had been the cause of all his misery. And now that he was old and broken, now that his ambition had destroyed him, Wolsey would be kind and full of tender reminiscence. But Percy also remembered!

'I have often thought of you,' he said, and that was true. When he had quarrelled with Mary, his wife, whom he hated and who hated him, he thought of the Cardinal's face and the stern words that he had used. 'Thou foolish boy . . .' Would he never forget the bitter humiliation? No, he never would; and because he would never cease to reproach himself for his own misery, knowing full well that had he shown sufficient courage he might have made a fight for his happiness, he hated this man with a violent hatred. He stood before him, trembling with rage, for well he knew that *she* had contrived this, and that she would expect him to show now that courage he had failed to show seven years ago.

Northumberland laid his hand on Wolsey's arm. 'My lord, I arrest you of High Treason!'

The Earl was smiling courteously, but with malice; the Cardinal began to tremble.

Revenge was a satisfying emotion, thought the Earl. He who had made others to suffer, must now himself suffer.

'We shall travel towards London at the earliest possible moment,' he said.

This they did; and, trembling with his desire for vengeance, the Earl caused the Cardinal's legs to be bound to the stirrups of his mule; thus did he proclaim to the world: 'This man, who was once great, is now naught but a common malefactor!'

About Cawood the people saw the Cardinal go; they wept; they called curses on his enemies. He left Cawood with their cries ringing in his ears. 'God save Your Grace! The foul evil take them that have taken you from us! We pray God that a very vengeance may light upon them!'

The Cardinal smiled sadly. Of late weeks, here in York, he had led that life which it would have become him as a churchman to have led before. Alms had he given to the people at his gates; his table had been over-flowing with food and wine, and at Cawood Castle had he entertained the beggars and the needy to whom he had given scarcely a thought at Hampton Court and York House; for Wolsey, who had once sought to placate his sense of inferiority, to establish his social standing, now sought a place in Heaven by his good deeds. He smiled at himself as he rode down to Leicester; his body was sick, and he doubted whether it would – indeed he prayed that it would not – last the journey to London. But he smiled, for he saw himself a man who has climbed high and has fallen low. Pride was my enemy, he said, as bitter an enemy as ever was the Lady Anne.

*　　*　　*

The rejoicing of the Boleyn faction at the death of Wolsey was shameless. None would have believed a year before that the greatest man in England could be brought so low. Wolsey, it was said, had died of a flux, but all knew he had died of a broken heart, for melancholy was as sure a disease as any other; and having lost all that he cared to live for, why should the Cardinal live? He to be taken to the Tower! He, who had loved his master, to be tried for High Treason!

Here was triumph for Anne. People sought her more than ever, flattered her, fêted her. To be favoured by Anne was to be favoured by the King. She enjoyed her triumph and gave special revels to commemorate the defeat of her enemy. She was led into the bad taste of having a play enacted which treated the great Cardinal as a figure of fun.

George was as recklessly glad about Wolsey's fall as she was. 'While that man lived, I trembled for you,' he said. He laughed shortly. 'I hear that near his end he told Kingston that had he served God as diligently as he had served the King, he would not have been given over in his grey hairs. I would say that had he served his God as diligently as he served himself, he would have gone to the scaffold long ere this!' People hearing this remark, took it up and laughed over it.

The King did not attend these revels of the Boleyns. Having given the order for the arrest of Wolsey, he wished to shut the matter from his mind. He was torn between remorse and gladness. Wolsey had left much wealth, and into whose hands should this fall but the King's!

Henry prayed: 'O Lord, thou knowest I loved that man. I would I had seen him. I would I had not let his enemies keep him from me. Did I not send him tokens of my regard? Did I not say I would not lose the fellow for twenty thousand pounds?'

But he could not stop his thoughts straying to the Cardinal's possessions. There was more yet that he must get his hands upon. Hampton Court was his; York House was his, for he had never given it back after Anne went to Suffolk House, liking it too well.

But he wept for the old days of friendship; he wept for Wolsey; and he was able to deplore his death whilst considering how much more there was in gold to come to him.

Soon after this there were two matters which caused Anne some misgiving. The first came in the form of a letter which the Countess of Northumberland had written to her father, the Earl of Shrewsbury. Shrewsbury had thought it wise to show this letter to the Duke of Norfolk, who had brought it to his niece with all speed.

Anne read the letter. There was no doubt of its meaning. Mary of Northumberland was leaving her husband; she told her father that in one of their more violent quarrels her husband had told her that he was not really married to her, being previously contracted to Anne Boleyn.

Anne's heart beat fast. Here was yet another plot to discredit her in the eyes of the King. She had been his mistress for nearly two years, and it seemed to her that she was no nearer becoming Queen than she had been on that first night in Suffolk House. She was becoming anxious, wondering how long she could expect to keep the King her obedient slave. For a long time she had watched for some lessening of his affection; she had found none; she studied herself carefully for some deterioration of her beauty; if she were older, a little drawn, there were many more gorgeous clothes and priceless jewels to set against that. But she was worried, and though she told herself that she longed for a peaceful life and would have been happy had she married Percy or Wyatt she knew that the spark of ambition inside her had been fanned into a great consuming fire; and when she had said to Anne Saville that she would marry the King, no matter what happened to herself, she meant that. She was quite sure that, once she was Queen, she would give the King sons, that not only could she delight him as his mistress, but as mother of the future Tudor King of England. Having tasted power, how could she ever relinquish it! And this was at the root of her fear. The delay of the divorce, the awareness of powerful enemies all about her – this was what had made her nervous, imperious, hysterical, haughty, frightened.

Therefore she trembled when she read this letter.

'Give it to me,' she commanded.

'What will you do with it?' asked her uncle. She was unsure. He said: 'You should show it to the King.'

She studied him curiously. Cold, hard, completely without sentiment, he despised these families which had sprung up, allied to his own house simply because the Norfolk fortunes were in decline at Henry the Seventh's accession on account of the mistake his family had made in backing Richard the Third. She weighed his words. He was no friend of hers; yet was he an enemy? It would be more advantageous to see his niece on the throne of England than another's niece.

She went to the King.

He was sitting in a window seat, playing a harp and singing a song he had written.

'Ah! Sweetheart, I was thinking of you. Sit with me, and I will sing to you my song . . . Why, what ails you? You are pale and trembling.'

She said: 'I am afraid. There are those who would poison your mind against me.'

'Bah!' he said, feeling in a merry mood, for Wolsey had left riches such as even Henry had not dreamed of, and he had convinced himself that the Cardinal's death was none of his doing. He had died of a flux, and a flux will attack a man, be he chancellor or beggar. 'What now, Anne? Have I not told you that naught could ever poison my mind against you!'

'You would not remember, but when I was very young and first came to court, Percy of Northumberland wished to marry me.'

The King's eyes narrowed. Well he remembered. He had got Wolsey to banish the boy from court, and he had banished Anne too. For years he had let her escape him. She was a bud of a girl then, scarce awake at all, but very lovely. They had missed years together.

Anne went on: 'It was no contract. He was sent from the court, being pre-contracted to my Lord Shrewsbury's daughter. Now they have quarrelled, and he says he will leave her, and she says he tells her he was never really married to her, being pre-contracted to me.'

The King let out an exclamation, and put aside his harp.

'This were not true?' he said.

'Indeed not!'

'Then we must put a stop to such idle talk. Leave this to me, sweetheart. I'll have him brought up before the Archbishop of Canterbury. I'll have him recant this, or 'twill be the worse for him!'

The King paced the floor, his face anxious.

'Dost know, sweetheart,' he said, 'I fear I have dolts about me. Were Wolsey here . . .'

She did not speak, for she knew it was unnecessary to rail against the Cardinal now; he was done with. She had new enemies with whom to cope. She knew that Henry was casting a slur on the new ministry of Norfolk and More; that he was reminding her that though Wolsey had died, he had had nothing to do with his death. She wished then that she did not know this man so well; she wished that she could have been as light-heartedly gay as people thought her, living for the day, thinking not of the morrow. She had set her skirts daintily about her, aware of her grace and charm, knowing that they drew men irresistibly to her, wondering what would happen to her when she was old, as her grandmother Norfolk. Then I suppose, she thought, I will doze in a chair and recall my adventurous youth, and poke my granddaughters with an ebony stick. I would like my grandmother to come and see me; she is a foolish old woman assuredly, but at least she would be a friend.

'Sweetheart,' said the King, 'I shall go now and settle this matter, for there will be no peace of mind until Northumberland admits this to be a lie.'

He kissed her lips; she returned his kiss, knowing well how to enchant him, being often sparing with her caresses so that when he received them he must be more grateful than if they had been lavished on him. He was the hunter; although he talked continually of longing for peace of mind, she knew that that would never satisfy him. He must never be satisfied, but always be looking for satisfaction. For two years she had kept him thus in difficult circumstances. She must go on keeping him thus, for her future depended on her ability to do so.

Fain would he have stayed, but she bid him go. 'For,' she said, 'although I know this matter to be a lie, until my lord of Northumberland admits it I am under a cloud. I could not marry you unless we had his full confession that there is no grain of truth in this claim.'

She surveyed him through narrowed eyes; she saw return to him that dread fear of losing her. He was easy to read, simple in his desires, ready enough to accept her own valuation of herself. What folly it would have been to have wept, to have told him that Northumberland lied, to have caused him to believe that her being Queen of England was to her advantage, not to his. While he believed she was ready to return to Hever, while he believed that she wished to be his wife chiefly because she had given way to his desires and sacrificed her honour and virtue, he would fight for her. She had to make him believe that the joy she could give him was worth more than any honours he could heap on her.

And he did believe this. He went storming out of the room; he had Northumberland brought before the Archbishops; he had him swear there had never been a contract with Anne Boleyn. It was made perfectly clear that Northumberland was married to Shrewsbury's daughter, and Anne Boleyn free to marry the King.

Anne knew that her handling of that little matter had been successful.

It was different with the trouble over Suffolk.

Suffolk, jealous, ambitious, seeking to prevent her marriage to the King, was ready to go to any lengths to discredit Anne, provided he could keep his head on his shoulders.

He started a rumour that Anne had had an affair with Thomas Wyatt even while the King was showing his preference for her. There was real danger in this sort of rumour, as there was no one at court who had not witnessed Thomas's loving attitude towards Anne; they had been seen by all, spending much time together, and it was possible that she had shown how she preferred the poet.

Anne, recklessly deciding that one rumour was as good as another, repeated something completely damaging to Suffolk. He had, she had heard, and she did not hesitate to say it in quarters where it would be quickly carried to Suffolk's ears, more than a fatherly affection for his daughter, Frances Brandon, and his love for her was nothing less than incestuous. Suffolk was furious at the accusation; he confronted Anne; they quarrelled; and the result of this quarrel was that Anne insisted he should absent himself from the court for a while.

This was open warfare with one who – with perhaps the exception of Norfolk – was the most powerful noble in the land, and the King's brother-in-law to boot. Suffolk retired in smouldering anger; he would not, Anne knew, let such an accusation go unpaid for, and she had always been afraid of Suffolk.

She shut herself in her room, feeling depressed; she wept a little and told Anne Saville that whoever asked for her was not to be admitted, even should it be the King himself.

She lay on her bed, staring at the ornate ceiling, seeing Suffolk's angry eyes wherever she looked; she pictured his talking over with his friends the arrogance of her who, momentarily, had the King's ear. Momentarily! It was a hideous word. The influence of all failed sooner or later. Oh, my God, were I but Queen! she thought. Were I but Queen, how happy I should feel! It is this perpetual waiting, this delay. The Pope will never give in; he is afraid of the Emperor Charles! And how can I be Queen of England while Katharine lives!

There was a tap on the door, and Anne Saville's head appeared.

'I told you I would see no one!' cried Anne impatiently. 'I told you – no one! No one at all! Not the King himself . . .'

'It is not the King,' said Anne Saville, 'but my Lord Rochford. I told him you might see him . . .'

'Bring him to me,' said Anne.

George came in, his handsome face set in a smile, but she knew him well enough to be able to see the worried look behind the smile.

'I had the devil's own job to get them to tell you I was here, Anne.'

'I had said I would see no one.'

He sat on the bed and looked at her.

'I have been hearing about Suffolk, Anne,' he said, and she shivered. 'It is a sorry business.'

'I fear so.'

'He is the King's brother-in-law.'

'Well, what if that is so? I am to be the King's wife!'

'You make too many enemies, Anne.'

'I do not make them! I fear they make themselves.'

220

'The higher you rise, sister, the more there will be, ready to pull you down.'

'You cannot tell me more than I know about that, George.' He leaned towards her.

'When I saw Suffolk, when I heard the talk . . . I was afraid. I would you had been more reasonable, Anne.'

'Did you hear what he said of me? He said Wyatt and I were, or had been, lovers!'

'I understand your need to punish him, but not your method.'

'I have said he shall be banished the court, and so he is. I have but to say one shall be banished, and it is done.'

'The King loves you deeply, Anne, but it is best to be wise. A queen will have more need of friends than Anne Rochford, and Anne Rochford could never have too many.'

'Ah, my wise brother! I have been foolish . . . that I well know.'

'He will not let the matter rest here, Anne; he will seek to work you some wrong.'

'There will always be those who seek to do me wrong, George, no matter what I do!'

'It is so senseless to make enemies.'

'Sometimes I am very weary of the court, George.'

'So you tell yourself, Anne. Were you banished to Hever, you would die of boredom.'

'That I declare I would, George!'

'If you were asked what was your dearest wish, and spoke truthfully, you would say "I would I were settled firmly on the throne of England." Would you not?'

'You know me better than I know myself, George. It is a glorious adventure. I am flying high, and it is a wonderful, exhilarating, joyous flight; but when I look down I am sometimes giddy; then I am afraid.' She held out a hand and he took it. 'Sometimes I say to myself "There is no one I trust but George." '

He kissed her hand. 'George you can always trust,' he said. 'Others too, I'll warrant; but always George.' Suddenly his reserve broke down, and he was talking as freely as she did.

'Anne, Anne, sometimes I too am afraid. Whither are we going, you and I? From simple folk we have become great folk; and yet ... and yet ... Dost remember how we scorned poor Mary? And yet ... Anne, whither are we going, you and I? Are you happy? Am I? I am married to the most vindictive of women; you contemplate marrying the most dangerous of men. Anne, Anne, we have to tread warily, both of us.'

'You frighten me, George.'

'I did not come to frighten you, Anne,'

'You came to reprove me for my conduct toward Suffolk. And I have always hated the man.'

'When you hate, Anne, it is better to hide your hatred. It is only love that should be shown.'

'There is nothing to be done about Suffolk now, George. In future I shall remember your words. I shall remember you coming to my room with a worried frown looking out from behind your smiles.'

The door opened and Lady Rochford came in. Her eyes darted to the bed.

'I thought to find you here.'

'Where is Anne Saville?' said Anne coldly, for she hated to have this *tête-à-tête* disturbed; there was much yet that she wished to say to her brother.

'Do you want to reprove her for letting me in?' asked Jane maliciously. 'Marry! I thought when my husband came into a lady's chamber, there should I follow him!'

'How are you, Jane?' said Anne.

'Very well, I thank you. You do not look so, sister. This affair of Suffolk must have upset you. I hear he is raging. You accused him of incest, so I heard.'

Anne flushed hotly. There was that in her sister-in-law to anger her even when she felt most kindly towards the world; now, the woman was maddening.

Jane went on: 'The King's sister will be most put about. She retains her fiery temper. . . . And what Frances will say I cannot think!'

'One would not expect you to think about any matter!'

said Anne cuttingly. 'And I do not wish you to enter my apartment without announcement.'

'Indeed, Anne, I am sorry. I thought there would be no need to stand on ceremony with your brother's wife.'

'Let us go, Jane,' said George wearily; and she was aware that he had not looked at her since that one first glance of distaste when she entered the room.

'Oh, very well. I am sure I know when I am not wanted; but do not let me disturb your pleasant conversation – I am sure it was most pleasant . . . and loving.'

'Farewell, Anne,' said George. He stood by the bed, smiling at her, his eyes flashing a message: 'Be of good cheer. All will be well. The King adores you. Hast forgotten he would make you Queen? What of Suffolk! What of any, while the King loves you!'

She said: 'You have done me so much good, George. You always do.'

He stooped and kissed her forehead. Jane watched jealously. When had he last kissed her – kissed her voluntarily, that was – a year ago, or more? I hate Anne, she thought, reclining there as though she were a queen already; her gowns beautifully furred – paid for by the King doubtless! Herself bejewelled as though for a state function, here in her private apartments. I hope she is never Queen! Katharine is Queen. Why should a man put away his wife because he is tired of her? Why should Anne Boleyn take the place of the true Queen, just because she is young and sparkling and vivacious and witty and beautifully dressed, and makes people believe she is more handsome than anyone at court? Everyone speaks of her; everywhere one goes one hears her name!

And he loves her . . . as he never loved me! And am I not his wife?

'Come, Jane!' he said, and his voice was different now that he spoke to her and not to his sister.

He led her out, and they walked silently through the corridors to their apartments in the palace.

She faced him and would not let him walk past her.

'You are as foolish about her as is the King!'

He sighed that weary sigh which always made her all but want to kill him, but not quite, because she loved him, and to kill him would be to kill her hopes of happiness.

'You will talk such nonsense, Jane!'

'Nonsense!' she cried shrilly, and then burst into weeping, covering her face with her hands, and waited for him to take her hands, plead with her to control herself. She wept noisily, but nothing happened; and taking down her hands, she saw that he had left her.

Then did she tremble with cold rage against him and against his sister.

'I would they were dead, both of them! They deserve to die; she for what she has done to the Queen; he for what he has done to me! One day . . .' She stopped, and ran to her mirror, saw her face blotched with tears and grief, thought of the cool, lovely face of the girl on the bed, and the long black hair which looked more beautiful in its disorder than it did when neatly tied. 'One day,' she went on muttering to herself, 'I believe I shall kill one of them . . . both of them, mayhap.'

They were foolish thoughts, which George might say were worthy of her, but nevertheless she found in them an outlet for her violent feelings, and they brought her an odd comfort.

*　　*　　*

A barge passed along the river. People on the banks turned to stare after it. In it sat the most beautiful lady of the King's court. People saw how the fading sunlight caught her bejewelled person. Her hair was caught up in a gold coif that sat elegantly on her shapely head.

'Nan Bullen!' The words were like a rumble of thunder among the crowd.

'They say the poor Queen, the true Queen, is dying of a broken heart . . .'

'As is her daughter Mary.'

'They say Nan Bullen has bribed the Queen's cook to administer poison unto Her Most Gracious Majesty . . .'

'They say she has threatened to poison the Princess Mary.'

'What of the King?'

'The King is the King. It is no fault of his. He is be-witched by this whore.'

'She is very lovely!'

'Bah! That is her witchery.'

' 'Tis right. A witch may come in any guise ...'

Women in tattered rags drew their garments about them and thought angrily of the satins and velvets and cloth of gold worn by the Lady Anne Rochford ... who was really plain Nan Bullen.

'Her grandfather was but a merchant in London town. Why should we have a merchant's daughter for our Queen?'

'There cannot be a second Queen while the first Queen lives.'

'I lost two sons, of the sweat ...'

They trampled through the muck of the gutter, rats scuttled from under their feet, made bold by their numbers and the lack of surprise and animosity their presence caused. In the fever-ridden stench of the cobbled streets, the people blamed Anne Boleyn.

Over London Bridge the heads of traitors stared out with glassy eyes; offal floated up the river; beggars with sore-en-crusted limbs asked for alms; one-legged beggars, one-eyed beggars and beggars all but eaten away with some pox.

' 'Tis a poor country we live in, since the King would send the rightful Queen from his bed!'

'I mind the poor lady at her coronation; beautiful she was then, with her lovely long hair flowing, and her in a litter of cloth of gold. Nothing too good for her then, poor lady.'

'Should a man, even if he be a king, cast off his wife be-cause she is no longer young?'

It was the cry of fearful women, for all knew that it was the King who set examples. It was the cry of ageing women against the younger members of their sex who would be-witch their husbands and steal them from them.

The murmurs grew to a roar. 'We'll have no Nan Bullen!'

There was one woman with deep cadaverous eyes and her

front teeth missing. She raised her hands and jeered at the women who gathered about her.

'Ye'll have no Nan Bullen, eh? And what'll ye do about it, eh? You'll be the first to shout "God save Your Majesty" when the King makes his whore our Queen!'

'Not I!' cried one bold spirit, and the others took it up.

The fire of leadership was in the woman. She brandished a stick.

'We'll take Nan Bullen! We'll go to her and we'll take her, and when we've done with her we'll see if she is such a beauty, eh? Who'll come? Who'll come?'

Excitement was in the air. There were many who were ever ready to follow a procession, ever ready to espouse a cause; and what more worthy than this, for weary house-wives who had little to eat and but rags to cover them, little to hope for and much to fear?

They had seen the Lady Anne Rochford in her barge, proud and imperious, so beautiful that she was more like a picture to them than a woman; her clothes looked too fine to be real . . . And she was not far off . . . her barge had stopped along the river.

Dusk was in the sky; it touched them with adventure, dangerous adventure. They were needy; they were hungry; and she was rich, and doubtless on her way to some noble friends' house to supper. This was a noble cause; it was Queen Katharine's cause; it was the cause of Princess Mary.

'Down with Nan Bullen!' they shouted.

She would have jewels about her, they remembered. Cupidity and righteousness filled their minds. 'Shall we let the whore sit on the throne of England? They say she carries a fortune in jewels about her body!'

Once, it was said, in the days of the King's youth when he feasted with his friends, the mob watched him; and so dazzled were they by his person, that they were unable to keep away from him; they seized their mighty King; they seized Bluff King Hal, and stripped him of his jewels. What did he do? He was a noble King, a lover of sport. What did he do? He did naught but smile and treat the matter as a joke. He was a bluff King! A great King! But momentarily he was in the hands of a witch. There were men who had picked up a fortune that night. Why should not a fortune be picked up from Nan Bullen? And she was no bluff, good king, but a scheming woman, a witch, a poisoner, a usurper of the throne of England! It was a righteous cause; it was a noble cause; it might also prove a profitable cause!

Someone had lighted a torch; another sprang up, and another. In the flickering glow from the flares the faces of the women looked like those of animals. Cupidity was in each face . . . cruelty, jealousy, envy. . . .

'Ah! What will we do to Nan Bullen when we find her? I will tear her limbs apart . . . I will tear the jewels off her. Nan Bullen shall not be our Queen. Queen Katharine for ever!'

They fell into some order, and marched. There were more flares; they made a bright glow in the sky.

They muttered, and each dreamed of the bright jewel she would snatch from the fair body. A fortune . . . a fortune to be made in a night, and in the righteous cause of Katharine the Queen.

'What means this?' asked newcomers.

'Nan Bullen!' chanted the crowd. 'We'll have no Nan Bullen! Queen Katharine for ever!'

The crowd was swollen now; it bulged and sprawled, but it went forward, a grimly earnest, glowing procession.

Anne, at the riverside house where she had gone to take supper, saw the glow in the sky, heard the low chanting of voices.

'What is it they say?' she asked of those about her. 'What is it? I think they come this way.'

Anne and her friends went out into the riverside garden, and listened. The voices seemed thousands strong.

'Nan Bullen . . . Nan Bullen. . . . We'll not have the King's whore . . .'

She felt sick with fear. She had heard that cry before, never at such close quarters, never so ominous.

'They have seen you come here,' whispered her hostess, and trembled, wondering what an ugly mob would do to the friends of Anne Boleyn.

'What do they want?'

'They say your name. Listen. . . .'

They stood, straining their ears.

'We'll have none of Nan Bullen. Queen Katharine for ever!'

The guests were pale; they looked at each other, shuddering. Outwardly calm, inwardly full of misery, Anne said: 'Methinks I had better leave you, good people. Mayhap when they find me not here they will go away.'

And with the dignity of a queen, unhurried, and taking Anne Saville with her, she walked down the riverside steps to her barge. Scarcely daring to breathe until it slipped away from the bank, she looked back and saw the torches clearly, saw the dark mass of people, and thought for a moment of what would have happened to her if she had fallen into their hands.

Silently moved the barge; down the river it went towards Greenwich. Anne Saville was white and trembling, sobbing, but Lady Anne Rochford appeared calm.

She could not forget the howls of rage, and she felt heavy with sadness. She had dreamed of herself a queen, riding through the streets of London, acclaimed on all sides. 'Queen Anne. Good Queen Anne!' She wanted to be respected and admired.

'Nan Bullen, the whore! We'll not have a whore on the throne. . . . Queen Katharine for ever!'

'I will win their respect,' she told herself. 'I must . . . I must! One day . . . one day they shall love me.'

Swiftly went the barge. She was exhausted when she reached the palace; her face was white and set, more haughty, more imperious, more queenly than when she had left to join the river-side party.

*   *   *

There was a special feast in the dormitory at Horsham. The girls had been giggling together all day.

'I hear,' said one to Catherine Howard, 'that this is a special occasion for you. There is a treat in store for you!'

Catherine, wide-eyed, listened. What? she wondered.

Isabel was smiling secretly; they were all in the secret but Catherine.

She had her lesson that day, and found Manox less adventurous than usual. The Duchess dozed, tapped her foot, admonished Catherine – for it was true she stumbled over her playing. Manox sat upright beside her – the teacher rather than the admiring and passionate friend. Catherine knew then how much she looked forward to the lessons.

She whispered to him: 'I have offended you?'

'Offended me! Indeed not; you could never do aught but please me.'

'Methought you seemed aloof.'

'I am but your instructor in the virginals,' he whispered. 'It has come to me that were the Duchess to discover we are friends, she would be offended; she might even stop the lessons. Would that make you very unhappy, Catherine?'

'Indeed it would!' she said guilelessly. 'More than most things I love music.'

'And you do not dislike your teacher?'

'You know well that I do not.'

'Let us play. The Duchess is restive; she will hear our talking at any moment now.'

She played. The Duchess's foot tapped in a spritely way; then it slowed down and stopped.

'I think of you continually,' said Manox. 'But with fear.'

'Fear?'

'Fear that something might happen to stop these lessons.'

'Oh, nothing must happen!'

'And yet how easily it could! Her Grace has but to decide that she would prefer you to have another teacher.'

'I would beg her to let you stay.'

His eyes showed his alarm.

'You should not do that, Catherine!'

'But I should! I could not bear to have another teacher.'

'I have been turning over in my mind what I would say to you today. We must go cautiously, Catherine. Why, if Her Grace knew of our . . . our friendship . . .'

'Oh, we will be careful,' said Catherine.

'It is sad,' he said, 'for only here do we meet, under the Duchess's eyes.'

He would talk no more. When she would have spoken, he said: 'Hush! Her Grace will awaken. In future, Catherine, I shall appear to be distant to you, but mistake me not, though I may seem merely your cold, hard master, my regard for you will be as deep as ever.'

Catherine felt unhappy; she thrived on caresses and demonstrations of affection, and so few came her way. When the Duchess dismissed her, she returned to the young ladies' apartments feeling deflated and sad at heart. She lay on her bed and drew the curtains round it; she thought of Manox's dark eyes and how on several occasions he had leaned close to her and kissed her swiftly.

In the dormitory she could hear the girls laughing together, preparing for tonight. She heard her own name mentioned amidst laughter.

'A surprise . . .'

'Why not . . .'

'Safer too . . .'

She did not care for their surprises; she cared only that Manox would kiss her no more. Then it occurred to her that he had merely liked her as a young and attractive man might like a little girl. It was not the same emotion as the older people felt for each other; that emotion of which Catherine thought a good deal, and longed to experience. She must live through the weary years of childhood before that could happen; the thought made her melancholy.

Through her curtains she listened to running footsteps. She heard a young man's voice; he had brought sweetmeats and dainties for the party tonight, he said. There were exclamations of surprise and delight.

'But how lovely!'

'I declare I can scarce keep my hands off them.'

'Tonight is a special occasion, didst know? Catherine's coming of age. . . .'

What did they mean? They could laugh all they liked; she was not interested in their surprises.

Evening came. Isabel insisted on drawing back the curtains of Catherine's bed.

'I am weary tonight,' said Catherine. 'I wish to sleep.'

'Bah!' laughed Isabel. 'I thought you would wish to join in the fun! Great pains have I taken to see that you should enjoy this night.'

'You are very kind, but really I would rather retire.'

'You know not what you say. Come, take a little wine.'

The guests began to arrive; they crept in, suppressing their laughter. The great room was filled with the erotic excitement which was always part of these entertainments. There were slapping and kisses and tickling and laughter; bed curtains pulled back and forth, entreaties for caution, entreaties for less noise.

'You'll be the death of me, I declare!'

'Hush! Her Grace . . .'

'Her Grace is snoring most elegantly. I heard her.'

'People are often awakened by their snores!'

'The Duchess is. I've seen it happen.'

'So has Catherine, has she not, when she is having her lesson on the virginals with Henry Manox!'

That remark seemed to be the signal for great laughter, as though it were the most amusing thing possible.

Catherine said seriously: 'That is so. Her snores do awaken her.'

The door opened. There was a moment's silence. Catherine's heart began to hammer with an odd mixture of fear and delight. Henry Manox came into the room.

'Welcome!' said Isabel. Then: 'Catherine, here is your surprise!'

Catherine raised herself, and turned first red, then white. Manox went swiftly to her and sat on her bed.

'I had no notion . . .' began Catherine breathlessly.

'We decided it should be a secret. . . . You are not displeased to see me?'

'I . . . of course not!'

'Dare I hope that you are pleased?'

'Yes, I am pleased.'

His black eyes flashed. He said: ''Twas dangerous, little

Catherine, to kiss you there before the Duchess. I did it because of my need to kiss you.'

She answered: 'It is dangerous here.'

'Bah!' he said. 'I would not fear the danger here . . . among so many. And I would have you know, Catherine, that no amount of danger would deter me.'

Isabel came over.

'Well, my children? You see how I think of your happiness!'

'This was your surprise, Isabel?' said Catherine.

'Indeed so. Are you not grateful, and is it not a pleasant one?

'It is,' said Catherine.

One of the young gentlemen came over with a dish of sweetmeats, another with wine.

Catherine and Manox sat on the edge of Catherine's bed, holding hands, and Catherine thought she had never been so excited nor so happy, for she knew that she had stepped right out of an irksome childhood into womanhood, where life was perpetually exciting and amusing.

Manox said: 'We can be prim now before Her Grace, and what care I! I shall be cold and aloof, and all the time you will know that I long to kiss you.' Thereupon he kissed her and she kissed him. The wine was potent; the sweetmeats pleasant. Manox put an arm about Catherine's waist.

Darkness came to the room, as on these occasions lights were never used for fear they should be detected in their revels.

Manox said: 'Catherine, I would be alone with you completely. . . . Let us draw these curtains.' And so saying he drew the curtains, and they were shut in, away from the others.

* * *

October mists hung over Calais. Anne was reminded of long ago feasting at Ardres and Guisnes, for then, as now, Francis and Henry had met and expressed their friendship; then Queen Katharine had been his Queen; now the chief lady from England was the Marchioness of Pembroke, Anne herself. Anne felt more at ease than she had for four years. Never had she felt this same certainty that her ambition would be realized. The King was ardent as ever, impatient with the long delay; Thomas Cromwell had wily schemes to present to His Majesty; there was something ruthless about the man; he was the sort one would employ to do any deed, however dangerous, however murky – and, provided the reward was great enough, one felt the deed would be done.

So, at the highest peak of glory she had so far reached, she could enjoy the pomp and ceremony of this visit to France, which was being conducted as a visit of a king and his queen. The King was ready to commit to the Tower any who did not pay her full honour. When, a month ago, she had been created Marchioness of Pembroke she had acquired with this high honour the establishment of a queen. She must have her train-bearer, her ladies of the bedchamber, her maids of honour, her gentlemen-in-waiting, her officers, and at least thirty domestics for her own use. What Henry wished the world to know was that the only thing that kept the Marchioness from being Queen in name was the marriage ceremony. 'By God!' said Henry to Anne. 'That shall take place before you are much older, sweetheart!'

They had stayed four days at Boulogne, and there Anne had met with some slight rebuff, being unable to attend the festivities which the French arranged for Henry, as the French ladies had not come with Francis. It was understandable that Francis's wife should not come, for, on the death of Claude he had married Charles's sister Eleanor, and Henry was known to have said, when the visit was being discussed, that he would rather see a devil than a lady in Spanish dress. The Queen of France therefore could not come. There remained Francis's sister, the Queen of Navarre, but she had pleaded illness. Consequently there were no ladies of the French court to greet Henry and his Marchioness. Doubtless it was a slight, but such slights would be quickly remedied once Anne wore a crown.

Now they were back at Calais and very soon, with her

ladies, Anne would go down to the great hall for the masked ball; she must however wait until supper was concluded, since the banquet was attended only by men. Contentedly she browsed, thinking of the past months, thinking of that state ceremony at Windsor, when the King had made her Marchioness of Pembroke – the first woman ever to be created a peer of the realm. What a triumph that had been! And how she, with her love of admiration and pomp, of which she was the centre, had enjoyed every minute of it! Ladies of noble birth, who previously had thought themselves so far above her, had been forced to attend her in all humility; Lady Mary Howard to carry her state robes; the Countesses of Rutland and Sussex to conduct her to the King; my lords of Norfolk and Suffolk with the French ambassador to attend the King in the state apartments. And all this ceremony that they might do honour to Anne Boleyn. She pictured herself afresh, in her surcoat of crimson velvet that was lined with ermine, her lovely hair flowing; herself kneeling before the King while he very lovingly and tenderly placed the coronet on the brow of his much loved Marchioness.

And then to France, with Wyatt in their train, and her uncle Norfolk and, best of all, George. With George and Wyatt there, she had felt secure and happy. Wyatt loved her as he ever did, though now he dared not show his love. He poured it out in his poetry.

> 'Forget not! O, forget not this!—
> How long ago hath been, and is,
> The mind that never meant amiss—
> Forget not yet!
>
> Forget not then thine own approved,
> The which so long hath thee so loved,
> Whose steadfast faith yet never moved:
> Forget not this!'

She quoted those words as her ladies helped to dress her. Wyatt would never forget; he asked her not to. She smiled happily. No, she would not forget Wyatt; but she was happy tonight for she was assured of the King's steadfastness in his intention to marry her. He had declared this, but actions speak so much louder than words; would he have created her Marchioness of Pembroke, would he have brought her to France if he were not even more determined to make her his Queen than he had been two years ago? She felt strong and full of power, able to bind him to her, able to keep him. How could she help but be happy, knowing herself so loved! George was her friend; Wyatt had said he would never forget. Poor Wyatt! And the King had met the disapproval of his people, even faced the possibility of a tottering throne, rather than relinquish her.

Courage made her eyes shine the brighter, made her cheeks to glow. Tonight she was dressed in masquing costume; her gown was of cloth of gold with crimson tinsel satin slashed across it in unusual fashion, puffed with cloth of silver and ornamented with gold laces. All the ladies were dressed in this fashion, and they would enter the hall masked, so that none should know who was who. And then, after the dancing, Henry himself would remove the masks, and the ladies would be exhibited with national pride, for they had been chosen for their beauty.

The Countess of Derby came in to tell her it was time they went down, and four ladies in crimson satin, who were to lead them into the hall, were summoned, and they descended the stairs.

There was an expectant hush as they entered the hall which at great cost Henry had furnished specially for this occasion. The hangings were of tissue of silver and gold; and the seams of these hangings had been decorated with silver, pearls and stones.

Each masked lady was to select her partner, and Anne chose the King of France.

Francis had changed a good deal since Anne had last seen him; his face was lined and debauched; she had heard alarming stories of him when she had been in France, and she remembered one of these was of the daughter of a mayor at whose house Francis had stayed during one of his campaigns. He had fancied the girl, and she, dreading his advances and knowing too well his reputation, had ruined her looks with acid.

Francis said he could think of no more delight to follow supper than the English King's idea of a ball in which the ladies were masked.

'One is breathless with suspense, awaiting that moment when the masks are removed.' He tried to peer lasciviously beneath hers, but laughingly she replied that she was surprised he should be breathless. 'It is the inexperienced, not the connoisseur, is it not, who is more likely to be reduced to such a state?'

'Even connoisseurs are deeply moved by masterpieces, Madam!'

'This is what our lord King would doubtless call French flattery.'

' 'Tis French truth nevertheless.'

Henry watched her, jealous and alert, knowing well the French King's reputation, distrusting him, disliking to see him in conversation with Anne.

Francis said: 'It is indeed exciting to contemplate that we have the Lady Anne here with us tonight. I declare I long to see the face that so enchants my brother of England.'

'Your curiosity will be satisfied ere long,' she said.

'I knew the lady once,' he said, feigning not to know it was with none other that he now danced.

'That must have been very long ago.'

'A few years. But such a lady, Madam, one would never forget, you understand.'

She said: 'Speak French, if you wish it. I know the language.'

He spoke French; he was happier in it. He told her she spoke it enchantingly. He told her that he would wager she was more fair than the Lady Anne herself, for he had never set eyes on such a lithesome figure, nor heard such a melodious voice; and he trusted she had the fairest face in England and France, for he would be disappointed if she had not!

Anne, feeling Henry's eyes upon her, rejoiced in Henry.

He was a king and a great king; she could not have endured Francis for all the kingdoms in the world.

Henry, impatient of watching, would now remove the masks; and did so, going first to Anne.

'Your Majesty has been dancing with the Marchioness of Pembroke,' he told Francis, who declared himself astonished and delighted. •

Henry moved on, leaving Anne with Francis.

'And what did I say of my old friend, little Anne Boleyn?' he said.

Anne laughed. 'Your Majesty was fully aware with whom he danced.'

'I should have known that one so full of grace, so pleasant to the eye and the ear, could be none other than she who will soon, I trust, be my sister of England. I congratulate myself that she chose to dance with me.'

'Ceremony, as Your Majesty will well understand, demanded it.'

'You were ever unkind, fair lady! That I well remember.'

'Tell me of your sister.'

They talked long together; Anne's laughter rang out now and then, for they had many reminiscences to share of the French court, and each could bring back memories to the other.

Henry watched, half proud, half angry. He had ever been jealous of Francis; he wondered whether to join them or leave them together. He did not care to see Anne in such close conversation with the lecher Francis, and yet it must be so for he was the King of France, and honour shown to Anne was honour shown to Henry. Francis's approval at Rome could mean a good deal, for though Charles was the most important man in Europe, might not Henry and Francis together carry more weight than Katharine's nephew?

The dance broke up; the ladies retired. Henry talked with his royal guest. Francis suggested he should marry Anne without the Pope's consent. Henry did not see how this could be, but enjoyed such talk; it was pleasant to think he had French support behind him.

He went to Anne's chamber, and dismissed her ladies.

'You were indeed a queen tonight!' he said.

'I trust I did not disgrace my King.'

She was gay tonight, savouring the success of the evening; adorable in her costume of cloth of gold and crimson.

He went to her and put his arms about her.

'The dresses were the same, but you stood out among them all. Had one not known who you were, it would have been easily seen that you were she who should be Queen.'

'You are very gracious to me.'

'And you are glad I love you, eh?'

She was so very happy this night that she wanted to shower happiness all about her; and on whom should it fall but on her royal benefactor!

'I was never happier in my life!' she said.

Later, when she lay in his arms, he confessed to jealousy of the French King.

'You seemed to like him too well, sweetheart.'

'Would you have had me ungracious to him? If I seemed to like him, it was because he was your guest.'

'Methought you appeared to coquette with him a little.'

'I did only what I thought would please you.'

' 'Twould never please me, Anne, to see your smiles given to another!'

'My smiles! Bah! If I smiled too warmly then 'twas because I compared him with you and was happy in the comparing.'

Henry was overjoyed.

'I declare he puts on years as one would put on state robes; he is weighed down with them. I never thought him handsome. . . .'

'Debauchery is apparent in his face,' said Anne.

Henry's prudish little mouth lifted into a smile.

'I would not care to own his reputation!'

Then she amused him with an imitation of the French King, recounting what he had said and what she had answered; and the King laughed and was very happy with her.

In the morning Francis sent Anne a jewel as a gift. Henry examined it, was delighted with its worth, and jealous that it had not come from himself.

He gave her more jewellery; he gave of his own and Katharine's and even his sister's, Mary of Suffolk. The King was more deeply in love than ever.

When it was time for them to leave Calais there was a high wind and it was unsafe to cross the Channel. Anne was reminded of that stay at Dover; but then she had been a seven-year-old girl of no importance whatever, trying to listen to those about her and learn something of life. Pleasant it was to think back, when one had come so far.

They beguiled the days with dice and cards, at which the King lost heavily and Anne almost always won; nor did it matter if she lost, for the King would pay her debts. One of the players was a handsome young man named Francis Weston, for whom Anne conceived a genuine liking, and he for her. They played by day and danced at night; they were hilarious over the cards; there was much fun to be had at 'Pope Julius', the favourite game of the court, with its allusions to matrimony, intrigue and the Pope – they all found it so apt in view of the pending divorce. Thus passed the days, with Anne happier than she had been since deciding to occupy the throne, more secure, more content.

* * *

The old year was dying, and Christmas came. Still the Pope was adamant; still action hung fire. Four years ago Anne had become the King's mistress, and now, at Christmas of the year 1532, still she waited to be his Queen.

She was pale and listless.

'Does aught ail thee, sweetheart?' the King asked her.

'Much ails me,' she told him.

The King was alarmed.

'Darling, tell me instantly. I would know what is wrong, and right it.'

She said very clearly: 'I fear he who should follow Your Majesty as King of England will after all be but a bastard.'

Henry was beside himself with the importance of this news. Anne was pregnant! A son was what he wanted more than anything – next to Anne herself – on Earth. Anne, who should have been the Queen long ere this – and had they married she would have given him a son by now, for it had ever been her wish that no children should be born to them until she was Queen – Anne was with child. His child! His *son*! He who should be King of England!

'And by God,' said the King, 'he shall be!' Now he was all tenderness, all loving care; that body which sheltered his son had become doubly precious. 'Fret not, sweetheart. Be done with fretting for evermore. I declare I'll endure this delay no longer. I'll be cut free from that canting Pope, or, by God, much blood will flow!'

Anne could smile; this was the happiest thing that could have happened; this would decide him. She was determined that her son should be born in wedlock; and so was Henry.

Well he remembered how he had looked with something like fury on his son, the Duke of Richmond – that fine boy so like himself, who, had he been born of Katharine instead of Elizabeth Blount would have spared him much heart-burning. No! There should be no repetition of that!

He called Cromwell to him; he would see Cranmer; he would leave nothing undone, no way out unexplored. Divorce he must have, and quickly, for Anne was pregnant with a son.

Henry's determination was vital; it swept all opposition before it; none who valued his future, or his head, dared go against him, whilst those who worked with him and were blessed with success were sure of favour.

Warham had died in August, and who should replace him but Cranmer, the man who, when the idea of divorce was first being considered, had the right sow by the ear! The Archbishopric of Canterbury could therefore be placed in good hands. Then Cromwell: Cromwell's daring scheme of separating England from Rome, which had on first hearing seemed too wild to be put into action, now presented itself as the only sure solution. Cromwell, unlike so many, suffered not at all from a superstitious dread of consequences; he was not by any means scrupulous; he could bring in evidence against Rome as fast as his master cared to receive it. What had Henry to lose by the separation? he demanded of his King. And see what he had to gain!

Henry's eyes glistened, contemplating the dissolution of those storehouses of treasure, the monasteries . . . treasures which would naturally be thrown into the King's chests. The state would be free of Rome; it would be strong, beholden to no one. Moreover, free from the Pope, why should Henry care for his verdict on the divorce? Henry, all-powerful, might make his own divorce! The Continent, in the grip of the reformation, had weakened the Church. Everywhere in Europe men were challenging the Pope's authority; a new religion was springing up. It was simple; it merely meant that the headship was transferred from the Pope to Henry. Henry had hesitated, turning this truly delightful plan over and over in his mind. He had to consider his conscience, which troubled him incessantly. He was afraid of isolation. How would it affect him politically? Wolsey – the wisest man he had ever known – would have opposed Cromwell's scheme; he did not like Cromwell, he considered him a knave. Was Cromwell right? Could Cromwell be trusted? Cromwell might be a knave, but was he a wise man?

Henry shilly-shallied. He had always considered his accession to be influenced by the Holy See, and through the Holy See, by God; but he was ever ready to support an idea he liked. He was superstitious to a great degree; he had looked upon the Pope as holy; it was not easy for a superstitious man with a conscience to overthrow a lifetime's tradition. He was afraid of God's wrath, although he did not fear the vacillating Clement. He had been proud of his title 'Defender of the Faith'. Who was it who had written the most brilliant denouncement of Luther? Henry of England. How could he then overthrow that which he had so ardently defended!

Cromwell had talked slyly and persuasively, for if he would keep in favour, this matter of the divorce must be settled, and he saw no way of settling it but this. He explained this was nothing to do with Lutherism; the religion of the country remained the same; it was merely the headship of the church that was involved. Was it not more seemly that a nation's great good King should lead its Church?

Henry tried to justify this procedure morally. Once he had

made a case for the break-away, it would be done. Warham had died at the most convenient moment; that was a sign perhaps. Who better to head a country's Church than its King! Anne was pregnant. This was a sign. He must have the divorce if he was to legitimize Anne's child. The time was short. There was no longer occasion for conferences, for shilly-shallying. Sir Thomas More, a few months previously, had retired from the office of Chancellor. More had ever been one to discountenance Henry. He liked the man, he could not help it, but he had been rather shaken when More had said, on taking office, that he would 'first look unto God and after God to his Prince,' for that was a most uncomfortable thing for a minister to say; but More was an uncomfortable man; he was beloved by the people, he was honest, religious in that true sense to which so few do, or even try to attain. He had calmly walked out and gone home to his family and friends; he begged to be allowed to do this on the plea of ill health, and Henry had to accept that plea; but he had always liked the man, and he knew his lack of ease was more mental than bodily. More could not reconcile himself to the divorce; that was why he had resigned and gone to the peace of his Chelsea home. The King had outwardly taken his resignation in good part; he had visited Chelsea; but at the same time he was disturbed on More's account, since More was known as a good man, and the King would have preferred him to be less arbitrary.

Cromwell was whispering in the King's ear. Cromwell was smart; Cromwell was cunning; any delicate job could be left to Cromwell.

Divorce! Why divorce? When a marriage has not been valid, what need of divorce? He had never been married to Katharine! She was his brother's wife, and therefore the ceremony was illegal.

Henry dared delay no longer. Anne's child must be legitimate. So, on a January day, he summoned one of his chaplains to a quiet attic of White Hall, and when the chaplain arrived, he found there – much to his astonishment, for he had been told he was merely to celebrate mass – the King attended by two grooms of the chamber, one of them being that Norris whose sympathy for Wolsey had lightened the Cardinal's last hours. The chaplain had not been there more than a few minutes when who should arrive but the Marchioness of Pembroke accompanied by Anne Saville!

The King then took the chaplain aside, and told him he would be required to marry him to the Marchioness.

The chaplain began to tremble at this, looking fearfully about him, at which the King stamped impatiently. Greatly did the chaplain fear the King, but more so did he fear Rome. Henry, seeing himself in a quandary, hastily told the man that the Pope had granted the divorce, and he need fear nothing. The ceremony was over before the light of morning, and all the party went secretly away.

Henry was disturbed and not a little alarmed; he had done a bold thing, and not even Cranmer knew he had intended to do it in this way. For, by marrying Anne as he had, he had irrevocably broken with Rome and placed himself at the head of the English Church. The Council could do nothing but accept this state of affairs; Henry was their King. But what of the people, that growling mass of the populace who had come through pestilence and poverty, and were less inclined to bend the knee than his courtiers? In the streets they murmured against Anne. Some murmured against the King.

If the King trembled, Anne was triumphant. She was Queen after four years of waiting; Queen of England. Already she carried the King's child within her. She was mentally exhausted by the long struggle, and only now did she realize what a struggle it had been, what nervous energy she had put into maintaining it, how she had feared she would never reach this pinnacle of power. She could now relax and remember that she was to be a mother. Love was not to be denied her then. She carried a child, and the child would inherit the throne of England. She slept peacefully, dreaming the child – a son – was already born, that her attendants laid it in her arms; and her heart was full of love for this unborn child. 'September!' she said on waking. 'But September is such a long way off!'

George Boleyn was preparing for a journey; he would leave

the palace before dawn. Jane came gliding to him as he buttoned his coat.

'George . . . where are you going?'

'A secret mission,' he said.

'So early?'

'So early.'

'Could I not accompany you?'

He did not answer such folly.

'George, is it very secret? Tell me where you go.'

He contemplated her; he always felt more kindly towards her when he was going to leave her.

'It is a secret, so if I tell you, you must keep it entirely to yourself.'

She clasped her hands, feeling suddenly happy because he smiled in such a friendly way.

'I will, George! I swear I will! I can see it is good news.'

'The best!'

'Tell me quickly, George.'

'The King and Anne were married this morning. I go to carry the news to the King of France.'

'The King . . . married to Anne! But the Pope has not given the divorce, so how can that be possible?'

'With God – and the King – all things are possible.'

She was silent, not wishing to spoil this slight friendliness he was showing towards her.

'So you are the Queen's brother now, George, and I am her sister-in-law!'

'That is so. I must away. I must leave the palace before the day begins.'

She watched him go, smiling pleasantly; then all her bitter jealousy burst forth. It was so unfair. So she was Queen of England, and she would be more arrogant than ever now. Why should a man displace his wife because he tired of her!

* * *

A marriage had been arranged for Isabel; she was leaving the Duchess's retinue. Catherine was not really sorry, never

244

having liked Isabel; and then she was too absorbed in Henry Manox to care much what happened to anyone else.

Manox had been to the dormitory on several occasions; he was recognized now as Catherine's lover. There was much petting and caressing and whispering, and Catherine found this a delightful state of affairs. She was grown up at last, revelling in intrigue, receiving little gifts from Manox; she never wrote to him, since she had never been taught how to write properly; but oral messages were exchanged between her and Manox by way of their friends.

During the lessons they were very conventional in their behaviour – which seemed to Catherine a great joke. The old Duchess might fall into a deep sleep, and all Manox and Catherine would do was exchange mischievous glances.

'I declare, Manox,' said the Duchess on one occasion, 'you are too stern with the child. You do nothing but scold!'

They would laugh at that when she lay in his arms in her bed with the curtains drawn. Catherine, though a child in years, was highly sexed, precocious, a budding woman; over-excitable, generous, reckless, this affair with Manox seemed the high spot of her life. He said he had loved her ever since he had first set eyes on her; Catherine was sure she had loved him ever since her very first lesson. Love was the excuse for everything they did. He brought her sweetmeats and ribands for her hair; they laughed and joked and giggled with the rest.

It was the Duchess who told Catherine that she was engaging another woman in place of Isabel.

'She is from the village, and her name is Dorothy Barwicke. She will take Isabel's place among the ladies. She is a serious young lady, as Isabel was, and I feel I can trust her to keep you young people in some sort of order. I'll whisper something else to you, Catherine . . . We really are going to Lambeth ere the month is out! I declare I grow weary of the country, and now that my granddaughter is in truth the Queen . . .'

She never tired of talking of Anne, but Catherine who had loved to hear such talk was hardly interested now.

'Imagine poor old Katharine's face when he took Anne to

France! If ever a king proclaimed his queen, he did then! And I hear she was a great success. How I should have loved to see her dancing with the French King! Marchioness of Pembroke, if you please! I'll warrant Thomas – I beg his pardon, the Earl of Wiltshire – is counting what this means in gold. Oh, Thomas, Earl of Wiltshire, who would not have beautiful daughters!'

'Grandmother, will you really go to Lambeth?'

'Don't look so startled, child. Assuredly I shall go. Someone must assist at the dear Queen's coronation. I feel sure I shall be invited, in view of my rank and my relationship to Her Majesty the Queen.'

'And . . . will you take the whole household?' asked Catherine, her voice trembling. But the Duchess was too absorbed by her thoughts and plans for the coronation to notice that.

'What foolish questions you ask, child! What matter . . .'

'You would take your musicians, would you not, Grandmother? You would take me?'

'Ah! So that is what you are thinking, is it? You fear to be left out of the excitement. Never fear, Catherine Howard, I doubt not the Queen your cousin will find a place at court for you when you are ready.'

There was no satisfaction to be gained from the Duchess; in any case she changed her plans every day.

'Isabel! Isabel!' said Catherine. 'Do you think the whole household will remove to Lambeth?'

'Ah!' cried Isabel, who in view of her coming marriage was not interested in the Duchess's household. 'You are thinking of your lover!' She turned to Dorothy Barwicke, a dark woman with quick, curious eyes and a thin mouth. 'You would think Catherine Howard but a child, would you not? But that is not so; she has a lover; he visits her in our bedroom of nights. He is a very bold young man, and they enjoy life; do you not, Catherine?'

Catherine flushed and, looking straight at Dorothy Barwicke, said: 'I love Henry and he loves me.'

'Of course you do!' said Isabel. 'And a very loving little girl she is, are you not, Catherine? She is very virtuous, and would not allow Manox in her bed an she did not love him!'

'And, loving him,' said Dorothy Barwicke, 'I'll warrant she finds it difficult to refuse his admittance.'

The two young women exchanged glances, and laughed. 'You will look after Catherine when I leave, will you not?' said Isabel.

'I do not need looking after.'

'Indeed you do not!' said Dorothy. 'Any young lady not yet in her teens, who entertains gentlemen in her bed at night, is quite able to look after herself, I'd swear!'

'Not gentle*men*,' said Isabel ambiguously. 'It is only Manox.'

Catherine felt they were mocking her, but she always felt too unsure of all the ladies to accuse them of so doing.

'I shall expect you to look after Catherine when I have gone,' said Isabel.

'You may safely leave that to me.'

Catherine lived in agony of fear while the Duchess set the household bustling with preparations for her journey to Lambeth. She talked perpetually of 'my granddaughter, the Queen', and having already heard that she was to attend the coronation – fixed for May – was anxious to get to Lambeth in good time, for there would be her state robes to be put in order, and many other things to be seen to; and she hoped to have a few informal meetings with the Queen before the great event.

Catherine was wont to lie in bed on those nights when there were no visitors to the dormitory and ask herself what she would do were the Duchess to decide not to take Manox. Catherine loved Manox because she needed to love someone; there were two passions in Catherine's life; one was music, and the other was loving. She had loved her mother and lost her; she had loved Thomas Culpepper, and lost him; now she loved Manox. And on all these people had she lavished unstintingly her capacity for loving, and that was great. Catherine must love; life for her was completely devoid of interest without love. She enjoyed the sensational excitement of physical love in spite of her youth; but her love for Manox was not entirely a physical emotion.

247

She loved to give pleasure as well as to take it, and there was nothing she would not do for those she loved. All that she asked of life was to let her love; and she was afraid of life, for it seemed to her that her love was ill-fated; first her mother, then Thomas Culpepper, now Manox. She was terrified that she would have to go to Lambeth without Manox.

There came a day when she could no longer bear the suspense. She asked her grandmother outright.

'Grandmother, what of my lessons at Lambeth?'

'What of them, child?'

'Shall Henry Manox accompany us, that he may continue to instruct me?'

The Duchess's reply sent a shiver down her spine.

'Dost think I would not find thee a teacher at Lambeth?'

'I doubt not that you would, but when one feels that one can do well with one teacher . . .'

'Bah! I know best who will make a good teacher. And why do you bother me with lessons and teachers? Dost not realize that this is to be the coronation of your own cousin Anne!'

Catherine could have wept with mortification, and her agony of mind continued.

Manox came often to the dormitory.

'Do you think I could ever leave you?' he asked. 'Why, should you go to Lambeth without me I would follow.'

'And what would happen to you if you so disobeyed?'

'Whatever the punishment it would be worth it to be near you, if but for an hour!'

But no! Catherine would not hear of that. She remembered the tales Doll Tappit had gleaned of Walter the warder. She remembered then that, though she ran wild through the house and her clothes were so shabby as to be almost those of a beggar, she was Catherine Howard, daughter of a great and noble house, while he was plain Henry Manox, instructor at the virginals. Though he seemed so handsome and clever to her, there would be some – and her grandmother and her dreaded uncle the Duke among them – who would consider they had done great wrong in loving. What if they, both, should be committed to the Tower! It was for Manox she trembled, for Catherine's love was complete. She could endure separation, but not to think of Manox's body cramped in the Little Ease, or rotting, and the food of rats in the Pit. She cried and begged that he would do nothing rash; and he laughed and said did she not think he did something rash every night that he came to her thus, for what did she think would happen to him if her grandmother were to hear of their love?

Then was Catherine seized with fresh fears. Why must the world, which was full of so many delights, hold so much that was cruel! Why did there have to be stern grandmothers and terrifying uncles! Why could not everybody understand what a good thing it was to love and be loved in this most exciting and sensational way which she had recently discovered!

Then Catherine found the world was indeed a happy place, for when she left for Lambeth in her grandmother's retinue, Manox was in it too.

* * *

Lambeth was beautiful in the spring, and Catherine felt she had never been so completely happy in her life. The fruit trees in the orchards which ran down to the river's brink were in blossom; she spent whole days wandering through the beautiful gardens, watching the barges go down the river.

With Manox at Lambeth, they were often able to meet out of doors; the Duchess was even more lax than she had been at Horsham, so busy was she with preparations for the coronation. Anne visited her grandmother, and they sat together in the garden, the Duchess's eyes sparkling to contemplate her lovely granddaughter. She could not resist telling Anne how gratified she was, how lucky was the King, and how, deep in her heart, she had ever known this must happen.

Catherine was brought to greet her cousin.

'Your Majesty remembers this one?' asked the Duchess. 'She was doubtless but a baby when you last saw her.'

'I remember her well,' said Anne. 'Come hither, Catherine, that I may see you more closely.'

Catherine came, and received a light kiss on her cheek. Catherine still thought her cousin the most beautiful person she had ever seen, but she was less likely to idealize, because all her devotion was for Manox.

'Curtsey, girl!' thundered the Duchess. 'Do you not know that you stand before your Queen?'

Anne laughed. 'Oh, come! No ceremony in the family . . . No, Catherine, please . . .'

Anne thought, Poor little thing! She is pretty enough, but how unkempt she looks!

'Perhaps Your Majesty will find a place for her at court . . .'

'Assuredly I will,' said Anne, 'but she is young yet.'

'On your knees, girl, and show some gratitude!'

'Grandmother,' laughed the Queen, 'I would have you remember this is but our family circle. I am weary of ceremony; let me drop it awhile. What do you like doing, Catherine? Are you fond of music?'

Catherine could glow when she talked of music. They remembered how they had once felt affection, which was spontaneous, for one another, and as they talked it came back to them.

After Catherine had been dismissed, Anne said: 'She is a sweet child, but a little gauche. I will send her some clothes; they could be altered to fit her.'

'Ah! You would dress up Catherine Howard! She is a romp, that child. And what a sheltered life she has led! I have kept her away in the country, perhaps too long.'

A new woman joined the Duchess's household while they were at Lambeth. Her name was Mary Lassells, and she was of lower birth than most of the Duchess's attendants; she had been nurse to Lord William Howard's first child, and on the death of his wife, the Duchess had agreed to take her in. During her first week in the Duchess's establishment, Mary Lassells met a young man who was dark and handsome with bold roving eyes, and to whom she felt immediately drawn. She was sitting on an overturned tree-trunk in the Lambeth orchard, when he strolled by.

'Welcome, stranger!' he said. 'Or am I wrong in calling you stranger? I declare I should recognize you, had I ever seen you before!'

And so saying he sat down beside her.

'You are right in supposing me to be a stranger. I have been in the Duchess's establishment but a few days. You have been here long?'

'I made the journey up from Norfolk.'

His bold eyes surveyed her. She was well enough, but not worth risking trouble with little Catherine, who, with her naïvety, her delight, her willingness, was giving him the most amusing and absorbing affair he had enjoyed for a long time.

'I rejoice to see you here,' he continued.

'Indeed, sir, you are very kind.'

'It is you who are kind, to sit thus beside me. Tell me, how do you like it here?'

She did not greatly like it, she told him; she found the behaviour of some of the ladies shocking. She was rather bitter, acutely feeling herself to be low-born, inexperienced in the ways of etiquette, having been merely a nurse before she entered the Duchess's household. She had been delighted when she was offered the position, and owing to the unconventional ways of the household Mary had been accepted into it without ceremony. But among these ladies she felt awkward – awkward in speech, awkward in manners; she fancied that they watched her, sneered at her behind her back. This was pure imagination on Mary's part, for in actual fact the ladies were much too absorbed in their own affairs to give much attention to her; but she nursed her grievances, aired them to herself with great bitterness, until they grew out of all proportion to the truth. She occupied a bed in the dormitory with the rest, but there had been no feasting nor love-making in her presence yet, as at the Lambeth house the dormitory was not so conveniently situated. Still, she could not help but notice the levity of the ladies; young gentlemen had looked in on some of them during the day; she had seen many a kiss and indications of greater familiarity. Mary had thought bitterly: And these are those who would look down on a good woman such as I am!

She told him that she did not like what she had so far seen of the conduct of those who were called ladies.

He raised his eyebrows.

'There is much familiarity between them and the young men.'

Manox laughed inwardly, thinking it would be amusing to lead her on. He feigned shocked surprise.

Warming to the subject, she went on: 'Gentlemen – or those who would call themselves gentlemen – look in at the dormitory at all hours of the day. I was never more startled in my life. There was one, who would doubtless call herself a lady, changing her dress, and a gentleman looked round the door and she pretended to hide herself by running behind a screen and was much delighted when he peeped over the top. I declare I wondered whether I should not go at once to Her Grace!'

Manox looked sharply at her. The severely practical head-dress, the thin disapproving lips, the pale eyes – all these belonged to a bearer of tales. She was a virgin, he doubted not – a virgin of necessity! he thought cynically; and of such material were made the tale-bearers, the really dangerous women.

He laid a hand over hers. She started, and a flush spread over her face, beginning at her modest collar and running swiftly to her flat and simply-arranged hair. She was nearer to being pretty at that moment than she would ever be.

He said gently: 'I understand . . . of course I understand. But would you take a word of advice?'

She turned her eyes upon him, smiling, thinking him the handsomest and most charming person she had met since entering the house.

'I am ever ready to take good advice,' she said.

'It would be most unwise to carry tales of this matter to Her Grace.'

'Why so?'

'You have told me that you were a nurse before you came

here. I am but a musician. I instruct ladies at whichever musical instrument it is decreed they shall learn to play.' His voice became caressing. 'You and I are but humble folk; do you think we should be believed? Nay! It is you who would be turned from the house, were you to tell Her Grace what you have seen!'

This was fuel to the bitterness in her; she had lived in noble houses, and had longed to be one of the nobility; she saw every situation from this angle. I am as good as they are . . . Why should I have to serve them, just because I was born in a humble house, and they in castles!

'Well I can believe that the blame would be put on me, rather than on those delinquents.'

He leaned closer to her. 'Depend upon it, it most assuredly would! That is the way of life. Be silent about what you see, fair lady.'

'I cannot tell you what it means to me to have met you,' she said. 'Your sympathy warms me, gives me courage.'

'Then I am indeed glad that I walked this way.'

Mary Lassells was trembling with excitement. No young man had ever taken notice of her before. The eyes of this one were warm and friendly, one might say bold. Mary began to feel very happy, very glad that she had joined the Duchess's retinue after all.

'Do you often walk this way?' she asked.

He kissed her hand. 'We shall meet again ere long.'

She was anxious to make it definite. 'I shall doubtless walk here tomorrow.'

'That is well to know,' he said.

They walked through the orchards down to the river's edge. It was a lovely spring day, and she thought there had never been any scene more beautiful than that of the river gliding by the blossoming trees. The sun, she was sure, was warmer today, and the birds seemed to sing more joyously. Manox sang too; he sang pleasantly; music was his passion, the only one to which he could remain faithful through his life. Mary thought: He means he is happy too, to sing thus.

They went into the house. That encounter had changed Mary; everything to her looked different, and people looked at her and thought her less plain than they had imagined. She hummed the song which Manox had sung; she was pleasant and smiling, forgetting the social barriers between her and most of the others. She smiled in a kindly way on the Duchess's little granddaughter. It is well, thought Mary, that I am not of noble birth; a musician would be a tolerable match for me.

In less than a week she was rudely awakened. She had seen Manox on several occasions, and on each he had continued to charm her. On this day she went to the dormitory in the middle of the morning, having been down to the orchards, having sat for a full hour on the overturned tree-trunk, waiting in vain. She opened the door of the dormitory; the curtains were drawn back from most of the beds, and on one in a corner – young Catherine Howard's – sat the little girl, and with her Henry Manox. They sat side by side, their arms about each other; he was caressing the child, and Catherine was flushed and laughing. It was a great shock to Mary; she stood still, staring at them. Then Manox rose and said: 'Ah! Here is Mistress Lassells!'

Mary stood, struggling with her emotions, thinking: How foolish of me! He likes children; he doubtless came here on some errand, saw the child, and made much of her. But what business could Henry Manox have in the ladies' dormitory? And had he not known that this was the hour when she would be waiting to see him in the orchards!

Manox was plausible. In his numerous love affairs he had found himself in many a delicate situation; with grace he had ever managed to set matters right, if only temporarily.

He went swiftly to Mary and said to her: 'I had a message to bring here; I am really but a servant; and when I came here, the little girl needed comforting.'

She accepted his explanation; because she felt Catherine to be but a child, it did not occur to her that they could possibly be lovers. She smiled again, quite happy. Manox thought, My God! She would be a vindictive woman! And he cursed himself for having light-heartedly indulged in this mild flirtation with her. She had been so prim, so seemingly virtuous, that he could not resist the temptation; he had wanted to show her that what she lacked was, not the desire to sin, but the opportunity.

He escaped, and the situation was saved; but this could not always be so, and he would not give up Catherine for Mary Lassells.

There came a night when Manox, unable to stay away longer, recklessly went to Catherine though he knew Mary would discover this. Mary pulled the curtains about her bed, and wept tears of bitter humiliation. If she had hated the world before she had met Manox, now she hated it a thousand times more; and her hatred was directed, not against Manox, but against Catherine Howard. The wanton! The slut! she thought. And she a great lady to be! A Howard! So much for the nobility – a cousin to the Queen! And who is the Queen? Another such as Catherine Howard. Why, in this wicked world does sin go unpunished and virtue unrewarded?

Her eyes were narrow with weeping. She would go to the Duchess at once, were it not that Manox would suffer. Catherine Howard would be beaten, possibly sent away, but they would hush the matter up so that scandal should not be brought to the house of Howard. It would be Manox who would suffer most, for he was low-born like herself, of no importance; it was such as they who suffered for the sins of the nobility.

Who knew that Manox might not come to his senses, that he might not learn to cherish virtue, that he might discard that vile slut, Catherine Howard, who was not yet in her teens and yet had sunk to the very depths of wickedness! Sexual immorality was surely the most violent form of sin; for such did one burn in hell. To steal and to murder were to commit evil crimes, it was true; but what crime could compare with the wickedness of Catherine Howard!

She would not tell though, for Manox's sake; she would hope that one day he would see his folly, that he would repent . . . that before the blossom gave way to leaves on the trees in the orchard, he would come to her and tell her he had been a fool.

He did not, and there was mockery in his eyes. One day

she met him by the river, and telling herself that she must save him from his folly, she went to him, and with burning eyes and lips that trembled demanded: 'Man, what meanest thou to play the fool of this fashion! Knowest thou not that an my lady of Norfolk knew of the love between thee and Mistress Howard she will undo thee? She is of a noble house; and if thou should'st marry her, some of her blood will kill thee.'

Manox threw back his head and laughed, knowing full well what had caused her to utter such warning, mocking her, laughing at her. He said that she need have no fear for him, since his intentions were strictly of a dishonourable nature.

Angry and humiliated, Mary went into the house. If Manox would not accept her warning against the folly of pursuing this affair, perhaps Catherine would. She found Catherine stitching at a piece of tapestry in the sewing-room.

'I would have speech with you, Mistress Howard.'

Catherine looked up; she knew little of Mary Lassells, and had not greatly liked what she did know, agreeing with most of the others that the woman was prudish and dull.

'Yes?' said Catherine.

'I have come to warn you. You are very young, and I do not think you realize what you do. What you do with Manox is . . . criminal!'

'I understand you not,' said Catherine haughtily, and would have moved away, but Mary caught her arm.

'You must listen. Manox is amusing himself with you. He jokes about your willingness.'

'You lie!' said Catherine.

'I have just come from him,' said Mary with a virtuous air, 'having wished – for indeed I feel it would be but Her Grace's pleasure – to beg him to cease his attentions to yourself. I pointed out to him what reckless folly this was, and how, if he married you, one of your house would surely work his ruin. He boasted that his intentions were only dishonourable.'

Catherine flushed hotly, hating the pale prim face of

Mary Lassells, suddenly afraid, suddenly seeing this beautiful love of hers in a different light. It was sordid now, not beautiful at all. She had been wrong to indulge in it. Manox despised her; many people would despise her; Heaven help her if what she had done should ever get to her grandmother's ears! But chiefly she suffered from Manox's words: His intentions were dishonourable! What a wicked thing for him to have said! Could it be that he was not the adoring, the faithful and gallant, the courteous lover she had believed him to be?

Catherine was hot with rage.

'Fie upon him!' she cried. 'Where is he now? I will go to him, and you shall come with me. I will demand of him whether you have spoken the truth.'

There was nothing Mary could do but conduct Catherine to him there in the orchards, where the thick trees helped to shield those who wished to meet clandestinely. Mary had one thought – and that to break up this foolish affair of Manox's with Catherine Howard. She visualized Manox's repentance, her own great understanding; a marriage between them would be so suitable.

Manox looked startled to see them both; Catherine flushed and angry, Mary smiling secretly.

'I would have you know,' said Catherine in such a fine temper that she could not control it, 'that I despise you, that I hate you, that I never wish to see you again!'

'Catherine!' gasped Manox. 'What does this mean?'

'I know what you have said to this ... woman, of me.'

He was shaken. There was something tremendously attractive about Catherine Howard; her complete enjoyment of physical contact made for his enjoyment; never had he known one so innocently abandoned and responsive; she was a lovely child; her youth was enchanting, and must add piquancy to the affair; he had never had such an experience. And he was not going to lose her if he could help it. He threw a venomous glance at Mary Lassells, which she saw, and which wounded her deeply.

'Catherine,' he said, and would have embraced her there in front of Mary Lassells, but she held off haughtily.

'Do not touch me! I would have you know that I shall never again allow you to do so.'

'I must make you understand,' said Manox, covering his face with his hands and forcing tears into his eyes. 'I love you entirely, Catherine. I have said nothing that could offend. How could I, when my only thought is for your happiness!'

She repeated what Mary had told her. Mary burst out spitefully: 'Thou canst not deny it, Manox, to my face!'

'I know not what I say,' said Manox, his voice shaking with anguish. 'All I know is that my passion for you so transports me beyond the bounds of reason that I wist not what I say!'

Catherine could never bear to see anyone in distress; her heart softened at once.

'I am very displeased,' she said, and it was obvious that she was weakening.

Ignoring Mary Lassells, Manox slipped an arm about Catherine; Mary, in bitter defeat, turned and ran into the house.

Catherine walked in friendly fashion through the orchards, listening to his protestations of love, but although she said she forgave him, it not being in her nature to harbour ill-feeling for long, as she was always ready to believe the best of people and could not happily see anyone suffer, she was shaken, and badly shaken.

Mary Lassells had made her see this love affair in a different light. She never felt the same towards Manox again; and, being Catherine, in need of love, she must look about her for a more worthy object on which to lavish her affection.

*   *   *

Every citizen who could find a boat to hold him was on the Thames that May morning; along the banks of the river the crowd thronged. Beggars had come into the city to view the procession, and pickpockets hoped to ensure a profitable day's work among the press of people. The taverns were full and over-flowing; at all points of vantage people stood, sat or knelt, mounted posts or one another's shoulders to get a good view of the celebrations in honour of Queen Anne's coronation.

From the river bank, Catherine watched with some of the ladies, among them Dorothy Barwicke and Mary Lassells. There was festivity and recklessness in the air today. All the ladies giggled and looked for someone with whom to flirt; they had decked themselves out in their gayest clothes in order to do honour to the new Queen. Most of the young people were ready to admire her; it was chiefly the old ones who continued to murmur against her, and even they were lethargic in their disapproval on this day. When she had been the King's mistress it was one thing; now she was Queen it was another. The King had married her; the Pope had not sanctioned the divorce; Rome considered the marriage illegal; but what matter! England was no longer under the Pope; it owed allegiance to none but its own great King. Weighty matters these, which the people did not fully understand; they worshipped in the same way as before, and the same religious rites were observed, so what matter! And even those who pitied sad Katharine and reviled flaunting, wicked Anne, enjoyed a day's pleasure. And this honour which the King would do to his newly made Queen was to be such a spectacle, so lavish in its display, as to outdo even Tudor splendour.

The Queen was to come from Greenwich to the Tower, and the coronation would take place at Westminster; there would be days of rejoicing, days of processions, and the citizens of London ever loved such occasions.

Mary Lassells would have liked to voice her opinions of the new Queen, but thought it wise to keep quiet. Here was another example of sin's being lauded and fêted; but she knew well enough the folly of talking too freely. The King was determined to have no opposition; already she had heard that the dungeons at the Tower of London were full of those who spoke rashly; well she knew that the instruments of torture were being over-worked. It was not for a humble person to run into danger.

Silly Catherine Howard was filled with childish glee, talking incessantly of her dear, beautiful cousin whom she loved devotedly. 'I declare I shall die of pride . . .' babbled Catherine Howard. 'I declare I can scarce wait for her royal barge . . .'

Mary Lassells talked with Dorothy Barwicke about the wickedness of Manox and Catherine. Dorothy listened and feigned disgust, not mentioning that she had carried many a message from Manox to Catherine, had helped to make their meetings easy, that she had taken over Isabel's task of advancing Catherine's love affair so that she, Catherine, might be involved in the practices which occurred in the ladies' apartments and thereby be prevented from carrying stories to her grandmother. Not, thought Dorothy, that Isabel need have feared. Catherine was no tale-bearer, but the last person in the world to wish to make trouble for others. With Mary Lassells it was quite another matter; Dorothy knew she must go cautiously with Mary.

Catherine's bright eyes had seen a little group of gentlemen along the river bank. The gentlemen looked interested in the party of young ladies, recognizing them as of the Duchess's retinue.

'I can tell you who they are,' whispered one laughing-eyed girl to Catherine, 'They are your uncle the Duke's young gentlemen.'

This was so, for the Duke of Norfolk kept in his household certain gentlemen of good birth and low fortune, most of whom could claim some connection – however distant – with himself. He called them his household troop; they were really pensioners; their only duty was to guard his interests wherever they might be, in time of war to follow him in the field, to back him in his quarrels, to be ever ready to defend him should the need arise. For this he paid them well, fed and clothed them, and gave them little to do – except when he should need them – but amuse themselves. The Earl of Northumberland had a similar retinue in his house; they had always had such, and found it difficult to discard this relic of the feudal system. The gentlemen, having nothing to do but amuse themselves, did this with gusto; they were a high-spirited group, reckless and daring, seeking adventure in any form.

It was a little band of these gentlemen who now found an opportunity of speaking to the ladies of the Duchess's household whom they had seen often, for the Duke's residence was close by his stepmother's, and its gardens and orchards also ran down to the river.

'Look!' cried Dorothy Barwicke, and Catherine's attention was taken from the young men to the river. Numerous barges, containing the chief citizens of London with their Lord Mayor, were passing by on their way to greet the Queen. The merchants presented a brilliant sight in their scarlet clothes and the great heavy chains about their necks. A band of musicians was playing in the city state barge.

Catherine began to sing, keeping time with the band; one of the young men on the river bank joined in. Catherine noticed that he was quite the handsomest of the group, and as she sang, she could not take her eyes from him. He pointed to a barge, calling her attention to what appeared to be a dragon which capered about the deck, shaking its great tail and spitting fire into the river, to the intense delight of all who beheld it. Catherine laughed gleefully, and the young man laughed; she believed he was urging his companions to get nearer to her and her friends. Catherine shrieked with excitement, watching the monsters who were helping the dragon to entertain the citizens. Catherine's eyes filled with ready tears as a barge came into view containing a choir of young girls, singing softly. Catherine could hear the words they sang, which were of the beauty and virtue of Queen Anne.

There was a long wait before the return of the procession bringing with it the Queen. There was however plenty with which to beguile themselves on such a day.

Sweetmeats were handed round; there was wine to drink and little cakes to nibble. It was all very pleasant, especially when Catherine found the handsome young man standing beside her, offering sweets.

'I watched you from the crowd,' he said.

'Indeed, sir, you need not tell me that, for I saw that you watched!'

She looked older than her years; she was flushed with

pleasure; her experience with Manox had matured her. Francis Derham judged her to be about fifteen – a delightful age, he thought.

'I thought you might care to sample these sweetmeats.'

'Indeed I do care.' She munched them happily, childishly. 'I long for the moment when the Queen comes by!'

'Have you ever seen Her Majesty? I hear she is wondrously beautiful.'

'Have I ever seen her! I would have you know, sir, that the Queen is first cousin to me.'

'Cousin to you! I know you are of my lady of Norfolk's house. Tell me, are you then her granddaughter?'

'I am.'

He was surprised that Her Grace of Norfolk should allow her granddaughter – so young and so attractive – to run wild in this way, but he suppressed his surprise. He said in tones of excitement: 'Then verily I believe you to be a kinswoman of mine!'

Catherine was delighted. They talked of their relations; he was right, there was a connection, though distant.

'Ah!' said Catherine. 'I feel safe then with you!'

That was a pleasant reflection, for she was realizing that she could feel safe no longer with Manox, that she was beginning to fear his embraces, that she sought excuses not to be with him. His sordid words to Mary Lassells had shocked and frightened her, and though she did not wish to hurt him, she had no desire to see him. Moreover, now that she had met Francis Derham, she felt more estranged from Manox than before, for Francis was an entirely different type – a gentleman, a man of good manners, good breeding – and being with him, even in those first hours, and seeing that he was attracted by her as Manox had been, she could not help but compare the two; and every vestige of admiration she had had for the musician vanished.

Francis thought: Her grandmother is waiting on the Queen, and that accounts for her freedom; but she is young to be abroad alone. He made up his mind to protect her.

He stayed at her side; they wandered along the bank of the river, they saw the Queen in her royal barge from which issued sweet music; and there followed the Queen, the barges of her father, the Duke of Suffolk, and all the nobility.

'She goes to the Tower!' said Derham.

'The Tower!' Catherine shivered, and he laughed at her. 'Why do you laugh?' she asked.

'Because you look afraid.'

Then she was telling him of her childhood, of Doll Tappit and Walter the warder, of the Little Ease and the Pit; and the screams the warder had heard coming from the torture chambers.

'I would,' said Catherine simply, 'that my sweet cousin were not going to the Tower.'

He laughed at this simplicity. 'Do you not know that all our sovereigns go to the Tower on their coronation? The state apartments there are very different from the dungeons and torture chambers, I'll warrant you!'

'Still, I like it not.'

'You are a dear little girl.' He thought again: She should not be allowed to run free like this! And he was angry towards those who were in charge of her. He liked her company; she was so youthful, so innocent, and yet ... womanly. She would attract men, he knew, perhaps too strongly for her safety. He said: 'You and I should see the celebrations together, should we not? We could meet and go together.'

Catherine was ever eager for adventure, and she liked this young man because he inspired her with trust. She wanted someone to think of affectionately, so that she might no longer brood on Manox.

'You are very kind.'

'You would need to wear your plainest garments, for we should mingle with the crowds.'

'My plainest! They are all plain!'

'I mean you would cease to be Catherine Howard of Norfolk in a crowd of citizens; you would be plain Catherine Smith or some such. How like you this plan?'

'I like it vastly!' laughed Catherine.

And so they made their plans, and it was with him that Catherine saw the Queen's procession after her sojourn at the Tower; it was with Derham that she watched the royal progress through the city. In Gracechurch Street, hung with crimson and scarlet, they mingled with the crowd; they marvelled at the sight of the Chepe decorated with cloth and velvet. They saw the Lord Mayor receive the Queen at the Tower Gate; they saw the French ambassador, the judges, the knights who had been newly honoured in celebration of the coronation; they saw the abbots and the bishops; they espied the florid Duke of Suffolk, who must bury his animosity this day, bearing the verge of silver which showed him to hold the office of High Constable of England.

Catherine looked at this man, and held Derham's hand more firmly. Her companion looked down at her questioningly.

'What ails Catherine Smith?'

'I but thought of his wife, the King's sister, who I have heard is dying. He shows no sorrow.'

'He shows nothing,' whispered Derham. 'Not his antagonism to the Queen. . . . But let us not speak of such matters.'

Catherine shivered, then burst into sudden laughter.

'I think it more pleasant to wear a plain hood and be of the crowd, than to be a queen. I trow I'm as happy as my cousin!'

He pressed her hand; he had begun by feeling friendship, but friendship was deepening into warmer feelings. Catherine Howard was so sweet, such a loving and entrancing little creature!

Catherine gasped, for now came none but the Queen herself, breath-takingly lovely, borne by two white palfreys in white damask in an open litter covered with cloth of gold. Her beautiful hair was flowing in her favourite style, and on her head was a coif whose circlet was set with precious stones. Her surcoat was of silver tissue, and her mantle of the same material lined with ermine. Even those who had murmured against her must stop their murmurings, for never had they beheld such beauty, and while she was among them they must come under her spell.

Catherine was entirely fascinated by her; she had no eyes for those following; she did not see the crimson-clad ladies nor the chariots that followed, all covered in red cloth of gold, until Derham pointed out her grandmother in the first of these with the Marchioness of Dorset. Catherine smiled, wondering what the old lady would say, could she see her in this crowd. But the old Duchess would be thinking of nothing but the lovely woman in the litter, her granddaughter Queen of England, and that this was the proudest day of her long life.

Through the city the pageant continued. In Gracechurch Street they fought their way through the crowd clustered round a fountain from which spurted most lavishly good Rhenish wine. The pageant of the white falcon was enchanting, thought Catherine, for the white falcon represented Anne, and it sat uncrowned among the red and white roses; and then, as the Queen came close, there was a burst of sweet music and an angel flew down and placed a golden crown on the falcon's head. In Cornhill the Queen must pause before a throne on which sat the Three Graces, and in front of which was a spring which ran continually with wine; and she rested there while a poet read a poem which declared that the Queen possessed the qualities represented by the three ladies on the throne. The conduits of Chepe Side ran at one end white wine, and at the other claret, during the whole of that afternoon.

All through this pageantry rode Anne, her eyes bright with triumph – this was the moment for which she had waited four long years – on to Westminster Hall to thank the Lord Mayor and those who had organized the pageantry. Weary and very happy, she ate, and changed from the state garments, staying there at Westminster with the King that night.

Next morning – the coronation day itself, the first of June and a glorious Sunday – Catherine and Derham were again together. They caught a glimpse of the Queen in her surcoat and mantle of purple velvet lined with ermine, with rubies glistening in her hair.

'There is my grandmother!' whispered Catherine. And so it was, for on this day it was the old Duchess's delight and joy to hold the train of her granddaughter. Following the Dowager Duchess were the highest ladies in the land, clad splendidly in scarlet velvet, and the bars of ermine which decorated their stomachers denoted by their number the degree of nobility possessed by each; after these ladies came the knights' wives and the Queen's gentlewomen all clad in gay scarlet. Neither Catherine nor Derham went into the Abbey to see Cranmer set the crown on Anne's head. Mingling with the crowd outside, they both thought they had never been so happy in their lives.

'This is a great adventure indeed for me!' said Derham. 'And glad I am I saw thee!'

'Glad I am too! '

They looked at each other and laughed. Then he, drawing her into an alley, laid his lips against hers. He was surprised by the warmth with which she returned his kiss. He kissed her again and again.

Passers-by saw them and smiled.

'The city is as full of lovers as pickpockets this day!' said one.

'Aye! All eager to follow the royal example doubtless!'

There was laughter, for who could but laugh at such a time, when these streets, in which but a few years before people had died of that plague called the sweating sickness, were now running with good wine!

*　　　*　　　*

There was one member of Anne's family who did not attend the coronation. Jane Rochford's jealousy had become uncontrollable, and in her mad rage against her sister-in-law she was even more indiscreet than was habitual with her.

She had said: 'This marriage ... it is no marriage. A man may not take a wife while he has another. Anne is still the King's mistress, no matter what ceremonies there may be. There is only one Queen, and she is Queen Katharine.'

There were many in support of Queen Katharine, many who shook their heads sadly over the melancholy fate which had befallen the woman whom they had respected as Queen for over twenty years; indeed even those who supported Anne through love or fear could have little to say against Queen Katharine. She must be admired for that calm and queenly dignity which had never deserted her throughout her reign; she had suffered deeply; she had been submitted to mental torture by her unfaithful husband, even before he had brutally told her he would divorce her since she was of no more use to him; she had, by her tactful behaviour, managed to endow the King with some of her own dignity, covering his blatant amours, saying and believing 'This is but the way of kings!' She who suffered bitter humiliations at the hands of Henry the Seventh during those years which had elapsed between Arthur's death and her marriage with Henry, bore few grudges; she was meek and submissive when she considered it her duty to be so; when she considered it her duty to be strong she could be as firm and tenacious as Henry himself. Duty was the keynote of her life. She would suffer the severest torture rather than deviate from what she considered right. She had been taught her religion by her mother, Isabella, who in her turn had been taught by that grim zealot, Torquemada.

In these great people – Katharine, Isabella, Torquemada – there burned fierce fires of fanaticism which purged them of fear. Their religion was the rock to which they clung; life on Earth was to them but a dream, compared with the reality to come. Katharine, bound irrevocably to Rome, believing there could be no divorce, was ready to go to the stake rather than give Henry what he demanded; for to her mind earthly torment was a small price to pay for that eternal bliss which was reserved only for those true servants of the Roman Catholic Faith. With all the strength she had possessed she had stood out against her blustering, furious husband, so nobly, so fearlessly, so assured of the right, that even in defeat she appeared to triumph, and there was none who could go into her presence and not treat her as a queen. There was her passionate devotion to her daughter to touch the hearts of all; to this daughter she had given all the affection her husband did not want; she lived for this daughter, and delighted in the belief that one day she would sit on the throne of England; she had superintended her education with the greatest care, had glowed with pleasure at Mary's aptitude for learning, at her youthful charm, at her father's affection for her.

The only earthly joy which had lighted Katharine's sombre life was in her daughter, the Princess Mary. Henry, raging against her, cursing her obstinacy, unable to believe she could not see what was so clear to his scrupulous conscience, cursing her because she would not admit having consummated her marriage with his brother, hating her because she could have solved the whole difficulty by going into a nunnery, had struck at her in the most effective way possible, when he had separated her from her daughter.

In doing this he had acted foolishly, for the sympathy of the great mass of people was ever ready to be given to the victim of injustice, and they were all for Katharine and Mary. Mothers wept for them and, with their own children beside them, though they might be humble fishwives, could well understand the sufferings of a queen.

Henry, whose nature demanded homage and admiration, was hurt and alarmed by the sympathy shown to Katharine. Previous to the time when the divorce was mooted, it was he who had strutted across the stage, he on whom all attention was focussed – he, large and magnificent, the goodliest of princes, the most handsome of princes, the most sporting of princes, the most loved and admired prince in the world. Katharine had been beside him, but only as a satellite shining with the reflected brilliance from his blazing personality. And now in the hearts of the susceptible and sentimental people she was enshrined as a saint, while he was looked upon as a bully, a promiscuous husband, a brutal man. He could not bear it; it was so unfair. Had he not told them he had merely obeyed the promptings of his conscience? They judged him as a man, not as a king. Then he grew angry. He had explained patiently; he had bared his soul; he had suffered the humiliation of a trial at Westminster Hall; and they did not understand! He had done with patience. He would have all these sullen people know who was their absolute master! A word, a look, would be enough to send any one of them, however high, however low, to the Tower.

Jane's motives were not of the highest, since it was her

jealousy which overcame her prudence. She was a little hysterical. George was so often with the Queen; she had seen emotion in his face at a fancied slight to his sister; he was alert, anxious for her, admonishing her for her impulsiveness, and ridiculously, as people do when they love, loving her the more for it. My faults, thought Jane tearfully, are treated as such; hers are considered virtues.

People were looking furtively at her. When she railed against the Queen, they moved away from her, not wishing to be involved in such recklessness. Jane was too unhappy to care what she said, and gave herself up to the bitter satisfaction of reviling Anne.

Now in her apartment at the palace, she felt about her an ominous calm; those of her associates who had been wont to chat with her or sit with her, were not to be found. Her jealousy burned out, she had time to be frightened, and as she sat and brooded, longing for the return of George that she might tell him of her fears – feeling that he, seeing her in danger, might find her at least worthy of his pity – she heard on the staircase close to her door the sound of footsteps. She leaped up, for there was something in those footsteps of precision and authority; they stopped outside her door; there was a peremptory knocking.

Suppressing a desire to hide, Jane called in a trembling voice: 'Come in!'

She knew him. His face was hard; he would have seen much suffering and grown accustomed to it; for he was Sir William Kingston, the Constable of the Tower of London.

Jane's fingers clutched the scarlet hangings. Her face was drained of colour, her lips trembled.

'Lady Jane Rochford, I am to conduct you to the Tower of London on a charge of High Treason.'

Treason! That dreaded word. And she was guilty of it, for it was treason to speak against the King, and in speaking against Anne, this was what she had done.

She felt the room swing round her; one of Sir William's attendants caught her. They held her head down until the blood rushed back, and they did this naturally, as though they expected it. The room righted itself, but there was a rushing sound in her ears, and the faces of the men were blurred.

She faltered: 'There is some mistake.'

'There is no mistake,' Sir William told her. 'Your ladyship is requested to leave immediately.'

'My husband . . .' she began. 'My sister the Queen . . .'

'I have a warrant for your ladyship's arrest,' she was told. 'I must obey orders. And I must ask your ladyship to accompany us at once.'

Quietly she went out, across the courtyard to the waiting barge. Silently they went up the river. She looked back at the sprawling palace on the river bank with its squat towers and its mullioned windows – the favourite palace of the King, for he was born there and he liked its situation which gave him a perfect view of the rising and falling of the river. When, wondered Jane, would she see Greenwich again?

Past the riverside houses of the rich went the barge until it came to that great fortress which now looked sullen in the grey light, forbidding and ominous. How many had passed through the Traitor's Gate and been swallowed up by that grey stone monster, and so lost to the world outside! It could not happen to me, thought Jane. Not to me! What have I done? Nothing . . . nothing. I did but voice an opinion.

Then she remembered some cynical remark of George's about those who voiced their opinions and those who were too nearly related to the King, deserving to die.

The barge was made fast; up the stone stairs Jane was led. She felt stifled by the oppressive atmosphere of the place. She was taken through a postern, across a narrow stone bridge, and was brought to the entrance of a grey tower. Trembling, Jane entered the Tower of London and was led up narrow spiral staircases, along cold corridors, to the room she would have to occupy. The door was locked on her. She ran to the window and looked out; below her was the dark water of the Thames.

Jane threw herself onto the narrow bed and burst into hysterical tears. This was her own folly! What did she care for Queen Katharine! What did she care for the Princess Mary! She wished to be no martyr. Well did she know that, had she tried to be Anne's friend, she could have been, for Anne did not look for enemies – she only fought those who stood against her. And how could poor little Jane Rochford stand against Queen Anne!

She was a fool. Looking back over her married life, she could see how foolish she had been. Oh, for another chance! She was humble, she was repentant, blaming herself. If she went to Anne, confessed her folly, asked for forgiveness, it would be granted, she knew well. She resolved that if she came out of the Tower she would overcome her jealousy of her brilliant sister-in-law; who knew, by so doing might she not gain a little of George's affection?

She was soothed and calmed, and so remained for some time, until that day which marked the beginning of the celebrations. And then, gazing from her window, she saw the arrival at the Tower, of Anne, dressed in cloth of gold and attended by many ladies; and at the sight of her, all Jane's enmity returned, for the contrast between herself and her sister-in-law was too great to be endured stoically. *She* had arrived by way of the Traitor's Gate, while Anne had come in triumph as the Queen. No! Jane could not endure it. Here in this very place was her sister-in-law, fêted and honoured, adored openly by that mighty and most feared man, Henry the Eighth. It was too much. Jane was overcome by fresh weeping.

'She has many enemies,' said Jane aloud. 'There is the true Queen and her daughter; there is Suffolk, Chapuys ... to name but a few, and all of them powerful people. But Anne Boleyn, though there are many who hate you,' she sobbed bitterly, 'none does so as whole-heartedly as your despised Jane Rochford!'

* * *

The King was not happy. All through the hot month of June he had been aware of his dissatisfaction with life. He had thought that when Anne became his Queen he would know complete happiness; she had been that for five months, and instead of his happiness growing it had gradually diminished.

The King still desired Anne, but he was no longer in love with her; which meant that he had lost that tenderness for her which had dominated him for six years, which had softened him and mellowed his nature. Never had the King loved any but himself, for even his love for Anne was based on his need of her. She had appeared on his horizon, a gay, laughing girl; to him she represented delightful youth; she was unique in her refusal to surrender; she appeared to be unimpressed by his kingship, and had talked of the need to love the man before the king. In his emotions Henry was as simple as a jungle lion; he stalked his quarry, and at these times stalking was his main preoccupation. The stalking of Anne was finished; she had managed to make it arduous; she had made him believe that the end of the hunt was not her surrender, but her place beside him on the throne; together they had stalked a crown for Anne; now it was hers, and they were both exhausted with the effort.

The relationship of mistress and lover was more exciting to a man of Henry's temperament than that of wife and husband; though his conscience would never allow him to admit this. The one was full of excitement, with clandestine meetings, with doubts and fears, and all the ingredients of romance; the other was prosaic, arranged, and – most objectionable of all – inescapable, or almost. Gradually the relationship had been changing ever since January. She could still arouse in him moments of wild passion; she would always do that, she would always be to him the most attractive woman in his life; but he was essentially polygamous, and he possessed a wonderful and elastic conscience to explain all his actions.

Anne was clever; she could have held him; she could have kept him believing he had achieved happiness. But she had always been reckless, and the fight had tired her far more than it had Henry; she had more to gain and more to lose; now she felt she had reached her goal and needed to rest. Moreover she was able now to see this man she had married, from a different angle. She was no longer the humble subject climbing up to the dizzy heights on which he stood secure as King; she was level with him now, not a humble knight's daughter, but a Queen looking at a King – and the closer view was less flattering to him. His youthful looks had gone. He was in his forties, and he had lived too well; he had done most things to excess, and this was apparent; stripped of his glittering clothes he was by no means wholesome; he had suffered the inevitable consequences of a promiscuous life. His oblique gaze at facts irritated Anne beyond endurance. She rebelled against his conscience; she looked at him too closely, and he knew she did. He had seen her lips curl at certain remarks of his; he had seen her face harden at some display of coarseness. This would enrage him, for he would remind himself that he was the son of a king, and that it was entirely due to him that she had gained her high eminence.

They quarrelled; they were both too easily roused to anger to avoid it; but so far the quarrels were little more than tiffs, for she could still enchant him, and moreover he did not forget that she carried the Tudor heir. Anne did not forget it either; in fact it absorbed her; she was experiencing the abandonment of the mother – all else was of small importance, set beside the life that moved within her. She was obsessed by it; she wished to be left alone that she might dream of this child, this son, for whom she must wait for three long dreary months.

This was all very right, thought Henry; the child *was* all-important, but there was no need for her to change so completely. He rejoiced to see her larger; it was a goodly sight. The boy was well and happy inside her, and God speed his coming! But . . . she should not forget the baby's father, as she appeared to do. She was languid, expressing no delight in the attentions he paid to her, preferring to talk of babies with her ladies than to have him with her. Henry was disappointed. He missed too their passionate love-making. He was in the forties; he could not expect to enjoy his manly vigour for many more years. Sometimes he felt quite old; then he would say to himself: 'What I have endured these last years for her has done this to me; brought me a few years nearer the grave, I trow!' Then he would be indignant with her, indignant that she, while carrying his child, must deny him those blissful moments which he could enjoy with none as he could with her. He would think back over his faithfulness to her. This was astonishing; it amazed him. Ah, well, a man must be faithful to a mistress if he wishes to keep her, but a wife is a different matter altogether!

The thought took hold of Henry, haunting his mind. He thought of the days before Anne had come to Suffolk House; they had a piquancy, a charm, since the excitement of adventure is in its unexpectedness. 'It is more pleasing to pluck an apple from the branch which you have seized, than to take one up from a graven dish.' There was truth enough in that, he assured himself, thinking of sudden amorous adventures.

There came a day in July when the rain was teeming down and there was little to do. One played the harp, one sang . . . but the day flagged, for he was uneasy in his mind. Affairs of state weighed heavily upon him. In spite of his separation from Rome, he was eager that the Pope should sanction his marriage; he was disappointed of this, for instead of the sanction there came an announcement that Cranmer's sentence on Henry's former marriage was to be annulled; unless, he was threatened, he left Anne before September and returned to Katharine, both he and she he called his new Queen would be excommunicated.

This was disquieting news which set Henry trembling; Anne's defiance of Rome, her lack of superstitious dread, angered him against her, for he did not care that she should show more courage than he; although his conscience explained that his feeling was not fear but eagerness to assure himself that he had acted within the will of God. Some priests, particularly in the North, were preaching against the new marriage. At Greenwich, Friar Peyto had even had the temerity to preach before Henry and Anne, hinting at the awful judgment that awaited them. Cardinal Pole, who had decided it would be well to live on the Continent owing to his close relationship to the King, wrote reproachful letters abusing Anne. Henry did not trust the Spanish ambassador; the man was sly and insolent and over-bold; he had dared to ask Henry if he could be sure of having children, making a reference to the state of the kingly body which was outwardly manifested by a malignant sore on the leg, which refused to heal.

Henry had reason to believe that Chapuys had reported to his master on the state of English defences; and if this were so, might he not advise the Emperor to make an attack?

Would a conquest of England be difficult for such a skilled general as Charles? Henry knew that most of his nobles – with perhaps the exception of Norfolk – would be ready to support Katharine's side; the Scots were ever eager to be troublesome. Why should not Charles, on the pretext of avenging an ill-treated aunt, do that which would be of inestimable advantage to himself – subdue England? There was one gleam of hope in this prospect; Charles was fully occupied in his scattered possessions, and he was too cautious to stretch his already overstrained resources in another cause. Henry raged and fumed and said he would send Chapuys home, but that was senseless, he knew well; better to have the spy whose evil ways were known to him than another sent in his place who might be possessed of even greater cunning. Henry bottled up his indignation temporarily, holding in his anger, but storing it, nourishing it. The only brightness on the political horizon was that Francis had sent congratulations to both himself and Anne; Henry had invited the French King to sponsor his son, which Francis had cordially agreed to do. Henry felt that, once his son was born, the mass of the people – the element he feared most – would be so over-joyed that it would be forgotten that various unorthodox methods had been followed in order to bring about such a joyous event. Astrologers and physicians had assured him that there could be no doubt of the sex of the child, so all Henry needed to do was to wait for September; but never had a month seemed so long in coming, and it was but July, and wet. The King therefore felt himself in need of diversion.

It came in the voluptuous form of one of the ladies attending Anne. This girl was in complete contrast to her mistress, round-faced, possessed of large baby blue eyes, plump and inviting. No haughtiness there; no dignity; Henry was ever attracted by change.

She glanced at him as she flitted about the chamber, and Anne, absorbed in maternity, did not at first notice what was going on. The girl curtseyed to him, glanced sideways at him; he smiled at her, forgetting Chapuys and astute Charles, and all those who preached against him.

He came upon her suddenly in the quiet of a corridor. She curtseyed, throwing at him that bold glance of admiration which he remembered so well from the days before his thoughts had been given entirely to Anne. He kissed the girl; she caught her breath; he remembered that too; as though they were overwhelmed by him! He felt a king again; pleasant indeed to bestow favours like a king, instead of having to beg for them like a dog.

He left her though, for Anne still largely occupied his thoughts. There was none to be compared with Anne, and he was afraid of her still, afraid of her reactions should she discover any infidelity. He could not forget how she had gone back to Hever; moreover she was to bear him a son. He felt sentimental towards her still; but a kiss was nothing.

The weather cleared, and he felt better. August came. Invitations to the christening of the prince were made ready. Anne, languid on her couch, watched the King obliquely, wondering what gave him that secret look, noting the sly glances of her attendant, noting a certain covert boldness in the girl's manner towards herself. Anne could not believe that he who had been faithful for so many years in the most difficult circumstances had so quickly lapsed, and at such a time, when she was to give him a son. But the secretiveness of him, that irritability towards herself which a man of his type would feel towards someone he had wronged or was about to wrong made her feel sure of what was afoot.

Anne was no patient Griselda, no Katharine of Aragon. She was furious, and the more so because her fury must be tinged with fear. What if history were to repeat itself! What if that which had happened to Queen Katharine was about to happen to Queen Anne! Would she be asked to admit that her marriage was illegal? Would she be invited to go into a nunnery? She must remember that she had no powerful Emperor Charles behind her.

She watched the King; she watched the girl. Henry was over-wrought; he drank freely; the days seemed endless to him; he was nervous and irritable sometimes, at others over-exuberant. But this was understandable, for the birth of a son was of the utmost importance since not only would it ensure the Tudor dynasty, but to Henry it would come like a sign from heaven that he had been right to displace Katharine.

Anne lived uncomfortably through the hot days, longing for the birth of her child. She felt upon her the eyes of all; she felt them to be waiting for that all-deciding factor, the birth of a male child. Her friends prayed for a son; her enemies hoped for a daughter or a still-born child.

One day at the end of August it seemed to her that the girl whom she watched with such suspicion was looking more sly and a trifle arrogant. She saw Henry give her a look of smouldering desire.

'Shall I endure this before my very eyes?' Anne asked herself. 'Am I not Queen?'

She waited until Henry was alone in the chamber with her; then she said, her eyes blazing: 'If you must amuse yourself, I would prefer you did not do it under my eyes and with one of my own women!'

Henry's eyes bulged with fury. He hated being caught; he had had this matter out with his conscience; it was nothing, this light little affair with a wench who had doubtless lost her virginity long ago; it was hardly worth confessing. It was a light and airy nothing, entered into after the drinking of too much wine, little more than a dream.

'Am I to be defied by one wife,' he asked himself, 'dictated to by another?'

He had had enough of this; he was the King, he would have her know. It was not for her to keep up her arrogance to him now.

As he struggled for words to express his indignation, one of Anne's attendants entered; that did not deter him. It should be known throughout the court that he was absolute

King, and that the Queen enjoyed her power through him.

He shouted: 'You close your eyes, as your betters did before you!'

Her cheeks flushed scarlet; she lifted herself in the bed; angry retorts rose to her lips, but something in the face of the King subdued her suddenly, so that her anger left her; she had no room for any other emotion than deadly fear. His face had lost its flushed appearance too; his eyes peered out from his quivering flesh, suddenly cold and very cruel.

Then he continued to speak, slowly and deliberately: 'You ought to know that it is in my power in a single instant to lower you further than I raised you up.'

He went from the room; she sank back, almost fainting. The attendant came to her hastily, ministering to her anxiously, knowing the deep humiliation that must have wounded one so proud. Had Anne been alone she would have retorted hotly; she would have flayed him with her tongue; but they were not alone – yet he had not cared for that! In the court her enemies would hear of this; they would talk of the beginning of the end of Anne Boleyn.

Her hands were cold and wet; she overcame a desire to burst into passionate tears. Then the child began to move inside her, reassuring her. Her son. Once he was born, she was safe, for Henry would never displace the mother of his son whatever the provocation.

Henry did not go near her again for several days. He found a fresh and feverish excitement in the knowledge that to be in lust was satisfying and more congenial to his nature than to be in love. The girl was a saucy wench, God knew, but ready enough, over-ready, to obey her King. To love was to beg and plead; to lust was but to demand satisfaction.

He thought of Anne often, sometimes when he was with the girl. His thoughts were so mixed he could not define them. Sometimes he thought, When the confinement's over, she'll be herself again. Then he thought of a lithesome girl leaning over a pond at Hever, a lovely woman entertaining him at Suffolk House. Anne, Anne . . . there is none on Earth as delightful as Anne! This is naught, Anne; this is forgotten once you are with me again.

Then at mass or confession his thoughts would be tinged with fear. Suppose the Almighty should show his displeasure by a daughter or a still-born child! Marriage with Katharine had been a succession of still-born children, because his marriage with Katharine had been no marriage. He himself had said that. What if his marriage with Anne should be no marriage either?

But God would show him, for God would always be ready to guide one who followed His laws and praised Him, as did Henry the Eighth of England.

*   *   *

Throughout the city the news was awaited. People in the barges that floated down the Thames called one to the other.

'Is the prince come yet then?'

There was scarcely a whisper against the new Queen; those who had been her most violent enemies thought of her now, not as the Queen, but as a mother.

'I heard her pains had started, poor lady . . .'

'They say his name will be Henry or Edward . . .'

Mothers remembered occasions when they had suffered as the Queen suffered now, and even those who cared nothing for motherhood were fond of pageantry. They remembered the coronation, when wine had flowed free from fountains. Pageants, feasting, rejoicing would mark the birth of a son to a king who had waited twenty-four years for it; it would be a greater event than a coronation.

'God save the little prince!' cried the people.

The Dowager Duchess of Norfolk scarcely slept at all, so eager was she for the event. She was full of pride and misgivings, assuring herself that Anne was a healthy girl, that the delivery must be effected efficiently, pushing to the back of her mind those fears which came from her knowledge of the King. Poor Katharine had had miscarriage after miscarriage; they said she was diseased, and whence did she come by such diseases? Might it not have been through close contact with His Majesty? One did not speak such thoughts, for it were treason to do so, but how could the most loyal subjects help their coming to mind! But Anne was a healthy girl; this was her first child. She had come safely through the nine months of pregnancy, and everything must be well.

* * *

In the orchard, sheltered by the trees whose fruit was beginning to ripen, Catherine Howard and Francis Derham lay in each other's arms with scarcely a thought for the momentous events which would shape the course of history.

Francis said: 'Why should they not consent to our marriage? It is true I am poor, but my birth is good.'

'They will assuredly consent,' murmured Catherine. 'They must consent!'

'And why should it not be soon? When the Duchess is recovered from this excitement, she will surely listen to me, Catherine. Do you think that I might approach her?'

'Yes,' said Catherine happily.

'Then we are betrothed!'

'Yes.'

'Then call me husband.'

'Husband,' said Catherine, and he kissed her.

'I would we were away from here, wife, that we were in our own house. I get so little opportunity for seeing you.'

'So little,' she sighed.

'And I hear that the Duchess's ladies are unprincipled in some ways, that they are over-bold with men. I like it not that you should be among them.'

'I am safe,' she said, 'loving thee.'

They kissed again, Catherine drew him closer, feeling that excessive excitement which physical contact with one who attracted her must always give her.

Derham kissed her fervently, enchanted by her as Manox had been; but he was genuinely in love with her, and his feelings were governed by affection as well as the need to gratify his senses. She was very young, but she was ready for passion. He was a reckless young man, courageous and virile; and Catherine's obvious longing to complete their intimacy was so alluring that he – while tenderly thinking of her age – must seek to arrange it.

He insisted they would marry. He could think of nothing more delightful. They were really married, he told her, because according to the law of the Church it was only necessary for two free people to agree to a contract and it was made. It soothed his fears that she was too young, when he called her wife; when she called him husband, he was transported with joy.

He meant to be tactful and kind. He knew nothing of her experience with Manox. Catherine did not tell him, not because she wished to hide it, but because Manox no longer interested her. She had asked her grandmother if she might have a new music teacher, and the old lady, too full of court matters to care what her granddaughter did, had nodded, and when Catherine had named an ascetic, middle-aged man, her grandmother had nodded again. In any case the Duchess no longer sat as chaperon during the music lessons. Manox had almost passed from Catherine's thoughts, except on those unpleasant occasions when he would try to see her – for he was furious that she had ended the affair so abruptly, blaming Mary Lassells for this and making no secret of his hatred and contempt for the girl. Catherine wished of course that she had never known Manox, but she was too blissful to think of much else but the completion of her love with Francis Derham.

'I have a plan,' said Derham.

'Tell me of it.'

'What if I were to ask Her Grace to take me into her house?'

'Dost think she would?' Catherine was trembling at the thought.

'I think she might.' He smiled complacently, remembering how on one occasion Her Grace had singled him out – as a most personable young man – for her special attention. 'I can but try. Then we shall be under the same roof; then I may speak for you. Oh, Catherine, Catherine, how I long for that day!'

Catherine longed for it with equal intensity.

He almost whispered to her that they need not wait; why should they, when they were husband and wife? Catherine was waiting for him to say that; but he did not . . . yet. They lay on the grass, looking up at the ripening fruit.

'I shall never forget the day you first called me husband,' he said. 'I shall remember it when I die!'

Catherine laughed, for death seemed far away and a most absurd topic for two young people in love.

'I shall never forget it either,' she told him, and turned her face to his. They kissed; they trembled; they yearned for each other.

'Soon,' he said, 'I shall be in the Duchess's house. Then I shall see you often . . . often.'

Catherine nodded.

*　　　*　　　*

On the gorgeous bed, which had been part of a French Prince's ransom, Anne lay racked with the agony of childbirth. The King paced up and down in an adjoining room. He could hear her groans. How he loved her! For her groaning set his heart beating with fear that she would die. He was that same lover to whom news of her illness had been brought during the pestilence. 'I would willingly endure half of what you suffer to cure you.' Memories of her came and went in his mind; her laughter, her gaiety; Anne, the centre of attraction at the jousts and masques; sitting beside him watching the jousts in the tiltyard, so beautiful, so apart from all others that he found it difficult to turn his attention from her to the jousting; he thought of her in his arms, his love and his Queen.

He was filled with remorse for that lapse, for the quarrel which had upset her, and – this made him break out into a clammy sweat – might have had some effect on the birth of his son.

He paced up and down, suffering with her. How long? How long? The veins stood out on his forehead. 'By God! If anything happens to her, blood will flow – that I swear!'

The girl with whom he had dallied recently, looked in at the door, smiling; she had been sent to soothe him. He looked at her without recognizing her.

Up and down he went, straining his ears and then putting

his hands over them to shut out the sound of Anne's pain. His fear was suddenly swept away, for distinctly he heard the cry of a child, and in a second he was at the bedside, trembling with eagerness. In the chamber there was a hushed silence. The attendants were afraid to look at him. Anne lay white and exhausted, aware neither of him, nor her room, nor perhaps herself.

'What is it?' he shouted.

They hesitated, one looking at another, hoping that some other would take on the delicate task of breaking unpleasant news.

His face was purple; his eyes blazing. He roared in his anguish.

'A daughter!' His voice was almost a sob; he was defeated; he was humiliated.

He stood, his hands clenched, words pouring from his mouth, abuse and rage; and his eyes were on Anne, lying still on the bed. This to happen to him! What had he done to deserve it? What had he ever done to deserve it? Had he not always sought to do right? Had he not spent hours of labour, studying theology; had he not written *A Glasse of the Truth*? Had he not delved deep into this matter before he had taken action? Had he not waited for the promptings of his conscience? And for whom had he worked and suffered? Not for himself, but for his people, to save them from the rigours of civil war which during the last century had distressed and ravaged the land. For this he had worked, sparing himself not at all, defying the wrath of his simple people who could not be expected to understand his high motives. And this was his reward ... a daughter!

He saw tears roll from Anne's closed eyes; her face was white as marble; she looked as though all life had gone from her; those tears alone showed him that she had heard. And then suddenly his disappointment was pushed aside. She too had suffered deeply; she was disappointed as he was. He knelt down and put his arms about her.

He said earnestly: 'I would rather beg from door to door than forsake you!'

When he had gone, she lay very still, exhausted by the

effort of giving birth to her daughter, her mind unable to give her body the rest it needed. She had failed. She had borne a daughter, not a son! This then was how Katharine of Aragon had felt when Mary was born. The hope was over; the prophecies of the physicians and the soothsayers had proved to be meaningless. 'It will be a boy,' they had assured her; and then . . . it was a girl!

Her heartbeats, which had been sluggish, quickened. What had he said? 'I would rather beg from door to door than forsake you!' Forsake you! Why should he have said that? He would surely only have said it if the thought of forsaking her had been in his mind! He had forsaken Katharine.

Her cheeks were wet; then she must have shed tears. I could never live in a nunnery, she thought, and she remembered how she had once believed that Katharine ought to have gone to such a place. How different the suggestion seemed when applied to oneself! She had never understood Katharine's case until now.

Someone bent over her and whispered: 'Your Majesty must try to sleep.'

She slept awhile and dreamed she was plain Anne Boleyn at Blickling; she was experiencing great happiness, and when she awoke she thought, Happiness then is a matter of comparison; I never knew such complete happiness, for my body was in agony and now I scarce know I have a body, and that in itself is enough.

Fully conscious, she remembered that she was no longer a girl at Blickling, but a queen who had failed in her duty of bearing a male heir. She remembered that throughout the palace – throughout the kingdom – they would now be talking of her failure, speculating as to what effect it would have upon her relationship with the King. Her enemies would be rejoicing, her friends mourning. Chapuys would be writing gleefully to his master. Suffolk would be smiling, well content. Katharine would pray for her; Mary would gloat: She has failed! She has failed! What will the King do now?

The sleep had strengthened her; her weakness of spirit

was passing. She had fought to gain her place, she would fight to keep it.

'My baby . . .' she said, and they brought the child and laid it in her arms.

The red, crumpled face looked beautiful to her, because the child was hers; she held it close, examining it, touching its face lightly with her fingers, murmuring: 'Little baby . . . my little baby!'

It mattered little to her now that the child was a girl, for, having seen her, she was convinced that there never had been such a beautiful child – so how could she wish to change it! She held her close, loving her and yet feeling fearful for her, for was not the child a possible Queen of England? No, there would be sons to follow. The first child had been a girl; therefore she would never sit on the throne of England, because Anne would have sons, many sons. Still, the mother must tremble for her child, must wish now that she were not the daughter of a king and queen. Suppose this baby had been born in some other home than royal Greenwich, where her sex would not have been a matter of such great importance. How happy she would have been then! There would have been nothing to think of but tending the child.

They would have taken the baby from her, but she would not let her go. She wanted her with her, to hold her close, to protect her.

She thought of Mary Tudor's fanatical eyes. How the birth of this child would add fuel to the fierce fires of Mary's resentment! Another girl to take her place, when she had lost it merely by being a girl! Before, there had been many a skirmish with Mary Tudor; now there must be deciding warfare between her and Queen Anne. For what if there were no more children! What if the fate of Queen Anne was that of Queen Katharine? Then . . . when the King was no more, there would be a throne for this child, a throne which would be coveted most ardently by Mary Tudor; and might not the people of England think Mary had the greater claim? Some considered that Katharine was still Queen, and that this newly born child was the bastard, not Mary Tudor.

'Oh, baby,' murmured Anne, 'what a troublesome world it is that you have been born into!' Fiercely she kissed the child. 'But it shall be as happy for you as I can make it. I would kill Mary Tudor rather than that she should keep from you that which is your right!'

One of the women bent over the bed.

'Your Majesty needs to rest. . . .'

Hands took the baby; reluctantly Anne let her go.

She said: 'She shall be called Elizabeth, after my mother and the King's.'

* * *

The court was tense with excitement. In lowered tones the birth of Elizabeth was discussed, in state apartments, in the kitchens; women weeding in the gardens whispered together. In the streets, the people said: 'What now? This is God's answer!' Chapuys was watchful, waiting; he sounded Cromwell. Cromwell was noncommittal, cool. He felt that the King was as yet too fond of the lady to desire any change in their relationship. He was unlike Wolsey; Wolsey shaped the King's policy while he allowed the King to believe it was his own; Cromwell left the shaping to the King, placing himself completely at the royal disposal. Whatever the King needed, Thomas Cromwell would provide. If he wished to disinherit Mary, Cromwell would find the most expeditious way of doing it; if the King wished to discard Anne, Cromwell would work out a way in which this could be done. Cromwell's motto was: 'The King is always right.'

The King still desired Anne ardently, but though he could be the passionate lover, he wished her to realize that it was not hers to command but to obey. A mistress may command, a wife must be submissive. Yet he missed his mistress; he even felt a need to replace her. He could not look upon Anne – young, beautiful and desirable – as he had looked on Katharine. And yet it seemed to him that wives are always wives; one is shackled to them by the laws of holy church, and to be shackled is a most unpleasant condition. There was an element of spice in sin, which virtue lacked; and even though a man had a perfectly good answer to offer his conscience, the spice was there. Anne could no longer threaten to return home; this was her home, the home of which she was indubitably master. She had given him a daughter – a further proof that she was not all he had believed her to be when he had pursued her so fanatically.

And so, in spite of his still passionate desire for her, when this was satisfied he would quickly change from lover into that mighty figure, King and master.

This was apparent very soon after Elizabeth's birth. Anne wanted to keep the child with her, to feed her herself, to have her constantly in her care. Apart from her maternal feelings which were strong, she feared ill might befall her daughter through those enemies whom the child would inherit from the mother.

Seeing his daughter's cradle in the chamber which he shared with Anne, the King was startled.

'How now!' he growled. 'What means this?'

'I would have her with me,' said Anne, used to command, continuing to do so.

'You would have her with you!' he repeated ominously.

'Yes. And I shall feed her myself, for I declare I shall trust no one else with this task.'

The King's face was purple with rage.

He stamped to the door and called to a startled maid of honour. She came in, trembling.

'Take the child away!' he roared.

The girl looked from the King to the Queen; the Queen's face was very pale, but she did not speak. She was trembling, remembering what he had said before the child's birth; at that time he had not waited until they were alone. 'You ought to know that it is in my power in a single instant to lower you further than I raised you up!' And later, 'I would rather beg from door to door than forsake you.' He cared not what he said before whom; he was so careless of her feelings that it mattered not to him if, in the court, people speculated as to whether her influence was waning. Therefore she watched the girl remove her baby, and said nothing.

'She would disturb our rest!' said the King.

When they were alone, Anne turned on him fiercely.

'I wished to keep her with me. I wished to feed her myself. What could it matter . . .'

He looked at her squarely. 'Remember,' he said slowly, 'that I lifted you up to be Queen of England. I ask that you do not behave as a commoner.'

His voice matched his eyes for coldness; she had never noticed how very cold they could be, how relentless and cruel was the small mouth.

Still trembling, she turned away from him, holding her head high, realizing that she, who a short while ago would have blazed at him demanding that her wishes be gratified, now dared do nothing but obey.

The King watched; her hair loose about her shoulders, she reminded him suddenly of the girl in the Hever rose garden. He went to her and laid a heavy hand on her shoulder.

'Come, Anne!' he said, and turning her face to his kissed her. Hope soared in her heart then; she still had power to move him; she had accepted defeat too easily. She smiled.

'You were very determined about that!' she said, trying to infuse a careless note into her voice, for she was afraid to insist on keeping Elizabeth with her, and realized the folly of showing fear to one who was naturally a bully.

'Come, sweetheart!' His voice was thick with the beginnings of passion; she knew him so well; she recognized his moods. 'A queen does not suckle her babes. Enough of this!' He laughed. 'We have a daughter; we must get ourselves a boy!'

She laughed with him. As he caressed her, her thoughts moved fast. She had believed that, with the birth of her child her great fight would be over; she would sink back, refreshed by new homage, into a security which could not be shaken. But Fate had been unkind; she had given the King, not that son who would have placed her so securely on the throne, but a daughter. The fight was not over; it was just beginning; for what had gone before must be a skirmish compared with what must follow. She would need all her skill now, since the very weapons which had won for her her first victories were grown blunt; and it was now not only for herself that she must fight.

How she pitied Katharine of Aragon, who had gone through it all before her! Who was still going through it; a veteran whose weapons were endurance and tenacity. Anne would have need of equal endurance, equal tenacity, for she fought in the opposite camp. She was a mother now; she was a tigress who sees her cub in mortal danger. Katharine of Aragon she had thought of as a pitiable woman, Mary as a wilful, outspoken girl; now they were her bitterest enemies, and they stood on their guard, waiting to dishonour her daughter.

She returned Henry's kisses.

He said: 'Anne, Anne, there's no one like you, Anne!'

And hot anger rose within her, for she sensed that he was comparing her with the woman whom he had dallied with before her delivery. Once she would have repulsed him, stormed at him, told him what she thought; now she must consider; she must lure him afresh, she must enchant him. It would be more difficult now, but she would do it, because it was imperative that she should.

As he lay beside her, she entwined her fingers in his.

'Henry,' she said.

He grunted.

Words trembled on her lips. What if she asked to have the baby in! No, that would be unwise; she could not make conditions now. She must tread very carefully; she was only the King's wife now. The Queen of England lacked the power of Anne Rochford and the Marchioness of Pembroke; but the Queen had all the cunning of those ladies, and she would laugh yet in the faces of her enemies who prophesied her destruction.

'Henry, now that we have a child, would it not be well to declare Mary illegitimate? We know well that she is, but it has never been so stated.'

He considered this. He was feeling a little hurt with Mary, who had applauded and supported her mother ever since the divorce had been thought of. Mary was an obstinate girl, an

289

unloving daughter who had dared to flout her father, the King.

'By God!' he said. 'I've been too lenient with that girl!'

'Indeed you have! And did I not always tell you so; you must announce her illegitimacy at once, and every man of note in the country must agree to it.'

'If they do not,' growled Henry, ''twill be the worse for them!'

She kissed his cheek; she had been foolish to worry. She still had the power to manage him.

He said: 'We must go cautiously. I fear the people will not like it. They have made a martyr of Katharine, and of Mary too.'

She did not attach over-much importance to the will of the people. They had shouted: 'We'll have no Nan Bullen!' And here she was, on the throne in spite of them. The people gathered together and grumbled; sometimes they made disturbances; sometimes they marched together with flaming torches in their hands. . . . Still, they should not pay too much attention to the people.

'Mary is a stupid, wayward girl,' said Anne. And as the King nodded in agreement, she added: 'She should be compelled to act as maid to Elizabeth. She should be made to understand who is the true Princess!'

Then she threw herself into his arms, laughing immoderately. He was pleased with her; he was sure that ere long they would have a healthy boy.

*　　*　　*

Sir Thomas More's daughter, Margaret Roper, was full of fear, for peace had been slowly filched from her home. April was such a pleasant month at Chelsea; in the garden of her father's house, where she had spent her happy childhood and continued to live with her husband Will Roper, the trees were blossoming; the water of the Thames lapped gently about the privy stairs; and how often had Margaret sat on the wooden seat with her father, listening to his reading to her and her brother and sisters, or watching him as he discoursed most wittily with his good friend Erasmus!

Change had crept into the house like a winter fog, and Margaret's heart was filled with a hatred alien to it; the hatred was for one whom she thought of as a brown girl, a girl with a sixth nail on her left hand and a disfiguring mark on her throat, a girl who had bewitched the King, who had cut off England from the Pope, and who had placed Margaret's father in mortal danger.

When Anne Boleyn had gone to court from Hever Castle, the first shadow had been cast over the Chelsea house. Her father would reprove her for her hatred, but Margaret could not subdue it. She was no saint, she reasoned. She had talked of Anne Boleyn most bitterly to her sisters, Elizabeth and Cecily; and now, sitting in the garden watching the river, calm today, bringing with it the mingled smells of tar and seaweed and rotting wood and fish, with the willow trees abudding and drooping sadly over it, she felt fear in the very air. When her adopted sister, Mercy, came running out to sit with her awhile, she had started violently and begun to tremble, fearing Mercy had brought news of some disaster. When her step-sister, Alice, appeared beside her, she felt her knees shake, though Alice had merely come to ask if Margaret would care to help her feed the peacocks.

Margaret recalled this house a few years back; she remembered seeing her father in the heart of his family, reading to them in long summer evenings out of doors, saying prayers in the house; and so often with a joke on his lips. Her father was the centre of his household; they all moved round him; were he removed, what then of the More family? 'Twould be like Earth without the sun, thought Margaret. She remembered writing letters to him when he was away from home on an embassy. He had been proud of her, showing her letters to the great scholar, Reginald Pole, who had complimented him on possessing such a daughter. He had told her this, for he knew well when a compliment might be passed to do the object good, and not to foster pride. He was a saint. And what so often was the end of saints? They became martyrs. Margaret wept softly, controlledly, for she dared not show the others she had wept; it would displease her father. Why must she now recall the memories of her childhood and all those sunny days in which her father moved, the centre of her life, the best loved one? Fear made her do it; fear of what was coming swiftly towards him. What was waiting for this adored father, tomorrow or the next day, or the next? Gloom had settled in the house; it was in the eyes of her step-mother, usually not eager to entertain it, usually eager to push it away; but it had come too close to be pushed away. Her sisters . . . were they over-gay? Their husbands laughed a little louder than was their wont; and in the garden, or from the windows of the house, their eyes would go to the river as though they were watching, watching for a barge that might come from Westminster or the Tower, and stop at the privy steps of Sir Thomas More's garden.

Her father was the calmest of the household; though often he would look at them all sadly and eagerly, as though he would remember the details of each face, that he might recall them after he would be unable to see them. A great calm had settled upon him of late, as though he had grappled with a problem and found the solution. He was a great, good man; and yet he was full of fun. One would have expected a saint to be a little melancholy, not fond of partaking of pleasure nor seeing those about him doing so. He was not like that; he loved to laugh, to see his children laugh; he was full of kindly wit. Oh, there was never such a one as Father! sighed Margaret.

He was fifty-six years of age now, and since he had given up the chancellorship he had looked every year of it. As a boy he had been taken into the household of Cardinal Morton who was then Archbishop of Canterbury; from thence he had gone to Oxford, become a lawyer, gone into Parliament, had lectured on the subject of theology, and was soon recognized as a brilliant young man. There was in him the stuff of the martyr; at one time he had come very near to becoming a monk, but he decided to marry. 'Did you ever regret that decision, Father?' Margaret once asked, and he laughed and pretended to consider; and she had been filled with happiness to know he did not. That was well, for if ever a man was meant to be a father, that man was Sir Thomas More. There was never such a family as ours, thought Margaret. We were happy . . . happy . . . before Anne Boleyn went to court. Wolsey had admired Sir Thomas, had made use of him; the King had met him, taken a liking to him, sought his help in denouncing the doctrines of Luther. Thus, when Wolsey was discarded, it was on this man that the King's choice fell. 'More shall be Chancellor. More shall have the Great Seal of England,' said the King. 'For rarely liked I a man better!' And so he achieved that high office; but he was never meant to go to court. Had he not remarked that he would serve God first, the Prince second? He would ever say that which would lead to trouble, because honesty was second nature to him. He was a saint; please God he need never show the world that he could be a martyr too! Margaret had been frightened when he became Chancellor, knowing his views on the divorce.

'Anne Boleyn will never be Queen,' she had said often enough to her husband, Will. 'How can she be, when the Pope will not sanction the divorce?'

'Indeed,' had answered Will, 'you speak truth, Meg. How can that be! A man who has one wife may not marry another.'

She had been afraid for Will then, for he was interested in the new Faith and would read of it secretly, being unsure in his mind; she trembled, for she could not have borne that her beloved father and her dear husband should not be in agreement on these matters. She had discussed Martin Luther and his doctrines with her father, for he was ever ready to talk with her on any serious subject, holding that though she was a woman she had the power to think and reason.

'Father,' she had said, 'there have been times when I have heard you discourse against the ways of Rome.'

'That I have done, Meg. But this is how I see it, daughter. Rome's ways are not always good, but I hold the things we value most in life may best be held to under Rome.'

She had not dared to tell him of Will's flirting with the new faith. She did not understand it fully. She supposed that

Will, being young, would prefer to try the new, and her father, being not so young, must like the old ways best. She had thought it a great tragedy when she discovered this tendency in Will; but what was that, compared with this which threatened!

The giving up of the Great Seal had been like the first clap of thunder that heralds an unexpected storm on a fine summer's day. After that there was quiet, until that April day a year ago, when three bishops came to the house one morning to bring twenty pounds for his dress, that he might attend the coronation of her who was set up as Queen, and who could never be accepted as Queen in this household. He had refused that invitation. She shivered at the memory. A few days later that refusal brought forth its results; he was charged with bribery and corruption. A ridiculous charge against the most honest man in England; but nothing was too ridiculous to bring against one so prominent who failed to do honour to Anne Boleyn. And recently there had come a further and more alarming charge; a mad nun of Kent, named Elizabeth Barton, had been shocking Anne's supporters and heartening those of Katharine with her lurid prophecies of the evil fates which would await the King and Anne, should they continue in their ungodly ways. The rightful Queen, declared the nun, was Katharine. She had seen visions; she went into trances and then gave voice to prophecies which she declared were put into her mouth by the Holy Ghost. As she had been in touch with Queen Katharine and the Emperor Charles, she was considered dangerous, but on her arrest and examination in the Star Chamber she had confessed she was an imposter. And Sir Thomas More was accused of having instigated this woman to pretend the future had been revealed to her, that she might frighten the King into taking back Katharine and abandoning Anne.

Margaret remembered how they had sat about the table, pretending to eat, pretending it would be well, telling each other that the innocence of the guiltless was their best defence. He had been taken before the Council; he had been questioned by the new Archbishop, by His Grace of Norfolk

– whom she feared for his cold eyes and his hard, cruel mouth – before Thomas Cromwell, whose thick hands looked as though they would not hesitate to turn on one slow to answer his questions; his fish-like eyes held no warmth, only cunning. But he was clever as well as good, this most loved father; he had outwitted them, for his wit was sharper than theirs; and she had heard that there was none equal to him apart from Cranmer, and on this occasion Cranmer was on the wrong side, so right must prevail. They had dismissed him in exasperation, for they could not trip him; and it was *his* arguments, she was sure, that had dumbfounded *them*, not theirs him.

Will had travelled down with him, and told her about this afterwards. Will had said that he knew all must be well, and rejoiced to see him so merry.

Her father had replied that truly he was merry, and would Will know why? He had taken the first step and the first step was the hardest. He had gone so far with those lords that without great shame he could never turn back.

This then had been the cause of his merriment. The step was taken down that path which he believed to be the right one; but what a path, where danger lurked at every turn! And what was at the end of it? That had happened a year ago, and now he had come far along that path; and this gloom which hung over them now – did it mean that he was nearing its end?

Mercy was running out to the garden now.

'Meg!' she called. 'Meg!' And Margaret dared not turn to look at her, so strong was her fear, so numbing the suspense.

Mercy's pleasant face was hot with running.

'Dinner, Meg! Of what are you thinking . . . dreaming here? We are all waiting for you. Father sent to call you. . . .'

She thought she had never heard more beautiful words than those, and their beauty was in their sweet normality. 'Father sent to call you.' She went with Mercy into the house.

They sat round the large table, her stepmother Alice, Cecily and her husband Giles, Elizabeth and her husband,

John and his wife, Mercy and Clement, Margaret and Will. And there at the head of the table he sat, his face more serene than any, as though he were unaware of the dark patches of sorrow that hung about his house. He was laughing, pretending to chide her for day-dreaming, giving her a lecture on the evils of unpunctuality which was spattered with fun; and she laughed with the rest, but not daring to meet his eyes for fear he should see the tears there. He knew why she would not look at him, for they were closer than any in the household, and though he loved well his family, it was his daughter Meg who was closest to his heart. So the others laughed, for he was a sorcerer where laughter was concerned, conjuring it up out of nowhere, but not for her; she was too close to the magician, she knew his tricks, she saw the sleight of hand; she knew the merry eyes watched the window, listened for a sign.

It came with a loud knocking on the outer door.

Gillian, their little maid, came running in, her mouth open. There was one outside who must see Sir Thomas.

Sir Thomas arose, but the man was already in the room. He carried the scroll in his hands. He bowed most courteously. His face was sad, as though he did not greatly love his mission, which was a command that Sir Thomas must appear next day before the Commissioners in order to take the Oath of Supremacy.

There was silence round the table; Margaret stared at the dish before her, at the worn wood of the table which she remembered so well, since she had sat at this particular place for as long as she could recall. She wished the birds would not sing so loudly, showing they did not know this was a day of doom; she wished the sun would not shine so hotly on her neck, for it made her feel she would be sick. She wanted perfect clarity of mind to remember for ever each detail of that well loved face.

Her stepmother had turned deathly pale; she looked as if she would faint. The whole family might have been petrified; they did not move; they sat and waited.

Margaret looked at her father; his eyes had begun to twinkle. No, no! she thought. Not now! I cannot bear that you should turn this into a joke. Not even for them. Not now!

But he was smiling at her, imploring her. Margaret! You and I, we understand. We have to help one another.

Then she arose from the table and went to the messenger, and looking closely at his face, she said: 'Why . . . Dick Halliwell! Mother . . . Everybody . . . 'Tis only Dick!'

And they fell upon her father, chiding him, telling him he went too far with his jokes. And there he was, laughing among them, believing that it is well not to look at unhappiness until it is close upon you, having often said that once you have passed it, every day lends distance between it and yourself.

Margaret went to her nursery where she stayed with her small daughter, finding solace in the charm of the child and thinking of the child's future when she would have children of her own, so that she might not think of this day and the days that would immediately follow it.

Later, hearing voices beneath her window, she looked out and saw her father walking below with the Duke of Norfolk who, she guessed, had come to have a word with him about the morrow. Margaret, her hand on her heart, as though she feared those below would hear its wild beating, listened to their voices which were wafted up to her.

' 'Tis perilous striving with princes,' said His Grace. 'I could wish you as a friend to incline to the King's pleasure.'

Then she heard her father's voice, and it seemed to her that it held little of sorrow. 'There will be only this difference between Your Grace and me, that I shall die today and you tomorrow.'

That night, she could not sleep. Death seemed already to be hovering over the house. She recalled what she had heard of those committed to the Tower; she thought of that gloomy prison and compared it with this happy home. He would say: 'All these years of happiness have I had; I should be grateful to have known them, not sorrowful that because I have loved them well I now must grieve the more to lose them.'

She wept bitter tears, and took her child in her arms, seeking comfort from that small body. But there was no comfort for Margaret Roper. Death hung over the house, waiting to snatch its best loved member.

He left next day. She watched him go down the privy steps with Will, his head held high; already he looked a saint. He did not cast a look behind him; he would have them all believe that soon he would be returning to them.

* * *

Catherine Howard was in the orchard, looking through the trees at the river. She was plumper than she had been almost a year ago when she had first met Francis Derham at the coronation. Now she deplored the state of her clothes, longed for rich materials, for ribands and flowers to adorn her hair.

She was not yet thirteen years old and looked seventeen – a plump, ripe, seventeen; she was very pretty, very gay, fond of laughter; in love with Francis.

Life was beautiful, she thought, and promised to be more so. Francis was husband to her, she wife to him. One day – and that not far distant – they would be so in earnest.

As she stood gazing at the river, a pair of hands were placed over her eyes; she gave a little cry of pleasure, assured this was Francis. Often he came to her, and they met here in the orchards, for he was still of her uncle's house.

'Guess who!' said the loved and familiar voice.

'Guess!' she cried shrilly. 'I do not have to guess – I know!'

She pulled away his hands and swung round to face him; they kissed passionately.

He said: 'Such good news I have today, Catherine! I can scarce wait to tell you.'

'Good news!'

'The best of news. I hope that you will agree that it is.'

'Tell me, tell me! You must tell me.'

He stood, surveying her, laughing, harbouring his secret, longing so deeply for the moment of revelation that he must keep it back, savouring afresh the pleasure it would give him to tell her.

'Very well, I will tell you, Catherine. Her Grace is to have a new gentleman usher. What do you think his name is?'

'Francis . . . you!'

He nodded.

'Then you will be here . . . under this very roof! This is wonderful news, Francis.'

They embraced.

'It will be so much simpler to meet, Catherine.'

She was smiling. Yes, indeed, it would be much easier to meet. There would be many opportunities of which he did not as yet dream.

She was flushed with pleasure, bright-eyed, dreaming of them.

Some young ladies and gentlemen came upon them kissing there. Among them was Francis's great friend Damport.

Francis and Catherine broke free on seeing them, and were greeted with laughter. One of the young men said in mock dismay: 'You often kiss Mrs Catherine Howard, Derham. Is it not very bold of you?'

Derham answered: 'Who should hinder me from kissing my wife?'

'I trow this matter will come to pass!' said one of the ladies.

'What is that?' asked Derham.

'Marry! That Mr Derham shall have Mrs Catherine Howard.'

Derham laughed with pleasure. 'By St John!' he cried. 'You may guess twice and guess worse!'

They were all laughing merrily, when Catherine broke up their mirth by pointing to a barge that went down the river.

'Look ye all!' she cried. 'Is that not Sir Thomas More!'

They all fell silent, thinking of the man. They knew he had come near to the block when the nun of Kent had burned for her heresies. What now? they wondered, and a gloom was cast over their merriment. They watched the barge pass along the river on its way to Westminster; and when it was out of sight, they sought to laugh again, but they found they had no mirth in them.

* * *

Jane Rochford's brief sojourn in the Tower had frightened her considerably. There, in her prison, as she looked down on the river at the pomp of the coronation, she had realized that only her own folly had brought her to this pass, and that in future she must be wiser. She would always hate Anne, but that was no reason why she should shout the dangerous fact abroad. Her short incarceration had been in the nature of a warning to herself and others, but she came out chastened, determined to curb her hysterical jealousy. She apologized to Anne, who accepted her apology, her dislike for Jane being but mild, and she thinking her too colourless to feel much interest in her. So Jane came back to court as attendant to Anne, and though they were never even outwardly friends, there was a truce between them.

It was about a year after the coronation when Jane, who had a habit of discovering the secrets of those around her, made a great discovery.

There was among Anne's attendants a young girl of some beauty, of modest, rather retiring demeanour, somewhat self-effacing; a member of what had come to be known as the anti-Boleyn faction – that set which had held out for Katharine, and were quiet now, though seeming to be watching and waiting for a turn in events.

Jane had intercepted a glance the King had given this girl, and she had felt a deep exultation. Could it be, wondered Jane, that the King was contemplating taking a mistress . . . that he had already been unfaithful to Anne? The thought made Jane laugh aloud when she was alone. How foolish she had been to murmur against Anne! What a poor sort of revenge, that merely put oneself into the Tower! Revenge should be taken subtly; she had learned that now.

How amusing to carry the news to Anne, to falter, to shed a tear, to murmur: 'I am afraid I have some terrible news for you. I am not certain that I should tell . . . I am grieved that it should fall to my lot to bring you such news . . .'

She must watch; she must peep; she must go cautiously. She listened at doors; she hid behind curtains. She was really very bold, for well she knew what the wrath of the King

300

could be like. But it was worth it; she discovered what she had hoped to discover.

She then must turn over in her mind how she would use this. She could go to Anne; she could have the story dragged from her seemingly reluctant lips; it would do her good to see the proud eyes flash, the anger burn in those cheeks, to see haughty Anne humiliated. On the other hand, what if she went to George with the news? She would have his complete attention; she would have his approval, as he would say she had done right in coming to him. She could not make up her mind what she wanted most, and she must do so quickly, for there were others in the court who pried and peeped, and would be only too glad to have the pleasure of doing that which she had worked for.

In the end she went to George.

'George, I have something to tell you. I am afraid. I hardly know what to do. Perhaps you can advise me.'

He was not very interested, she noticed with a sudden jealous rage; he thought it was her own affair. But wait until he learned it concerned his sister Anne!

'The King is indulging in a love affair with one of Anne's ladies.'

George, who had been writing when she came in, hardly looked up from his work. He was perturbed by this news, but not greatly. Knowing the King, he considered such affairs inevitable; they were bound to come sooner or later. The main point was that Anne should realize this and not irritate the King further than he was already irritated by the birth of a daughter. If she remained calm, understanding, she could keep her hold on him; if she were jealous, demanding, she might find herself in a similar position to that of Katharine. He would warn her to treat this matter with the lightness it deserved.

'Well,' said Jane, 'do you not think it was clever of me to have discovered this before most?'

He looked at her with distaste. She could not hide the triumph in her eyes. He pictured her, spying; he discovered early in their married life that she had a gift for spying. And now she was all excitement, happy – and showing it – because she had knowledge which was certain to hurt Anne.

'I am sure,' he said, 'that you enjoyed making the discovery and were clever in doing so.'

'What mean you?' she demanded.

'Just what I say, Jane.'

He stood up, and would have walked past her; she stopped him, putting her hands on his coat.

'I thought to please you, George. I wish I had gone straight to Anne now.'

He was glad she had not done that. Anne was nervous; she was irritable; she was inclined to do the first rash thing that came into her head these days.

He forced himself to smile at Jane. He patted her hand.

'I am glad you told me first.'

She pouted.

'You seemed angry with me a moment ago. Why, George? Why? Why does everything I do anger you?'

He could feel blowing up, one of those scenes which he dreaded. He said: 'Of course I was not angry. You imagine these things.'

'You were angry because you think she will be hurt. It does not matter that *I* risk my life . . .'

'To spy on the King!' he finished. He burst into sudden laughter. 'By God, Jane, I should like to have seen His Majesty, had he come upon you peeping through a crack in the door!'

She stamped her foot; her face was white with rage.

'You find this comic!' she said.

'Well, in a measure. The King, taking his guilty pleasure, and you doing that for which you have a perfect genius . . . spying, congratulating yourself . . .'

'Congratulating myself!'

'Oh, come! I swear I never saw you so pleased with anything.'

Her lips trembled; tears came into her eyes.

'I know I'm not clever, but why should you laugh at everything I do!'

'Everything?' he said, laughing. 'I assure you, Jane, that it is only on rare occasions that I can laugh at what you do.'

She turned on him angrily.

'Perhaps you will not find this such a laughing matter when I tell you who the lady is!'

He was startled now, and she had the joy of seeing that she had all his attention.

'I forget her name. She is so quiet, one scarcely notices her. She is a friend of Chapuys; she is of those who would very gladly see the Queen displaced from the throne...'

She saw now that he was deeply perturbed; this was not merely a king's light love affair; this was high politics. It was very likely that the girl had been primed to do this by the enemies of Anne.

George began to pace up and down; Jane sat in a window seat, watching him. Quite suddenly he went towards the door, and without a glance at Jane strode from the room. Jane wanted to laugh; but there was no laughter in her; she covered her face with her hands and began to cry.

George went to Anne. She was in her room, reading quietly, making marks with her thumbnail at those passages which she meant Henry to read. She was interesting herself in theology, because the subject interested him. She was trying now to bind him to her in every way she knew; she was uneasy; she thought often of Katharine and what had happened to her; she now wondered why she had not previously been more sympathetic towards Henry's first Queen. Bitterly she would laugh at herself; did she not understand the old Queen's case because her own was becoming distressingly similar?

'You look alarmed, George,' she said, laying aside her book.

'I have alarming news.'

'Tell me quickly.' She gave a somewhat hysterical laugh. 'I think I am prepared for anything.'

'The King is philandering.'

She threw back her head and laughed.

'I cannot say I am greatly surprised, George.'

'This is no ordinary philandering. It is important, when we consider who the girl is.'

'Who?'

'Jane does not remember her name.'

'Jane!'

They exchanged glances of understanding.

'Jane made it her affair to discover this matter,' said George. 'This time I think Jane has done us a service. She described the girl as meek and mild as milk.'

'Ah!' cried Anne. 'I can guess who she is!'

'She is of our enemies,' said George. 'It may well be that she has been made to do this to work your ruin, Anne.'

Anne stood up, her cheeks flaming.

'She shall be banished from the court! I myself will see her. She shall come to me at once . . . I . . .'

He lifted a restraining hand.

'Anne, you terrify me. These sudden rages . . .'

'Sudden! Rages! Have I not good cause . . .'

'You have every cause in the world, Anne, to go carefully. You must do nothing rash; everything you do is watched; everything you say is listened to. The throne shakes under you! You must say nothing of this to the King; you must feign ignorance for awhile. We must go secretly and in great quiet, for this is no ordinary light flirtation.'

'There are times,' she said, 'when I feel I should like nothing better than to walk out of the palace and never set eyes on the King again.'

'Be of good cheer. We'll think of something. There is one point you must not forget: Give no sign to the King that you know anything. We will, between us, think of a plan.'

'It is so . . . humiliating!' she cried. 'By my faith! I have suffered more indignities since I have been the Queen than I ever did before.'

'One of the penalties of being Queen, Anne! Promise . . . promise you will go cautiously!'

'Of course, of course! Naturally I shall . . .'

'No,' he said, with a little grimace, 'not naturally, Anne; most unnaturally! Remember Mary . . .'

'What of Mary?'

'You know well to what I refer. How could you have been so wild, so foolish, as to say that if the King went to France and you were Regent, you would find a reason for putting Mary out of the way!'

'This girl maddens me. She is foolish, obstinate . . . and . . .'

'That we well know, but the greater foolishness was yours, Anne, in making such unwise statements.'

'I know . . . I know. And you do well to warn me.'

'I warn you now. Remember previous follies, and keep in good temper with the King.'

'I had thought he seemed more tender of late,' she said, and began to laugh suddenly. 'To think it was naught but his guilty conscience!'

'Ah!' said George. 'He was ever a man of much conscience. But, Anne, he is simple; you and I know that, and together we can be frank. He has great pride in himself. His verses . . . If he thought we did not consider them the best ever written in his court, he would be ready to have our heads off our shoulders!'

'That he would! He has indeed great pride in himself and all his works. George . . .' She looked over her shoulder. 'There is none other to whom I could say this.' She paused, biting her lips, her eyes searching his face. 'Katharine had a daughter, and then . . . all those miscarriages! George, I wonder, might it not be that the King cannot breed sons?'

He stared at her.

'I understand not,' he said.

'Not one son,' she said, 'but Richmond. And Richmond . . . have you noticed? There is a delicate air about him; I do not think he will live to a great age. He is the King's only son. Then there is Mary who is normal, but Mary is a girl and they say that girls survive at birth more easily than boys. There is my own Elizabeth; she is also a girl . . .' She covered her face with her hands. 'And all those stillborn boys, and all those boys who lived to breathe for an hour or so before they died . . . George, was it due to any weakness in Katharine, think you, or was it . . . ?'

He silenced her with a look. He read the terror behind her words.

She said in a whisper: 'He is not wholly well . . . The place on his leg . . .' She closed her eyes and shivered. 'One feels unclean . . .' She shivered again. 'George, what if . . . he . . . cannot have sons?'

He clenched his hands, begging her with his eyes to cease such talk. He got up and strode to the door. Jane was in the corridor, coming towards the room. He wondered, Had she heard that? Had she heard him rise from his seat and stride to the door? Had she retreated a few paces from the door, and then, just as it opened, commenced to walk leisurely towards it? He could not tell from her face; her eyes glistened; she had been weeping. It seemed to him that she was always weeping. He would have to be careful with her; he was sure she could be dangerous.

'Oh . . . Jane . . . I was just telling Anne . . .'

Anne threw a haughty glance at her sister-in-law, but Jane did not care, as George was smiling at her.

'Come inside,' said George.

Jane went in, and the three of them sat together; but Anne would not speak of this matter before Jane. She wondered at her brother's show of friendship for his wife. Could it be that he was reconciling himself to his unhappy marriage, trying to make something out of it at last?

*   *   *

The King hummed a snatch of a song. Anne watched him. He sparkled with jewels; he looked enormous; he was getting corpulent, he was no longer the handsomest prince in Christendom; he was no longer the golden prince. He was a coarse man whose face was too red, whose eyes were bloodshot, and whose leg was a hideously unwholesome ulcer. His eyes were gleaming; he was the lover now, and she remembered the lover well. How often had she seen that look in his eyes! Always before, the look had been for her. Strange indeed to know his desires were fixed on someone else – strange and terrifying.

She said: 'The song is charming. Your own?'

He smiled. She was reclining on the bed he had given her before her confinement. It was a beautiful bed, he thought. By God, she should think herself lucky to have such a fine bed! He doubted whether there was such another bed in the world. Its splendour suited her, he thought indulgently. Anne! There was no one like her, of course; not even little . . . Well, he had never thought she was, but she was sweet, and Anne was fractious and could be maddening – and a man needed a change, if but to prove his manhood. He felt tender towards Anne at moments like this, when she said: 'The song is charming. Your own?' It was when those great black eyes of hers seemed to look right through him and see more of his mind than he cared for anyone to see, that he was angry with her. She was more clever than a woman ought to be! Learned foreigners delighted to talk to her of the new Lutheran theories, and did great homage to her because she could converse naturally and easily with them. He liked that not. Any glory that came to a queen should come through her king. Her beauty might be admired; the splendid clothes she wore, also; but her cleverness, her sharp retorts that might be construed as gibes . . . No, no; they angered him.

He would have her keep in mind that he had raised her up, that she owed all she now enjoyed to him. By God, there were moments when she would appear to forget this! She could please him still, could make him see that there never had been any like her, nor ever would be. That in itself irritated him; it bound him, and he did not like to be bound. He could think with increasing longing of the days before he had known Anne, before this accursed leg began to trouble him, when he was a golden-haired, golden-bearded giant of a man, excelling all others in any sport that could be named; riding hard, eating, drinking, loving, all in a grander manner than that of other men; with Wolsey – dear old Wolsey – to take over matters of state. She had killed Wolsey as surely as if she had slain him with her own hands, since but for her Wolsey would have been alive to this day.

More was in the Tower. And she had done this. And yet . . . there was none could satisfy him as she could; haughty, aloof, as she well knew how to be, always he must feel the longing to subdue her. Sometimes his feeling for her was difficult to explain; sudden anger and fury she aroused in him, and then as suddenly desire, blinding desire that demanded satisfaction at any price. Nay, there was no one like her, but she had cut him off from the days of his glowing manhood. He had met her and changed from that bright youth; during the years of his faithfulness he had been steadily undergoing a change; now he would never be the same man again.

But enough of introspection! He was trying hard to regain his youth. There was one – and she soon to be in his arms, looking up at him with sweet humility – who would assure him that he was the greatest of men as well as the mightiest of kings; who asked for nothing but the honour of being his mistress. Sweet balm to the scorching wounds the black-eyed witch on the bed had given him. But at the moment the witch was sweetly complimenting him, and he had ever found her irresistible in that mood. The other could wait awhile.

'My own, yes,' he said. 'You shall hear me sing it, but not now.'

'I shall await the hearing with pleasure.'

He looked at her sharply. Did she mock? Did she like his songs? Did she compare them with her brother's, with Wyatt's, with Surrey's? Did she think they suffered by comparison?

She was smiling very sweetly. Absently she twirled a lock of her hair. Her eyes were brilliant tonight, and there was a flush in her cheeks. He was taken aback at the contemplation of her beauty, even though he had come to know it too familiarly.

The little one would be awaiting him. Her homage was very sweet. He would sing his song to her, and have no doubts of her approval – but for that reason it was not as sweet as Anne's. She thought him wonderful. She was not clever; a woman should not be clever; her mission in life was to please her lord. And yet . . . he was proud of his Queen. But what matter? It was but manly to love; there was little harm in a dash of light loving here and there; the ladies expected it, and a king should please his subjects.

'Henry . . .' she said. He paused, patting the diamond

which was the centre button of his coat. 'There is something I would say to you.'

'Can it not wait?'

'I think you would rather hear it now.'

'Then tell me quickly.'

She sat up on the bed and held out her hands to him, laughing.

'But it is news I would not care to hurry over.' She was watching his face eagerly.

'What!' said the King. 'Anne ... what meanest thou?'

He took her hands, and she raised herself to a kneeling position.

'Tell me,' she said, putting her face close to his, 'what news would you rather I gave, what news would please you more than any?'

His heart was beating wildly. Could it be what he had longed to hear? Could it really be true? And why not? It was the most natural ... it was what all expected, what all were waiting for.

'Anne!' he said.

She nodded.

He put his arms about her; she slid hers about his neck.

'I thought to please you,' she said.

'Please me!' He was hilarious as a schoolboy. 'There could be naught to give me greater pleasure.'

'Then I am happy.'

'Anne, Anne, when ... ?'

'Not for eight long months. Still ...'

'You are sure?'

She nodded, and he kissed her again.

'This pleases me more than all the jewels in the world,' he told her.

'It pleases me as much as it pleases you. There have been times of late ... when I have felt ...'

He stopped her words by kissing her.

'Bah! Then thou wert indeed a foolish girl, Anne!'

'Indeed I was. Tell me, were you about to go on an important mission? For I would fain talk of this ...'

He laughed. 'Important mission! By God! I would desert the most important of missions to hear this news!'

He had forgotten her already, thought Anne exultantly. Here was the tender lover returned. It had only needed this.

He did not leave her, not that night, nor the next. He had forgotten the demure little girl; he had merely been passing the time with her. Anne was with child. This time a son; certainly a son. Why not! All was well. He had done right to marry Anne. This was God's answer!

* * *

Henry felt sure of his people's joy, once his son was born. It would but need that to have done with the murmuring and grumbling. He forgot the girl with whom he had been pleasing himself; he was the loyal husband now; the father of a daughter, about to be the father of a son. He gave up the idea of going to France, and instead went on a tour through the midlands with Anne – belligerent and mighty. This is the Queen I have chosen. Be good subjects, and love her – or face my wrath!

Subjects *en masse* were disconcerting. A king might punish a few with severity, but what of that? The Dacres affair was proof that the people were not with Anne. Dacres was devoted wholeheartedly to the Catholic cause, and thus to Katharine; and for this reason, Northumberland – still a great admirer of Anne – had quarrelled with the man and accused him of treason. To Cromwell and Cranmer it seemed a good moment to conduct Lord Dacres to the block, so they brought him to London, where he was tried by his peers. The Lords, with unexpected courage and with a defiance unheard of under Henry's despotic rule, had acquitted Dacres. This would seem to Henry like treason on the part of the peers, but it was much more; it meant that these gentlemen knew they had public support behind them, and that was backed up by hatred of Anne – whether she was with child or not made no difference. It shook Henry; it shattered Anne and her supporters. It seemed that everyone was waiting now for the son she promised to produce; that of course would make all the difference; Henry could never displace the mother of his son. Once Anne gave birth to a boy, who showed some promise of becoming a man, she was safe; until then she was tottering.

Anne was very uneasy; more so than anyone, with perhaps the exception of George, could possibly guess. She would wander in the grounds around Greenwich, and brood on the future. She wished to be alone; sometimes when she was in the midst of a laughing crowd she would steal away. Anne was very frightened.

Each day she hoped and prayed for some sign that she might be pregnant; there was none. She had planned boldly, and it seemed as if her plan had failed. What will become of me? she wondered. She could not keep her secret much longer.

She had believed, when she told the King that she was with child, that soon she must be. Why was it that she was not? Something told her the fault lay with him, and this idea was supported by Katharine's disastrous experiences and her own inability to produce another child. There was Elizabeth, but Elizabeth would not do. She murmured: 'Oh, Elizabeth, my daughter, why wast thou not born a boy!'

She watched the clouds drifting across the summer sky; she looked at the green leaves on the trees and murmured: 'Before they fall I shall have to tell him. A woman cannot go on for ever pretending she is pregnant!'

Perhaps by then . . . Yes, that had been the burden of her thoughts. . . . Perhaps by then that which had been a fabrication of her tortured mind would be a reality. Perhaps by then there would be a real child in her womb, not an imaginary one.

The days passed. Already people were glancing at her oddly. Is the Queen well? How small she is! Can she really be with child? What think you? Is something wrong? Is this her punishment for the way she treated poor Queen Katharine?

She sat under the trees, praying for a child. How many women had sat under these trees, frightened because they were to bear a child! And now here was one who was terrified because she was not to bear one, because she, feeling herself in a desperate situation, had seen in such a lie a possible way out of her difficulties.

Her sister Mary came and sat beside her. Mary was plumper, more matronly, but still the same Mary although perhaps over ripe now. Still unable to say No, I'll warrant, thought Anne, and was suddenly filled with sharp envy.

'Anne,' said Mary, 'I am in great trouble.'

Anne's lips curled; she wondered what Mary's trouble was, and how it would compare with her own.

'What trouble?' asked Anne, finding sudden relief as her thoughts necessarily shifted from herself to her sister.

'Anne, dost know Stafford?'

'What!' cried Anne. 'Stafford the gentleman usher?'

'The very one,' said Mary. 'Well . . . he and I . . .'

'A gentleman usher!' said Anne.

'All the world seemed to set so little by me, and he so much,' said Mary. 'I thought I could take no better way out but to take him and forsake all other ways.'

'The King will never consent,' said Anne.

'Perhaps when he knows I am to have a child . . .'

Anne turned on her sister in horror. Mary had been a widow for five years. Naturally one would not expect her to live a nun's life, but one did expect her to show a little care. Oh, thought Anne, how like Mary! How like her!

Mary hastened to explain. 'He was young, and love overcame us. And I loved him as he did me. . . .'

Anne was silent.

'Ah!' went on Mary, 'I might have had a man of higher birth, but I could never have had one who could have loved me so well . . . nor a more honest man.'

Anne looked cold, and Mary could not bear coldness now; she did not know of her sister's trials; she pictured her happy and secure, rejoicing in her queenly state. It seemed unkind to have from her no word of reassurance.

Mary stood up. 'I had rather be with him than I were the greatest queen!' she cried, and began to run across the grass into the palace.

Anne watched her. Mary – a widow – was with child, and afraid because of it. Anne – a queen and a wife – was not, and far, far more afraid than Mary could understand, because of it! Anne threw back her head and laughed immoderately; and when she had done, she touched her cheeks and there were tears upon them.

*   *   *

When Anne told Henry there was not to be a child, he was furious.

'How could such a mistake occur!' he demanded suspiciously, his little eyes cold and cruel.

'Simply!' she flared back. 'And it did, so why argue about it!'

'I have been tricked!' he cried. 'It seems that God has decreed I shall never have a son.'

And he turned away, for there was a certain speculation in his eyes which he did not wish her to see. He went to the demure little lady-in-waiting.

'Ha!' he said. 'It seems a long time since I kissed you, sweetheart!'

She was meek, without reproaches. How different from Anne! he thought, and remembered resentfully how she had commanded him during the days of his courtship, and how when she had become his mistress she continued to berate him.

By God, he thought, I'll have none of that. Who brought her up, eh? Who could send her back whence she came? Women should be meek and submissive, as this one was.

Anne watched angrily, trying to follow her brother's advice and finding herself unable to do so.

'Madge,' she said to her cousin, a lovely girl of whom she was very fond, 'go to that girl and tell her I would see her this minute.'

Madge went, and awaiting the arrival of the girl, Anne paced up and down, trying to compose herself, trying to rehearse what she would say to her.

The girl came, eyes downcast, very frightened, for Anne's eyes were blazing in spite of her efforts to remain calm.

'I would have you know,' said Anne, 'that I have been hearing evil reports of my ladies. I am sending you back to your home. Be ready to start as soon as you hear from me that you are to do so.'

The girl scarcely looked at Anne; she blushed scarlet, and her lips quivered.

Sly creature! thought Anne angrily. And she the King's mistress! What he can see in the girl I do not understand, except that she is a trifle pretty and very meek. Doubtless she tells him he is wonderful! Her lips twisted scornfully, and then suddenly she felt a need to burst into tears. Here was she, the Queen, and must resort to such methods to rid herself of her rivals! Was everyone in this court against her? Her father was anxious now, she knew, wondering how long she would retain her hold on the King; Norfolk no longer troubled to be courteous; they had quarrelled; he had stamped out of the room on the last occasion she had seen him, muttering that of her which she would prefer not to remember; Suffolk watched, sly, secretly smiling; the Princess Mary was openly defiant. And now this girl!

'Get you gone from my presence!' said Anne. 'You are banished from court.'

The girl's reply was to go straight to the King, who immediately countermanded the Queen's order.

He left the girl and went to Anne.

'What means this?' he demanded.

'I will not have you parade your infidelities right under my nose!'

'Madam!' roared the King. 'I would have you know I am master here!'

'Nevertheless,' she said, 'you cannot expect me to smile on your mistresses and to treat them as though they were the most faithful of my attendants.'

He said coarsely: 'If that is what I wish, you shall do it . . . as others did before you!'

'You mistake me,' she answered.

'I mistake you not. From where do you derive your authority if not from me! Consider from what I lifted you. I have but to lift my finger to send you back whence you came!'

'Why not lift it then?' she blazed. 'Your pretty little mistress doubtless would grace the throne better than I. She is so brilliant! Her conversation is so witty! The people would acclaim her. But, Henry, do you not think she might put you a little in the shade. . . . Such wit . . . such brilliance!'

He looked at her with smouldering eyes; there were occasions when he could forget he was a king and put his hands about that little neck, and press and press until there was no breath left in her. But a king does not do murder; others do it for him. It was a quick thought that passed through his mind and was gone before he had time to realize it had been there.

He turned and strode out of the room.

Jane Rochford had overheard that quarrel. She was excited; it gave her a pleasurable thrill to know that Anne was having difficulties with her husband, just as she herself had with George, though with a difference.

Jane crept away and came back later, begging a word with the Queen. Could the ladies be dismissed? Jane whispered. What she had to say was for Anne's ear alone.

She expresssed her sympathy.

'Such a sly wench! I declare she deliberately sets out to trap the King. All that modesty and reluctance . . .' Jane glanced sideways at Anne; had her barb struck a vulnerable spot? Oh, how did it feel, when you have shown reluctance to a king and complete indifference to the feelings of his wife, to find your position suddenly reversed; yourself the neglected wife, and another careless of your feelings? Jane was so excited she could scarcely talk; she wanted to laugh at this, because it seemed so very amusing.

'But I have not come to commiserate with you, dear sister. I want to help. I have a plan. Were I to let her people know that she is in danger of disgracing herself – oh, I need not mention His Majesty – it might be a friendly warning. . . . I would try. I trow that, were she removed from court, the King would be the most loyal of husbands; and how can a woman get children when her husband has no time for her, but only for other women!'

Jane spoke vehemently, but Anne was too sick at heart to notice it. Everywhere she looked, disaster was threatening.

315

She was young and healthy, but her husband was neither so young nor so healthy; she could not get a child, when the most urgent matter she had ever known was that she should first get with child, and that the child should be a son. The King's health was doubtless to blame, but the King never blamed himself; when he was in fault he blamed someone else. There was evidence of that all about him, and had been for years. Francis had made an alarming move; he had begun to talk once more of a match between his son and Mary. What could that mean, but one thing! Mary was a bastard; how could a bastard marry the son of the King of France?

There was only one answer: The King of France no longer regarded Mary as a bastard. Her hopes had soared when Clement died and Paul III took his place; Paul had seemed more inclined to listen to reason, but what did she know of these matters? Only what it was deemed wise to tell her! Francis, whom she had regarded as a friend to herself, who had shown decided friendship when they had met at Calais, had decided it was unsafe to quarrel with Charles and with Rome. France was entirely Catholic – that was the answer. Francis could not stand out against his people; his sympathy might be with Anne, but a king's sympathy must be governed by diplomacy; Francis was showing a less friendly face to Anne. She saw now that the whole of Europe would be against the marriage; that would have meant nothing, had Henry been with her, had Henry been the devoted lover he had remained during the waiting years. But Henry was turning from her; this sly, meek, pretty girl from the opposite camp was proof of that. She was filled with terror, for she remembered the negotiations which had gone on before news of a possible divorce had reached Katharine. Everyone at court had known before Katharine; they had whispered of The King's Secret Matter. Was the King now indulging once more in a secret matter? Terrified, she listened to Jane; she was ready to clutch at any straw. That was foolish – she might have known Jane was no diplomatist. Jane's art was in listening at doors, slyly setting one person against another.

Henry discovered what Jane was about.

'What!' he shouted. 'This is the work of Rochford's wife. She shall be committed to the Tower by the Traitor's Gate.' She wept and stormed, cursing herself for her folly. To think she had come to this by merely trying to help Anne! What would become of her now? she wondered. If ever she got out of the Tower alive, she would be clever, subtle. . . . Once before she had been careless; this time she had been equally foolish, but she had learned her lesson at last. George would bear her no gratitude for what she had done; he would say: 'What a clumsy fool you are, Jane!' Or if he did not say it, he would think it.

All this she had done for George really . . . and he cared not, had no feeling for her at all. 'Methinks I begin to hate him!' she murmured, and looked through her narrow windows onto the cobbles beneath.

George came to see his sister; he was secretly alarmed.

'Jane has been sent to the Tower!' he said. Anne told him what had happened. 'This grows mightily dangerous, Anne.'

'You to tell *me* that! I assure you I know it but too well.'

'Anne, you must go very carefully.'

'You tell me that persistently,' she answered pettishly. 'What must I do now? I have gone carefully, and I have been brought to this pass. What is happening to us? Mary in disgrace, our father quite often absenting himself from court, shamefaced, hardly looking at me! And Uncle Norfolk becoming more and more outspoken! You, alarmed that I will not be cautious, and I . . .'

'We have to go carefully, that is all. We have to stop this affair of the King's with this girl; it must not be allowed to go on.'

'I care not! And it were not she, it would be another.'

'Anne, for God's sake listen to reason! It matters not if it were another one; it only matters that it should be *she*!'

'You mean . . . there is more in this than a simple love affair?'

'Indeed I do.'

Madge Shelton looked in at the door.

'I beg your pardon. I had thought Your Majesty to be

alone.' She and George exchanged cousinly greetings, and Madge retired.

'Our cousin is a beautiful girl,' said George.

Anne looked at him sharply.

He said: 'You'll hate what I am about to say, Anne. It is a desperate remedy, but I feel it would be effective. Madge is delightful, so young and charming. The other affair may well be beginning to pall.'

'George! I do not understand. . . .'

'We cannot afford to be over-nice, Anne.'

'Oh, speak frankly. You mean – throw Madge to the King, that he may forget that other . . .'

'It is not a woman we have to fight, Anne. It is a party!'

'I would not do it,' she said. 'Why, Madge . . . she is but a young girl, and he . . . You cannot know, George. The life he has lived. . . .'

'I do know. Hast ever thought we are fighting for thy life?'

She tried to throw off her fears with flippancy. She laughed rather too loudly; he noticed uneasily that of late she had been given to immoderate laughter.

'Ever since I had thought to be Queen, there have been those ready to thrust prophecies under my eyes. I mind well one where I was depicted with my head cut off!' She put her hands about her throat. 'Fret not, George. My husband, after the manner of most, amuses himself. He was all eagerness for me before our marriage; now?' She shrugged her shoulders and began to laugh again.

'Be silent,' said George. 'What of Elizabeth?'

She stopped laughing.

'What of Elizabeth?'

'It has been decreed that Mary Tudor is a bastard, because the King tired of her mother and decided – as she could no longer hope to give him a son – that he was no longer married to her. Oh, we know of his conscience, we know of his treatise . . . we know too well the story. But, Anne, we are alone and we need not fear each other. . . . Ah! What a good thing it is to have in this world one person of whom you need not cherish the smallest fear! Anne, I begin to think we are not so unlucky, you and I.'

'Please stop,' she said. 'You make me weep.'

'This is no time for tears. I said Mary has been decreed a bastard, though her mother is of Spain and related to the most powerful man in Europe. Anne, you are but the daughter of the Earl of Wiltshire – Sir Thomas Boleyn not long since – and he was only raised to his earldom to do honour to you; he could be stripped of that honour easily enough. He is no Emperor, Anne! Dost see what I mean? Mary was made a bastard; what of Elizabeth? Who need fear *her* most humble relations?'

'Yes,' said Anne breathlessly. 'Yes!'

'If the King has no sons, Elizabeth will be Queen of England . . . or Mary will! Oh, Anne, you have to fight this, you have to hold your place for your daughter's sake.'

'You are right,' she said. 'I have my daughter.'

'Therefore . . .'

She nodded. 'You are right, George. I think you are often right. I shall remember what you said about our being lucky. Yes, I think we are; for who else is there, but each other!'

The next day she sent Madge Shelton with a message to the King. From a window she watched the girl approach him, for he was in the palace grounds. Yes, he was appreciative; who could help being so, of Madge! Madge had beauty; Madge had wit. She had made the king laugh; he was suggesting they should take a turn round the rose garden.

Anne soothed her doubts with the reflection that Madge was a saucy wench, able to take care of herself, and had probably had love affairs before. Besides . . . there was Elizabeth!

*   *   *

The Dowager Duchess of Norfolk was uneasy. Rumours came from the court, and one could not ignore them. All was not well with the Queen. She herself had quarrelled with her stepson, the Duke, because he had spoken as she did not care to hear him speak, and it had been of the Queen. I never did like the man, she mused. Cruel, hard, opportunist! One could tell which way the wind was blowing, by what he would have to say. Which way was the wind blowing? She liked not these rumours.

She was to be state governess to the Princess Elizabeth, a further sign of Anne's friendship for her. 'I do hope the dear child is well and happy. It is a terrible trial to be a queen, and to such a king!' she murmured to herself.

The Duchess was fractious in her own household. Those girls were noisy in their room at night, and she had heard it whispered that they were over-free with the young men.

She sent for Mary Lassells, whom she did not like over-much. The girl was of humble birth, apt to look sullen; she was really a serving-maid, and should not be with the ladies. I must see to that one day, thought the duchess, and filed the matter away in that mental pigeon-hole which was crammed full of forgotten notes.

'Mary Lassells,' she said, when the girl came to her, 'there is much noise in the ladies' sleeping apartments at night. These ladies are under my care, and as since my grand-daughter's coronation I find myself with less and less leisure, I am going to take a few precautions to make sure of correct behaviour on the part of these young people.'

The girl was smiling primly, as though to indicate that there was every reason for the Duchess to take precautions. This angered the Duchess; she did not wish to be reminded that she had been lax; she would have preferred the girl to look as though this were a quite unnecessary precaution being taken by an over-careful duenna.

'It will be your duty, Mary Lassells, every night when the ladies have retired, to see that the key of their apartment is placed in the lock outside the door. Then at a fixed hour I shall send someone to lock the door, and the key will be brought to me.'

The Duchess sat back in her chair, well pleased.

'I think that will be a very excellent plan, Your Grace,' said Mary Lassells unctuously.

'Your opinion was not asked, Mary Lassells,' said the Duchess haughtily. 'That will do. Now remember please, and I will send someone for the key this very night.'

Mary said nothing. It was shocking to consider what

went on in that room at night. Catherine Howard behaved quite shamelessly now with Francis Derham; he would bring fruit and wine for her, and they would sit on her bed and laugh and chatter, telling everyone that as they were really married there was no harm in what they were doing. Derham was very much in love with the child – that was obvious – and she with him; he salved his conscience by pretending they were married. It was very silly, thought Mary Lassells, and certainly time such wickedness was stopped.

They were planning for tonight. Let them plan! What a shock for them, when they were waiting to receive their lovers, to find the door locked, keeping them out! And so would it be every night. No more games, no more of such wicked folly.

Though Manox never came to the room now, she often thought of him. Some said he was sorely troubled because he had lost little Catherine Howard. And she not fourteen! Thirteen at the most. Was ever such crass wickedness allowed to go unpunished! She will go to hell and suffer eternal torment when she dies, I'll swear! And Mary Lassells felt happier at the thought.

They were all laughing, chattering in their silly way, when Mary Lassells went to the door to obey the Duchess's instructions. 'Where go you?' asked one girl.

'Merely to act on Her Grace's orders.' Mary put the key in the outer lock. Inside the room they heard her exchanging a few words with someone outside the door. Mary came back into the room, and the door was immediately locked on the outside.

There was a chorus of excitement. 'What means this?' 'Is it a joke?' 'What said you, Mary Lassells?' 'Why did you take the key?'

Mary Lassells faced them, her prim mouth working. 'Her Grace the Duchess is much displeased. She has heard the laughing and chatter that goes on here of nights. She has taken me on one side and told me what she will do. Every night the door of this apartment is to be locked and the key taken to her.'

There were cries of rage.

'Mary Lassells! You have been bearing tales!'

'Indeed I have not!'

'What can one expect of a cook's daughter!'

'I am not a cook's daughter.'

'Oh, well ... something such!'

'This is shameful. Her Grace merely asked me to put the key outside. .... I suppose because she sees I am more virtuous than the rest of you.'

Dorothy Barwicke said: 'Do you swear, Mary Lassells, that you have said nothing to Her Grace of what happens in this room?'

'I swear!'

'Then why ... ?'

'She has heard the noise in here. She says too that she has heard whispers of what goes on. . . . Doubtless the servants. . . .'

'They may have heard the gentlemen creeping up the stairs!' said one girl with a giggle. 'I declare Thomas made one devil of a row last time.'

'The truth remains,' said Mary Lassells, 'that you are under suspicion. I only hope Her Grace does not think I have been a party to your follies!'

'Impossible!'

'You would find it difficult, Mary, to discover one who would be a partner.'

The girls were rocking on their beds, laughing immoderately.

'Poor Mary!' said Catherine. 'I am sure Manox likes you very well.'

Everyone shrieked with laughter at that. Catherine was hurt; she had not meant to be unkind. She had seen Manox and Mary together before she had broken with him, and she had thought they seemed friendly. She would have liked Manox to find someone he could care for. Mary too. It seemed a satisfactory settlement, to Catherine.

Mary threw her a glance of hatred.

'Well,' said Dorothy Barwicke, 'this is an end of our little frolics ... unless ...'

'Unless what?' cried several voices.

'There are some very rash and gallant gentlemen among our friends; who knows, one might find a way of stealing the keys!'

'Stealing the keys!' The adventures would have an additional spice if keys had first to be stolen.

The young ladies settled into their beds and talked for a long time. Mary Lassells lay in hers, trembling with rage against them all, and particularly against Catherine Howard.

*   *   *

In his prison room in the Tower of London, Margaret Roper stood before her father. He was hollow-eyed, but he was smiling bravely, and she saw that he was more serene in his mind than he had been for a long time. Margaret flung herself at him, reproaches on her lips for those who had brought him to this, for her hatred of them she could not express in his presence, knowing it would disturb him.

They could only look at each other, drinking in each detail of the well-loved faces, knowing that only with the greatest good luck could they hope for another interview. He was braver than she was. Perhaps, she thought, it is easier to die than to be left. He could laugh; she could not. When she would have spoken, tears ran from her eyes.

He understood her feelings. Had he not always understood her?

'Let me look at thee, Meg! Thou hast been too long in the sun. There are freckles across thy nose. Look after the children, Meg. Let them be happy. Meg, thou and I may speak frankly together.'

She nodded. She knew that all pretence between them was at an end. He would not say to her, as he might have said to any of the others: 'This will pass!' They were too close; they could hide nothing. He knew that it was but a matter of time before he must lay his head on the block.

'Take care of the children, Meg. Frighten them not with gloomy tales of death. Tell them of bright chariots and of beauty. Make them see death as a lovely thing. Do this for me, Meg. Grieve not that I must leave this gloomy prison.

My spirit is enclosed in a shell. It longs for the hatching. It longs to be born. Oh, let that shell be cracked. What matter by whom, by the King or his mistress!'

'Speak not of her, Father . . . But for her . . .'

He must lay his hands on her lips, and say a word for the creature.

'Judge her not, Meg. For how do we know what she may be suffering at this moment?'

She burst out: 'At the court there is sport and dances. What do they care that you – the noblest of men – shall die! They must amuse themselves; they must destroy those who would stand in the way of their pleasure. Father, do not ask me not to curse them . . . for I do, I do!'

'Poor Anne Boleyn!' he said sadly. 'Alas, Meg, it pitieth me to consider what misery, poor soul, she will shortly come to. These dances of hers will prove such dances that she will spurn our heads off like footballs, but 'twill not be long ere her head will dance the like dance.'

He was saint indeed, thought Margaret, for he could defend her who was to cause his death; he could be sorry for her, could weep a little for her. He talked of the King more frankly than she had ever heard him spoken of. He said there was always cruelty in a man who cannot restrain his passions.

'Be not troubled, sweet daughter, even when you see my head on London Bridge. Remember it is *I* who will look down on *thee* and feel pity.'

He asked of family affairs, of the garden, of the house, of the peacocks. He could laugh; he could even jest. And sick at heart, yet comforted, she left him.

After his trial she saw him brought back to the Tower. He walked with his head erect; though she noticed his clothes were creased and looked shabby; well she remembered the gold chain ornamented with double roses, the dark green coat with its fur collar and big sleeves which he favoured as his hands were of awkward shape; she looked at his hands, loving him afresh for his one vanity. Anger surged through her that they should have made him walk between the guards, their bills and halberts ready lest he should attempt an escape. Fools, to think he would try to escape! Did they not know he welcomed this, that he had said to Will: 'I am joyful because the first step which is the worst and most difficult, is taken!' Had he not said that to stand out against the King was to lose one's body, but to submit to him was to lose one's soul!

She ran to him, breaking through the guards; she flung her arms about his neck. And the guards turned away that they might not see this which brought tears to their eyes.

'Meg!' he whispered. 'For Christ's sake don't unman me!'

She remembered nothing more until she was lying on the ground while those about her chafed her hands and whispered words of comfort; she was conscious of nothing but the hateful sultry July heat, and the fact that she would never see him alive again.

From the Tower he wrote to her, using a piece of coal, to tell her which day he would be executed. He could not forbear to jest even then. 'It will be St. Thomas's Eve, a day very meet and convenient for me. And I never liked your manners better than when you kissed me last. For I like when daughterly love and dear charity hath no leisure to look to worldly courtesy.'

She was to go to his burial. The King had given written consent – and this was a privilege – providing that at his execution Sir Thomas would promise not to use many words.

So he died; and his head was impaled on London Bridge to show the people he was a traitor. But the people looked at it with anger; they murmured sullenly; for these people knew they looked at the head of one who was more saint than traitor.

* * *

Henry was uneasy; he was tired of women. Women should be a pleasant diversion; matters of state should be those affairs to claim the attention of a king.

The French King was trying to renew negotiations for a marriage with Mary. More was in prison awaiting execution; so was Fisher. He had postponed execution of these men, knowing of the popular feeling towards them. He had ever been afraid of popular feeling.

Anne coloured all his thoughts; he was angry with her who had placed him in this position; angry with his desire for her, brief though it might be, without which his life would be incomplete. Anne had brought him to this pass; he could wish she had never entered his life, yet he could not imagine it without her. He hated her; he loved her. She was a disturbance, an irritation; he could never escape from her; he fancied he never would; worse still, he was not entirely sure that he wanted to. Obviously a most unfortunate state of affairs for a mighty king to find himself in. He had broken with Rome for Anne's sake; the Pope's name had been struck from the prayer books, and it was not mentioned at Divine Service; yet in the streets the people never ceased to talk of the Pope, and with reverence. Wolsey was gone, and with his going, the policy of England was changed. Wolsey it was who had believed that England must preserve the balance of power in Europe; Henry had pursued a new policy, he had cut off England from Europe. England stood alone.

Those matters, which had once been the concern of the Cardinal's, were now the King's. Cromwell was sly and cunning, but a servant, no leader; Cromwell did what he was told. Why should a man with so much on his shoulders be pestered by women! Madge Shelton was a bright wench, but he had had enough of her. Anne was Anne . . . none like her, but a witch – a nagging witch at that. Too clever, trying to dictate to England through him; advising rashness here, there and everywhere. This state of affairs was such as to make a man's blood – which was ever ready to simmer – bubble and boil over.

He was going to be firm. Anne could not get children; he would be better without Anne; she disturbed him, distracted him from state matters. Women were for bedtime, not to sidle between a king and his country.

The people were dissatisfied. There were too many noble lords ready to support the Catholic cause, possibly conspiring with Chapuys. These were not dangerous at the moment, but there were inevitable perils in such a situation. He had his daughter Mary watched; he believed there was a plot afoot to smuggle her out of the country to the Emperor. What if that warrior thought to raise an army against the King, with the replacement of Katharine and Mary as its cause! How many nobles of England, who now did honour to its King, would slip over to the Emperor's banner? Henry asked himself uneasily. His conscience told him that he had embarked on this matter of divorce that he might produce a son and save England from civil war, but he had produced no son, and his actions had put England nearer to civil war than she had been since the conflicts between the houses of York and Lancaster.

He sounded a few of his most trusted counsellors on a new line of action. What if he divorced Anne? It looked as if she could not have a son. Might not this be a sign from Almighty God that the union with Anne had not found favour in the sight of heaven? It was astonishing; a healthy girl to be so barren. One daughter! One pretended pregnancy! His lips curled. How she had fooled him! How she continued to fool him! How, when he was thinking he would be better without her, she would lure him and tempt him, so that instead of occupying his mind with plans to rid himself of her, he found himself making love to her.

His counsellors shook their heads at the suggestion of a second divorce. There were points beyond which even the most docile men could not go, and the most despotic of kings could not carry them with him. Perhaps these men were thinking of Sir Thomas More and John Fisher, awaiting death stoically in the Tower; perhaps they were thinking that the people were murmuring against the doings of the King.

Divorce Anne he might, his counsellors thought, but only on condition that he took Katharine back.

Katharine! That made the King roar like a wounded animal. Katharine back! Anne angered him, Anne plagued him, but at least she excited him. Let matters rest. Not for anything would he have Katharine back.

These matters all tended to arouse the wrath of the King.

The new Pope aggravated him still further, by raising John Fisher – a man who was in prison for treason – to cardinal's rank. When Henry heard the news, he foamed with rage.

'I'll send the head to Rome for the cap!' he cried fiercely. He had had enough. Fisher was executed. Sir Thomas More was to follow. Nor were these the only traitors; those monks of the Charterhouse who had refused to acknowledge him Supreme Head of the Church, were to be punished with the utmost severity. This should be a sign to the people that all those who would not do the will of Henry the Eighth of England should suffer thus. He would have the people heartily aware of this. There should be public executions; there should be hangings; there should be burnt flesh offerings to the supremacy of the King. Murder was in the King's heart; he murdered now with a greater ferocity than when he had murdered men like Empson, Dudley, and Buckingham; the murders of these men were calculated, cold blooded; now he murdered in revenge and anger. The instruments of torture in those gloomy dungeons of pain beneath the grey buildings of the Tower should be worked night and day. The King was intent on the complete subjugation of all who raised a voice against him.

A pall of smoke hung over London. The people huddled together, watching the mutilation, listening to the shrieks and groans of martyrs.

The Continent was aghast at the news of the death of Fisher and More; the Church infuriated by the murder of Fisher, the political world shocked beyond expression by that of More. The Vatican found its voice, and sent forth vituperation against the monster of England. The Emperor, astonished at the stupidity of a king who could rid himself of the ablest man in the country, said: 'Had we been master of such a servant, we would rather have lost the fairest city in our dominion than such a counsellor.'

Europe mourned wise men, but London mourned its martyrs, and the King was shaken, afraid. But his blood was up; he was shrewd enough to know that any sign of weakness would not help him now; he had gone too far to retrace his steps. When More had said that a man who cannot restrain his passions is essentially cruel, he spoke the truth. The real Henry emerged from behind the fair, flushed, good-tempered hail-fellow-well-met personality which his people – as good Englishmen – had admired so long. The cold, cruel, implacable, relentless egoist was exposed.

But there was still the conscience, which could make him tremble. 'What I have done,' he told it, 'has been done for Anne.' He did not say 'I am a great hater!' but 'I am a great lover.'

They brought the news of Thomas More's execution to him while he played at the tables with Anne; as he sat opposite her, he pictured beside her brilliant beauty the calm ascetic face of the man whose death he had just brought about.

He stood up. He had no stomach for the game now. He knew that he had murdered a great man, a good man; and he was afraid.

Then he saw Anne sitting there opposite him. The answer to his conscience was clear; he knew how to stifle that persistent voice inside him.

He said: 'Thou art the cause of this man's death!'

Then he left the table and shut himself in his private chamber in sudden fright which nothing would allay.

* * *

Crossing London Bridge, people could not look up without seeing the ghastly sights exhibited there. The heads of brave men dripped blood; to this pass had their bravery brought them, since it was unwise to be brave in the reign of bluff King Hal.

On the lips of all were the names of More and Fisher. These men were saints enshrined in the hearts of the people; there could be no open worship of such saints. Many of the monks of the Charterhouse preferred death to admitting that Henry was Supreme Head of the Church. A large number of them went to the Tower; some were tortured on the rack, that they might betray their friends; many found their way into the embrace of the Scavenger's Daughter, that vile instrument recently invented by Thomas Skevington, which contracted the body in a manner exactly opposite to that of the rack, so that blood was forced from the nose and ears; some were hung from the ceilings of dungeons by their wrists, which were encased in gauntlets, until their hands were bleeding and paralysed; some had their teeth forced out by the brakes; some were tortured with the thumb-screws or the bilboes. People whispered together of the dreadful things that befell these saintly men in the Tower of London. Some were chained in airless dungeons, and left to starve; some were paralysed by continued confinement in one of those chambers called the Little Ease, the walls of which were so contrived that its inmate could neither walk, nor sit, not lie full length; some were put into the Pit, a noisome deep cavern in which rats were as ferocious as wild beasts and lived on those human wrecks who, chained and helpless, standing knee deep in filthy water, must face them while being unable to defend themselves. Some of the more obstinate monks were given an execution which was public and shameful; taken to Tyburn, they were half-hanged, cut down, and while they were conscious their abdomens were ripped open and their bowels dragged forth from their muti-lated bodies and burned. Even after death their bodies were further desecrated.

This, the King would have the people know, might be the fate of any who questioned his supremacy. The people of London heard the screams of the Anabaptists as the flames leaped from the faggots at their feet, scorching and frizzling their bodies. In Europe the people talked of the terror which had befallen England; they talked in hushed, shocked whis-pers. When Henry heard this he laughed savagely, calling to mind the Spaniards' way of dealing with heretics, and how, but a few months before, Francis and his family had marched through Paris chanting piously while Lutherans were burned before the doors of Notre-Dame.

Henry knew how to suppress rebellion; he knew how to make the people knuckle under. 'I will have this thing an it cost me my crown!' he had been known to say, and he meant it. He was strong and ruthless; all men trembled be-fore him. He was no longer the young and lusty boy seeking pleasure while a cardinal ruled; he was master. He would force all to recognize that, however much blood should flow.

He had a plan now which intrigued him; it was to make Thomas Cromwell his Vicar-general, and as such let him visit all the churches and monasteries of England. The Supreme Head of the church would know the state of these monasteries; it worried his conscience that stories he had heard from time to time of the profligacy of the monks and nuns might have some truth in them! What if these monasteries were the bawdy houses he had often heard it whispered that they were! What if there were men living licentious lives, sheltered by their monks' robes! Those nuns, wrapped up in the garments of piety – what of them? He remembered the case of Eleanor Carey, that relative of Anne's who had had two illegitimate children by a priest. These things had come to light, and if there was one thing the Supreme Head of the Church of England would not tolerate in his land, it was immorality! He would suppress it, he would stamp it out! Once it had been no concern of his, but now by God's will he was the head of the Church, and by God, he would put an end to all evil practices.

Thomas Cromwell should go to these places; he should bring back evidence of what he found – and Thomas Cromwell could always be relied upon to bring back the evidence that was expected of him – and if that evidence warranted the dissolution of these places, then dissolved they should be! A list of their valuables, should Thomas bring back; it was said they had some fine treasures in their chests – jewels, works of art only suited to a king's palace. This was a good plan; later he would talk with Cromwell.

From his palace he saw the smoke over London. This was done in the name of righteousness. The Anabaptists denied the divinity of Christ; they deserved to die.

In the courtyards of the palace men talked together in whispers. Something was afoot. The King was nervous to-day; there had been a time in the days of his youth when he had gone among his people unafraid, but now it was not so. If he stayed in a house, even for a night, he took a locksmith with him that new bolts might be put on the door of his sleeping apartment; he had the straw of his bed searched every night for hidden daggers.

'Now what?' he said, and leaning from his windows roared down to be told what fresh news was exciting them.

A little group of courtiers looked up at him in some alarm.

'There is some news. Hide it not!' he shouted.

''Tis naught, Your Majesty, but that the head of Sir Thomas More is no longer on the bridge.'

'What!' cried the King, roaring, that none might guess his voice shook. 'Who moved it then?'

There was no answer.

'Who moved it then?' he roared again.

''Tis not known, Your Majesty . . . 'Tis but known that it is gone.'

He shut the window. His knees trembled; the whole of his great body shook. The head of More the martyr had been removed from the bridge, where it should have remained with the heads of other traitors. What meant this? What meant it? A miracle, was it? There had been One who had risen from the dead; what if this man, More, were such another!

He could see the shrewd, kind face, did he but close his eyes; he could recall the humour, the mocking kindliness. He remembered the man so well; often had he walked in the Chelsea garden, his arms about the fellow's neck. He remembered when he had written his book denouncing Luther, who had worked with him, whose lucid style, whose perfect Latin knowledge had largely made the book. And because he had had need to show this man he could not disobey his master, he had murdered him. True he had not wielded the axe; true he had not been the one to place the head among the heads of traitors; but he was the murderer nevertheless. His old friend More – the brightest light in his realm! He remembered how the man had walked with him and Katharine on the terraces of the palace, and talked of the stars, pointing them out to the royal pair, for he and Katharine had been interested in astronomy then. Now he was dead, he who had never wanted to sun himself in the brilliance of court life; who would have preferred to live quietly in the heart of his family with his books. He was dead; and his head had disappeared. This might be a miracle, a sign!

Anne came in, saw that he was distressed, and was unusually soft and ready to comfort him.

'You have had some shock.'

He looked at her eagerly; she thought he had the air of a frightened boy who is afraid to be left in the dark.

'More's head has gone from London Bridge!'

She was taken aback; she looked at him, wide-eyed; and they were drawn together in their fear.

'Anne,' he said, groping for her hand, 'what means this, thinkest thou?'

She took his hand and pressed it firmly; she forgot the miracle of the missing head, since the fear which had been with her night and day was evaporating. Henry needed her; at moments such as this, it was to her he turned; she had been too easily humiliated, too ready to show her humiliation. She had nothing to fear. She was the wife of a man who, having absolute power, would have his way, but a clever woman might manage him still. She could see her folly stretching right back to her coronation; she thought she saw why she had appeared to lose her power over him. Now here he was, trembling and afraid, superstitious in an age of superstition, lacking that courage which had made her the reckless creature she was.

She smiled at him.

'My lord, someone has removed the head.'

'But who would dare?'

'He was a man who had many friends, and one of these might be ready to take his head from where it belonged.'

'I see that, Anne.' He was feeling better already; he looked at her through softly sentimental eyes. She was very beautiful, and now she was gentle and very reassuring; she was clever too; the others palled quickly. When Anne reassured, there was a good deal that was truth in the reassurance; the others flattered; it was good to be with Anne. 'That was where the head belonged,' he said fiercely. 'He was a traitor, Anne.'

'As all who seek to disobey Your Majesty's commands,' she said.

'Thou speakest truth. 'Twas a friend of his that took the head. By God, that in itself was a traitorous act, was it not!'

She stroked his hand.

'Indeed it was. There will be those simple people who ever look on traitors as saints. Mayhap it would be well to leave this matter. Why should it worry us? We know the man deserved to die.'

'By God, you're right!' he cried. ''Tis a matter of small importance.'

He did not wish to leave her; she distracted his thoughts from the memory of that severed head with its kindly mocking eyes.

It was reconciliation. In the court it was said: 'She has a power over him, which none other could exercise.'

Her enemies cursed her. If she but give him a son, they said, she is Queen of England till her death.

Chapuys wrote home to the Emperor, Charles, telling him that the King of England was over and over again unfaithful, but that the concubine was cunning and knew how to manage the King. It would be unwise to attach too much importance to his brief infatuations for court ladies.

*   *   *

Anne was preparing the most splendid banquet the court had yet seen. She was feverish with delight. She felt as though she had come through a nightmare of terror, and now here was the morning to prove that the shadows had been conjured up out of her imagination, that they had no existence in truth. How could she have been so foolish; how could she have believed that she who had held the King so well in check, could have lost control now! She was supreme; his need of her was passionate and lasting; now that – as her husband – he was conscious of the shackles that held him to her, all she need do was lengthen the tether. Her fault had been in trying to keep it as tight as a mistress might. All a wife needed was a little more subtlety, and it had taken her two years of doubts and nightmares to realize this. Let him wander away from her, let him dally with others – it would but be to compare them with his incomparable Queen.

She was gayer than she had ever been. She designed new costumes; she called to her the most brilliant courtiers to arrange an entertainment that should enchant the King; Witty Wyatt, subtle George, gentle Harry Norris, amusing Francis Bryan, Henry Howard, those gay courtiers Francis Weston and William Brereton; others too, all the brightest stars of the court clustered about her, and she the dazzling centre as it used to be. The King was with her constantly; she planned and thrilled to her plans.

One day she found one of the youngest of the musicians sitting alone playing, and she paused to listen, delighting in his delicate touch, thinking, He is more than ordinarily good. She had Madge Shelton bring him to her. He was young and slender, a rather beautiful boy with long tapering fingers and dreamy, dark eyes.

'Her Majesty heard your music,' said Madge. 'She thought it good.'

The boy was overcome with the honour of being noticed by the Queen, who smiled on him most graciously.

'I would have you play awhile,' she said. 'I feel you could be of use to us in the revels, for it would seem to me that we have not so many musicians of your talent in the court that we can afford to leave out one who plays as you do.'

She was charming, because she at once saw that his admiration was not merely that which he would give to his Queen. Her long sleeves hung over the hand with its slight malformation; the other, with long, white, jewel-decked fingers, rested lightly on her chair. He could not take his wondering eyes from her, for he had never been so close to her before.

'What is his name?' she asked, when he had been dismissed.

'It is Smeaton, Your Majesty. Mark Smeaton.'

'He was poorly clad,' she said.

'He is one of the humbler musicians, Your Majesty.'

'See that he has money with which to procure himself clothes. He plays too well to be so shabbily attired. Tell him

335

he may play before me; I will have a part for him to take at the entertainment.'

She dismissed him from her mind, and gave herself over to fresh plans. There was an air of lightheartedness among her friends; George seemed younger, excessively gay. The Queen herself was as sparkling as she had ever been when she was the King's mistress. She was the centre of the brilliant pageant, the pivot round which the wit and laughter revolved; she was the most lovely performer. The King watched the entertainment, his eyes for her alone. Anne! he thought, inwardly chuckling. By God, she was meant to be a Queen. She could amuse him, she could enchant him, she could divert him, she could cast unpleasant thoughts from his mind.

He had forgotten Fisher; More too almost, for the removal of his head from London Bridge had been no miracle but the bold action of his daughter, Margaret Roper, who had gone stealthily and by night. Anne had learned this, and brought him the news.

'By God!' he had cried. ' 'Tis a treasonable offence to go against the King's command!' She had soothed him. 'Let be! Let be! 'Twas a brave action. Doubtless the girl loved her father well. People are full of sentiment; they would not care that a girl should be punished because she loved her father well. Let us have done with this gruesome affair of a traitor's head. To please me, I would ask Your Majesty not to pursue the matter.'

He had frowned and feigned to be considering it, knowing full well that his people would not care for interference with Margaret Roper; then she had wheedled, and kissed him, and he had patted her thighs and said: 'Well then, sweetheart, since you ask it, it shall be done. But I like not treason ... I like it not at all!' She had smiled, well pleased, and so had he. An unpleasant business was done with.

He watched her now – the loveliest woman in the court – and too many of these young profligates had their eyes upon her, ready to be over-bold an they dared. He liked to know that they fancied her, even while it filled him with this smouldering rage. He could laugh. None dared to give her more than covert looks, for it would be treason to cast over-desirous eyes on what belonged to the King; and well they knew this King's method of dealing with traitors! He called to her, would have her sit by him, would let his hands caress her.

It was borne home to the Queen's enemies that their hopes had been premature, and to her friends that they had feared too soon.

* * *

Catherine Howard was joyous as a lark; like the lively young grasshopper, she danced all through the summer months without a thought of winter. She was discovering that she was more than ordinarily pretty; she was the prettiest of all the ladies; she had, said some, a faint resemblance to her cousin the Queen. She developed a love of finery, and being kept short of decorative clothes or the money with which to provide herself with even the smallest addition to her wardrobe, she looked to her lover to provide these. Derham was only too delighted. He was enchanted by the lovely child, who was so very youthful at times, at others completely mature. He would provide her with many little luxuries besides – wines and sweetmeats, fruit and flowers. So when Catherine yearned to possess an ornament called the French Fennel, which was being worn by all the court ladies who would follow the latest fashion, Derham told her that he knew a little woman in London with a crooked back who was most skilled in the making of flowers of silk. Catherine begged him to get this done for her. 'I will pay you when I have the means,' she told him, which set him smiling and begging her that it should be a present. And so it was, but when she had the precious ornament, she was afraid to wear it until she had let it be known that one of the ladies had given it to her, for the Duchess was more watchful than she had been at Horsham.

It was tiresome of the old lady to have taken that precaution of locking the chamber door each night. Derham was an adventurous young man; he was passionately in love. He was not going to let a key separate him from

Catherine. A little planning, a little scheming, a little nodding and looking the other way by those who liked to see good sport, and it was not such a difficult matter to steal the key after it had been brought to the Duchess.

There was the additional spice of planning what should be done, should there be a sudden intrusion.

'You would have to hurry into the gallery and hide there!' said Catherine.

'That I could do with the greatest of ease!' said Derham.

He would come to the chamber at any hour of the night; it was a highly exciting adventure they were both enjoying.

The others watched, rather wistfully. Derham was such a handsome young man and so much in love with the child; there were some, such as Dorothy Barwicke and a newcomer, Jane Acworth, who whispered to each other that Catherine Howard was the sort who would always find men to love her. What use to warn her? She was too addicted to physical love to heed any warning. If she realized that the path she was treading might be dangerous, she might try to reform, but she would surely slip back. She was a lusty little animal, irresistible to men because she found them irresistible. Mary Lassells thought the Duchess should be told, in secret so that she could come up and catch them in the act, but the others were against this. They wanted no probings, no inquiries. They pointed out that they would all be implicated – even Mary Lassells, since she had been months in the house and had not seen fit to warn Her Grace before.

The Duchess was less comfortable in her mind than she had been. Apart from the rumours she heard at court, she sensed the presence of intrigue in her own household. She watched Catherine, flaunting her new French Fennel. Heaven knew there were plenty of men all too eager to take advantage of a young girl. She saw something in Catherine's face, something secret and knowledgeable, and the memory of it would recur in her uneasy thoughts. Her other granddaughter, she believed, was not happy; the Duchess preferred not to think of what might be happening at court; better to turn her attention to her own house. Were the young men too free with the girls? She would have to be arranging a marriage for young Catherine soon; when she next saw the Queen, she would have a word with her about this. In the meantime the greatest care must be exercised.

Sometimes the Duchess did not sleep very well; sometimes she would wake in the night and fancy she heard footsteps on the stairs, or a muffled burst of laughter overhead. She knew now that for some time she had been suspicious of what went on in the girls' apartments; there were some over-bold wenches there, she believed. I must bestir myself; I must look into this. There is my little granddaughter, Catherine to be considered. That French Fennel . . . She had said she got it from Lady Brereton. Now did she? Would her ladyship give such a handsome gift? What if one of the young gentlemen was seeking Catherine's favours by offering gifts! It was not a very pleasant reflection.

Forced by a sense of impending danger both at court and at Lambeth, she roused herself one night soon after twelve, and went to the place where the key of the ladies' apartment should be. It was not there. Puffing and panting with the fear of what she would find if she went to the room, she nevertheless could make no excuse for not going. It had ever been her habit to avoid the unpleasant, but here was something for the avoidance of which it would be most difficult to find an adequate excuse.

She put on a robe and went out of her sleeping apartment to the corridor. Slowly she mounted the staircase. She was distressed, for she was sure she could hear muffled voices coming from that room; she paused outside the door. There was no sound inside the room now. She opened the door and stood on the threshold. All the ladies were in their beds, but there was in that room an atmosphere of such tenseness that she could not but be aware of it, and she was sure that, though they had their eyes shut, they but feigned sleep.

She went first to Catherine's bed. She drew off the clothes and looked at the naked body of her granddaughter. Catherine feigned sleep too long for innocence.

The Duchess thought she heard the faintest creak of boards in the gallery which ran along one side of the room.

She had an alarmed feeling that if she had that gallery searched, the search would not be fruitless. It would set tongues wagging though, and she dared not let that happen.

Her panic made her angry; she wished to blame someone for the negligence of which she knew herself to be guilty. Catherine was lying on her back; the Duchess rolled her over roughly and brought her hand across the girl's buttocks. Catherine yelled; the girls sat up in bed, the curtains were drawn back.

'What has happened? What is this?'

Did their exclamations ring true? wondered the old lady.

Catherine was holding her bruised flesh, for the Duchess's rings had cut into her.

'I would know,' said the Duchess sharply, 'who it was who stole my keys and opened this door.'

'Stole Your Grace's keys. . . .'

'Opened the door. . . .'

Oh, yes! The sly wenches . . . they knew well enough who it was. Thank God, she thought, I came in time!

Mary Lassells was trying to catch her eye, but she would not look at the sly creature. Didn't the fool realize that what she just did not want to hear was the truth . . . providing of course that the truth was disturbing!

'Tomorrow,' said the Duchess, 'I shall look into this matter. If any of you had aught to do with this matter of my keys, you shall be soundly whipped and sent home in disgrace. I shall make no secret of your sins, I warn you! I thought I heard noises here. Let me warn you that if I hear more noises it will be the worse for you.'

She went out and left them.

'There!' she said, as she settled down to sleep. 'I have done my duty. I have warned them. After such a threat, none of them would dare to misbehave herself, and if any of them have already done so, they will take good care to keep quiet about it.'

In the morning she found her keys; they were not in their rightful place, which led her to hope and believe that they must have been there all the time, and that there had been an oversight, the doors having been left unlocked all that night.

Still, she was resolved to keep an eye on the young women, and particularly on Catherine.

There came a day when, entering what was known as the maids' room, she saw Catherine and Derham together. The maids' room was a long, pleasant, extremely light room in which the ladies sat to embroider, or to work tapestry, or to spin. Such a room was certainly forbidden to gentlemen.

The Duchess had come to the room, taking her usual laboured steps, and had Derham and Catherine not been noisily engaged in a romp, they would assuredly have heard her approach.

Derham had come in to talk to Catherine, and she feigning greater interest in her piece of needlework than in him, had goaded him to snatch it from her; after which, Catherine immediately sought to retrieve it. They were not interested in the piece of needlework, except as an excuse for titillating their senses by apparent haphazard physical contacts. Derham ran round the room, flourishing the piece of needlework, and Catherine gave chase. Cornering him behind the spinning wheel, she snatched it from him, but he caught her round the waist and she slid to the floor, at which he did likewise. They rolled on the floor together, he with his arms about her, Catherine shrieking her delighted protests. And thus the Duchess found them.

She stood in the doorway, shouting at them for some seconds before they heard her angry voice.

Then she stalked over to them. They saw her and were immediately quiet, standing abashed before her.

She was trembling with rage and fury. Her granddaughter to be guilty of such impropriety! The girl's gown was torn at the neck, noted Her Grace, and that doubtless on purpose! She narrowed her eyes.

'Leave us at once, Derham!' she said ominously. 'You shall hear further of this.'

He threw Catherine a glance and went out.

The Duchess seized her frightened granddaughter by her sleeve and ripped the clothes off her shoulders.

'You slut!' she cried. 'What means this behaviour . . . after all my care!'

She lifted her ebony stick, and would have brought it down on Catherine's head had she not dodged out of the way. The Duchess was growing a little calmer now, realizing it would not do to make too violent a scene.

She cornered Catherine, pushed her onto a couch and, bending over her, said: 'How far has this gone?'

'It was nothing,' said Catherine, fearful for Derham as well as for herself. 'It was just that he . . . stole my piece of needlework, and I . . . sought to retrieve it . . . and then . . . you came in.'

'His hands were on your neck!'

'It was to retrieve the needlework which I had snatched from him.'

The Duchess preferred to believe it was but a childish romp. She wanted no scandal. What if it came to the hard-faced Duke's ears, of what went on in her house, what tricks and pranks those under her care got up to! He would not hesitate to whisper it abroad, the wicked man, and then would she be considered the rightful state governess for the Princess Elizabeth!

It must go no further than this room; but at the same time she must make Catherine understand that she must have no dangerous friendships with young men under her roof.

She said: 'An I thought there was aught wrong in this romping between thee and Derham, I would have thee sent to the Tower; him too! As it is, I will content myself with giving you the biggest beating you have ever had in your life, Catherine Howard!'

She paused, horror-stricken; sitting in a corner, quietly trembling with fear, was one of her attendants, and she must have witnessed the whole scene.

The Duchess turned from Catherine and went over to her

'Jane Acworth! You think to sit there and allow such behaviour! What do you think your task is? To watch young men make free with Catherine Howard?'

The girl, trembling, said: 'Your Grace, it was naught . . .'

But a stinging blow at the side of her head silenced the girl. The Duchess continued to slap her for some seconds.

'Let me hear no more of this, girl, or you shall feel a whip across your shoulders. Catherine, go to my private chamber; you shall receive your punishment there!'

She went puffing from the room, very ill at ease. But having beaten Catherine, while Catherine writhed and shrieked, she felt she had done her duty.

She summoned one Margaret Morton, when she had done with Catherine.

'I would have speech with Francis Derham. Send him to me without delay!'

He came. She did not know how to punish him. She should banish him of course. But she had always liked him; he was quite the most charming young man of her household. If anything, he was over-bold, but there is something very attractive about over-boldness. He was a distant kinsman too . . . so perhaps it would be enough to warn him.

'I would have you know that you are without prospects. You could not marry my granddaughter. I would have you remember your position in this house, Francis Derham!'

'Your Grace, I must humbly apologize. It was but animal spirits. . . .'

The animal spirits of youth, she thought. There was something delightful about them. Memories came back, softening her. Suppose she allowed him to stay this time! She had warned him; he would not dare to presume again. He was such a handsome, courtly, charming boy!

*　　*　　*

With the coming of the autumn, Anne's spirits soared, for she discovered that at last she was pregnant. The King was overjoyed. He was sure that if he would but show the people a male heir, everything that had gone to the producing of it might be forgotten.

Anne, eager to be brought to bed of a healthy child, gave up her life of gaiety and spent a good deal of time reading and thinking of the past. She could not look back with much pride on the two years which had seen her Queen. It seemed to her that much of her time had been spent in worthless machinations and sordid subterfuge. The affair of Madge Shelton stood out from those years, filling her with shame. She herself was now with child again; should she be delivered of a son, her dearest wish would be granted; she would then ask nothing more of life.

She was thoughtfully sitting over her tapestry with her ladies, asking questions about the poor of London. She said: 'Would it not be better if, instead of stitching this fine tapestry, we made shirts and suchlike garments for the poor?'

It was strange to see her who had been known to occupy herself at great length with the planning of her own gowns, to see her who had given orders how should be cut and made yards of black satin and gold arras, now stitching contentedly at garments for the poor. She had changed, and the change had a good deal to do with the terrible fear which had beset her and which had been removed, first by the King's returning affection for her, and then by her pregnancy.

Hugh Latimer had been largely instrumental in her change of heart. She had been interested in the great reformer ever since she had heard of him, and when Stokesley, Bishop of London, had had him committed to the Tower, she used all her influence to get him released. The King, reluctant and yet unable in a fresh return of his passion to refuse what she asked, agreed on the release, and thus postponed Latimer's martyrdom for twenty-five years. On his release, Anne had desired to hear him preach and forthwith did so, when, much to her astonishment, instead of receiving the gratitude she might have expected from the man, he delivered for her benefit a stormy lecture advising those who placed too much reliance on treasures upon Earth to turn from their folly and repent. Anne saw the man afterwards and characteristically asked him where he thought she had erred. He answered unflinchingly that she should by her morality and piety set an example to those under her command. Greatly impressed by his honesty – a virtue by which she set great store – she appointed him one of her chaplains and began to veer towards a more spiritual way of life. Always generous in the extreme, she delighted in looking into deserving cases about her, and helping those whom she considered would benefit by such help. She had always done this when cases were brought to her notice, but now she looked for them systematically.

Although less superstitious than the King, she was not entirely free from this weakness. As she stitched at garments for the poor, she asked herself if she were not doing this in return for a healthy boy. Was she placating the Powers above, as Henry did? Was she, she wondered, getting a little like him? She had her moments of fear. Was Henry capable of begetting a healthy boy? His body was diseased. What if this were the reason Katharine had failed, and she too, so far! Perhaps she was, in a way, placating Providence, making conditions.

She was worried about the Princess Mary. She was still afraid of the Princess and of Katharine. It had seemed to her that if these two were together they might plot something against her, and through her against Elizabeth. Chapuys she feared. She knew well there were many powerful nobles who deeply resented the break with Rome. They were all only waiting to rise up and destroy her. She must not allow her new favour with the King to blind her to this.

And as she stitched, she prayed for a son.

The King prayed too. He was pleased with the change in Anne. It was well to see her calmer, quieter; it was well to feel this peace stealing over him because at last their union was flavoured with hope. He needed such hope; the people were being difficult once more. They were saying that it had not rained since More had died; they would always find a reason for a bad harvest, and the crops had failed once more. The Flanders trade was not good. In fact it looked as if the country was getting together a collection of grievances and irritations in order to make trouble.

The King needed distraction. It suddenly dawned on him that one of his wife's attendants was – well, not so much an attractive girl as a different kind of girl. Perhaps he meant that she was quite different from Anne; she was so quiet, she moved about like a little mouse; she was very fair; she had a prim little mouth and quick, glancing eyes. She would never be leader of the revels, she would never shine, she would never outwit a man with her sharp tongue! She was as different from Anne as any woman could be. That was why he first noticed her.

If she caught his eyes upon her, she would drop hers quickly; a soft rose-pink blush would steal into her cheeks. She was very demure.

On one occasion he was sitting alone, thinking that it was a long time before his son could be born, and wondering if there was some holy relic the soothsayers could give him as protection against another girl child. He had some holy water, a tear which Christ had shed over Lazarus, and a phial of the sweat of St Michael; all of which he had purchased at great cost during the sweating sickness. But in spite of these, Anne's first child had been a girl, and he wondered whether he should buy something especially which might ensure the birth of a boy. As he considered this, the demure maid of honour came into the room and, seeing him, curtseyed in a frightened way and would have hurried off had he not detained her with a 'Hi, there! What want you?'

'Her Grace, the Queen . . .' said the girl, so low that he could scarcely hear her.

'What of Her Grace, the Queen?' He studied her from head to toe. Small where Anne was tall; slow of movement where Anne was quick; meek where Anne sparkled; slow of speech instead of bright; modest instead of coquettish; willing to listen humbly rather than disconcert a man with her wit.

'I had thought to find her . . .'

'Come hither!' said the King. 'And are you very disturbed to come upon the King when you looked for the Queen?'

'Yes, Your Majesty . . . I mean no, Your Majesty . . . .'

'Well,' said Henry pleasantly, 'make up your mind.'

She would not come too close. He did not force her, liking suddenly her demureness, since there were so many of them who were too ready.

She could think of nothing to say, which pleased him and made him remember that Anne was over-ready with her retorts.

'Sit there awhile and I will play. You may listen. Bring my lute to me.'

She brought it, cautiously. He tried to touch her fingers over the lute, but she was quick; she had leaped back as though he had tried to sting her. He was not angry. His thoughts were chiefly of his son, and therefore with Anne. But he liked the girl; he was, he told himself, always touched by modesty; he liked and respected it in the young people about his court.

He commanded her to sit; she did so, modestly letting her hands fall into her lap; her mild eyes watched him, and then seemed full of admiration.

When he had finished he saw that her eyes were filled with tears, so moved was she by his music, and he realized that he had not felt so gratified for a long time.

He asked her name. She told him it was Jane Seymour.

He dismissed her then. 'You may go. We shall meet again. I like you, Jane!'

It was not a quarrel with Anne, just a slight irritation. A petty argument, and she, in her overpowering way, had proved herself right. Jane Seymour would never be one to prove herself right. She's all woman, thought Henry. And that's how a woman should be. Women are women, and men are men. When the one will dabble with that which is solely within the province of the other, it is a sad thing.

He sent for Jane Seymour. She should have the honour of hearing his new song before he allowed anyone else to hear it. She sat listening, her feet scarce reaching the floor; which made her seem helpless. She was very meek.

He made inquiries about her. She was the daughter of Sir John Seymour of Wolf Hall in Wiltshire; he was by no means a powerful nobleman, but it was interesting to discover that there was a tiny root of royalty in his family tree, provided one dug deep enough to find it. Henry stored such knowledge. And as he played his lute, he thought about Jane; a quiet, mild bed-fellow, he thought, pleasant enough,

347

and white-skinned; unawakened and virginal. He grew sentimental; virtue had that effect on him. All women, he told himself, should be virtuous.

The court noticed his preoccupation with the maid of honour. Chapuys and the French ambassador laughed together. They were cynical. The King had been noted of late to extol virginity. 'He refers to Jane Seymour!' said the French ambassador, to whom the Spanish ambassador replied that he greatly doubted Jane possessed that quality, having been some time at court. He added that the King might be pleased though that she did not, for then he could marry her on condition that she was a virgin, and when he needed a divorce he could then find many witnesses to the contrary.

But the King continued to view Jane through sentimental eyes. She had been primed by her father and her brothers, when dazzling possibilities had occurred to the minds of these very ambitious men who had the example of the Earl of Wiltshire and the young Lord Rochford before their eyes. They advised Jane: 'Do this . . .' 'On no account do that . . .' Jane herself was not without ambition. She had watched many a quarrel between the King and Queen, and she understood the King more than he would have thought from the demure eyes that met his with such seeming sincerity.

When he tried to kiss her, she was overcome with blushes; she ran away and hid herself, and the King, having become the champion of virtue, could not satisfy his conscience if he forced the girl to anything. His mind began to scheme with his conscience once again. What if this marriage with Anne had been wrong? What if God should show his disapproval over the child? The plans were not very well shaped as yet – they were misty shadows of thought, which allowed him to dally with Jane, while respecting her virtue.

He gave her a locket bearing his picture; she wore it on a chain round her throat, intending this to be a sign that were she not of such unbending virtue she would readily consider his advances, having the greatest admiration for his person. He wanted Jane; he could not have her; and this made her seem very desirable to him.

The story of Anne was to Jane a long object lesson: what to do before, what not to do after. But though Jane knew what she must do, she was not very intelligent, and she could not prevent a new haughtiness creeping into her manner, which Anne was quick to notice. She saw the locket which Jane was wearing, and asked mildly enough if she might see it.

Jane flushed guiltily, and put her hand over the locket; whereat Anne's suspicions flared up. She took the locket, breaking its chain as she did so, and on snapping it open beheld the smiling face of the King crowned in a jewelled cap.

A year ago she would have raged against him; now she was silent and undecided. She saw in sly Jane Seymour, with her much-paraded virtue, a more deadly enemy than any other woman who had taken the King's fancy.

She prayed urgently. A son! I must have a son!

*   *   *

At Kimbolton Castle, Katharine lay dying. She had lived wretchedly during her lingering illness, for money due to her was not paid. She was full of sorrow; not only had she been separated from her beloved daughter, but when she had asked that she might see the Princess before she died, even this request was denied her. She was deeply disturbed by the fate of her former confessor, Father Forrest, who though an old man had, through his allegiance to her, been cruelly treated at the hands of the King; he had been imprisoned and tortured in such a manner that she could not bear to contemplate; she longed to write and comfort him, but she feared that if a letter from her was intercepted, it might cause the old man's execution, and though, in his case, death might be the happiest release from his misery, she could not bring it about. Abell, her other confessor, was treated with equal cruelty; it was unbearable that her friends should suffer thus.

Chapuys had got the King's reluctant permission to visit

her, and arrived on New Year's Day. She was delighted to see one whom she knew to be her friend. She was very ill, and looked ten years older than her fifty years. He sat by her bed and she, while expressing genuine sorrow for all those who had suffered in her cause, said that she had never thought for one instant that she had been wrong in her struggle against the King.

To the man who had caused the chief miseries of her life she had no reproaches to offer. She was the daughter of a king and queen, and she believed in the divine right of royalty. The King would bastardize a princess, because he was bewitched; he would, she believed, emerge from that witchery and see the folly of his ways. It was her duty in the interests of royalty to uphold herself and her daughter – not for any personal reasons, but because they were Queen and Princess. Katharine was adamant now as ever, and would have suffered any torture rather than admit that her daughter was not the legitimate heir to the throne of England.

She talked with tears of Fisher, with regret of More; she talked of Abell and Forrest, mercifully knowing nothing of the more horrible deaths that awaited these two of her faithful adherents.

Chapuys, the cynic, thought, She is dying by his hand as surely as More and Fisher did. He thought of the years of misery this woman had endured, the mental torture that had been inflicted on her by her husband. Here was yet another victim of the murderer's hand. What though the method was different!

Chapuys had no real comfort to give her. His master would not wish to be embroiled in a war with England for the sake of Katharine of Aragon and her daughter, since he had his hands full elsewhere.

To comfort her though, he hinted at some action from outside on her behalf. She brightened. His visit did much to revive her; it was so rarely that the King allowed her to be visited by her friends.

After he left, another incident occurred which helped to lighten her grief in being denied the comfort of her daughter's presence.

It was evening of a bitterly cold day, when through the castle there echoed the sound of loud knocking. Her maid came to tell her that it was a poor woman who, making a journey across country, had lost her way and begged to be allowed to spend the night at the castle for fear she and her attendant should freeze to death.

Katharine bade them bring in the poor souls and give them food.

She was dozing, when her bedroom door was opened and a woman came in. Katharine looked at the newcomer in astonishment for one moment, and then the tears began to flow from her eyes. She held out her arms, feeling that she was a girl again, riding the rough seas of the Bay of Biscay, thinking fearfully of the fate which awaited her in an unknown country where she was to marry a boy husband; she was young again, watching the land grow less blurred, as she sailed into Plymouth. With her there had been a band of beautiful Spanish girls, and there was one among them who, during the unhappy years which England had given her, had ever been her faithful friend. This girl had married Lord Willoughby; and they had been together until, by the King's command, Katharine had been banished from the court and cut off from all those she loved. And here was Lady Willoughby coming by stealth, as a stranger lost in the snow, that she might be with Katharine during her last hours in England as she had been during her first.

This was wonderful; she was almost happy.

'If I could but have seen my little daughter . . .' she murmured.

But the coming of her friend had put her in high spirits, and she revived so much that she was well enough to sit up in her bed, though she was too far gone in sickness of body, which had grown out of sickness of mind, to make any real recovery. During the first week of January her condition grew worse. She had mass said in her room on the afternoon of the sixth, and then, ill as she was, asked for materials that she might write a last letter to the King. She did not blame him; she accepted her fate meekly; she only asked that he should be a good father to their daughter Mary, and that he should do right by her servants.

Henry was hilarious when he heard the news of Katharine's death; there followed one moment of apprehension when in a blurred fashion he remembered her sad, pale face, heard her strong voice pleading for justice. He did then what he ever did when remorse touched him; he made the persecution of Katharine someone else's burden, not his own; he assured himself that he had acted from the highest and most disinterested of motives.

'Praise be to God!' he cried. 'We are delivered from all fear of war. The time has come for me to manage the French better than before, because in wondering whether I may now ally myself to the Emperor, they will do all I want.'

He would now show that he had never been married to Katharine. He dressed himself in yellow, having a white feather set in his cap, for why should a man go into mourning for one not his wife!

'Bring me my daughter!' he cried, and the nurses brought Elizabeth to him. Although little more than two years old, she was already a very bright and intelligent child who enjoyed being exhibited, and surveyed her great dazzling father with the utmost interest.

He called for all the musical instruments to play; the courtiers must dance. He went from one to the other, demanding they do homage to their little Princess. 'For,' he exclaimed again and again, 'we are now delivered from the evil threat of war!'

Anne rejoiced when she heard the news. It was a great relief. For the first time, she thought, I can feel myself to be really Queen; there is no shadowy Queen in the background to whom some could still look. I am Queen. There is no other Queen but me!

She was inordinately gay; she imitated the King's action, and dressed in yellow.

She did not know that he had once discussed the question of divorcing her, with his most trusted counsellors; she did not know that he had refrained from doing so because they had said he might divorce her, but if he did, he would surely have to take back Katharine.

*   *   *

Now that Katharine was dead, and Anne felt more secure, she decided she could be less harsh to the Princess Mary, so she sent one of her ladies to the girl with a message. Would Mary come to court? Could they not be friends?

'Tell her,' said Anne, 'that if she will be a good daughter to her father, she may come to court and count me her friend. Tell her she may walk beside me, and I shall not need her to hold my train.'

Mary, grief-stricken by the death of her mother, broken-hearted so that she cared not what became of her, sent back word that if being a good daughter to her father meant denying that for which martyrs' blood had been shed, she could not accept Anne's offer.

'The foolish girl!' said Anne. 'What more can I do?'

Then she was angry, and at the root of her anger was the knowledge that she herself had helped to make this motherless girl's unhappy lot harder than it need have been. She could not forget what she had heard of Katharine's miserable death, and in her new and chastened mood she felt remorse as well as anger.

She tried again with Mary, but Mary was hard and stubborn, neither ready to forgive nor forget. Mary was fanatical; she would have all or nothing. She wanted recognition: Her mother to be recognized as the true Queen, Anne to be displaced, Elizabeth to be acknowledged a bastard. And on these terms only, would Mary come to court.

Anne shrugged impatient shoulders, really angry with the girl because she would not let her make amends. When my son is born, thought Anne, I shall be in such a strong position that she will do as I say. If I say she shall come to court, she shall come to court, and it will not be so easy for her to find favour with the King when she is forced to do that which she might have done more graciously.

The beginning of that year was disastrously eventful for

Anne. The first disturbance was when Norfolk came hurrying into her chamber to tell her that the King had taken such a toss from his horse that he feared he was killed. This upset Anne – not that the King, during their married life, had given her any reasons to love him – but in her condition she felt herself unable to cope adequately with the situation which must inevitably arise if he died. She had the interests of her daughter and the child as yet unborn, to look to, and she was greatly disturbed. This however proved to be a minor accident; the King's fall had done scarcely any harm, and he was too practised a horseman to suffer much shock from such a fall.

After this escape, the King was in excellent spirits. He found Jane Seymour alone in one of the Queen's apartments. People had a way of disappearing from Jane Seymour's side when the King approached. Demure as she was, she had permitted certain liberties. He was somewhat enamoured of the pretty, pale creature, and she was a pleasant diversion for a man who can scarcely wait to hear that his son is born.

'Come hither, Jane!' he said in the soft, slurred voice of a lover, made husky with good ale and wine. And she came to him most cautiously, until he, seizing her, pulled her on to his knee.

'Well, what did you think, Jane, when that fool Norfolk ran around telling the world I was done for, eh?'

Jane's eyes filled with tears.

'There, there!' he said. ' 'Tis no matter for weeping. Here I am, hale and hearty as ever, except for a sore leg ...'

He liked to talk of his leg; he spent a good deal of time thinking about it.

'Every physician in London has had a go at it, Jane! And to no avail. I've tried charms and potions ... no avail ... no avail.'

Jane was timidly sympathetic; he stroked her thighs caressingly.

He liked Jane; he could sit thus happily with her, feeling a mild pleasure in her, without that raging desire which must put a man in torment till it was slaked; it was just pleasant, stroking and patting and going so far and then drawing back.

The door opened, and Anne was watching them. All the fears which she had successfully pushed away came rushing back. She knew Jane Seymour . . . sly, waiting, watchful of her opportunities. Anne suddenly realized why they waited, why Henry could be content to wait. They were waiting to see whether she bore a son. If she did, then Jane Seymour would be the King's mistress. If not. . . .

Anne's self-control broke. She began to storm and rage. She now said to the King all those things which had been in her mind and which, even in her most frank moments, she had never mentioned before. It was as though she dragged him away from that bright and pleasant picture he had made of himself, and held up her picture of him. She was laughing at his conscience, at his childish method of putting himself right. Did he not think she saw through that! Did he not think that the great men about him did not either!

She was maddened with rage and grief and terror, so that she knew not what she said.

Henry's one idea was to calm her, for he must think of the son, whom she was so soon to bear.

'Be at peace, sweetheart,' he pleaded, 'and all shall go well for thee.'

But Anne was not at peace. Jane Seymour ran and hid herself behind the hangings, covering her face with her hands and audibly murmuring: 'Oh, what have I done!' while she rejoiced at what she had done.

For what could she have done to suit herself and her supporters more, since, after that sudden shock, prematurely Anne's son was born dead!

*　　　*　　　*

Trembling, they brought the news to the King. He clenched his hands; his eyes seemed to sink into the flesh about them, while the veins stood out knotted on his forehead. In uncontrollable rage he strode into Anne's room. He stood over her as she lay limp, exhausted and defeated.

Words flowed from that cruel little mouth. She had done this! She had humiliated him! She had deceived him into thinking she would give him sons! She was a witch, a sorceress . . .

Enfeebled as she was by hours of agony, yet she answered with spirit: 'There was none to blame but yourself. This is due to the distress of mind you caused me through your philanderings with that sly Seymour wench!'

Henry roared back wrathfully: 'You shall have no more boys by me!' And then, cunning and pious: 'I see well that God does not wish to give me male children.'

But he did not really believe this, not seeing how he himself could possibly be at fault in this matter.

'When you are on your feet, I will speak to you,' he said coldly.

Then he went from the room, his thoughts with Jane Seymour. It might well be that this marriage was a mistake, he was thinking. By God, I was forced into it by sorcery! She was irresistible, with her long hair and her wicked little pointed face. It was beyond the power of man to say nay to her. Sorcery! This is why God does not permit me to have male children. Might it not be that I should make a new match?

* * *

Jane Seymour sat in her apartments at the palace, awaiting the King. These apartments which were splendid and hung with rich arras and cloth of gold, had a short while before belonged to Thomas Cromwell, but he had vacated them that Jane might use them, because adjoining those of the King they could most easily and secretly be reached by His Majesty.

Jane was rather frightened by the great happenings which had come about ever since that day when the King had glanced in her direction. Her brothers, Thomas and Edward, had planned ambitiously, and their plans, they told their sister, were all for her. Edward was clever, subtle and ambitious; Thomas was fascinating, dashing and also ambitious. Look what came to Anne Boleyn! said these two.

Why not to Jane Seymour? True, Jane had not the obvious attractions of Anne Boleyn, but men were strange in their fancies, and was it Anne's beauty and wit that had charmed the King as much as her reluctance? If Jane had not beauty and wit, she could be as reluctant as Anne, and in all probability with more effect, for shyness would seem more natural in Jane than it ever could be in Anne.

So Jane must bow to the wishes of her family. Chapuys and the imperialists were with Jane too, eager to support any who would bring disfavour on the partisans of Martin Luther.

So here was Jane, meek and mild, yet not being entirely without ambition, feeling that it would be somewhat pleasant to wear a crown, and that to discountenance the haughty Anne Boleyn would be most gratifying. She was therefore ready enough to step into her mistress's shoes, yet a little frightened, for she could not but be aware that this role which was being forced upon her – even though she was not altogether reluctant to take it – was a very dangerous one. Anne was losing her place; Anne who had wit and beauty; Anne who had kept the King for five long years after she had become his mistress; and when she remembered this, Jane dared not think more than a month or two ahead. Her brothers had assured her that all she need do was obey their orders. She admired her brothers; they were clever, which Jane had never been; they were men, whereas Jane was just a weak woman. She was afraid of the King; when he put his face near hers and she smelt the wine on his breath, when she looked at the great face with its purple veins, when the little bloodshot eyes twinkled at her, she did not have to feign a desire to run. Jane, without pity, thought of the Queen who would have to be displaced if she were to sit on the throne; it was not that Jane was cruel or hard-hearted, but merely that she was without imagination. Children could move her a little; they were small and helpless like Jane herself, and she understood their doubts, their fear of their elders, their gropings for enlightenment. She had wept a little for the Princess Mary, for surely that child had suffered a very hard fate; if Jane were ever Queen, she would do her best to see that even little Elizabeth was treated fairly, for bastard though she was, she was at least a child, and a little child at that.

Jane's thoughts went back to that important day when the King's messenger had come to her with a letter and purse of gold from the King. Her brothers had been expecting some such approach from the King, and had primed her as to what she must do. Jane was ever obedient; her nature demanded that she should be; so she obeyed her brothers. She kissed the letter to show how greatly she esteemed the King's person, how if he were but free to pay honourable courtship to her, she would so willingly have linked her fortune with his. The purse she refused.

'Kneel to His Grace the King,' said Jane, 'beseeching him to consider that I am a gentlewoman of good and honourable family. I have no greater wealth than mine honour, and for a thousand deaths I would not sully it. If my lord the King desires to make me a present of money, I pray it shall be when God sends me a good offer of marriage.'

The King had evidently not been displeased with this response. Jane had made it tremblingly, doubting whether her brothers had not gone too far and might have displeased His Majesty. But no! Her brothers had been right; the King was enchanted by such modesty and virtue. He would have the world know that the virtue of the ladies of his court was their most admired possession in the eyes of their King. The Seymours were honoured; they should have apartments in the palace near the King, for with Jane's family and friends he was more at ease than with Anne and hers. He was never sure of Anne's friends; they were too clever, too subtle. In future, give him good practical jokes; give him hearty humour that all could understand; he had done with mockery and smartness, and people who wrote and talked in a manner that he was not at all sure did not put him in the shade. No, he liked the company of the Seymours; they soothed him, and it was pleasant to contemplate a good and virtuous woman who appealed to him without arousing too insistent a passion.

He knew what the Seymours were after. Well, well, Anne could not have boys. A daughter from Katharine, a daughter from Anne! He wondered what he would get from Jane. With Anne he had scarcely thought of children at first, so greatly had he desired her, but he would not marry Jane on the chance that she might have a child; he would have to make sure that she was capable of doing so, before he committed himself again. This was a delicate situation for the Seymours, which while it was full of the most dazzling possibilities, was rampant with danger. Jane's strength had been in her aloofness, and how could she remain aloof and at the same time prove to the King that she was capable of bearing his child? The Seymours had to act with extreme tact; the had to take a risk, and they took it boldly. Hence the apartments close to those of His Majesty; hence the secret visits of the King, when he found Edward Seymour and his wife discreetly absent, and Jane alone and not so demure, waiting to receive him.

His courtship of her was a sober matter when he compared it with his courtship of Anne Boleyn. There was something restful about Jane; he never forgot for a moment when he was with her that he was the King, and never did he lose sight of the real meaning of this love-making. If Jane was unlike Anne, she was also unlike the King; he looked at their reflections, side by side in the mirror; himself large and red, she small and white; he completely master of the situation, she shrinking, a little afraid. She did not shrink from his coarseness as Anne had often done; cleverly she feigned such innocence as not to understand it; if she made a false move, if she said anything to arouse his anger, she would be meekly apologetic. With Jane Seymour he was enjoying a period of domestic peace which he had not enjoyed since he had banished Katharine and taken Anne to live beside him. In the turbulent years he had longed for that peace which would be brought about by what he thought of as Anne's sweet reasonableness; it had been a goal to which he, in his sentimental hours, had reached out with yearning hands, and never did he succeed in attaining it. Now here was Jane, offering it to him; he could lie back, close his eyes, enjoy it, say what he liked, and be sure of approbation.

The girl was a bit insipid though; he realized that, after the first few nights with her. She was too passive; neither eager nor repulsing him; just meek and submissive. All that a Queen should be to a King of course, but . . . Ah! he thought, I think of Anne. I gave too much of myself to that witch, for witch she is, with the devil's own power over me, so that even when I lie with another I cannot forget her. There will be no peace for me, while Anne lives, for the power of a witch is far-reaching, and she can cast spells even when her victim is in a good woman's arms.

Jane was not a little troubled by this most secret love affair between herself and the King; she was terrified of the Queen, whose rages could be awful; she had been maid of honour long enough to witness many a scene between their Majesties, and at these scenes the Queen had been known to outwit the King. The Queen was more physically attractive than any woman at court; it was impossible to be near her and not see the effect she could have on those about her. There were men who, conceiving passions for her ladies, would visit them, and on the coming of the Queen would be unable to take their eyes from her; she had but to throw a stray word in their direction, or a quick smile, and they were ready to do anything for her. She had that power. There might be those who said the King was tired of her; and so he was . . . at times. There might be those who would say that her only hope of holding the King was to give him a son; that was true in part, but not wholly. Jane had seen the many and conflicting moods that had come to the King as he watched this woman; anger and hatred had been there, strong enough to let in murder; but something else too, passionate hunger which Jane could not understand but vaguely feared. 'What if through Your Majesty's visits I should be with child?' she had asked. He had patted her thigh indulgently. 'Then, my Jane, you would please me mightily; you would show yourself worthy to be my Queen.' 'But how may I be your Queen when you have already a Queen?' His eyes glinted like tiny diamonds. 'Let not thy head bother with matters too big for it, Jane!' A warning, that had been; Do not meddle in state affairs, child. It is a dangerous thing for a woman to do.

All the same, Jane was uneasy. She would tell herself that the King was bewitched, the Queen had sorcery in her eyes; it was not necessary to be clever to see that. Those huge, black, flashing eyes had more witchery than was natural for a woman to have; and the Queen was careless of what she said, as though she had some hidden power to protect her; she could draw men to her with a speed and an ease that had magic in their roots. She would weave spells round the King who, having realized her wickedness and his folly in submitting to it, would now escape. She had brought evil into the court when she entered it. She had brought misery and great humiliation to the true Queen and her daughter Mary. Jane could weep to think of the child. And now her spells were less potent, for though she could weave them about men, she could bring no son to the King, since children were of heaven and Anne's powers came from hell. This was how Jane saw it. When the King caressed her, she would close her eyes tightly and say to herself: 'I must endure this, for in this way can I save our lord the King from a witch.' She prayed that her body might be fruitful, for she saw that thus could she fulfil her mission.

She thought continually of the Princess Mary. She had known her when she had been a maid to Katharine, before the coming of Anne Boleyn; she had ever deplored the King's mad infatuation for Anne; she had secretly adhered to Katharine all through the dangerous years, and so had she won the approval of Chapuys and many of the nobles who condemned the break with Rome. Thus they had been pleased when the King's fancy had lighted on her, and had sought to help and advise her.

She said to the King when he came to her: 'I have been thinking of the Princess Mary.'

'What of her?' he asked indifferently.

'I but thought of the hardship of her life, and how sad it is that she should be banished from the court. I wondered if Your Majesty would most graciously allow her to be brought back; I fear she suffers deeply from the humiliation which has been heaped upon her.'

The King looked at Jane with narrowed eyes. He said with exasperation: 'You are a fool! You ought to solicit the advancement of the children we shall have between us, and not others.'

When he left her Jane assured herself that her duty was to rescue the Supreme Head of the English Church from a wanton witch who would never release him in this life. And as Jane did not know how she could rescue him, except by bearing him a child, she knelt down by her bed and prayed that her union with the King might bring forth fruit.

* * *

The Queen was gay, recklessly so. Her eyes were enormous in her pale face; she was almost coquettish; she was lavish with the smiles she bestowed on those about her. The King was spending more and more time with the Seymours, and there was no doubt in Anne's mind that Jane was his mistress; moreover she knew this to be no light affair; there was deep meaning behind it. Those two brothers of Jane's were eager and apprehensive; they watched, they waited; indeed all the court was watching and waiting for something to happen. The loss of her boy, they whispered, had finished Anne. Cynical courtiers murmured together: 'Is he trying out Jane? If the King is waiting to produce a child before divorcing Anne, he may wait a very long time!'

It would have been a humiliating position for anyone; for Anne it was agonizing. She thought, This happened to Katharine while we tried for the divorce; it happened to Wolsey when he awaited his downfall; this is how More and Fisher must have waited in their homes . . . waited for a doom they felt coming to them, but knew not from which direction it would come. She was not the sort to show her fear; if during the lonely nights she would awake startled, the sweat on her forehead, having dreamed some nightmare in which the doom was upon her; if she lay awake for hours staring into darkness, thinking of the King with Jane Seymour, wondering if he ever thought of her, she never showed this. After such nightmares, such nocturnal wondering, she would be gayer than ever. Her clothes were still the talk of the court; she would throw herself feverishly into the planning of a new gown; she could no longer sit silently stitching for the poor, though she did not forget them. She would gather round her the most brilliant of the young men and women. Just as there had been Katharine's sober friends in the old days who had held aloof from that set over which she and the King ruled together, so now there was yet another set, and this time it was the Seymour party, but the King was of the Seymour party. Round Anne fluttered the poets and the wits, not seeming to care that they scorched their wings. Her revels were still the wittiest; the Seymours' were heavy and clumsy in comparison, but the King could not be lured from them. Handsome Henry Norris, who was supposed to be in love with Madge Shelton, had eyes for none but the Queen; people smiled at this man who was supposed to be engaging himself to Madge but was for ever postponing his marriage. 'What good does that do poor Norris?' they asked. 'Surely he cannot hope to marry the Queen!' Francis Weston and William Brereton, younger and more sophisticated, were equally enamoured of her; Wyatt was faithful as ever. She encouraged their attentions, finding great solace in the love of these men, finding a balm to her pride which had been so deeply wounded when she discovered that the King preferred dull Jane Seymour. She was reckless; she accepted the homage of those who loved her; she would dance and laugh immoderately; she was wittier than ever, and the wildness of her looks gave her beauty a new strangeness that for some augmented it. It would seem that she wished to lure all to her side, that only when she was surrounded by those who admired her did she feel safe. She sought to build up a wall of friendship round her. She had with her, in addition to Madge Shelton, those two friends, Margaret Lee and her sister Mary Wyatt, in whom she placed the greatest trust. Her own sister Mary came to attend her, and it was good to contemplate the serene happiness of Mary who, happy in her love for Stafford whom she had married, was as comfortable to be near as a glowing fire in winter. Anne felt secure with these people. Even Mark Smeaton, whom she had raised to be one of her chief musicians, might show his passionate admiration of her, and go unreproved.

There were always those to watch her slyly. The black eyes of the Spanish ambassador would meet those of the King's vicar-general, and the Spaniard would guess what thoughts went round and round in Cromwell's ugly shaven head. Jane Rochford was now openly unsympathetic towards Anne, not caring if she did invite her husband's disapproval.

As for George, he seemed to have caught his sister's recklessness; he rarely warned Anne now; he was like a man who had been running from danger and, feeling suddenly there is no escape, turns to face it.

It was pleasant to sit with George and Mary, Margaret Lee, Mary and Thomas Wyatt, talking of childhood days before they had been scattered and lost touch with each other.

'Well I remember,' said Anne on one occasion, 'how we all played together in Norfolk, and then again in Kent, how we all talked of our ambitions and what we would do.'

'Ambition,' laughed George, 'is like the moon; it looks so close, so easy to grasp, but the nearer knowledge takes you to it, the more unattainable you realize it to be. Ambition is a pernicious thing!'

'You said you would be a great poet,' said Anne. 'Wyatt too.'

'And he at least achieved his ambition,' said George.

'Much good did it do him!' said Wyatt, looking meaningly at Anne.

'We hoped for too much,' she said; 'all of us except Margaret and my sister Mary and your sister Mary. They are the happiest ones.'

They could look at those three. Margaret who was happily married to Sir Henry Lee, Mary Wyatt who had no husband but a serene countenance, Mary Boleyn who had many lovers, not for gain but for pleasure. The ambition of these three was happiness; they had found it. For the other three it had been power, and in a measure they had realized it too. There they were – Wyatt whose joy was in his verses and yet, being never satisfied with them, they could not give him complete happiness; Anne who would be a queen and had achieved her ambition and now listened for some sign to herald in disaster, as she scanned people's faces and tried to read behind their eyes; George who through the fortunes of his sisters had come to fame. Three of those children who had played together – the ordinary ones who were not clever or brilliant, or made for great-ness – had succeeded; it was the clever ones who had asked for much – though in a measure they had found what they desired – to whom failure had come.

Anne said: 'We chose the wrong things; they chose the right. . . .' And none answered her, for this was a matter which it was unwise to discuss.

Mary would talk to her comfortingly.

'The King . . . ah! How well I knew him! Almost as well as you do, Anne.' Mary would smile at the memory. 'He is wayward; none dare stand between him and his desires, but an a woman pleases she need fear naught.'

Ah, but Mary had known him as a mistress; Anne knew him as a wife.

The winter of that year passed into spring. Anne danced and sang as though she had not a care in the world; she would wander through the park at Greenwich, would watch the barges on the river, would sit under the trees; some-times she would romp with the dogs, laughing gaily at their antics, throwing herself about in a frenzy of enjoyment, but her heart was sad and heavy; she would weep some-times and mingle her tears with her laughter; this was a dangerous mood, for in it she cared nothing for what she said or what she did, and so laid herself open to attack from all her enemies. She would call Smeaton to her and bid him play, play something gay, something to which she could dance, something to make her gay and joyous; play music that told of love and laughter, not of sorrow. And the musician's great dark eyes watched her passionately, and his long tapering fingers played for her, soothing her.

She gave him a fine ring, for his talent, she said, was great, and those with talent should not go unrewarded. She thought, He may sell it and buy himself clothes, poor man; he has little reward for his labours. But she knew he would never sell the ring, since she had worn it on her finger; and she laughed and was pleased that though the King appeared to be indifferent to her, a poor musician was deep in hopeless love for her.

'Come!' she would cry suddenly. 'Let us have a masque. Let us do a witty play. Thomas, you and George shall put your heads together; I would be amused. Mark, you shall play for the dancing; you shall play for my singing. Let us dance and be merry.... I am tired of melancholy.'

*　　*　　*

Cromwell had retired from court life for several days, on the plea of sickness. Cromwell needed solitude; he had to work out his next moves in this game of politics most carefully. He was no inspired genius; everything that had come to him had been the result of unflagging labour, of cautiously putting one foot forward and waiting until it was securely in its rightful place before lifting the other. He was fully aware that now he faced one of the crises of his career. His master commanded, and he obeyed, though the command of course was not given in so many words. Henry was too conscience-ridden to mention his more vile thoughts, so it was the duty of a good servant to discover his master's wishes though not a word be spoken between them. Murder is a dangerous business, and Cromwell must consider whilst carrying out the King's wishes, not what was good for the King and the country, but what was good for Cromwell. Cromwell had a very good head on a pair of sturdy shoulders, and he did not intend that those should part company. The farther one climbed, the more steep the road, the easier it was to slip; one false step now, and Cromwell would go slipping down to the dark valley where waited the block and the executioner's axe.

It had seemed to Emperor Charles that, on the death of Katharine, new friendship with Henry might be sought, and for this reason Chapuys came to Greenwich for a special audience with the King. But how could Henry become the ally of Charles, when Henry had broken so definitely with Rome, and Charles supported Rome? Rome, it seemed, stood between the Emperor and Henry. Cranmer trembled; he got as near blazing forth his anger as Cranmer could get; he preached a reckless sermon. Cromwell did not feel so deeply. Cranmer made up his mind which course he would take, and was loyal to that course; Cromwell was ready to examine any course; he would use any members of any sect if necessary; he would support them one day, burn them at the stake the next. Cromwell could see that there was some advantage to accrue from a new bond of friendship with the Emperor; therefore he was ready to explore this course of action. Cromwell was at this time very busily engaged in ransacking the monasteries, but he could see that if the Emperor and Henry should cease to be enemies, this could easily be held up for a time. He was prepared for anything. Anne was furious; naturally she would be. A possible reconciliation with the Emperor was a direct insult to her; she had not been over-cautious in her treatment of Cromwell, never liking nor trusting him. Until now Cromwell had been meek enough, but he did not believe that he need now treat the Queen with over-much humility. The King had hinted that Jane Seymour was with child, and Cromwell must think of this matter very seriously. What if this were so? What if there was need for Henry to marry the girl quickly in order to legitimize a possible heir to the throne? Cromwell would be expected to bring this about, and if Cromwell failed to do it in the time at his disposal, what then? It was not so long ago when the King had desired a divorce most urgently, and Cromwell's late master had blundered. Cromwell was ready to profit by the Cardinal's mistakes, for he was resolved that he should not be caught as Wolsey had been. Cromwell would be ready. It was easy to see – and this applied particularly if Jane

Seymour was really pregnant – that he need fear nothing from the wrath of Queen Anne. This secret matter of the King's was conducted rather differently from that other secret matter. This was a series of hints and innuendoes: the lady was so demure, so shy, that the King must respect her reserve. She must not suffer – nor the King through her – the pain and scandal of divorce. How did one rid oneself of a wife one no longer wants, if not by divorce?

Cromwell knew a great deal about that peculiar burden of the King's – his conscience. Cromwell knew that it was capable of unexpected twists and turns; Cromwell knew that it must always be placated, and how comparatively easy it was to placate it; how one turned a subject to show the side which the conscience might like and approve; how one carefully covered that which was unpleasant. The conscience was obliging; it could be both blind and deaf when the need arose; therefore, he did not propose to lose much sleep over that accommodating creature.

Cromwell decided to favour alliance with Spain. The Emperor was a better ally than Francis; alliance with the French had never brought gain to England. Henry had been very difficult at the meeting – which had seemed to Cromwell and to most of the counsellors deplorable. It showed cunning Cromwell one thing – the King was still under the influence of Anne. In spite of Jane Seymour, he would listen to Anne; in spite of her failure to give him an heir, he still hankered after her. It was an alarming state of affairs; Cromwell knew his master well enough to realize that if something was not soon done, he would have Henry throwing aside Jane Seymour, buying fresh holy relics, reconciling himself to his black-browed witch, in one more effort to get himself a son. Were the Queen secure again, what would happen to Thomas Cromwell? What had happened to Thomas Wolsey! It was not so long ago that one could forget.

There must be alliance with Spain, for it meant the downfall of Anne; how disconcerting therefore, when the King must abuse the Emperor before Chapuys himself, must recall all he had done to delay the divorce, must announce here and now that not for a hundred alliances would he give way to Rome! He had made himself head of the Church, and head of the Church he would stay. If there was any humility to be shown, then Emperor Charles must show it. He even went so far as to tell Chapuys that he believed Francis had first claim on Burgundy and Milan.

This seemed to Cromwell sheer folly. The King was not acting with that shrewdness a statesman must always display. Henry was smarting under insults which he had received from Clement and Paul and Charles. He was not thinking of the good of England; he could only think: 'They want my friendship – these people who have been against me, who have worked against me, who have humiliated me for years!'

Anne had said: 'Ah! So you would be friends with your enemies as soon as they whistle for you, would you! Have you forgotten the insults of Clement? And why did he insult us? Would Clement have dared, had he not been supported? And by whom was he supported? By whom but this Charles who now comes and asks for your friendship, and in a manner that is most haughty! Oh, make friends, accept your humble rôle, remember not the insults to your kingship, to your Queen!'

He had ever been afraid of her tongue; it could find his weakness. Well he knew that she feared alliance with Spain more than anything, for it would mean her personal defeat; and yet he knew there was something in what she said; they had humiliated him and her, and as he had made her Queen, insults to her were insults to him. They had doubly insulted him!

This he remembered as he paced the floor with Chapuys, as he talked to Cromwell and Audley – that chancellor who had followed More – both of whom were urging him to sink his grievances and snatch a good thing while he could. But no! It was the Emperor who must come humbly to him. The egoist was wounded; he needed the sweet balm of deference from one he feared to be more mighty than himself, to lay upon his wounds.

Cromwell, for the first time in a long obsequious association, lost his temper; his voice cracked as he would explain; Cromwell and the King shouted at each other.

'Danger, Cromwell! Danger!' said a small voice inside the man, and he had to excuse himself and move away that he might regain control of his temper. He was trembling from head to foot at his folly; he was sick with fear and anger. How simple to abandon his quarrel with Rome! What need to continue it now Katharine was dead. Only the gratification of Henry's personal feelings came into this. Anne and her supporters were at the bottom of it; they would keep alive the King's anger. Could it be that Anne's falling into disfavour really was but a temporary thing? Such thoughts were fraught with great terror for Thomas Cromwell. For the first time in his career with the King, he must act alone; thus he feigned sickness that he might shut himself away from the King, that he might make a plan, study its effect, its reverberations, from all sides before daring to put it into practice.

He emerged from his isolation one mild April day, and asked for permission to see the King.

The King scowled at him, never liking him, liking him less remembering the man's behaviour when he had last seen him. He, who had ever been meek and accommodating, daring to shout at him, to tell him he was wrong! Was this secretary – whom he had made his vicar-general – was humble Thomas Cromwell a spy of Chapuys!

'Sir,' said Thomas Cromwell, 'I am perplexed.'

His Majesty grunted, still retaining his expression of distaste.

'I would have Your Majesty's permission to exceed the powers I now enjoy.'

Henry regarded his servant with some shrewdness. Why not? he wondered. He knew his Cromwell – cunning as a fox, stealthy as a cat; since he had attained to great power, he had his spies everywhere; if one wanted to know anything, the simplest way was to ask Cromwell; with speed and efficiency he would bring the answer. He was the most feared man at court. A good servant, thought Henry, though a maddening one; and there'll come a day, was the royal mental comment, when he'll anger me so much by his uncouth manners and his sly, cunning ways, that I'll have his head off his shoulders . . . and doubtless be sorry afterwards, for though he creeps and crawls and is most wondrous sly, I declare he knows what he is about.

Cromwell should have his special powers. Cromwell bowed low and retired well pleased.

A few nights later, he asked Mark Smeaton to come up to dinner at his house at Stepney.

*   *   *

When Mark Smeaton received an invitation to dine at the house of the King's secretary, he was delighted. Here was great honour indeed. The Queen had shown him favour, and now here was Master Secretary Thomas Cromwell himself seeking his company!

It must be, thought Mark, my exceptional skill at music – though he had not known that Master Cromwell was fond of music. He knew very little of Cromwell; he had seen him now and then at the court, his cold eyes darting everywhere, and he had shivered a little, for he had heard it said that none was too insignificant to be of interest to that man. He would know a good deal of most people, and usually of matters they would prefer to keep secret; and every little piece of information he gathered, he would store, cherishing it until he might lay it beside another bit of information, and so make up a true picture of what was happening at court.

Mark had never been so happy as he had this last year or so. He had begun life most humbly in his father's cottage; he had watched his father at work on his bench, mending chairs and such things as people brought to him to be mended. He had heard music in his father's saw and plane; he had heard music in his mother's spinning wheel. Mark had been born with two great gifts – beauty and a love of music. He had a small pointed face with great luminous dark eyes, and hair that hung in curls about his face; his hands were delicate, his fingers tapering; his skin was white. He had danced gracefully from the time he was a small boy, though he had never been taught to dance. He was noticed, and taken to the house of a neighbouring knight where he had taught the knight's daughter to play various musical instruments; and when she had married, his benefactor had found him a place at court – a very humble place, it was true – so that Mark thought himself singularly blessed, which indeed he was, to have gained it. He had seen poor beggars wander past his father's door with never a bite to eat, and their feet sore and bleeding; no such fate for clever Mark! An opening at court; what next?

What next, indeed! He had never known how beautiful a thing life could be until one day when the Queen had passed so close to him that he had seen her long silken lashes lying against her smooth skin, and had heard her sing in the most exquisite voice he had ever heard, very softly to herself. Then she had caught sight of him, noticed his beauty of face, would have him play to her. He had wondered how he had been able to play, so deep had been his emotion.

Not only was she his idol, she was his benefactress. He was in his teens, at that age when it is possible to worship from afar some bright object, and to be completely happy in such worship, to be amply rewarded by a smile; and the Queen was generous with her smiles, especially to those who pleased her – and who could please her more readily than those who played excellently the music she loved!

Sometimes she would send for him and have him play to her when she was sad; he had seen her eyes fill with tears, had seen her hastily wipe them. Then he had yearned to throw himself at her feet, to say: 'Let Your Majesty command me to die for you, and gladly will I do it!'

But that was foolish, for what good could his death do her? There were rumours in the court, and thinking he knew the cause of her unhappiness, he longed to comfort her. He could do so by his music, and he played to the Queen as he had never played before in his life. So pleased was she that she gave him a ring with a ruby in it, a most valuable ring which never, never would he remove from his finger.

That was some weeks ago, and it seemed to him as he

considered this invitation to dine at Stepney, that events were moving so fast that he could not guess to what they pointed.

There were many about the Queen who loved her and made no great effort to hide their love; playing the virginals close by, he had heard their conversation with her. There was Sir Henry Norris whose eyes never left her, and whom she baited continually, pretending to scold him because he was a careless lover – since he was supposed to be in love with her cousin, Madge Shelton, yet was ever at the Queen's side. There were Brereton and Weston too, whom she scolded happily enough as though the scolding was not meant to be taken seriously. There was Wyatt with whom she exchanged quips; they laughed together, those two, and yet there was such sadness in their eyes when they looked on each other, that Mark could not but be aware of it. As for Mark himself, he was but humbly born, unfit to be the companion of such noble lords and their Queen, but he could not help his emotions nor could he hide them completely, and those lovely black eyes must see his feelings and regard him with more indulgence because of them.

Two days before Mark had received the invitation, Brereton did not come to the presence chamber. He heard the nobles' speculating on what had happened to him. He had been seen in his barge – going whither? None could be sure.

'On some gay adventure, I'll warrant,' said the Queen. 'We shall have to exact a confession from gay William, when he again presents himself!' And she was piqued, or feigned to be so; Mark was not sure; he could never be sure of the Queen; when she laughed most gaily, he sensed she was most near tears.

She found him sitting in the window seat, his lute idle in his hands.

She said softly: 'Mark, you look sad! Tell me why.'

He could not tell her that he had been thinking he was but a foolish boy, a boy whose father was a carpenter, a boy who had come far because of his skill in music, and he at the height of his triumph must be melancholy because he loved a queen.

He said that it was of no importance that he was sad, for how could the sadness of her humblest musician affect so great a lady!

She said then that she thought he might be sad because she may have spoken to him as an inferior person, and he would wish her to speak to him as though he were a nobleman.

He bowed low and, overcome with embarrassment, murmured: 'No, no, Madam. A look sufficeth me.'

That was disturbing, because she was perhaps telling him that she knew of his ridiculous passion. She was clever; she was endowed with wit and subtlety; how was it possible to keep such a mighty secret from her!

The next day he took barge to Stepney. Cromwell's house stood back from the river, which lapped its garden. Smeaton scrambled out and ascended the privy steps to the garden. A few years ago he would have been overawed by the splendour of the house he saw before him, but now he was accustomed to Greenwich and Windsor and Hampton Court; he noted it was just a comfortable riverside house.

He went through the gates and across the courtyard. He knocked, and a servant opened the door. Would he enter? He was expected. He was led through the great hall to a small chamber and asked to sit. He did so, taking a chair near the window, through which he gazed at the sunshine sparkling on the river, thinking what a pleasant spot this was.

The door must have been opened some time before he realized it, so silently was it done. In the doorway stood Thomas Cromwell. His face was very pale; his eyes were brilliant, as though they burned with some excitement. Surely he could not be excited by the visit of a humble court musician! But he was. This was decidedly flattering. In the court there were many who feared this man; when he entered a room, Mark had noticed, words died on people's lips; they would lightly change a dangerous subject. Why had the great Thomas Cromwell sent for Mark Smeaton?

Mark was aware of a hushed silence throughout the house. For the first time since he had received the invitation, he began to wonder if it was not as a friend that Cromwell had asked him. He felt the palms of his hands were wet with sweat; he was trembling so much that he was sure that if he were asked to play some musical instrument he would be unable to do so.

Cromwell advanced into the room. He said: 'It was good of you to come so promptly and so punctually.'

'I would have you know, my lord,' said Mark humbly, 'that I am by no means insensible of the honour . . .'

Cromwell waved his thick and heavy hands, as though to say 'Enough of that!' He was a crude man; he had never cultivated court graces, nor did he care that some might criticize his manners. The Queen might dislike him, turning her face from him fastidiously; he cared not a jot. The King might shout at him, call him rogue and knave to his face; still Thomas Cromwell cared not. Words would never hurt him. All he cared was that he might keep his position in this realm, that he might keep his head safely in the place where it was most natural for it to be.

He walked silently and he gave the impression of creeping, for he was a heavy man. Once again Mark was aware of the silence all about him, and he felt a mad desire to leap through the window, run across the gardens to the privy stairs and take barge down the river . . . no, not back to court where he could never be safe from this man's cold gaze, but back to his father's cottage, where he might listen to the gentle sawing of wood and his mother's spinning-wheel.

He would have risen, but Cromwell motioned him to be seated, and came and stood beside him.

'You have pleasant looking hands, Master Smeaton. Would they not be called musician's hands?' Cromwell's own hands were clammy as fish skin; he lifted one of Mark's and affected to study it closely. 'And what a pleasant ring! A most valuable ring; a ruby, is it not? You are a very fortunate young man to come by such a ring.'

Smeaton looked at the ring on his finger, and felt that his

375

face had flushed almost to the stone's colour; there was something so piercing in the cold eyes; he liked not to see them so close. The big, clumsy fingers touched the stone.

'A gift, was it, Master Smeaton?'

Mark nodded.

'I should be pleased to hear from whom.'

Mark tried to conceal the truth. He could not bear those cold hands to touch the ring; he could not bear to say to this crude man, 'It was a gift from the Queen.' He was silent therefore, and Cromwell's fingers pressed into his wrist.

'You do not answer. Tell me, who gave you that most valuable ring?'

'It was . . . from one of my patrons . . . one who liked my playing.'

'Might I ask if it was a man . . . or a lady?'

Mark slipped his hands beneath the table.

'A man,' he lied.

His arms were gripped so tightly that he let out a shriek for Cromwell's hands were strong, and Mark was fragile as a girl.

'You lie!' said Cromwell, and his voice was quiet and soft as silk.

'I . . . no, I swear . . . I . . .'

'Will you tell me who gave you the ring?'

Mark stood up. 'Sir, I came here on an invitation to dine with you. I had no idea that it was to answer your questions.'

'You came here to dine,' said Cromwell expressionlessly. 'Well, when you dine, boy, will depend on how readily you answer my questions.'

'I know not by what authority . . .' stammered the poor boy, almost in tears.

'On the authority of the King, you fool! Now will you answer my questions?'

Sweat trickled down Smeaton's nose. He had never before come face to face with violence. When the beggars had passed his father's door, when he had seen men in the pillory or hanging from a gibbet, he had looked the other way. He could not bear to look on any distressing sight. He was an artist; when he saw misery, he turned from it and tried to conjure up music in his head that he might disperse his unhappy thoughts. And now, looking at Cromwell, he realized that he was face to face with something from which it was not possible to turn.

'Who gave you the ring?' asked Cromwell.

'I . . . I told you. . . .' Smeaton covered his face with his hands, for tears were starting to his eyes, and he could not bear to look longer into the cold and brutal face confronting him.

'Have done!' said Cromwell. 'Now . . . ready?'

Mark uncovered his eyes and saw that he was no longer alone with Cromwell. On either side of him stood two big men dressed as servants; in the hands of one was a stick and a rope.

Cromwell nodded to these men. One seized Smeaton in a grip that paralysed him. The other placed the rope about his head, making a loop in the rope through which was placed the stick.

'Tighten the rope as I say,' commanded Cromwell.

The boy's eyes were starting in terror; they pleaded with Cromwell: Do not hurt me; I cannot bear it! I could not bear physical pain . . . I never could. . . .

The eyes of Cromwell surveyed his victim, amused, cynical. One of the thick fingers pulled at his doublet.

'Indeed it is a fine doublet . . . a very fine doublet for a humble musician to wear. Tell me, whence came this fine doublet?'

'I . . . I . . .'

'Tighten the rope,' said Cromwell. It cut into the pale skin of Mark's forehead. He felt as though his head was about to burst.

'The doublet . . . whence did it come?'

'I . . . I do not understand. . . .'

'Tighter . . . tighter! I have not all the day to spend on such as he.'

Something was trickling down his face, something warm and thick. He could see it on his nose, just below his eyes.

'Who gave you the doublet? Tighten the rope, you fools!'

Mark screamed. His head was throbbing; black spots, like notes of music, danced before his eyes.

'Please . . . stop! I . . . will tell you . . . about the doublet . . . Her Majesty . . .'

'Her Majesty!' said Cromwell, smiling suddenly. 'Loosen the rope. Bring him a little water. Her Majesty?' he prompted.

'Her Majesty thought I was ill-clad, and since I was to be her musician, she gave money for the doublet. . . .'

'The Queen gave you money. . . .' One large cold finger pointed to the ruby. 'And the ring. . . ?'

'I . . .'

'The rope, you fools! Tighten it! You were too soft before. . . .'

'No!' screamed Mark. 'You said . . . water . . .'

'Then who gave you the ring?'

'The Queen . . .'

'Give him water. The Queen then gave you the ruby ring.'

Mark drank; the room was swimming round and round; the ceiling dipped. He could see the river through the window – it looked faint and far away; he heard the sound of singing on a passing barge. Oh, were I but there! thought Mark.

'I would know why the Queen gave you the ruby.'

That was easy. 'She was pleased with my playing . . . She is a most generous lady . . .'

'Over-generous with her favours, I'll warrant!'

He felt sick. This was no way to speak of the Queen. He wanted to stand up, push aside that bland, smiling face, run out into the fresh air, run to the Queen.

'You were most friendly with the Queen?'

'She was most gracious . . .'

'Come, no evasions! You know full well my meaning. The Queen gave you money, clothes, and a ruby ring. Well, why not? She is young, and so are you. You are a handsome boy.'

'I understand not . . .'

'Subterfuge will not help you. You are here, on the King's command, to answer questions. You are the Queen's lover!'

The shock of those words set his head throbbing anew; he

could still feel the tight pressure of the rope about his head, although in actual fact it was quite loose now; the torture had stopped for awhile. He felt very ill; the blood was still trickling down his face from the cut which the rope had made. Oh, why had he accepted an invitation to dine with Thomas Cromwell! Now he knew what people meant when they talked with fear of Cromwell. Now he knew why they would suddenly stop talking when Cromwell appeared.

Cromwell rapped on the table with his knuckles.

'Tighten the rope.'

'No!' screamed Mark.

'Now. Speak the truth, or it will be worse for you. You are the Queen's lover. You have committed adultery with the Queen. Answer! Answer yes!'

'No!' sobbed Mark.

He could not bear this. He was screaming with the pain; it seemed to him that his blood was pounding against the top of his head, threatening to burst it. It gushed from his nose. He alternately moaned and screamed.

Cromwell said: 'You must tell the truth. You must admit this crime you and she have committed.'

'I have committed no crime! She ... she ... is a queen ... No, no! Please ... please ... I cannot bear it ... I cannot ...'

One of the men was putting vinegar beneath his nose, and he realized that he had enjoyed a second or two of blessed unconsciousness.

Cromwell gripped his chin and jerked his head up violently, so that it seemed as if a hundred knives had been plunged into his head.

'This is nothing to what will follow, if you do not answer my questions. Admit that you have committed adultery with the Queen.'

' 'Twould be but an untruth ...'

Cromwell banged on the table; the noise was like hammer blows on his aching head.

'You committed adultery with the Queen ... Tighten up ... Tighter, you fools! Tighter ...'

'No!' screamed Mark. And then the smell of vinegar,

mingling with that of blood, told him he had lost consciousness again.

He sobbed: 'I cannot . . . I cannot . . .'

'Listen,' snarled Cromwell, 'you committed adultery with the Queen . . .' The great hand shot up and seized the stick from the hands of his servant 'There! There! You committed adultery with the Queen. You committed adultery with the Queen . . . Admit it! Admit it!'

Mark screamed. 'Anything . . . anything . . . Please . . . I cannot . . . I cannot . . . endure . . . my head . . .'

'You admit it then?'

'I admit . . .'

'You committed adultery with the Queen . . .'

He was crying, and his tears mingled with the blood and sweat . . . and that hateful smell of vinegar would not let him sink into peace. He had longed to die for her, and he could not bear a little pain for her. A little pain! Oh, but it was such exquisite torture; his head was bursting, bleeding; he had never known there could be agony like this.

Cromwell said: 'He admits adultery with the Queen. Take him away.'

They had to carry him, for when he stood up he could see nothing but a blur of panelled walls, and light from the window, and a medley of cruel faces. He could not stand; so they carried him to a dark chamber in which they left him, locked in. And as he sank to the floor, he lost consciousness once more.

He lay there, half fainting, not aware of the room nor even what had gone before. He knew nothing except that there was a pain that maddened him, and that it was in his head. In his mouth he tasted blood; the smell of vinegar clung to his clothes, devilishly not allowing him to rest in that dark world for which he longed.

He was semi-conscious, thinking he was in his father's cottage, thinking he sat at the feet of the Queen, and that darkness for which he longed was her eyes, as black as night, as beautiful as forgetfulness.

But now someone was beating with a hammer on his head, and it was hurting him abominably. He awakened screaming, and knew suddenly that he was not in his father's cottage, nor at the feet of the Queen; he was in a dark room in Thomas Cromwell's house at Stepney, and he had been tortured . . . and what had he said? What *had* he said?

He had lied; he had lied about her for whom he would have died! Sobs shook his slender body. He would tell them . . . he would tell them he lied; he would explain. It hurt me so that I knew not what I said. She is a great, good lady. How could I have said that of her! How could I so demean her . . . and myself! But I could not bear the pain in my head; it was maddening. I could not endure it, Your Most Gracious Majesty! For that reason I lied.

He must pray for strength. He must do anything, but he must explain that he had lied. He could not let them believe . . .

He lay groaning in the dark, misery of body forgotten because he mourned so sincerely what he had done. Even though I assure them it is not so, I said it . . . I failed her.

He was almost glad when they came to him. That cruel man was with them.

Mark stammered: 'I lied . . . It was not so. The pain was too much for me.'

'Can you stand?' asked Cromwell in a voice that was almost solicitous.

He could stand. He felt better. There was a terrible throbbing in his head, but the frightening giddiness had passed. He felt strengthened. No matter what they did to him, he would tell no more lies. He was ready to go to the scaffold for the Queen.

'This way,' said Cromwell.

The cool air fanned his burning face, setting his wounds to smart. He reeled, but there were those to support him. He was too dazed to wonder where he was going. They led him down the privy stairs to a barge.

He could feel the river breeze; he could smell the river, tar and sea salt mingling with blood and vinegar. He felt steady with purpose; he pictured himself going to the scaffold for her sake; but first though, he must make it clear that he had lied, that only such frightening, maddening torture could have made him lie about her.

The river was shot with darkness, for evening was advancing. The barge was being moored; he was prodded and told to get out. Above him loomed a dark, grey tower; he mounted the steps and went over the stone bridge. They were going to put him in the Tower! He was suddenly sick; the sight of the Tower had done that to him. What now? Why should they take him to the Tower? What had he done? He had accepted money, he had accepted a ring; they were gifts from a queen to one whose music had pleased her. He had committed no crime.

'This way,' said Cromwell. A door was unlocked; they passed through it. They were in a dark passage whose walls were slimy; and there was a noisome smell coming up from below the dismal spiral staircase which they were descending.

A man with a lanthorn appeared. Their shadows were grotesque on the walls.

'Come along,' said Cromwell, almost gently.

They were in one of the many passages which ran under the great fortress. The place was damp and slimy; little streams trickled across the earthen floor, and rats scuttled away at their approach.

'You are in the Tower of London, Smeaton.'

'That I have realised. For what reason have I been brought here?'

'You will know soon enough. Methought I would like to show you the place.'

'I would rather go back. I would have you know that when I said ... when I said what I did ... that I lied ...'

Cromwell held up a thick finger.

'An interesting place, this Tower of London. I thought you would enjoy a tour of inspection before we continue with our cross-examination.'

'I ... I understand not ...'

'Listen! Ah! We are nearer the torture chambers. How that poor wretch groans! Doubtless 'tis the rack that stretches his body. These rogues! They should answer questions, and all would be well with them.'

Mark vomited suddenly. The smell of the place revolted him, his head was throbbing, he was in great pain, and he felt he could not breathe in this confined space.

'You will be better later,' said Cromwell. 'This place has a decided effect on those who visit it for the first time . . . Here! Someone comes . . .'

He drew Mark to one side of the loathsome passage. Uncanny screams, like those of a madman, grew louder, and peering in the dim light, Mark saw that they issued from the bloody head of what appeared to be a man who was coming towards them; he walked between two strong men in the uniform of warders of the Tower, who both supported and restrained him. Mark gasped with horror; he could not take his eyes from that gory thing which should have been a head; blood dripped from it, splashing Mark's clothes as the man reeled past, struggling in his agony to dash his head against the wall and so put an end to his misery.

Cromwell's voice was silky in his ear.

'They have cut off his ears. Poor fool! I trow he thought it smart to repeat what he'd heard against the King's Grace.'

Mark could not move; it seemed to him that his legs were rooted to this noisome spot; he put out a hand and touched the slimy wall.

'Come on!' said Cromwell, and pushed him.

They went on; Mark was dazed with what he had seen. I am dreaming this, he thought. This cannot be; there could never be such things as this!

The passages led past cells, and Cromwell would have the man shine his lanthorn into these, that Mark might see for himself what befell those who saw fit to displease the King. Mark looked; he saw men more dead than alive, their filthy rags heaving with the movement of vermin, their bones protruding through their skin. These men groaned and blinked, shutting their eyes from that feeble light, and their clanking chains seemed to groan with them. He saw what had been men, and were now mere bones in chains. He saw death, and smelt it. He saw the men cramped in the Little Ease, so paralysed by this form of confinement that when Cromwell called to one of them to come out, the man, though his face lit up with a sudden hope of freedom, could not move.

The lanthorn was shone into the gloomy pits where rats swam and squeaked in a ferocious chorus as they fought one another over dying men. He saw men, bleeding and torn from the torture chambers; he heard their groans, saw their bleeding hands and feet, their mutilated fingers from which the nails had been pulled, their poor, shapeless, bleeding mouths from which their teeth had been brutally torn.

'These dungeons have grown lively during the reign of our most Christian King,' said Cromwell. 'There will always be fools who know not when they are fortunate . . . Come, Master Smeaton, we are at our destination.'

They were in a dimly lighted chamber which seemed to Mark's dazed eyes to be hung with grotesque shapes. He noticed first the table, for at this table sat a man, and set before him were writing materials. He smelt in this foul air the sudden odour of vinegar, and the immediate effect of this – so reminiscent of his pain – was to make him retch. In the centre of this chamber was a heavy stone pillar from which was projected a long iron bar, and slung around this was a rope at the end of which was a hook. Mark stared at this with wonder, until Cromwell directed his gaze to that ponderous instrument of torture nick-named The Scavenger's Daughter; it was a simple construction, like a wide iron hoop, which by means of screws could be tightened about its victim's body.

'Our Scavenger's Daughter!' said Cromwell. 'One would not care for that wench's embrace. Very different, Smeaton, from the arms of her who is thought by many to be the fairest lady of the court!'

Mark stared at his tormentor, as a rabbit stares at a stoat. He was as if petrified, and while he longed to scream, to run to dash himself against the walls in an effort to kill himself – as that other poor wretch had done – he could do nothing but stand and stare at those instruments of torture which Cromwell pointed out to him.

'The gauntlets, Smeaton! A man will hang from these . . . Try them on? Very well. I was saying . . . they would be fixed on yonder hook which you see there, and a man would hang for days in such torture as you cannot . . . yet imagine. And all because he will not answer a few civil questions. The folly of men, Smeaton, is past all believing!'

Mark shuddered, and the sweat ran down his body.

'The thumbscrews, Smeaton. See, there is blood on them. The Spanish Collar . . . see these spikes! Not pleasant when pressed into the flesh. How would you like to be locked into such a collar and to stay there for days on end? But no, you would not be unwise, Smeaton. Methinks you are a cultured man; you are a musician; you have musician's hands. Would it not be a pity were those beautiful hands fixed in yon gauntlets! They say men have been known to lose the use of their hands after hanging from that beam.'

Mark was trembling so that he could no longer stand.

'Sit here,' said Cromwell, and sat with him. Regaining his composure to some small extent, Mark looked about him. They were sitting on a wooden frame shaped like a trough, large enough to contain a human body. At each end of this frame were fixed windlasses on which rope was coiled.

Smeaton screamed aloud. 'The rack!' he cried.

'Clever of you, Smeaton, to have guessed aright. But fear not. You are a wise young man; you will answer the questions I ask, and you will have no need of the rack nor her grim sister, the Scavenger's Daughter.'

Mark's mouth was dry, and his tongue was too big for it.

'I . . . I cannot . . . I lied . . .'

Cromwell lifted a hand. Two strong men appeared and, laying hands on the shivering boy, began stripping off his clothes.

Mark tried to picture the face of the Queen; he could see her clearly. He must keep that picture before him, no matter what they did to him. If he could but remember her face . . . if . . .

He was half fainting as they laid him in the frame and fastened the loops of the ropes to his wrists and ankles.

Cromwell's face was close to his.

'Smeaton, I would not have them do this to you. Dost know what happens to men who are racked? Some lose their reason. There are some who never walk again. This is pain such as you cannot dream of, Smeaton. Just answer my questions.' He nodded to his attendants to be ready. 'Smeaton, you have committed adultery with the Queen.'

'No!'

'You have admitted it. You admitted it at Stepney; you cannot go back on that.'

'I was tortured . . . The pain . . . it was too much . . .'

'So you admitted the truth. Did I not tell you that what you have known so far was naught? You are on the rack, Smeaton. One sign from me, and those men will begin to work it. Will you answer my questions?'

'I lied . . . I did not . . .'

He could see her face clearly, smiling at him; her eyes were great wells of blessed darkness; to lose oneself in that darkness would be to die, and death was the end of pain.

'Begin,' said Cromwell. The windlasses turned outwards . . . Smeaton felt his body was being torn apart; he screamed, and immediately lost consciousness.

Vinegar. That hateful smell that would not let a man rest.

'Come, Smeaton! You committed adultery with the Queen.'

He could still see her face, but it was blurred now.

'You committed adultery with the Queen . . .'

There was nothing but pain, pain that was a thousand red hot needles pressing into the sockets of his arms and legs; he could feel his joints cracking; he felt they must be breaking. He began to groan.

'Yes, yes . . . yes . . . anything . . . But . . .'

'Enough!' said Cromwell, and the man at the table wrote.

Mark was sobbing. It seemed to him that they poured the accursed vinegar over his face. They sprinkled it on with the brush he had seen hanging on the wall, adding fresh smarts to his bleeding head; causing him to shrink, which in its turn made him scream afresh, for every movement was acute torture.

Cromwell's voice came from a long way off.

'There were others, beside yourself, Smeaton.'

Others? He knew not what the man meant. He knew nothing but pain, pain, excruciating pain that shot all over his flesh; this was all the pain he had ever thought there could be; this was all the pain in the world. And more than pain of the body – pain of the mind. For he would have died for her, and he had betrayed her; he had lied; he had lied about her; he had said shameful things of her because . . . he . . . could not bear the pain.

'Their names?' said Cromwell.

'I know . . .no names.'

Not vinegar again! I cannot bear it . . . I cannot bear pain and vinegar . . . not both! He broke into deep sobs.

'You shall rest if you but tell us their names.'

How could he know of what the man was speaking? Names? What names? He thought he was a little boy at his mother's spinning-wheel. 'Little Mark! He is a pretty boy. Here is a sweetmeat, Mark . . . And he sings prettily too. And he plays the virginals . . . Mark, how would you like a place at court? The King loves music mightily . . .'

'Begin again!' ordered Cromwell.

'No!' shrieked Mark.

'The names,' murmured Cromwell.

'I . . . I . . . know . . . not . . .'

It was coming again, the agony. There was never agony such as this. Burning pincers . . . the wrenching apart of his muscles . . . the wicked rack was tearing off his limbs. Vinegar. Accursed vinegar.

'Mark Smeaton, you have committed adultery with the Queen. Not you alone! You were not to blame, Mark; the Queen tempted you, and who were you, a humble musician, to say nay to the Queen! But you were not alone in this, Mark; there were others. There were noble gentlemen, Mark . . . Come now, you have had enough of this rack; men cannot be racked forever – you know that, Mark. It drives men mad. Just say their names, Mark. Come! Was it Wyatt?'

'There was none . . . I know not. I lied. Not I . . . I . . .'

No, not again. He was going mad. He could not endure more. Her face was becoming blurred. He must stop, stop. He was going mad. He would not say what they told him to. He must not say Wyatt's name . . .

They were putting vinegar under his nose. They were going to turn the rack again.

He saw the court, as clearly as though he were there. She was smiling, and someone was standing beside her.

'Norris!' he screamed. 'Norris!'

Cromwell's voice was gentle, soothing.

'Norris, Mark. That is good. That is right. Who else, Mark? Just whisper . . .'

'Norris! Brereton! Weston!' screamed Mark.

He was unconscious as they unbound him and carried his tortured body away.

Cromwell watched them, smiling faintly. It had been a good day's work.

*　　　*　　　*

The next day was the first of May. May Day was a favourite court festival which the King never failed to keep. At one time he had been the hero of the tiltyard, but now that his leg was troublesome, he must sit back and watch others take the glory of the day. The chief challenger on this day would be Lord Rochford, and the chief of the defenders, Henry Norris. It was not pleasant, when one had been more skilful than they, to realize age was creeping on, turning one into a spectator instead of a brilliant performer who had held the admiration of the entire court.

Cromwell came to see the King before he went to the tilt-yard. Henry frowned on the man, not wishing to see him now, but for once Cromwell would not be waved aside; he had news, disturbing news, news which should not be with-held from His Majesty one second longer than necessary. Cromwell talked; the King listened. He listened in silence, while his eyes seemed to sink into his head and his face grew as purple as his coat.

Down in the tiltyard they were awaiting the arrival of the

King. The Queen was already in her place, but obviously the jousts could not start without the King. He went to the yard, and took his place beside her. The tilt began.

He was aware of her beside him; he was trembling with jealous rage. He was thinking. This is the woman to whom I have given everything; the best years of my life, my love, my throne. For her I broke with Rome; for her I risked the displeasure of my people. And how does she reward me? She betrays me with any man that takes her fancy!

He did not know who tilted below; he did not care. Red mist swam before his eyes. He glanced sideways at her; she was more beautiful than she had ever seemed, and more remote than she had been in her father's garden at Hever. She had tricked him; she had laughed at him; and he had loved her passionately and exclusively. He was a king, and he had loved her; she was a nobody, the daughter of a man who owed his advancement to the favour of his king . . . and she had flouted him. Never had she loved him; she had loved a throne and a crown, and she had reluctantly taken him because she could not have them without him. His throat was dry with the pain she had caused him; his heart beat wildly with anger. His eyes were murderous; he wanted her to suffer all the pain she had inflicted on him – not as he had suffered, but a thousand times more so. It galled him that even now she was not one half as jealous of Jane Seymour as he was of Norris down there in the yard.

He looked at Norris – one of his greatest and most intimate friends – handsome, not as young as those others, Weston, Brereton and Smeaton, but with a distinguished air, a charm of manner, a gracious, gentle, knightly air. He loathed Norris, of whom a short while ago he had been very fond. There was her brother, Rochford; he had liked that young man; he had been glad to raise him for his own sake as well as his sister's; gay, amusing, devilishly witty and attractive . . . and now Cromwell had discovered that Rochford had said unforgivable, disloyal, treasonable things of his royal master; he had laughed at the King's verses, laughed at the King's clothes; he had most shamefully – and for this he deserved to die – disparaged the King's manhood, had laughed at him and whispered that the reason why the King's wives could not have children successfully was that the King himself was at fault.

Smeaton . . . that low-born creature who had nothing to recommend him but his pretty face and his music had pleased her more than he himself had. He, King of England, had begged her, had implored her, had bribed her with offers of greatness, and reluctantly she had accepted – not for love of him, but because she could not refuse a glittering crown.

He was mad with rage, mad with jealousy; furious with her that she could still hurt him thus, and that he was so vulnerable even now when he planned to cast her off. He could leap on her now . . . and if he had a knife in his hand he would plunge it into her heart; nothing would satisfy him, nothing . . . nothing but that her blood should flow; he would stab her himself, rejoicing to see her die, rejoicing that no one else should enjoy her.

The May sunshine was hot on his face; the sweat glistening across his nose. He did not see the jousts; he could see nothing but her making such voluptuous love with others as she had never given him. He had been jealous of her before; he had been ready to torture those who had glanced at her, but that had been complacent jealousy; now he could be jealous by reason of his knowledge, he could even fill in the forms of her lovers – Norris! Weston! Brereton! Wyatt? And that Smeaton! How dare she, she whom he had made a Queen! Even a humble boy could please her more than he could!

His attention was suddenly caught, for her handkerchief had fluttered from her hand; she was smiling, smiling at Norris; and Norris picked up the handkerchief, bowed, handed it to her on the point of his lance while they exchanged smiles that seemed like lovers' smiles to Henry's jealous eyes.

The joust continued. His tongue was thick, his throat was dry; he was filled with mad rage which he knew he could not continue to control. If he stayed here he would shout at her, he would take her by the beautiful hair which he had

390

loved to twine about his fingers, and he would twist it about that small white neck, and tighten it and tighten it until there was no life left in the body he had loved too well.

She spoke to him. He did not hear what she said. He stood up; he was the King, and everything he did was of importance. How many of those people, who now turned startled eyes on him, had laughed at him for the complaisant husband he had appeared to be, had laughed at his blind devotion to this woman who had tricked him and deceived him with any man she fancied in his court!

It was the signal for the jousting to end. How could it go on, when the King no longer wished to see it? Anne was not so surprised, that she would attach too much importance to the strange behaviour of the King; he had been curt with her often enough of late; she guessed he had left Greenwich for White Hall, as he often went to London to see Jane Seymour.

The King was on his way to White Hall. He had given orders that Rochford and Weston should be arrested as they were leaving the tiltyard. Norris he had commanded to ride back with him.

He could not take his eyes from that handsome profile; there was a certain nobility about Norris that angered the King; he was tall and straight, and his gentle character was apparent in the finely cut profile and the mobile mouth. He was a man to be jealous of. The King had heard that Norris was about to engage himself to Madge Shelton who at one time – and that not so long ago – had pleased the King himself. Henry had wished him well of Madge; she was a very attractive woman, lively and clever and good-looking. The King had tired of her quickly; the only woman he did not tire of quickly was Anne Boleyn. And she . . . The anger came surging up again. The wanton! The slut! To think that he, who had always admired virtue in women, should have been cursed with a wife who was known throughout his court for her wanton ways! It was too much. She had known that he admired virtue in those about him; and she had laughed at him, jeered at him . . . with her brother and Weston and Brereton and Norris . . .

He leaned forward in his saddle and said, his voice quivering with rage: 'Norris, I know thee for what thou art, thou traitor!'

Norris almost fell from the saddle, so great was his surprise.

'Your Majesty . . . I know not . . .'

'You know not! I'll warrant you know well enough. Ha! You start, do you! Think you not that I am a fool, a man to stand aside and let his inferiors amuse themselves with his wife. I accuse you of adultery with the Queen!'

'Sir . . . this is a joke . . .'

'This is no joke, Norris, and well you know it!'

'Then it is the biggest mistake that has ever been made.'

'You would dare to deny it?' foamed the King.

'I deny it utterly, Your Majesty.'

'Your lies and evasions will carry little weight with me, Norris.'

'I can only repeat, Sir, that I am guiltless of that of which you accuse me,' said Norris with dignity.

All the rich blood had left the King's usually florid face, showing a network of veins against a skin grown pallid.

' 'Twill be better if you do not lie to me, Norris. I am in no mood to brook such ways. You will confess to me here and now.'

'There is naught I can confess, my lord. I am guiltless of this charge you bring against me.'

'Come, come! You know, as all in the court know, how the Queen conducts herself.'

'I assure Your Most Gracious Majesty that I know naught against the Queen.'

'You have not heard rumours! Come, Norris, I warn you I am not in the mood for dalliance.'

'I have heard no rumours, Sir.'

'Norris, I offer you pardon, for you know that I have loved you well, if you will confess to your adultery.'

'I would rather die a thousand deaths, my lord, than accuse the Queen of that which I believe her, in my conscience, innocent.'

The King's fury almost choked him. He said no more until

they reached Westminster. Then, calling to him the burly bully Fitzwilliam, whom Cromwell had chosen to be his lieutenant, he bade the man arrest Norris and despatch him to the Tower.

*   *   *

Anne, sitting down to supper in Greenwich Palace, felt the first breath of uneasiness.

She said to Madge Shelton: 'Where is Mark? He does not seem to be in his accustomed place.'

'I do not know what has happened to Mark, Your Majesty,' answered Madge.

'If I remember aright, I did not notice him last night. I hope he is not sick.'

'I do not know, Madam,' said Madge, and Anne noticed that her cousin's eyes did not meet hers; it was as though the girl was afraid.

Later she said: 'I do not see Norris. Madge, is it not strange that they should both absent themselves? Where is Norris, Madge? You should know.'

'He has said nothing to me, Madam.'

'What! He is indeed a neglectful lover; I should not allow it, Madge.'

Her voice had an edge to it. She well knew, and Madge well knew that though Norris was supposed to be in love with Madge, it was the Queen who received his attention. Madge was charming; she could attract easily, but she could not hold men to her as her cousin did. Weston had been attracted by Madge once, until he had felt the deeper and irresistible attraction of the Queen.

'I know not what is holding him,' said Madge.

Anne said: 'You know not *who* is holding him, you mean!' And when she laughed, her laughter was more than usually high-pitched.

It was a strange evening; people whispered together in the corridors of the palace.

'What means this?'

'Did you see the way His Majesty left the tiltyard?'

'They say Norris, Weston and Brereton are missing.'

393

'Where is Mark Smeaton? Surely they would not arrest little Mark!'

The Queen was aware of this strange stillness about her; she called for the musicians, and while they played to her, sat staring at Mark's empty place. Where was Norris? Where was Weston? Why did Brereton continue to absent himself?

She spent a sleepless night, and in the early morning fell into a heavy doze from which she awakened late. All during the morning the palace abounded in rumour. Anne heard the whispering voices, noted the compassionate glances directed at her, and was increasingly uneasy.

She sat down to dinner, determined to hide the terrible apprehension that was stealing over her. When she did not dine with the King, His Majesty would send his waiter to her with the courteous message: 'Much good may it do you!' On this day she waited in vain for the King's messenger; and as soon as the meal was over and the surnap was removed, there came one to announce the arrival at Greenwich of certain members of the council, and with them, to her disgust, was her uncle the Duke of Norfolk.

Her uncle looked truculent and self-righteous, pleased with himself, as though that which he had prophesied had come to pass. He behaved, not as a courtier to a queen, but as a judge to a prisoner.

'What means this?' demanded Anne.

'Pray be seated,' said Norfolk.

She hesitated, wanting to demand of him why he thought he might give her orders when to sit and when to stand; but something in his eyes restrained her. She sat down, her head held high, her eyes imperious.

'I would know why you think fit to come to me at this hour and disturb me with your presence. I would know . . .'

'You shall know,' said Norfolk grimly. 'Smeaton is in the Tower. He has confessed to having committed adultery with you.'

She grew very pale, and stood up, her eyes flashing.

'How dare you come to me with such vile accusations!'

'Tut, tut, tut!' said Norfolk, and shook his head at her.

'Norris is also in the Tower.' He lied: 'He also admits to adultery with you.'

'I will not believe that he could be guilty of such false-hood! I will not believe it of either. Please leave me at once. I declare you shall suffer for your insolence.'

'Forget not,' said Norfolk, 'that we come by the King's command to conduct you to the Tower, there to abide His Highness's pleasure.'

'I must see the King,' said Anne. 'My enemies have done this. These stories you would tell me would be tragic, were they not ridiculous. . . .'

'It is not possible for you to see the King.'

'It is not possible for *me* to see the King. You forget who I am, do you not? I declare you will wish . . .'

'You must await the King's pleasure, and he has said he does not wish to see you.'

She was really frightened now. The King had sent these men to arrest her and take her to the Tower; he had said he did not wish to see her. Lies were being told about her. Norris? Smeaton? Oh, no! Not those two! They had been her friends, and she would have sworn to their loyalty. What did this mean. . . . George, where was George? She needed his advice now as never before.

'If it be His Majesty's pleasure,' she said calmly, 'I am ready to obey.'

In the barge she felt very frightened. She was reminded of another journey to the Tower, of a white falcon which had been crowned by an angel, of the King, waiting to receive her there . . . eager that all the honour he could give her should be hers.

She turned to her uncle. 'I am innocent of these foul charges. I swear it! I swear it! If you will but take me to the King, I know I can convince him of my innocence.'

She knew she could, if she could but see him . . . if she could but take his hands. . . . She had ever been able to do with him what she would . . . but she had been careless of late. She had never loved him; she had not much cared that he had strayed; she had thought that she had but to flatter him and amuse him, and he would be hers. She had never thought that this could happen to her, that she would be removed from him, not allowed to see him, a prisoner in the Tower.

Norfolk folded his arms and looked at her coldly. One would have thought he was her bitterest enemy rather than her kinsman.

'Your paramours have confessed,' he said, shrugging his shoulders. ' 'Twould be better if you did likewise.'

'I have naught to confess. Have I not told you! What should I confess? I do not believe that these men have made confessions; you say so to trap me. You are my enemy; you always have been.'

'Calm yourself!' said Norfolk. 'Such outbursts can avail you nothing.'

They made fast the barge; they led her up the steps; the great gate opened to admit her.

'Oh, Lord, help me,' she murmured, 'as I am guiltless of that whereof I am accused.' Sir William Kingston came out to receive her, as he had on that other occasion. 'Mr Kingston,' she asked, 'do I go into a dungeon?'

'No, Madam,' answered the constable, 'to your own lodgings where you lay at your coronation.'

She burst into passionate weeping, and then she began to laugh hysterically; and her sobs, mingling with her laughter, were pitiful to hear. She was thinking of then and now – and that in but three short years. A queen coming to her coronation; a queen coming to her doom.

'It is too good for me!' she cried, laughing as the sobs shook her. 'Jesus have mercy on me!'

Kingston watched her until her hysteria passed. He was a hard man but he could not but be moved to pity. He had seen some terrible sights in these grey, grim buildings, but he thought that this girl, laughing and crying before him, presented one of the most pathetic he had ever witnessed. He had received her on her first coming to the Tower, thought her very beautiful in her coronation robes with her hair flowing about her; he could not but compare her then with this poor weeping girl, and so was moved in spite of himself.

She wiped her eyes, controlled her laughter, and her dignity returned to her. She listened to a clock strike five, and such a familiar, homely sound reminded her of ordinary matters. Her family – what of them?

She turned to the members of the council, who were about to leave her in Kingston's care.

'I entreat you to beseech the King in my behalf that he will be a good lord unto me,' she said; and when they had taken their leave, Kingston conducted her to her apartments.

She said: 'I am the King's true wedded wife.' And added: 'Mr Kingston, do you know wherefore I am here?'

'Nay!' he answered.

'When saw you the King?'

'I saw him not since I saw him in the tiltyard,' he said.

'Then Mr Kingston, I pray you tell me where my lord father is.'

'I saw him in the court before dinner,' said Kingston.

She was silent awhile, but the question she had longed to ask, now refused to be kept back longer. Oh, where is my sweet brother?'

He could not look at her; hard as he was he could not face the passionate entreaty in her eyes which pleaded with him to tell her that her brother was safe.

Kingston said evasively that he had last seen him at York Place.

She began to pace up and down, and as though talking to herself, she murmured: 'I hear say that I shall be accused with three men, and I can say no more than "Nay!"' She began to weep softly, as if all the wildness had been drained out of her, and there was only sadness left. 'Oh, Norris, hast thou accused me? Thou art in the Tower, and thou and I shall die together; and Mark, thou art here too? Oh, my mother, thou wilt die for sorrow.'

She sat brooding awhile, and then turning to him asked: 'Mr Kingston, shall I die without justice?'

He tried to comfort her. 'The poorest subject the King hath, has that,' he assured her.

She looked at him a moment before she fell into prolonged and bitter laughter.

*   *   *

Silence hung over the palace; in the courtyards men and women stood about whispering together, glancing furtively over their shoulders, fearful of what would happen next. Wyatt was in the Tower; who next? No man in the Queen's set felt safe. In the streets the people talked together; they knew that the Queen was a prisoner in the Tower; they knew she was to be tried on a charge of adultery. They remembered how the King had sought to rid himself of Katharine; did he seek to rid himself of Anne? Those who had shouted 'Down with Nan Bullen!' now murmured 'Poor lady! What will become of her?'

Jane Rochford, looking from her window, watched the courtiers and the ladies crossing the courtyard. She had expected trouble, but not such trouble. Anne in the Tower, where she herself had spent many an uneasy hour! George in the Tower! It was Jane's turn to laugh now, for might it not be that her whispered slander had put Cromwell on the scent? Had she not seen grave Norris and gay Weston cast their longing glances at the Queen? Yes, and she had not hesitated to laugh at these matters, to point them out to others. 'Ah! The Queen was born gay, and my husband tells me that the King . . . no matter, but what is a woman to do when she cannot get children. . . .' Proud George was in the Tower now, though it was whispered that no harm could come to him. It was those others, who had been her lovers, who would die.

Jane threw back her head, and for some moments she was weak with hysterical laughter. Poor little Jane! they had said. Silly little Jane! They had not bothered to explain their clever remarks to her; they had cut her out, considering her too stupid to understand. And yet she had had quite a big part to play in bringing about this event. Ah, Anne! she thought, when I was in the Tower you came thither in your cloth of silver and ermine, did you not! Anne the Queen, and Jane the fool whose folly had got her accused of treason. Now, who is the fool, eh, Anne? You, you and your lovers . . . dear sister! Not Jane, for Jane is free, free of you all . . . yes, even free of George, for now she does not cry and fret for him; she can laugh at him and say 'I hate you, George!'

And he will be freed, for what has he done to deserve death! And he was ever a favourite with the King. It is only her lovers who will die the deaths of traitors. . . . But he loved her as well as any.

Her eyes narrowed; her heart began to pound against her side, but her mind was very calm. She could see his face clearer in her mind's eye—calm and cynical, ever courageous. If he could stand before her, his eyes would despise her, would say 'Very well, Jane, do your worst! You were always a vindictive, cruel woman.' Vindictive! He had used that word to describe her. 'I think you are the most vindictive woman in the world!' He had laughed at her fondness for listening at doors.

Her cheeks flamed; she ran down the staircase and out into the warm May sunshine.

People looked at her in a shamefaced way, as they looked at those whose loved ones were in danger. They should know that George Boleyn meant nothing to her; she could almost scream at the thought of him. 'Nothing! Nothing! He means nothing to me, for if I loved him once, he taught me to hate him!' She was a partisan of the true Queen Katharine. Princess Mary was the rightful heir to the throne, not the bastard Elizabeth!

She joined a little group by a fountain.

'Has aught else happened?'

'You have heard about Wyatt. . . .' said one.

'Poor Wyatt!' added another.

'Poor Wyatt!' Jane's eyes flashed in anger. 'He was guilty if ever one was!'

The man who had spoken moved away; he had been a fool to say 'Poor Wyatt!' Such talk was folly.

'Ah! I fear they will all die,' said Jane. 'Oh, do not look to be sorry for me. She was my sister-in-law, but I always knew. My husband is in the Tower, and he will be released because ... because ...' And she burst into wild laughter.

'It is the strain,' said one. 'It is because George is in the Tower.'

'It is funny,' said Jane. 'He will be released ... and he ... he is as guilty as any. ...'

They stared at her. She saw a man on the edge of that group, whom she knew to be Thomas Cromwell's spy.

'What mean you?' he asked lightly, as though what she meant were of but little importance to him.

'He was her lover as well as any!' cried Jane. 'He adored her. He could not keep his hands from her ... he would kiss and fondle her ...'

'George ... ?' said one, looking oddly at her. 'But he is her brother. ...'

Jane's eyes flashed. 'What mattered that ... to such ... monsters! He was her lover. Dost think I, his wife, did not know these things? Dost think I never saw? Dost think I could shut my eyes to such obvious evidence? He was for ever with her, for ever shut away with her. Often I have surprised them ... together. I have seen their lovers' embrace. I have seen ...'

Her voice was shrill as the jealousy of years conjured up pictures for her.

She closed her eyes, and went on shouting. 'They were lovers, I tell you, lovers! I, his wife, meant nothing to him; he loved his sister. They laughed together at the folly of those around them. I tell you I know. I have seen ... I have seen ...'

Someone said in a tone of disgust: 'You had better go to your apartment, Lady Rochford. I fear recent happenings have been too much for you; you are overwrought.'

She was trembling from head to foot. She opened her eyes and saw that Cromwell's spy had left the group.

* * *

The King could not stop thinking of Anne Boleyn. Cromwell had talked to him of her; Cromwell applied enthusiasm to this matter as to all others; he had closed his eyes, pressed his ugly lips together, had begged to be excused from telling the King of all the abominations and unmentionable things that his diligent probing had brought to light. The King dwelt on these matters which Cromwell had laid before him, because they were balm to his conscience. He hated Anne, for she had deceived him; if she had given him the happiest moments of his life, she had given him the most wretched also. He had, before Cromwell had forced the confession from Smeaton, thought of displacing Anne by Jane Seymour; and Jane was with child, so action must take place promptly. He knew what this meant; it could mean but one thing; he was embarking on no more divorces. There were two counts which he could bring forward to make his marriage with Anne null and void; the first was that pre-contract of hers with Northumberland; the second was his own affinity with Anne through his association with her sister Mary. Both of these were very delicate matters, since Northumberland had already sworn before the Archbishop of Canterbury that there had been no pre-contract, and this before he himself had married Anne; moreover he was in full knowledge of the matter. Could he now say that he believed her to have been pre-contracted to Northumberland when he had accepted her freedom and married her? Not very easily. And this affair with Mary; it would mean he must make public his association with Anne's sister; and there was of course the ugly fact that he had chosen to forget about this when he had married Anne. It seemed to him that two opportunities of divorcing Anne were rendered useless by these very awkward circumstances; how could a man, who was setting himself up as a champion of chastity, use either? On the other hand how – unless he could prove his marriage to Anne illegal – could he marry Jane in time to make her issue legitimate?

There was one other way, and that was the way he wanted. He wanted it fiercely. While she lived he would continue to think of her enjoyed by and enjoying others; he could never bear that; she had meant too much to him, and still did. But their marriage had been a mistake; he had been completely happy with her before it, and he had never known a moment's true peace since; and it was all her fault.

She could not get a male child, which meant that heaven disapproved of the marriage. He could see no other way out of this but that that charming head should be cut from those elegant shoulders. His eyes glistened at the thought. Love and hatred, he knew, were closely allied. None other shall have her! was his main thought. She shall enjoy no more lovers; she shall laugh at me no more with her paramours! She shall die . . . die . . . die, for she is a black-browed witch, born to destroy men; therefore shall she be destroyed. She was guilty of adultery, and, worse still, incest; he must not forget that.

Ah, it grieved him that one he had once loved dearly should be too unworthy to live; but so it was . . . so it was. It was his painful duty to see justice done.

He said to Cranmer: 'This is painful to me, Cranmer. I would such work as this had not fallen to my bitter lot!'

Cranmer was grieved too; he was terrified that this might turn back the King towards Rome. And then what of those who had urged the break? Cranmer imagined he could smell the pungent smell of burning faggots and feel the hot flames creeping up his legs.

He said that he was hurt and grieved as was His Majesty, for next to the King's Grace he was most bound unto her of all creatures living. He would ask the King's permission to pray for her; he had loved her for the love he had supposed her to bear to God and the gospel. He hastened to add that all who loved God must now hate her above all others, for there could never have been one who so slandered the gospel.

Poor chicken-hearted Cranmer went in fear and trembling for the next few weeks. He could wish his courage was as strong as his beliefs. What if he who had been helped by the Queen, whose duty really lay towards her now, were clapped into the Tower! Those who were high one day, were brought low the next. He thought of a girl he had loved and married in Nuremberg, whither he had gone to study Lutheran doctrines, and whom he had left in Nuremberg because he had been called home to become Archbishop of Canterbury. It had been heartbreaking to leave her behind;

she was sweet and clinging; but Henry believed in the celibacy of priests, and what would he have said to a priest who had married a wife? He had left her for Henry; had left a bride for an archbishopric, had sacrificed love for a high place at court. What if he should fall from that high place to a dungeon in the Tower! From the Tower to the stake or the block was a short step indeed.

Henry found it comforting to talk with Cranmer; Cranmer was eager as he himself to do what was right.

'If she has done wrong,' said Cranmer, 'then Your Grace will punish her through God.'

'Through God,' said Henry. 'Though I trust she may yet prove her innocence. I would say to you, my lord, that I have no desire in the world to marry again unless constrained to do so by my subjects.'

'Amen!' said Cranmer, and tried not to show by his expression that he must think of Jane Seymour and those reports he had heard that she was already with child.

Henry patted the Archbishop's shoulder, called him his good friend; and Cranmer begged that this sad matter should not cause the King to think less of the gospel.

'I but turn to it more, good Cranmer.'

Cranmer left happier, and the King was relieved by his visit.

He called to his son, the young Duke of Richmond, and would have him stand before him that he might embrace him.

'For I feel tender towards you this night, my son.'

He was thinking of Anne even as he spoke. How often had she discountenanced him! How often had she disturbed him! And she, laughing at him . . . in the arms of his courtiers. . . . Norris . . . Weston. . . . Their faces leaped up in his mind, and were beside Anne's, laughing at him.

Fiercely he embraced his son; tears of self-pity came into his eyes and brimmed over onto the boy's head.

'Your Majesty is deeply disturbed,' said the young Duke.

Henry's voice broke on a sob. He remembered a rumour that when he had thought of going to France and leaving

Anne as Regent, she had talked wildly of getting rid of Mary; some had said she meant to poison her.

He held the boy against his chest.

'You and your sister Mary ought to thank God for escaping that cursed and venomous whore who tried to poison you both!' he declared.

* * *

Anne was desolate. The weary days were passing. There were with her two women, day and night, whom she hated and knew to be her enemies. These had been sent as her attendants by command of the King. They were a certain Mrs Cosyns, a spy and a talebearer, and her aunt, Lady Boleyn, who was the wife of her uncle, Sir Edward. This aunt had always been jealous of her niece, right from the time when she was a precocious child considered in the family to be clever. These two, at Cromwell's instigation, wore her down with their questions as they tried to trap her into admissions; they were sly-faced, ugly women, envious, jealous women who enjoyed their position and were made most gleeful by the distress of the Queen. Every chance remark that fell from her lips was repeated with some distortion to make it incriminating. This was just what Cromwell wanted, and he was therefore pleased with these two women. Those ladies whom she would have liked to have beside her, were not allowed to come to her. She longed to talk with Margaret Lee and Mary Wyatt, with her own sister Mary, with Madge; but no, she must be followed, no matter where she went, by these two odious females or by Lady Kingston who was as cold as her husband and had little sympathy, having seen too much suffering in her capacity of wife of the Constable of the Tower to have much to spare for one who, before this evil fate had befallen her, had enjoyed in plenty the good things of life.

But news filtered through to Anne. Her brother had been arrested. On what charge? Incest! Oh, but this was grotesque! How could they say such things! It was a joke; George would laugh; they could not hurt George. What had George done to deserve this? 'For myself,' she cried, 'I have been foolish and careless and over-fond of flattery. I have been vain and stupid. . . . But oh, my sweet brother, what have you ever done but help me! I would die a thousand deaths rather than you should suffer so through me.'

The sly women nodded, carefully going over what she had said. By eliminating a word here, a sentence there, they could give a very good account of themselves to Thomas Cromwell.

'Wyatt here!' she exclaimed. 'Here in the Tower?' And she wept for Wyatt, calling him Dear Thomas, and was over-wrought, recalling the happy days of childhood.

'Norris is here. Norris accused me. . . . Oh, I cannot believe it of Norris. . . . Oh, I cannot! He would never betray me.'

She could not believe that Norris would betray her! Then, argued Cromwell, if she cannot believe he would betray her, is not that an admission that there is something to betray?

When she was tired, they would pretend to soothe her, laying wily traps.

'What of the unhappy gentlemen in the Tower?' she wanted to know. 'Will any make their beds?'

'No, I'll warrant you; they'll have none to make their beds!'

She showed great solicitude for the comfort of her paramours, they reported.

'Ballads will be made about me,' she said, smiling suddenly. 'None can do that better than Wyatt.'

She spoke with great admiration and feeling of Thomas Wyatt, they then told Cromwell.

She wept bitterly for her baby. 'What will become of her? Who will care for her now? I feel death close to me, because I know of her whom the King would set up in my place, but how can he set up a new queen when he has a queen already living? And what of my baby? She is not yet three. It is so very young, is it not? Could I not see her? Oh, plead for me please! Have you never thought how a mother might long for a last glimpse of her daughter! No, no. Bring her not to me. What would she think to see me thus! I should weep over her and frighten her, since the thought of her frightens me, for she is so very young to be left alone in a cruel world. . . . Say not that I wish to see my baby.'

Her eyes were round with fear. They would be so clever at thinking up fresh mental torture for her to bear. Not that though! Not Elizabeth!

'She will be playing in her nursery now. What will become of her? After all, is she not the King's daughter?'

Then she began to laugh shrilly, and her laughter ended in violent weeping. For she thought, They will call her bastard now perhaps . . . and this is a judgment on me for my unkindness to Katharine's daughter Mary. Oh, Katharine, forgive me. I knew not then what it meant to have a daughter. And what if the King . . .

But she could not think; she dared not. Oh, but she knew him, cold and relentless and calculating, and having need to rid himself of her. Already she was accused with five men, and one of them her own, and so innocently loved, brother. What if he said Elizabeth were not his child? What will he care for her, hating her mother? And if he marries Jane Seymour . . . if she is Queen, will she be kind to my baby daughter . . . as I was to Mary? Jesus, forgive me. I was wicked. I was wrong . . . and now this is my punishment. It will happen to me as it happened to Katharine, and there will be none to care for my daughter, as there was none to care for Mary.

Such thoughts must set her weeping; then remembering that when she had become Henry's Queen she had chosen as her device 'Happiest of Women', she laughed bitterly and long.

'How she weeps! How she laughs!' whispered the women. 'How unstable she is . . . hysterical and afraid! Does not her behaviour tend to show her guilt?'

She talked a good deal; she did not sleep; she lay staring into the darkness, thinking back over the past, trying to peer into the future. Despair enveloped her. The King is cruel and cold; he can always find a righteous answer when he wishes to do some particularly cruel deed. I am lost.

There is naught can save me now! Hope came to her. But he loved me once; once there was nothing he would not do for me. Even to the last I could amuse him, and I tried hard enough. . . . I could delight him more than any an I gave myself up to it. He does this but to try me. He will come to me soon; all will be well.

But no! I am here in the Tower and they say evil things of me. My friends are here. George, my darling, my sweet brother, the only one I could truly trust in the whole world. And they know that! That is why they have sent you here, George; that is why they imprison you; so that I shall have none to help me now.

She asked for writing materials. She would write; she would try to forget his cruel eyes; she would try to forget him as he was now and remember him as he used to be when he had said the name of Anne Boleyn was the sweetest music in his ears.

The words flowed impulsively from her pen.

'Your Grace's displeasure and my imprisonment are things so strange unto me, that what to write or what to excuse, I am altogether ignorant. . . .'

She wrote hastily, hope coming back to her as her pen moved swiftly along.

'Never a prince had wife more loyal in all duty, and in all true affection, than you have ever found in Anne Boleyn – with which name and place I could willingly have contented myself if God and your Grace's pleasure had so been pleased. Neither did I at any time so far forget myself in my exaltation, or received queenship, but that I always looked for such alteration as I now found; for the ground of my preferment being on no surer foundation than your Grace's fancy, the least alteration was fit and sufficient (I knew) to draw that fancy to some other subject.'

She paused. Was she over-bold? She felt death close to her and cared not.

'You have chosen me from low estate to be your Queen and companion, far beyond my desert or desire; if then you found me worthy of such honour, good your Grace, let not any light fancy or bad counsel of my enemies, withdraw your princely favour from me, neither let that stain – that unworthy stain – of a disloyal heart towards your good Grace, ever cast so foul a blot on me and on the infant Princess your daughter Elizabeth.

'Try me, good King, but let me have a lawful trial and let not my sworn enemies sit as my accusers and as my judges; yea, let me receive an open trial, for my truth shall fear no open shames; then shall you see either my innocency cleared, your suspicions and conscience satisfied, the ignominy and slander of the world stopped, or my guilt openly declared. So that whatever God and you may determine of, your Grace may be freed from an open censure, and mine offence being so lawfully proved, your Grace may be at liberty, both before God and man, not only to execute worthy punishment on me, as an unfaithful wife, but to follow your affection already settled on that party, for whose sake I am now as I am; whose name I could, some good while since, have pointed unto; your Grace being not ignorant of my suspicion therein.'

Her cheeks burned with anger as her pen flew on.

'But if you have already determined of me, and that not only my death, but an infamous slander, must bring you the joying of your desired happiness, then, I desire of God that he will pardon your great sin herein, and, likewise, my enemies, the instruments thereof, and that He will not call you to a strait account of your unprincely and cruel usage of me, at his general judgment seat, where both you and myself must shortly appear; and in whose just judgment I doubt not (whatsoever the world may think of me) mine innocency shall be openly known, and sufficiently cleared.'

She laid down her pen, a bitter smile about her lips. That would touch him as she knew so well how to touch him, and as she, among all those around him, alone had the courage to touch him. She was reckless of herself, and though she may have been foolish and vain she clung to her magnificent courage. If he ever read those words with their reference to the judgment of God he would tremble in his shoes, and no matter how he might present them to his conscience, they would disturb him to the end of his days. He would think of them when he lay with Jane Seymour; and she exulted in that power over him which she would wield from the grave. She was sure that he intended to murder her; in cold blood he planned this, as any commoner might plan to put away a wife of whom he had tired, by beating her to death or stabbing her with a knife or throwing her body into the dark river. She was terrified, experiencing all the alarm of a woman who knows herself to be followed in the dark by a footpad with murder in his heart. Such women, who were warned of an impending fate, might call for help; but there was none who could come to her aid, for her murderer would be the mightiest man in England whose anger none could curb, for whose crimes the archbishops themselves would find a righteous excuse.

She began to cry in very fear, and her thoughts went from her own troubles to those of the men who would be required to shed their blood with her, and she blamed herself, for was it not her love of flattery that had led them to express their feelings too openly? Was it not her desire to show the King that though he might prefer others, there were always men to prefer her, which had brought about this tragedy?

She took up her pen once more.

'My last and only request shall be, that myself may only bear the burden of your Grace's displeasure, and that it may not touch the innocent souls of those poor gentlemen, who, as I understand, are likewise in strait imprisonment for my sake.

'If ever I have found favour in your sight – if ever the name of Anne Boleyn have been pleasing in your ears – then let me obtain this request; and so I will leave to trouble your Grace any further : with mine earnest prayer to the Trinity to have your Grace in his good keeping, and to direct you in all your actions.

'From my doleful prison in the Tower, the 6th of May.

ANNE BOLEYN.'

She felt better after having written that letter; she would keep the writing materials with her that she might write now and then. She was wretched though, wondering how her letter would reach the King. She pictured its falling into Cromwell's hands, which was likely, for he had his spies all about her, and it could hardly be hoped that the letter would find its way through them to the King. If by good luck it did, he could not be unmoved by her words, she felt sure. He who had once upbraided her for not writing frequently enough, surely would read this last letter.

But she was afraid, sensing her doom, knowing her husband too well, knowing how he was placed, how he must find a way to marry Jane Seymour and appease his conscience; and thinking on these matters, hope, which had come to her through the writing of the letter, was swallowed up once more in deepest despondency.

*   *   *

Smeaton lay in his cell. He was no longer a beautiful boy; his dark curls were tangled and matted with blood and sweat; his delicate features were swollen with pain and grief. It seemed to him that there were but two emotions in the world – that of suffering pain and that of having no pain. One was agony; the other bliss.

He had scarcely been aware of the solemn atmosphere of the courtroom of the men who stood on trial with him; he had answered when he had been questioned, answered mechanically as they wanted him to answer, for he knew that not to do so would be to invite pain to come to him once more.

'Guilty!' he cried. 'Guilty! Guilty!' And before his eyes he saw, not the judge and the jurymen, but the dark room with the smell of blood and death about it, mingling with the odour of vinegar; he saw the dim light, heard the sickening creak of rollers, felt again the excruciating pain of bones being torn from their sockets.

He could but walk slowly to the place assigned to him; every movement was agony; he would never stand up straight again; he would never walk with springy step; he would never let his fingers caress a musical instrument and draw magic from it.

A big bearded man came to him as he lay in his cell and

would have speech with him. He held a paper in his hand. He said Mark must sign the paper.

'Dost know the just reward of low born traitors, Mark?' a voice whispered in his ear.

No! He did not know; he could not think; pain had robbed him of his power to use both his limbs and his mind.

Hung by the neck, but not to die. Disembowelled. Did Mark wish him to go on? Had not Mark seen how the monks of the Charterhouse had died? They had died traitors' deaths, and Mark was a traitor even as they had been.

Pain! He screamed at the thought of it; it was as though every nerve in his body cried out in protest. A prolongation of that torture he had suffered in that gloomy dungeon? No, no! Not that!

He was sobbing, and the great Fitzwilliam, leaning over him, whispered: ' 'Tis not necessary, Mark. 'Tis not necessary at all. Just pen your name to this paper, and it shall not happen to you. You shall have naught to fear.'

Paper? 'Where is it?' asked Mark, not What is it? He dared not ask that, though he seemed to see the Queen's beautiful black eyes reproaching him. He was not quite sure whether he was in the cell or in her presence chamber; he was trying to explain to her. Ah, Madam, you know not the pains of the torture chamber; it is more than human flesh can stand.

'Sign here, Mark. Come! Let me guide your hand.'

'What then? What then?' he cried. 'No more . . . no more. . . .'

'No more, Mark. All you need do is sign your name. Subscribe here, Mark, and you shall see what will come of it.'

His hand guided by Fitzwillian, he put his name to the statement prepared for him.

Sir Francis Weston, the beautiful and very rich young man, whose wife and mother offered the King a very large ransom for his freedom, could face death more stoically. So it was with Sir William Brereton. Handsome, debonair, full of the spirit of adventure they had come to court; they had seen others go to the block on the flimsiest of excuses. They lived in an age of terror and had been prepared for the

411

death sentence from the moment they entered the Tower. Guiltless they were, but what of that? Their jury was picked; so were the judges; the result was a foregone conclusion and the trial a farce; and they were knowledgeable enough to know this. They remembered Buckingham who had gone to the block ostensibly on a charge of treason, but actually because of his relationship to the King; now they, in their turn, would go to the block on a charge of treason, when the real reason for their going was the King's desire to rid himself of his present Queen and take another before her child was born. It was brutal, but it was simple. Court law was jungle law, and the king of beasts was a roaring man-eating lion who spared none – man nor woman – from his lustful egoistical demands.

They remembered that they were gentlemen; they prayed that no matter what befell them, they might go on remembering it. Mark Smeaton had perjured his soul and sullied his honour; they trusted that whatever torment they were called upon to face, they would not sink so low. They took their cue from their older companion, Norris, who, grave and stoical, faced his judges.

'Not guilty!' said Norris.

'Not guilty!' echoed Weston and Brereton.

It mattered not; they were found guilty, and sentenced to death, all four of them – the block for three of them and the hangman's noose for Mark on account of his low birth.

The King was angry with these three men. How dared they stand up in the courtroom, looking such haughty heroes, and pronounce in ringing tones that they were not guilty! The people were sentimental, and he thanked God that Anne had ever been disliked and resented by them. They would not have a word to say in favour of her now; they would be glad to see the end of her, the witch, the would-be-poisoner, the black-browed sorceress, the harlot. He thanked God there would be none ready to defend her. Her father? Oh, Thomas, Earl of Wiltshire, was not very much in evidence these days. He was sick and sorry, and ready to obey his King, fearful lest he should be brought in to face trial with his wicked daughter and son. Norfolk?

There was none more pleased than Norfolk to see Anne brought low. They had been quarrelling for years. Suffolk, her old enemy, was rubbing his hands in glee. Northumberland? A pox on Northumberland! Sick and ailing! A fine champion, he! He should be appointed one of her judges and he should see what would happen to him were he to oppose his King. He had been in trouble over Anne Boleyn before; doubtless he would be so again. There was none to fear. My Lord Rochford, that foul, unnatural monster, was safe under lock and key, and what had he with which to defend himself and his sister but a tongue of venom! Anne should see what price she would pay for laughing at the King, first bewitching him and then deceiving him. No one else, girl, he said viciously, shall kiss your pretty lips, unless they like to kiss them cold; nor would they find the head of you so lovely without the body that goes with it!

But a pox on these men, and all would-be-martyrs! There they stood, side by side, on trial for their lives, and though Cromwell could be trusted to find evidence against them, though they were traitors, lechers, all of them, people would murmur: 'So young to die! So handsome! So noble! Could such bravery belong to guilty men? And even if they are guilty, who has not loved recklessly in his life? Why, the King himself . . .'

Enough! He called Cromwell to him.

'Go to Norris!' he commanded. 'I liked that man. Why, he was an intimate friend of mine. Tell him I know the provocation of the Queen. Tell him I know how she could, an she wished it, be wellnigh irresistible. Go to him and tell him I will be merciful. Offer him his life in exchange for a full confession of his guilt.'

Cromwell went, and returned.

'Ah, Your Most Clement Majesty, that there should be such ungrateful subjects in your realm!'

'What said he then?' asked Henry, and he was trembling for the answer. He wanted to show Norris's confession to his court; he would have it read to his people.

'His reply is the same as that he made Your Majesty before. He would rather die a thousand deaths than accuse the Queen who is innocent.'

Henry lost control.

'Hang him up then!' he screamed. 'Hang him up!'

He stamped out of the room and he seemed to see the bodyless head of More and there was a mocking smile about the mouth.

'A thousand curses on all martyrs!' muttered Henry.

*   *   *

The room in which Anne and her brother would be tried had been hastily erected within the great hall of the Tower. Courageously she entered it, and faced that row of peers who had been selected by the King to try her, and she saw at once that he had succeeded in confronting her with her most bitter enemies. Chief among them was the Duke of Suffolk, his hateful red face aglow with pleasure; there was also the young Duke of Richmond who was firmly against her, because he had had hopes of the throne, illegitimate though he might be; he was influenced by his father the King, and the Duke of Norfolk who had become his father-in-law when he had married the Lady Mary Howard, the Duke's daughter.

Anne had schooled herself for the ordeal; she was determined that she would not break down before her enemies; but she almost lost control to see Percy among those whom the King had named Lord-Triers. He looked at her across the room, and it seemed to them both that the years were swept away and that they were young and in love and from the happiness of a little room in Hampton Court were taking a terrified peep into a grim future. Percy, weak with his physical defects, turned deathly pale at the sight of her; but she lifted her head higher and smiled jauntily, shaming him with her readiness to face whatever life brought her. Percy was not of her calibre. He crumpled and fell to the floor in a faint. How could he condemn her whom he had never been able to forget? And yet, how could he not condemn her, when it was the King's wish that she should be condemned? Percy could not face this, as years before he had not been able to face the wrath of Wolsey, his father and the King. He was genuinely ill at the prospect and had to be carried out of the courtroom.

Thank God, thought Anne, that her father was not among those who were to try her! She had feared he would be, for it would have been characteristic of Henry to have forced him to this and characteristic of her father that he would have obeyed his King and sent his daughter to her death. She had escaped the shame of seeing her father's shame.

She listened to the list of crimes for which she was being tried. She had, they were saying, wronged the King with four persons and also with her brother. She was said to have conspired with them against the King's life. Cromwell's ingenuity had even supplied the dates on which the acts had taken place; she could smile bitterly at these, for the first offence – supposed to have been committed with Norris – was fixed for an occasion when she, having just given birth to Elizabeth, had not left the lying-in chamber.

As she faced her accusers she seemed to see the doubts that beset them. There could not be any of these men who did not know that she was here because the King wished to replace her with Jane Seymour. Oh, justice! she thought. If I could but be sure of justice!

The decision of the peers was not required to be unanimous; a majority was all that was necessary to destroy her. But Suffolk's hot eyes were surveying those about him as though to tell them he watched for any who would disobey the King's desires.

Outside in the streets, where men and women stood about in groups, the atmosphere was stormy. If Anne could have seen these people her spirits would have been lightened. Many eyes wept for her, though once their owners had abused her. At the height of her power they had called her whore; now they could not believe that one who carried herself with such nobility and courage could be anything but innocent. Mothers remembered that she had a child scarcely three years old. A terrible, tragic fate overhung her, and she had the pity of the people as Katharine and Mary had had it before her.

Suffolk knew what people were thinking; he knew what some of the Lord-Triers were thinking. This was a reign of terror. Bluff Hal had removed his mask and shown a monster who thought nothing of murder and of inhuman torture to herald it in. A man would be a fool to run his body into torment for the sake of Anne Boleyn. Suffolk won the day and they pronounced her guilty.

'Condemned to be burnt or beheaded, at the King's pleasure!' said the Duke of Norfolk, savouring each word as though it held a flavour very sweet to his palate.

She did not change colour; she did not flinch. She could look into the cruel eyes of her enemies and she could say, her voice firm, her head high, her eyes imperious: 'God hath taught me how to die, and he will strengthen my faith.'

She smiled haughtily at the group of men. 'I am willing to believe that you have sufficient reasons for what you have done, but then they must be other than those which have been produced in court.'

Even Suffolk must squirm at those words; even Norfolk must turn his head away in shame.

But her voice broke suddenly when she mentioned her brother.

'As for my brother and those others who are unjustly accused, I would willingly suffer many deaths to deliver them.'

The Lord Mayor was very shaken, knowing now for certain what he had before suspected, that they had found nothing against her, only that they had resolved to make an occasion to get rid of her.

*　　　*　　　*

Back in her room, Anne relived it over and over again; she thanked God for the strength which had been hers; she prayed that she might have sustained courage.

Lady Kingston unbent a little now that she had been condemned to die and Mary Wyatt was allowed to come to her.

'You cannot know what comfort it is to me to see you here, Mary,' she said.

416

'You cannot know what comfort it gives me to come,' answered Mary.

'Weep not, Mary. This was inevitable. Do you not see it now? From the first moments in the garden of Hever. . . . But my thoughts run on. You know not of that occasion; nor do I wish to recall it. Ah, Mary, had I been good and sweet and humble as you ever were, this would never have befallen me. I was ambitious, Mary. I wanted a crown upon my head. Yet, looking back, I know not where I could have turned to tread another road. You must not weep, dear Mary, for soon I shall be past all pain. I should not talk of myself. What of George, Mary? Oh, what news of my sweet brother?'

Mary did not answer, but the tears which she could not restrain, were answer enough.

'He defended himself most nobly, that I do not need to be told,' said Anne. Her eyes sparkled suddenly. 'I wonder he did not confound them. Mary, dost remember old days at Blickling and Hever! When he had done aught that merited punishment, could he not always most convincingly defend himself? But this time . . . what had he done? He had loved his sister. May not a brother love his sister, but there must be those to say evil of him? Ah, George, this time when you were truly innocent, you could not save yourself. This was not Blickling, George! This was not Hever! This was the wicked court of Henry, my husband, who now seeks to murder me as he will murder you!'

'Be calm,' said Mary. 'Anne, Anne, you were so brave before those men. You must be brave now.'

'I would rather be the victim of a murderer, Mary, than be a murderer. Tell me of George.'

'He was right noble in his defence. Even Suffolk could scarce accuse him. There was much speculation in court. It was said: "None could name this man guilty!"'

'And what said they of . . . me and George?'

'They said what you would have expected them to say! Jane was there . . . a witness against him.'

'Jane!' Anne threw back her head and laughed. 'I would not be in Jane's shoes for years of life. Liar and perjurer that she is. She . . . out of jealousy, to bear false witness against her husband! But what could she say of him and me? What *could* she say?'

'She said that on one occasion he did come to your chamber while you were abed. He came to make some request and he kissed you. There seemed little else. It was shameful. They had naught against him. They could not call him guilty, but he . . .'

'Tell me all, Mary. Hold nothing back from me. Know you not what this means to me to have you here with me at last, after my dreary captivity with them that hate me? Be frank with me, Mary. Hold nothing back, for frankness is for friends.'

'They handed him a paper, Anne, for on it was a question they dared not ask and he . . .'

'Yes? What did he?'

'He, knowing how it would sorely discountenance them, should he read aloud what was written, read it aloud, in his reckless and impulsive way.'

'Ah! I know him well. For so would I have done in an unguarded moment. He had nothing but contempt for that group of selected peers – selected by the King whose one object is to destroy us – and he showed it by reading aloud that which was meant to be kept secret. It was of the King?'

Mary nodded. 'That the King was not able to have children; that there was no virtue or potency in him. He was asked if he had ever said such things. And he read that aloud. No man could be allowed to live after that. But he meant to show his contempt for them all; he meant to show that he knew he had been condemned to die before the trial began. He asked then to plead Guilty, solely that he might prevent his property passing into the hands of the King. The King could have his life but he should not have his goods.'

'Oh, George!' cried Anne. 'And you to scold me for reckless folly! Mary, I cannot but weep, not for myself but for my brother. I led the way; he followed. I should go to the block for my careless ambition, for my foolish vanity. But that I should take him with me! Oh, Mary, I cannot bear that, so I weep and am most miserable. Oh, Mary, sit by me.

Talk to me of our childhood. Thomas! What of Thomas? I cannot bear to think on those I have loved and brought to disaster.'

'Grieve not for Thomas. He would not have it so. He would not have you shed one tear for him, for well you know he ever loved you dearly. We hope for Thomas. He was not tried with the rest. Perhaps he will just be a prisoner awhile, for it is strange that he should not be tried with the others.'

'Pray for him, Mary. Pray that this awful fate may not befall him. Mayhap they have forgotten Thomas. Oh, pray that they have forgotten Thomas.'

When Mary left her she lay on her bed. She felt happier. Rather my lot, she thought, than the King's. Rather my lot, than Jane Rochford's. I would rather mine were the hapless head that rolled in the straw, than mine the murderous hand that signs the death warrant.

* * *

She was preparing herself for a journey. A summons had been brought to her that she was to make ready to go to the Archbishop at Lambeth. She was to go quietly; this was the King's order. He wanted no hysterical crowds on the river's bank to cheer her barge. He himself had received a copy of the summons, but he would not go; he would send his old proctor, Doctor Sampson, to represent him. Come face to face with Anne Boleyn! Never! There were too many memories between them. What if she tried her witcheries on him once more!

He felt shaken and ill at ease. He was sleeping badly; he would wake startled from bad dreams, calling her name and, with the daze of sleep still on him, think she was there beside him. He had despatched Jane Seymour to her father's house, since that was the most seemly place for her to be in. He did not wish to have her with him during the critical days, as he had announced that he was deeply grieved at the falseness of his wife and would not take another unless his people wished it. Jane should therefore not attract much attention. Her condition – early in pregnancy though she was – must be considered. So Henry sat alone, awaiting news from Lambeth; whilst Anne, who would have liked to refuse to answer the summons, left the Tower and went quietly up the river.

She was conducted to the crypt of the Archbishop's residence and awaiting her there were Cranmer, looking troubled but determined to do his duty, Cromwell, looking more sly and ugly than ever, Doctor Sampson, to represent the King, and two doctors Wotton and Barbour, who, most farcically, were supposed to represent her.

She had not been there for more than a few moments when she realized their cunning purpose.

Cranmer's voice was silky. There was no man who could present a case as he could. His voice almost caressed her, expressing sympathy for her most unhappy state.

She was under the sentence of death, he said, by beheading . . . or burning.

Did he mean to stress that last word, or did she imagine this? The way in which he said it made her hot with fear; she felt as though the flames were already scorching her flesh.

The King's conscience, went on Cranmer, troubled him sorely. She had been pre-contracted to Northumberland! That, she would understand, would make her marriage with the King illegal.

She cried: 'Northumberland was brought before you. You yourself accepted . . .'

Cranmer was quiet and calm, so capable of adjusting his opinion, so clever, so intellectual, so impossible to confound.

The King himself had been indiscreet. Yes, His Majesty was ready to admit it. An association with Anne's sister. An affinity created.

Cranmer spread his hands as though to say, Now, you see how it is. You were never really married to the King!

She could hold her head high in the crypt at Lambeth as she had in that other court where they had condemned her. They would need her acknowledgment of this, would they not? Well, they should never get it.

Cranmer was pained and sad. He had loved her well, he said.

She thought, How I hate all hypocrites! Fool I may be but I am no hypocrite. How I hate you, Cranmer! I helped you to your present position. You too, Cromwell. But neither of you would think of helping me! But Cranmer I hate more than Cromwell for Cranmer is a hypocrite, and perhaps I hate this in men because I am married to the most shameless one that ever lived.

Cranmer was talking in his deep sonorous voice. He had a gift for making suggestions without expressing actual statements. She was thinking, I have my little daughter to consider. She shall never be called bastard.

Cranmer's voice went droning on. He was hinting at her release. There was a pleasant convent at Antwerp. What of the young men whose fate she deplored and whose innocence she proclaimed? All the country knew how she esteemed her brother, and he her. Was he to go to the block? What of her daughter? The King would be more inclined to favour a child whose mother had impressed him with her good sense.

Anne's mind was working quickly. It was painfully clear. She must make a choice. If her marriage to the King were proved null and void then that was all he need ask of her. He could marry Jane Seymour immediately if his marriage with Anne Boleyn had been no marriage at all. The child Jane carried would be born in wedlock. And for this, Anne was offered a convent in Antwerp, the lives of her brother and those innocent men who were to die with him. And if not . . . Once more she was hot with the imaginary fire that licked her limbs. And what would her refusal mean in any case? If the King had decided to disinherit Elizabeth, he would surely do so. He had ever found excuses for what he wished to do.

She had something to gain and nothing to lose, for if she had not been married to the King, how could she have committed adultery? The affairs of Lady Anne Rochford and the Marchioness of Pembroke could not be called treason to the King.

Her hopes were soaring. She thought, Oh, George, my darling, I have saved you! You shall not die. Gladly I will throw away my crown to save you!

Cromwell went back to his master rubbing his ugly hands with pleasure. Once more he had succeeded. The King was free to take a new wife whenever he wished, for he had never been married to Anne Boleyn. She herself had agreed upon it.

* * *

It was over. They had tricked her. At the King's command she had stood and watched them as they passed by her window on their way to Tower Hill. She had sacrificed her own and her daughter's rights in vain. Although she was no queen, these men had died. It was not reasonable; it was not logical; it was simply murder.

She herself had yet another day to live through. Mary Wyatt came to tell her how nobly these men had died, following the example of George, how they had made their speeches, which etiquette demanded, on the scaffold, how they had met their deaths bravely.

'What of Smeaton?' she asked. She thought of him still as a soft-eyed boy, and she could not believe that he would not tell the truth on the scaffold. Mary was silent and Anne cried out: 'Has he not cleared me of the public shame he hath done me!' She surveyed Mary's silent face in horror. 'Alas,' she said at length and in great sorrow, 'I fear his soul will suffer from the false witness he hath borne.'

Her face lightened suddenly.

'Oh, Mary,' she cried, 'it will not be long now. My brother and the rest are now, I doubt not, before the face of the greater King, and I shall follow tomorrow.'

When Mary left her her sadness returned. She wished they had not given her fresh hope in the Lambeth Crypt. She had resigned herself to death, and then they had promised her she should live, and life was so sweet. She was twenty-nine and beautiful; and though she had thought herself weary of living, when they had given her that peep into a possible future, how eagerly she had grasped at it!

She thought of her daughter, and trembled. Three is so very young. She would not understand what had happened to her mother. Oh, let them be kind to Elizabeth.

She asked that Lady Kingston might come to her, and when the woman came she locked the door and with tears running down her cheeks, asked that Lady Kingston would sit in her chair of state.

Lady Kingston herself was moved in face of such distress.

'It is my duty to stand in the presence of the Queen, Madam,' she said.

'That title is gone,' was the answer. 'I am a condemned person, and I have no estate left me in this life, but for the clearing of my conscience, I pray you sit down.'

She began to weep, and her talk was incoherent, and humbly she fell upon her knees and begged that Lady Kingston would go to Mary, the daughter of Katharine, and kneel before her and beg that she would forgive Anne Boleyn for the wrong she had done her.

'For, my Lady Kingston,' she said, 'till this be accomplished, my conscience cannot be quiet.'

After that she was more at peace and did not need to thrust the thought of her daughter from her mind.

The news was brought to her that her death should not take place at the appointed hour; there had been a postponement. She had been almost gay, and to learn that she was to have a few more hours on Earth was a disappointment to her.

'Mr Kingston,' she said, 'I hear I shall not die afore noon, and I am very sorry therefore, for I thought to be dead by this time and past my pain.'

'The pain will be little,' he told her gently, 'it is so subtle.'

She answered: 'I have heard say the executioner is very good, and I have a little neck.'

She embraced it with her hands and laughed; and when her laughter had subsided, a great peace came to her. She had another day to live and she had heard that the King wished the hour of her execution to be kept secret, and that it was not to take place on Tower Hill where any idle spectator might see her die, but on the enclosed green; for the King feared the reactions of the people.

The evening passed; she was gay and melancholy in turns; she joked about her end. 'I shall be easily nick-named – "Queen Anne . . . *sans tête*".'

She occupied herself in writing her own dirge.

> '*Oh death, rock me asleep,*
> *Bring on my quiet rest,*
> *Let pass my very guiltless ghost*
> *Out of my careful breast.*
> *Ring out the doleful knell*
> *Let its sound my death tell;*
> *For I must die,*
> *There is no remedy,*
> *For now I die . . .*'

*　　　*　　　*

She dressed herself with such care that it might have been a state banquet to which she was going instead of to the scaffold. Her robe of grey damask was trimmed with fur and low cut; beneath this showed a kirtle of crimson. Her head-dress was trimmed with pearls. She had never looked more beautiful; her cheeks were flushed, her eyes brilliant, and all the misery and fear of the last weeks seemed to have been lifted from her face.

Attended by four ladies, among them her beloved Mary Wyatt, with much dignity and grace she walked to the green before the church of St Peter ad Vincula. Slowly and calmly she ascended the steps to that platform which was strewn with straw; and she could smile because there were so few people to witness her last moments, smile because the hour and place of her execution had had to be kept secret from the people.

Among those who had gathered about the scaffold she saw the Dukes of Suffolk and Richmond, but she could feel no enmity towards these two now. She saw Thomas Cromwell whose eldest son was now married to Jane Seymour's sister. Ah, thought Anne, when my head has rolled into the sawdust, he will feel an impediment lifted and his relationship to the King almost an accomplished fact.

She called to her one whom she knew to be of the King's privy chamber, and said she would send a message by him to the King.

'Commend me to His Majesty,' she said, 'and tell him that he hath ever been constant in his career of advancing me; from a private gentlewoman, he made me a marchioness, from a marchioness a queen, and now he hath left no higher degree of honour, he gives my innocency the crown of martyrdom.'

The messenger trembled for she was a woman about to die, and how could he dare carry such a message to the King!

Then she would, after the etiquette of the scaffold, make her dying speech.

'Good Christian people,' she said, 'I am come hither to die, according to law, for by the law I am judged to die, and therefore I will speak nothing against it . . .'

Her ladies were so overcome with weeping that she, hearing their sobs, was deeply moved.

'I come hither to accuse no man,' she continued, 'nor to speak anything of that whereof I am accused, as I know full well that aught that I say in my defence doth not appertain to you . . .'

When she spoke of the King, her words were choked. Cromwell moved nearer to the scaffold. This was the moment he and the King had most feared. But with death so near she cared nothing for revenge. All the bitterness had gone out of her. Cromwell would arrange the words she spoke, not only as they should best please the King, but also that they should mislead the public into thinking she had died justly. The people must be told that at the end she had only praise for the King, that she spoke of him as a merciful prince and a gentle sovereign lord.

Her voice cleared and she went on: 'If any person will meddle with my cause I require them to judge the best. Thus I take my leave of the world and of you, and I heartily desire you all to pray for me.'

It was time for her now to lay her head upon the block and there was not one of her attendants whose hands were steady enough to remove her headdress; they could only turn from her in blind misery. She smiled and did this herself; then she spoke to each of them gently, bidding them not to grieve and thanking them for their services to her. Mary she took aside and to her gave a little book of devotions as a parting gift and whispered into her ear a message of good cheer that she might give it to her brother in the Tower.

Then she was ready. She laid her head upon the block. Her lips were murmuring her own verses.

> 'Farewell my pleasures past,
> Welcome my present pain,
> I feel my torments so increase
> That life cannot remain.
> Sound now the passing bell,
> Rung is my doleful knell,
> For its sound my death doth tell.
> Death doth draw nigh,
> Sound the knell dolefully,
> For now I die.'

She was waiting now, waiting for that swift stroke, that quick and subtle pain.

'Oh, Lord God have pity on my soul. Oh, Lord God . . .'

Her lips were still moving as her head lay on the straw.

*   *   *

The Dowager Duchess of Norfolk was weeping bitterly as she went about the Lambeth House. Catherine Howard flung herself onto her bed and wept. Over the city of London hung silence. The Queen was dead.

At Richmond the King waited for the booming of the gun which would announce the end of Anne Boleyn. He waited in anxiety; he was terrified of what she might say to those watching crowds. He knew that the people who had never accepted her as their Queen, were now ready to make of her a martyr.

His horse was restive, longing to be off; but not more so

than he. Would he never hear the signal! What were they at, those fools? What if some had planned a rescue! He was hot at the thought. There had been men who loved her dearly and none knew better than he did, how easy it was to do that. She had changed his life when she came into it; what would she do when she went out of it?

He pictured her last moments; he knew she would show great courage; he knew she would show dignity; he knew she would be beautiful enough to stir up pity in the hearts of all who beheld her. It was well that but few were sure of hour and place.

Around him were hounds and huntsmen. This night the hunt would end at Wolf Hall whether the stag led them there or not. But the waiting was long, and try as he might he could not forget Anne Boleyn.

He spoke to his conscience, 'Thank God I can now leave Mary without constant fear that she will meet a horrible end. Thank God I discovered the evil ways of this harlot.'

He had done right, he assured himself. Katharine had suffered through her; Mary had suffered. Thank God he had found out in time! Thank God he had turned his affections on a more worthy object!

What would the people say when they heard the gun booming from the Tower? What would they say of a man who went to a new bride before the body of his wife was cold?

Along the river came the dismal booming of the gun. He heard it; his mouth twisted into a line of mingling joy and apprehension.

'The deed is done!' he cried. 'Uncouple the hounds and away!'

So he rode on, on to Wolf Hall, on to marriage with Jane Seymour.

THE DOWAGER DUCHESS of Norfolk was in bed and very sad. A new queen reigned in the place of her granddaughter; a pale-faced creature with scarcely any eyebrows so that she looked for ever surprised, a meek, insipid, vapid woman; and to put her on the throne had the King sent beautiful Anne to the block. The Duchess's dreams were haunted by her granddaughter, and she would awaken out of them sweating and trembling. She had just had such a dream, and thought she had stood among those spectators who had watched Anne submit her lovely head to the Executioner's sword.

She began to weep into her bedclothes, seeing again Anne at court, Anne at Lambeth; she remembered promised favours which would never now be hers. She could rail against the King in the privacy her bedchamber offered her. Fat! Coarse! Adulterer! And forty-five! While Anne at twenty-nine had lost her lovely head that that slut Seymour might sit beside him on the throne!

'Much good will she do him!' murmured the Duchess. 'Give the King a son quickly, Mistress Seymour, or your head will not stay on your shoulders more than a year or two, I warrant you! And I'll be there to see the deed done; I swear it!' She began to chuckle throatily, remembering that she had heard but a week or so after his marriage to Jane had been announced, the King, on meeting two very beautiful young women, had shown himself to be – and even mentioned this fact – sorry that he had not seen them before he married Jane. It had not been so with Anne. She had absorbed his attention, and it was only when she could not produce a son that her enemies had dared to plot against her. 'Bound to Serve and Obey.' That was the device chosen by Jane. 'You'll serve, my dear!' muttered the Duchess. 'But whether you produce a son or not remains to be seen, and if you do not, why then you must very meekly obey, by laying your head on the block. You'll have your enemies just as my sweet Anne did!' The Duchess dried her eyes and set her lips firmly together as she thought of one of the greatest of those enemies, both to Anne and herself, and one with whom she must continually be on her guard – her own stepson and Anne's uncle, the Duke of Norfolk.

Some of the Duchess's ladies came in to help her dress. Stupid girls they were. She scolded them, for she thought their hands over-rough as they forced her bulk into clothes too small for it.

'Katharine Tylney! I declare you scratch me with those nails of yours. I declare you did it apurpose! Take that!'

Katharine Tylney scowled at the blow. The old Duchess's temper had been very bad since the execution of the Queen, and the least thing sent it flaring up. Katharine Tylney shrugged her shoulders at Mistress Wilkes and Mistress Baskerville, the two who were also assisting with the Duchess's toilet. When they were beyond the range of the Duchess's ears they would curse the old woman, laughing at her obscenity and her ill-temper, laughing because she who was so fat and old and ugly was vain as a young girl, and would have just the right amount of embroidered kirtle showing beneath her skirt, and would deck herself in costly jewels even in the morning.

The Duchess wheezed and scolded while her thoughts ran on poor Anne and sly Jane and that absurd fancy of the King's, which had made him change the one for the other; she brooded on the cunning of that low-born brute Cromwell, and the cruelty of Norfolk and Suffolk, until she herself felt as though she were standing almost as near the edge of that active volcano as Anne herself had stood.

She dismissed the women and went slowly into her presence chamber to receive the first of her morning callers. She was fond of ceremony and herself kept an establishment here at Lambeth – as she had at Norfolk – like a queen's. As she entered the chamber, she saw a letter lying on a table, and going to it, read her own name. She frowned at it, picked it up, looked at the writing, did not recognize this, unfolded it and began to read; and as she read a dull anger set her limbs shaking. She re-read it.

'This is not true!' she said aloud, and she spoke to re-assure herself, for had she not for some time suspected the possibility of such a calamity! 'It is not true!' she repeated fiercely. 'I'll have the skin beaten off the writer of this letter. My granddaughter to behave in this way! Like some low creature in a tavern!'

Puffing with that breathlessness which the least exertion aroused in her, she once more read the letter with its sly suggestion that she should go quietly and unannounced to the ladies' sleeping apartments and see for herself how Catherine Howard and Francis Derham, who called themselves wife and husband, behaved as such.

'Under my roof!' cried the Duchess. 'Under my roof!' She trembled violently, thinking of this most sordid scandal's reaching the ears of her stepson.

She paced up and down not knowing what it would be best for her to do. She recalled a certain night when the key of the ladies' apartment had not been in its rightful place, and she had gone up to find the ladies alone, but seeming guilty; she remembered hearing suspicious creaking noises in the gallery. There had been another occasion when going to the maids' room she had found Catherine and Derham romping on the floor.

She sent for Jane Acworth, for Jane had been present and had had her ears boxed in the maids' room for looking on with indifference while Catherine and Derham behaved so improperly.

Jane's eyes glinted with fear when she saw the wrath of the Duchess.

'You know this writing?'

Jane said she did not, and a slap on her cheek told her that she had better think again; but Jane Acworth, seeing Catherine's and Derham's names on that paper, was not going to commit herself. The writing, she said, was doubtless disguised, and she knew it not.

'Get you gone then!' said the Duchess; and left alone once more began her pacing up and down. What would this mean? Her granddaughter, Catherine Howard, had been seduced by a young man, who, though of good family, being a connection of the Howards, was but a member of an obscure branch of theirs. Catherine, for all her illiteracy, for all that she had been allowed to run wild during her childhood, was yet the daughter of Lord Edmund Howard; and she had been so reckless and foolish, that she had doubtless ruined her chances of making a good marriage.

'The little slut!' whispered the Duchess. 'To have that young man in her bed! This will cost him his life! And her ... and her ...' The Duchess's fingers twitched. 'Let her wait till I lay hands on her. I'll make her wish she had never been so free with Mr Derham. I'll make her wish she had never been born. After all my care of her... ! I always told myself there was a harlot in Catherine Howard!'

Jane Acworth sought Catherine Howard and found her on the point of going to the orchard to meet Derham.

'A terrible thing has happened,' said Jane. 'I would not care to be in your shoes!'

'What mean you, Jane?'

'Someone has written to Her Grace, telling her what you and Derham are about.'

Catherine turned pale.

'No!'

'Indeed yes! Her Grace is in a fury. She showed me the letter and asked if I knew the handwriting. I swore I did not, nor could I be sure, but to my mind ...'

'Mary Lassells!' whispered Catherine.

'I could not swear, but methought. Let us not waste time. What do you think is going to happen to you and Derham and to us all?'

'I dare not think.'

'We shall all be brought into this. I doubt not but that this is the end of our pleasant days and nights. The Duchess cannot ignore this, much as she may wish to do. I would not be you, Catherine Howard; and most assuredly I would not be Derham.'

'What dost think they will do to him?'

'I could not say. I could only guess. They will say what he

has done to you is criminal. Mayhap he will go to the Tower. Oh, no, it will not be the block for him, because then it would be known that he had seduced Catherine Howard. He would be taken to the dungeons and allowed to rot in his chains, or perhaps be tortured to death. The Howards are powerful, and I would not be in the shoes of one who had seduced a member of their house!'

'Please say no more. I must go!'

'Yes. Go and warn Derham. He must not stay here to be arrested and committed to the Tower.'

Fear made Catherine fleet; tears gushed from her eyes and her childish mouth was trembling; she could not shut from her mind terrible pictures of Francis in the Tower, groaning in his chains, dying a lingering death for her sake.

He was waiting in the orchard.

'Catherine!' he cried on seeing her. 'What ails thee, Catherine?'

'You must fly,' she told him incoherently. 'You must wait for nothing. Someone has written to Her Grace, and you will be sent to the Tower.'

He turned pale. 'Catherine! Catherine! Where heard you this?'

'Jane Acworth has seen the letter. Her Grace sent for her that she might tell her who wrote it. It was there . . . all about *us* . . . and my grandmother is furious.'

Bold and reckless, very much in love with Catherine, he wished to thrust such unpleasantness aside. He could not fly, and leave Catherine?'

'Dost think I would ever leave thee?'

'I could not bear that they should take thee to the Tower.'

'Bah!' he said. 'What have we done? Are we not married – husband and wife?'

'They would not allow that to be.'

'And could they help it? We are! That is good enough for me.'

He put his arms about her and kissed her, and Catherine kissed him in such desire that was none the less urgent because danger threatened, but all the more insistent. She took his hand and ran with him into that part of the orchard where the trees grew thickest.

'I would put as far between us and my grandmother as possible,' she told him.

He said: 'Catherine, thou hast let them frighten thee.'

She answered: 'It is not without cause.' She took his face into her hand and kissed his lips. 'I fear I shall not see thee for a long time, Francis.'

'What!' he cried, throwing himself onto the grass and pulling her down beside him. 'Dost think aught could keep me from thee?'

'There is that in me that would send thee from me,' she sighed, 'and that is my love for thee.'

She clung to him, burying her face in his jerkin. She was picturing his young healthy body in chains; he was seeing her taken from him to be given to some nobleman whom they would consider worthy to be her husband. Fear gave a new savour to their passion, and they did not care in those few moments of recklessness whether they were discovered or not. Catherine had ever been the slave of the moment; Derham was single-minded as a drone in his hymeneal flight; death was no deterrent to desire.

The moment passed, and Catherine opened her eyes to stare at the roof of branches, and her hand touched the cold grass which was her bed.

'Francis . . . I am so frightened.'

He stroked her auburn hair that was turning red because the sun was glinting through the leaves of the fruit tree onto it.

'Do not be, Catherine.'

'But they know, Francis. They know!'

Now he seemed to feel cold steel at his throat. What would the Norfolks do to one who had seduced a daughter of their house? Assuredly they would decide he was not worthy to live. One night at dusk, as he came into this very orchard, arms mayhap would seize him. There would be a blow on the head, followed by a second blow to make sure life was extinct, and then the soft sound of displaced water and the ripples would be visible on the surface of the river at the spot where his body had fallen into it. Or would it be a charge of treason? It was simple enough for the Norfolks to find a poor man guilty of treason. The Tower ... the dreaded Tower! Confinement to one who was ever active! Living a life in one small cell when one's spirit was adventurous; one's limbs which were never happy unless active, in heavy chains.

'You must fly from here,' said Catherine.

'Thou wouldst have me leave thee?'

'I shall die of sorrow, but I would not have them hurt thee. I would not have thee remember this love between us with aught but the utmost delight.'

'I could never think on it but with delight.'

She sat up, listening. 'Methought I heard ...'

'Catherine! Catherine Howard!' It was the voice of Mistress Baskerville calling her.

'You must go at once!' cried Catherine in panic. 'You must leave Lambeth. You must leave London.'

'And leave you! You know not what you ask!'

'Do I not! An you lose me, do I not lose you? But I would rather not keep you with me if it means that they will take you. Francis, terrible things happen to men in the Tower of London, and I fear for you.'

'Catherine!' called Mistress Baskerville. 'Come here, Catherine!'

Her eyes entreated him to go, but he would not release her.

'I cannot leave you!' he insisted.

'I will come with you.'

'We should then be discovered at once.'

'An you took me,' she said sagely, 'they would indeed find us. They would search for us and bring me back, and oh, Francis, what would they do to you?'

Mistress Baskerville was all but upon them.

'I will go to her,' said Catherine.

'And I will wait here until you come back to me.'

'Nay, nay! Go now, Francis. Do not wait. Something tells me each moment is precious.'

They embraced; they kissed long and broken-heartedly.

'I shall wait here awhile and hope that you will come back to me, Catherine,' he said. 'I cannot go until we are certain this thing has come to pass.'

Catherine left him and ran to Mistress Baskerville.

'What is it?' asked Catherine.

'Her Grace wants you to go to her at once . . . you and Derham. She is wellnigh mad with rage. She has had a whip brought to her. Some of us have been questioned. I heard Jane Acworth crying in her room. I believe she has been whipped . . . and it is all about you and Derham.'

Catherine said: 'What do you think they will do to Derham?'

'I know not. It is a matter of which one can only guess. They are saying he deserves to die.'

Catherine's teeth began to chatter. 'Please help me,' she pleaded. 'Wait here one moment. Will you give me one last moment with him?'

The girl looked over her shoulder. 'What if we are watched?'

'Please!' cried Catherine. 'One moment. . . . Stay here. . . . Call my name. Pretend that you are still looking for me. I swear I will be with you after one short minute.'

She ran through the trees to Derham. 'It is all true!' she cried. 'They will kill thee, Francis. Please go. . . . Go now!'

He was thoroughly alarmed now, knowing that she did not speak idly. He kissed her again, played with the idea of taking her with him, knew the folly of that, guessing what hardships she would have to face. He must leave her; that was common sense; for if he disappeared they might not try very hard to find him, preferring to let the matter drop, since with him gone, it would be easier to hush up the affair. Besides, he might be able to keep in touch with Catherine yet.

'I will go,' said Francis, 'but first promise me this shall not be the end.'

'Dost think I could bear it an it were?' she demanded tearfully.

'I shall write letters, and thou wilt answer them?'

She nodded. She could not wield a pen very happily, but that there would be those to help her in this matter she doubted not.

'Then I leave thee,' he said.

'Do not return to the house for aught, Francis. It would not be safe. Where shall you go?'

'That I cannot say. Mayhap I shall go to Ireland and turn pirate and win a fortune so that I may then come back and claim Catherine Howard as my wife. Never forget, Catherine, that thou art that.'

The tears were streaming down Catherine's cheeks. She said with great emotion: 'Thou wilt never live to say to me "Thou hast swerved!"'

One last kiss; one last embrace.

'Not farewell, Catherine. Never that. *Au revoir*, sweet Catherine. Forget not the promise thou hast made to me.'

She watched him disappear through the trees before she ran back to Mistress Baskerville. Fearfully they went into the house and to the Duchess's rooms.

When the old woman saw Catherine, her eyes blazed with rage. She seized her by the hair and flung her against the wall, shouting at her, after first shutting the door: 'You little harlot! At your age to allow such liberties! What dost think you have done! Do not look at me so boldly, wench!'

The whip came down on Catherine's shoulders while she cowered against the wall, covering her face with her hands. Across her back, across her thighs, across her legs, the whip descended. There was not much strength behind the Duchess's blows, but the whip cut into Catherine's flesh, and she was crying, not from the infliction of those strokes, but for Derham, since she could know no pain that would equal the loss of him.

The Duchess flung away the whip and pushed Catherine onto a couch. She jerked the girl's head up, and looked into her grief-swollen face.

'It was true then!' cried the Duchess in a fury. 'Every word of it was true! He was in your bed most nights! And when you were disturbed he hid in the gallery!' She slapped Catherine's face, first one side, then the other. 'What sort of marriage do you expect after this? Tell me that! Who will want Catherine Howard who is known for a slut and a harlot!' She slapped Catherine's face. 'We shall marry you to a potman or a pantler!'

Catherine was hysterical with the pain of the blows and the mental anxiety she suffered concerning Derham's fate.

'You would not care!' stormed the Duchess. 'One man as good as another to you, eh? You low creature!'

The slapping began again. Catherine had wept so much that she had no more tears.

'And what do you think we shall do with your fine lover, eh? We will teach him to philander. We shall show him what happens to those who creep stealthily into the beds of their betters... or those who should be their betters....'

Down came the heavy ringed hands again. Catherine's bodice was in tatters, her flesh red and bruised; and the whip had drawn blood from her shoulders.

The Duchess began to whisper of the terrible things that would be done to Francis Derham, were he caught. Did she think she had been severely punished? Well, that would be naught compared with what would be done to Francis Derham. When they had done with him, he would find himself unable to creep into young ladies' beds of night, for lascivious wenches like Catherine Howard would find little use for him, when they had done with him ... when they had done with him...!

Saliva dripped from Her Grace's lips; her venom eased her fear. What if the Duke heard of this? Oh, yes, his own morals did not bear too close scrutiny and there were scandals enough in the Norfolk family and to spare. What of the washerwoman Bess Holland who was making a Duchess of Norfolk most peevish and very jealous! And the late Queen herself had had Howard blood in her veins and stood accused of incest. But oddly enough it was those who had little cause to judge others who most frequently and most loudly did. The King himself who was over-fond of wine and women was the first to condemn such excesses in others; and did not courtiers ever take their cue from a king! If the Duke heard of this he would laugh his sardonic laugh and doubtless say evil things of his old enemy his step-mother. She was afraid, for this would be traced to her neglect. The girl had been in her charge and she had allowed irreparable harm to be done. What of Catherine's sisters? Such a scandal would impair their chances in the matrimonial field. Then, there must be no scandal, not only for Catherine's sake, but for that of her sisters – and also for the sake of the Dowager Duchess of Norfolk. She quietened her voice and her blows slackened.

'Why,' she said slyly, 'there are those who might think this thing had gone farther than it has. Why, there are those who will be ready to say there was complete intimacy between you and Francis Derham.' She looked earnestly into Catherine's face, but Catherine scarcely heard what she said; much less did she gather the import of her words. 'Derham shall suffer nevertheless!' went on the Duchess fiercely; and she went to the door and called to her Mary Lassells and Katharine Tylney. 'Take my granddaughter to the apartment,' she told them, 'and put her to bed. She will need to rest awhile.'

They took Catherine away. She winced as they removed her clothes. Katharine Tylney brought water to bathe her skin where the Duchess's ring had broken it.

While Catherine cried softly, Mary Lassells surveyed with satisfaction the plump little body which had been so severely beaten. Her just deserts! thought Mary Lassells. It was a right and proper thing to have done, to have written to the Duchess. Now this immorality would be stopped. No more petting and stroking of those soft white limbs. Mary Lassells did not know how she had so long borne to contemplate such wickedness.

In her room the Duchess was still shaking with agitation. She must have advice, she decided, and she asked her son, Lord William Howard, to come to see her. When he arrived she showed him the letter and told him the story. He grumbled about mad wenches who could not be merry among themselves without falling out.

'Derham,' said Her Grace, 'has disappeared.'

Lord William shrugged. Did his mother not attach too much importance to a trifling occurrence, he would know. Young men and women were lusty creatures and they would always frolic. It need not necessarily mean that although

438

Derham had visited the girl's sleeping apartment, there was anything to worry about.

'Forget it! Forget it!' said Lord William. 'Give the girl a beating and a talking to. As for Derham, let him go. And pray keep all this from my lord Duke.'

It was sound advice. There was no harm done, said the Duchess to herself, and dozed almost serenely in her chair. But out of her dozes she would awake startled, worried by dreams of her two most attractive granddaughters, one dead, and the other so vitally alive.

Then the Duchess made a resolution, and this she determined to keep, for she felt that it did not only involve the future of Catherine Howard, but that of her own. Catherine should be kept under surveillance; she should be coached in deportment so that she should cease to be a wild young hoyden and become a lady. And some of those women, whose sly ways the Duchess did not like over-much, should go.

On this occasion the Duchess carried out her resolutions. Most of the young ladies who had shared the main sleeping apartment with Catherine were sent to their homes. Jane Acworth was among those who remained, for a marriage was being arranged for her with a Mr Bulmer of York, and, thought the Duchess, she will soon be going in any case.

The Duchess decided to see more of Catherine, to school her herself, although, she admitted ruefully, it was hardly likely that Jane Seymour would find a place at court for Anne's cousin. Never mind! The main thing was that Catherine's unfortunate past must be speedily forgotten, and Catherine prepared to make the right sort of marriage.

* * *

It seemed to the Princess Mary that the happiest event that had taken place since the King had cast off her mother, was the death of Anne Boleyn. Mary was twenty years old, a very serious girl, with bitterness already in her face, and fanaticism peering out through her eyes. She was disappointed and frustrated, perpetually on the defensive and whole-heartedly devoted to Roman Catholicism. She was proud and the branding of illegitimacy did not make her less so. She had friends and supporters, but whereas, while Anne Boleyn lived, these did not wish to have their friendship known, they now were less secretive. The King had put it on record that not in any carnal concupiscence had he taken a wife, but only at the entreaty of his nobility, and he had chosen one whose age and form was deemed to be meet and apt for the procreation of children. His choice had been supported by the imperialists, for he had chosen Jane Seymour who was one who still clung to the old catholicism; moreover Jane was known to be kindly disposed towards Mary.

It was, as ever, necessary to tread very cautiously, for the King had changed since the death of Anne; he was less jovial; he had aged considerably and looked more than his forty-five years; he did not laugh so frequently, and there was a glitter in his eyes, which could send cold shivers down the spine of a man though he might have no knowledge of having displeased the King. His matrimonial adventures had been conspicuously unsuccessful, and though Jane had been reported to be pregnant before the death of Anne – well, Katharine of Aragon had been pregnant a good many times without much result; and Anne had had no success either. Young Richmond, on whom the King doted, as his only son, had ever since the death of Anne been spitting blood. 'She has cast a spell on him,' said Mary. 'She would murder him as she tried to murder me, for Richmond has death in his face if ever one had.' And what if Richmond died and Jane Seymour was without issue! Elizabeth was a bastard now, no less then Mary.

'It is time,' said her friends to Mary, 'that you began to woo the King.'

'And defame my mother!' cried Mary.

'She who was responsible for your mother's position is now herself cast off and done with. You should try to gain His Majesty's friendship.'

'I do not believe he will listen to me.'

'There is a way of approaching him.'

'Which way is that?'

'Through Cromwell. It is not only the best, but the only possible way for you.'

The result was that Cromwell came to visit Mary at Hunsdon whither she had been banished. Cromwell came eagerly enough, seeing good reasons for having Mary taken back into favour. He knew that the King would never receive his daughter unless she agreed that her mother's marriage had been unlawful and incestuous; and if Mary could be brought to such admission, she would cease to have the sympathy of the people. There were many nobles in the land who deplored the break with Rome; who were silently awaiting an opportunity to repair the link. If they were ever able to do this, what would happen to those who had worked for the break! And was not the greatest of them Thomas Cromwell! Cromwell could therefore see much good in the King's reconciliation with his daughter.

Henry's eyes were speculative regarding the prospect laid out before him by Cromwell. How he loathed that man! But what good work he was doing with the smaller abbeys, and what better work he would do with the larger ones! If there was to be a reconciliation with Mary, Cromwell was right in thinking this was the time to make it. Many people considered Mary had been badly treated; the common people were particularly ready to be incensed on her behalf. He had separated her from her mother, had not allowed her to see Katharine on her death-bed. He could not help feeling a stirring of his conscience over Mary. But if he effected a reconciliation at this moment, he himself would emerge from the dangerous matter, not as a monster but as a misguided man who had been under the influence of a witch and a sorceress. Anne, the harlot and would-be-poisoner, could be shown to have been entirely responsible for the King's treatment of his daughter. 'Why,' people would say, 'as soon as the whore was sent to her well-deserved death, the King becomes reconciled to his daughter!' A well-deserved death! Henry liked that phrase. He had suffered many disturbed nights of late; he would awaken and think she lay beside him; he would find sleep impossible for hours at a time; and once he dreamed of her looking into a pool

441

at Hever: and when he looked too, he saw her head with its black hair, and blood was streaming from it. A well-deserved death! thought Henry complacently, and he sent Norfolk to see his daughter at Hunsdon.

'Tell the girl,' he said, 'that she is wilful and disobedient, but that we are ever ready to take pity on those who repent.'

Mary saw that she was expected to deny all that she had previously upheld, and was frightened by the storm that she had aroused.

'My mother was the King's true wife,' she insisted. 'I can say naught but that!'

She was reminded ominously that many had lost their heads for saying what she had said. She was not easily frightened and she tried to assure herself that she would go to the block as readily as More and Fisher had done.

Mary could see now that she had been wrong in blaming Anne for her treatment. Norfolk was brusque with her, insulting even; she had never been so humiliated when Anne was living. It was Anne who had begged that they might bury their quarrel, that Mary should come to court, and had told her that she should walk beside her and need not carry her train. Lady Kingston had come to her with an account of Anne's plea for forgiveness and Mary had shrugged her shoulders at that. Forgiveness! What good would that do Anne Boleyn! When Mary died she would look down on Anne, burning in hell, for burn in hell she assuredly would. She had carried out the old religious rites until her death, but she had listened to and even applauded the lies of Martin Luther and so earned eternal damnation. Mary was not cruel at heart; she knew only two ways, the right and the wrong, and the right way was through the Roman Catholic Church. No true Catholic burned in hell; but this was a fate which those who were not true Catholics could not possibly escape. But she saw that though Anne would assuredly burn in hell for her responsibility in the severance of England from Rome, she could not in all truth be entirely blamed for the King's treatment of his elder daughter. Mary decided that although she could not forgive Anne, she would at least be as kind as she could to Anne's daughter.

Henry was furious at the reports brought back to him. He swore that he could not trust Mary. He was an angry man. It was but a matter of days since he had married Jane Seymour and yet he was not happy. He could not forget Anne Boleyn; he was dissatisfied with Jane; and he was enraged against Mary. A man's daughter to work against him! He would not have it! He called the council together. A man cannot trust those nearest to him! was his cry. There should be an inquiry. If he found his daughter guilty of conspiracy she should suffer the penalty of traitors.

'I'll have no more disobedience!' foamed Henry. 'There is one road traitors should tread, and by God, I'll see that they tread it!'

There was tension in court circles. It was well known that, while Anne lived, Mary and her mother had had secret communications from Chapuys; and that the ambassador had had plans for – with the Emperor's aid – setting Katharine or Mary on the throne.

The King, as was his custom, chose Cromwell to do the unpleasant work; he was to go secretly into the houses of suspected persons and search for evidence against the Princess.

The Queen came to the King.

'What ails thee?' growled the newly married husband. 'Dost not see I am occupied with matters of state!'

'Most gracious lord,' said Jane, not realizing his dangerous mood, 'I would have speech with you. The Princess Mary has ever been in my thoughts, and now that I know she repents and longs to be restored in your affections ...'

Jane got no further.

'Be off!' roared the King. 'And meddle not in my affairs!'

Jane wept, but Henry strode angrily from her, and in his mind's eye, he seemed to see a pair of black eyes laughing at him, and although he was furious he was also wistful. He growled: 'There is none I can trust. My nearest and those who should be my dearest are ready to betray me!'

Mary's life was in danger. Chapuys wrote to her advising her to submit to the King's demands, since it was unsafe for her not to do so. She must acknowledge her father Supreme

Head of the Church; she must agree that her mother had never been truly married to the King. It was useless to think that as his daughter she was safe, since there was no safety for those who opposed Henry. Let her think, Chapuys advised her, of the King's last concubine to whom he had been exclusively devoted over several years; he had not hesitated to send her to the block; nor would he hesitate in his present mood to send his own daughter.

But the shrewd man Henry had become knew that the unpopularity he had incurred, first by his marriage with Anne and then by his murder of her, would be further increased if he shed the blood of his daughter. The enmity of the people, ever a dark bogey in his life since he felt his dynasty to be unsafe, seemed as close as it had when he broke from the Church of Rome. He told Cromwell to write to her telling her that if she did not leave all her sinister councils she would lose her chance of gaining the King's favour.

Mary was defeated, since even Chapuys was against her holding out; she gave in, acknowledged the King Supreme Head of the Church, admitted the Pope to be a pretender, and agreed that her mother's marriage was incestuous and unlawful. She signed the papers she was required to sign and she retired to the privacy of her rooms where she wept bitterly, calling on her saintly mother to forgive her for what she had done. She thought of More and Fisher. 'Ah! That I had been brave as they!' she sobbed.

Henry was well pleased; instead of a recalcitrant daughter, he had a dutiful one. Uneasy about the death of Anne, he wished to assure himself and the world that he had done right to rid himself of her. He was a family man; he loved his children. Anne had threatened to poison his daughter, his beloved Mary. Did his people not now see that Anne had met a just fate? Was not Mary once more his beloved daughter? It mattered not that she had been born out of wedlock. She was his daughter and she should come to court. With the death of the harlot who had tried to poison his daughter, everything was well between her and her father.

Jane was jubilant.

'You are the most gracious and clement of fathers,' she told Henry.

'You speak truth, sweetheart!' he said and warmed to Jane, liking afresh her white skin and pale eyelashes. He loved her truly, and if she gave him sons, he would love her all the more. He was a happy family man.

Mary sat at the royal table, next in importance to her step-mother, and she and Jane were the best of friends. Henry smiled at them benignly. There was peace in his home, for his obstinate daughter was obstinate no longer. He tried to look at her with love, but though he had an affection for her, it was scarcely strong enough to be called love.

When Jane asked that Elizabeth should also come to court, he said he thought this thing might be.

'An you wish it, sweetheart,' he said, making it a favour to Jane. But he liked to see the child. She was attractive and spirited, and there was already a touch of her mother in her.

'The King is very affectionate towards the young Elizabeth,' it was said.

*   *   *

When his son the Duke of Richmond died, Henry was filled with sorrow. Anne, he declared, had set a spell upon him, for it was but two months since Anne had gone to the block, and from the day she died, Richmond had begun to spit blood.

Such an event must set the King brooding once more on the succession. He was disturbed because young Thomas Howard, half brother to the Duke of Norfolk had dared to betroth himself, without Henry's permission, to Lady Margaret Douglas, daughter of Henry's sister Margaret of Scotland. This was a black crime indeed. Henry knew the Howards – ambitious to a man. He was sure that Thomas Howard aspired to the throne through this proposed marriage with Henry's niece and he was reminded afresh of what a slight hold the Tudors had upon the throne.

'Fling young Howard into the Tower!' cried Henry, and this was done.

He was displeased with the Duke also, and Norfolk was

terrified, expecting that at any moment he might join his half brother.

If the Howards were disturbed so was Henry; he hated trouble at home more than trouble abroad. The Henry of this period was a different person from that younger man whose thoughts had been mainly occupied in games and the hunting of women and forest creatures. He had come into the world endowed with a magnificent physique and a shrewd brain; but as the former was magnificent and the latter merely shrewd, he had developed the one at the expense of the other. Excelling as he did in sport, he had passed over intellectual matters; loving his great body, he had decked it in dazzling jewels and fine velvets and cloth of gold; for the glory of his body he had subdued his mind. But at forty-five he was well past his active youth; the ulcer in his leg was bad enough to make him roar with pain at times; he was inclined to breathlessness being a heavy man who had indulged too freely in all fleshly lusts. His body being not now the dominating feature in his life, he began to exercise his mind. He was chiefly concerned in the preservation and the glorification of himself, and as this must necessarily mean the preservation and the glorification of England, matters of state were of the utmost interest to him. Under him, the Navy had grown to a formidable size; certain monies were set aside each year for the building of new ships and that those already built might be kept in good fighting order; he wished to shut England off from the Continent, making her secure; while he did not wish England to become involved in war, he wished to inflame Charles and Francis to make war on one another, for he feared these two men; but he feared them less when they warred together than when they were at peace. His main idea was to have all potential enemies fighting while England grew out of adolescence into that mighty Power which it was his great hope she would one day be. If this was to happen, he must first of all have peace at home, for he knew well that there was nothing to weaken a growing country like civil war. In severing the Church of England from that of Rome, he had done a bold thing, and England was still shaking

446

from the shock. There were many of his people who deplored the break, who would ask nothing better than to be reunited with Rome. Cleverly and shrewdly, Henry had planned a new religious programme. Not for one moment did he wish to deprive his people of those rites and ceremonies which were as much a part of their lives as they were of the Roman Catholic faith. But their acceptance of the King as Supreme Head of the Church must be a matter of life and death.

Peace at home and peace abroad therefore, was all he asked, so that England might grow in the best possible conditions to maturity. Wolsey had moulded him into a political shape very like his own. Wolsey had believed that it was England's task to keep the balance of power in Europe, but Wolsey had been less qualified to pursue this than was Henry. Wolsey had been guilty of accepting bribes; he could never resist adding to his treasures; Henry was not so shortsighted as to jeopardize England's position for a gift or two from foreign Powers. He was every bit as acquisitive as Wolsey, but the preservation of himself through England was his greatest need. He had England's treasures at his disposal, and at this moment he was finding the dissolution of the abbeys most fruitful. Wolsey never forgot his allegiance to Rome; Henry knew no such loyalty. With Wolsey it was Wolsey first, England second; with Henry, England and Henry meant the same thing. Cromwell believed that England should ally herself with Charles because Charles represented the strongest Power in Europe, but Henry would associate himself with neither Charles nor Francis, clinging to his policy of preserving the balance of power. Neither Wolsey nor Cromwell could be as strong as Henry, for there was ever present with these two the one great fear which must be their first consideration, and this was fear of Henry. Henry therefore was freer to act; he could take advantage of sudden action; he could do what he would, without having to think what excuse he should make if his action failed. It was a great advantage in the subtle game he played.

Looking back, Henry could see whither his laziness had

led him. He had made wars which had given nothing to England, and he had drained her of her strength and riches, so that the wealth so cautiously and cleverly amassed by his thrifty father, had slowly dwindled away. There was the example of the Field of the Cloth of Gold, on which he could now look back through the eyes of a wiser and far more experienced man, and be shocked by his lack of state-craft at that time. Kings who squandered the treasure and the blood of their subjects also squandered their affections. He could see now that it was due to his father's wealth that England had become a Power in Europe, and that with the disappearance of that wealth went England's power. By the middle of the twenties England was of scarcely any importance in Europe, and at home Ireland was being trouble-some. When Henry had talked of divorcing his Queen, and was living openly with Anne Boleyn, his subjects had murmured against him, and that most feared of all calamities to a wise king – civil war – had threatened. At that time he had scarcely been a king at all, but when he had broken from Rome he had felt his strength, and that was the beginning of Henry VIII as a real ruler.

He would now continue to rule, and brute strength would be his method; never again should any other person than the King govern the country. He was watchful; men were watchful of him. They dreaded his anger, but Henry was wise enough to realize the wisdom of that remark of his Spanish ambassador's: 'Whom many fear, must fear many.' And Henry feared many, even if many feared him.

His great weakness had its roots in his conscience. He was what men called a religious man, which in his case meant he was a superstitious man. There was never a man less Christian; there was never one who made a greater show of piety. He was cruel; he was brutal; he was pitiless. This was his creed. He was an egoist, a megalomaniac; he saw himself not only as the centre of England but of the world. In his own opinion, everything he did was right; he only needed time to see it in its right perspective, and he would prove it to be right. He took his strength from this belief in himself; and as his belief was strong, so was Henry.

One of the greatest weaknesses of his life was his feeling for Anne Boleyn. Even now, after she had died at his command, when his hands were stained with her innocent blood, when he had gloated over his thoughts of her once loved, now mutilated body, when he knew that could he have her back he would do the same again, he could not forget her. He had hated her so violently, only because he had loved her; he had killed her out of passionate jealousy, and she haunted him. Sometimes he knew that he could never hope to forget her. All his life he would seek a way of forgetting. He was now trying the obvious way, through women.

Jane! He was fond enough of Jane. What egoist is not fond of those who continually show him he is all that he would have people believe he is! Yes, he liked Jane well enough, but she maddened him; she irritated him because he always knew exactly what she would say; she submitted to his embraces mildly, and he felt that she did so because she considered it her duty; she annoyed him because she offered him that domestic peace which had ever been his goal, and now having reached it, he found it damnably insipid; she angered him because she was not Anne.

Moreover, now she had disappointed him. She had had her first miscarriage, and that very reason why he had been forced to get rid of Anne so speedily, to resort to all kinds of subterfuge to pacify his subjects, and to tell his people that it was his nobles who had begged him to marry Jane before Anne's mutilated body was cold, had proved to be no worthwhile reason at all. He could have waited a few months; he could have allowed Cromwell and Norfolk to have persuaded him; he could have been led self-sacrificingly into marriage with Jane instead of scuffling into it in the undignified way he had done. It was irritating.

It was also uncanny. Why did all his wives miscarry? He thought of the old Duke of Norfolk's brood, first with one wife, then with another. Why should the King be so cursed? First with Katharine, then with Anne. Katharine he had discarded; Anne he had beheaded; still, he was truly married to Jane, for neither of these two had been living when he married Jane; therefore he could have done no wrong. If he had displeased God in marrying Anne while Katharine was alive, he could understand that; but he had been a true widower when he had married Jane. No, he was worrying unduly; he would have children yet by Jane, for if he did not ... why, why had he got rid of Anne?

In his chamber at Windsor, he was brooding on these matters when he was aware of a disturbance in the courtyard below his window; even as he looked out a messenger was at his door with the news that certain men had ridden with all speed to the King as they had alarming news for him.

When they were brought in they fell on their knees before him.

'Sir, we tremble to bring such news to Your Majesty. We come hot speed to tell you that trouble has started, so we hear, in Lincoln.'

'Trouble!' cried Henry. 'What mean you by trouble?'

'My Lord, it was when the men went into Lincoln to deal with the abbeys there. There was a rising, and two were killed. Beaten and roughly handled, please Your Majesty, unto death.'

Henry's face was purple; his eyes blazed.

'What means this! Rebellion! Who dares rebel against the King!'

Henry was astounded. Had he steered the country away from civil war, only to find it breaking out at last when he had been congratulating himself on his strength. The people, particularly those in the north, had been bewildered by the break with Rome; but by the pillaging of the abbeys, they had been roused to action. Already bands of beggars were springing up all over the country; they who had been sure of food and shelter from the monks were now desolate, and there was but one sure way for a destitute man to keep himself fed in Tudor England, and that was to rob his fellow men. Over the countryside there roamed hordes of desperate starving men, and to their numbers were added the displaced monks and nuns. There was more boldness in the north than in the south because those far removed from his presence could fear Henry less. So they, smarting from the break with Rome, sympathizing with the monks, resenting the loss of the monasteries, decided that something should be done. They were joined by peasants who, owing to the enclosure acts, and the prevailing policy of turning arable into pasture land, had been rendered homeless. Lords Darcy and Hussey, two of the most powerful noblemen of the north, had always supported the old Catholic faith; the rebels therefore could feel they had these men behind them.

Henry was enraged and apprehensive. He felt this to be a major test. Should he emerge from it triumphant, he would have achieved a great victory; he would prove himself a great King. Two ways lay before him. He could return to Rome and assure peace in his realm; he could fight the rebels and remain not only head of the Church but truly head of the English people. He chose the second course. He would risk his crown to put down the rebels.

It meant reconciliation with Norfolk, for whenever there was a war to be fought, Norfolk must be treated with respect. He would send Suffolk to Lincoln. He stormed against those of his counsellors who advised him against opposing the rebels. Fiercely he reminded them that they were bound to serve him with their lives, lands and goods.

Jane was afraid. She was very superstitious and it seemed to her that this rising was a direct reproach from heaven because of Cromwell's sacrilegious pillaging of the monasteries.

She came to the King and knelt before him, and had her head not been bent she would have seen her danger from his blazing eyes.

'My lord husband,' she said, 'I have heard the most disquieting news. I fear it may be a judgment on us for ridding ourselves of the abbeys. Could not Your Most Gracious Majesty consider the restoring of them?'

For a few seconds he was speechless with rage; he saw Jane through the red haze in his eyes, and when he spoke his voice was a rumble of thunder.

'Get up!'

She lifted terrified eyes to his face and stood. He came

closer to her, breathing heavily, his jowls quivering, his lower lip stuck out menacingly.

'Have I not told you never to meddle in my affairs!' he said very slowly and deliberately.

Tears came into Jane's eyes; she was thinking of all those people who were wandering homeless about the country; she thought of little babies crying for milk. She had pictured herself saving the people from a terrible calamity; moreover, her friends who longed for the return of the old ways, would rejoice in the restoration of the monasteries, and would be very pleased with Queen Jane. Therefore she felt it to be her duty to turn the King back to Rome, or at least away from that wickedness which had sprung up in the world since Martin Luther had made himself heard.

The King gripped her shoulder, and put his face to hers.

'Dost remember what happened to your predecessor?' he asked meaningly.

She stared at him in horror. Anne had gone to the block because she was guilty of high treason. What could he mean?

His eyes were hot and cruel.

'Forget it not!' he said, and threw her from him.

*　　*　　*

The men of the north had followed the example of the men from Lincolnshire. This was no mob rising; into the ranks of the Pilgrimage of Grace went sober men of the provinces. The most inspiring of its leaders was a certain Robert Aske, and this man, whose integrity and honesty of purpose were well known, had a talent for organization; he was a born commander, and under him, the northern rebels were made into a formidable force.

Henry realized too well how very formidable. The winter was beginning; he had no standing army. He acted with foresight and cunning. He invited Aske to discuss the trouble with him.

It did not occur to Aske that one as genial as Henry appeared to him could possibly not be as honest as Aske himself. On the leader, Henry unloosed all his bluffness, all his honest down-to-earth friendliness. Did Aske wish to spread bloodshed over England? Aske certainly did not. He wanted only hardship removed from the suffering people. Henry patted the man affectionately. Why then, Aske and the King had the same interests at heart. Should they quarrel! Never! All they must do was to find a way agreeable to them both of doing what was right for England.

Aske went back to Yorkshire to tell of the King's oral promises, and the insurgents were disbanded; there was a truce between the north and the King.

There were in the movement less level-headed men than such leaders as Aske and Constable, and in spite of Aske's belief in the King's promises he could not prevent a second rising. This gave Henry an excuse for what followed. He had decided on his action before he had seen Aske; his promises to the leader had meant that he wished to gain time, to gather his strengh about him, to wait until the end of winter. He had never swerved from the policy he intended to adopt and which he would continue to follow to the end of his reign. It was brute strength and his own absolute and un-questioned rule.

He decided to make a bloody example and show his people what happened to those who opposed the King. Up to the north went Norfolk and the blood-letting began. Darcy was beheaded; Sir Thomas Percy was brought to Tyburn and hanged; honest men who had looked upon the Pilgrimage of Grace as a sacred movement were hanged, cut down alive, disembowelled, and their entrails burned while they still lived; then they were beheaded. Aske learned too late that he had accepted the promises of one to whom a promise was naught but a tool to be picked up and used for a moment when it might be useful and then to be laid aside and forgotten. In spite of his pardon, he was executed and hanged in chains on one of the towers of York that all might see what befell traitors. Constable was taken to Hull and hanged from the highest gate in the town, a grim warning to all who beheld him.

The King licked his lips over the accounts of cruelties done in his name. 'Thus shall all traitors die!' he growled, and warned Cromwell against leniency, knowing well that he could leave bloody work in those ugly hands.

The Continent, hearing of his internal troubles, was on tiptoe waiting and watching. Henry's open enemy Pope Paul could state publicly his satisfaction; Henry's secret enemies, Charles and Francis, though discreetly silent, were none the less delighted.

The Pope, deeply resenting this King who had dared set an example which he feared others might follow, began to plan. What if the revolt against Henry were nourished outside England? Reginald Pole was on the Continent; he had left England for two reasons; he did not approve of the divorce and break with Rome; and he being the grandson of that Duke of Clarence who was brother to Edward IV, was too near the throne to make residence in England safe for him. He had written a book against Henry, and Henry feigning interest suggested Pole return to England that they might discuss their differences of opinion. Pole was no careless fly to walk into the spider's web. He declined his sovereign's offer and went to Rome instead where the Pope made him a Cardinal and discussed with him a plan for fanning the flames which were at this time bursting out in the North of England. If Pole succeeded in displacing Henry, why should he not marry the Princess Mary, restore England to the papacy and rule as her king?

Henry acted with cunning and boldness. He demanded from Francis, Pole's extradition, that he might be sent to England and stand his trial as a traitor. Francis, who did not wish to defy the Pope not to annoy Henry, ordered Pole to leave his domains. Pole went to Flanders, but Charles was as reluctant as Francis to displease the King of England. Pole had to disguise himself.

The attitude of the two great monarchs showed clearly that they were very respectful towards the island lying off the coast of Europe, for never had a papal legate been so humiliated before.

Henry could purr with pleasure. He was treated with respect abroad and he had crushed a revolt which threatened his throne. The crown was safe for the Tudors, and England was saved from civil war. He knew how to rule his country. He had been strong and he had emerged triumphant from the most dangerous situation of his reign.

There was great news yet. The Queen was paler than usual; she had been sick; she had fancies for special foods.

Henry was joyful. He once more had hopes of getting a son.

* * *

While Henry was strutting with pleasure, Jane was beset with fear. There were many things to frighten Jane. Before her lay the ordeal of childbirth. What if it should prove unsuccessful? As she lay in those Hampton Court apartments which the King had lovingly planned for Anne Boleyn, she brooded on these matters. From her window she could see the initials entwined in stone work – J and H, and where the J was there had once been an A, and the A had had to be taken away very suddenly indeed.

The King was in high humour, certain that this time he would get a son. He went noisily about the palace, eating and drinking with great heartiness; and hunting whenever his leg was not too painful to deter him. If Jane gave him a son, he told himself, he would at last have found happiness. He would know that he had been right in everything he had done, right to rid himself of Katharine who had never really been his wife, right to execute Anne who was a sorceress, right to marry Jane.

He jollied the poor pale creature, admonishing her to take good care of herself, threatening her that if she did not, he would want to know the reason why; and his loving care was not for her frail body but for the heir it held.

The hot summer passed. Jane heard of the executions and shuddered, and whenever she looked from her windows she saw those initials. The J seemed to turn into an A as she looked, and then into something else, blurred and indistinguishable.

Plague came to London, rising up from the fetid gutters and from the dirty wash left on the river banks with the fall of the tide. People died like flies in London. Death came close to Jane Seymour during those months.

She was wan and sickly and she felt very ill, though she dared not mention this for fear of angering the King; she was afraid for herself and the child she carried. She had qualms about the execution of Anne, and her dreams became haunted with visions. She could not forget an occasion when Anne had come upon her and the King together. Then Anne must have felt this sickness, this heaviness, this fear, for she herself was carrying the King's child at that time.

Jane could not forget the words the King had used to her more than once. 'Remember what happened to your predecessor!' There was no need to ask Jane to remember what she would never be able to forget.

She became more observant of religious rites, and as her religion was of the old kind, both Cranmer and Cromwell were disturbed. But they dared not approach the King with complaints for they knew well what his answer would be. 'Let the Queen eat fish on Fridays. Let her do what she will an she give me a son!'

All over the country, people waited to hear of the birth of a son. What would happen to Jane, it was asked, if she produced a stillborn child? What if she produced a girl?

Many were cynical over Henry's matrimonial affairs, inclined to snigger behind their hands. Already there were Mary and Elizabeth – both proclaimed illegitimate. What if there was yet another girl? Perhaps it was better to be humble folk when it was considered what had happened to Katharine of Aragon and Anne Boleyn.

The Dowager Duchess of Norfolk waited eagerly for the news. Her mouth was grim. Would Jane Seymour do what her granddaughter had failed to do? That pale sickly creature succeed, where glowing, vital Anne had failed! She thought not!

Catherine Howard fervently hoped the King would get a son. She had wept bitterly at the death of her cousin, but unlike her grandmother she bore no resentment. Let poor Queen Jane be happy even if Queen Anne had not. Where was the good sense in harbouring resentment? She scarcely listened to her grandmother's grim prophecies.

Catherine had changed a good deal since that violent beating her grandmother had given her. Now she really looked like a daughter of the house of Howard. She was quieter; she had been badly frightened by the discovery. She had received lectures from Lord William who insisted on looking on the episode as a foolish girlish prank; she had received a very serious warning from her grandmother who, when they were alone, did not hide from her that she knew the worst. Catherine must put all that behind her, must forget it had happened, must never refer to it again, must deny what she had done if she were ever questioned by anyone. She had been criminally foolish; let her remember that. Catherine did remember; she was restrained.

She was growing very pretty and her gentle manners gave a new charm to her person. The Duchess was ready to forget unsavoury incidents; she hoped Catherine was too. She did not know that Catherine was still receiving letters from Derham, that through the agency of Jane Acworth, whose pen was ever ready, the correspondence was being kept up.

Derham wrote: 'Do not think that I forget thee. Do not forget that we are husband and wife, for I never shall. Do not forget you have said, "You shall never live to say I have swerved." For I do not, and I treasure the memory. One day I shall return for you. . . .'

It appealed strongly to Catherine's adventure-loving nature to receive love letters and to have her replies smuggled out of the house. She found it pleasant to be free from those women who had known about her love affair with Derham and who were for ever making sly allusions to it. There were no amorous adventures these days, for the Duchess's surveillance was strict. Catherine did not want them; she realized her folly and she was very much ashamed of the freedom she had allowed Manox. She still loved Francis, she insisted; she still loved receiving his letters; and one day he would return for her.

October came, and one morning, very early, Catherine

was awakened by the ringing of bells and the sound of guns. Jane Seymour had borne the King a son.

* * *

Jane was too ill to feel her triumph. She was hardly aware of what was going on in her chamber. Shapes rose up and faded. There was a huge red-faced man, whose laughter was very loud, drawing her away from the peaceful sleep she sought. She heard whispering voices, loud voices, laughter.

The King would peer at his son anxiously. A poor puny little thing he was, and Henry was terrified that he would, as others of his breed before him, be snatched from his father before he reached maturity. Even Richmond had not survived, though he had been a bonny boy; this little Edward was small and white and weak.

Still, the King had a son and he was delighted. Courtiers moved about the sick room. They must kiss Jane's hand; they must congratulate her. She was too tired? Nonsense! She must rejoice. Had she not done that which her predecessors had failed to do, given the King a son!

Fruit and meat were sent to her, gifts from the King. She must show her pleasure in His Majesty's attentions. She ate without knowing what she ate.

The ceremony of the christening began in her chamber. They lifted her from her bed to the state pallet which was decorated with crowns and the arms of England in gold thread. She lay, propped on cushions of crimson damask, wrapped in a mantle of crimson velvet furred with ermine; but Jane's face looked transparent against the rich redness of her robes. She was exhausted before they lifted her from the bed; her head throbbed and her hands were hot with fever. She longed to sleep, but she reminded herself over and over again that she must do her duty by attending the christening of her son. What would the King say, if he found the mother of his prince sleeping when she should be smiling her pleasure!

It was midnight as the ceremonial procession with Jane in its midst went through the draughty corridors of Hampton Court to the chapel. Jane slipped into unconsciousness, recovered and smiled about her. She saw the Princess Mary present the newly born Prince at the font; she saw her own brother carrying the small Elizabeth, whose eyes were small with sleepiness and in whose fat little hands was Edward's crysom; she saw Cranmer and Norfolk who were the Prince's sponsors; she saw the nurse and the midwife; and so vague was this scene to her that she thought it was but a dream, and that her son was not yet born and her pains about to begin.

Through the mist before her eyes she saw Sir Francis Bryan at the font, and she was reminded that he had been one of those who had not very long ago delighted in the wit of Anne Boleyn. Her eyes came to rest on the figure of a grey old man who carried a taper and bore a towel about his neck; she recognized him as Anne's father. The Earl looked shamefaced, and had the unhappy air of a man who knows himself to be worthy of the contempt of his fellow-men. Was he thinking of his brilliant boy and his lovely girl who had been done to death for the sake of this little Prince to whom he did honour because he dared do nothing else?

Unable to follow the ceremony because of the fits of dizziness which kept overwhelming her, Jane longed for the quiet of her chamber. She wanted the comfort of her bed; she wanted darkness and quiet and rest.

'God, in His Almighty and infinite grace, grant good life and long, to the right high, right excellent, and noble Prince Edward, Duke of Cornwall and Earl of Chester, most dear and entirely beloved son of our most dread and gracious Lord Henry VIII.'

The words were like a rushing tide that swept over Jane and threatened to drown her; she gasped for breath. She was only hazily aware of the ceremonial journey back to her chamber.

A few days after the christening, Jane was dead.

'Ah!' said the people in the streets, 'His Majesty is desolate. Poor dear man! At last he had found a queen he could love; at last he has his heart's desire, a son to follow him; and now this dreadful catastrophe must overtake him.'

Certain rebels raised their heads, feeling the King to be too sunk in grief to notice them. The lion but feigned to sleep. When he lifted his head and roared, rebels learned what happened to those who dared raise a voice against the King. The torture chambers were filled with such. Ears were cut off; tongues were cut out; and the mutilated victims were whipped as they were driven naked through the streets.

Before Jane was buried, Henry was discussing with Cromwell whom he should next take for a wife.

* * *

Henry was looking for a wife. Politically he was at an advantage; he would be able to continue with his policy of keeping his two enemies guessing. He would send ambassadors to the French court; he would throw out hints to the Emperor; for both would greatly fear an alliance of the other with England.

Henry was becoming uneasy concerning continental affairs. The war between Charles and Francis had come to an end; and with these two not at each other's throats, but in fact friends, and Pole persisting in his schemes to bring about civil war in England with the assistance of invasion from the Continent, he had cause for anxiety. To be able to offer himself in the marriage market was a great asset at such a time and Henry decided to exploit it to the full.

Although Henry was anxious to make a politically advantageous marriage, he could not help being excited by the prospect of a new wife. He visualized her. It was good to be a free man once more. He was but forty-seven and very ready to receive a wife. There was still in his mind the image of Anne Boleyn. He knew exactly what sort of wife he wanted; she must be beautiful, clever, vivacious; one who was high-spirited as Anne, meek as Jane. He reassured himself that although it was imperative that he should make the right marriage, he would not involve himself unless the person of his bride was pleasing.

He asked Chatillon, the French ambassador who had taken the place of du Bellay at the English court, that a selection of the most beautiful and accomplished ladies of the French court be sent to Calais; Henry would go there and inspect them.

'Pardie!' mused Henry. 'How can I depend on any but myself! I must see them myself and see them sing!'

To this request, Francis retorted in such a way as to make Henry squirm, and he did not go to Calais to make a personal inspection of prospective wives.

There were among others the beautiful Christina of Milan who was a niece of Emperor Charles. She had married the Duke of Milan who had died leaving her a virgin-widow of sixteen. Henry was interested in reports of her, and after the snub from Francis not averse to looking around the camp of the Emperor. He sent Holbein to make a picture of Christina and when the painter brought it back,. Henry was attracted, but not sufficiently so to make him wish to clinch the bargain immediately. He was still keeping up negotiations with the French. It was reported that Christina had said that if she had had two heads one should be at the English King's service, but having only one she was reluctant to come to England. She had heard that her great-aunt Katharine of Aragon had been poisoned; that Anne Boleyn had been put innocently to death; and that Jane Seymour had been lost for lack of keeping in childbirth. She was of course at Charles's command, and these reports might well have sprung out of the reluctance of the Emperor for the match.

Henry's uneasiness did not abate. He was terrified that the growing friendship between Charles and Francis might be a prelude to an attack on England. He knew that Pope Paul was trying to stir up the Scots to invade England from the North; Pole was moving slyly, from the Continent.

Henry's first act was to descend with ferocity on the Pole family in England. He began by committing Pole's young brother Geoffrey to the Tower and there the boy was tortured so violently that he said all Henry wished him to say. The result was that his brother Lord Montague and his cousin the Marquis of Exeter were seized. Even Pole's mother, the ageing Countess of Salisbury, who had been governess to the Princess Mary and one of the greatest friends of Katharine of Aragon, was not spared.

These people were the hope of those Catholics who longed for reunion with Rome, and Henry was watching his people closely to see what effect their arrest was having. He had had enough of troubles within his own domains, and with trouble threatening from outside he must tread very cautiously. At this time, he selected as his victim a scholar named Lambert whom he accused of leaning too far towards Lutheranism. The young man was said to have denied the body of God to be in the sacrament in corporal substance but only to be there spiritually. Lambert was tried and burned alive. This was merely Henry's answer to the Catholics; he was telling them that he favoured neither extreme sect. Montague and Exeter went to the block as traitors, not as Catholics. Catholic or Lutheran, it mattered not. No favouritism. No swaying from one sect to another. He only asked allegiance to the King.

Francis thought this would be a good moment to undermine English commerce which, while he and Charles had been wasting their people's energy in war, Henry had been able to extend. Henry shrewdly saw what was about to happen and again acted quickly. He promised the Flemish merchants that for seven years Flemish goods should pay no more duty than those of the English. The merchants – a thrifty people – were overjoyed, seeing years of prosperous trading stretching before them. If their Emperor would make war on England he could hardly hope for much support from a nation benefiting from good trade with that country on whom Charles wished them to make war.

This was a good move, but Henry's fears flared up afresh when the Emperor, visiting his domains, decided to travel through France to Germany, instead of going by sea or through Italy and Austria as was his custom. This seemed to Henry a gesture of great friendship. What plans would the two old enemies formulate when they met in France? Would England be involved in those plans?

Cromwell, to whose great interest it was to turn England from the Catholics and so make more secure his own position, seized this chance of urging on Henry the selection of a wife from one of the German Protestant houses. Cromwell outlined his plan. For years the old Duke of Cleves had wanted an alliance with England. His son had a claim to the Duchy of Guelders, which Duchy was in relation to the Emperor Charles very much what Scotland was to Henry, ever ready to be a cause of trouble. A marriage between England and the house of Cleves would therefore seriously threaten the Emperor's hold on his Dutch dominions.

Unfortunately, Anne, sister of the young Duke, had already been promised to the Duke of Lorraine, but it was not difficult to waive this. Holbein was despatched; he made a pretty picture of Anne, and Henry was pleasurably excited and the plans for the marriage went forward.

Henry was impatient. Anne! Her very name enchanted him. He pictured her, gentle and submissive and very very loving. She would have full awareness of her duty; she was no daughter of a humble knight; she had been bred that she might make a good marriage; she would know what was expected of her. He could scarcely wait for her arrival. At last he would find matrimonial happiness, and at the same time confound Charles and Francis.

'Anne!' he mused, and eagerly counted the days until her arrival.

* * *

Jane Acworth was preparing to leave.

'How I shall miss you!' sighed Catherine.

Jane smiled at her slyly. 'It is not I whom you will miss but your secretary!'

'Poor Derham!' said Catherine. 'I fear he will be most unhappy. For I declare it is indeed a mighty task for me to put pen to paper.'

Jane shrugged her shoulders; her thoughts were all for the new home she was to go to and Mr Bulmer whom she was to marry.

'You will think of me often, Jane?' asked Catherine.

Jane laughed. 'I shall think of your receiving your letters. He writes a pretty letter and I dare swear seems to love you truly.'

463

'Ah! That he does. Dear Francis! How faithful he has always been to me.'

'You will marry him one day?'

'We are married, Jane. You know it well. How else . . .'

'How else should you have lived the life you did together! Well, I have heard it whispered that you were very lavish with your favours where a certain Manox was concerned.'

'Oh, speak not of him! That is past and done with. My love for Francis goes on for ever. I was foolish over Manox, but I regret nothing I have done with Francis, nor ever shall.'

'How lonely you will be without me!'

'Indeed, you speak truthfully.'

'And how different this life from that other! Why, scarce anything happens now, but sending letters to Derham and receiving his. What excitement we used to have!'

'You had better not speak of that to Mr Bulmer!' warned Catherine; and they laughed.

It was well to laugh, and she was in truth very saddened by Jane's departure; the receiving and despatching of letters had provided a good deal of excitement in a dull existence.

With Jane's going the days seemed long and monotonous. A letter came from Francis; she read it, tucked it into her bodice and was aware of it all day; but she could not read it very easily and it was not the same without Jane, for she, as well as being happy with a pen was also a good reader. She must reply to Derham, but as the task lacked appeal, she put it off.

The Duchess talked to her of court matters.

'If the King would but take him a wife! I declare it is two years since Queen Jane died, and still no wife! I tell you, Catherine, that if this much talked of marriage with the Duchess of Cleves materializes, I shall look to a place at court for you.'

'How I wish I could go to court!' cried Catherine.

'You will have to mind your manners. Though I will say they have improved since . . . since . . .' The Duchess's brows were dark with memory. 'You would not do so badly now at court, I trow. We must see. We must see.'

Catherine pictured herself at court.

'I should need many new clothes.'

'Dost think Lord William would allow you to go to court in rags! Why even His Grace the Duke would not have that! Ha! I hear he is most angry at this proposed marriage. Master Cromwell has indeed put my noble stepson's nose out of joint. Well, all this is not good for the Howards, and it is a mistake for a house to war within its walls. And so ... it may not be so easy to find you a place at court. And I know that the King does not like the strife between my stepson and his wife. It is not meet that a Duke of noble house should feel so strongly for a washer in his wife's nurseries that he will flaunt the slut in the face of his lady Duchess. The King was ever a moral man, as you must always remember. Ah! Pat my back, child, lest I choke. Where was I? Oh, yes, the Howards are not in favour while Master Cromwell is, and this Cleves marriage is Cromwell-made. Therefore, Catherine, it may not be easy to find you a place at court, for though I dislike my lord Duke with all my heart, he is my stepson, and if he is out of favour at court, depend upon it, we shall be too.'

On another occasion the Duchess sent for Catherine. Her old eyes, bright as a bird's, peered out through her wrinkles.

'Get my cloak, child. I would walk in the gardens and have you accompany me.'

Catherine obeyed, and they stepped out of the house and strolled slowly through the orchards where Catherine had lain so many times with Derham. She had ever felt sad when she was in the orchards being unable to forget Derham, but now she scarcely thought of him, for she knew by the Duchess's demeanour that she had news for her, and she was hoping it was news of a place at court.

'You are an attractive child,' wheezed the Duchess. 'I declare you have a look of your poor tragic cousin. Oh ... it is not obvious. Her hair was black and so were her eyes, and her face was pointed and unforgettable. You are auburn-haired and hazel-eyed and plump-faced. Oh, no, it is not in your face. In your sudden laughter? In your quick movements? She had an air of loving life, and so have you. There was a little bit of Howard in Anne that looked out from her eyes; there is a good deal of Howard in you; and there is the resemblance.'

Catherine wished her grandmother would not talk so frequently of her cousin, for such talk always made her sad.

'You had news for me?' she reminded her.

'Ah, news!' The Duchess purred. 'Well, mayhap it is not yet news. It is a thought. And I will whisper this in your ear, child. I doubt not that the stony-hearted Duke would give his approval, for it is a good match.'

'A match!' cried Catherine.

'You do not remember your dear mother, Catherine?'

'Vaguely I do!' Catherine's large eyes glistened with tears so that they looked like pieces of topaz.

'Your dear mother had a brother, and it is to his son, your cousin, whom we feel you might be betrothed. He is a dear boy, already at court. He is a most handsome creature. Thomas Culpepper, son of Sir John, your mother's brother . . .'

'Thomas Culpepper!' whispered Catherine, her thoughts whirling back to a room at Hollingbourne, to a rustle of creeper, to a stalwart protector, to a kiss in the paddock. She repeated: 'Thomas Culpepper!' She realized that something very unusual was about to happen. A childhood dream was about to come true. 'And he . . . ?' she asked eagerly.

'My dear Catherine, curb your excitement. This is a suggestion merely. The Duke will have to be consulted. The King's consent will be necessary. It is an idea. I was not to tell you yet . . . but seeing you so attractive and marriageable, I could not resist it.'

'My cousin . . .' murmured Catherine. 'Grandmother . . . when I was at Hollingbourne . . . we played together. We loved each other then.'

The Duchess put her finger to her lips.

'Hush, child! Be discreet. This matter must not be made open knowledge yet. Be calm.'

Catherine found that very difficult. She wanted to be

alone to think this out. She tried to picture what Thomas would be like now. She had only a hazy picture of a little boy, telling her in a somewhat shame-faced way that he would marry her.

Derham's letter scraped her skin. The thought of Thomas excited her so much that she had lost her burning desire to see Francis. She was wishing that all her life had been spent as she had passed the last months.

The Duchess was holding her wrists and the Duchess's hands were hot.

'Catherine, I would speak to you very seriously. You will have need of great caution. The distressing things which have happened to you . . .'

Catherine wanted to weep. Oh, how right her grandmother was! If only she had listened even to Mary Lassells! If only she had not allowed herself to drift into that sensuous stream which at the time had been so sweet and cooling to her warm nature and which now was so repulsive to look back on. How she had regretted her affair with Manox when she had found Francis! Now she was beginning to regret her love for Francis as her grandmother talked of Thomas.

'You have been very wicked,' said her grandmother. 'You deserve to die for what you have done. But I will do my best for you. Your wickedness must never get to the Duke's ears.'

Catherine cried out in misery rather than in anger: 'The Duke! What of him and Bess Holland!'

The Duchess was on her dignity. She might say what she would of her erring kinsman, not so Catherine.

'What if his wife's washerwoman be his mistress! He is a man; you are a woman. There is all the difference in the world.'

Catherine was subdued; she began to cry.

'Dry your eyes, you foolish girl, and forget not for one instant that all your wickedness is done with, and it must be as though it never was.'

'Yes, grandmother,' said Catherine, and Derham's letter pricked her skin.

Derham continued to write though he received no answers. Catherine had inherited some of her grandmother's capacity for shifting her eyes from the unpleasant. She thought continually of her cousin Thomas and wondered if he remembered her, if he had heard of the proposed match and if so what he thought of it.

One day, wandering in the orchard, she heard a rustle of leaves behind her, and turning came face to face with Derham. He was smiling; he would have put his arms about her but she held him off.

'Catherine, I have longed to see thee.'

She was silent and frightened. He came closer and took her by the shoulders. 'I had no answer to my letters,' he said.

She said hastily: 'Jane has married and gone to York. You know I was never able to manage a pen.'

'Ah!' His face cleared. 'That was all then? Thank God! I feared . . .' He kissed her on the mouth; Catherine trembled; she was unresponsive.

His face darkened. 'Catherine! What ails thee?'

'Nothing ails me, Francis. It is . . .' But her heart melted to see him standing so forlorn before her, and she could not tell him that she no longer loved him. Let the break come gradually. 'Your return is very sudden. Francis . . .'

'You have changed, Catherine. You are so solemn, so sedate.'

'I was a hoyden before. My grandmother said so.'

'Catherine, what did they do to thee?'

'They beat me with a whip. There never was such a beating. I was sick with the pain of it, and for weeks I could feel it. I was locked up, and ever since I have scarce been able to go out alone. They will be looking for me ere long, I doubt not.'

'Poor Catherine! And this you suffered for my sake! But never forget, Catherine, you are my wife.'

'Francis!' she said, and swallowed. 'That cannot be. They will never consent, and what dost think they would do an you married me in actual fact?'

'We should go away to Ireland.'

'They would never let me go. We should die horrible deaths.'

'They would never catch us, Catherine.'

He was young and eager, fresh from a life of piracy off the coast of Ireland. He had money; he wished to take her away. She could not bear to tell him that they were talking of betrothing her to her cousin, Thomas Culpepper.

She said: 'What dost think would happen to you if you showed yourself?'

'I know not. To hold you in my arms would suffice for anything they could do to me afterwards.'

Such talk frightened her. She escaped, promising to see him again.

She was disturbed. Now that she had seen Derham after his long absence, she knew for truth that which she had begun to suspect. She no longer loved him. She cried herself to sleep, feeling dishonoured and guilty, feeling miserable because she would have to go to her cousin difiled and unclean. Why had she not stayed at Hollingbourne! Why had her mother died! What cruel fate had sent her to the Duchess where there were so many women eager to lead her into temptation! She was not yet eighteen and she had been wicked . . . and all so stupidly and so pointlessly.

She determined to break with Francis; there should be no more clandestine meetings. She would marry Thomas and be such a good wife to him, that when set against years and years of the perfect happiness she would bring him, the sinful years would seem like a tiny mistake on a beautifully written page.

Francis was hurt and angry. He had come back full of hope; he loved her and she was his wife, he reminded her. He had money from his spell of piracy; he was in any case related to the Howards.

She told him she had heard she was to go to court.

'I like that not!' he said.

'But I like it,' she told him.

'Dost know the wickedness of court life?' he demanded.

She shrugged her shoulders. She hated hurting people and being forced to hurt Francis who loved her so truly was a terrible sorrow to her; she found herself disliking him because she had to hurt him.

'You . . . to talk of wickedness . . . when you and I . . .'

He would have no misunderstanding about that.

'What we did, Catherine, is naught. Thou art my wife. Never forget it. Many people are married at an early age. We have done no wrong.'

'You know we are not husband and wife!' she retorted. 'It was a fiction to say we are; it was but to make it easy. We have sinned, and I cannot bear it. I wish we had never met.'

Poor Derham was heartbroken. He had thought of no one else all the time he had been away. He begged her to remember how she had felt towards him before he went away. Then he heard the rumour of her proposed betrothal to Culpepper.

'This then,' he said angrily, 'is the reason for your change of heart. You are going to marry this Culpepper?'

She demanded what right he had to ask such a question, adding: 'For you know I will not have you, and if you have heard such report, you heard more than I do know!'

They quarrelled then. She had deceived him, he said. How could she, in view of their contract, think of marrying another man? She must fly with him at once.

'Nay, nay!' cried Catherine, weeping bitterly. 'Francis, please be reasonable. How could I fly with you? Dost not see it would mean death to you! I have hurt you and you have hurt me. The only hope for a good life for us both is never to see each other again.'

Someone was calling her. She turned to him imploringly. 'Go quickly. I dare not think what would happen to you were you found here.'

'They could not hurt me, an they put me on the rack, as you have hurt me.'

Such words pierced like knives into the soft heart of Catherine Howard. She could not be happy, knowing she had hurt him so deeply. Was there to be no peace for her, no happiness, because she had acted foolishly when she was but a child?

The serving-maid who had called her told her her grandmother would speak to her at once. The Duchess was excited.

'I think, my dear, that you are to go to court. As soon as

the new queen arrives you will be one of her maids of honour. There! What do you think of that? We must see that you are well equipped. Fear not! You shall not disgrace us! And let me whisper a secret. While you are at court, you may get a chance to see Thomas Culpepper. Are you not excited?'

Catherine made a great effort to forget Francis Derham and think of the exciting life which was opening out before her. Court . . . and Thomas Culpepper.

* * *

Henry was on his way to Rochester to greet his new wife. He was greatly excited. Such a wise marriage this was! Ha! Charles! he thought. What do you think of this, eh? And you, Francis, who think yourself so clever? I doubt not, dear Emperor, that Guelders is going to be a thorn in your fleshy side for many a long day!

Anne! He could not help his memories. But this Anne would be different from that other. He thought of that exquisite miniature of Holbein's; the box it had arrived in was in the form of a white rose, so beautifully executed, that in itself it was a fine work of art; the carved ivory top of the box had to be unscrewed to show the miniature at the bottom of it. He had been joyful ever since the receipt of it. Oh, he would enjoy himself with this Anne, thinking, all the time he caressed her, not only of the delights of her body, but of sardonic Francis and that Charles who believed himself to be astute.

He had a splendid gift of sables for his bride. He was going to creep in on her unceremoniously. He would dismiss her attendants, for this would be the call of a lover rather than the visit of a king. He chuckled. It was so agreeable to be making the right sort of marriage. Cromwell was a clever fellow; his agents had reported that the beauty of Anne of Cleves exceeded that of Christina of Milan as the sun doth the moon!

Henry was fast approaching fifty, but he felt twenty, so eager he was, as eager as a bridegroom with his first wife. Anne was about twenty-four; it seemed delightfully young when one was fifty. She could not speak very much English; he could not speak much German. That would add piquancy to his courtship. Such a practised lover as himself did not need words to get what he wanted from a woman. He laughed in anticipation. Not since his marriage to Anne Boleyn, said those about him, had the King been in such high humour.

When he reached Rochester, accompanied by two of his attendants he went into Anne's chamber. At the door he paused in horror. The woman who curtseyed before him was not at all like the bride of his imaginings. It was the same face he had seen in the miniature, and it was not the same. Her forehead was wide and high, her eyes dark, her lashes thick, her eyebrows black and definitely marked; her black hair was parted in the centre and smoothed down at the sides of her face. Her dress was most unbecoming with its stiff high collar resembling a man's coat. It was voluminous after the Flemish fashion, and English fashions had been following the French ever since Anne Boleyn had introduced them at court. Henry started in dismay, for the face in the miniature had been delicately coloured so that the skin had the appearance of rose petals; in reality Anne's skin was brownish and most disfiguringly pock-marked. She seemed quite ugly to Henry, and as it did not occur to him that his person might have produced a similar shock to her, he was speechless with anger.

His one idea was to remove himself from her presence as quickly as possible; his little scheme to 'nourish love' as he had described it to Cromwell, had failed. He was too upset to give her the sables. She should have no such gift from his hands! He was mad with rage. His wise marriage had brought him a woman who delighted him not. Because her name was Anne, he had thought of another Anne, and his vision of his bride had been a blurred Anne Boleyn, as meek as Jane Seymour. And here he was, confronted by a creature whose accents jarred on him, whose face and figure repelled him. He had been misled. Holbein had misled him! Cromwell had misled him. Cromwell! He gnashed his teeth over that name. Yes, Cromwell had brought about this unhappy state of affairs. Cromwell had brought him Anne of Cleves.

'Alas!' he cried. 'Whom shall men trust! I see no such thing as hath been shown me of her pictures and report. I am ashamed that men have praised her as they have done, and I love her not!'

But he was polite enough to Anne in public, so that the crowds of his subjects to whom pageantry was the flavouring in their dull dish of life, did not guess that the King was anything but satisfied. Anne in her cloth of gold and rich jewellery seemed beautiful enough to them; they did not know that in private the King was berating Cromwell, likening his new bride to a great Flanders mare, that his conscience was asking him if the lady's contract with the Duke of Lorraine did not make a marriage between herself and the King illegal.

Poor Anne was deliberately delayed at Dartford whilst Henry tried to find some excuse for not continuing with the marriage. She was melancholy. The King had shown his dislike quite clearly; she had seen the great red face grow redder; she had seen the small eyes almost disappear into the puffy flesh; she had seen the quick distaste. She herself was disappointed, such accounts had she had of the once handsomest prince in Christendom; and in reality he was a puffed-out, unwieldy, fleshy man with great white hands overloaded with jewels, into whose dazzling garments two men could be wrapped with room to spare; on his face was the mark of internal disease; and bandages bulged about his leg; he had the wickedest mouth and cruellest eyes she had ever seen. She could but, waiting at Dartford, remember stories she had heard of this man. How had Katharine met her death? What had she suffered before she died? All the world knew the fate of tragic Anne Boleyn. And poor Jane Seymour? Was it true that after having given the King a son she had been so neglected that she had died?

She thought of the long and tiring journey from Dusseldorf to Calais, and the Channel crossing to her new home; she thought of the journey to Rochester; until then she had been reasonably happy. Then she had seen him, and seeing him it was not difficult to believe there was a good deal of truth in the stories she had heard concerning his treatment of his wives. And now she was to be one of them, or perhaps she would not, for, having seen the distaste in his face, she could guess at the meaning of this delay. She did not know whether she hoped he would marry her or whether she would prefer to suffer the humiliation of being sent home because her person was displeasing to him.

Meanwhile Henry was flying into such rages that all who must come into contact with him went in fear for their lives. Was there a previous contract? He was sure there was! Should he endanger the safety of England by producing another bastard? His conscience, his most scrupulous conscience, would not allow him to put his head into a halter until he was sure.

It was Cromwell who must make him act reasonably, Cromwell who would get a cuff for his pains.

'Your most Gracious Majesty, the Emperor is being fêted in Paris. An you marry not this woman you throw the Duke of Cleves into an alliance with Charles and Francis. We should stand alone.'

Cromwell was eloquent and convincing; after all he was pleading for Cromwell. If this marriage failed, Cromwell failed, and he knew his head to be resting very lightly on his shoulders, and that the King would be delighted to find a reason for striking it off. But Henry knew that in this matter, Cromwell spoke wisely. If Henry feared civil war more than anything, then next he feared friendship between Charles and Francis, and this was what had been accomplished. He dared not refuse to marry Anne of Cleves.

'If I had known so much before, she should not have come hither!' he said, looking menacingly at Cromwell, as though the meetings between Charles and Francis had been arranged by him. Henry's voice broke on a tearful note. 'But what remedy now! What remedy but to put my head in the yoke and marry this . . .' His cheeks puffed with anger and his eyes were murderous. . . . 'What remedy but to marry this great Flanders mare!'

There followed the ceremony of marriage with its gorgeously apparelled men and women, its gilded barges and banners and streamers. Henry in a gown of cloth of gold raised with great silver flowers, with his coat of crimson satin decorated with great flashing diamonds, was a sullen bridegroom. Cromwell was terrified, for he knew not how this would end, and he had in his mind such examples of men who had displeased the King as would make a braver man than he was tremble. The Henry of ten years ago would never have entered into this marriage; but this Henry was more careful of his throne. He spoke truthfully when he had said a few hours before the ceremony that if it were not for the sake of his realm he would never have done this thing.

Cromwell did not give up hope. He knew the King well; it might be that any wife was better than no wife at all; and there were less pleasant looking females than Anne of Cleves. She was docile enough and the King liked docility in women; the last Queen had been married for that very quality.

The morning after the wedding day he sought audience with the King; he looked in vain for that expression of satiety in the King's coarse red face.

'Well?' roared Henry, and Cromwell noticed with fresh terror that his master liked him no better this day than he had done on the previous one.

'Your Most Gracious Majesty,' murmured the trembling Cromwell, 'I would know if you are any more pleased with your Queen.'

'Nay, my lord!' said the King viciously, and glared at Cromwell, laying the blame for this catastrophe entirely upon him. 'Much worse! For by her breasts and belly she should be no maid; which, when I felt them, strake me so to the heart that I had neither will nor courage to prove the rest.'

Cromwell left his master, trembling for his future.

*   *   *

Catherine Howard could not sleep for excitement. At last she had come to court. Her grandmother had provided her with the garments she would need, and Catherine had never

475

felt so affluent in the whole of her eighteen years. How exciting it was to peep through the windows at personages who had been mere names to her! She saw Thomas Cromwell walking through the courtyards, cap in hand, with the King himself. Catherine shuddered at the sight of that man. 'Beware of the blacksmith's son!' her grandmother had said. 'He is no friend of the Howards.' Always before Catherine had seen the King from a great distance; closer he seemed larger, more sparkling than ever, and very terrifying, so that she felt a greater urge to run from him than she did even from Thomas Cromwell. The King was loud in conversation, laughter and wrath, and his red face in anger was an alarming sight. Sometimes he would hobble across the courtyards with a stick, and she had seen his face go dark with the pain he suffered in his leg, and he would shout and cuff anyone who annoyed him. His cheeks were so puffed out and swollen that his eyes seemed lost between them and his forehead, and were more like the flash of bright stones than eyes. This King made Catherine shiver. Cranmer she saw too – quiet and calm in his archbishop's robes. She saw her uncle and would have hidden herself, but his sharp eyes would pick her out and he would nod curtly.

Catherine was enjoying life, for Derham could not pester her at court as he had done at the Duchess's house, and when she did not see him she could almost forget the sorrow that had come to her through him. She loved the Queen, and wept for her because she was so unhappy. The King did not love her; he was with her only in public. The ladies whispered together that when they went to the royal bedchamber at night the King said Good night to the Queen and that nothing passed between them until the morning when he said Good morning. They giggled over the extraordinary relationship of the King and Queen; and Catherine was too inexperienced and too much in awe of them not to giggle with them, but she was really sorry for the sad-eyed Queen. But Catherine did refrain from laughing with them over the overcrowded and tasteless wardrobe of the Queen.

'Ah!' whispered the ladies. 'You should have seen the other Queen Anne. What clothes she had, and how she knew the way to wear them! But this one! No wonder the King has no fancy for her. Ja, ja, ja! That is all she can say!'

Catherine said: 'But she is very kind.'

'She is without spirit to be otherwise!'

But that was not true. Catherine, who had been often beaten by the hard-handed Duchess, was susceptible to kindness; she sat with the Queen and learned the Flemish style of embroidery, and was very happy to serve Anne of Cleves.

There was something else that made Catherine happy. Thomas Culpepper was at court. She had not yet seen him, but each day she hoped for their reunion. He was, she heard, a great favourite with the King himself and it was his duty to sleep in the royal apartment and superintend those who dressed the King's leg. She wondered if he knew she was here, and if he were waiting for the reunion as eagerly as she was.

Gardiner, the Bishop of Winchester, gave a banquet one evening. Catherine was very excited about this, for she was going to sing, and it would be the first time she had ever sung alone before the King.

'You are a little beauty!' said one of the ladies. 'What a charming gown!'

'My grandmother gave it to me,' said Catherine, smoothing the rich cloth with the pleasure of one who has always longed for beautiful clothes and has never before possessed them.

'If you sing as prettily as you look,' she was told, 'you will be a successful young woman.'

Catherine danced all the way down to the barge; she sang as they went along the river; she danced into the Bishop's house. Over her small head smiles were exchanged; she was infectiously gay and very young.

'Mind you do not forget your words.'

'Oh, what if I do! I feel sure I shall!'

'Committed to the Tower!' they teased her, and she laughed with them, her cheeks aglow, her auburn curls flying.

She sat at the great table with the humblest of the ladies.

The King, at the head of the table, was in a noisy mood. He was eating and drinking with great heartiness as was his custom, congratulating the Bishop on his cook's efforts, swilling great quantities of wine, belching happily.

Would His Most Gracious Majesty care for a little music? the Bishop would know.

The King was ever ready to be entertained, and there was nothing he liked better, when he was full of good food and wine, than to hear a little music. He felt pleasantly sleepy; he smiled with benevolent eyes on Gardiner. A good servant, a good servant. He was in a mellow mood; he would have smiled on Cromwell.

He looked along the table. A little girl was singing. She had a pretty voice; her flushed cheeks reminded him of June roses, her hair gleamed gold; she was tiny and plump and very pretty. There was something in her which startled him out of his drowsiness. It was not that she was the least bit like Anne. Anne's hair had been black as had her eyes; Anne had been tall and slender. How could this little girl be like Anne? He did not know what could have suggested such a thought to him, and yet there it was ... but elusive, so that he could not catch it, could not even define it. All he could say was that she reminded him. It was the tilt of her head, the gesture of the hands, that graceful back bent forward, and now the pretty head tossed back. He was excited, as for a long time he had wanted to be excited. He had not been so excited since the early days of marriage with Anne.

'Who is the girl now singing?' he asked Gardiner.

'That, Your Majesty, is Norfolk's niece, Catherine Howard.'

The King tapped his knee reflectively. Now he had it. Anne had been Norfolk's niece too. The elusive quality was explained by a family resemblance.

'Norfolk's niece!' he said, and growled without anger, so that the growl came through his pouched lips like a purr. He watched the girl. He thought, By God, the more I see of her the more I like her!

He was comparing her with his pock-marked Queen. Give him English beauties, sweet-faced and sweet-voiced. He liked sonorous English on the tongue, not harsh German. Like a rose she was, flushed, laughing and happy.

'She seems little more than a child,' he said to Gardiner.

Norfolk was beside the King. Norfolk was cunning as a monkey, artful as a fox. He knew well how to interpret that soft look in the royal eyes; he knew the meaning of the slurring tones. Norfolk had been furious when the King had chosen Anne Boleyn instead of his own daughter, the Lady Mary Howard. Every family wanted boys, but girls, when they were as pleasant to the eye as Anne Boleyn and Catherine Howard, had their uses.

'We liked well your little niece's playing,' said the King.

Norfolk murmured that His Majesty was gracious, and that it gave him the utmost delight that a member of his family should give some small pleasure to her sovereign.

'She gives us much pleasure,' said the King. 'We like her manners and we like her singing. Who is her father?'

'My brother Edmund, sir. Your Majesty doubtless remembers him. He did well at Flodden Field.'

The King nodded. 'I remember well,' he said kindly. 'A good servant!' He was ready to see through a haze of benevolence, every member of a family which could produce such a charming child as Catherine Howard.

'Doubtless Your Most Gracious Majesty would do my little niece the great honour of speaking to her. A royal compliment on her little talents would naturally mean more to the child than the costliest gems.'

'Right gladly I will speak to her. Let her be brought to me.'

'Your Majesty, I would humbly beg that you would be patient with her simplicity. She has led but a sheltered life until recently she came to court. I fear she may seem very shy and displease you with her gaucherie. She is perhaps too modest.'

'Too modest!' The King all but shouted. 'How is it possible, my lord, for maidens to be too modest!' He was all impatience to have her close to him, to study the fresh young skin, to pat her shoulder and let her know she had pleased her King. 'Bring her to me without delay.'

Norfolk himself went to Catherine. She stopped playing and looked at him in fear. He always terrified her, but now his eyes glittered speculatively and in the friendliest manner.

Catherine stood up. 'Have I done aught wrong?'

'Nay, nay!' said his Grace. 'Your singing has pleased His Majesty and he would tell you how much. Speak up when he talks to you. Do not mumble, for he finds that most irritating. Be modest but not shy.'

The King was waiting impatiently. Catherine curtseyed low and a fat, white, jewelled hand patted her shoulder.

'Enough!' he said, not at all unkindly, and she rose and stood trembling before him.

He said: 'We liked your singing. You have a pretty voice.'

'Your Majesty is most gracious. . . .' she stammered and blushed sweetly. He watched the blood stain her delicate cheeks. By God, he thought, there never has been such a one since Anne. And his eyes filled with sudden self-pity to think how ill life had used him. He had loved Anne who had deceived him. He had loved Jane who had died. And now he was married to a great Flanders mare, when in his kingdom, standing before him so close that he had but to stretch out his hands and take her, was the fairest rose that ever grew in England.

'We are glad to be gracious to those who please us,' he said. 'You are lately come to court? Come! You may sit here . . . close to us.'

'Yes, please Your Majesty. I . . . I have lately come . . .'

She was a bud just unfolding, he thought; she was the most perfect creature he had ever seen, for while Anne had been irresistible, she had also been haughty, vindictive and demanding, whereas this little Catherine Howard with her doe's eyes and gentle frightened manner, had the beauty of Anne and the docility of Jane. Ah, he thought, how happy I should have been if instead of that Flemish creature I had found this lovely girl at Rochester. How I should have enjoyed presenting her with costly sables; jewels too; there is naught I would not give to such a lovely child.

He leaned towards her; his breath, not too sweet, warmed

her cheek, and she withdrew involuntarily; he thought this but natural modesty and was enchanted with her.

'Your uncle has been talking to me of you.'

Her uncle! She blushed again, feeling that the Duke would have said nothing good of her.

'He told me of your father. A good man, Lord Edmund. And your grandmother, the Dowager Duchess is a friend of ours.'

She was silent; she had not dreamed of such success; she had known her voice was moderately good, nothing more, certainly not good enough to attract the King.

'And how do you like the court?' he asked.

'I like it very much, please Your Majesty.'

'Then I am right glad that our court pleases you!' He laughed and she laughed too. He saw her pretty teeth, her little white throat, and he felt a desire to make her laugh some more.

'Now we have discovered you,' he said, 'we shall make you sing to us often. How will you like that, eh?'

'I shall find it a great honour.'

She looked as if she meant this; he liked her air of candid youth.

He said: 'Your name is Catherine, I know. Tell me, how old are you?'

'I am eighteen, sir.'

Eighteen! He repeated it, and felt sad. Eighteen, and he close fifty. Getting old; short of breath; quick of temper; often dizzy; often after meals suffering from divers disorders of the body; his leg getting worse instead of better; he could not sit his horse as once he had done. Fifty . . . and eighteen!

He watched her closely. 'You shall play and sing to us again,' he said.

He wanted to watch her without talking; his thoughts were busy. She was a precious jewel. She had everything he would look for in a wife; she had beauty, modesty, virtue and charm. It hurt him to look at her and see behind her the shadow of his Queen. He wanted Catherine Howard as urgently as once he had wanted Anne Boleyn. His hunger for Catherine was more pathetic than that he had known for Anne, for when he had loved Anne he had been a comparatively young man. Catherine was precious because she was a beacon to light the dark days of his middle-age with her youthful glow.

Sweetly she sang. He wanted to stretch out his hands and pet her and keep her by him. This was cold age's need of warm youth. He thought, I would be a parent and a lover to her, for she is younger than my daughter Mary, and she is lovely enough to make any but the blind love her, and those she would enchant with her voice.

He watched her and she played again; then he would have her sit with him; nor did she stir from his side the evening through.

*   *   *

A ripple of excitement went through the court.

'Didst see the King with Mistress Catherine Howard last night?'

'I declare I never saw His Majesty so taken with a girl since Anne Boleyn.'

'Much good will it do her. His mistress? What else since he has a Queen?'

'The King has a way with queens, has he not?'

'Hush! Dost want to go to the Tower on a charge of treason?'

'Poor Queen Anne, she is so dull, so German! And Catherine Howard is the prettiest thing we have had at court for many years!'

'Poor Catherine Howard!'

'*Poor*, forsooth!'

'Would *you* change places with her? Remember ...'

'Hush! They were unfortunate!'

Cromwell very quickly grasped the new complications brought about by the King's infatuation for Catherine Howard, and it seemed to him that his end was in sight. Norfolk could be trusted to exploit this situation to the full. Catherine was a Catholic, a member of the most devout Catholic family in England. Continental events loomed up darkly for Cromwell. When the Emperor had passed through France there were signs that his friendship with Francis was not quite as cordial as it had been. Charles was no longer thinking of attacking England, and it was only when such plans interested him that he would be eager to take Francis as an ally. Trouble was springing up over Charles's domains and he would have his hands tied very satisfactorily from Henry's point of view if not from Cromwell's. When the Duke of Cleves asked for help in securing the Duchy of Guelders, Henry showed that he was in no mood to give it.

Cromwell saw the position clearly. He had made no mistakes. He had merely gambled and lost. When the marriage with Anne of Cleves had been made it was necessary to the safety of England; now England had passed out of that particular danger and the marriage was no longer necessary, and the King would assuredly seize an excuse to rid himself of his most hated minister. Cromwell had known this all the time. He could not play a good game if he had not the cards. With Charles and Francis friendly, he had stood a chance of winning; when relations between these two were strained, Cromwell was unlucky. On Cromwell's advice Henry had put a very irritating yoke about his neck. Now events had shown that it was no longer necessary that the yoke should remain. And there was Norfolk, making the most of Cromwell's ill luck, cultivating his niece, arranging meetings between her and the King, offering up the young girl as a sacrifice from the House of Howard on that already blood-stained altar of the King's lusts.

Henry's mind was working rapidly. He must have Catherine Howard. He was happy; he was in love. Catherine was the sweetest creature in the world, and there was none but Catherine who could keep him happy. She was delightful; she was sweetly modest; and the more he knew her, the more she delighted him. Just to see her skipping about the Hampton Court gardens which he had planned with her cousin Anne, made him feel younger. She would be the perfect wife; he did not want her to be his mistress – she was too sweet and pure for that – he wanted her beside him on the throne, that he might live out his life with none other but her.

She was less shy with him now; she was full of laughter, but ready to weep for other people's sorrows. Sweet Catherine! The sweetest of women! The rose without a thorn! Anne had perhaps been the most gorgeous rose that ever bloomed, but oh, the thorns! In his old age this sweet creature should be beside him. And he was not so old! He could laugh throatily, holding her hand in his, pressing the cool, plump fingers against his thigh. He was not so old. He had years of pleasant living in front of him. He did not want riotous living, he told himself. All he had ever wanted was married happiness with one woman, and he had not found her until now. He must marry Catherine; he must make her his Queen.

His conscience began to worry him. He realized that Anne's contract with the Duke of Lorraine had ever been on his mind, and it was for this reason that he had never consummated the marriage. So cursed had he been in his matrimonial undertakings, that he went cautiously. He had never been Anne's true husband because of his dread of presenting another bastard to the nation. Moreover the lady was distasteful to him and he suspected her virtue. Oh, he had said naught about it at the time, being over-merciful perhaps, being anxious not to accuse before he was sure. He had not been free when he entered into the marriage; only because he had felt England to be defenceless against the union of Charles and Francis had he allowed it to take place. England owed him a divorce, for had he not entered into this most unwelcome engagement for England's sake? And he owed England children. He had one boy and two girls – both of these last illegitimate; and the boy did not enjoy the best of health. He had failed to make the throne secure for Tudors; he must have an opportunity of doing so. Something must be done.

*   *   *

The Dowager Duchess of Norfolk could scarcely believe her ears when she heard the news. The King and her granddaughter! What a wonderful day this was to bring her such news!

She would bring out her most costly jewels. 'If Catherine could attract him in those simple things,' she babbled, 'how much more so will she when I have dressed her!'

For once she and the Duke were in agreement. He visited her, and the visit was the most amiable they had ever shared. The Dowager Duchess had never thought she and the Duke would one day put their heads together over the hatching of a plot. But when the Duke had gone, the Duchess was overcome with fears, for it seemed to her that another granddaughter looked at her from out of the dark shadows of her room and would remind her of her own tragic fate. How beautiful and proud that Queen Anne had been on the day of her coronation! Never would the Duchess be able to forget the sight of her entering the Tower to be received by her royal lover. And then, only three years later....

The Duchess called for lights. 'I declare the gloom of this house displeases me. Light up! Light up! What are you wenches thinking of to leave me in the dark!'

She felt easier when the room was lighted. It was stupid to imagine for a moment that the dead could return. 'She cannot die for what was done before,' she muttered to herself; and she set about sorting out her most valuable jewels – some for Catherine in which to enchant the King; and some for herself when she should go to another coronation of yet another granddaughter.

*   *   *

The Earl of Essex, who had been such a short time before plain Thomas Cromwell, was awaiting death. He knew it was inevitable. He had been calculating and unscrupulous; he had been devilishly cruel; he had tortured men's bodies and sacrificed their flesh to the flames; he had dissolved the monasteries, inflicting great hardship on their inmates, and he had invented crimes for these people to have committed, to justify his actions; with Sampson, Bishop of Chichester, he had worked out a case against Anne Boleyn, and had brought about her death through the only man who would talk against her, a poor delicate musician who had had to be violently tortured first; all these crimes – and many others – had he committed, but they had all been done at the command of his master. They were not Cromwell's crimes; they were Henry's crimes.

And now he awaited the fate which he had so many times prepared for others. It was ten years since the death of Wolsey, and they had been ten years of mounting power for Cromwell; and now here was the inevitable end. The King had rid himself of Wolsey – for whom he had had some affection – because of Anne Boleyn; now he would rid himself of Cromwell – whom, though he did not love him, he knew to be a faithful servant – for Catherine Howard. For though this young girl, whom the King would make his Queen, bore no malice to any, and would never ask to see even an enemy punished but rather beg that he should be forgiven, yet was it through her that Cromwell was falling; for cruel Norfolk and Gardiner had risen to fresh power since the King had shown his preference for Norfolk's niece, and these two men, who represented Catholicism in all its old forms, would naturally wish to destroy one who, with staunch supporters like Thomas Wyatt, stood more strongly for the new religion than he would dare admit. Whilst he was despoiling the monasteries, he had been safe, and knowing this he had left one very wealthy institution untouched, so that in an emergency he might dangle its treasure before the King's eyes and so earn a little respite. This he had done, and in throwing in this last prize he had earned the title of Earl of Essex.

It was a brief triumph, for Cromwell's position was distressingly similar to that in which Wolsey had found himself. Had not Wolsey flung his own treasure to the King in a futile effort to save himself? Hampton Court and York House; his houses and plate and art treasures. Cromwell, as Wolsey before him, if it would please the King, must rid his master of a wife whom he, Cromwell, supported; but if he succeeded in doing this, he would put on the throne a member of the Howard family who had sworn to effect his destruction.

When the King realized that Cromwell was hesitating to choose between two evils, since he could not be certain as to which was the lesser, he lost patience, and declared that Cromwell had been working against his aims for a settlement of the religious problem, and this was, without a doubt, treason.

Now, awaiting his end, he recalled that gusty day when as he travelled with the members of the privy council to the palace a wind had blown his bonnet from his head. How significant had it been when they, discourteously, did not remove their bonnets, but had kept them on whilst he stood bareheaded! And their glances had been both eager and furtive. And then later he had come upon them sitting round the council chamber, talking together, insolently showing him that they would not wait for his coming; and as he would have sat down with them, Norfolk's voice had rung out, triumphant, the voice of a man who at last knows an old enemy is defeated. 'Cromwell! Traitors do not sit with gentlemen!'

He had been arrested then and taken to the Tower. He smiled bitterly, imagining the King's agents making inventories of his treasures. How often had he been sent to do a similar errand in the King's name! He had gambled and lost; there was a small grain of comfort in the knowledge that it was not due to lack of skill, but ill luck which had brought about his end.

A messenger was announced; he came from the King. Cromwell's hopes soared. He had served the King well; surely His Majesty could not desert him now. Perhaps he could still be useful to the King. Yes! It seemed he could. The King needed Cromwell to effect his release from the marriage into which he had led him. Cromwell must do as he was bid. The reward? The King was ever generous, ever merciful, and Cromwell should be rewarded when he had freed the King. Cromwell was a traitor and there were two deaths accorded to traitors. One was the honourable and easy death by the axe. The other? Cromwell knew better than most. How many poor wretches had he condemned to die that way? The victim was hanged but not killed; he was

487

disembowelled and his entrails were burned while the utmost care was taken to keep him alive; only then was he beheaded. This should be Cromwell's reward for his last service to his master: In his gracious mercy, the most Christian King would let him choose which way he would die.

Cromwell made his choice. He would never fail to serve the King.

* * *

Anne had been sent to Richmond. It was significant that the King did not accompany her. She was terrified. This had happened before, with another poor lady in the rôle she now must play. What next? she wondered. She was alone in a strange land, among people whose language she could not speak, and she felt that death was very close to her. Her brother the Duke of Cleves was far away and he was but insignificant compared with this great personage who was her husband, and who thought little of murder and practised it as lightly as some people eat, drink and sleep.

She had endured such mental anguish since her marriage that she felt limp and unequal to the struggle she would doubtless have to put up for her life. Her nights were sleepless; her days were so full of terror that a tap on a door would set her shivering as though she suffered from some ague.

She had been Queen of England for but a few months and she felt as though she had lived through years of torment. Her husband made no attempt to hide his distaste for her. She was surrounded by attendants who mimicked her because they were encouraged in this unkindness by the King who was ready to do any cruel act to discredit her, and who found great satisfaction in hurting her – and inspiring others to hurt her – as he declared her unpleasant appearance hurt him. The Lady Rochford, one of her ladies, who had been the wife of another queen's late brother, was an unpleasant creature, who listened at doors and spied upon her, and reported all that she said to the other ladies and tittered unkindly about her; they laughed at her clothes which she was ready to admit were not as graceful as those worn in

England. The King was hinting that she had led an immoral life before she came to England; this was so unjust and untrue that it distressed her more than anything else she had been called upon to endure, because she really believed Henry did doubt her virtue. She did not know him well enough to realize that this was characteristic of him, and that he accused others of his own failings because he drew moral strength from this attitude and deceived himself into thinking that he could not be guilty of that which he condemned fiercely in others. So poor Queen Anne was a most unhappy woman.

There was one little girl recently come to court whom she could have loved; and how ironical it was that this child's beauty and charm should have increased the King's animosity towards herself. The King would rid himself of me, she thought, to put poor little Catherine Howard on the throne. This he may well do, and how I pity that poor child, for when I am removed, she will stand in my most unhappy shoes!

As she sat in the window seat a message was brought to her that my lords Suffolk and Southampton with Sir Thomas Wriothesley were without, and would speak with her.

The room began to swing round her; she clutched at the scarlet hangings to steady herself. She felt the blood drain away from her head. It had come. Her doom was upon her!

When Suffolk with Southampton and Wriothesley entered the room they found the Queen lying on the floor in a faint. They roused her and helped her to a chair. She opened her eyes and saw Suffolk's florid face close to her own, and all but fainted again; but that nobleman began to talk to her in soothing tones and his words were reassuring.

What he said seemed to Anne the happiest news she had ever heard in her life. The King, out of his regard for her – which meant his regard for the house of Cleves, but what did that matter! – wished to adopt her as his sister, providing she would resign her title of Queen. The King wished her no ill, but she well knew that she had never been truly married to His Majesty because of that previous contract with the Duke of Lorraine. This was why His Most Cautious

Majesty had never consummated the marriage. All she need do was to behave in a reasonable manner, and she should have precedence at court over every lady, excepting only the King's daughters and her who would become his Queen. The English taxpayers would provide her with an income of three thousand pounds a year.

The King's sister! Three thousand pounds a year! This was miraculous! This was happiness! That corpulent, perspiring, sullen, angry, spiteful, wicked monster of a man was no longer her husband! She need not live close to him! She could have her own establishment! She need not return to her own dull country, but she could live in this beautiful land which she had already begun to love in spite of its King! She was free.

She almost swooned again, for the reaction of complete joy after absolute misery was overwhelming.

Suffolk and Southampton exchanged glances with Wriothesley. The King need not have been so generous with his three thousand pounds. It had not occurred to him that Anne would be so eager to be rid of him. They would keep that from the King; better to let His August Majesty believe that their tact had persuaded the woman it would be well to accept.

Anne bade her visitors a gay farewell. Never had Henry succeeded in making one of his wives so happy.

* * *

Catherine was bewildered. Quite suddenly her position had changed. Instead of being the humblest newcomer, she was the most important person at court. Everyone paid deference to her; even her grim old uncle had a pleasant word for her, so that Catherine felt she had misjudged him. The Dowager Duchess, her grandmother, would deck her out in the most costly jewels, but these were poor indeed compared with those which came from the King. He called her 'The Rose without a Thorn'; and this he had had inscribed on some of the jewels he had given her. He had chosen her device which was 'No other Will but His.'

Catherine was sorry for the poor Queen, and could not

bear to think that she was displacing her; but when she heard that Anne appeared to be happier at Richmond than she had ever been at court, she began to enjoy her new power.

Gifts were sent to her, not only from the King, but from the courtiers. Her grandmother petted, scolded and warned at the same time. 'Be careful! No word of what has happened with Derham must ever reach the King's ears.'

'I would prefer to tell him all,' said Catherine uneasily.

'I never heard such folly!' Her Grace's black eyes glinted. 'Do you know where Derham is?' she asked. And Catherine assured her that she did not know.

'That is well,' said the Duchess. 'I and Lord William have spoken to the King of your virtues and how you will make a most gracious and gentle queen.'

'But shall I?' asked Catherine.

'Indeed you shall. Now, no folly. Come let me try this ruby ring on your finger. I would have you know that the King, while liking well our talk, would have been most displeased with us had we done aught but sing your praises. Oh, what it is to be loved by a king! Catherine Howard, I declare you give yourself graces already!'

Catherine had thought that she would be terrified of the King, but this was not so. There was nothing for her to fear in this great soft man. His voice changed when he addressed her, and his hard mouth could express nothing but kindness for her. He would hold her hand and stroke her cheek and twine her hair about his fingers; and sometimes press his lips against the flesh on her plump shoulders. He told her that she would mean a good deal to him, that he wished above all things to make her his Queen, that he had been a most unhappy man until he had set eyes on her. Catherine looked in wonder at the little tear-filled eyes. Was this the man who had sent her beautiful cousin to her death? How could simple Catherine believe ill of him when she stood before him and saw real tears in his eyes?

He talked of Anne, for he saw that Anne was in Catherine's thoughts; she was, after all, her own cousin, and the two had known and been fond of one another.

'Come and sit upon my knee, Catherine,' he said, and she sat there while he pressed her body against his and talked of Anne Boleyn. 'Wert deceived as I was by all that charm and beauty, eh? Ah! but thou wert but a child and I a man. Didst know that she sought to take my life and poison my daughter Mary? Dost know that my son died through a spell she cast upon him?'

'It is hard to believe that. She was so kind to me. I have a jewelled tablet she gave me when I was but a baby.'

'Sweet Catherine, I too had gifts from her. I too could not believe ...'

It was easier for Catherine to believe the King who was close to her, when Anne was but a memory.

It was at this time that she met Thomas Culpepper. He was one of the gentlemen of the privy chamber, and had great charm of manner and personal beauty which had pleased the King ever since he had set eyes upon him. Thomas's intimate duties of superintending the carrying out of the doctor's orders regarding the King's leg kept him close to Henry, who had favoured him considerably, and had given him several posts which, while they brought little work, brought good remuneration; he had even given him an abbey. He liked Culpepper; he was amused by Culpepper. In his native Kent, the boy had involved himself in a certain amount of scandal, for it seemed he was wild and not over-scrupulous, but the King was as ready to forgive the faults of those he wished to keep around him, as he was to find fault with those he wished removed.

The knowledge that his cousin was at court soon reached Thomas Culpepper, for since her elevation, everyone was discussing Catherine Howard. Seeing her in the pond garden one afternoon, he went out to her. She was standing by a rose tree, the sun shining on her auburn hair. Thomas immediately understood the King's infatuation.

'You would not remember me,' he said. 'I am your cousin, Thomas Culpepper.'

Her eyes opened very wide and she gave a little trill of pleasure; she held out both her hands.

'Thomas! I had hoped to see you.'

They stood holding hands; studying each other's faces.

How handsome he is! thought Catherine. Even more handsome than he was as a boy!

How charming she is! thought Thomas. How lovable – and in view of what has happened to her during the last weeks, how dangerously lovable! But to Thomas nothing was ever very interesting unless it held an element of danger.

He said greatly daring: 'How beautiful you have grown, Catherine!'

She laughed delightedly. 'That is what everyone says to me now! Do you remember the stick you gave me with which to tap on the wall?'

They were laughing over their memories.

'And the adventures you used to have . . . and how we used to ride in the paddock . . . and how you . . .'

'Said I would marry you!'

'You did, you know, Thomas, and then you never did anything about it!'

'I never forgot!' he lied. 'But now . . .' He looked across the garden and over the hedge to the windows of the palace. Even now, he thought, little hot jealous eyes might have caught sight of him. Living close to the King he knew something of his rages. Dangerously sweet was this contact with Catherine.

'It is too late now,' she said soberly, and she looked very sad. She saw Thomas as the lover to whom she had been betrothed for many years; she forgot Manox and Derham and believed that she had loved Thomas always.

'Suppose that we had married when it was suggested a year or so ago,' said Thomas.

'How different our lives would have been then!'

'And now,' he said, 'I risk my life to speak to you.'

Her eyes widened with terror. 'Then we must not stay here.' She laughed suddenly. They did not know the King, these people who were afraid of him. His Majesty was all kindness, all eagerness to make people happy really. As if he would hurt her cousin if she asked him not to!

'Catherine,' said Thomas, 'I shall risk my life again and again. It will be worth it.'

493

He took her hand and kissed it, and left her in the pond garden.

They could not resist meeting secretly. They met in dark corridors; they feared that if it reached the ears of the King that they were meeting thus, there would be no more such meetings. Sometimes he touched her fingers with his, but nothing more; and after the first few meetings they were in love with each other.

There was a similarity in their natures, both were passionate, reckless people; they were first cousins and they knew now that they wished to enjoy a closer relationship; and because, when they had been children, they had plighted their troth in the paddock of Hollingbourne, they felt life had been cruel to them to keep them apart and bring them together only when it was too late for them to be lovers.

Catherine had little fear for herself, but she feared for him. He, a reckless adventurer who had been involved in more than one dangerous escape, was afraid not for himself but for her.

They would touch hands and cry out to each other: 'Oh, why, oh, why did it have to happen thus!'

She would say to him: 'I shall be passing along the corridor that leads to the music room at three of the clock this afternoon.'

He would answer: 'I will be there as if by accident.'

All their meetings were like that. They would long for them all day, and then when they reached the appointed spot, it might be that someone was there, and it was impossible for them to exchange more than a glance. But to them both this danger was very stimulating.

There was one occasion when he, grown more reckless by the passing of several days which did not bring even a glimpse of her, drew her from the corridor into an antechamber and shut the door on them.

'Catherine,' he said, 'I can endure this no longer. Dost not realize that thou and I were meant one for the other from the first night I climbed into thy chamber? We were but children then, and the years have been cruel to us, but I have a plan. Thou and I will leave the palace together. We will hide ourselves and we will marry.'

She was pale with longing, ever ready to abandon herself to the passion of the moment, but it seemed to her that she heard her cousin's voice warning her. Catherine would never know the true story of Anne Boleyn, but she had loved her and she knew her end had been terrible. Anne had been loved by the same huge man; those eyes had burned hotly for Anne; those warm, moist hands had caressed her. Anne had had no sad story of a cousin to warn her.

Culpepper was kissing her hands and her lips, Catherine's healthy young body was suggesting surrender. Perhaps with Manox or Derham she would have surrendered; but not with Culpepper. She was no longer a lighthearted girl. Dark shadows came pursuing her out of the past. Doll Tappit's high voice. 'The cries of the torture chambers are terrible. . . .' Catherine knew how the monks of the Charterhouse had died; she could not bear to think of others suffering pain, but to contemplate one she loved being vilely hurt was sufficient to stem her desire. She remembered how Derham had run for his life; but then she had been plain Catherine Howard. What of him who dared to love her whom the King had chosen for his Queen!

'Nay, nay!' she cried, tears falling from her eyes. 'It cannot be! Oh, that it could! I would give all my life for one year of happiness with you. But I dare not. I fear the King. I must stay here because I love you.'

She tore herself away; there must be no more such meetings.

'Tomorrow . . .' she agreed weakly. 'Tomorrow.'

She ran to her apartment, where, since Anne had left for Richmond, she enjoyed the state of a queen. She was greeted by one of her attendants, Jane Rochford, widow of her late cousin George Boleyn. Lady Rochford looked excited. There was a letter for Catherine, she said.

'A letter?' cried Catherine. 'From whom?'

Catherine did not receive many letters; she took this one and opened it; she frowned for she had never been able to read very easily.

Jane Rochford was at her side.

'Mayhap I could assist?'

Jane had been very eager to ingratiate herself with Catherine; she had not liked the last Queen; Jane had decided to adhere to the Catholic cause and support Catherine Howard against Anne of Cleves.

Catherine handed her the letter.

'It is from a Jane Bulmer,' said Jane, 'and it comes from York.'

'I remember. It is from Jane Acworth who went to York to marry Mr Bulmer. Tell me what she says.'

Jane Bulmer's letter was carefully worded. She wished Catherine all honour, wealth and good fortune. Her motive in writing was to ask a favour of Catherine, and this was that she should be found a place at court. Jane was unhappy in the country; she was desolate. A command from the future Queen to Jane's husband to bring his wife to court would make Jane Bulmer very happy, and she begged for Catherine's help.

The threat was in the last sentence.

'I know the Queen of Britain will not forget her secretary....'

Her secretary! Jane Bulmer it was who had written those revealing, those intimate and passionate letters to Derham; Jane Bulmer knew everything that had happened.

Catherine sat very still as Jane Rochford read to her; her face was rosy with shame.

Jane Rochford was not one to let such signs pass unnoticed. She, as well as Catherine, read into those words a hint of blackmail.

*　　*　　*

On a hot July day Cromwell made the journey from the Tower to Tyburn. Tyburn it was because it was not forgotten that he was a man of lowly origins; he could smile at this, though a short while ago it would have angered him; but what does a man care when his head is to be cut off, whether it be done at Tower Hill or Tyburn?

He had obeyed his master to the last; he had been more than the King's servant; he had been the King's slave. But to his cry for mercy, had his most gracious Prince been deaf. He had done with Cromwell. He had not allowed Cromwell to speak in his own defence. Cromwell's fall would help to bring back Henry's popularity, for the people of England hated Cromwell.

His friends? Where were they? Cranmer? He could laugh at the thought of Cranmer's being his friend. Only a fool would expect loyalty in the face of danger from weak-kneed Cranmer. He knew that the Archbishop had declared himself smitten with grief; he had told the King that he had loved Cromwell, and the more for the love he had believed him to bear His Grace the King; he had added that although he was glad Cromwell's treason was discovered, he was very sorrowful, for whom should the King trust in future?

He had said almost the same words when Anne Boleyn had been taken to the Tower. Poor Cranmer! How fearful he was. He must have faced death a thousand times in his imagination. There was never a man quicker to dissociate himself from a fallen friend!

Crowds had gathered to see Cromwell's last moments. He recognized many enemies. He thought of Wolsey who would have faced this, had he lived long enough. He had walked in the shadow of Wolsey, had profited by his example, by his brilliance and his mistakes; he had followed the road to Power and had found it led to Tyburn.

There was one in the crowd who shed a tear for him. It was Thomas Wyatt who had been as eager as Cromwell himself that the Lutheran doctrines should be more widely understood. Their eyes met. Cromwell knew that Wyatt was trying to reassure him, to tell him that cruelties he had inflicted on so many had been done at Henry's command and that Cromwell was not entirely responsible for them. This young man did not know of the part Cromwell had played in the destruction of Anne Boleyn. Cromwell hoped then that he never would. His heart warmed to Wyatt.

'Weep not, Wyatt,' he said, 'for if I were not more guilty

than thou wert when they took thee, I should not be in this pass.'

It was time for him to make his last speech, to lay his head upon the block. He thought of all the blood he had caused to be shed, and tried to pray, but he could think of nothing but blood, and the screams of men in agony and the creaking of the rack.

Onto his thick neck, the axe descended; his head rolled away from his body as four years before, had Anne Boleyn's.

* * *

The King was enchanted with his bride. In the great hall at Hampton Court, he proclaimed her Queen. None had known the King in such humour for years; he was rejuvenated.

A few days after the proclamation, he took her from Hampton Court to Windsor, and astonished everyone by cutting himself off from the court that he might enjoy the company of his bride in private. Catherine seemed doubly pleasing in the King's eyes, coming after Anne of Cleves; she was gentle yet ever ready to laugh; she had no disconcerting wit to confound him; her conversation held not a trace of cleverness, only kindness. She was a passionate creature, a little afraid of him, but not too much so; she was responsive and womanly; and never had the King felt such drowsy and delicious peace. If she had a fault it was her generosity, her kindness to others. She would give away her clothes and jewels, explaining, her head a little on one side, her dewy lips parted, 'But it becomes her so, and she had so little. . . .' Or, 'She is poor, if we could but do something for her, how happy I should be!' She was irresistible and he could not bring himself to reprimand her for this overlavishness; he liked it; for he too came in for his share of her generosity. He would kiss her and stroke her and tickle her; and have her shrieking with laughter. Never had he dreamed of such blessedness.

Anne of Cleves was ordered to come to court to pay homage to the new Queen. There was a good deal of speculation in the court as to how the displaced queen would feel when kneeling to one who had but a short time ago been her maid of honour. It was expected that Catherine would demand great homage from Anne of Cleves to prove to herself and to the court that she was safely seated on the throne and had command of the King's affection. But when Anne came and knelt before the new Queen, Catherine impulsively declared that there should be no ceremony.

'You must not kneel to me!' she cried, and the two Queens embraced each other with tears of affection in their eyes, and it was Anne of Cleves who was moved to pity, not Catherine Howard.

Catherine would do honour to her cousin's daughter, Elizabeth, partly because she was her cousin's daughter, and partly because, of all her step-children, she loved Elizabeth best.

Mary was disposed to be friendly, but only because Catherine came from a family which adhered to the old Catholic faith, and Mary's friendship for people depended entirely on whether or not they were what she called true Catholics. Mary was six years older than her father's wife, and she thought the girl over-frivolous. Catherine accepted Mary's disapproval of her at first because she knew the Princess had suffered so much, but eventually she was goaded into complaining that Mary showed her little respect; she added that if only Mary would remember that although she was young she was the Queen, she would be ready to be friendly. This resulted in a sharp reprimand to Mary from the King; but friendship was not made that way, and how could poor, plain, frustrated Mary help feeling certain twinges of jealousy for sparkling Catherine whose influence over the King appeared to be unlimited. Mary was more Spanish than English; she would often sink into deepest melancholy; she would spend hours on her knees in devotion, brooding on her mother's dreary tragedy and the break with Rome; preferring to do this rather than sing and dance and be gay. On her knees she would pray that the King might come back to the true faith in all its old forms, that he might follow the example of her mother's country and earn the approval of heaven by setting up an Inquisition in this careless island

and torturing and burning all those who deserved such a fate, since they were heretics. How could soft-hearted, frivolous Catherine ever bring the King to take this duty upon himself! No, there could be no real friendship between Catherine and Mary.

Little Edward was not quite two years old; pale of face; solemn-eyed, he was watched over by his devoted nurse, Mrs Sibell Penn, who was terrified that some cold breath of air might touch him and end his frail life.

Of course it was Elizabeth whom Catherine must love most, for the child already had a look of Anne, for all that she had inherited her father's colouring. She would have Elizabeth at the table with them, occupying the place of honour next to Mary. She begged privileges for Elizabeth.

'Ah!' said Henry indulgently. 'It would seem that England has a new ruler, and that Queen Catherine!'

'Nay!' she replied. 'For how could I, who am young and foolish, rule this great country? That is for one who is strong and clever to do.'

He could not show his love sufficiently. 'Do what thou wilt, sweetheart,' he said, 'for well thou knowest, I have heart to refuse thee naught.'

He liked to watch them together – his favourite child and his beloved Queen. Seeing them thus, he would feel a deep contentment creep into his mind. Anne's child is happy with my new Queen, he would tell himself; and because it would seem to him that there might be a plea for forgiveness in that thought, he would hastily assure himself that there was nothing for Anne to forgive.

He and Catherine rode together in the park at Windsor. He had never wandered about so unattended before; and he enjoyed to the full each day he shared with this lovely laughing girl. It was pleasant to throw off the cares of kingship and be a lover. He wished he were not so weighty, though he never could abide lean men; still, to puff and pant when you were the lover of a spritely young girl was in itself a sad state of affairs. But Catherine feigned not to notice the puffing and looked to it that he need not exert himself too much in his pursuit of her. She was perfect; his rose without a single thorn.

He was almost glad that the low state of the treasury would not allow for ceremony just at this time, for this enabled him to enjoy peace with his young bride.

They made a happy little journey from Windsor to Grafton where they stayed until September, and it was while they were at Grafton that an alarming incident took place.

Cranmer noted it and decided to make the utmost use of it, although, knowing the amorous nature of the King, he could hope for little from it yet. Cranmer was uneasy, and had been since the arrest of Cromwell, for they had walked too long side by side for the liquidation of one not to frighten the other seriously. Norfolk was in the ascendant, and he and Cranmer were bitterly engaged in the silent subtle warring of two opposing religious sects. Such as Catherine Howard were but counters to be moved this way and that by either side; and the fight was fierce and deadly. Cranmer, though a man of considerable intellectual power, was at heart a coward. His great aim was to keep his head from the block and his feet from the stake. He could not forget that he had lost his ally Cromwell and had to play this wily Norfolk single-handed. Cranmer was as determined to get Catherine Howard off the throne as the Catholics had been to destroy Anne Boleyn. At this time, he bowed before the new Queen; he flattered her; he talked of her in delight to the King, murmuring that he trusted His Majesty had now the wife his great goodness deserved. And now, with this incident coming to light and the marriage not a month old, Cranmer prayed that he might be able to make the utmost use of it and bring Catherine Howard to ruin and so serve God in the way He most assuredly preferred to be served.

It had begun with a few words spoken by a priest at Windsor. He had talked slightingly of the Queen, saying that he had been told once, when she was quite a child, she had led a most immoral life. This priest was immediately taken prisoner and put into the keep of Windsor Castle, while

Wriothesley, at the bidding of the Council, was sent to lay these matters before the King.

Catherine was in a little antechamber when this man arrived; she heard the King greet him loudly.

'What news?' cried Henry. 'By God! You look glum enough!'

'Bad news, Your Majesty, and news it grieves me greatly to bring to Your Grace.'

'Speak up! Speak up!' said the King testily.

'I would ask Your Majesty to be patient with me, for this concerns Her Majesty the Queen.'

'The Queen!' Henry's voice was a roar of fear. The sly manner and the feigned sorrow in the eyes of the visitor were familiar to him. He could not bear that anything should happen to disturb this love idyll he shared with Catherine.

'The dribblings of a dotard doubtless,' said Wriothesley. 'But the Council felt it their duty to warn Your Majesty. A certain priest at Windsor has said that which was unbefitting concerning the Queen.'

Catherine clutched the hangings, and felt as though she were about to faint. She thought, I ought to have told him. Then he would not have married me. Then I might have married Thomas. What will become of me? What will become of me now?

'What's this? What's this?' growled the King.

'The foolish priest – doubtless a maniac – referred to the laxity of Her Majesty's behaviour when she was in the Dowager Duchess's care at Lambeth.'

The King looked at Wriothesley in such a manner as to make that ambitious young man shudder. The King was thinking that if Catherine had been a saucy wench before he had set eyes on her, he was ready to forget it. He wanted no disturbance of this paradise. She was charming and good-tempered, a constant delight, a lovely companion, a most agreeable bedfellow; she was his fifth wife, and his fourth had robbed him of any desire to make a hasty change. He wanted Catherine as he had made her appear to himself. Woe betide any who tried to destroy that illusion!

'Look ye here!' he said sternly. 'I should have thought you would have known better than to trouble me with any foolish tale of a drunken priest. You say this priest but repeated what he had heard. You did right to imprison him. Release him now, and warn him. Tell him what becomes of men who speak against the King . . . and by God, those who speak against the Queen speak against the King! Tongues have been ripped out for less. Tell him that, Wriothesley, tell him that. As for him who spoke these evil lies to the priest, let him be confined until I order his release.'

Wriothesley was glad to escape.

Catherine, trembling violently, thought: I must speak to my grandmother. I must explain to the King.

She half expected the King to order her immediate arrest, and that she would be taken to the Tower and have to lay her head on the block as her cousin had done. She was hysterical when she ran out to the King; she was flushed with fear; impulsively she threw her arms about his neck and kissed him.

He pressed her close to him. He might still be doubtful, but he was not going to lose this. By God, he thought, if anyone says a word against my Queen, he shall pay for it!

'Why, sweetheart?' he said, and turned her face to his, determined to read there what he wished to read. Such innocence! By God, those who talked against her deserved to have their heads on London Bridge – and should too! She was pure and innocent, just as Lord William and her grandmother had assured him. He was lucky – even though he were a King – to have such a jewel of womanhood.

The happy honeymoon continued.

*   *   *

The Dowager Duchess was closeted with the Queen.

'I declare,' said Catherine, 'I was greatly affrighted. I heard every word, and I trembled so that I scarce dared go out to the King when the man had gone!'

'And the King, said he naught to you?'

'He said naught.'

'He has decided to ignore this, depend upon it.'

503

'I feel so miserable. I would prefer to tell him. You understand, with Derham, it was as though we were married...'

'Hush! Do not say such things. I am an old woman and an experienced one; you are young and unwise. Take my advice.'

'I will,' said Catherine. 'Of course I will. It was yours I took when I did not tell the King before my marriage.'

'Pish!' said the Duchess, and then dropping her voice to a whisper: 'I have heard from Derham.'

'From Derham!'

'I said from Derham. He is back in my house. He is such a charming boy and I could not find it in my heart to keep up my anger against him. He still speaks of you with indiscreet devotion, and he has asked for something which I cannot advise you to refuse him. He says that he must see you now and then, that you have nothing to fear from him. He loves you too well to harm you.'

'What does he ask?'

'A place at court!'

'Oh, no!'

'Indeed yes; and I feel that you would be very unwise to refuse it. Do not look so frightened. Remember you are the Queen.'

Catherine said slowly: 'I have Jane Bulmer here and Katharine Tylney as well as Margaret Morton. I would that I had refused them.'

'Refuse them! You speak without thought. Have you forgotten that these people were at Lambeth and actually witnessed what took place between you and Derham!'

'I had rather they were not here. They are inclined to insolence as though they know I dare not dismiss them.'

She did not tell the Duchess that Manox had approached her too, that he had demanded a place at court. There was no need to disturb the Duchess further, and tell her that Manox, now one of the court musicians, had once been Catherine's lover.

'Now,' said the Duchess, 'you must listen to me. Derham must come to court. You cannot refuse him.'

'I see that you are right,' said Catherine wearily.

So came Derham.

* * *

The King's delight in his Queen did not diminish with the passing of the months. They left Ampthill for More Park where they could enjoy an even more secluded life; Henry was impatient with any minister who dared disturb him, and gave special instructions that no one was to approach him; any matter which was urgent was to be set out in writing. He was happy, desperately warming himself by the fire of Catherine's youth; he doted on her; he caressed her even in public, declaring that at last he had found conjugal happiness. He felt this to be a reward for a life of piety. There was one further blessing he asked, and that was children. So far, there was little success, but what matter? Catherine in herself was as much as any man could reasonably ask.

She was such a soft-hearted little thing and could bear to hurt no one. She hated to hear of the executions which were taking place every day; she would put her plump little fingers into her ears, and he would pet her and murmur; 'There, there, sweetheart, wouldst have me fête these traitors?'

'I know traitors must be severely dealt with,' she said. 'They must die, but let them die by the axe or the rope, not these lingering, cruel deaths.'

And he, forgetting how he had spurned Jane Seymour and threatened her when she would meddle, could deny his new Queen little.

Those Catholics who still hoped for reunion with Rome thought the moment ripe to strike at the men who had supported Cromwell, and Wyatt, among others, was sent to the Tower. He, bold as ever, had dared defend himself, and Catherine angered her uncle Norfolk by pleading for leniency towards Wyatt. She took warm clothes and food to the old Countess of Salisbury who was still in the Tower.

The King remonstrated with her.

'It will not do, sweetheart, it will not do.'

'Would you have me leave such a poor old lady to starve?'

He took her onto his knee, and touched her cheek in a

manner meant to reprove her, but she, with a characteristic gesture, seized his finger and bit it softly, which amused him, so that he found himself laughing instead of scolding.

He could not help it. She was irresistible. If she would take clothes and food to the old Countess, then she must. He would try pleading with her again concerning the greater indiscretion of asking pardon for Wyatt.

'Now listen to me,' he said. 'Wyatt is a traitor.'

'He is no traitor. He is a brave man. He does not cringe nor show fear, and is not afraid to state his opinions.'

'Aye!' said the King slyly. 'And he is the handsomest man in court, you are about to add!'

'He is assuredly, and I am certain he is a true friend to Your Majesty.'

'So you find him handsomer than your King, eh?'

'The handsomest *man*, you said. We did not speak of *kings*!' She took his great face in her hands and surveyed him saucily. 'Nay,' she said, 'I will say that Thomas Wyatt is the handsomest man in the court, but I would not include the King in that!' Which made him laugh and feel so gratified that he must kiss her and say to himself, A plague on Norfolk! Does he think to rule this realm! Wyatt is indeed a bold spirit and I was ever one to look for boldness in a man. If he is too anti-Catholic, he is at least honest. How does a King know when men will plot against him? Wyatt is too pleasant a man to die; his head is too handsome to be struck off his shoulders. Doubtless we can pardon Wyatt on some condition.

Norfolk was furious over the affair of Wyatt. He quarrelled with his step-mother.

'What means the Queen? Wyatt is our enemy. Has she not sense enough to know that!'

'Speak not thus of the Queen in my presence!' said the Dowager Duchess. 'Or 'twill go ill with thee, Thomas Howard.'

'You are an old fool. Who put the wench on the throne, I would ask you?'

'You may ask all you care to. I am willing to answer. The

King put Catherine Howard on the throne because he loves her sweet face.'

'Bah! You will go to the block one day, old woman, and that wench with you.'

'This is treason!' cried Her Grace.

'Tut, tut,' said the Duke and left her.

The Duchess was so furious that she went straight to the Queen.

'He was but feigning friendship for us,' said Catherine. 'I believe I ever knew it . . .'

'I fear him,' said the Duchess. 'There is that in him to terrify a woman, particularly when . . .'

They looked at each other; then glanced over their shoulders. The past was something they must keep shut away.

'Tread warily with the Duke!' warned the Duchess.

But it was not in Catherine's nature to tread warily. She showed her displeasure in her coolness to the Duke. The King noticed it and was amused. He liked to see proud Norfolk slighted by this vivacious Queen of his whose power flowed from himself.

Norfolk was filled with cold fury. This Catherine was every bit as unruly as his niece Anne Boleyn. If there was anything in that rumour which had risen up within a few weeks of her marriage, by God, he would not be the one to hold out a helping hand to Catherine Howard.

Sly Cranmer watched the trouble between Norfolk and his niece, and was pleased by it, for Norfolk was a worthy ally, and that they, enemies to one another, should be joined in common cause against Catherine Howard, was not an unsatisfactory state of affairs. But even if he had a case against Catherine, he would have to wait awhile, since it would be folly to present it to the King in his present amorous state. How much longer was the fat monarch going on cooing like a mating pigeon?

There was no sign of a change in the King's attitude towards Catherine. All through spring and summer as they journeyed from place to place, he was her devoted husband.

He preferred comparative retirement in the country to state balls and functions.

Henry was, however, jolted out of his complacency by news of a papist revolt in the north. This was headed by Sir John Neville and there was no doubt that it had been strongly influenced from the Continent by Cardinal Pole. Up rose Henry, roaring like a lion who has slumbered too long. He would restrain his wrath no longer. He had, in his newly found happiness, allowed himself to be over-lenient. How could he go on enjoying bliss with Catherine if his throne was imperilled and snatched from him by traitors!

The old Countess of Salisbury could no longer be allowed to live. Her execution had been delayed too long. Catherine had pleaded for her, had conjured up pitiful pictures of her freezing and starving in the Tower. Let her freeze! Let her starve! So perish all traitors! She was the mother of a traitor – one of the greatest and most feared Henry had ever known. Cardinal Pole might be safe on the Continent, but his mother should suffer in his stead.

'To the block with her!' shouted Henry, and all Catherine's pleas could not deter him this time. He was gentle with her, soothing her. 'Now now, sweetheart, let such matters rest. She is not the poor old lady you might think her to be. She is a traitor and she has bred traitors. Come, come, wouldst thou have thy King and husband tottering from his throne? Thrones have to be defended now and then with blood, sweetheart.'

So the old Countess was done to death in cruel fashion, for she, the last of the Plantagenets, kept her courage to the violent end. She refused to lay her head on the block, saying the sentence was unjust and she no traitor.

'So should traitors do,' she said, 'but I am none, and if you will have my head, you must win it if you can.'

Of all murders men had committed at the King's command this was the most horrible, for the Countess was dragged by her hair to the block, and since she would not then submit her head peaceably, the executioner hacked at her with his axe until she, bleeding from many wounds, sank in her death agony to the ground, where she was decapitated.

Such deaths aroused Henry's wrath. The people loved to gloat over bloody details; they whispered together, ever fond of martyrs.

It had always been Henry's plan, since the break with Rome, to play the Catholics off against the Lutherans, just as he played Charles against Francis. The last insurrection had put the Catholics out of favour, and his conscience now gave him several twinges about Cromwell. He replied to his conscience by mourning that, acting on false accusations which those about him had made, he had put to death the best servant he had ever had. Thus could he blame the Catholics for Cromwell's death and exonerate himself. Norfolk was out of favour; Cranmer in the ascendant. Henry left the administration of his affairs in the hands of a few chosen anti-papists headed by Cranmer and Chancellor Audley, and proceeded North on a punitive expedition, accompanied by the Queen.

* * *

Henry was whole-hearted in most things he undertook. When he set out to stamp the impression of his power on his subjects, he did so with vigour; and as his method was cruelty, Catherine could not help being revolted by that tour to the north.

Loving most romantically the handsome Culpepper, she must compare him with Henry; and while she had been prepared to do her best and please the indulgent man she had so far known, she was discovering that this was not the real man, and she was filled with horror. There was no kindness in him. She was forced to witness the grovelling of those who had rebelled because they wished to follow what they believed to be true. As they went through county after county and she saw the cruelty inflicted, and worse still was forced to look on his delight in it, it seemed to her, that when he came to her, his hands dripped blood. She wished the King to be a loving monarch; she wished the people to do homage to him; but she wanted them to respect him without fearing him, as she herself was trying so desperately to do.

There had been many compensations which had come to her when she forsook Culpepper to marry Henry. Mary, Joyce and Isabel, her young sisters, had been lifted from their poverty; indeed, there was not one impecunious member of her family who had not felt her generosity. This did not only apply to her family but to her friends also. She wanted to feel happiness about her; she wanted to make the King happy; she wanted no one worried by poverty, inconvenienced by hardship, smitten with sorrow. She wanted a pleasant world for herself and everyone in it.

When they came to Hull and saw what was left of Constable, a prey to the flies, hanging on the highest gate where Norfolk had gleefully placed him full four years ago, she turned away sickened, for the King had laughingly pointed out this grim sight to her.

'There hangs a traitor . . . or what is left of him!'

She turned from the King, knowing that however she tried she would never love him.

'Thou art too gentle, sweetheart!' The King leaned towards her and patted her arm, showing that he liked her gentleness, even though it might make her shed a tear for his enemies.

Often she thought of Thomas Culpepper who was in the retinue accompanying them. Often their eyes would meet, exchanging smiles. Jane Rochford noted this, and that peculiar twist of her character which had ever made her court danger though through doing so she could bring no gain to herself, made her say: 'Your cousin Culpepper is a handsome young man. He loves you truly. I see it there in his eyes. And methinks Your Majesty is not indifferent to him, for who could be to such a handsome boy! You never meet him. You are over-cautious. It could be arranged. . . .'

This was reminiscent of the old days of intrigue, and Catherine could not resist it. She felt that only could she endure Henry's caresses if she saw Thomas now and then. She carried in her mind every detail of Thomas's face so that when the King was with her, she could, in her imagination, put Thomas in his place, and so not show the repugnance to his caresses which she could not help but feel.

Derham came to her once or twice to write letters for her. He watched her with smouldering, passionate eyes, but she was not afraid of harm coming from Derham. He was devoted as ever, and though his jealousy was great, he would never do anything, if he could help it, to harm the Queen. Derham knew nothing of her love for Culpepper, and Catherine, not wishing to cause him pain, saw to it that he should not know, and now and then would throw him soft glances to show that she remembered all they had been to each other. In view of this Derham could not forbear to whisper to his friend Damport that he loved the Queen, and he was sure that if the King were dead he might marry her.

During that journey there were many meetings with Culpepper. Lady Rochford was in her element; she carried messages between the lovers; she listened at doors. 'The King will be in council for two hours more. It is safe for Culpepper to come to the apartment. . . .' Catherine did not know that her relations with Culpepper were becoming a sly joke throughout the court and were discussed behind hands with many a suppressed giggle.

When they were at Lincoln she all but surrendered to Culpepper. He would beg; she would hesitate; and then be firm in her refusals.

'I dare not!' wept Catherine.

'Ah! Why did you not fly with me when I asked it!'

'If only I had done so!'

'Shall we go on spoiling our lives, Catherine?'

'I cannot bear this sorrow, but never, never could I bear that harm should come to you through me.'

Thus it went on, but Catherine was firm. When she felt weak she would seem to feel the presence of Anne Boleyn begging her to take care, warning her to reflect on her poor cousin's fate.

Because no one showed that the love between them was known, they did not believe it was known, and they grew more and more reckless. There was a time at Lincoln when they were alone until two in the morning, feeling themselves safe because Lady Rochford was keeping guard. They revelled in their secret meetings with ostrich-like folly. As long as they denied themselves the satisfaction their love demanded, they felt safe. No matter that people all around them were aware of their intrigue. No matter that Cranmer was but waiting an opportunity.

On this occasion at Lincoln, Katharine Tylney and Margaret Morton had been loitering on the stairs outside the Queen's apartment in a fever of excitement lest the King should come unexpectedly, and they be involved.

'Jesus!' whispered Katharine Tylney as Margaret came gliding into the corridor, 'is not the Queen abed yet?'

Margaret, who a moment before had seen Culpepper emerge, answered: 'Yes, even now.' And the two exchanged glances of relief, shrugging their shoulders and smiling over the Queen's recklessness and frivolity, reminding each other of her behaviour at Lambeth.

Many such dangerous meetings took place, with Lady Rochford always at hand, the Queen's trusted attendant, always ready with suggestions and hints. Catherine had been indiscreet enough to write to Culpepper before this journey began. This was an indication of the great anxiety she felt for him, because Catherine never did feel happy with a pen, and to write even a few lines was a great effort to her. She had written this letter before the beginning of the tour when she and the King were moving about close to London and Culpepper was not with them. It was folly to write; and greater folly on Culpepper's part to keep the letter; but being in love and inspired by danger rather than deterred by it, they had done many foolish things and this was but one of them.

> 'I heartily recommend me unto you, praying you to send me word how that you do,' wrote Catherine. 'I did fear you were sick and I never longed for anything so much as to see you. It makes my heart to die when I think that I cannot always be in your company. Come to me when Lady Rochford be here for then I shall be best at leisure to be at your commandment. . . .'

And such like sentences all written out laboriously in Catherine's untrained hand.

She lived through the days, waiting for a glimpse of Culpepper, recklessly, dangerously, while the foolish Lady Rochford sympathized and arranged meetings.

The King noticed nothing. He felt pleased; once more he was showing rebels what happened to those who went against their King. He could turn from the flattery of those who sought his good graces to the sweet, youthful charm of Catherine Howard.

'Never was man so happy in his wife!' he said; and he thought that when he returned he would have the nation sing a Te Deum, for at last the Almighty had seen fit to reward his servant with a perfect jewel of womanhood.

* * *

Cranmer was so excited he could scarcely make his plans. At last his chance had come. This was too much even for the King to ignore.

There was a man at court who was of little importance, but towards whom Cranmer had always had a kindly feeling. This man was a Protestant, stern and cold, a man who never laughed because he considered laughter sinful, a man who had the makings of a martyr, one who could find more joy in a hair-shirt than in a flagon of good wine. This man's name was John Lassells, a protégé of Cromwell's who had remained faithful to him; he preached eternal damnation for all those who did not accept the teachings of Martin Luther.

This John Lassells came to Cranmer with a story which set Cranmer's hopes soaring, that made him feel he could embrace the man.

'My lord,' said Lassells most humbly, 'there is on my conscience that which troubles me sorely.'

Cranmer listened half-heartedly, feeling this was doubtless some religious point the man wished explained.

'I tremble for what this may mean,' said Lassells, 'for it concerns Her Grace the Queen.'

Gone was Cranmer's lethargy; there was a flicker of fire in his eyes.

'My lord Archbishop, I have a sister Mary, and Mary being nurse to Lord William Howard's first wife, was after her death taken into the service of the Dowager Duchess of Norfolk.'

'Where the Queen was brought up,' said Cranmer eagerly.

'I asked my sister Mary why she did not sue for service with the Queen, for I saw that many who had been in the Dowager Duchess's household now held places at court. My sister's answer was most disturbing. "I will not," she said. "But I am very sorry for the Queen." I asked why, and she answered, "Marry, for she is both light in living and behaviour." I asked how so, and she did tell me a most alarming story.'

'Yes, yes?'

'There was one Francis Derham who had slept in bed with her for many nights, and another, Manox, had known her.'

'Derham!' cried Cranmer. 'Manox! They are both in the Queen's household.'

He questioned Lassells further, and when he had learned all the man had to tell, he dismissed him after telling him he had indeed done the King a great service.

Cranmer was busy, glad of the absence of the King to give him a free hand. He sent Southampton to question Mary Lassells. Manox was arrested and brought before him and Wriothesley. Derham went to the Tower. Cranmer was going to garner each grain he gleaned, and when they were laid side by side he doubted not he would have a good harvest. He waited impatiently for the return of the royal pair.

Henry was filled with satisfaction when he returned to Hampton Court. He was full of plans which he would lay before his confessor. A public thanksgiving should be prepared that the whole country might know, and thank God, that he had been blessed with a loving, dutiful and virtuous wife.

But Henry's satisfaction was shortlived. He was in the chapel at Hampton Court when Cranmer came to him; Cranmer's eyes were averted and in his hand he carried a paper.

'Most Gracious King,' said Cranmer, 'I fear to place this grave matter set out herein in your hands, and yet the matter being so grave I dare do naught else. I pray that Your Grace will read it when you are alone.'

Henry read the report on Catherine; his anger was terrible, but it was not directed against Catherine but those who had given evidence against her. He sent for Cranmer.

'This is forged!' he cried. 'This is not truthful! I have conceived such a constant opinion of her honesty that I know this!'

He paced up and down so that Cranmer's chicken heart was filled with fear. It was too soon. The King would not give up the Queen; rather he would destroy those who sought to destroy her.

'I do not believe this!' cried the King, but Cranmer had heard the quiver of doubt in his master's voice and rejoiced. 'But,' went on the King, 'I shall not be satisfied until the certainty is known to me.' He glowered at Cranmer. 'There must be an examination. And . . . no breath of scandal against the Queen.'

The King left Hampton Court, and Catherine was told to stay in her rooms. Her musicians were sent away and told that this was no time for music.

Over Hampton Court there fell a hush of horror like a dark curtain that shut away gaiety and laughter; thus it had been at Greenwich less then six years ago when Anne Boleyn had looked in vain for Brereton, Weston, Norris and Smeaton.

Catherine was chilled with horror; and when Cranmer with Norfolk, Audley, Sussex and Gardiner, came to her, she knew that the awful doom she had feared ever since she had become the King's wife was about to fall upon her.

* * *

Wriothesley questioned Francis Derham in his cell.

'You may as well tell the truth,' said Wriothesley, 'for others have already confessed it for you. You have spent a hundred nights naked in the bed of the Queen.'

'Before she was Queen,' said Derham.

'Ah! Before she was Queen. We will come to that later.

You admit that there were immoral relations between you and the Queen?'

'No,' said Derham.

'Come, come, we have ways of extracting the truth. There were immoral relations between you and the Queen.'

'They were not immoral. Catherine Howard and I regarded each other as husband and wife.'

Wriothesley nodded slowly.

'You called her "wife" before others?'

'Yes.'

'And you exchanged love tokens?'

'We did.'

'And some of the household regarded you as husband and wife?'

'That is so.'

'The Dowager Duchess and Lord William Howard regarded you as husband and wife?'

'No; they were ignorant of it.'

'And yet it was no secret.'

'No, but . . .'

'The entire household knew, with the exception of the Dowager Duchess and Lord William?'

'It was known among those with whom it was our custom to mix.'

'You went to Ireland recently, did you not?'

'I did.'

'And there were engaged in piracy?'

'Yes.'

'For which you deserve to hang, but no matter now. Did you not leave rather abruptly for Ireland?'

'I did.'

'Why?'

'Because Her Grace had discovered the relationship between Catherine and me.'

'Was there not another occasion when she discovered you with her granddaughter?'

'Yes.'

'It was in the maids' room and she entered and found you romping together, in arms kissing?'

516

He nodded.

'And what were Her Grace's reactions to that?'

'Catherine was beaten; I was warned.'

'That seems light punishment.'

'Her Grace believed it to be but a romp.'

'And you joined the Queen's household soon after her marriage with the King? Mr Derham, I suggest that you and the Queen continued to live immorally, in fact in adultery, after the Queen's marriage with His Majesty.'

'That is not true.'

'Is it not strange that you should join the Queen's household, and receive special favours, and remain in the rôle of Queen's attendant only?'

'It does not seem strange.'

'You swear that no immoral act ever took place between you and the Queen after her marriage with the King?'

'I swear it.'

'Come, Mr Derham. Be reasonable. Does it seem logical to you in view of what you once were to the Queen?'

'I care not what it may seem. I only know that no act of immorality ever took place between us since her marriage.'

Wriothesley sighed. 'You try my patience sorely,' he said, and left him.

He returned in half an hour accompanied by two burly men.

'Mr Derham,' said the King's secretary softly, 'I would ask you once more to confess to adultery with the Queen.'

'I cannot confess what is not so.'

'Then I must ask you to accompany us.'

Derham was no coward; he knew the meaning of that summons; they were going to torture him. He pressed his lips together, and silently prayed for the courage he would have need of. He had led an adventurous life of late; he had faced death more than once when he had fought on the rough sea for booty. He had taken his chances recklessly as the inevitable milestones on the road of adventure; but the cold-blooded horror of the torture chamber was different.

In the corridors of the Tower was the sickening smell of death; there was dried blood on the floor of the torture rooms. If he admitted adultery, what would they do to Catherine? They could not hurt her for what was done before. They could not call that treason, even though she had deceived the King into thinking her a virgin. They could not hurt Catherine if he refused to say what they wished. He would not swerve. He would face all the torture in the world rather than harm her with the lies they wished him to tell. She had not loved him since his return from Ireland; but he had continued to love her. He would not lie.

They were stripping him of his clothes. They were putting him on the rack. Wriothesley, one of the cruellest men in all England, was standing over him implacably.

'You are a fool, Derham. Why not confess and have done!'

'You would have me lie?' asked Derham.

'I would have you save yourself this torture.'

The ropes were about his wrists; the windlasses were turned. He tried to suppress his cries, for it was more cruel than his wildest imaginings. He had not known there could be such pain. He shrieked and they stopped.

'Come, Derham. You committed adultery with the Queen.'

'No, no.'

Wriothesley's cruel lips were pressed together; he nodded to the tormentors. It began again. Derham fainted and they thrust the vinegar brush under his nose.

'Derham, you fool. Men cannot endure much of this.'

That was true; but there were men who would not lie to save themselves from death, even if it must be death on the rack; and Derham, the pirate, was one of them.

When it would have been death to continue with the torture they carried him away; he was fainting, maimed and broken; but he had told them nothing.

*　　*　　*

When the Dowager Duchess heard what had happened at Hampton Court she shut herself into her chamber and was sick with fear. The Queen under lock and key! Derham in the Tower! She remembered her sorrow when Anne was sent to the Tower; but now side by side with sorrow went fear, and out of these two was born panic.

She must not stay idle. She must act. Had she not assured His Majesty of Catherine's purity and goodness! And yet had she not beaten Catherine for her lewdness! Had she not warned Derham first, and had he not, later, run away to escape her anger when it had been discovered that he and Catherine had been living as husband and wife in her house!

She paced up and down her room. What if they questioned her! Her teeth chattered. She pictured the terrible end of the Countess of Salisbury, and saw herself running from the headsman's axe. She was rich; her house was chock-full of treasure. Was not the King always ready to despatch those who were rich, that their goods might fall into his hands! She pictured the Duke's sly eyes smiling at her. 'That wench will go to the block!' he had said; and she had berated him, telling him he had better take care how he spoke of the Queen. Her stepson was her most deadly enemy and now he would have a chance of working openly against her.

She must waste no time. She must act. She went down to the great hall and called a confidential servant to her. She told him to go to Hampton Court, glean the latest news, and come back to her as fast as he could. She waited in mental anguish for his return, but when he came he could only tell her what she knew already. The Queen and Derham were accused of misconduct, and some of the Queen's attendants were accused of being in the guilty secret.

She thought of Derham's friend Damport, who doubtless knew as much of Derham's secrets as any. She had some hazy plan of bribing him to silence on all he knew.

'I hear Derham is taken,' she said plaintively, 'and also the Queen; what is the matter?'

Damport said he thought Derham had spoken with indiscretion to a gentleman usher.

Her Grace's lips quivered; she said that she greatly feared that in consequence of evil reports some harm should fall the Queen. She looked fearfully at Damport and said she would like to give him a little gift. Thereupon she presented him with ten pounds. It was stupid and clumsy, but she was too frightened to know what she did. She murmured something about his saying nothing of Catherine Howard's friendship with Derham.

Her fear becoming hysterical, the Dowager Duchess paced from room to room. What if Catherine and Derham had exchanged letters when he had gone away to Ireland!

There were here in her house some trunks and coffers of Derham's, for before he had gone to court she had taken him back into her house; several of the trunks were those which he had left behind when he fled. He had not removed them when he went to court, for his lodging there was not large enough to accommodate them. What if in Derham's trunks and coffers there was some incriminating evidence?

Her legs shaking, her voice high with hysteria, she called to some of her most trusted servants. She told them that she feared a visit from the King's ambassadors at any moment; the Queen was in danger; all Derham's belongings must be searched for fear there might be something in them to incriminate the Queen; she implored her attendants to show their loyalty and help her.

There was a great bustling throughout the house; trunks were forced open; coffers were rifled. There were found some of those letters written by Jane Bulmer on Catherine's behalf, and which had been preserved by Derham; of these there was made a bonfire; the Duchess even destroyed articles which she suspected had been gifts from Catherine to Derham.

When this work was done she retired to her chamber, feeling old and very weary. But there was no rest for her. A knocking on her door heralded the advent of fresh trouble, the worst possible trouble.

'His Grace the Duke is below,' said her frightened maid, 'and he demands to see you immediately.'

*   *   *

Catherine, facing those five dreaded men, was numb with terror. Her limbs trembled so much, and her countenance was so wild, that they thought she would lose her reason. She had had a wild fit of laughing which had ended in weeping; she was more hysterical than had been her cousin, for Anne had not had a terrible example in her mind all the time.

There was one thing which terrified her beyond all others, and gave her great agony of mind. She could think of no way of warning Culpepper. She was almost mad with anxiety on his behalf.

Norfolk's cold eyes mocked her, seeming to say – So you thought yourself so clever, did you! You are another such as your cousin Anne Boleyn. Oh, did ever a man have such a pair of nieces!

Her uncle was more terrifying than the other four.

'Compose yourself! Compose yourself!' said Norfolk. 'Think not to drown your guilt in tears!'

Cranmer seemed much kinder; he was ever cautious, knowing well the King's great tenderness for her; he was determined to go cautiously for fear he had to retrace his steps. It was to Cranmer whom she would talk if she talked at all.

In his soft voice he told her how grieved he was that this should have befallen her. Francis Derham had confessed to having lived with her as her husband. Manox had also known her. It would be better for her to tell the truth, for the King, heartbroken at her deception, was inclined towards leniency.

Her answers were scarcely audible. She caught her breath every time one of them spoke, terrified that she would hear Culpepper's name. But when they did not speak of him, she came to the conclusion that they knew nothing of her love for him and his for her; and this so lightened her spirits that she seemed suddenly happy. She confessed readily to what she had done before her marriage to the King. Yes, Derham had called her wife; she had called him husband. Yes . . . yes. . . .

Norfolk, with never a thought of his own adultery with Bess Holland, tut-tutted in horror at such wickedness; but in comparison with him, the others seemed almost kind, and her hysteria was passing. They knew nothing against Thomas. They could send her to the block as they had her cousin, but Thomas Culpepper should not suffer through his love for her.

The council of five left her, and Cranmer prepared a report of the examination that he might show it to the King.

Henry was awaiting the report in feverish impatience. He could not hide his agitation. He had changed since he had read that paper containing the news which Cranmer had declared he was too moved to give his master by word of mouth. His usually purple face had gone a shade of grey the colour of parchment, and the veins, usually so full of rich red blood, now looked like brown lines drawn upon it.

Cranmer's voice took on those pained tones he could always assume on certain occasions. He talked of the abominable, base, and carnal life of the Queen; voluptuous and vicious were the words he used to describe her; and this woman had led the King to love her, had arrogantly coupled herself in marriage with him.

Norfolk watched the King and Cranmer uneasily. After all the wanton wench was his niece, and it was he who had helped to recommend her to the King. Norfolk was worried. He was possessed of great worldly riches. When a queen was found guilty of treason, members of her family often found themselves in like trouble. He had spoken with disgust of his niece whenever he could; he had whispered slander about her; his great wish was to dissociate himself from her. He was grieved, he told all; his house was plunged into deepest mourning because it had produced two such wanton and abandoned women as Anne Boleyn and Catherine Howard. He said he thought the only just fate that should be meted out to Catherine Howard was death by burning. He would be there to savour every one of her screams as she had a foretaste of the torment that would be eternally hers. His pity, he had announced, went to the King whom he loved and whom he hoped would not hold him in any way responsible for the vile creatures his house had produced to deceive his most loved monarch. He had quarrelled with his

'Why, Damport, that is a very fine set of teeth you have, and doubtless you are very proud of them!'

Damport looked about him as though seeking escape from such a situation, but the dark and slimy walls had no suggestion to offer; there was nothing to learn from them except that within them men had descended for many many years to the level of the lowest animals. It seemed to Damport that the evil shadows that hung about the dim chamber were the ghosts of those who, having died in agony, had returned to watch the anguish of those doomed to follow them. These cruel tormentors, these examiners, felt not the presence of those sad ghosts; cruelty was commonplace to them; they had learned indifference to the groans of tortured men; one had but to look into their brute faces to know this.

Damport whimpered: 'An I knew aught, I would tell it.'

'We were saying those teeth were fine, Damport. Let us see whether they will look as fine when the brakes have done with them!'

It seemed that his head was being torn from his body; he felt a sickening crunch; his jerkin was wet and he felt its damp warmness on his chest; he smelt his own blood, and swooned. Words were like the beating of the blunt end of an axe on his head.

'Come, Damport, you know Derham committed adultery with the Queen.'

They had torn out most of his teeth and all he could remember was that Derham had said that if the King were dead he would marry Catherine Howard. He told them this, fearing further torture. They were disappointed, but the man was bleeding badly and he could not stand for the pain; and his mouth was so swollen that if he would, he could not speak.

They led him from the torture chamber. They would have to tell Cranmer that they could get nothing from Damport and believed he had nothing to tell. Cranmer would be filled with that cold fury that was more terrifying than the hot rage of some men.

From Manox they could get nothing of interest. There

was not sufficient evidence against him; he had been one of the humblest musicians, and there was really nothing against him; he had not been in the Queen's presence, even while her ladies were with her. As for his relations with her at Horsham and Lambeth he was ready enough to talk of these. He was such an obvious rogue, that torture would be wasted on him.

But Cranmer was not angry. He was in fact delighted. The King of France had sent condolences to Henry, telling him how grieved he was to hear news of the faults of her, so recently his Queen. That was good; but there was better still.

Why, thought Cranmer, should the Queen wish to surround herself with those who had helped her in her wantonness before her marriage, if it was not to help her in the same capacity after marriage? He would examine thoroughly all those women at the court of the Queen who had been in the service of the Dowager Duchess of Norfolk. There were several of them – Katharine Tylney, Margaret Morton, Jane Bulmer, and two named Wilkes and Baskerville being the chief among them. It was from Katharine Tylney and Margaret Morton that Cranmer learned of a certain night at Lincoln; Thomas Culpepper's name was mentioned. Lady Rochford had arranged interviews. There had been several meetings before the tour to the north and during it.

'Bring in Culpepper!' ordered Cranmer, and they brought in Culpepper.

He was a bold youth, fearless and courageous, such as Francis Derham.

A plague on courageous, gallant men! thought Cranmer, the coward. What trouble they give us!

Head held high, Culpepper admitted his love for the Queen, admitted that he would have married her if he could. No wrong, he said, had passed between them.

Cranmer laughed at that. He must admit that wrong had passed between them! How else could Cranmer be sure of enraging this love-sick King.

'Rack him until he confesses!' he ordered.

Derham had been a pirate; he had faced death more than once, and it held less horror for him than for a man like

Cranmer who had never seen it come close to himself; it was with Culpepper as with Derham. Culpepper was a wild boy and had ever been a plague to his father; he was a rebellious, unruly boy with a taste for adventure and getting into trouble. There was one quality he had in common with Derham and that was bravery.

They put him on the rack. He endured that excruciating pain, that most exquisite of tortures, pressing his lips firmly together, and only now and then, and most shamefacedly, let out a groan of pain. He even smiled on the rack and tried to remember her face, anxious for him. 'Oh, take care, Thomas. Take care lest thou shouldst suffer for love of me.'

He thought she was with him, talking to him now. In his thoughts he answered her. 'Sweet Catherine, dost think I would do aught that might hurt thee? Thou shalt never suffer through me, Catherine. Let them do what they will.'

'Culpepper! Culpepper, you young fool! Will you speak?'

He gasped, for the pain was such as to make speech difficult.

'I have spoken.'

'Again! Again! Work faster, you fools! He *has* to confess!'

But he did not confess, and they carried his poor suffering body away most roughly, for they had worked themselves weary over him in vain.

*   *   *

The King's rage was terrible when he heard that Culpepper was involved. Rage, misery, jealousy, self-pity, humiliation maddened him. He wept; he shut himself up; he would see no one. This . . . to happen to the King of England.

His face was clothed in grief; his sick leg throbbed with pain; his youth was gone, taking with it his hope of happiness. He was an old sick man and Culpepper was a young and beautiful boy. He himself had loved to watch the grace of Culpepper; he had favoured the lad; he had winked at his wickedness and had said that what happened in Kent need not be remembered at court. He had loved that boy –

loved him for his wit and his beauty; and this same boy, fair of face and clean of limb had looked frequently on the unsightly weeping sore on the royal leg, and doubtless had laughed that all the power and riches in England could not buy youth and health such as he enjoyed.

Mayhap, thought the King angrily, he is less beautiful now his graceful limbs have been tortured; The King laughed deep sobbing laughter. Culpepper should die the death of a traitor; he should die ignobly; indignities should be piled upon his traitor's body; and when his head was on London Bridge, would she feel the same desire to kiss his lips? The King tormented himself with such thoughts of them together that could only come to a very sensual man, and the boiling blood in his head seemed as if it would burst it.

'She never had such delight in her lovers,' he said, 'as she shall have torture in death!'

Catherine, in those apartments which had been planned for Anne Boleyn and used so briefly by Jane, and briefer still by Anne of Cleves, was in such a state of terror that those who guarded her feared for her reason. She would fling herself onto her bed, sobbing wildly; then she would arise and walk about her room, asking questions about her death; she would have those who had witnessed the death of her cousin come to her and tell her how Anne had died; she would weep with sorrow, and then her laughter would begin again for it seemed ironical that Anne's fate should be hers. She was crazy with grief when she heard Culpepper was taken. She prayed incoherently. 'Let them not harm him. Let me die, but let him be spared.'

If I could but see the King, she thought, surely I could make him listen to me. Surely he would spare Thomas, if I asked him.

'Could I have speech with His Majesty? Just one moment!' she begged.

'Speech with His Majesty!' They shook their heads. How could that be! His Majesty was incensed by her conduct; he would not see her. And what would Cranmer say, Cranmer who would not know real peace until Catherine Howard's head was severed from her body!

She remembered the King as he had always been to her, indulgent and loving; even when he had reprimanded her for too much generosity, even when he, angered by the acts of traitors, had listened to her pleas for leniency, he had never shown a flicker of anger. Surely now he would listen to her.

She made plans. If she could but get to the King, if she could but elude her jailors, she would know how to make herself irresistible.

She was calm now, watching for an opportunity. One quick movement of the hand to open the door, and then she would dash down the back stairs; she would watch and wait and pray for help.

The opportunity came when she knew him to be at mass in the chapel. She would run to him there, fling herself onto her knees, implore his compassion, promise him life-long devotion if he would but spare her and Culpepper and Derham.

Those who were guarding her, pleased with her calmness, were sitting in a window seat, conversing among themselves of the strange happenings at court. She moved swiftly towards the door; she paused, threw a glance over her shoulder, saw that their suspicions had not been aroused, turned the handle, and was on the dark staircase before she heard the exclamation of dismay behind her.

Fleet with fear she ran. She came to the gallery; she could hear the singing in the chapel. The King was there. She would succeed because she must. Culpepper was innocent. He must not die.

Her attendants were close behind her, full of determination that her plan should not succeed, fully aware that no light punishment would be meted out to them should they let her reach the King. They caught at her gown; they captured her just as she reached the chapel door. They dragged her back to the apartment. Through the gallery her screams rang out like those of a mad creature, mingling uncannily with the singing in the chapel.

A few days later she was taken from Hampton Court; she sailed down the river to a less grand prison at Sion House.

* * *

The Dowager Duchess lay in bed. She said to her attendants: 'I cannot get up. I am too ill. I feel death approaching fast.'

She was sick and her disease was fear. She had heard that Culpepper and Derham had been found guilty of treason. She knew that they had had no true trial, for how could men be sentenced to death for what could not be proved, and for that which they would not admit under the vilest torture! But these two brave men had not convinced their torturers that they would not eventually respond to the persuasions of the rack, and even after their sentence, daily they were taken to the torture chambers to suffer fresh agonies. But not once did either of them swerve from their protestations of the Queen's innocence since her marriage.

Never in the Dowager Duchess's memory, had men been tried like this before. For those accused with Anne Boleyn there had been a trial, farcical as it was. Culpepper and Derham had been taken to Guildhall before the Lord Mayor but on either side of the Lord Mayor had sat Suffolk and Audley. Sentence had been quickly pronounced, and the two were judged guilty and condemned to die the horrible lingering death assigned to traitors.

The Dowager Duchess thought of these matters as she lay abed, staring up in terror when she heard the least sound from below. She knew inventories had been made of her goods, and she knew they could not fail to arouse the covetousness of the King, for they were great in value.

What hope had she of escaping death? Even the Duke, old soldier that he was, had shown that he thought the only safe thing for a Howard to do was retreat. He had gone into voluntary retirement, hoping that the King would forget him awhile, until the fortunes of the Howard family were in a happier state.

And as she lay there, that which she dreaded came to

pass. Wriothesley, accompanied by the Earl of Southampton, had come to see her.

Her face was yellow when they entered; they thought she was not malingering but really suffering from some terrible disease. They dared not approach too near the bed, the fear of plague being ever in their minds.

'We but called to see how Your Grace does,' said Wriothesley artfully, never taking his eyes from her face. 'Do not distress yourself, this is but a visit; we would condole with you on the sad happenings which have befallen your family.'

The colour returned slightly to her face. The men could see hope springing up. They exchanged glances. Their little ruse had succeeded, for she had always been a foolish woman ready to believe what she wished rather than what she should have known to be the truth; and she could not hide the wonderful feeling that after all she might be safe. The Dowager Duchess, these two men knew, suffered from no plague, but only from the qualms of a guilty conscience.

They questioned her. She wept and talked incoherently.

She knew nothing . . . nothing! she assured them. She had thought the attraction between Derham and her granddaughter but an affection between two who were united by the bonds of kinship. She had not thought to look for wickedness in that. But had she not found them together, in arms kissing? Had she thought that meet and proper in her whom the King had chosen to honour? Oh, but Catherine had been such a child, and there had been no harm. . . no harm that she had known of. But had she not been told of these things? Had she not beaten the girl, and had not Derham fled for his life?

'I knew it not! I knew it not!' she sobbed.

Wriothesley's cunning eyes took in each rich detail of the room.

'Methinks,' he said, 'Your Grace is well enough to be transported to the Tower.'

*　　*　　*

At Tyburn a crowd had gathered to see the death of the Queen's lovers. Culpepper first. How could the Queen have

531

loved such a man? His face was emaciated; his lips drawn down; his skin like bad cheese; his eyes had sunk into black hollows. The people shuddered, knowing that they saw not the Queen's lover, but what the tormentors had made of him. Lucky Culpepper, because he was of noble birth, and was to be but beheaded!

Derham could say Lucky Culpepper! He was of not such noble birth, and although he begged the King for mercy, which meant that he asked to die by the axe or the rope, the King was in no mood for mercy. He saw no reason why sentence should not be carried out as ordained by the judges.

Derham's eyes were dazed with pain; he had suffered much since his arrest; he had not known there could be such cruelty in men; truly, he had known of those grim chambers below the fortress of the Tower of London, but to know by hearsay and to know by experience were two very different matters. He did not wish to live, for if he did he would never forget the gloomy dampness of grey stone walls, the terrible shrieks of agony, pain and the smell of blood and vinegar, and those awful great instruments, like monsters without thought, grimly obedient to the evil will of men.

This he had suffered and he had to suffer yet; he had been submerged in pain, but mayhap he had not yet tested its depth. Nature was more merciful than men, providing for those who suffered great pain such blessedness as fainting; but men were cruel and brought their victims out of faints that the pain might start again.

He clung to the glorious memory of unconsciousness which must inevitably follow an excess of pain. There was another joy he knew, and it was this: He had not betrayed Catherine. They might kill Catherine, but not a drop of her blood should stain his hands. He had loved her; his intentions towards her had been ever honest. In the depth of his passion he had been unable to resist her; but that was natural; that was no sin. He had called her wife and she had called him husband, and it had been the dearest wish of his life that he should marry her. Now, here at Tyburn with the most miserable ordeal yet before him, he could feel lightness of spirit, for his end could not be far off, however they would revive him that he might suffer more. These men, whose cruel eyes were indifferent to his suffering, these monsters who were but hirelings of that spiteful murderer who stood astride all England and subdued her with torture and death, were to be pitied, as was Henry himself. For one day they must die, and they would not die as Derham died; they would not know his agony of body, but neither would they know his peace of mind.

The noose was about his neck; he swung in mid-air. There was a brief jolting pain, and the next he knew was that he was lying on hard wood and he could not breathe; he was choking; but they were tending him solicitously, that he might return to life and suffer more pain.

Now he was sufficiently recovered to smell the Tyburn crowd, to hear a faint hum of voices, to feel a man's hands on his body, to see a flash of steel, to be aware of agony. He felt the knife cold against his flesh. A searing hot pain ran through him. He writhed and screamed, but he seemed to hear a voice close to his ear murmur: 'Soon now, Derham. Not long now, Derham. It cannot last. Remember they are helping you out of this wicked world.'

He could smell the smoke. 'Oh, God!' he moaned, and twisted and groaned afresh in his agony. He could smell his burning entrails. A thousand white hot knives were surely being plunged into him. He tried to raise himself. He tried to sob out to them to have pity. He could not speak. He could do nothing but endure, but give his tortured body up to a million gnawing devils. He had touched pain's depth, for there was never agony such as that endured by men who were hanged by the neck, and then revived that they might feel the knife that ripped their bodies, that they might feel the agony of their burning entrails.

Blessed blackness closed in on him, and the stroke of the axe which severed his head was like a gentle caress.

*　　　*　　　*

Jane Rochford was back in the Tower. She had been

533

calm enough when they took her there, but now her eyes were wild, her hair hung loose about her face; she did not know why she was there; she talked to those who were not there.

'George! You here, George!' She went into shrieks of crazy laughter. 'So we meet here, George. It is so just that we should . . . so just.'

She paused as though listening to the conversation of another; then she went into wild laughter that was followed by deep sobbing. Lady Rochford had gone mad.

She looked from her window and saw the Thames.

She said: 'Why should you come in your pomp and I be here a prisoner? You have everything; I have nothing. The King loves you. George loves you. Oh, George, do not stand there in the shadows. Where is your head, George? Oh, yes, I remember. They took it off.'

There was none who dared stay with her. It was uncanny to hear her talking to those who were not there. It was eerie to watch her eyes as she looked into space.

'Is it the ghost of George Boleyn she talks to?' it was whispered. 'Is he really there and we see him not? Is he haunting her because she sent him to his death?'

Her shrieks terrified all those who heard them, but after a while a calmness settled on her, though the madness was still in her eyes.

She said quietly: 'He has come to mock me now. He says that all my wickedness has but led me to the block. He puts his hands to his head and lifts it off to show me that he is not really George but George's ghost. He says the axe that killed him was wielded by me and it was called vindictiveness. And he says that the axe that will kill me will be wielded by me also and it is called folly. He says I am twice a murderess because I killed him and now I kill myself.'

She flung herself against the window seat, her hands held up in supplication to an empty space.

Her attendants watched her fearfully; they were frightened by the uncanny ways of the mad.

* * *

Out of Sion House and down the river to the Tower passed the Queen's barge. She was composed now and looked very beautiful in her gown of black velvet. She thanked God that darkness had fallen and that she might not see the decomposing, fly-pestered heads of the men who had loved her. The suspense was over. Thomas was dead; Francis was dead; there but remained that Catherine should die. She thought with deep compassion of her poor old grandmother who was suffering imprisonment in the Tower. She thought of Manox and Damport and Lord William, who, with members of her family and her grandmother's household had come under suspicion through her. She had heard that Mary Lassells had been commended for her honesty in bringing the case against the Queen to light; she had heard that the King, whose grief and rage had been great, was now recovering, and that he was allowing himself to be amused with entertainments devised by the most beautiful ladies of the court.

Catherine felt calm now, resenting none except perhaps her uncle Norfolk, who now, to save himself, was boasting that it was due to him that the old Dowager Duchess had been brought to her present state. For him, Catherine could feel little but contempt; she remembered her grandmother's telling her how cruel he had been to Anne Boleyn.

Lady Rochford was with Catherine; her madness had left her for awhile though it would keep returning, and it was never known when she would think she saw visions. But there was some comfort for Catherine in having Jane Rochford with her, for she had been a witness of, and participator in, Anne's tragedy. She would talk of that sad time which was but six years ago, and Catherine gained courage in hearing how Anne had nobly conducted herself even to the block.

Sir John Gage, who had taken the place of Sir William Kingston as Constable of the Tower, came to her on the second day in the fortress.

'I come to ask that you prepare yourself for death,' he told her solemnly.

She tried to be brave but she could not. She was not quite

535

twenty years old, so young, so beautiful and in love with life; she was overtaken with hysteria, and wept continually and with such violence as was verging on madness.

In the streets people were murmuring against the King.

'What means this? Another Queen – and this time little more than a child – to go to the block!'

'It is whispered that she has never done aught against even her enemies.'

'Is it not strange that a man should be so cursed in his wives?'

Gage returned to her and told her she would die the next day.

She said: 'I am ready!' And she asked that they should bring the block to her that she might practise laying her head upon it.

'My cousin died most bravely I hear. I would follow her example. But she was a great lady and I fear I am not, nor ever were. What she could do naturally, I must practise.'

It was a strange request but he could not deny it, and the block was brought to her room, where she had them place it in the centre thereof, and graciously she walked to it, looking so young and innocent that it was as though she played some child's game of executions. She laid her head upon it, and kept it there a long time so that the wood was wet with her tears.

She said she was tired and would sleep awhile, and she fell into a deep, peaceful sleep almost as soon as she lay down. In sleep, her auburn hair fell into disorder, her brow was smooth and untroubled; her mouth smiling.

She dreamed she saw her cousin Anne who caressed her as she had done when she was a baby, and bid her be of good cheer for the death was easy. A sharp subtle pain and then peace. But Catherine could not be reassured, for it seemed to her that though she was innocent of adultery, she was in some measure to blame because of what had happened before her marriage. But her cousin continued to soothe her, saying: 'Nay, I was more guilty than you, for I was ambitious and proud, and hurt many, while you never hurt any but yourself.'

She was comforted, and clung to her dream. She knew now that she, like Anne, was innocent of any crime deserving of death. Anne had been murdered; she was about to be. But the death was quick and there was nothing to fear.

In the early morning, when they aroused her, she said almost calmly: 'I had forgotten what the day was. Now I know. Today I am to die.'

* * *

She walked with that slow dignity, which she had rehearsed last evening in her room, to the spot before the church where, six years before, Anne had died. She was dressed in black velvet, and was very pale. Her eyes were wide, and she tried to believe she saw her cousin, smiling at her from beyond the haze through which she herself must step. She thought as she walked, I must die like a queen, as Anne died.

She was accompanied by Jane Rochford who was to die with her. Jane's dignity was as complete as that of the Queen. Her eyes were calm, and all the madness had passed from her now; she could face death gladly, for it seemed to her that only by dying could she expiate the sin she had committed against her husband.

The early morning February air was cold and river-damp; the scene was ghostly. Catherine looked for her uncle's face among those of the people gathered there to see her die, and felt a rush of gratitude to know she would be spared seeing him there.

She muttered a little prayer for her grandmother. She would not pray for Thomas and Francis for they were now at peace. Had Anne felt this strange lightening of the heart when her death had been but a moment away; had she felt this queer feeling which had a touch of exultation in it?

She said she would speak a few words. Tears were in the eyes of many who beheld her, for she had none of that haughtiness which had characterized her tragic cousin. In her black velvet gown she looked what she was, a very young girl, innocent of any crime, whose tragedy was that she had had the misfortune to be desired by a ruthless man whose power was absolute. Some remembered that though Anne had been found guilty by a picked jury, she had had an opportunity of defending herself, and this she had done with a clarity, dignity and obvious truthfulness so that all unprejudiced posterity must believe in her innocence; but little Catherine Howard had had no such opportunity; contrary to English law she would be executed without an open trial, and there was but one word for such an execution, and that the ugly one of murder. Some must ask themselves what manner of man was this King of theirs, who twice in six years had sent a young wife to the block! They remembered that this Henry was the first King of England to shed women's blood on the block and burn them at the stake. Was the King's life so moral, they must ask themselves, that he dared express such horror at the frailty of this child?

But she was speaking, and her voice was so low that it was difficult to hear her, and as she spoke tears started from her eyes and ran down her smooth cheeks, for she was speaking of her lover Culpepper, the grisly spectacle of whose head all might see when crossing London Bridge.

She was trying to make these people understand her love for that young man, but she could not tell them how she had met and loved him when at Hollingbourne he had first come into her lonely life.

'I loved Culpepper,' she said, and she tried to tell them how he had urged her not to marry the King. 'I would rather have him for husband than be mistress of the world. . . . And since the fault is mine, mine also is the suffering, and my great sorrow is that Culpepper should have to die through me.'

Her voice faltered; now her words grew fainter and the headsman looked about him, stricken with sorrow at what he must do, for she was so young, but a child, and hardened as he was, it moved him deeply that his should be the hand to strike off her head.

She turned her brimming eyes to him and begged he would not delay. She cried: 'I die a queen, but I would rather die the wife of Culpepper. God have mercy on my soul. Good people . . . I beg you pray for me. . . .'

She fell to her knees and laid her head on the block not so neatly as she had done it in her room, but in such a way as to make many turn away and wipe their eyes.

She was praying when the headsman, with a swift stroke, let fall the axe.

Her attendants, their eyes blinded with tears, rushed forward to cover the mutilated little body with a black cloth, and to carry it away where it might be buried in the chapel, close to that spot where lay Anne Boleyn.

There was none to feel much pity for Lady Rochford. This gaunt woman was a striking contrast to the lovely young Queen. Jane mounted the scaffold like a pilgrim who has, after much tribulation, reached the end of a journey.

She spoke to the watching crowd and said that she was guiltless of the crime for which she was paying this doleful penalty; but she deserved to die, and she believed she was dying as a punishment for having contributed to the death of her husband by her false accusation of Queen Anne Boleyn. Almost with exultation she laid her head on the block.

'She is mad,' said the watchers. 'None but the insane could die so joyfully.'

Jane was smiling after the axe had fallen and her blood gushed forth to mingle with that of the murdered Queen.

*　　*　　*

In his palace at Greenwich, the King stood looking over the river. He felt himself to be alone and unloved. He had lost Catherine. Her mutilated body was now buried beside that of another woman whom he had loved and whom he had killed as he had now killed Catherine.

He was afraid. He would always be afraid. Ghosts would haunt his life . . . myriads of ghosts, all the men and women whose blood he had caused to be shed. There were so many that he could not remember them all, although among their number there were a few he would never forget. Buckingham. Wolsey. More. Fisher. Montague. Exeter and the old Countess of Salisbury. Cromwell. These, he could tell his conscience he had destroyed for England's sake. But there were others he had tried harder to forget. Weston. Brereton. Norris. Smeaton. Derham. Culpepper. George Boleyn. Catherine . . . and Anne.

He thought of Anne whom he had once loved so passionately; never had he loved one as he had her; nor ever would he; for his love for Catherine had been an old man's selfish love, the love of a man who is done with roving; but his love for Anne had had all the excitement of the chase, all the urgency of passionate desire; all the tenderness, romance and dreams of an idyll.

A movement beside him startled him and the hair was damp on his forehead, for it seemed to him that Anne was standing beside him. A second glance told him that it was but an image conjured up by the guilty mind of a murderer, for it was not Anne who stood beside him, but Anne's daughter. There were often times when she reminded him of her mother. Of all his children he loved her best because she was the most like him; she was also like her mother. There were times when she angered him; but then, her mother had angered him, and he had loved her. He loved Elizabeth, Elizabeth of the fiery hair and the spirited nature and the quick temper. She would never be the dark-browed beauty that her mother had been; she was tawny-red like her father. He felt sudden anger sweep over him. Why, oh, why had she not been born a boy!

She did not speak to him, but stood quite still beside him, her attention caught and held, for a great ship – his greatest ship – was sailing towards the mouth of the river, and she was watching it, her eyes round with appreciation. He glowed with pride and warmed further towards her because she so admired the ships he had caused to be built.

To contemplate that ship lifted his spirits. He needed to lift his spirits, for he had been troubled, and to think one sees a ghost is unnerving to a man of deep-rooted superstitions. He found himself wondering about this man who was Henry of England, who to him had always seemed such a mighty figure, so right in all that he did.

He was a great king; he had done much for England, for he *was* England. He was a murderer; he knew this now and then; he knew it as he stood looking over the river, Anne's daughter beside him. He had murdered Anne whom he had loved best, and he had murdered Catherine whom he had also loved; but England he had begun to lift to greatness, because he and England were one.

He thought of this land which he loved, of April sunshine and soft, scented rain; of green fields and banks of wild flowers; and the river winding past his palaces to the sea. It was no longer just an island off the coast of Europe; it was a country becoming mighty, promising to be mightier yet; and through him had this begun to happen, for he would let nothing stand in the way of his aggrandisement, and he was England.

He thought backwards over bloodstained years. Wales subdued; but a few weeks ago he had assumed the title of King of Ireland; he planned to marry his son Edward to a Scottish princess. As he reached out for treasure so should England. He would unite these islands under England and then . . .

He wanted greatness for England. He wanted people, in years to come, when they looked back on his reign, not to think of the blood of martyrs but of England's glory.

There were dreams in his eyes. He saw his fine ships. He had made that great Navy into the finest ever known. He had thought of conquering France, but he had never done so. France was powerful, and too much of England's best blood had been shed in France already. But there were new lands as yet undiscovered on the globe. Men sailed the seas from Spain and Portugal and found new lands. The Pope had drawn a line down the globe from pole to pole and declared that all lands discoverable on the east side of that line belonged to Portugal and west of it to Spain. But England had the finest ships in the world. Why not to England? War? He cared not for the shedding of England's blood, for that would weaken her and weaken Henry, for never since Wolsey had left him to govern England did he forget that England was Henry.

No bloodshed for England, for that was not the way to greatness. What if in generations to come England took the place of Spain! He had ever hated Spain as heartily as he loved England. What if English ships carried trade to the new lands, instead of war and pillage, instead of fanaticism and the Inquisition! He had the ships. . . . If Spain were weak. . . . What a future for England!

He thought of his pale, puny son, Jane's son. No! It should have been Anne's son who carried England through these hazy dreams of his to their reality. He looked at Anne's girl – eager, vital, with so much of himself and so much of Anne in her.

Oh, Anne, why did you not give me a son! he thought. Oh, had this girl but been a boy!

What would scholarly Edward do for England? Would he be able to do what this girl might have done, had she been a boy? He looked at her flushed face, at her eyes sparkling as she watched the last of the ship, at her strong profile. A useless girl!

He was trembling with the magnitude of his thoughts, but his moment of clarity was gone. He was an old and peevish man; his leg pained him sorely, and he was very lonely, for he had just killed his wife whose youth and beauty were to have been the warm and glowing fire at which he would have warmed his old body.

He reminded his conscience – better preserved than his body – that Anne had been an adulteress, a traitress, that her death was not murder, only justice.

He scowled at Elizabeth; she was too haughty, too like her mother. He wished he could shut from his mind the sound of screaming, mingling with the chanting voices in the chapel. Catherine was a wanton, a traitress, an adulteress, no less than Anne.

The ship was passing out of sight, and he was no longer thinking of ships, but of women. He pictured one, beautiful and desirable as Anne, demure and obedient as Jane, young and vivacious as Catherine. His hot tongue licked his lips, and he was smiling.

He thought, I must look for a new wife . . . for the sake of England.

I wish to acknowledge most gratefully the help I have had from the following:

Froude's *History of England, Henry VIII*, and *The Divorce of Katharine of Aragon*.
Strickland's *Lives of the Queens of England*.
Trevelyan's *History of England*.
MacDonald's *History of France*.
Salzman's *England in Tudor Times*.
The Quennells' *History of Everyday Things in England*.
Sergeant's *Life of Anne Boleyn*.
Cavendish's *Life of Wolsey*.
Hackett's *Henry VIII*.
Pollard's *Henry VIII*.
Collected Letters of Henry VIII.
Miss Manning's *Household of Sir Thomas More*.
Etc.

Where the authorities differ on various points I have used my own discretion, endeavouring to keep as near to the truth as possible.

J.P.